W9-AEW-572

# THE NON-RELIGION
# OF THE FUTURE

KANSAS SCHOOL OF RELIGION
University of Kansas
1300 Oread Avenue
LAWRENCE, KANSAS 66044

Sociology of relig.
Individualism

# M. Guyau

# THE NON-RELIGION
# OF THE FUTURE

## A SOCIOLOGICAL
## STUDY

*Introduction by Nahum N. Glatzer*

SCHOCKEN BOOKS · NEW YORK

Copyright © 1962 by Schocken Books Inc.

This edition is reprinted in its entirety from
the original edition of 1897 with the exception
of the author's introduction, which has been
replaced with a new introduction by the editor.

*First* SCHOCKEN PAPERBACK *edition 1962*

Library of Congress Catalog Card No. 62-19393

Manufactured in the United States of America

# TABLE OF CONTENTS.

### CHAPTER III.

### RELIGIOUS MORALS.

## Part Second.

## THE DISSOLUTION OF RELIGIONS IN EXISTING SOCIETIES.

### CHAPTER I.

### DOGMATIC FAITH.

## CHAPTER II.

### SYMBOLIC AND MORAL FAITH.

## CHAPTER III.

### DISSOLUTION OF RELIGIOUS MORALITY.

## CHAPTER IV.

### RELIGION AND NON-RELIGION AMONG THE PEOPLE.

## CHAPTER V.

### RELIGION AND NON-RELIGION AND THE CHILD.

## CHAPTER VI.

### RELIGION AND NON-RELIGION AMONG WOMEN.

*CHAPTER II.*

ASSOCIATION.   THE PERMANENT ELEMENT OF RELIGIONS IN
SOCIAL LIFE.

*CHAPTER III.*

THEISM.

## CHAPTER IV.

### PANTHEISM.

#### REVIEW OF THE PRINCIPAL METAPHYSICAL HYPOTHESES WHICH WILL REPLACE DOGMA.—*Continued.*

## CHAPTER V.

### IDEALISM, MATERIALISM, MONISM.

#### REVIEW OF THE PRINCIPAL METAPHYSICAL HYPOTHESES WHICH WILL REPLACE DOGMA.—*Concluded.*

# INTRODUCTION

## by N. N. Glatzer

### I

While he was browsing in a bookstore, Friedrich Nietzsche's attention was provoked by an unusual title: *Esquisse d'une morale sans obligation ni sanction,* by Jean Marie Guyau. He bought a copy, read the book and scribbled his reactions in the margins. Guyau stated: "The compassionate love for all men must be the final goal to which all our striving is directed." Nietzsche noted: *Incredibile.* Again Guyau: "The richer one's life, the stronger will be the desire to surrender, to sacrifice, to give of oneself." Nietzsche: "What perversion. Life is concerned with power." Guyau: "Thinking is truly impersonal and selfless." Nietzsche jotted down his disagreement.

As representative thinkers in the second half of the nineteenth century, the two men have much in common. The work of both combines philosophy with poetry, intellectual passion with passion for life; both are critics of stagnant, dogmatic religion and envision a new humanity; both conceive of ethics as a body of concepts engendered by the intensity of life; both live in the tragic awareness of the closeness of death. Yet each is representative of different attitudes to life. Nietzsche stands for self-assertion, the will to power, dominion; Guyau, for sympathy, altruism, service. Guyau, the opponent of established religion, is, simultaneously, a critic of what the atheist Nietzsche was about to propound. And much of what Guyau, the fellow-iconoclast, fought for sounded to Nietzsche as *incredibile.* The richness and diversity of late nineteenth-century free thought is symbolized by the similarities and dissonances between these two philosopher-poets.

## II

Jean Marie Guyau was born in Laval Mayenne, on October 28, 1854. The education of the exceptionally gifted boy was directed by his stepfather, the philosopher Alfred Fouillée. He studied Plato and Kant, ethics, aesthetics, and the history and philosophy of religions. His family practiced no form of Christianity. At the age of twenty, he won the French Academy of Science prize for a history of Utilitarianism from Epicurus to the present, and accepted an appointment as lecturer in philosophy at the Lycée Condorcet in Paris. His teaching career was soon interrupted by a pulmonary disease; he moved to the Riviera, to find some relief in the mild, southern, climate. In the short period before his death in the spring of 1888 he wrote *La Morale anglaise contemporaine,* a continuation and completion of his first book; a volume of poetry (*Vers d'un philosophe*); *Les Problèmes de l'esthétique contemporaine;* the above-mentioned *Esquisse,* an English rendition of which appeared in London in 1898; and his magnum opus, *L'Irréligion de l'avenir.* His *L'Art au point de vue sociologique,* edited by A. Fouillée, appeared posthumously. In this rich literary and scholarly output, Guyau delineated both his critical stance towards the intellectual movements of modern times and his own concepts of ethics, aesthetics, metaphysics, and religion. The thirty-four year old thinker died with the words, "I have fought bravely."

## III

*L'Irréligion de l'avenir* appeared in 1887; the English translation was published in New York in 1897. The author calls his work "a sociological study." He considers religion to be "the outcome of an effort to explain all things—physical, metaphysical, and moral—by analogies drawn from human society." Man, accustomed to living in a social structure, extends the concept of a social bond "till it reaches to the stars." He conceives the existence, beyond human society, of a broader, universal, cosmic society. Human relations, friendly or hostile, serve as a pattern for the explanation first of natural phenomena, then for a comprehension of the creation, conservation, and government of the world. Sociological laws are universalized. At the basis of all religions lies "the mythic or mystic sociology." Religious orientation in the world calls not only for anthropomorphism, that is, seeing the gods in the image of man, but also for what Guyau terms "sociomorphism," that is, an explanation of the universe and the gods in the image of human society. For this entire complex Guyau employed the designation "sociality," or "sociability," a term borrowed from Fouillée.

In his book *La Science sociale contemporaine,* Alfred Fouillée, convinced of the close relationship of biology and sociology (as taught by Herbert Spencer), suggested that the laws that are common to them should be expected to point to still more universal laws of nature and thought. He felt that the universe, in its effort to transmute the reign of mechanics into a reign of justice, is but a society in process of formation. Sociability, therefore, "is the immanent power at the heart of beings." Guyau felt that this theory, which Fouillée extended to ethics and metaphysics, could be applied equally to religion.

The author was aware of the classical definition of Schleiermacher, who saw at the core of religion man's feeling of dependence—a theory accepted and modified by the German religious historian David Friedrich Strauss, the philosopher Hermann Lotze, and others. Guyau also knew Ludwig Feuerbach's interpretation that man's needs and desires were the origin of religion. These and similar theories appeared to Guyau to contain some relevance but not the full explanation of the phenomenon of religion. For, he declared, in addition to a primary feeling of limitation, weakness, and dependence (and, in reaction to it, a desire for deliverance and liberation), there is in religious man a social need, a factor no less important than the above: the need for affection. "Our sensibility, developed by hereditary instincts of sociality . . . instinctively seeks for a person, a commanding figure to lean on, to confide in." Man cannot accept as fact that the universe spins in a void, that no one cares for him, that his voice dies away in an unconcerned, neutral nowhere. The imperfect, limited, forgetful human society appears rectified by the belief in a divine and omnipresent Being, in Whom "the society, which is constantly broken by death, [is] once more reunited." God is more than a master and a guardian; He is a friend, a father. Man in search of affection (as the deepest expression of social life) "fills out the bosom of infinity by the addition of a heart."

## IV

Guyau wanted his readers to realize the close relation of this, his book on religion, to his previously published volumes on aesthetics and morals. He believed the aesthetic notion to refer to life that is "conscious of its own subjective intensity and harmony"; the moral notion he understood as reference to "consciousness of the powers and possibilities in the sphere of practice of a life ideal in intensity and breadth of interest." Religion appears when this awareness of the social aspect of life is "extended to the totality of conscious beings," both living and ideal. Thus the individual and social manifestations of life itself reveal the basic unity of aesthetics with ethics and religion. Equally, Guyau recognized the relationship between religion and metaphysics. Need for protection and affection—the domain of religion—leads inevitably to questions concerning the destiny of man and the world, he maintained. Thus religion, "nearly physical in origin, issues in systems of metaphysics."

From the phenomenon of religion we turn to its history. Every positive and historically identifiable religion presents, according to Guyau, three essential elements. First, myths, as attempts to account for natural phenomena or historical facts. Second, a system of dogmas—beliefs not verifiable scientifically or philosophically but "imposed upon one's faith as absolute verities." Third, a fixed system of ritual practices to which a supernatural efficacy is ascribed. A so-called natural religion, that is to say, a faith without myth, dogma, and cult, is a system of metaphysical hypotheses, but no religion.

These elements of positive religion are, in Guyau's opinion, historically conditioned. A religion overcomes its crudities, religious ideas become more subtle and sublime, mythology undergoes a transformation into mysticism. But ultimately, with the rise of science, industry, independent ethics, and individualism, religious forces fail; decline of ritual sets in, dissolution of dogma: a religion has ceased to exist, unless the term is being applied to a brand of metaphysics (Herbert Spencer) or to a trend in philosophy (Eduard von Hartmann).

The French fascination with logic and linguistic precision revolted, in Guyau, against the use of the time-honored term "religion" for intellectual movements that, in the natural course of history, have replaced religion. Thus, for example, the scientific explanation of natural phenomena has superseded the mythical interpretation; this, in effect, constitutes the dissolution of one of the elements of religion as Guyau defines it. What follows is a scientific and no longer religious orientation.

If the term "religion" was to be retained beyond the pre-scientific era in history, one could with equal justification include science in a definition of philosophy, since scientific research was originally undertaken by philosophy. Philosophy, in turn, could be considered a part of religion, for originally religion included aspects of thought and of science. Lack of precision in terminology is proof of confusion in the thinker's mind. True, the Reformation and Protestantism constituted progress in religious thought and rendered services to liberty of conscience; but Protestantism, in rejecting some dogmas, retained others, and even strengthened their relevance for the faithful. In Guyau's view, the belief in original sin, the redemptive character of the Crucifixion, predestination, grace, election, and hell, testifies to the half-way measures of orthodox Protestantism; Luther preached and practiced the same intolerance as the Catholics, and Calvin burned the Unitarian Michael Servetius. Modern criticism indicates a trend towards abolition of all dogmatism, all "crystallization of faith." While institutional religion, in pursuit of unity, demands a belief in infallibility—the dogma of papal infallibility was proclaimed in 1870—modern man, convinced of the relativity and fallibility of human knowledge, moves toward what Guyau calls "religious individualism" (as opposed to dogmatic universalism).

Guyau gave close attention to Matthew Arnold's *Literature and Dogma,* which appeared in 1873 and was much discussed in England and elsewhere. In Arnold's interpretation, God becomes a symbol of morality. Not satisfied with a purely philosophic system of morals, he postulated a symbolic interpretation of the classical religious texts; in so doing, he preserved the ancient forms while imbuing them with a content close to the heart of the present; he attempted to reconcile loyalty to the past with concern for the situation in the modern world.

Upon reflection, Guyau rejected Arnold's reasoning, just as he refused to accept the "domestication" of God by Kant and the Hegelians, by Renouvier in France and Coleridge and John Stuart Mill in England. The various novel theories—all centering on the supremacy of morals—appeared to Guyau as a degradation rather than an elevation of "the eternally Just, the Omnipotent who squares reality with justice . . . the God of . . . Judaism, as he ultimately appears in the midst of the unknown." Basically, he opines, "liberal Christians suppress religion." Let us face the truth, he argues; myth, dogma, and cult are of the past; the term "religion" cannot honestly be employed as designating the intellectual forces of the future, or those of the present which are expected to have a future.

Before expounding his view of the future, Guyau formulated his opinion on the faith, professed by many among his contemporaries, in the eventual unification of existing religions into a single religion of the future, "either a perfected Judaism, or a perfected Christianity, or a perfected Buddhism." He viewed this aspiration to universality as pretension. To him, the element of dogma and myth, central to religion (again, in his definition), was irreconcilable with universality, for different minds are attracted in different directions. Therefore, a plurality of beliefs, or what Guyau designates as "religious individualism," was the sign of the future. Intellectual progress must proceed from the homogeneous to the heterogeneous and express itself in ever increasing variety. The future will bring the extinction of religious dogma, "but the best elements of religious life will be propagated, and augmented in intensity and extent," assuming the form of diverse religious associations.

## V

His choice of the title *Non-Religion* the author explains as a protest against the various attempts to define the religion of the future. For he has demonstrated that such a future religion is "no more than a somewhat hypocritical compromise with some form of positive religion," under cover of misleading symbolism. But Guyau takes pains to state that non-religion is not synonymous with impiety. "To be non-religious or a-religious is not to be anti-religious." By non-religion he means negation of dogma, supernatural authority, miracle, myth, formalized ritual. The non-religion of the future will, however, retain all that is pure in the religious sentiment: "an admiration for the cosmos and for the infinite powers which are there displayed; a search for an ideal not only individual, but social, and even cosmic, which shall overpass the limits of actual reality." The absence of dogmatic religion will facilitate "religious independence, or anomy, or individualism." He who searches for truth, he who loves the truth, "he alone is religious, in the philosophical sense of the word."

Articles of faith are today anachronisms, Guyau continues; but, as practical and philosophical conceptions, religious ideas, like all works of art, are, in a measure, imperishable. "The poetry of religion may survive the dogmatism of religion." He envisages a religion that has become a metaphysics of immanent finality, and in which God is the term for "what renders the movement of the world toward a state of peace, concord, and harmony *possible.*" He considers doubt a product of the religious sentiment, and doubt about God "a form of the sense of the divine." Human inquiry, provoked by doubt, does not preclude "the erection of an altar to the unknown God." His "religious anomy" implies suppression of an external revelation, but does not exclude "a subjective and personal intuition of divinity."

Though Guyau foresaw scientific induction ultimately triumphant over natural intuition, and probability over faith, his own over-all world-view appears to be a metaphysics of a religious nature. Although the title he has chosen points one-sidedly in the direction of criticism of established religions, the books offers much more. It relates the epic of mankind's ceaseless striving for orientation in the world and in the cosmos, its trials and errors, and the engagement of both mind and heart in the search for a measure of truth. The treatment of the vast source materials and of the views of other thinkers displays genuine sympathy throughout. His polemics, vigorous and pointed, never become destructive. "There is an anti-religious fanaticism which is almost as dangerous as religious fanaticism," Guyau asserted, and acted accordingly.

## VI

What distinguishes Guyau from the classical men of faith is not his rejection of myth, dogma, and cult, but his opposition to the idea

of Creation in whatever form or version, and his demand for an impersonal attitude to the universe. The two are essentially one. The
idea of Creation implies a conscious relationship of the Creator to
the universe; it is this relationship, rather than an attempt to explain the origin of the world, that is central in the Western, mono-
theistic, religions. The personality of God is responded to by the
personality of man. In a mechanical, deterministic, universe a
Creator-God is, indeed, "worse than superfluous," as Guyau says.
However, in the infinity of such a universe it would be presump-
tuous to attach undue significance to the personal element in man.
Our author is consistent enough to urge man, especially man who
is aware of his mortality, to consider "one's self and one's progress
toward the unknown in a sense impersonally." He acknowledges
the limitation of our freedom and our will ("If God gave us liberty
He was very miserly about it"). In these respects, is Guyau, therefore, justified in speaking of *l'absence finale de religion* in the
classical sense of the word.

Guyau recognized the charm of the pantheism of Spinoza, that
modern substitute for religion, that vast synthesis in which "the mystic Hebrew and Christian idea proves one with the moral theories
of antiquity." He must have felt the attraction of a doctrine according to which the individual is absorbed in universal being and the
organic unity of the cosmos is affirmed. He admired Spinoza and
his *amor dei intellectualis;* in Guyau's poem "Unity," Spinoza's cosmic pathos merges with his, Guyau's, own passionate faith in the
power of love. But in an incisive analysis he refutes both what he
calls the optimistic trend in pantheism, as represented by Spinoza,
and the pessimistic school, as represented by Schopenhauer and
Eduard von Hartmann. In addition, the scientist in Guyau realized
that the pantheistic concept of unity is but a projection of human
reasoning without correspondence in reality. And the metaphysician
and moralist in him demanded "not only the presence of life in all
things but of life in pursuit of an ideal of goodness and universal
sociality."

## VII

The fifth and final chapter of the book presents Guyau's own view of man and the world. It is an impassioned confession of faith by a dogma-free thinker.

Of the three metaphysical systems: idealism, materialism, monism, Guyau advocated idealism. He excluded "subjective idealism"—especially as represented by the English, for example, Thomas Henry Huxley—which reduces the external world to subjective terms, and chose objective, impersonal, or moral, idealism. It is an idealism that regards the will as the ever-present, fundamental element in man and in the universe. This will, immanent in all things, is further defined as the will to goodness, with a tendency to indefinite self-expansion. Man is endowed with radical goodness of will, but the germ of such goodness is found in a more or less conscious form throughout the entire universe. Evil remains, but assumes a spiritualized nature. Inverting Schleiermacher's definition of religion, Guyau considered the universe as depending upon the determination that goodness shall prevail, a goodness "of which we are conscious in ourselves and which we conceive to be or to be capable of becoming the directing principle of universal evolution." Mind and matter are not to be resolved one into the other; both are united in a synthesis known as life. Life progresses with the progress of consciousness; it develops toward sensation and thought. The law of life is not egoism (which is a diminution and mutilation of self) but expansion; the individual aspires to become both social and moral. Life is the source of metaphysical thought and moral deed. "To live is to become a conscious, a moral, and ultimately a philosophical being." On the highest level of ethics and metaphysics, man lives "in a sort of sacred league with the universe"—for the advancement of what is good.

Guyau, the idealist, naturalist, and romantic, believed in the existence of consciousness in other parts of the universe and conceived the possibility of consciousness radiating through space. He spoke of a possible "society of consciousnesses," freely communicating throughout the whole expanse of space, and of a kind of "intercosmic consciousness," to arise in an infinity of ages. And, conscious of his unity with the totality of things and of his membership in the "brotherhood of living things," and living in a *"solidarité intime et universelle,"* man is eternal.

Eternal and immortal. It is love that gives every conscious being a right to immortality. Love is "a protest against death," against the dissolution of the individual. Are, then, eternity and immortality to be understood as the preservation of personality and individuality? Science is inclined to sacrifice the individual; love strives to preserve him. But the antagonism disappears in a higher synthesis: "Death closes one's eyes, but love stands by to open them again." Yet love (to the affirmation of which Guyau devoted a passionately beautiful chapter in the central part of his book) inspires man with a deep faith not only in himself and in others, but also "in this mysterious and mute universe." As one who has gained knowledge and love, he will consider "his self and his progress toward the unknown in a sense impersonally."

Religions of the past extended the concept of a social bond among men into the universe and explained the cosmos in human, personal, and social terms. Guyau's non-religion of the future sees man *sub specie* of the universe; its impersonality and indifference permeate his soul and subdue his "rebellious individuality." Death becomes "a most mysterious incident in life," but mortal man, knowing, loving, active, participating in the totality of life, is "conscious of indifference to death."

Guyau considered man's faculty of "impersonalizing himself" to be the most durable element in religion and philosophy. His book attempted to safeguard this element. It is a confession of a new faith. To Nietzsche, who considered himself the first perfect nihilist of Europe, and whose religion of life spelled a display of power, Guyau's humility was *incredibile.* But Guyau's neo-Stoic and neo-Jobean *Credo* may, in the long run, emerge as the more genuine and authentic of those of the late nineteenth century European poet-philosophers who ventured to penetrate the future.

Brandeis University
June 1962

# THE NON-RELIGION
# OF THE FUTURE

## Part First.

### THE GENESIS OF RELIGIONS IN PRIMITIVE SOCIETIES.

### CHAPTER I.

#### RELIGIOUS PHYSICS.

<small>IMPORTANCE OF THE PROBLEM OF THE ORIGIN OF RELIGION—UNIVERSALITY OF RELIGIOUS BELIEFS OR SUPERSTITIONS—VARIABILITY OF RELIGIONS AND RELIGIOUS EVOLUTION.</small>

    I. Idealist Theory which Attributes the Origin of Religion to a Notion of the Infinite—Henotheism of Max Müller and Von Hartmann—M. Renan's Instinct for Divinity.

    II. Theory of a Worship of the Dead and of Spirits—Herbert Spencer—Spencer's Objections to the Theory of the Attribution of a Soul to Natural Forces.

    III. Answer to Objections—Religious Physics Sociological in Form, and the Substitution of Relations between Malevolent or Beneficent Conscious Beings for Relations between Natural Forces—Socio-morphism of Primitive Peoples.

THE question of the genesis of religion is more important than any other historical inquiry. It involves not only the truth or falsity of past events, but the value or the reverse of our ideas and present beliefs. Each of us has something at stake in this investigation. The causes which formerly gave rise to a belief are still, in the majority of cases, those which maintain it in existence in our days, and to take stock of these causes is, whether one intends it to be so or not, to pass judgment on the belief itself. History, if it should ever be complete, would possess here the power of effacing in the future what it had failed to justify in the past. Perfectly to

*Importance of inquiry into genesis of religion.*

ascertain the origin of religions would be at the same time either to condemn them or to fortify and preserve them.

One point may legitimately be regarded as attained by contemporary criticism.    After the labours of Herr Roskoff, M. Réville, and M. Girard de Rialle, it is impossi-ble to maintain that there exist nowadays on the surface of the earth whole peoples absolutely without religion or superstition, which among non-civilized people amount to the same thing.[1]    The reason why man is a superstitious or religious being is simply that he possesses a high degree of intelligence.    Megalithic monu-ments (menhirs, cromlechs, dolmens), sepulchres, amulets, are trustworthy evidence of the existence of religion in prehistoric times ; and those fragments of bone detached from the skull and pierced with holes to pass a string through—" cranial rounds "—belong, no doubt, to the same category.[2]    Manifes-tations of the religious spirit date back thus to the age of polished stone.    And to pass from facts to hypotheses it is conceivable that at the beginning of the quaternary period, perhaps two hundred and fifty thousand years ago, man was already feeding upon vague and elementary superstitions, though he does not appear to have felt sufficient respect for his dead to have dug sepulchres, and although no fetiches belonging to that period have been discovered.

*Established fact that every known race of people is religious.*

A second point which may be regarded as equally estab-lished, and which results in important consequences in the matter of method of research, is that religion, being of natural origin, must have developed slowly and in accordance with universal and regular laws ; it must have · originated in simple and vague notions of some sort, accessible to the most primi-tive intelligence.    And from that starting point it must have risen by gradual evolution to the complex and precise concep-tions which characterize it to-day.    It is in vain for religions

*Established fact that religion is of natural origin.*

[1] Herr Roskoff, *Das Religionswesen der rohesten Naturvoelker* (Leipzig, 1880) ; M. Girard de Rialle, *Mythologie comparée* (Paris, 1878); M. Réville, *Les religions des peuples non civilisés* (Paris, 1880).

[2] See M. G. De Mortillet, *Le préhistorique.    Antiquité de l'homme* (Paris, 1883).

to believe themselves immutable; they have all of them been borne forward unwittingly by the movement of universal evolution. The great Egyptian Sphinx, who has not changed her position in the desert these four thousand years, might believe herself to be stationary, but she has never ceased for an instant to whirl through space, borne along by the earth's motion around the sun.

It remains to determine what these primary notions that lay at the bottom of all religions were. And here begins the disagreement among the principal authorities on Two contrasted theories of its the science of religion. Some of them explain origin. the birth of religion by a sort of mysterious intuition of supra-sensible verity, by a divination of God; others regard it as an intellectual error, a false hypothesis, which was natural, however, and perhaps inevitable to primitive intelligence. The first look upon religion as an immense leap on the part of the human mind over and beyond the limits of the physical world in which we are confined, the second believe it to be born in the beginning of an inexact interpretation of the commonest phenomena of the world, of objects of our senses or of our consciousness; for the first, religion is more than science; for the second, religion is pseudo-science. All idealists—Strauss, Renan, Matthew Arnold—discover in every religion the germ of their own especial form of refined idealism, and bow down before it with a respect that might well appear ironical if they did not affirm themselves to be quite sincere; they see in religions generally the noblest and most lasting product of the human mind. Their extreme adversaries, on the contrary, see no more in the origin of religions than, as Auguste Comte would have said, the expression of a gross fetichism.

It is evident that the problem of the origin of religion, in the new form in which it presents itself to-day, is quite as grave as ever it was; formerly the question was Is religion a species of illu- whether religion is revealed or natural; to-day sion? the question is whether religion is or is not true— whether it is or is not the product of an intellectual error, of a sort of inevitable optical illusion which it is the business of science to explain and to correct ; whether, in effect, the god of mythical and symbolical religion is not simply a magnified idol.

The positivist theory of religion seemed some years ago close upon its ultimate triumph.[1]    Many had accepted it, but without having fully perceived all of its con-

*The positivist theory no longer in possession of the field.*

sequences.    At the present moment it is, on the contrary, strongly contested.    New elements have been introduced into the problem and the whole question must be gone over again.    Max Müller in especial has made what might be almost called a desperate effort to make out a case for the objectivity and essential rationality of religion, which had both been compromised by positivism.[2]    From a different point of view Herbert Spencer also, in his " Sociology," has criticised theories which regard fetichism or naturism as the principle of religion.

According to Max Müller some notion of divinity, in especial in the form of a notion of the infinite, must have preceded the conception of God.  Gods are

*Max Muller's theory.*

simply subsequent personifications of this great innate idea ; our ancestors kneeled in worship long before they possessed a name for Him before whom they were kneeling.  Even at the present day we recognize in the last resort the vanity of all the titles of the unknown God whom we must adore really in silence.  Religion, which is responsible for the origin of the gods of history, may therefore well survive them.  We say religion ; for in effect, according to Max Müller, all religions amount in the end to one, since they may all be traced back through the long course of their development to a single original conception, that namely of the infinite, which from the very beginning was present in the mind of man.  This universal conception, however, Max Müller does not regard as in any sense mystical or innate, in the old acceptation of that word.  He willingly

---

[1] We find it adopted or almost so even by spiritualists, like M. Vacherot, *La religion*, Paris, 1869.

[2] See *Origin and Development of Religion*, by F. Max Müller, M. A.

adopts the axiom: *Nihil in fide quod non antea fuerit in sensu.*[1] But in his opinion some perception of the infinite is logically involved in a perception of the finite, and this conception of infinity, with its basis at once in sense and reason, is the true foundation of religion. Given the five senses of a savage, Max Müller undertakes to make him sensible of or at least experience some presentiment of the infinite, make him desire it, feel some aspiration toward it. Take the sense of sight for example : " Man sees, he sees to a certain point ; and then his eyesight breaks down. But exactly where his eyesight breaks down there presses upon him, whether he likes it or not, the perception of the unlimited or the infinite." " It may be said," he adds, " that this is not perception in the ordinary sense of the word. No more it is, but still less is it mere reasoning." " If it seems too bold to say that man actually sees the invisible, let us say that he *suffers* from the invisible, and the invisible is only a special name for the infinite." Man not only necessarily divines the infinite as existing beyond the limits of the finite, and as it were enveloping it ; he perceives it within the limits of the finite, and as it were penetrating it ; the infinite divisibility of matter is manifest to the senses, the fact that science seems to demand the existence of an irreducible atom as a necessary postulate to the contrary notwithstanding. And what is true of space is equally true of time, applies equally to quality and quantity. " Beyond, behind, beneath, and within the finite, the infinite is always present to our senses. It presses upon us, it grows upon us from every side. What we call finite in space and time, in form and word, is nothing but a veil or net which we ourselves have thrown over the infinite." And let it not be objected that primitive languages supply no means of expressing the idea of infinity, of the beyond, which is given in every finite sensation. Do the languages of antiquity supply a means of designating the infinite shades and variety of colour ? Democritus was acquainted with but four colours : black, white, red, and yellow. Shall **we** say, therefore, that the ancients did not perceive the blue of

[1] *Origin and Development of Religion*, p. 210.

heaven? The sky was as blue for them as it is for us, but they had not yet established a conventional designation for the sensation it afforded them. And similarly in the case of the infinite for the primitive man ; it existed for him although he had not as yet invented a name for it. Well, what is this infinite, in the last resort, but the object to which every religion addresses itself? A religious being is essentially one who is not satisfied with such and such a finite sensation ; who looks everywhere for the beyond—looks for it in life, in death, in nature, in himself. To be divinely aware of a vague somewhat that one cannot quite understand, to feel a veneration for it and then to endeavour to fit it with a name, to call to it stammeringly, these are the beginnings of every system of religious worship. The religion of the infinite comprehends and precedes all others, and since the infinite itself is given in sensation, it follows that "Religion is simply another development of sensuous perception, quite as much as reason is." [1]

Max Müller is equally critical in his attitude toward positivists, who regard fetichism as the primitive religion, and toward the orthodox, who find in monotheism the natural uncorrupted type of religion. In his opinion, to name a god or gods implies antecedently the possession of a notion of the divine, of the infinite ; gods are simply the different forms, more or less imperfect indeed, in which divers peoples have bodied forth one and the same idea; religion is, so to speak, a language into which men have endeavoured to translate one and the same internal aspiration—that of comprehending the great unknown; if man's tongue and intelligence have gone astray, if the diversity and inequality of religions are comparable to the diversity and inequality of languages, that does not necessarily mean that at bottom the veritable principle and object of all these different religions, as of all these different languages, are not very nearly the same. According to Max Müller a fetich, in the proper sense of the word (*factitius*), is no more than a symbol which presupposes an

*Equally opposed to positivists and orthodox monotheists.*

[1] *Origin of Religion,* p. 25.

idea symbolized; the idea of God cannot come out of a fetich unless it has already been put there. Casual objects, such as stones, shells, the tail of a lion, a tangle of hair, or any such rubbish, do not possess in themselves a theogonic or god-producing character. The phenomena of fetichism, therefore, are always historically and psychologically secondary. Religions do not begin in fetichisms, it is truer to say that they end in it; not one of them has shown itself capable of maintaining its original purity in connection with fetichism. Portuguese Catholics who reproach negroes with the *feitiços* were the first (were they not?) to have their rosaries, their crosses, their sacred images, blessed by the priests, before their departure from their native land.

If fetichism, understood as Max Müller understands it, is not the primitive form of religion, if self-conscious monotheism is equally incapable of maintaining its claim to be so, it is more exact to say that the

*Henotheism.*

earliest religion, at least in India, consisted in the worship of different objects, accepted one after the other as representing *a* god ($\varepsilon \tilde{\iota}\varsigma$) and not the unique and sole God ($\mu \acute{o} \nu o \varsigma$). It is this that Max Müller calls by a word invented by him: henotheism ($\varepsilon \tilde{\iota}\varsigma$, $\dot{\varepsilon}\nu \acute{o}\varsigma$, in opposition to $\mu \acute{o}\nu o \varsigma$), or better, kathenotheism.[1] In ordinary polytheism the gods are arranged in hierarchies, belong to different ranks; order reigns in heaven; but in the beginning no such system of subordination could have existed. Each god must have seemed in turn the most powerful to whoever invoked him; Indra, Varuna, Agni, Mitra, Somah were accustomed to hear the same epithets addressed to them; religious anarchy preceded religious monarchy. "Among you, O Gods," says Rishi Manu Vaivasvata, "there is none that is large, there is none that is small, there is none that is old nor young: you are all great indeed." They are all but different symbols of the same idea, of an adoration for that which overpasses the limits of the human mind, for the mysterious infinite whose existence our senses prove by their very incapacity of taking cognizance of it.

[1] This word has met with success in Germany. Hartmann also adopts a theory of henotheism.

Max Müller endeavours to trace the evolution of Hindu thought from a period long previous to the birth of Buddhism, which was the Protestantism of India. The learned philologist sees in the development of religion in India one of the essential types of the development of human religions generally. It may be even, he thinks, that the Hindus, who started from as low a plane as we, have in some respects reached a more considerable height. Let us follow him in this inquiry, which has nowhere been conducted more anxiously and indefatigably than in the great country which may almost be called the home of meditation. Let us take with him a "bird's-eye view" of what may be regarded as an epitome of human history.

*The evolution of the Hindu faith typical.*

Πάντες δὲ Θεῶν χατέουσ' ἄνθρωποι, said Homer. It was not within the domain of the wholly tangible that India sought for its gods; understanding by *tangible* whatever one can touch on all sides, stones, shells, bones, etc.; and Max Müller sees in this fact (which, by the way, may be contested) a fresh argument against the fetich theory. On the contrary, in the presence of his great, snow-capped mountains, of which our comparatively level Europe can scarcely afford us even an idea, in the presence of his immense beneficent rivers with their rumbling cataracts, their eddies, their unknown sources, in the presence of the ocean, stretching away beyond the line of vision, the Hindu found himself surrounded by things, of which he could touch and understand but some inconsiderable portion—of which the origin and destiny baffled him. It was in the domain of the *semi-tangible* that India found its *semi-deities*. One step beyond, Hindu thought domesticated itself in the region of the intangible, that is to say, in the region of things which, though visible, lie entirely beyond our reach—the visible heaven, the stars, the sun, the moon, the dawn, which were regarded in India, as also elsewhere, as true divinities. Add to these thunder, which for the Hindus also descends from heaven with a "howl," the wind sometimes so terrible, which, however, in the hot days of summer "pours

*Progress from the semi-tangible to the intangible.*

honey" upon man, and the rain, sent by the beneficent rain god, Indra. Having thus created their deities and peopled heaven somewhat at haphazard, the Hindus were not slow to distribute them into classes and families—to invent for them a necessary background of genealogy. There is a record of certain efforts to establish in the Hindu heaven, as in the Olympus of the Greeks, a system of government, a supreme authority; in a number of hymns the notion of the one God, Creator and Master of the world, is clearly expressed: He is " the Father that begat us, the Ruler who knows the laws and the worlds, in Him alone all creatures repose."

But the Hindu mind was destined to rise at a bound above Greek polytheism and Hebrew monotheism. It is

And from the intangible to the unreal.

well to see God in nature. There lies still a step beyond: to ignore nature. A firm belief in the reality of this world, in the value of this life, enters as an essential element into the belief in a personal God, superior to the world and distinct from it, like the Javeh of the Hebrews. The distinguishing characteristic of the Hindu mind is precisely a certain scepticism in regard to the world, a persuasion of the vanity of nature; so that the Hindu god possesses and can possess nothing in common with Jupiter or Javeh. He who sees no more in material force than a play of the senses, will see no more in the power which is supposed to direct that force than a play of the imagination; faith in a Creator shares the fate of faith in a creation. It is in vain for Hindu poets to vindicate *sraddhâ* faith, for the gods. Indra in especial, the most popular of the divinities, to whom the supreme epithet of Visvakarman, the maker of all things, is given, is of all others most subject to be doubted. "There is no Indra. Who has seen him? Whom shall we praise?" (Rig. vii. 89, 3.) It is true that the poet after these bitter words represents Indra as appearing in person, as in the book of Job. "Here I am, O worshipper! behold me here. In might I overcome all creatures." But the faith of the poet and of the thinker takes fire but for a moment; we enter into a period of doubt which Max Müller designates by the name of adevism and which he carefully

distinguishes from atheism properly so called. And in effect
Hindus did not reject the very notion of a god, the Greek
Θεός; they sought God simply back of and beyond the personal and capricious deities that up to that time they had
adored; such deities became for them names simply, but
names of some thing, of some being, unknown. " There is
only one being, although the poets call him by a thousand
names." Buddhism itself, which came later and did no more
than develop tendencies already existing in Brahmanism,
was not, in Max Müller's judgment, originally atheistic.
Adevism was no more for India, with some slight exceptions,
than a period of transition; the Hindu mind passed it as a
step toward a higher level. And yet what anxiety, what
incertitude, is expressed in certain hymns which belong, no
doubt, to this unhappy epoch. The Vedic poets no longer
glorify the sky nor the dawn, they do not celebrate the powers
of Indra, nor the wisdom of Visvakarman and Pragâpati. They
move about, as they themselves say, " as if enveloped in mist
and idle speech." Another says : " My ears vanish, my eyes
vanish, and the light also which dwells in my heart; my mind
with its far off longing leaves me ; what shall I say, and what
shall I think? . . . Who knows from whence this great
creation sprang? and whether it is the work of a Creator or
not? The most High Seer, that is in the highest heaven, he
knows it, or perchance even he knows not." (Rig. x. 129.)
There is profoundness in these last words, and how the
problem of the creation has been probed by the human intellect since that epoch ! The evolution of the ideas indicated
in the passages of the hymns reaches its climax in what are
called the Upanishads, the last literary compositions which
still belong to the Vedic period, where all the philosophy of
the time is found condensed, and where one catches glimpses of
the modern doctrine of Schopenhauer and of Von Hartmann.
After having meditated a long time the Hindu believed himself to have succeeded. Max Müller cites the surprising
dialogue between Pragâpati and Indra, in which the latter acquires, after a long effort, an acquaintance with the " self hidden
within the heart," the Atman, what Kant would call " the

transcendental ego." In the beginning Indra supposed this ego to be the visible reflection of his body, covered with its splendid raiment, in the water. But no; for when the body suffers or perishes, Atman would perish. "I see no good in this doctrine." Indra then entertained the hypothesis that the Atman reveals itself in dreams, when the mind is given over to the control of one knows not what invisible power, and forgets the pains of life. But no, for in dreams one still weeps, still suffers. Or may not the Atman, the supreme ego, be simply the man in dreamless sleep, in perfect repose? The ideal of repose, forgetfulness, of profound and sweet sleep, has always possessed great charm for the Orient. But no, "for he who sleeps does not know himself (his self), that he is I, nor does he know anything that exists. He is gone to utter annihilation. I see no good in this doctrine." It is only after passing through all these successive stages, that the Hindu mind comes at last to formulate what seems to it altogether the most profound truth and the supreme ideal. Atman is the self, leaving the body and freeing itself from pleasure and pain, taking cognizance of its own eternity (Upan. viii. 7–12); recognizing the Old, who is difficult to be seen, who has entered into darkness. . . It is smaller than small, greater than great; hidden in the heart of the creature. (ii. 12, 20.) Atman the "highest person," whom the sage finally discovers in himself, lies also at the bottom of all other beings than himself. Atman, the subjective ego, is identical with Brahma, the objective ego. Brahma is in us, and we are in all things, the distinction between individuals vanishes, nature and its gods are absorbed in Brahma, and Brahma is "the very ether of our hearts." "Thou art it, *tat tvam*, is the word of life and of the whole world." To find one's self in everything, to feel the eternity of everything, is the supreme religion; it is the religion of Spinoza. "There is one eternal thinker, thinking the non-eternal thoughts; he, though one, fulfils the desires of many. . . Brahma cannot be reached by speech, by mind, or by eye. He cannot be apprehended, except by him who says: He is." This Brahma in whom everything vanishes as a dream, "is a great terror, like a drawn sword"; but he is also the highest joy to him who has once found him; he is the appeaser of desire and intelligence. " Those who know him become immortal."

We have at last reached with Max Müller " the end of the long journey which we undertook to trace." We have seen the Hindu religion, which is typical of human religions, develop gradually, endeavour to cope with the infinite in its various forms, until it attains the height of conceiving it as Brahma, the eternal thinker, of whom the world is no more than a transitory thought. The gods are dead; sacrifices, rites, observances of all sorts are useless; the sole rite which is appropriate as an offering to the infinite is meditation and detachment. Do the débris therefore of the earlier stages of the faith disappear and the temples fall in dust, and Agni, Indra, and all these splendid titles pass into oblivion? Not at all, and here, following Max Müller, we may find in the history of the religions of India a lesson for ourselves in tolerance and generosity. The Brahmans understood that, as man grows from infancy to old age, the idea of the divine must grow in him from the cradle to the grave; a religion which does not live and grow is a dead religion. The Hindus accordingly have divided the life of the individual into distinct periods—Âsramas, as they say; in the earlier Âsramas the believer invokes gods, offers sacrifices, puts up prayers; it is only later, when he has accomplished these naïve duties and tempered his soul by long contact with the juvenile aspects of the faith, that in his mature reason he rises above the gods, and regards all sacrifices and ceremonies as vain forms, and thenceforth finds his cult in the highest science which is to him the highest religion, the Vedânta. Thus in the life of the individual the various stages of religion exist in an harmonious hierarchy. Even in our days in a Brahman family one may see the grandfather at the summit of the intellectual ladder looking down without disdain upon his son, who fulfils each day his sacred duties, and at his grandson learning by heart the ancient hymns. All generations live in peace, side by side. The different castes, each of

*Hindu tolerance.*

which follows a system of belief adapted to its degree, do the same. All adore, at bottom, the same god, but this god takes care to make himself accessible to everyone, to stoop for those whose station does not lift them above the earth. " It is thus," says Max Müller, " that every religion, if it is a bond of union between the wise and the foolish, the old and the young, must be pliant, must be high, and deep, and broad ; bearing all things, believing all things, enduring all things." Let us be as tolerant as our fathers in India, let us not be indignant against the superstitions above which we ourselves have risen and which served us in their day as stepping stones. Let us learn how to discover the element of good-ness and truth in all the creeds of humanity. It may be that all human religions, if they could once be freed from the legends which drape them, would unite to furnish for the cultivated portion of mankind a religion really complete. " Who knows but that their very foundation may serve once more, like the catacombs, or like the crypts beneath our old cathedrals, for those who, to whatever creed they may belong, long for something better, purer, older, and truer than what they can find in the statutable sacrifices, services, and sermons of the days in which their lot on earth has been cast."

Is this elevated theory exact ? In the first place it seeks erroneously to find in Hindu civilization the type of primi-tive religion ; more than that, it inverts the order of evolution by presupposing at the beginning the existence of complex notions and profound symbols which have been misconceived, it holds, by later generations only through an inability correctly to interpret the language in which they lay embalmed.[1] The capital defect in the theory, however, is that it discovers the origin of religion in the vaguest and most modern of metaphysical

Criticism of Max Müller's theory.

---

[1] Max Müller, as is well known, goes the length of believing that the authors of the first myths were perfectly conscious that they were speaking in parables ; and that subsequent generations misunderstood them, because they personified the fig-ures and the names by which the Divine was referred to ; so that mythology becomes literally the science of a disease of language.

ideas, that namely of the infinite. Max Müller holds that this idea is furnished even by the senses; his system presents itself to us as an effort at a reconciliation between the sensualists and the idealists. But the doctrine rests upon a confusion. A perception of relativity is one thing, a perception of infinity is another; some objects are great, some are small, and any object is great or small according to the standard of comparison—that is what the senses, or rather the memory, informs us of; and unless the metaphysical subtlety of a modern scholar whispers something in their ear, that is all they tell us. Max Müller seems to believe that the perception of space supplies us directly with a perception of infinity; but over and above any question of the psychological inexactitude of this account, it is irreconcilable with the historical facts. The infinity of space is an idea which metaphysicians alone, and that too in comparatively late times, have succeeded in realizing. The horizon is, on the face of it, a physical limit. The child fancies that he can go close up to the horizon and touch the beginnings of the celestial dome with his finger; the ancients conceived the heavens as an inverted bowl of hard crystal, sown with luminous points.[1]  For us who have been told since we were children that the stars are greater than the earth, and are separated from us by a distance unimaginably great, the spectacle of the heavens by a necessary association gives rise to a feeling

---

[1] Among the most ingenious and least contestable of Max Müller's suggestions, we cite the paragraph devoted to the Vedic deity Aditi, one of the names of the dawn : " You will be as surprised as I certainly was surprised when the fact first presented itself to me, that there really is a deity in the Veda who is simply called the boundless or the infinite, in Sanscrit A-*diti*. *Aditi* is derived from *diti*, and the negative particle *a*. *Diti*, again, is regularly derived from a root DÂ (dyati), to bind, from which *dita*, the participle, meaning bound, and *diti*, a substantive, meaning binding and bound. *Aditi*, therefore, must originally have meant without bounds, not chained nor inclosed, boundless, infinite, infinitude."

This etymology, on the contrary, seems to us rather to be calculated to show precisely that the conception of infinity is not primitive, and that the first time the Hindus invoked the dawn under the name of Aditi, they were far from possessing any distinction between finite and infinite. The night was for them a prison-house, the return of day was their deliverance. It is well known that they represented day as a luminous cow, which moved slowly out of the stable at night

of the incommensurable and the infinite. There is no reason to suppose that anything analogous took place in the mind of primitive man when he lifted his eyes on high. Primitive man has not the least idea that the power of vision is limited, that the vault of heaven is the vault of his incapacity and that infinite space stretches beyond; habitually, primitive man locates the end of the world at the extremity of his line of vision, which forms on all sides of him a visible and motionless sphere. It is difficult for him to understand that heavenly space is greater than the visible world. He finds it equally difficult to conceive the infinitely little; the infinite divisibility of matter of which, according to Max Müller, the senses take cognizance, is a conception which results only from the most abstract reasoning. Man's natural belief is that the divisibility of matter stops at the same point that his power of taking cognizance of it does—at the visible atom.

As to this "suffering from the invisible" of which Max Müller speaks, it is an altogether modern disease, which, instead of giving rise to the idea of the infinite, "Suffering from the invisible," a modern malady. is, on the contrary, a late product of this notion which was itself acquired by force of knowledge and of reasoning; far from marking the point from which religions spring, the "suffering from the unknown" stamps their insufficiency, is the beginning of their end. Primitive man troubles himself little about the infinity of

and stepped across the fields of heaven and of earth. Sometimes these cows are represented as stolen and confined in sombre caverns. Aurora herself is retained in the depths of *Rita;* night threatens to reign without end, but the gods set out in search of her, Indra discovers and delivers her, and with her aid, the cows bellowing for liberty are discovered in their cavern. It seems to us that for one who enters into the spirit of these primitive legends, it is easy to determine the primitive sense of Aditi. Aditi is the dawn who, confined one knows not where, succeeds at last in breaking bonds and appears radiantly in the open heaven, delivering and delivered, breaking the jail in which the hours of darkness have confined the world. Aditi is the dawn, freed and giving freedom. And, by an extension of meaning, it comes to signify the immortal and imperishable light which no power can veil or hide for more than a day. Whereas, Diti signifies what is mortal and perishable and prisoned in the bounds of matter. This construction is simple, and what is more, is confirmed by the legends to which we have just alluded; after having advocated it in the *Revue philosophique* (December, 1879), we find it adopted by M. Réville, *Prolégomènes à l'histoire des religions,* 1881.

nature and the eternal silence of infinite space ; he constructs
a world after the model of his own houses and shuts himself
safely up in it.   It is only the visible world that troubles him ;
he finds in it an object more than sufficient for his utmost
physical and intellectual activity ; he does not go far afield in
search of his gods ; he finds them, so to speak, under his hand,
touches them with his finger, lives in their company.   The
essence of their power over him lies in the fact that they are
neighbours of his.   To his gross intelligence the greatness of
the gods is not commensurate with their intrinsic infinity, but
with their power over him ; if heaven neither lighted him nor
warmed him with its sun, it would not be the universal father,
the Dyaush-pitâ, the Ζεύς, the Jupiter.   We do not mean to
say with Feuerbach that religion strikes root in gross self-
interest and brutal egoism simply ; in his relations with the
gods, as in his relations with his fellows, man is partly selfish,
partly unselfish : what we maintain is that primitive man is
not an advanced rationalist of the type of Max Müller, that
the conception of infinity was attained independently of
religious faith, and, more than that, is in conflict with
religious faith and will ultimately destroy it.   When in the
progress of human thought the universe is once conceived as
infinite, it overpasses the gods and unseats them.   This happened in Greece at the time of Democritus and Epicurus.
Positive religion demands a finite world : primitive people
did not rear temples to the Infinite in the hopes of domesti-
cating Him.   Max Müller pronounces a eulogy upon the
Hindus for their adevism ; was it really to their conception
of the infinite that they owed their wisdom, and might not
the idea of infinity alone have quite as well led them to
atheism ?   When one learns to contemplate the world as an
eternally lengthening chain of phenomena, one no longer
hopes, by a futile prayer, to stop or to modify the march
of such inflexible determinism ; one contents one's self with
investigating it by science or entering into it in some field
of action.   Religion disappears in science or morality.   There
remains, it is true, a final hypothesis that one may maintain : one may apotheosize the infinite, make over to it,

after the manner of the Brahmans, of the ancient and modern Buddhists, of the Schopenhauers and the Hartmanns, a donation of some mysterious unity of essence; but if so, prayer expires in meditation, in ecstasy, in a monotonous rocking of the cradle of thought to the rhythm of the phenomenal world, and religion becomes a religion of monism. But this religion does not spring in any proper sense from the notion of infinity, it, so to speak, hooks on to it rather; it is another example of man's need, if not to personify, at least to individualize and to unify the infinite—so great is man's need to project his individuality by main force, if need be, into the world! One is bent on endowing this great material body that one calls nature with some sort of a soul, one is bent on conceiving it in some fashion or other on the model of the human organism; and is not that, too, a species of anthropomorphism?

It is only later that human thought, carried away upon an endless voyage of discovery analogous to the migration of a primitive people, after having traversed the length of visible space and leaped the bound of its own intellectual horizon, attains the presence of the unfathomable ocean of the infinite. The infinite is for the human mind such a discovery as the ocean was for peoples who had wandered to its shores from the mountains and the plains. Just as for the newborn child the different planes of vision are indistinct and equally near; just as it is by the sense of touch that one learns little by little to recognize the depth of space and to acquire the conception of distance; just as, so to speak, it is with one's own hand that one opens the horizon before one; in the same way to the uncultivated intelligence everything seems finite and limited; and it is only by moving forward that it perceives the breadth and depth of its domain. It is only to a mind upon the march that the great perspective of the infinite is thrown open. At bottom this conception of infinity is less due to any direct experience of mere things than to a sense of one's own personal activity, to a belief in the perpetual progress open to human thought; action, as somebody has said,[1] is the real infinite or at least what appears

*The conception of infinity a scientific discovery.*

[1] Alfred Fouillée, *La liberté et le déterminisme,* 2e *partie.*

as such.   In this sense it may be admitted that there is in every human thought some vague presentiment of infinity, for there is a consciousness of a fund of activity which will not be exhausted in any given act nor in any given thought; to be conscious that one lives is thus in some sort to be conscious that one is infinite: illusion or reality, this notion forms a part of all our thoughts, turns up in every proposition of science; but it does not produce science, it is, on the contrary, born of it; it does not produce religion, which is the science of primitive ages, but descends from it.   The conception of infinity in many respects resembles the ignorance of Socrates, the refined ignorance which was really in disguise the last development of intelligence.   One of the antiscientific traits of existing religions is precisely that they display no sufficient sentiment of our ignorance in the presence of the unknowable, that the window they have open upon the infinite is decidedly too contracted.   If, as we have seen, religious physics tends little by little to transform itself into a metaphysics; if the gods have retreated from phenomenon to phenomenon, to the region of the supersensible; if heaven has separated itself from earth, positive religion nevertheless still lives in fear of throwing open to human thought a perspective really infinite.   Its eyes are always fixed upon a more or less determinate being, a creator, a unity in which the spirit may find repose and safety from the infinite.   Religious metaphysics, like religious physics, has remained more or less anthropomorphic, and rests more or less on a foundation of miracle; a foundation, that is to say, which limits and suspends the exercise of intelligence.   And as the object of adoration, in the majority of religions, is anything rather than the infinite, in the same way religious faith itself leads to a disposition to arrest the march of thought and impose upon it an immutable barrier; it leads to the negation of infinity and of the indefinite progress of human research.   Stricken by an arrest of development the majority of positive religions settled once for all on the first formulæ that occurred to them; they erected them into the practical object of a cult and left the intangible infinite unmolested in outer vagueness.

Over and above the conception of the infinite there is another and a similar notion that it is equally impossible to discover at the roots of religious thought ; it is that of unity in plurality, of totality. This pantheistic, monistic concept Von Hartmann believes to be the starting-point of all religions. As a partial disciple of Hegel and of Schopenhauer, Von Hartmann inevitably attributes to humanity and applies to the interpretation of history the formulæ of his dialectic. " Henotheism," he says, " is founded on a recognition of the positive identity at bottom of all the divinities of nature ; an identity which permits one to adore in the person of every god individually, and principally in the person of each of the leading gods, absolute divinity, the divine god. It becomes therefore a matter of indifference, in some measure, under which of its particular aspects one worships Divinity ; when Indra is represented imaginatively in the form of a buffalo, the right to represent him immediately afterward in the form of an eagle, or a falcon, is not for an instant abrogated ; when henotheism offers its homage to the supreme deity under the name of Indra, god of the tempest, it does not incapacitate itself from adoring him a moment afterward under the name of Surya, god of the sun ; or of Rudra-Varuna, god of the heavens. Henotheism does not owe its origin, therefore, to a failure in the association of ideas, and to a chance forgetfulness, an incredible lapse of memory on the part of polytheists, when they were addressing their homage to Surya as the supreme god, that there were still other gods in existence who were adored by other people, and even sometimes by themselves." Imagine primitive humanity " up " in the latest developments of the philosophy of monism, with its symbolism and its notion of conceiving diverse powers as metaphorical manifestations of the fundamental unity of things ! Even for India, the home of pantheistic metaphysics, such a philosophy is the reluctant product of a civilization already refined. People never take the first steps in thought by means of abstractions. To conceive divinity in general, and subsequently represent it by Indra, Surya, or Rudra-Varuna, as by aspects,

*Conception of an all-embracing unity, also modern.*

no one of which exhaust the totality of it—by a sort of litany in which the unity of things appears successively under diverse names and forms—implies a subtlety of intelligence and a mastery of the henotheistic conception of the universe that is one of the latest products of metaphysical speculation.   In the beginning the form and figure of the god was not distinguished from the god himself.   The distinction between body and mind was one that humanity attained with great difficulty ; and, *a fortiori*, any notion of a unity of the supreme and world soul, existing under a multiplicity of forms, must of necessity have made its appearance much later.

Another and later form of this vague idealism, that Max Müller and Von Hartmann, and also Strauss, have advocated, is presented in the theory of M. Renan concerning the " religious instinct," or the " revelation of the ideal."   By religious instinct M. Renan understands something mysterious and mystical, a heavenly voice in one's bosom, a sudden and almost sacred revelation.   " The construction of a religion," he cries, " is for humanity what the construction of a nest is for a bird.   A mysterious instinct awakens in the heart of a being, who heretofore has lived totally unaware of the existence in himself of any such possibilities.   The bird which has never itself laid an egg nor seen an egg laid, possesses a secret foreknowledge of the natural function which it is going to perform.   It lends itself with a species of pious and devoted joy to an end which it does not understand.   The birth of the religious idea in man is something quite analogous.   Mankind is moving forward unsuspectingly in its allotted course, and suddenly a little period of silence comes upon it, a lapse of sensation, and it cries to itself : ' O God, how strange is the destiny of man! Is it indeed true that I exist? What is the world ? Am I the sun, and does its heat and light feed upon my heart? . . . O Father, I see thee beyond the clouds,' and the noise of the outer world begins again, and the window, open out upon the infinite, closes once more, but, from that moment, a being to all appearance egoistic will perform inexplicable deeds and will experience

*M. Renan's religious instinct.*

a need to bow the knee and to adore." This charming passage, set off by the unction and the ecstasy of Gerson and Fénelon, is a capital instance of the mental attitude of a number of people nowadays who are endeavouring to transmute a reverence for some tottering religion into a reverence for the religious sentiment. Unhappily, M. Renan's account is purely mythological; primitive man never experienced anything of the kind. M. Renan completely confounds the ideas and sentiments which he, the historian of religion, the refined thinker, might have experienced himself, with those which primitive man was really subject to. This species of supreme doubt on the matter of our own existence and that of the world, this sentiment of the strangeness of our destiny, this communion of the soul with the totality of nature, this outbreak of refined sensibility, excited and tormented by modern life, possesses nothing in common with the sentiment of primitive religion, with its robust and crude faith reposing upon palpable fact and visible miracle. Mysticism, far from explaining the origin of religion, marks rather its period, its decomposition. A mystic is a person, who, feeling vaguely the insufficiency, the void, of a positive and finite religion, endeavours to compensate himself for the narrowness and poverty of established dogma by superabundance of sentiment. Mystics, substituting a more or less personal sentiment and spontaneous outburst of emotion for a faith in authority, have always played the rôle in history of unconscious heretics. Sentimental epochs are epochs of inaction, of concentration upon one's self, of comparative independence of thought. On the contrary, there presided nothing sentimental or meditative at the origin of religion, there was a stampede simply of a multitude of souls in mortal terror or hope, and no such thing as independence of thought; it is less of sentiment properly so-called, than of sensation and of action, that religions have been born. Primitive religion was not a means of escape out of this world, a port-hole into the blue; the earliest gods were not in the least ethereal, they were possessed of solid muscles, of arms capable of dealing blows. To explain the origin of primitive beliefs by a nascent idealism, is to explain them by their precise opposite.

One becomes an idealist when one is on the point of ceasing to believe; after having rejected a multitude of alleged realities one consoles one's self by adoring, for a time, the figments of one's own imagination; the spirit of early times is much more positive, as the Comtists say. A preoccupation with the infinite, a divine vertigo, a sentiment of the abysses of life, are wanting to man in early times. The modern mind with its intenser vision now and again perceives in nature an endless perspective down which we look with agony; we feel ourselves carried forward to the verge of a chasm; we are like navigators who, in the Antilles, under the intense light of the sun, can see the bottom and the depth of the sea and measure the gulf above which they hang suspended. But for less enlightened intelligences nature is opaque, vision is limited to the surface of things, and one floats upon the rhythm and pulse of the sea without asking what lies beneath.

Before the need for mystical belief can occur to one, one must have been reared in an atmosphere of faith, or else in an atmosphere of doubt; and both these states of mind are equally unknown to the earlier and simpler races of humanity. Or, more accurately, they are perfectly acquainted with faith, but it is the naïve faith of eye and ear; they possess the perfect confidence that every sentient being has in his five senses, and in all that there is nothing religious properly so-called. I remember the astonishment I felt in my infancy when I first saw the words doubt and faith; it was in some verses, and the poet was singing, with much eloquence, all the horrors of doubt. I perfectly understood what it was to doubt a fact, or to believe in it, but I bothered my head in vain to discover what one meant by doubt simply: What was there so terrible about being in doubt on matters with which one was insufficiently acquainted? The word faith was equally unintelligible to me, for I had as yet no conception of believing in anything except what was certain. The case of primitive man is exactly the same. He no more experiences a mystical need to believe than he experiences a mystical need to get drunk before having tasted wine. Religious sentiment does not make its

*A late phenomenon.*

appearance in him suddenly, does not simply step out on the stage. There are no lacunæ in the human soul, it is a prey to invincible continuity. Such a sentiment must come gradually by a slow adaptation of the spirit to the inexact ideas supplied to one by the senses. Man, imagining himself to live in the bosom of a society of gods, inevitably accommodates himself to so novel a habitat. Every society, human or divine, creates the individual member in its own image; draft the labourer for a soldier, let the villager become a citizen, they acquire of necessity new gestures and sentiments which, upon their return to their former habitat, they once more in a measure lose. The case is inevitably the same for mankind and religion. As the most sociable of beings, man is also the most readily subject to the influence of those with whom he lives or believes himself to live. The gods, whom we create more or less in our own image, thereupon, by an inevitable reaction, return the compliment. A religious instinct, such as M. Renan describes, is in a large part the work of this sort of reaction and of education; if it possesses profound roots in our being, the reason is that it was planted in us in our infancy, that it speaks to us with the voice of our childhood, and takes us back to our earliest years; often a word, a thought with which we have been struck at some former time, without, however, having understood it, unexpectedly reawakens in us, reverberates in our memory; it is but an echo, and it appeals to us as if it were a voice. The rôle played by heredity in the formation of one's character has been noticeably exaggerated ; the influence of education is at the present day not estimated at its full value.[1] Even among animals, instinct amounts to little without education. A bird, no doubt, does not actually need to see an egg laid to acquit itself with "devotion" of that new function; but when it is a question of building the nest, the case is not so simple : birds reared in a cage, who have never seen a nest, are often at a loss what to do ; instinct whispers indeed to them still, but its voice is no longer clear, no definite image of the ideal nest presents itself to their eyes. Nature's "devotion" is at fault. Add that these instincts, so

[1] See the authors *Morale anglaise contemporaine*, 2e *partie*.

"mysterious" in M. Renan's opinion, act on the individual by means of a somewhat gross mechanism, and that it suffices to tamper with the mechanism, to excite the instinct or to suspend it. To transform, for example, a capon into a setting hen, it suffices simply to pluck the feathers off the belly ; it then squats upon eggs—or upon pebbles—with pleasure. Really there is mystery enough in nature without going out of one's way to add to it; it is not philosophic to trace everything back to instinct, and then presently to regard these instincts as unconscious intentions, and in these intentions to see the proof of a plan, and in this plan the proof of a god. With a logic so accommodating as that, M. Renan might well find in the religious instinct a peremptory demonstration of the existence of God.

In our judgment there was, in the beginning, no other instinct involved than the instinct of self-preservation, and the instinct of sociality, which is closely allied to the former. More than that, the intellectual procedure upon which primitive men relied was no other than a simple association by contiguity and similarity, together with such reasoning by induction or analogy as is inseparably bound up with association. This species of intellectual procedure is precisely that which, in its highest stages, gives birth to the scientific explanation of things. Religion, as we shall show presently, originates as science does, in a certain astonishment that an intelligent being experiences in the face of certain phenomena and in the fears and desires which result therefrom, and in the consequent voluntary reaction.

*The only instincts involved the instincts of self-preservation and sociability.*

II. Herbert Spencer, who is almost at the antipodes from Max Müller, by a conscious return to euhemerism regards the gods simply as heroes transfigured in the memories of their descendants, reduces religion to an ancestor worship, and thus implicitly denies that a presentiment of the divine or of the infinite has played any part in its origin. Nevertheless, Max Müller and Herbert Spencer, in spite of such divergences, agree in reject-

*Muller and Spencer agree in rejecting the fetich hypothesis.*

ing the theory which attributes the birth of religion to the mingled astonishment and fear of an intelligent being in the face of certain natural phenomena, and to the need of explanation and protection that he experiences before what is puisant and powerful.

We willingly concede to Mr. Spencer that ancestor worship has played its part in the genesis of human beliefs; heroes have been deified not only after their death, but even in their lifetime. But why rely upon this single principle for the explanation of so complex a phenomenon as religion? Why wish to see in every detail a realization of it, even when no positive fact seems to authorize one's doing so? Spencer's system, which resolves the whole body of our beliefs into one, reminds one a little of Genesis, and of the theory that all mankind are descended from the first couple, Adam and Eve, after Eve had herself been fashioned out of one of Adam's ribs. If it is an excellent characteristic of Mr. Spencer's to look for the origin of heterogeneous and later beliefs in some vague and homogeneous conception, this primitive conception must at least be sufficiently ample to be able fairly to accommodate within its own limits the whole body of its successors, and Mr. Spencer is somewhat too much inclined to confound the homogeneity of a notion with its amplitude; it is only by a prodigy of artifice that he succeeds in extracting from his principle a completely furnished religious theory of the universe.

*Necessity of relying upon a number of principles.*

Mr. Spencer endeavours, first, to prove, by *three* examples, that a cult for the dead exists among three tribes of savages very low in the scale of civilization and not possessed, so far as has been observed, of any other form of religion; he thereupon infers that a cult for the dead is the earliest form of worship. These examples are open to discussion, but even if they were not, it in nowise follows that all other forms of religion spring from a cult for the dead. Death is, no doubt, so frequent and brutal a fact that it early engages the attention of primitive peoples; some germ of the notion of burial may be discovered among animals. Ants have frequently been observed, after

*Spencer's theory wantonly clever.*

their battles, carrying off the corpses of their soldiers ; but from the fact that human intelligence must necessarily have been engaged in one direction, does it follow that it can have been engaged in no other?   For the manufacture of a god Mr. Spencer requires first a corpse, second the conception of a spiritual double of the corpse, third a belief that this spirit is capable of inhabiting, not only the body, that it has just quitted, but another body, an inanimate effigy, a bee, a stone, etc.   What a complication!   One knows Mr. Spencer's ingenious device for explaining tree-worship; sometimes he would have us conceive trees as the resting-places of departed souls, who for some reason or other have taken a notion to inhabit them; sometimes he would have us rely on a theory of misinterpreted legend : a tribe that in former years inhabited the forest, a tribe *come from the forest*, ultimately believes itself to be descended from trees, ultimately believes that its ancestors were trees.   Really, all that strikes us as particularly artificial.   A tall tree is venerable in and of itself.   A certain "sacred horror" is an essential attribute of a dense forest. Night and obscurity play a notable part in the genesis of religion; well, a forest is the very incarnation of eternal night with its element of the unforeseen, its terrors, the sigh of the wind in the branches like a voice, the cry of the wild beast which seems sometimes to come from the trees themselves. And what intense and silent life in and about a tree, if one but studies it closely !   An animal does not observe with sufficient attention to see plants grow and the sap rise; but how astonished man must have been when first he remarked that the roots of trees make their way even into rock, that their trunks break all bonds : that they rise year by year, and are at the very beginnings of their maturity at an age when man is old !   Forest vegetation is alive, but with a life so different from ours that it must naturally have filled our ancestors with surprise and reverence.   Remember, too, that the sap of certain trees, when it flows from a wound, is of the colour of blood, or of the colour and almost of the taste of milk.

Similarly, why resort to an ancestor worship to explain zoolatry?   What is more natural, for example, than the universal veneration for the snake? This mysterious creature which glides away among the shadows, appears, and dis-appears, and carries with it power of life and death? Or instead of a serpent, consider the lion, or any other ferocious animal. He makes his appearance in a country and creates havoc among the flocks; one pursues him, but for some reason or other no shot reaches him; he is invulnerable. He becomes increasingly audacious and terrible; he disappears for weeks together, nobody knows where; he reappears suddenly, nobody knows why; he defies the hunters with the majesty that wild beasts sometimes show, in perfect consciousness of their power. Behold! a veritable god.

*Superfluity of effort to explain zoolatry by ancestor worship.*

It is well known that the aborigines worshipped the horses which the Spaniards imported into America; according to Prescott, they preferred to attribute the invention of firearms to the horses rather than to the Spaniards. The fact is simply that the Spaniards were men like themselves, and that the aborigines took their measure accordingly; but an unknown animal came to them armed with an indefinite power. Men adore nothing but what they are comparatively ignorant of, and it is for that reason, whatever Mr. Spencer may say, that nature, so long imperfectly known, afforded to religion a more generous and inexhaustible aliment than humanity.

At bottom what Mr. Spencer regards as the true confirmation of his doctrine is the relation it bears to the rest of his system; it is for him an example simply of a universal law, a consequence of evolution. According to this doctrine, everything seems to spring from a primordial unity, from a single homogeneous belief—the belief in a power more or less vague, exercised by the souls of the dead; this belief, once given, undergoes a complete series of integrations and differentiations, and ultimately becomes a belief in the regular action of an unknown and universal power. Mr. Spencer seems to us to be right in pitching upon the one homogeneous belief from which all others arise by a process of evolution; but the

*Narrowness and insufficiency of Spencer's formula.*

formula of this belief that he presents us with seems to us altogether too narrow and insufficient. If one wishes to discover the idea which dominates both the cult for the dead and the cult for the gods, one will find in it a natural persuasion that nothing is absolutely and definitively inanimate, that everything lives and possesses, therefore, intentions and volitions. Man has deified the phenomena of nature, as he has immortalized his ancestors, for the sole and only reason that, as a living being possessed of a will, the most difficult thing in the beginning for him to understand is the invincible determinism and absolute inertia of the phenomena of the external world.

The adoration of natural forces, conceived as more or less analogous to powerful living beings possessed of volition, has been denominated sometimes fetichism, sometimes naturism. Messrs. Müller and Spencer are agreed that fetichism is one of the later forms of religion, and decline to treat it as primitive.

Criticism of fetichism commonly a play on words.

On both sides of this interesting discussion one desideratum seems to us to be beautifully conspicuous by its absence, namely, precision of formula and agreement as to the exact sense of terms. The words *fetich, animate being, inanimate being*, and so forth, seem to us to have given rise to a number of misunderstandings, on the part both of those who are defending the fetich theory and of those who are attacking it. Let us cite some examples: Max Müller has undertaken to define the word fetichism; as was natural for a philologist he went in search of an etymology, and he found, relying on Tylor, that fetichism (from the Portuguese *feitiço*, derived from the Latin *factitius, artificial*) could not designate anything but a superstitious reverence felt or shown for certain knick-knacks that possessed no apparent title to any such honourable distinction. The definition of Tylor and of Max Müller may be philologically exact; unhappily, none of the philosophers who have regarded fetichism as the basis of religion have ever employed that word in the narrow and rigorous sense which Max Müller puts upon it; they understood by

[1] See our *Morale anglaise contemporaine*, p. 579.

it, as de Brosses and A. Comte did, the primitive tendency to conceive external objects as animated by a life analogous to that of man. They comprehended also, under the title of fetichism, what Max Müller distinguishes from it so carefully under the names of *physiolatry*, or the worship rendered to natural objects other than gimcracks, and of *zoolatry*, or the worship of animals. The result is that Max Müller's refutations really do not concern the doctrine which they are designed to combat, and over against which he sets up his own doctrine. Similarly in regard to the definitions of M. Réville.[1] To demonstrate that a cult for knick-knacks is not the primitive and unique original of all human religions does not help us forward; the problem remains where it was. Let us consider, therefore, not the words, but the theory itself of the animation of nature, and let us examine the objections that have been urged against it.

According to Messrs. Spencer and Müller the savage may legitimately be compared to a child who mistakes a well-dressed doll for a living being, or who punishes a door against which he has stumbled; the savage is not so naïve. The very child is far from possessing all the naïveté that is ascribed to him, in general he perfectly distinguishes between the animate and the inanimate; and when he talks to his playthings, and conducts himself before them as if they were alive he is not a dupe of his own words, he is composing a diminutive drama simply, in which he is an actor; he is making poetry and not mythology. " If his doll should step up to him

*Children and even animals distinguish between animate and inanimate.*

---

[1] Fetichism, M. Réville also says, is logically a later belief. "A fetich is a vulgar object, possessing no value in itself, but which a negro preserves, venerates, adores, because *he believes that it is the dwelling place of a spirit.* And the choice of the said object is not absolutely arbitrary. A fetich possesses this very special distinction, that it is the property of the person who adores it. It is in this element of individual ownership—ownership by the tribe or the family—that the difference clearly appears between the object of a naturist religion, and the fetich, properly so called. However humble it may be—tree, rock, or rivulet—the first is independent, is accessible to all, to strangers as to indigenes, on the sole condition that they conform to the exigencies of the ritual or the cult. The sun shines for everybody, the mountain is accessible to all who scale its sides, the spring refreshes the passer-by, whatever be his tribe ; the very tree which rises in the midst of the

and bite him, he would be the first person to be astonished."[1]
In the same way, a dog plays with a stick—the comedy of
the chase—he bites it, he tears it into pieces, he warms to
his game, which is still for him, when all is said, no more than
a game. Even the famous example of a child's rage at
inanimate objects against which it has stumbled, an example
which has done service in the pages of all those who have
written on religion,[2] is seriously damaged by Mr. Spencer;
according to him, mothers and nurses suggest to the child
absurd ideas which, but for them, it would not have; it is
they, who, if it has hurt itself against an inanimate object,
affect to be angry; and, to distract its attention from the
pain, endeavour to excite its anger also. The little comedy
of the inanimate object is one in which the child displays no
initiative. In any event the example deals with an ill-observed
psychological phenomenon, which, for the present, can be
employed to support no theory whatever.

Similarly, according to Mr. Spencer, no employment can
be made of the mistakes committed by a savage in the
Savages mis- presence of certain complex products of the arts
taking a watch, and of civilization; he believes these objects to
etc., for animate
lends no sup- be alive, but how should he do otherwise? If
port to fetichism. he is deceived, it is rather due to the degree
of perfection attained by our art than to any defect in
his own intelligence. When the indigenes of New Zeal-
and saw Cook's ship, they took it for a sailing whale.
Anderson relates that the Bushmen supposed that a carriage
was an animate being and must be provided with fodder; the
complexity of its structure, the symmetry of its parts, its
moving wheels, naturally suggested no fragment of their own
experience of inanimate things. Just so the Esquimaux

desert asks of the traveller some mark of deference, and does not trouble itself
about his origin. One cannot appropriate a natural object. It is otherwise with
a fetich. Once adopted by a family, it is in some sort in the service of that
family and has nothing to do with others." This definition of fetichism is quite
special, and in no wise concerns *primitive fetichism*, conceived as an ascription
of something analogous to the human will in all inanimate things.

[1] Spencer, *Principles of Sociology.*
[2] See, among others, M. Vacherot, *La religion.*

believed that a music-box and a hand-organ were living beings. All these errors are in a measure rational, but they are errors of a kind that really primitive man would have no opportunity to commit. To suppose that he was dominated by a natural tendency to assign life to things which were not alive, to imagine that he went out of his way to confound things which animals of a lesser degree of intelligence perfectly distinguish, is to invert the whole course of evolution.

There are, in Mr. Spencer's opinion, still other prejudices relative to primitive man from which we should free ourselves. We believe him to be voluntarily and incessantly

**Primitive man incurious.** occupied, as the modern infant is, with the *why* of things ; we fancy him perpetually endeavouring to satisfy a restless curiosity. Unhappily, if we are to trust our experience of the lower races of man, it appears that the sentiment of curiosity decreases directly as one approaches the savage state. To awaken curiosity demands surprise ; Plato was correct in regarding astonishment as the beginning of philosophy. Well, what produces astonishment is an unexpected breach in the chain of causation ; but for a primitive intelligence which has not yet achieved scientific maturity, there is no such thing as natural causation and no such thing as rational surprise.[1] The Fuegians, the Australians, show the most complete indifference in the presence of matters for them absolutely new and essentially surprising. According to Dampier, the Australians whom he took on board paid no attention to anything in the vessel except what was given them to eat. The very mirrors did not succeed in astonishing savages of inferior race ; they were amused with them, but evinced neither surprise nor curiosity. When Park inquired of the negroes, " What becomes of the sun at night ? Is it the same sun that rises the next day or another ? "—they made him no reply and found the question puerile. Spix and Martius report, that the minute one begins to question a Brazil Indian about his language he shows signs of impatience, complains of headache, and proves himself incapable of mental labour. Similarly the Abipones, when they find themselves unable to

[1] Spencer, *Principles of Sociology.*

understand anything at a glance, soon become fatigued and cry, "What, after all, does it amount to?" "It seems," Sir John Lubbock says, "as if the mind of the savage lives in a perpetual come and go of pure feebleness, incapable of fixing itself upon anything. He accepts what he sees as an animal does; he adapts himself to the world about him spontaneously; astonishment, admiration, the very conditions of worship are above him. Accustomed to the regularity of nature he patiently awaits the succession of such phenomena as he has observed, mechanical habit overbears all intelligence in him."

In effect, according to Mr. Spencer, all of the observed facts upon which the old fetichistic theory was founded are chargeable with inexactitude; they were taken from the narratives of the earlier travellers, who rarely came into contact with any but races already debauched and half civilized. Little by little, he says, the idea that fetichism is primordial took possession of men's minds and, as prepossession constitutes nine-tenths of belief, it has rested master of the field almost without a contest; I myself accepted it, although, as I remember, with a vague feeling of discontent. This discontent became positive doubt when I was better informed with regard to the ideas of the savage. From doubt I passed to negation when I had once tabulated the whole body of the facts relating to the most degraded races.

*Inexactitude of facts on which the fetich theory is founded.*

Mr. Spencer undertakes even to demonstrate *a priori* the falsity of the fetich theory. What, he asks, is a fetich? An inanimate object supposed to contain a being, of which the senses do not take cognizance; such a conception is extremely complex, and above the reach of primitive minds. The savage is so incapable of abstraction that he can neither conceive nor express a colour as distinct from some coloured object, a light as distinct from some light object—star or fire, an animal which shall be neither a dog nor a cow nor a horse; and he is asked to imagine an animate being in the heart of an inanimate thing, an invisible power in the heart of a visible object,

*A priori demonstration of the priority of animism.*

in effect, a soul! Nothing less than the conception of a soul, in Mr. Spencer's judgment, will serve the fetich hypothesis; and primitive man certainly could not attain the notion of a soul by mere observation of nature. Before projecting this complex idea into the heart of things, he must previously have constructed it, and as preparation for that, Mr. Spencer says, he must have supplied himself with a theory of death, and conceived the mind as surviving the body, and therefore as separable from the body and as the motive principle of the body. It is to his notions on death that man must look for any conception of life in inanimate nature. Every fetich is a spirit, no spirit can be for a primitive intelligence anything else than the spirit of someone who is dead. Necessarily, therefore, a cult for the dead, spiritism, must precede fetichism; the latter is no more than an extension, a by-product, of the former.[1]

III. Such is the theory of Mr. Spencer. And he would be right if the partisans of primitive fetichism understood by

Spencer's attack not against a vital spot.

fetich, as he does, a material object at the heart of which the adorer imagines the existence of a mysterious agent *distinct from this object itself*. But is this notion of distinctness a necessary part, at least in the beginning, of fetichism, or, as one says to-day, of naturism? Imagine a rock which should detach itself unexpectedly from the mountain side, and roll down to the hut of a savage; it stops suddenly just as it is on the point of crushing his dwelling, it remains there pendent, menacing, to all appearance ready at an instant's notice to begin rolling again; the savage fairly trembles at the sight of it. Do you believe that he needs really to suppose the presence of some foreign agent, of a soul, of an ancestral spirit in that stone to regard it as an object of fear and of respect? Not at all. It is the rock itself which constitutes his fetich, it is to the rock that he bows; he venerates it precisely because he is far from supposing it, as you do, essentially and eternally inert and passive; he ascribes to it possible inten-

[1] Mr. Spencer's *Principles of Sociology.*

tions, a maleficent or beneficent will. He says to himself : " It is asleep to-day, but it was awake yesterday ; yesterday it could have killed me, and it did not want to." Let the lightning strike a savage's hut three times in succession within a month, and he will easily recognize that the thunder is ill-disposed toward him and, quite without any preliminary need of personification in the way of endowing it with a departed soul, he will set about adoring the thunder and con-juring it not to do him harm. Mr. Spencer does not perceive that, at the very beginning of his exposition, he ascribes to primitive man a conception of nature analogous to the abstract mechanism of Descartes. Such a conception once pre-sup-posed, it is plain that to regard an object or a natural phe-nomenon as the centre of a cult, some new conception must be added to it, and this new conception may well be that of a spirit. Mr. Spencer, as he himself admits, looks upon fetich-ism as quite analogous to modern spiritualism, which sees in turning tables and oscillating chairs the work of disembodied souls ; but nothing could be more arbitrary than this analogy. It is quite impossible that primitive man should stand in the same position that we do in the face of any natural phe-nomenon ; as he does not possess the modern metaphysical idea of inert matter, he experiences no need to invent an indwelling spirit before he can ascribe volition to it. If a savage should see a table turn, he would say simply that the table was turning, no doubt, because it wanted to turn, and that, for him, would be the end of it ; and if by chance it should be a matter of interest to him whether the table turned or not, it would immediately become a fetich to him. The concep-tion of a fetich does not in the least presuppose, as Mr. Spencer maintains, the conception of a soul ; there is no such meta-physical element in fetichism, and it is precisely on that account that this form of religion must have preceded spirit-ism, which is always founded on a more or less rudimentary metaphysics.

For animals and savages, as for very young children, nature is absolutely the opposite of what it appears to be nowadays to the scholar and the philosopher : for them it is not a cold

and neuter habitat, in which man alone possesses aims and
bends everything to the fulfilment of his wishes; it is not
a physical laboratory full of inert instruments
for the service of man. On the contrary, nature
is a society; primitive people see intention in
everything. Friends or enemies surround them on all sides;
the struggle for existence is one long pitched battle with
imaginary allies against adversaries not infrequently only too
real. How should they understand that there is a profound
unity in nature which rigidly excludes from the chain of
things anything like individuality or independence? The
only cause of movement with which they are acquainted is
desire; they reckon desire or intention as the cause of every
movement in nature, as of every movement in their fellow-
men and in animals; and they conceive that the intentions
of all of the diverse beings by which they find themselves
surrounded may be equally modified by prayer and offerings.
Their conception of nature is at once anthropomorphic and
sociomorphic, as is subsequently their conception of God.
Nothing is more natural and inevitable than this fashion of
modeling the external world on the internal, and the relations
of things on the relations of men.

*For savages and children nature a society.*

If the word fetichism is too vague to designate this primitive state of mind and gives rise to confusion, take another
word; if the word *panthelism* were not a little
barbarous it would better express this stage of
human intelligence in which one is inclined to ascribe to all the
phenomena of nature not indeed souls, as distinct from bodies,
but simply intentions, desires, volitions, as naturally inhering
in the objects themselves.

*Panthelism.*

But here we shall perhaps be reminded that, as Mr. Spencer
says, the distinction between things animate and inanimate
is quite clear even to the brute, and, *a fortiori*, to
primitive man; so that primitive man will not
attribute desire or volition to a thing which he
knows to be inanimate—*animate, inanimate;* how we do come
back to the vague! Under each of these terms the modern
man ranges a group of ideas absolutely inaccessible to primi-

*English classifi-cation of things.*

tive man and to the lower animals.  Personally we deny that
the distinction between animate and inanimate was present
in the earliest stages of intellectual evolution.  Certainly both
the animal and the savage recognized a division of the phenomena of nature into two classes; one is composed of the
things which are disposed to do them good or evil, the other
is composed of those which ignore them simply; that is the
primitive distinction.  As to an acquaintance with animate
and inanimate they are innocent of anything of the kind; on
this point, as on all others, they confine themselves to the
grossest sense-experience.  Their senses inform them that
certain objects are beings who are altogether inoffensive, who
eat nobody and are not themselves good to eat; one gives
them no further attention; practically they do not exist.  I
one day asked a peasant woman the name of a small plant.
She looked at me with frank astonishment and replied, with a
shake of the head, " *Ce n'est rien*—it is nothing; it is not good
to eat!"  That woman was on a level with primitive man.
In the eyes of the latter, as in the eye of an animal, one-half
the phenomena of nature are *nothing*—they do not count; one
scarcely sees them.  The fruits on a tree, on the contrary, are
*good to eat*.  The savage, however, perceives immediately that
the fruit makes no active resistance, does not cry out when he
bites into it; and he considers it, therefore, as on all accounts
absolutely indifferent, except that it is good to eat.  But given
a fruit that poisons him, he promptly fears it and venerates it.
Similarly with animals : stones and vegetation hold equally
aloof from the carnivora, are practically as distant as the
moon and the stars.  The herbivora, on the contrary, pay no
attention to anything but vegetation.  Natural objects being
thus parcelled off into two classes, the class of the indifferent
and inoffensive, and the class of the useful and hurtful, the
animal soon learns to recognize that in the second class the
most important objects are those which possess spontaneity
of movement.  But in his eyes—and this is a fact of capital
importance—spontaneity of movement is not the exclusive
sign of *life*, of interior activity; it is a sign simply of utility,
or of heightened danger for him.  He is wholly preoccupied

with personal and practical consequences; he indulges in no superfluity of inference in regard to the object itself; he does not speculate. Moreover, a moving object which in nowise affects his sensibility rapidly becomes quite as indifferent to him as a motionless object. Animals soon become accustomed to the passage of railway trains: cows browse tranquilly, partridges on the brow of a hill scarcely lift their heads; and why? Because they have recognized in the locomotive an inanimate mechanism?[1] Not in the least; they observe simply that the locomotive never goes out of its way to damage them.

This being the primitive conception of the world, we believe that the more incapable an uncivilized being is of observing and reasoning the more natural it should be for him to acquire the conviction that objects which at first struck him as indifferent are not genuinely inanimate, but are sometimes malevolent in their intentions toward him, sometimes benevolent; that they possess in effect over him a quite respectable degree of power. In other words the more intelligent an animal or a savage becomes, the more superstitious he will be, and thus by the very progress of mental evolution the primitive distinction of objects into two classes will become dim—the distinction of objects into those which are altogether indifferent and outside of the society in which one lives, and those which are more or less worthy of attention, more or less closely in practical relations with us. Mental evolution has proceeded, believe us, in precisely the opposite direction to that imagined by Mr. Spencer.

Let us speak first of the more intelligent animals, before

*Belief that all things are animate natural to animals.*

[1] According to Mr. Spencer, the movement of a train does not appear spontaneous to animals because it is continuous; and therein lies the ground of their exemption from fright. On this reasoning, animals who live in the neighbourhood of stations should display fright at the arrival and departure of trains. Nothing of the kind is observable. They are equally incurious in regard to horses harnessed to wagons on a high-road. Speculative disinterestedness is altogether lacking in animals and savages; they live locked in the arms of sensation and desire; they spontaneously draw a circle about their ego, and whatsoever lies beyond lies beyond their intelligence.

passing to man. The more intelligent animals are often obliged to give their attention to a class of objects in appear-

Motion a mate-
rial sign of life
in them.

ance indifferent to them and to modify the imperfect ideas which they had at first conceived in regard to them. Generally speaking, objects of this sort are motionless; if immobility be not their essential distinguishing characteristic, it is at least one of their principal distinguishing characteristics. The instinct of self-preservation in a being inevitably bestirs itself in the presence of every movement that looks like a menace. Well, an animal is soon obliged to recognize that indifferent objects possess in certain circumstances the attribute of spontaneous movement, an attribute which is for him so vitally interesting. I remember the surprise a kitten once showed when it perceived the dead leaves rise in the wind and circulate about it; at first it ran away, and then came back and pursued the leaves, and smelt them, and touched them with its paw. Darwin relates that a dog was one day lying near an open parasol on the lawn; the parasol moved in the breeze, the dog began to bay, to growl furiously, and, every time that the parasol moved again, began to growl afresh. Evidently it was a new thing to Darwin's dog that such an object as a parasol might change its place without the visible intervention of some person; all the dog's classifications were thrown into disorder, he was no longer certain whether he must class the parasol with things indifferent or with things harmful. He would have experienced an analogous impression if he had seen a paralytic patient, always theretofore motionless in his armchair, suddenly rise and walk. An animal's surprise is still more strong when an object regarded as till then indifferent approaches him and manifests its activity by an infliction of sudden pain. I witnessed the astonishment of a cat which, having seen a red-hot coal roll out of the stove door, leaped forward to play with it; he caught it simultaneously with snout and paw, gave a cry of pain, and fled in such fear that it was two days before he returned to the house. Mr. Spencer himself cites another example which he has observed. The beast was a formidable creature, half mastiff, half hound, who was playing with a canè; he was leaping and gambolling, and holding it by the ferule end. Suddenly the handle of the cane touched the ground and the ferule was pushed forcibly back toward the dog's palate. The animal groaned, let the cane fall, and fled some distance away; and there he manifested, it appears, a degree of alarm truly comic in a beast apparently so ferocious. It was only after many cautious approaches and much hesitation that he yielded to the temptation of taking hold of the cane. Mr. Spencer, who supplies us with this fact, with great impartiality concludes from it, as we also do, that it was the unusual conduct of the cane which suggested to the dog the notion that it was animate; but he hastens to add that before the vague idea of animation thus given rise to in an animal could become definite in a man, the intervention of some spiritualistic theory would be absolutely necessary. One may well ask one's self what spiritualism has to do with the case.[1]

One may learn from the preceding example something like what animals conceive the inert instruments to be which they

**Instruments supposed to be animate by animals.** see us handling and with which we sometimes strike them. The notion of an instrument, as such, is relatively modern and was altogether unknown in the early stages of evolution. An instrument, in the eyes of an animal as in the eyes of primitive man, is almost a companion and an accomplice; neither the one nor the other possesses any other notion in especial of causation than that of a co-operation, mute agreement between two associated beings. A lion, which Livingstone shot at and did not hit, ran first to bite the stone which the bullet had struck; it was only subsequently that he threw himself upon the hunter; the ball, the gun, the hunter, were so many distinct and separate enemies that he was bent on punishing in succession. Similarly, in an ancient list of pains and penalties, one finds that the warrior is to lose his hand, the blasphemer his tongue, the spy his ears. At this moment my dog is at my side; the whip with which I corrected him this morning lies upon a chair; the dog walks about that chair sniffing the air with defiance and respect, and I do not believe he would

[1] *Principles of Sociology.*

have the courage to touch it, He is aware, however, that when the whip hurt him, the circumstances were quite different, that I was holding that dangerous object in my hand, and that I was, in a sense, the first cause of his chastisement. Still he is not perfectly reassured, as he would be in the presence of an inert object. The impression he seems to have got strikes me as comparable to that which a child receives from a serpent behind a pane of glass; the child knows perfectly that under the actual circumstances he is safe, but he cannot help saying to himself, "If the circumstances were otherwise!"[1] Recollect that the Australian savage treats the white man's gun as a living and powerful being which he adores and crowns with flowers and supplicates not to kill him. Legend attributes a magic power to the swords of great captains, to Joyeuse or to Durandal. In our own days, even, one sees combatants spend their force not only against their

---

[1] Add that when an animal or primitive man has recognized that a certain object possesses a particular attribute, he often finds it difficult to recognize that simply analogous objects possess the same attribute. I was one day making a kitten run after a wooden ball as a dog would do ; the ball struck it and hurt it ; it cried out and I petted it and then wanted to begin playing once more ; it would run willingly even after large stones when I threw them, but obstinately refused to run after the ball. So that it evidently conceived that the ball alone possessed the attribute of power to injure it ; the kitten looked upon the ball, no doubt, with an evil eye, regarded it perhaps as an evil being who was unwilling to play; by a fault of generalization the kitten created for itself a sort of fetich which it did not adore indeed, but which it feared, and fear is a step toward adoration.

Mr. Spencer himself admits in savages a certain inaptitude for generalization. This opinion, paradoxical as it may seem, is perhaps an important truth. If primitive intelligences, as M. Taine among others remarked, are especially prompt at noticing the superficial resemblances of things, that fact is not always a mark of genuine perspicacity, for the resemblance perceived between two sensations may be explicable less as an intelligent generalization than as a sort of confusion of the sensations themselves ; if sensations are analogous or indistinct, they may naturally be mistaken for each other without any exercise whatsoever of intelligence. Thence the comparative insignificance of many examples taken from the case of language. True generalization seems to consist, more than anything else, in the reduction of facts to law ; that is to say, in a conscious abstraction of differences, in a conscious recognition of the fundamental determinism which binds things up together and which precisely eludes both savages and animals.

Note finally that the majority of animals and of savages, when they have once been deceived, are slow to recover from their error, are for a long time distrustful

enemies but against everything which pertains to them ; it is as if something were supposed to have passed from the man into everything he possesses. Nothing is more difficult to recognize than the profound indifference of nature.

Mr. Spencer, who denies that the child spontaneously strikes the table which has wounded him, is not, however,

Conduct gener-
ates beliefs that
justify it.

unaware that a savage—the Indian Tupis, for example—if he has bruised his foot against a stone, leaps against it in fury and bites it like a dog. Mr. Spencer sees in such facts a phenomenon wholly physical, the need for spending one's rage in violent muscular action ; but this very need can but favour the birth of a psychological illusion, of which the tenacity will be proportionate to the intensity of the sentiment. The physical and the moral are too closely bound up together for a physical expression of anger not to be accompanied by a

toward the object which has deceived them. A dog, coming home one evening, perceived an empty cask in an unusual place. He was extremely frightened and barked for a long time ; it was only by day that he dared approach near the object of his alarm, and he examined and moved about it, and finally, like the frog in La Fontaine's fable, recognized that the thing was inoffensive. If the cask in question had disappeared during the night, the dog would evidently have remembered it as a redoubtable being seen the evening before in the yard. A monkey, which I left in the room with a cardboard sheep one entire day, proved unable to the end entirely to satisfy itself that the sheep was inanimate. I believe, however, that this persuasion was ultimately achieved, for the monkey began finally to pluck the sheep's wool and to treat it something too familiarly. But nature seldom permits us equally extended *tête-à-tête* with objects that alarm us.

Messrs. Spencer and Müller will call our attention to the fact, it is true, that cardboard sheep, no more than hand-organs or watches, exist *in rerum natura*. We reply that nature supplies primitive man with things much more astonishing : with rocks, and forests which can talk (the echo), with springs of hot water, with intermittent fountains. Mr. Fergusson (*Tree and Serpent Worship*) relates that in India he saw with his own eyes a tree which saluted the rising and setting sun, by lifting or lowering its boughs. Temples had formerly been reared in its neighbourhood. People came from all sides to see the marvellous tree. This tree was an old date-palm, half decayed, which hung above the road ; in order to pass below it, it had been held back by a rope ; but during this operation the fibres which composed the trunk were twisted like the threads in a rope. These fibres contracted toward midday in the heat of the sun ; the tree untwisted and rose. It relaxed under the dew at evening and once more bowed down. (See M. Girard de Rialle, *Mythologie comparée*, t. i.)

moral belief corresponding to the action; if a powerful instinct induces us to treat a stone as an enemy, we shall very really see an enemy in this stone.

Mr. Romanes made some observations, of the same kind as those of Mr. Spencer, upon a very intelligent Skye terrier. This terrier, like many other dogs, was accustomed to play with dried bones, throwing them into the air and endowing them with an appearance of life, for the pleasure of chasing them afterward. Mr. Romanes attached a long slender thread to a dried bone which he gave the dog to play with. After he had played for some time Mr. Romanes chose an opportune moment, when the bone had fallen to the ground some distance away, and the terrier was approaching it; he drew the bone gently away, by means of the thread attached to it. The attitude of the terrier changed entirely. The bone, which he had been pretending to regard as living, appeared to him to be really so, and his surprise knew no bounds. He approached it nervously and cautiously, as Mr. Spencer describes in the observation which he made; but the slow motion of the bone continued, and the dog became more and more certain that the movement could not be explained as resulting from the impulsion which he had communicated; his surprise became terror, and he ran away and hid himself under the table, to study from a distance the disconcerting spectacle of dried bones coming to life again !

*Romanes' experiments.*

Another of Mr. Romanes' experiments on the same dog shows that the sentiment of the mysterious was, in this animal, quite powerful enough to serve as an explanation of his conduct. Having taken the terrier into a carpeted room, Mr. Romanes rolled some soap-bubbles which an unsteady draft of air blew about the carpet. The dog took a great interest in the matter, and seemed unable to decide whether the bubbles were alive or not. At first he was very prudent, and followed the bubbles at a distance, but as he was encouraged to examine them more closely, he approached them with his ears up and his tail down, in evident apprehension ; the instant the bubble moved

*Soap-bubble experiment.*

he drew back. After a time, however, during which there was at least one bubble on the floor, he took courage, and, the scientific spirit gaining the upper hand over the sentiment of mystery, he became brave enough to draw slowly near one of them and to put his paw upon it, not without anxiety. Naturally the bubble burst, and his astonishment was vivid in the extreme. Mr. Romanes made other bubbles, but could not persuade the dog to approach them for a long time. After a while, however, he started again in pursuit of one, and endeavoured with much caution to put his paw upon it. The result was the same as before. After the second attempt it was impossible to induce him to make a third, and he ultimately ran out of the room and could not be coaxed back. The same experiment, tried by Professor Delbœuf on his dog Mouston, gave a still more striking result. At the blowing of the fourth bubble, his wrath knew no bounds, but he no longer sought to seize it, he contented himself with barking at it, in all the accents of rage, until it burst. Professor Delbœuf wished to continue the experiment, and attempted to do so, but, to his great regret, was obliged to break off because of the frenzy into which the dog had worked himself. The moment that Professor Delbœuf laid his hand upon the vessel containing the soap-suds, the dog was no longer under his control. His condition was evidently due, Professor Delbœuf says, to a contradiction between the fact and his experience, that everything which is coloured is tangible. He was in the presence of the unknown, with all its mysteries and menaces; the unknown, which is the source of fear and of superstition.

According to Mr. Romanes the fear that many animals have of thunder is due, in some sort, to a sentiment of mystery. He once possessed a setter, which, he says, had not heard thunder until it had reached the age of eighteen months, when it almost died of fear. He has observed the same phenomenon in other animals, in diverse circumstances. The fright of the setter in question was so strong that, subsequently, when he heard some artillery practice and mistook it for thunder, his aspect

*Fear of thunder in animals due to sense of mystery.*

was positively pitiable, and in the midst of the chase he endeavoured to hide himself, or to gain the house.  After two or three experiences of thunder his horror of cannon became greater than ever, so much so that, in spite of his love for the chase, it was impossible to coax him out of his kennel, so great was his fear that the artillery practice might recommence and he be distant from the house.  But the keeper, who had had a wide experience of dogs, assured Mr. Romanes that, if the dog were once taken to the battery and shown the veritable cause for a noise analogous to that of thunder, he would become once more fit for the hunt.  Mr. Romanes does not doubt that such would have been the case, for once, when sacks of apples were being emptied, it made a noise in the house like distant thunder ; the setter was very restless, but when Mr. Romanes took him where the sacks were being opened and showed him the real cause of the noise, his terror left him, and on his return to the house he listened to the low rumbling in perfect quietude.

When one looks close one is surprised to see how many causes would naturally lead one to attribute life, and life of an

All natural phenomena tend to seem artificial to primitive man. extraordinary and mysterious character, to such and such really passive objects.  Such causes act evidently with greatly additional power upon the savage, the primitive man, the man of the quaternary epoch, or upon the anthropoid, as yet undiscovered, whose instruments have been found in the tertiary period.  Common animals, in effect, are almost lacking in attention ; from which it results that to produce any durable mental effect on them, a prolonged repetition of the same sensation is necessary ; they must be accustomed to it.  Moreover their crude intelligence takes no impression from evanescent facts, they are unaquainted with the external world except by averages.  Exceptional facts strike them for an instant, but presently glance off into oblivion.  In this imperfect machine, wear and tear is very rapid and the traces of phenomena inevitably blur and become confounded.  If animals possess a memory for sensations, they lack an intellectual memory altogether ; they are capable of surprise, but not of remembering a surprise. To produce in them a tenacious memory demands a setting of pain or pleasure, and even then, if they recollect the sensation they experienced, they readily forget the grounds of it. They feel passively, instead of observing. From the moment where, with man, the spirit of observation enters upon the scene everything is different; an exceptional fact, for the same reason that it becomes rapidly effaced in an animal intelligence, penetrates the more deeply into the memory of a man. Moreover, man's sphere of action is much wider than that of any animal, and consequently the field of his experience is much more vast; the more he modifies, voluntarily, the face of nature, the more capable he becomes of recognizing and observing the variations which it presents, independently of his interventions. Man possesses a notion unknown to animals, the notion of *artificial* things, of results deliberately attained by self-conscious volition. One remembers that *fetich* comes from *factitius*, artificial. Man, being acquainted with the use of fire, will regard, for example, a forest set ablaze by lightning from entirely a different point of view from what any animal could : the animal will flee without any other sentiment than that of alarm ; the man will naturally suppose the existence of some person who set it on fire—who was acting, who was doing on a grand scale what he himself sometimes does. Similarly with a boiling spring ; this phenomenon lies too far beyond the limits of animal intelligence to be especially striking ; but a man, on the other hand, who habitually goes to some trouble to provide himself with boiling water, infers the existence of some subterranean person who is heating water for purposes of his own. All natural phenomena tend thus to appear artificial to the eyes of a being who has once familiarized himself with the notion of artifice. I was present recently among some members of the lower classes at the flowing of an intermittent spring ; not one of them was inclined to believe the phenomenon a natural one, they regarded it as an effect of some mechanism, of some artifice. The same belief is evidently common among primitive people, with this difference, that artificial, instead of suggesting mechanics, implies the notion of a superhuman and marvellous power.

Just as the animal finds the rationale of all things in a notion of life and of activity, man tends to find a rationale of all things in a conception of art and of scheming intelligence. For the one, surprising phenomena are simply inexplicable conduct; for the other, they are the complex effects of deliberative intelligence, they are master-pieces. But the notion of activity, far from becoming effaced in the progress of evolution, becomes simply more definite and more precise. Given his incomplete experience, primitive man is perfectly logical in attributing intelligence and consciousness to nature, he could not rationally do otherwise; his mind is imprisoned in a blind alley, and superstition is the sole outlet. At a given moment in human evolution, superstition was perfectly rational.

*Fetichism a logical theory to primitive man.*

Even in our days, men of science are greatly embarrassed by their inability to point out the precise line of demarcation between the animate and the inanimate; and how should primitive man have grappled with this problem? How distinguish, for example, between sleep and death during one entire portion of life; during sleep, living bodies lie inert, and why should not inert bodies sometimes prove to be alive? At night especially, the whole becomes transformed, everything becomes animate, a breath of wind suffices to make everything palpitate; it seems as if all nature awakened after its day's sleep; it is the hour when wild beasts go in search of prey, and mysterious noises fill the forest. The calmest imagination, under such circumstances, yields to a temptation to see fantastic objects that are not. One night I was walking on the sea-shore, and saw distinctly a gigantic beast moving some distance away; it proved to be a perfectly motionless rock, in the midst of others like it, but the waves, which alternately covered and discovered it in part, lent it, to my eyes, some portion of their own mobility. How many things in nature borrow thus from some circumstance—from the wind, from a more or less uncertain light—an appearance of life![1]

*Seeming immanence of conscious life in nature.*

[1] Mr. H. Russell, the explorer of the Pyrenees, remarks 'the fantastic effects produced by the moonlight in the mountains. As the moonlight replaced the

Even when the eyes themselves would be incapable of self-deception, the influence of the foolish terrors so frequent among children and beings habituated to savage life would count enormously. Emotional susceptibility is the more highly developed among savages, in that it forms for them frequently a means of safety. And primitive man is much more subject than we are to hallucinations of the sort that are due to terror, and are not wholly fantastic, but result from a fantastic interpretation of some genuine sense stimulus. The traveller Park met two negroes on horseback; they fled from him at a gallop in extreme terror, and meeting his followers in the course of their flight reported that they had seen him dressed in the floating robes of some redoubtable spirit. One of them affirmed that at sight of Park he had felt himself enveloped in a breath of cold air from heaven, which was like a jet of cold water. Suppress the word spirit in this passage, which implies a pre-existing belief in the soul, and you will perceive how hallucinations due to terror may well give birth to beliefs all the more tenacious for the element of truth they contain.

Dreams also have played a considerable rôle in the genesis of superstitions, as Epicurus and Lucretius remarked, and the

*Dreams.* labours of Messrs. Tylor and Spencer have proved. Primitive language supplies no means of saying, " I dreamt that I saw "; one must say simply, " I saw." Well, in the dreams which the savage himself can scarcely distinguish from reality, he sees nothing but a perpetual series of metamorphoses, of the transformation of men

previous shadow on the faces and the angles of the rocks, he says, in an account of the ascension of the peak of Eriste, they seemed so plainly to move that once he mistook one of them for a bear and cocked the revolver at his side. The same explorer remarks also the surprising transformations which natural objects undergo at nightfall and at daybreak. At dawn, he says, there is a sort of universal shiver which seems to animate everything ; the sound of the neighbouring cascade changed frequently ; at break of day, after having groaned and thundered alternately, it begins to scold. For in the morning in the mountains, he says, sounds gain magnitude, they swell, and torrents in especial lift their voices as if angry ; with the arrival of the day the air becomes sonorous and sound carries farther. He has experienced this, he says, frequently, but does not understand the cause.—*Alpine Club*, 1887.

into ferocious beasts, and of ferocious beasts into men ; he dreams that he picks up a stone, and that it comes to life in his hand ; he looks out upon a motionless lake, and it becomes suddenly a crawling mass of crocodiles and of serpents.[1] How can Mr. Spencer maintain, after that, that primitive man can distinguish with some degree of certainty the animate from the inanimate ? Not only during dreams, but during wakefulness, everything suggests to primitive man the notion of changes of substance and magic metamorphoses. Eggs, which are inanimate, change into birds or insects ; dead flesh becomes living worms ; an effigy, under the influence of memory, seems to live again and to respire.[2]

An animal is not sufficiently master of its sensations to follow their course throughout their successive modifications ; it is not in any proper sense a witness, as man is, of the progress, of the perpetual movement and transformation of all things ; nature is, for it, a series of detached pictures of which it does not seize the contrasts. When man, on the contrary, follows attentively the more or less slow evolution of things, he perceives the effacement of every fundamental difference between the animate and the inanimate, he observes a process of blind mechanical labour, which produces life in objects in appearance quite inert. Is there not something rationally profound and justifiable in the very naïveté with which he interprets nature? Poetry is often philosophy in its most penetrating form.

*Primitive man humanizes nature.*

---

[1] Spencer's *Sociology.*

[2] Savages imagine that they see the eyes of portraits move. I myself saw a child of two years old, accustomed to play with engravings, one day in a great fright snatch away its grandmother's finger, which was resting on the picture of a ferocious beast. " Big beast bite grandmamma ! " These ideas, which totally ignore the profound and definitive difference between animate and inanimate, are fixed in the human mind. A man of distinguished education once maintained to me quite seriously that certain petrifactive springs in the Pyrenees possessed the power of changing sticks into serpents. For one capable of imagining that a bit of wood might thus become a serpent, what difficulty would there be in believing that the bit of wood is alive (even a bit of dead wood), that the spring is alive (in especial a spring with such marvellous properties), and finally that the mountain itself is alive ; everything is animate to eyes like that, and possessed of magic power.

Who has not asked himself sometimes if a puissant and hidden spring of life does not circulate unknown to us in the high mountains, in the still trees, and in the restless ocean, and if mute nature does not live in one long course of meditation upon themes unknown to us? And since even nowadays we ourselves are full of such vague doubts as that, do we imagine that it would be easy to convince one of these primitive men of his error, when he fancies that he feels the beating of what the Germans call the "heart of nature"? After all is the primitive man wrong? Everything about us does live, nothing is inanimate except in appearance, inertia is a word simply; all nature is one universal aspiration, modern science alone can measure with some approach to accuracy the activity with which all things are saturated, and show it to us, here existent in a state of diffusion, there in a state of concentration, and self-conscious, and make us acquainted with the difference between the higher organisms and the lower organisms, and between the latter and mechanisms and rudimentary groupings of bits of matter. For primitive man, to whom all these distinctions, all the gradations are impossible, there is but one thing evident, and that is that the whole of nature lives; and he naturally conceives this life on the model of his own, as accompanied by self-consciousness, by an intelligence the more astonishing in that it is mysterious. Moreover he is a man, and *humanizes* nature; he lives in society with other men, and conceives all things in terms of social relations of friendship or of enmity.

From the humanization to the divinization there is but one step; let us endeavour to make it. Whoever says *god*, means And divinizes it. a living and powerful being worthy, in some especial degree, of fear, of respect, or of gratitude. Primitive man possesses already, let us suppose, some notion of life; he needs now to be supplied with some notion of power, which alone is capable of inspiring him with reverence, and this notion it does not seem difficult for a being to obtain, who sees in all nature an expression of a manifold conscious life, and who must recognize in certain great phenomena the manifestation of a will much more powerful

than that of any man, and consequently more redoubtable
and worthy of respect. Here also, however, we encounter
serious objections from Mr. Spencer and from anthropolo-
gists like M. Le Bon; the question becomes more complex.

According to Mr. Spencer, as we have seen, the most
important phenomena of nature, and among others the rising

Natural phe-<br>nomena quite<br>striking enough<br>to be adored on<br>their own account. and the setting of the sun, are precisely those
which must be least striking to primitive man;
they cannot appear to him to be *extraordinary*
because they happen every day; so that he
experiences before them neither surprise nor admiration.
This argument is very ingenious, but is it not also a
little sophistical? If it were pushed to the end it would
amount simply to the fact that there is nothing surprising
or unusual in nature, nothing which breaks with the preconceived association of ideas, nothing which seems to manifest the sudden intervention of strong or violent powers. The
fact, however, is quite the contrary; nature is full of surprises
and of terrors. The day may be fine; suddenly the clouds
gather and the thunder rolls—the fear of thunder felt by animals
has already been spoken of; in the mountains especially the
rumbling, re-echoing, fills them with unspeakable terror.
Droves of cattle lose all control of themselves and throw themselves headlong down precipices. It is with great difficulty that
the herdsman by his presence and exhortations keeps his herd
in order; probably the beasts see in the herdsman a powerful
friend, capable of protecting them against this terrible being
whom the Hindus call the "howler." If animals tremble
thus before the thunder, it is unlikely that primitive man
should see nothing in it abnormal and extraordinary. Similarly with the hurricane, which seems like an enormous
respiration, as of a universe out of breath. Similarly with the
tempest: one knows the Basque proverb: "If you want to
learn to pray, go to sea." Everyone who finds himself in the
hands of a victorious enemy is naturally inclined to beg for
mercy. Let there supervene a sudden calm; at the moment
when the tempest was about to break, let the sun reappear
like a great smiling face, chasing away the cloud with his

arrow of gold, and will it not seem a benevolent auxiliary; will it not be received with cries of joy and enthusiasm? Nature is incessantly showing us thus some unexpected change of scene, producing some theatrical effect which inevitably suggests some anthropomorphic drama, in which the elements and the stars are the actors. How many strange things happen in the sky when once the attention is directed thither! Eclipses of the moon and of the sun, and the very phases of the moon, are abundantly calculated to astonish the very savages whom Messrs. Spencer and Müller declare to be incapable of astonishment. Note, too, that the simple view of the stars at night provokes a lively admiration in any-one who is accustomed to sleep under a roof. I remember still my surprise, when, as a child, I was awake for the first time in the night and lifted my eyes by chance on high and perceived the heaven glittering with stars; it was one of the most striking impressions of my life.[1]

In effect, earth and sky incessantly furnish mankind with

[1] Let us remember in this connection that, according to Wuttke, J. G. Müller, and Schultze, a cult for the moon and nocturnal stars must have preceded that of the sun, contrary to the weight of opinion heretofore. The moon's phases were calculated to take the attention of primitive people, and must early have done so. One must, however, in this connection be on one's guard against generalizing too quickly and believing that the evolution of human thought has in all places followed the same route. Habitats differ too widely for there not to have been in the beginning an infinite diversity in the religious conceptions entertained by different peoples. In Africa, for example, it is evident *a priori* that the sun does not possess all the characteristics of a divinity. It is never desired or regretted, as in a northern country; it is, to all appearance at least, rather maleficent than beneficent; and the Africans adore by preference the moon and stars, the gentle radiance of which affords them light without oppressive heat, refreshes and reposes them from the fatigues of the day. The moon is considered by them as a male and all-powerful being, of which the sun is the female. It is when the new moon arises, after its period of absence from the heavens, and begins once more the round of its visible phases, that it is received and saluted with an especial demonstration of cries and dances. The Congo blacks go the length of seeing in the moon a symbol of immortality (M. Girard de Rialle, *Mythologie comparée*, p. 148). America, on the contrary, has been the centre of the worship of the sun. In general it seems that agriculture must of necessity result in the triumph of sun worship over moon worship, for the labourer is more dependent upon the sun than the hunter or the warrior. According to J. G. Müller, savage and warlike races have displayed a preference for the moon.

new impressions capable of stimulating the most torpid imagination, and of appealing to the whole round of human and social sensibilities: fear, respect, gratitude. With these three elements it is easy to account for the genesis of the religious sentiment.[1] If, then, our ancestors adored the dawn, we do not believe, with Max Müller, that it was because it seemed to open the gates of heaven and reveal to them a vision of the infinite ; we do not admit, with Mr. Spencer, that a cult for the stars is reducible in the last resort to a simple confusion of names, and was originally but an off-shoot from ancestor worship due originally to the soul of some ancestor, who was metaphorically called in his lifetime by the name of the sun or of some star. It seems to us that one might quite well worship the sun and the stars on their own account, or rather on account of the relation they bear to us.

To sum up, the simplest, the most primitive conception that man can form of nature is to regard it, not as a manifold of interdependent phenomena, but as a multitude of

Summary.

conscious and voluntary beings, more or less independent and endowed with extreme power, capable of acting upon each other and upon mankind. Scientific determinism cannot but be a much later conception, incapable of suggesting itself in the early stages of human thought. The world once conceived thus as a collection of physically powerful, voluntary beings, man comes, in the course of time, to endow these beings, morally and socially, with qualities according to the manner in which they conduct themselves toward him. "The moon is naughty this evening," a child said to me ; "it will not show itself." Primitive man said also that the hurricane was naughty, the thunder was naughty, and so forth, whereas the sun, the moon, the fire, when they gave him pleasure, were good and beneficent.

---

[1] As has been remarked, the adoration of natural forces has been observed under two forms. It has been addressed sometimes to regular and calm phenomena (Chaldeans, Egyptians), sometimes to changing and portentous phenomena (Jews, Indo-Europeans). It almost always results in the personification of these forces.

Well, given a world of voluntary beings sometimes good, sometimes evil, armed with irresistible power, easy to irritate, prompt to take vengeance as man is himself, are they not gods? And if primitive man thus possesses gods, does he not also possess a religion as the ceremonial which regulates his social relations with the gods? To create a religion we need, in effect, to add but one idea to those already dealt with—the idea that it is possible by such and such conduct, by offerings, by supplications, to influence the superior beings with which nature is peopled; but this idea, which seems to us quite simple, did not, however, appear before a relatively advanced stage of int llectual evolution. A savage animal is scarcely acquainted with any other means of influencing other beings than biting, growling, and menacing; if these means fail, he counts on flight. A mouse has no hope of influencing a cat in any manner whatsoever; once between the cat's paws, it knows there is but one resource, to run away; still the animal ultimately, and in especial at the period of courtship, learns to recognize the power of caresses and attentions; it does not, however, occur to him to employ these means toward any but individuals of the same species. Moreover, the animals must be social before the language of manners can attain even a very humble degree of development; the animal confines itself generally to caresses with the tongue, with the head, with the tail. Evidently, also, such means would be inappropriate in regard to beings which did not possess a hide and coat of hair; an animal would not lick a tree or a stone, even if it attributed to them an unwonted degree of power. So that even if the brute, as Auguste Comte supposed, really possessed fetichistic conceptions more or less vague, it would experience a complete inability to manifest its goodwill in any manner whatsoever toward its rudimentary fetiches.

Superstitious fear is one of the elements of religion which, after all, is well within the capacity of an animal, but this fear cannot in an animal produce even the first steps of an embryo cult. An animal is ignorant of the means of touching, of captivating, of the infinitely complex language of affection and reverence. Comparatively inaccessible to pity himself, he has no notion how to act to excite pity in another; the conception of a gift, of an offering, so essential to the relations of men to each other and to their gods is, save in rare instances, to it unknown.   The most primitive cult is always essentially a counterfeit of an advanced social state; an imitation, in an imaginary commerce with the gods, of a commerce already existing among men united by complex ties.   Religion implies a nascent art of sociability, an elementary acquaintance with the springs which regulate the conduct of beings in society; there is a certain rhetoric in prayer, in genuflections and pros- trations.   Everything of that kind is far beyond the range of the lower animals.   One may discover among them, however, some traces of the process of evolution which man must have followed.   It is, in especial, under domestication that an ani- mal's manners reach their highest development.   Their asso- ciation with a superior being resembles, more closely than anything else in nature, the state in which primitive man believed himself to live with his gods.   The dog seems at times to put up a veritable prayer to the master who is beat- ing it, when it crawls at his feet and whimpers.   This attitude, however, provoked by the fear of a blow, is perhaps in a large measure instinctive and not reflectively designed to excite pity.   The true prayer of the dog consists in licking the hand which wounds him; the story is well known of the dog that licked the fingers of his master while the latter was pitilessly practising upon him an experiment in vivisection.   I myself observed an analogous fact in an enormous dog from the Pyrenees whose eye I had to cauterize; he might have crushed my hand, and he simply licked it feverishly.   It is almost an example of religious submission; the sentiment which is observable in embryo in the dog is the same as that which in its complete development appears in the Psalms and the book of Job.   The lower animals display such a sentiment toward no other being but man.   As to man himself, he displays it only toward his gods, toward an absolute chief or a father. Profound, however, as this sentiment is in some animals, their expression of it is quite imperfect; though I remember a case in which the action of licking, so habitual with dogs, was almost like a human kiss. I was embracing my mother, at the door of the house, before leaving for a journey, when my Pyrenees dog ran up to us, and, placing his paws upon our shoulders literally kissed both of us. From that time on (we have tried the experiment) he never sees us embrace each other without coming to demand his kiss.

Another well-known fact, and worthy of remark, is the following: when a dog or even a cat has committed some reprehensible act, has eaten the roast or done something clumsy, it comes toward one with a thousand little attentions; in so much that I have found myself able to divine when my dog had committed a peccadillo simply by observing his unwonted demonstrations of friendship. The animal hopes therefore, by force of his social graces and attentions, to prevent his master from holding a grudge against him, to deprecate the wrath that his culpable conduct ought legitimately to arouse, and to awaken in its stead some degree of benevolence by his demonstrations of submission and affection. This notion of compensation becomes later an important element in the religious cult. The Neapolitan brigand who dedicates a wax candle to the altar of the Virgin; the mediæval lord, who, after having killed his next of kin, rears a chapel to some saint, the hermit who lacerates his chest with his hair shirt in order to avoid the more redoubtable pangs of hell, reason precisely after the same fashion as my dog, they are endeavouring, like him, to conciliate their judge, and, to be quite frank, to corrupt him, for superstition rests in a great measure upon the belief that it is possible to corrupt God.

*Notion of Compensation.*

The most difficult notion to discover among animals is that of the voluntary and conscious gift; the solidarity observed among certain insects, for example the ant, which causes them to hold all their goods in common, is something too instinctive and irreflective; a veritable gift must address itself to some determinate person, and not to an entire society; it must possess a degree of spontaneity that excludes any hypothesis of pure instinct; and finally, it must be as far as possible a sign of affection,

*Notion of conscious gift.*

a symbol. And the more symbolic its character, the more religious, properly speaking, it will be ; religious offerings are more than anything else a symbolic testimony of respect ; piety scarcely plays a part in them, one does not in general believe that they answer to any real need on the part of the gods, one believes that they will be rather accepted by them than seized upon with avidity. The notion of a gift, therefore, presupposes a certain delicacy and refinement. Some germ of this sentiment, however, we discover precisely in a dog observed by Mr. Spencer. This dog, a very intelligent and very valuable spaniel, met one morning, after an absence of some hours, a person of whom he was very fond. He amplified his ordinary greeting by an addition which was not habitual ; he drew back his lips in a sort of smile, and, once out of doors, offered other demonstrations of fidelity. As a hunter he had been trained to bring game to his master. He no doubt regretted that there was no game at the moment for him to bring as a means of expressing his affection ; however he rummaged about, and seizing presently a dead leaf, carried it to his master with a multitude of caressing gestures.[1] Evidently the leaf possessed for the dog no more than a symbolic value ; he knew that it was his duty to retrieve game, and that the action of retrieving gave pleasure to his master, and he wished to accomplish this action under his eyes, as to the object itself it made little difference ; it was his goodwill that he wished to show    The dead leaf was a veritable offering, it possessed a sort of moral value.

Thus animals may acquire, by contact with man, a certain number of sentiments which enter later into human religion.

Elements of which religion is compounded within the reach of the lower animals.

The monkey in this respect, as in all others, seems much in advance of the other animals. Even in the savage state a number of simiæ display gestures of supplication to deprecate the firing of a gun at them :[2] They possess the sentiment of pity, since they ascribe it to others. Who knows but that there may be in this mute prayer more of real relig-

[1] H. Spencer, *Appendix to the Principles of Sociology.*
[2] Brehm, *Revue scientifique*, p. 974, 1874.

ious sentiment than exists sometimes in the psittacism of certain believers? Animals in general employ in their relations
with man the maximum of the means of expression at their
disposal, and it is not their fault if the means are limited; they
seem to consider man as a really royal being, a thing apart in
nature.[1] Must one conclude, as is sometimes done, that man
is a god in the eyes of the rest of the animal kingdom? Not
altogether; the lower animals see man too close; even in
an embryonic religion one must not be able to touch God
with one's finger; in religion as in art, there is an advantage in
perspective. My dog and I are companions; sometimes he is
jealous, sometimes he pouts. I am unhappily in no respect,
in his eyes, on a pedestal. There are, however, evidently
exceptions, cases in which the master seems to preserve his
prestige. I believe that under certain circumstances man has
appeared to some members of the lower animals as endowed
with a power so extraordinary that he must have awakened
some vague religious sentiments; if man is sometimes a god
to his fellow-men, he may well be so to the lower animals. I
am aware that in the judgment of certain philosophers, and
even of certain men of science, religion is the exclusive appan-
age of the human race, but up to this point we have found in
primitive religion no more than a certain number of simple
ideas, not one of which, taken separately, is above the reach of
the lower animals. Just as industry, art, language, and reason,
so religion also has its roots in the nebulous and confused consciousness of the animal. The animal, however, rises to such
ideas only at moments. He is unable to maintain himself at
their level, to synthesize them, to reduce them to a system.
His attention is too mobile for him to regulate his conduct by
them. Even if an animal were quite as capable of conceiving a god as is the lowest of savages, he would remain forever
incapable of a religious cult.

We have seen that the birth of religion is not a species of
theatrical effect in nature, that preparation is being made for
it among the higher animals, and that man himself achieves it

[1] Espinas, *Sociétés animales*, p. 181.

gradually, and without shock.   In this rapid effort to trace the
genesis of primitive religions, we have found no need to rely
upon the conceptions of the soul, of spirit, of the
infinite, of a first cause, nor upon any metaphysical sentiment.   These ideas are of later date;

they are the product of religion, rather than the roots of it.
The basis of religion was in the beginning quite positive and
natural; religion is simply a mythical and sociomorphic
theory of the physical universe, and it is only at its summit,
at an advanced degree of evolution, that it comes into contact
with metaphysics.   Religion lies beyond and at the side of
science.   Superstition, in the strict sense of the word, and
primitive religion were one, and it is not without reason that
Lucretius compares the two : *relligio, superstitio.*   To be present at the birth of religion is to perceive an erroneous scientific conception, gathering other errors or incomplete verities
to itself, entering into one body of belief with them, and ultimately, little by little, subordinating them.   The earliest
religions were systematized and organized superstitions.   Be
it added that in our judgment superstition consists simply in
an ill-conducted scientific induction, in a mistaken effort of
human reason ; and we do not wish to be understood as intending by that the mere play of the imagination ; we do not
wish to be understood as holding that religion is founded in the
last resort on a species of recreation of the mind.   How often
the birth of religion has been attributed to an alleged appetite
for the marvellous, for the extraordinary, which is supposed to
seize upon young peoples as upon infants !   A singularly artificial explanation for a very natural and profound tendency.
To say the truth, what primitive peoples were in search of
when they built up their different religions was an explanation, and the least surprising explanation possible, the explanation most in harmony with their rude intelligence, the most
rational explanation.   It was infinitely less marvellous for an
ancient to suppose that the thunder came from the hand of
Indra or of Jupiter, than to believe it to be the product of a
certain force called electricity ; the myth was for him a much
more satisfying explanation ; it was the most plausible one

that he could hit upon, given his intellectual habitat. So that if science consists in relating things, Jupiter and Jehovah may be regarded as rudimentary scientific conceptions. If they are no longer such, the reason is simply that we have discovered the natural and regular laws which supersede them. When a task, so to speak, begins to perform itself, one dismisses the employee who had previously been charged with it ; but one should be careful not to say that he was previously good for nothing, that he had been stationed there by caprice or by favour. If our gods seem nowadays to be purely honorary, the fact was otherwise at a previous period. Religions are not the work of caprice ; they correspond to an invincible tendency in man, and sometimes in the lower animals, to try to understand what passes before his eyes. Religion is nascent science, and it was with purely physical problems that it at first essayed to grapple. It was a physics *à côté*, a paraphysics, before becoming a science *au delà*, a metaphysics.

# CHAPTER II.

## RELIGIOUS METAPHYSICS.

## I. Animism.

THE upshot of the preceding chapter is that every religion in its beginning consisted of a mistaken system of physics; and

Legitimate and illegitimate metaphysics. between a mistaken system of physics and certain forms of metaphysics there is often no difference but one of degree simply. Magnify some scientific error, reduce it to a system, explain heaven and earth by it, and it will be a metaphysics—in the bad sense. Whatever one universalizes—error or truth—acquires metaphysical significance, and possibly it is more easy to universalize in this way the false than the true ; truth possesses always a greater concreteness than error, and therefore offers greater resistance to arbitrary fashioning. Let a modern man of science develop his knowledge as he will, and enlarge the circle of known phenomena ; so long as he holds vigorously by scientific methods he will never be able to pass at a bound from the sphere of phenomena to the sphere of things in themselves. The conscientious man of science is prisoned within the limits of knowledge, his thought has no outlet. But let him once break the chain of logic which confines him, and behold him free. His false hypothesis grows without obstacle or check from reality ; he lands at a bound up to his neck in metaphysics. The fact is, one may arrive at a system of metaphysics in two ways—incontinently, by a logical solecism and an exaggeration of some false premise *ad infinitum*, or by following the chain of known truth to the point at which it disappears in eternal night, and by endeavouring to peer into the darkness by the light of hypothesis : in the first case metaphysics is simply a logically developed mistake which gains in magnitude what it loses in reality, an illegitimate negation of science ; in the second case it is a hypothetical extension of truth, in some sort a legitimate supplement to science.

We are approaching the moment when religious physics became transformed into metaphysics ; the period when the gods retreated from phenomenon to phenomenon, and took refuge ultimately in the supersensible ; the period when heaven and earth first became distinct and separate ; although, to be quite accurate, the distinguishing characteristic of religion even at the present day is an incoherent mixture of physics and metaphysics, of anthropomorphic or sociomorphic theories in regard to nature and to the supernatural. The foundation of every primitive religion is reasoning by analogy, that is to say, the vaguest and least sound of logical methods. At a later date the mass of naïve analogies constituting any one religion is criticised and systematized and completed by tentative induction or regular deduction.

Man, as we have seen, begins by creating a natural society, including animals, plants, and even minerals, which he endows with a life similar to his own : he believes himself to be in communication with them in matters of volition and intention, just as he is in communication with other men and animals. But in thus projecting something analogous to his own life, to his power of volition and of his social relations and responsibilities, into the exist-

Primitive metaphysics a fetichistic monism.

ence of external things, he does not, at first, dream of any distinction between the animating principle and the body which it animates; he conceives as yet no such distinction in his own case. The earliest stage of religious metaphysics, therefore, is not a sort of vague monism relative to the divine principle, the indwelling divinity of things, τὸ 9εῖον, as Messrs. Müller and Von Hartmann affirm, but a vague monism in regard to the soul and body, which at first are conceived as one. The whole world is a society of living *bodies*.

The conception which is most analogous to the preceding is that of distinct and separate souls animating each its body, of spirits capable of quitting each its dwelling-place. It is this that historians of religion mean by animism. What is remarkable in this conception is its dualistic character. It contains the germ of the opposition between soul and body. The dualistic conception arises slowly from a number of naïve analogies. The first are borrowed from the fact of respiration. Does not one fairly hear the departure of the breath animating a living body, in what one calls the last gasp? Other analogies are borrowed from the physical fact of the shadow cast by the sun ; one seems to see the spirit marching side by side with the body, and even changing its place when the body is motionless. Shadow has played a large rôle in the paraphysics of primitive peoples; shadows people the other world. In the third place, during sleep it is incontestable, on the premises that primitive man has at his disposal, that the spirit sometimes makes long journeys, for the sleeper often recollects wandering, hunting, or making war in distant countries, at a time when his companions are perfectly aware that his body has lain motionless. Fainting also seems to be a case in which something dwelling in us suddenly leaves and presently comes back again. Lethargy is a more striking example of the same thing. Visions in delirium, hallucinations in madness, or even in dreams, deal with beings who are invisible to others ; fantastic beings who appear to savages as real as any others. Also it is well known that fools and innocents were regarded, until modern times, as inspired and sacred. Other

*Becomes a dualistic animism. Separate existence of the soul.*

nervous maladies—hysteria, "possession," somnambulism—add their quota of precision to the conception of a spirit animating the body, dwelling in it, quitting it more or less at will, tormenting it, etc.

Thus, by degrees, there arises the conception of a subtle mode of being eluding touch, and commonly vision even, capable of a life independent of the body it inhabits, and more powerful than the body. Man comes to believe himself to be living in a society with beings other than those who appeal directly and grossly to his senses; he believes himself to be living in a society of spirits.

That is not all. The problem of death early engaged the attention of primitive people. They considered it altogether as a physical affair; they explained it, as Messrs.

**Ghosts.**

Tylor and Spencer (following Lucretius) have shown, by a number of inductions drawn from observations on sleep, lethargy, and dream. A sleeping body awakes, it seems to follow that a dead body will awake; that is the line of reasoning. Moreover, the dead come back in dreams, or in the demi-hallucinations of the night and of fear. The modern conception of pure spirit is an indirect and later consequence of a belief in immortality, it is not itself the principle of it. A cult for the dead, for the manes, as the Romans said, is partly explicable on moral or psychological grounds, as, for example, by a prolongation of filial respect and fear, and partly on grounds altogether material and gross. A cult for the dead rests on a naïve theory based on sentiment; it is semi-physical and semi-psychological. The nature of a departed soul has been conceived in very different ways. Among the Dakota Indians of North America, one's double goes up into the air, one's *third* rejoins the spirits, one's fourth and last soul stays by the body; an instance of a very complicated theory formed out of elements altogether primitive. In general, the belief is that the souls of the dead go to join ancestral souls in another world, which is commonly a distant land from which the tribe has migrated in former times—affording an example of a social tie which survives death. The Greeks and Romans believed that, if the body was deprived of sepulture, its shadow could not penetrate into its proper place of abode; it remained on earth and haunted the living—a remnant of former beliefs in the necessity of sepulture and the maintenance of friendly relations with the society of the dead.[1]

The dead were to be conciliated by the same means as the living, by supplications and gifts. The gifts were the same as those which are acceptable to the living—food,

*Analogies between ghosts and living people.* arms, costumes, horses, servants. In Dahomey, when a king dies, a hundred of his soldiers are immolated on his tomb as a body guard. Much the same thing was done among the Incas of Peru. At Bali all the women of the harem are immolated upon the grave of the defunct sultan. In Homer, Achilles slaughtered his Trojan prisoners on the funeral pyre of Patroclus, together with the horses and the dogs of his dead friend. The Fiji islanders used to immolate a man at the foot of each pillar in the home of a chief, as a guard for the edifice. In our days, spirits are still so numerous, in the eyes of certain people, that an Arab, for example, when he throws a stone, breathes an apology to such spirits as he may strike.[2] The universe is populated by anthropomorphic societies.

It was to spirits that the care of one's vengeances was confided. According to Tylor, two Brahmans, believing that

*Care of vengeance committed to ghosts.* a man had robbed them of fifty rupees, took their own mother and, with her consent, cut off her head in order that her shadow might torment and pursue the robber till death. Among the Alfourous of Moluccas children are buried alive up to the neck, and left there under the scorching sun with their mouths full of pepper and salt, so that, dying in an agony of thirst, their souls may go in a state of fury in search of the enemy against whom they have been sent. It is always some social exigency, some hatred, some vengeance, some punishment, that leads one to enter into commerce with spirits.

[1] See the author's *Morale d'Epicure* (*Des idées antiques sur la mort*) 3d edition, p. 105.

[2] See Le Bon, *L'Homme et les Sociétés*, t. ii.

In effect, all historical treatises unite to show that animism or polydemonism has at one time or other been universal. It immediately succeeded fetichism or concrete naturism, the primitive belief, in which animating soul and animated body were not distinguished.

Summary.

A belief in separately existing spirits, or spiritism, as Mr. Spencer calls it, which contains the germ of the belief in revisitants from the other world, constitutes the primitive origin of the more refined metaphysical system called spiritualism. This last system, founded also upon the notion of the fundamental duality of man, and of every living being, leads to the notion of a society of spirits.

Let us now consider the inherent necessity under which animism lies of developing into theism.

## II. *Providence and Miracles.*

From the notion of a spirit to that of a divinity is but one step. It suffices to conceive the spirit as sufficiently powerful and redoubtable to reduce us in some considerable measure to a state of dependence. Spirits, manes, gods, subsist in the beginning on an indistinct sentiment of terror. The instant that spirits can separate themselves from the body and perform mysterious actions of which we are incapable, they begin to be divine; it is for this reason that death may change a man into a species of god.

From ghosts to divinity a single step.

Spirits are not only powerful, however; they are also clairvoyant, prevoyant—they are acquainted with things that lie beyond our knowledge. More than that, they are benevolent or hostile; they are related to us in various social or antisocial ways. Here we have the elements of the notion of divine providence. The second semi-metaphysical idea, which lies in germ at the bottom of every religion, is, therefore, this of perspicacious spirits, of favouring or unfavouring deities, of providences. " This being is well or ill disposed toward me ; he may work me good or harm." Such is the first naïve formulation of the theory of divine providence. One must not expect to

Development of notion of special providence.

find, in the beginning, the notion of a general, directing intelligence, but simply that of a social tie between particular voluntary, well-disposed or ill-disposed beings. The notion of providence, like all other religious notions, was at first a superstition. A savage, on his way to some undertaking, meets a serpent and succeeds in his enterprise; it was the serpent that brought him luck: behold a providential accident! Gamblers at the present time are quite as superstitious. The fetich theory of providence still subsists, in the belief in medals, scapularies, and so forth.[1] Observation inevitably results in the perception of causal relations among phenomena; the trouble is, simply, that to the primitive mind every coincidence appears to be a cause ; *post hoc, ergo propter hoc.* Any object that is a party to any such coincidence is a lucky object, good to have in one's power, a portable provi-

---

[1] A belief in relics, pushed so far by the earlier Christians and by so many Catholics to-day, is, too, a sort of faith in fetiches or amulets. From the earliest period of Christianity the faithful were accustomed to go to the Holy Land to obtain water from the Jordan, and gather dust from the soil that the feet of Christ had trod, and to break pieces from the true cross, which St. Paulin of Nole says, "possesses in all its parts a vital force in so much that although its wood be every day clipped off by innumerable pilgrims, it remains intact." Relics are supposed not only to cure the body, but the soul of those who touch them : Gregory sent to a barbarous king the chains that had served to manacle the apostle Paul ; assuring him that the same chains which had manacled the body of the saint could deliver the heart from sin.

This superstition for relics, common in the Middle Ages, was held in all its naïveté by Bishop Gregory of Tours. He relates that one day when he was suffering from a pain in the temples, a touch from the hangings about the tomb of St. Martin cured him. He repeated the experiment three times with equal success. Once, he tells, he was attacked by a mortal dysentery ; he drank a glass of water in which he had dissolved a pinch of dust scraped up on the tomb of the saint, and his health was restored. One day a bone stuck in his throat, he began praying and groaning, and kneeled before the tomb ; he stretched out his hand and touched the hangings and the bone disappeared. "I do not know," he says, "what became of it, for I neither threw it up nor felt it pass downward into my stomach." At another time his tongue became swollen and tumefied ; he licked the railing of the tomb of St. Martin and his tongue became of its natural size. St. Martin's relics go the length even of curing toothache. "Oh, ineffable theriac !" cries Gregory of Tours, "ineffable pigment ! admirable antidote ! celestial purge ! superior to all the drugs of the faculty ! sweeter than aromatics, stronger than all unguents together ! Thou cleanest the stomach like scammony, the lungs like hyssop ; thou purgest the head like pyrethrig."

dence, so to speak. Thus there arises the notion of a destiny, a bias in phenomena toward good or evil, which imposes itself upon the previously existing conception of nature as animated or peopled by spirits. The *post hoc, ergo propter hoc*—that is to say, the belief in the influence of phenomena immediately preceding or concomitant to the main event, and in the influence of a present action upon some future event—is the germ of superstitions both in regard to providence and to destiny. And out of the idea of destiny, of fortune, of necessity, grows in process of time the scientific notion of determinism and universal reciprocity.

Little by little, by the growth of experience, man achieves the conception of an orderly subordination among the different voluntary beings with whom he peoples the earth, a sort of unification of special providences, a more or less regular organization of the world. Responsibility for current events retreats from cause to cause into the distance, from powerful being to still more powerful being ; primitive man still insists on believing that every event is still the sign, the expression of a volition. Once more his faith is dualistic : he conceives the world as dependent upon the will of some one or more superior beings who direct it, or suspend at need the ordinary course of things.

It is at this stage in the evolution of religion that the conception of miracles appears. The notion of miracles is at first very vague in primitive religions ; the period at which this notion begins to become definite marks the initiation of a further step in the development of religion. If, in effect, the marvellous has in all times formed a necessary element in the constitution, it did not possess in the beginning the same character as nowadays ; it was not so definitely distinguished from the natural order of things. Human intelligence had not yet distinguished scientific determinism and supernaturalism. A natural phenomenon ! The bare idea is almost modern ; that is to say, the idea of a phenomenon subject to immutable laws, bound up together with the whole body of other phenomena and forming with them a single unit. What a complex conception,

*Systematic subordination among the gods.*

*Development of belief in miracle.*

and how far above the reach of primitive intelligence ! What we call a miracle *is* a natural phenomenon to a savage, he sees miracles every hour ; properly speaking, he sees nothing else but miracles, that is to say, surprising events. Primitive man, in effect, takes no notice of what does not surprise him (surprise, it has been said, is the father of science), and one of the immediate characteristics, in his opinion, of what surprises him, is that it is intentional.[1] That it should be so no more shocks him, than a paradox shocks a philosopher. The savage is not acquainted with the laws of nature, he has no notion of their being universal to prevent his admitting exceptions to them. A miracle is simply to him a sign of a power like his own, acting by methods unknown to him and producing effects above the limits of his own capacity. Are such effects *infinitely* above his capacity ? No such notion enters into the question ; it suffices that they be above it at all to make him bow down and adore.

The belief in miracles, so anti-scientific nowadays, marks a considerable progress in the intellectual evolution. It amounts, in effect, to a limitation of divine intervention to a small number of extraordinary phenomena. A conception of universal determinism is, in fact, beginning to make its appearance. The belief in dualism, in the separation between spirit and body, becoming constantly more marked, ends in the belief in distinct and separate powers.

Marks a degree of intellectual progress.

Belief in a power miraculously distributing good and evil, in a Providence, is the most vital element in religion. The most important act in every religion, indeed, is propitiation and entreaty ; well, this act is not simply directed toward God as such, but toward God as a presiding divinity, a power capable of favouring or disfavouring us. And the great Oriental religions have reached their present state of per-

Conception of God as Providence more essential than that of Him as First Cause.

---

[1] Etymologically, miracle signifies simply surprising. The Hindus do not even possess a special word for a supernatural event ; miracle and spectacle in their language are one. The supernatural, that is to say, is for them simply an object of contemplation and admiration, an event which stands out prominently from the general monotony which attracts the eye.

fection without any special effort to make the notion of God precise, without specially insisting upon any of his distinguishing attributes except such as are subsidiary to this notion of a Providence awarding good and evil; and popular fancy hastens to ascribe the accomplishment of this distribution to genii, to good and evil spirits; it need go no further, it need not penetrate to the Great Being, to the infinite, so to speak, to the noumenon, and to the abyss which, in effect, is to it a comparative matter of indifference. Even in religions of Christian origin—in especial, in Catholicism, and the Greek Church—God is not always addressed directly; saints, angels, the Virgin, the Son, the Holy Spirit, are much more frequently invoked as mediators. There is something vague, and obscure, and terrible, in God the Father; He is the creator of heaven and hell, the great and somewhat ambiguous principle of goodness, and, in some dim way, of evil. One may see in Him the germ of an indirect personification of nature, which is so indifferent to man, so hard, so inflexible. Christ, on the contrary, is the personification of the best elements of humanity. The responsibility for ferocious laws, maledictions, eternal punishments, is laid upon the shoulders of the Old Testament Deity hidden behind His cloud, revealed only in the lightning and the thunder, reigning by terror, and demanding the life even of His Son as an expiatory sacrifice. At bottom, the real God adored by the Christians is Jesus, that is to say, a mediating Providence whose function is to soften down the asperities of natural law, a Providence who distributes nothing but good and happiness, whereas nature distributes good and evil with equal indifference. It is Jesus we invoke, and it is to the personification of Providence rather than to that of the first cause of the world that humanity has kneeled these two thousand years.

A belief in miracles and in a Providence comes, in the course of its development, into sharper and sharper conflict with a belief in the order of nature. Man gives himself up to an exclusive preoccupation with what he supposes to be the means of ameliorating his destiny and that of his fellows: providential interference with the course of nature, sacrifice, and prayer

are his great means of action on the world.  He lives in
the supernatural.  There exists always, in the early stages of
*Increasing oppo-* every religion, a certain sentiment of evil, of
*sition between* suffering, of terror; and to correct it the believer
*notion of Provi-* takes refuge in miracles.  Providence is thus the
*dence and science.* primitive means of progress, and man's first hope
lay in the superhuman.

Fear of evil, and belief that it can be cured by divine intervention, were the origin of prayer.  A positive religion, even
*Practical evil of* in our days, can scarcely rest content with the
*belief in Provi-* conception of a God who simply sits at a dis-
*dence.* tance and watches the march of a world which
he regulated, once for all, at the beginning of time.  He
must absolutely show himself from time to time in our
midst, we must feel the proximity of his hand ready to
sustain us, he must be able to suspend the course of nature
to our profit.  Piety requires the stimulus of a belief in the
immediate and present possibility of miracles, in their past
existence, in their present existence even, and in one's power
of invoking them by prayer.  Thus the believer opposes to the
conception of ordinary determinism, as the regulating principle of the external world, a faith in a being capable at any
moment of tampering with it; and he counts upon this
power being exercised, he counts upon invoking it, he puts
his hope in supernatural means not less than in natural means,
and sometimes even to the neglect of the latter.

As Littré remarked, the mind may behave in three ways in
regard to miracles: adore them, reject them as a mystifica-
*Miracles not* tion, or explain them by natural means.  Primi-
*frauds.* tive times, Antiquity, and the Middle Ages adored
miracles; the eighteenth century rejected them
as impostures and made game of them.  It was then that the
theory, that the founders of religion were impostors simply,
was generally prevalent.  One of the most necessary and most
serious incidents in the human drama was simply mistaken
for a bit of comedy.  It was forgotten that men do not devote
a whole lifetime to falsehood; the theory of imposture was a

psychological as well as historical error. A man—even an actor or a politician—is always sincere on some side or other; at some period or other a man inevitably says what he thinks, even if only by mistake. Even certain palinodes, provoked by self-interest, are explicable by an unconscious deviation, under the influence of some passion, rather than by an altogether conscious and brazen determination to deceive; and even when one lies with all one's heart, one inevitably believes, or soon comes to believe, some part of one's own falsehood. The reproach of hypocrisy, of comedy and false-hood, has been uttered a hundred times in the course of his-tory, and it has usually been a mistake. In the eighteenth century the same men who prepared and achieved the French Revolution were fond of accusing the prophets and Apostles, the revolutionists of an early date, of insincerity and fraud. To-day such an accusation can no longer be sustained against the sacred books, and the men of the eighteenth century are themselves accused of hypocrisy. For M. Taine, for example, almost all the leaders of the French Revolution lie under the reproach of insincerity, and the very people who sustained them were not, in his judgment, moved by the ideas which they proclaimed, but by the grossest self-interest. The fact is, there are always two points of view from which historic events may be regarded: that of personal inter-ests, which come to the surface as seldom as possible, and that of the general and generous ideas which, on the contrary, are complacently given prominence in public speeches and writings. If it is useful for the historian to divine the inter-ested motives which contributed to the production of a his-torical event, it is irrational to refuse to lend some measure of credence to the higher motives which justified it and which may well have lent their influence to that of self-interest. The human heart is not a one-stringed instrument. The revolutionists had faith in the Revolution, in the rights which they were vindicating, in equality and fraternity; they even believed, sometimes, in their own disinterestedness, as the Protestants believed in the Reformation, as Christ and the prophets believed in their own inspiration; as even in our days, by a belated superstition, the Pope believes in his own infallibility. There is in every faith some element of the naïveté which a child shows in its little semi-conscious hypocrisies, in its caresses which mask a demand and its smiles which are the efflorescence of satisfied desire. But without a certain element of genuineness, a certain element of real naïveté in the faith of the believers, no religion could exist, no revolution would be achieved, no important change would be produced in the life of humanity. Intellectual affirmation and action are always proportionate: to act is to believe and to believe is to act.

In our days, miracles are beginning to be scientifically explained. They are phenomena simply; frequently they were witnessed and described in good faith, but with insufficient knowledge. Everyone is acquainted, for example, with the biblical miracle according to which Isaiah " brought again the shadows of the degrees, which was gone down in the sun dial of Ahaz, ten degrees backward "; indeed the miracle has been reproduced. Mr. Guillemin [1] demonstrates by geometrical reasonings that, by inclining the dial slightly toward the horizon, the shadow may be made gradually to creep a certain distance backward. In the same way, the successive appearances of Jesus after his burial have been paralleled by a recent event in the United States : a criminal, at whose execution all his fellow-prisoners were present, appeared to all of them successively the next day, or the day after. The latter is a remarkable instance of collective hallucination, which shows that a group of individuals living in, so to speak, the same emotional habitat may well be struck at the same time by the same vision, without there being, on their part, either conscious or unconscious fraud or collusion. A third miracle, of an altogether different kind, has also been scientifically explained : I mean the colouring of the fleece of the flocks of Laban and of Jacob ; the effect was obtained by a process well-known to the Egyptians, and mentioned by Pliny. Matthew Arnold believes that the miraculous cures also are not pure legend simply,

*But illusions.*

[1] *Actes de la Societe helvét. des sc. nat.*, August, 1877.

that they bear witness to the great influence of mind over matter. Jesus really aid exorcise devils, that is to say, the mad passions which howled about him. And thus may be understood in their true sense the words : " What does it matter whether I say, *Thy* sins are forgiven thee! or whether I say Arise and walk?" and again : " Thou art made whole ; sin no more, lest a worse thing befall thee." Jesus himself must have known, as Socrates and Empedocles did, though even in a more extraordinary degree, that he possessed a moral and physical power, a virtue, which he himself did not understand and which seemed to him a divine gift. He knew himself to be morally and symbolically the healer of the deaf, the blind, the paralytic, a physician of souls ; and the cures that he wrought in cases of hysteria, more or less temporary but real, forced him to attribute to himself a superhuman power over the body also.

The science of the nervous system, which dates almost entirely from our days, may be taken as a perpetual running commentary on the history of miracles. Perhaps a full quarter of the marvellous facts observed and revered by humanity fall into place within the limits of this new science. A physician, or observer, in the midst of his subjects is like a prophet ; those who surround him are incessantly obliged to recognize in him an occult power, which he himself does not understand ; physician and patient, observer and observed, live equally in the realm of the extraordinary. The facts of partial insensibility, of catalepsy followed by a reawakening like a rising from the dead, of mental suggestion taking place even at a distance, all these facts, which are well known, and are each day becoming more and more explicable, are even for us at the present moment on the confines of the miraculous ; they are detaching themselves, under our very eyes, from the sphere of religion, and falling within the compass of science. The observer who notices for the first time that he can transmit an almost compulsive command by a look, by a pressure of the hand, and even, it appears nowadays, by a simple tension of his will, must experience a species of surprise, even of

*Usually explicable by the science of nervous phenomena.*

fright, of almost religious disquietude at finding himself armed with such a power.   He must begin to understand that the mythical and mystical interpretation of such facts is an affair of delicate discrimination, that lay beyond the stretch of primitive intelligence.

Even the miracles which do not belong simply to the less explicable phenomena of the nervous system tend increas-

Often by less recondite knowl- edge.

ingly to appear to the historian as having been possessed of some foundation in fact.   All that was subjective in them is the element of the marvellous and the providential.   The miracles really were produced, but in the human heart; and instead, in any proper sense, of engendering faith they proceeded from it and are explicable by it.   An English missionary [1] who made a journey in Siberia relates that at the moment of his arrival at Irkutsk a fire was consuming three-fourths of the town; a chapel, however, had been spared and the Russian clergy saw in this fact a miracle; the English missionary explained it very simply by the observation that the rest of the town had been built up of wood, and that the chapel was of brick.   But the missionary, who denies anything like providential intervention in the above mentioned case, admits providential intervention the same day in regard to another point; for he relates that but for one of his horses having run away he would have arrived too soon at Irkutsk, and would have had his baggage burned in the fire, and offers thanks to God because his horse had been inspired to break the traces.   The same natural causes which suffice, according to this excellent gentleman, to explain why the Russian church was spared, suffice no longer when the luggage of an Anglican missionary, the special *protégé*, is involved.   Every believer is inclined thus to interpret miraculously the mercies that have been shown to him. From the height of a stall or the pulpit of a church one sees the events of this world at a particular angle ; from the stall or pulpit of another church one sees them at another angle,

---

[1] *Through Siberia*, by Henry Lansdell, with illustrations and maps ; London, 1882.

and for purposes of scientific verity the events must be looked down upon from the stalls and pulpits of every church —unless one rejects churches altogether.

Religions create miracles by the very need that they themselves feel for them, they create them as evidence in their own support; miracles enter as a necessary element into the process of mental evolution which engenders religion. The distinguishing mark of the word of God is that it alters the order of natural phenomena. Mohammedanism alone made its way in the world without the assistance of visible and gross evidence in its favour, appealing not to the eyes but to the spirit, as Pascal would say; and in this respect it may perhaps claim an intellectual elevation that Judaism and Christianity cannot. But if Mohammed refused the gift of miracles, with a good faith that Moses seems not to have possessed, his disciples hastened to force it upon him, and have supplied his life and death with an appropriate setting of marvellous legend. Ground of belief must be had; the messenger of God must present some visible sign by which he may be recognized.

*Miracles essential to religion.*

It is evident that divine providence or protection must have been conceived in the beginning as quite *special*, and not as acting by general laws. The course of the world was one continual series of divine interventions in the natural order of things, and in the affairs of men; divinities lived in the midst of mankind, in the midst of the family, in the midst of the tribe. This result may be explained as due to the very character of primitive humanity. Primitive man, who is the most credulous, is evidently also the least responsible of mankind; incapable of governing himself, he is always willing to abandon himself to the management of somebody else; in every circumstance of life he needs to share some part of his burden. If a misfortune happens to him, he relies on anybody or anything rather than on himself. This characteristic, which has been remarked in a number of races of mankind, is especially visible in infants and in infant peoples. They lack patience to follow without skipping a link in the chain of cause and effect; they do not understand

*Prevalence of belief in special providence.*

how any human action can produce any great effect, and are, in general, much astonished at the disproportion which exists between effects and their causes—a disproportion which is only explicable in their eyes by the intervention of some foreign cause. Hence the need, so remarkable in feeble minds, to discover some other than the real explanation for a phenomenon ; the real explanation is never, in their eyes, truly sufficient. For a vanquished soldier, the defeat is never sufficiently explained by scientific grounds ; for example, by his own cowardice, by the ill-management of the men on the field, by the ignorance of the leaders ; before the explanation is complete the notion of treason must always be added. Just so, if one of the lower classes has an attack of indigestion, he will not admit that he has eaten too much ; he will complain of the quality of the food, and perhaps even suggest that somebody has tried to poison him. In the Middle Ages, when there was pestilence, it was the fault of the Jews ; at Naples the people beat the images of the saints when the harvest is not good. All these facts are explicable in the same way ; an uncultivated mind cannot bring itself to accept a result which is disagreeable to it, cannot resign itself to having been unexpectedly disconcerted by the mere brute course of things, to say with Turenne, when he was asked how he lost a battle : " By my own fault." The notion of a special providence allies itself with his natural disposition ; it permits man to wash his hands of all responsibility, no matter what happens. A result which it would be too much trouble to foresee, and to obtain by mere natural means, can always be demanded at the hand of Providence ; one waits for it instead of working for it ; and if one is deceived in one's expectations one lays the blame on the Deity. In the Bible, kings are never guilty except toward God, their incapacity is simply impiety ; but it is always easier to be pious than to be capable.

At the same time that the naïve irresponsibility of primitive people thus accommodates itself to the providential government of the world, it accommodates itself no less to the despotic government of a monarch or of an aristocracy. The principle of despotism is at bottom identical with that of a

supernatural, external providence; the latter also demands a
certain renunciation or abdication in the direction of events.

Belief in Provi-
dence tames
people for abso-
lute monarchy.

One lets one's self go, one confides one's self to
someone else, and by this means one winks at the
cruellest of frauds, the defraudment of one's own
volition; another wills and determines in one's
stead. One limits one's self to desiring and hoping, and prayers
and supplications take the place of action and of work. One
floats with the stream in a state of relaxation; if things turn
ill there is always someone for one to blame, to curse, or to
wheedle; if, on the contrary, things turn out well, one's heart
overflows with benedictions, not to mention that one secretly
attributes some part (man is so made) of the result obtained to
one's self. Instead of saying, " I determined that it should be
so," one says, " I asked, I prayed for it." It is so easy to
believe that one is helping to manage the state, or govern the
earth, when one has murmured two words into the ear of a
king or a god—when, like the fly in the fable, one has simply
buzzed an instant about the great rolling wheel of the world.
Propitiatory prayer possesses a power which is great in proportion to its vagueness; it seems to be able to do everything
precisely because it cannot ever do anything in especial. It
exalts man in his own eyes because it enables him to obtain
the maximum of effect with the minimum of effort. What
a penchant the people have always felt for destiny and
men of destiny! How every appeal to the people, in
behalf of men of destiny, has in all times succeeded in
taking the suffrage of the masses! A sentiment of submission to the decrees of Providence, who is destiny personified, has been the excuse of every form of indolence,
of every cowardly adherence to custom. And if one carries it to its logical conclusion, to what else does the indo-
lent sophism of the Orientals amount? It is true that the
precept, " Heaven will aid thee," is habitually corrected by
the precept, " Aid thyself." But efficiency to aid one's self
demands initiative, and audacity, and a spirit of revolt against
an unwelcome course of things; efficiently to aid one's self one
must not say, " God's will be done," but " My will be done";

one must be a rebel in the midst of the passive multitude, a sort of Prometheus or Satan. It is difficult to say to one, " Whatever happens, whatever exists, is what it is, by the irresistible and special will of God," and nevertheless to add, " Do not submit to the accomplished facts." In the Middle Ages men consoled themselves in the midst of tyranny and poverty by thinking that it was God himself who was oppressing them, and dared not rise against their masters for fear they might be rising really against God. To preserve social injustice it had to be apotheosized. What was really no more than a human right had to be made divine.

The sentiment of personal initiative, like that of personal responsibility, is quite modern and incapable of being developed in the atmosphere of bigotry and narrowness in which man has long lived with his gods. To say to one's self, " I can undertake something new ; I shall have the audacity to introduce a change into the world ; to make an advance ; in the combat against brute nature I shall shoot the first arrow, without waiting, like the soldier of antiquity, till the auspices have been consulted "—would have looked like an enormity to men of former times ; to men who did not take a step without consulting their gods and carrying their images before them to show the way. Personal initiative was, on the face of it, a direct offence against Providence, an encroachment on His rights ; to strike the rock as Moses did, before having received the order to do so from God, would have been to expose one's self to His wrath. The world was the private property of the Most High. It was not permitted to a man to employ the forces of nature without special leave ; man was in the position of a child, who is not allowed to play with the fire ; except that the reason for prohibiting the child is not the same—we do not prohibit children from playing with the fire because we are " jealous " of them. The jealousy of the gods is a conception which has survived till the present day, although it is incessantly retreating before the progress made by human initiative. Machinery, the product of modern times, is the most powerful enemy that the notion of a Providence has ever had to wrestle with. One

*Personal initiative a defiance of the gods.*

knows how the innocent winnowing machine was cursed by
the priests, and looked upon with an eye of hatred by the
peasants, because it imprisoned and employed in the service of
man an essentially providential force—that of the wind. But
malediction was useless, the wind could not refuse to winnow
the wheat ; the machine vanquished the gods. There, as
everywhere, human initiative carried the day. Science found
itself in direct opposition to the special intervention of Providence, and appropriated and subdued the forces of nature to
an end, in appearance, not divine but natural. A man of
science is a disturbing element in nature, and science an anti-
providence.

Before the earliest developments of science, primitive
man found himself, as a result of his imagination, in a state
of domesticity in the world, analogous to that
to which he had himself reduced certain
animals ; and this state exerted a profound influence upon the character of such animals,
deprived them of certain capacities and endowed
them, in turn, with others. Some of them—certain birds, for
example—become under domestication almost incapable of
finding and providing themselves with their necessary food.
More intelligent animals like the dog, who might in a case
of absolute necessity rely upon himself for indispensables, contract nevertheless a habit of subjection to man which creates
a corresponding need : my dog is not at ease except when he
knows that I am near ; if anything causes me to go away, he
is restless and nervous ; in the presence of danger he runs
between my legs, instead of taking refuge in flight, which
would be the primitive instinct. Thus every animal which
knows itself to be watched and protected in the details of its
life by a superior being, necessarily loses its primitive independence, and if its primitive independence should be once
more restored, it would be unhappy, would experience an
ill-defined fear, a vague sentiment of enfeeblement. Just so
in the case of primitive and uncultivated man : once he is
habituated to the protection of the gods, this protection
becomes for him a veritable need ; if he is deprived of it, he

*Side note:* Man practically a domestic animal in the house of the gods: resulting enfeeblement of character.

falls into a state of inexpressible discomfiture and inquietude. Add that, in this case, he will soon provide himself with a substitute ; to escape from the intolerable solitude which doubt creates within him, he will take refuge in his gods or his fetiches, under the influence of a sentiment identical with that which sends the dog to take refuge between the legs of his master. To attain some idea of the force of such a sentiment among primitive human beings, one must remember that the surveillance of the gods is much more extended and more scrupulous even than that of man over domestic animals, or of a master over his slaves. Primitive man feels his god or his genii at his side at every step, in all the circumstances of life ; he is accustomed to being never alone, to the presence of someone by him keeping step with him ; he believes that every word that he says and every act that he does is witnessed and judged. No domestic animal is accustomed to so high a degree of subjection ; he knows perfectly that our protection is not always efficacious and that we are sometimes mistaken about him, that we caress him when he ought to be punished, etc. Cats, for instance, know that man cannot see in the dark : one evening a white cat made ready to commit an abominable misdemeanour within two steps of me, not suspecting that its colour would betray it to an attentive eye, even in the obscurity. Primitive men sometimes practised an analogous cunning in regard to their gods ; they did not yet believe in the complete sovereignty, in the absolute ubiquity, of Providence. But by a process of logical development, Providence is ultimately believed to extend to everything, to envelop one's whole life ; the fear of God becomes to man a perpetual prohibition against his passions, a hope in God's aid his perpetual recourse. Religion and science possess this much in common, that they result in enveloping us equally in a network of necessities ; but what distinguishes science is that it makes us acquainted with the real order and causes of phenomena, and by that fact permits us to modify that order at will ; by showing us the fact and nature of our dependence, science supplies us with the means of conquering a comparative independence. In religion, on the contrary, the mythical and miraculous element introduces an unforeseen factor, the divine will, a special providence, into the midst of events, and by that fact deceives one as to the true means of modifying the real course of things. The instant one believes one's self to be dependent upon Jupiter or Allah, one ascribes a greater efficacy to propitiation than to action; and it follows that the greater one perceives one's dependence to be the more completely one believes one's self to be without defence against it; the more complete the submission is to God, the more complete one's resulting submission becomes to the established fact. The feeling of an imaginary dependence upon supernatural beings thus increases the general dependence of man in relation to nature. Thus understood, the notion of a special providence, of a divine tutelage, has resulted in the protracted maintenance of the human soul in a state of genuine minority; and this state of minority, in its turn, has rendered the existence and surveillance of divine protectors a necessity. When, therefore, the believer refuses an offer of emancipation from the dependence which he has voluntarily accepted, the reason is that he feels a vague sentiment of his own insufficiency, of his irremediably belated coming of age; he is a child, who does not dare stray far from the paternal roof; he does not possess the courage to walk alone. The child who should show a precocious independence, and should early learn to go its own road, would not improbably become simply dissipated; his precocity might well be depravity in disguise. Similarly in history, the irreligious, the sceptics, the atheists, have been frequently spoiled children, precocious in the bad sense; their freedom of spirit was only a high form of mischief. The human race, like the individual, long needed surveillance and tutelage; so long as it experienced this need it leaned inevitably upon a belief in a providence external to itself and to the universe, capable of interfering in the course of things, and of modifying the general laws of nature by particular acts of volition. Subsequently, by the progress of science, Providence has been deprived day by day of some of its special and miraculous powers, of its supernatural prerogatives. By the evolution of human thought piety has been transformed; it tends to-day to regard as an object of filial affection what was formerly an object of terror, of deprecation, of propitiation. Science, enveloping Providence in a network of inflexible laws, is day by day reducing it to a state of immobility and, so to speak, paralyzing it. Providence is becoming like an old man whom age has rendered incapable of movement—who but for our aid could not raise a hand or foot, who lives with our assistance, and who, nevertheless, is only the more beloved, as if his existence became to us more precious in proportion to its uselessness.

### III. Creation.

After the notion of Providence one must deal, in running through the metaphysical principles of religion, with the notion of a creator, which has acquired in our days an importance that it did not possess formerly. This conception, like that of the soul and of a special providence, presented itself originally under the form of dualism. Man conceived in the beginning a god as fashioning a world more or less independent of himself, out of some pre-existing material. It was only later that this crude dualism was refined into the notion of creation *ex nihilo*, which represented the traditional duality as produced by a primitive unity—God, who had at first existed alone, created out of nothing a world distinct and separate from himself.

*Conception of creation dualistic.*

The following conversation, of which I can guarantee the authenticity, affords an example of naïve metaphysic. The two interlocutors were a little peasant girl, four years old, who had always lived in the country, and a young girl from town, the daughter of the owner of the farm. They had gone out into the garden where a number of flowers had opened that morning; the little peasant girl admired them enthusiastically, and addressing her companion, for whom she had long entertained a species of cult: " It is you, mistress, is it not," she cried, " who makes these flowers?" This interrogation did not embody an incipient speculation in a sphere of physics; the child sim-

*Conception of creation natural.*

ply attributed an unknown power to a visible and palpable being. Her mistress replied laughingly, "No, not I. I haven't the power." "Who does it then?" the child asked. One perceives the persistence, in primitive intelligences, of the impulse to explain things by the direct action of somebody's volition, the impulse to place somebody behind every event. "It is God," replied the elder girl. "And where is God? Have you ever seen Him?" No doubt the little peasant, who regarded the city as a very surprising place, supposed one might meet God there, face to face, and God did not, as yet, represent to her anything supra-physical. But how admirably disposed she was for the reception of a more or less illegitimate metaphysic! "I have never seen God," replied her mistress, "and nobody has ever seen Him. He lives in heaven, and at the same time lives among us; He sees us and hears us; it is He who made the flowers, who made you and me, and everything that exists." I shall not report the child's replies, for I believe that she was too much astonished really to say anything. She was in a situation such as a savage finds himself in when a missionary comes and talks with him about God, the supreme being, creator of all things, a spirit existing without a body. Savages sometimes refuse to understand, and point to their heads and declare that they suffer; sometimes they believe that one is making fun of them, and even among our children there is a good deal of persistent and mute astonishment, which wears off slowly with the lapse of time. What is striking in the little conversation reported above, is the way in which the metaphysical myth necessarily rises out of the scientific error. An inexact induction first gives rise to the notion of a human being acting by means to us unknown and mysterious; this notion, once obtained, fastens upon the body of such and such an individual, the object antecedently of especial veneration ; from this individual it retreats in course of time to another more distant, from country to town, from earth to heaven, from visible heaven to the invisible essence of things, the omnipresent substratum of the world. Simultaneously with this retrograde movement, the being endowed with marvellous powers becomes increasingly vague and abstract.   The human intelligence, in developing its conception of the supernatural being, employs what theologians call *the negative method*, which consists in abstracting one known attribute after another.   If men and races of men have always followed this procedure, it is less because of any refinement of thought on their part than in obedience to the pressure of an external necessity.   Directly as man becomes acquainted with nature, he sees all traces of his god fly before him; he is like a miner who, thinking that he recognizes the presence of gold in the soil beneath his feet, begins to dig, and finding nothing, cannot make up his mind to believe that the earth contains no treasure; he sinks his shafts deeper and deeper in an eternal hopefulness.   Just so, instead of breaking with his gods, man exiles them to a greater and greater distance as he advances in knowledge.   What nature excludes tends to take on a metaphysical character; every error which persists in spite of the progress of experience takes refuge in heaven, in some sphere more and more completely inaccessible.   Thus the somewhat gross origins of religions are not irreconcilable with the refined speculations incident to their period of development.   Human intelligence, once launched into infinite space, inevitably describes a wider and wider orbit about reality.   A mythical religion is not a completely rational and *a priori* construction; it always rests upon alleged experience, upon observations and analogies, which are tainted with error; it is, therefore, false *a posteriori*, and therein lies the explanation of the invincible and increasing divergence between myth and verity.

In the beginning men conceived God rather as an orderer of the universe, as a workman fashioning a pre-existing matter, than

God conceived as orderer rather than as creator.

as a creator; we find this notion still predominant among the Greeks.   Its genesis was probably something as follows:   Whoever supposes the existence of God regards the world as an instrument in His hands; God employs the thunder, the wind, the stars for purposes of his own, as man employs his arrows and his hatchet.   Does it not naturally result from that conception that God fashions these marvellous instruments just as man fashions his arrows and hatchet ? If the little peasant girl, of whom we spoke above, had not seen her father repair or make his tools, make a fire, make bread, till the soil, she would never have asked who made the flowers in the garden. The child's first *why* involves the following reasoning : Somebody has acted on this thing as I myself have acted on such and such another thing ; who, then, in the present case is it ? The abstract notion of causality is a consequence of the practical development of our own causality ; the greater the number of things that one can make one's self, the greater one's astonishment at seeing things done by other people with greater rapidity or on a larger scale. The more bound down one is one's self, to the employment of tedious artifice, the more one admires what is produced suddenly by a power which is apparently extraordinary. So that the notion of a miracle thus more naturally arose from one's experience of the practical arts, than, so to speak, from brute experience, and for the rest contained no element which was contradictory to the naïve science of the earliest observers. Every question presupposes a certain kind and amount of action on the part of the questioner ; one does not demand the cause of an event until one has one's self been the conscious cause of such and such another event. If man possessed no influence in the world, he would not ask himself who made the world. The mason's trowel and carpenter's saw have played a considerable part in the development of religious metaphysics.

Remark, also, how easy it is, even at the present day, to confound the word make with the word create, which indeed did not exist in primitive times. How should one distinguish precisely what one fashions from what one creates? There is a certain element of creation in fashioning ; and this element sometimes positively assumes a magical character, seems to rise *ex nihilo*. What a marvel, for example, is a spark of fire obtained from stone or wood ! The Hindus see in it the symbol of generation. In fire the earliest races of men laid their fingers on the miraculous. In appearance the pebble one strikes or the dried wood one rubs to produce a spark is not itself consumed; it

Notion of creation ex nihilo of empirical origin.

gives without loss, it creates. The first man who discovered the secret of producing fire seemed to have introduced something genuinely new into the world, to have ravished the power of creation from the gods. In general, what distinguishes the artist, properly so called, from the simple workman is the feeling that he possesses a power which he does not understand, that he produces in some sense more than he aims at, that he is lifted above himself; genius is not fully conscious, as simple talent is, of its resources; it contains an element of the unforeseen, a force which is not calculable in advance, a creative power; and therein lies the secret of the true artist's personal pride. Even in a matter of purely physical power a superexcitation of the nervous system may place at one's disposal an amount of muscular energy one did not suppose one possessed: the athlete, no more than the thinker, at such times knows the limits of his own strength and the marvels of which he is capable. Each of us possesses thus, during certain hours of his existence, the consciousness of a more or less creative power, of the direct production of something out of nothing. One feels that one has produced by force of will a result that one's intelligence cannot wholly account for, that one cannot rationally explain. Therein lies the foundation and in a measure the justification of a belief in miracles, in the extraordinary power of certain men, and, in the last analysis, in a power of creating. This indefinite power that man sometimes feels well up within him, he naturally ascribes to his gods. Since he conceives them as acting upon the world in a manner analogous to himself, he conceives them as capable of giving rise to new elements in the world; and this notion of creative power once introduced continuously develops till the day when it leads one, from induction to induction, to the belief that the entire world is the work of a divinity, that the earth and the stars have been fashioned and created by a supernatural volition. If man can strike fire out of a stone, why might not God strike a sun out of the firmament? The conception of a creator, which seems at first a remote consequence from a chain of abstract reasoning, is thus one of the innumerable manifestations of anthropomorphism; one of the ideas which, at least originally, seems to have been rather paraphysical than metaphysical. It rests at bottom upon an ignorance of the possible transformation and actual equivalents of forces, owing to which every apparent creation is resolvable into a substantial equivalence and every apparent miracle into an exemplification of immutable order.

To sum up, the creative power once ascribed to God is in our opinion an extension of the notion of special Providence,

Summary.

which itself is of empirical origin. When theologians nowadays begin by establishing the creation, in order therefrom to deduce a special Providence, they are precisely inverting the order of things as they appeared in the beginning. It is only through the continually increasing preoccupation of abstract thought and metaphysical speculation with the question of the first cause, that the idea of a creative deity has acquired thus a sort of preponderance, and constitutes in our day an essential element in religion. Dualism, as we have seen, is of the essence of this notion; dualism is the principal form under which the union of souls and bodies, the relation of a special providence to natural laws, the relation of creator to created has been conceived. The notion, however, of a supreme unity running through all things has been caught more or less vague glimpses of, from remote times down to the present day. And it is on this notion that pantheistic and monistic religions, principally those of India, are based. Brahmanism and Buddhism tend to what has been called "absolute illusionism" for the benefit of a unity in which the supreme being takes for us the form of non-existence.

The temptation is natural systematically to class diverse systems of religious metaphysics and to represent them as

Dangers of effort to classify systems of religious metaphysics.

evolving, one after the other in a regular order, conformable to a more or less determinate scheme; but one must be on one's guard here against two things: first, the seduction of a system, with the metaphysical abstractions to which it leads; second, the pretense of finding everywhere a regular progress constantly headed toward religious unity. Religious philosophers have erred in both these respects; Hegel, for example, yielded to the temptation of imposing upon the history of religion his monotonous trilogy, of thesis, antithesis, and synthesis. In Von Hartmann the Hegelian spirit, influenced by Schopenhauer, still survives. We have seen Von Hartmann borrowing from Max Müller the abstract conception of a divinity at once unified and multiple, a species of primitive synthesis out of which historical religions were to arise by a process of differentiation: out of henotheism, as out of matter still void and without form, was to arise polytheism, and then by a process of degenerescence was to arise polydemonism or animism, and finally fetichism.[1] This order of development, as we have seen, is contrary to matter of fact.

Fetichism, understood simply as the ascription of life to natural objects, is primitive. Animism, or the conception of indwelling spirit, arises subsequently. Polytheism, or the worship of a certain number of analogous objects, such as the trees of a forest, implies some distinction between the deity and the forest, whereas fetichism limits itself strictly to the animation of each particular tree, and finally henotheism, or

---

[1] " Henotheism," says Von Hartmann, " rests upon a contradiction. Man goes forth in search of divinity, and finds gods. He addresses each of these divinities in succession in the hope that he may be the divinity sought for, and confers upon him a multitude of predicates which call in question the divinity of the other gods. Obliged, however, as he is to look to different gods for the fulfilment of his respective demands he is unable to remain faithful to any one of them ; he changes his object of adoration repeatedly and each time acts toward the god he is addressing as if he were god *par excellence*, without indeed himself observing at the time that he is denying the supreme divinity of any god by attributing it in turn to each of them. What renders the origin of religion possible is that this contradiction is not at first remarked ; a persistent failure to recognize such a contradiction would not be possible in the midst of the progress of civilization, except in the case of an extreme intensity of religious sentiment, which shields all religious subjects from rational criticism. Such intensity of religious sentiment neither exists in all places nor at all times, and a spirit of intellectual criticism, operating intermittently, suffices in the long run to render the point of view of henotheism untenable. Two ways of avoiding the contradiction in question offer themselves. One may maintain the unity of God at the expense of the plurality, or, on the contrary, plurality of God at the expense of the unity. The first way leads to abstract monism, the second to polytheism ; and out of polytheism, by a process of degeneration, arise polydemonism or animism and then fetichism."

the vague conception of an indwelling divinity in all things, is ulterior and derivative. Monistic pantheism or monism lies but one step beyond.

Remark also that Von Hartmann, who endeavours to prove that a vague monism is the primitive form of religion, regards Logically pos- the Vedas as a fair example of the earliest form terior often his- of natural religion, traces of which remain more torically prior. or less distinctly manifest in all mythologies. But this is positively to forget that for an anthropologist the Vedas are quite modern compositions, and that Hindu literature belongs to a period of high refinement and civilization. Monistic metaphysics may be the ultimate goal toward which all religions tend, but it is at least not the point of departure. Finally, Von Hartmann endeavours to establish the fact of a certain logical order in religious development, a *progress*. This progress does not exist in history nor anywhere outside of the abstract system constructed by Von Hartmann ; it is dialectic, not historic. The divers religious points of view have often coincided in history ; and sometimes a logically superior point of view has even preceded an inferior.

Another classification, not less open to suspicion than that of Von Hartmann, is the celebrated Comtist progression from Comte's classifi- fetichism to polytheism and from polytheism to cation logical, not monism. In this classification the framework no psychological. longer consists of metaphysical abstractions, but of numbers. But numbers also possess their artificial and superficial side ; they do not express the most fundamental aspects of religion. In the first place, it is a matter of extreme difficulty to perceive any radical difference between naturistic fetichism and polytheism. Multiplicity of divinities is a characteristic common to both. The sole difference that Comte was able to establish is that in polytheism a whole class of objects, for example all the trees of a forest, or a whole class of phenomena, as lightning and storm, is represented by one divinity. But this species of abstraction and generalization is much less important, much more exterior and purely logical, than the psychological and metaphysical progression from a grossly unitarian and concrete naturism to a dualistic animism. This latter line of development is in the direction of naturalistic and spiritualistic metaphysics, which possess a deeper significance than a system of mathematical enumeration and logical generalization. The passage from polytheism to monotheism is also conceived by Comte somewhat too mathematically. Polytheism early resulted in a certain hierarchy and subordination of the whole body of individual deities to some one powerful god: Jupiter, Fate, etc. On the other hand, monotheism has always provided some place for secondary divinities—angels, devils, spirits of every kind, to say nothing of the trinitarian conception of the Godhead itself. Mathematical terms, in this connection, obscure profound problems which belong really to metaphysics and to morals.

From the point of view of metaphysics the great question is that of the relation which exists between the divinity and the world and mankind; a relation of immanence or of transcendence, of duality or of unity.

The real classification.

We have seen that, from this point of view, religions have passed from an extremely vague primitive immanence to a relation of transcendence and of separation, ultimately to return, sometimes with comparative rapidity (as in India), sometimes very slowly (as among Christian nations), to the notion of an immanent God in whom we live and move and have our being.

Along with this difference of conception there necessarily goes a corresponding difference in the parts ascribed respectively to determinism and natural law, and to the

Progressive encroachment of deterministic conception.

arbitrary will of the deity or deities. That is to say, the conflict between religion and science, or what will one day become such, exists implicitly in the earliest conceptions of the world. In the beginning, to be sure, there being no such thing as science properly so called, no conflict is apparent; one explains whatever one chooses as the product of an arbitrary will, then little by little the regularity, the determinism, the orderliness of certain phenomena are remarked. Divinities cease to be

absolute princes, and become more or less constitutional
sovereigns. Therein lies the law of religious evolution, which
is much more significant than the law promulgated by Comte ;
humanity tends progressively to restrict the number of the
phenomena with the natural course of which the gods are
supposed to interfere ; the sphere of natural law tends progressively to become more and more nearly all-comprehensive.
The Catholic nowadays no longer believes that a goddess
brings his crops to maturity or that a particular god launches
a thunder-bolt, though he is still profoundly inclined to imagine that God blesses his fields or punishes him by destroying
his house by a flash of lightning ; arbitrary power tends to
be concentrated in a single being placed on a height above
nature. At a still further stage in the course of evolution,
the will of this being is conceived as expressed in the laws of
nature themselves without allowing for the existence of
miraculous exceptions ; Providence, the Divinity, becomes
*immanent* in the scientific ordering and determinism of the
world. In this respect the Hindus and the Stoics are far
in advance of the Catholics.

The absorption of the respective worships of a number of
deities into the worship of one deity has been an incidental
consequence of the progress of science. Humanity began by offering up a multitude of
special services to a multitude of special gods.
If one were to believe certain linguists, it is true,
natural objects—the sun, fire, the moon—were at first adored
as impersonal entities ; their subsequent personification being
due to a too literal interpretation of figurative impressions
habitually employed to designate them, such as Ζεύς, the
brilliant. Certain myths, no doubt, did spring from this source :
*nomina, numina ;* but humanity does not usually progress from
the general to the particular. Primitive religion, on the contrary, was at first subdivided or rather simply divided into cults
of all sorts ; it was only later that simplifications and generalizations arose. The passage from fetichism to polytheism and
to monotheism was simply the consequence of a progressively
scientific conception of the world ; of the progressive absorp-

*Unification of
creeds incidental
to that encroach-
ment.*

tion of the several transcendent powers into a single power immanent in the laws of the universe.

More important still than this metaphysical and scientific evolution of religion is the sociological and moral evolution. What is really important in a religious theory

**Development of sociological and moral sides of religion.** is less the conceived relation of the primary substance to its manifestations in the universe, than the attributes ascribed to this substance and to the inhabitants of the universe. In other words, what sort of a society does the universe constitute? What sort of social relation more or less moral between the various members are derivable from the fundamental tie which binds them to the principle which is immanent in all of them? That is the great problem for which the others simply constitute a preparation. The problem is to interpret the true foundation of beings and of being, independently of numerical, logical, and even metaphysical relations. Well, such an interpretation cannot be other than psychological and moral. Psychologically, power was the first and essential attribute of divinity, and this power was conceived as redoubtable. Intelligence, knowledge, foreknowledge, were only at a later period ascribed to the gods. And finally, divine morality, under the twofold aspects of justice and goodness, is a very late conception indeed. We shall see it develop side by side with the development of the systems of practical morals that are incident to religion.

# CHAPTER III.

## RELIGIOUS MORALS.

I. The laws which regulate the social relations between gods and men—Morality and immorality in primitive religions—Extension of friendly and hostile relations to the sphere of the gods—Primitive inability in matters of conscience, as in matters of art, to distinguish the great from the monstrous.

II. The moral sanction in the society which includes gods and men—Patronage—That divine intervention tends always to be conceived after the model of human intervention and to sanction it.

III. Worship and religious rites—Principles of reciprocity and proportionality in the exchange of services—Sacrifice—Principle of coercion and incantation—Principle of habit and its relation to rites—Sorcery—Sacerdotalism—Prophecy—The externals of worship—Dramatization and religious æsthetics.

IV. Subjective worship—Adoration and love; their psychological origin.

*I. The laws which regulate the social relations between gods and men.*

We are to-day inclined to see everywhere a very intimate relation between religion and morals, since Kant recognized in ethics the aim and sole foundation of the conception of God. In the beginning nothing of the sort existed. It is plain from the preceding chapters that religion was at first a physical explanation of events, and above all of events in their relation to the interests of mankind, by a theory of causes acting for ends of their own after the manner of the human will; an explanation, that is to say, by causes at once efficient and final; and theology is the development of a primitive teleology. Man imagined himself to be living in society with beneficent or maleficent beings, at first visible and tangible, then progressively invisible and separate from the objects

Religion and morals not originally related.

they inhabited.   Therein, as we have said, lay the first step of religion.   Religion was in the beginning nothing more than an imaginative extension of human society; the explanation of things by a theory of volitions analogous to the volitions by means of which man himself acts on the world, but of another order, of a higher degree of power.   Well, these volitions are sometimes good, sometimes evil, sometimes friendly, sometimes hostile: friendship and hatred are the two categories under which man inevitably classified the superior powers with whom he believed himself to be in relations.   Morality was in no sense one of the distinguishing characteristics of these powers; man was quite as naturally inclined to attribute to them wickedness as goodness, or rather he felt vaguely that the rules of conduct by which he was himself bound were not necessarily those by which these beings, at once analogous to men and so different from them, were themselves bound.   Also in his relations with the gods, with the powers of nature, man in nowise believed that the rules of mere human society, of the family, of the tribe, of the nation, were always and in every respect applicable.   Thence it came that to render the gods propitious, man had recourse to practices which he would have blamed in mere human morals: human sacrifices, anthropophagy, sacrifices of virginity, etc.[1]

If one stops to recollect that moral laws are in a great measure the expression of the very necessities of human life, and that the generality of certain rules is due to the uniformity of the conditions of life on the surface of the globe, one will understand why it was that one's relations to the gods, that is to say to creatures of the imagination, were not dominated so directly as one's

Religion much less moral than society.

---

[1] It has been remarked that peoples who for centuries have renounced anthropophagy have long persisted in human sacrifices: that thousands of women in certain sanctuaries have offered the painful sacrifices of their chastity to gods of a furious sensuality.   The gods of paganism are dissolute, arbitrary, vindictive, pitiless, and still their adorers rise little by little to a conception of moral purity, of clemency, and of justice.   Javeh is vindictive and ferocious, and yet it is in the midst of his people that the religion *par excellence* of benignity and forgiveness took its rise.   Also the real morality of men was never proportionate to the frequently fanatic intensity of their religious sentiments.   See M. Réville (*Prolégomènes*, p. 281).

relations to one's fellow-men by the exigencies of practical life, but were regulated by much more variable and fantastic laws containing often a visible germ of immorality. The divine society was an imaginary extension of human society, not an imaginative perfection of it. It was physical fear, *timor*, and not moral reverence, which gave being to the first gods. The human imagination, labouring thus under the empire of fear, naturally gave birth to a prodigy more often than to an ideal. For the primitive conscience, as for primitive art, the distinction between the great and the monstrous was by no means sufficiently marked. The germ of immorality, therefore, not less than of morality lies at the root of every religion. Once more, it would be an error to believe that religions are immoral in that they are anthropomorphic, or sociomorphic; rather the contrary is true, they are not moral except in so far as they are sociomorphic. Mutilation, for example, cruelty, obscenity are foreign to the conceptions which dominate human conduct. One may verify in every religion what is observed in Christianity, that the truly moral God is precisely the man-God, Jesus, whereas God the Father, who pitilessly sacrifices his own son, is anti-human and immoral, precisely in that he is superhuman.

In effect we find our fundamental proposition confirmed afresh : religion is a sociology conceived as a physical, meta-

Summary. physical, and moral explanation of all things ; it is the reduction of all natural, and even supernatural forces to a human type, and the reduction of their relations to social relations. Also the progress of religion has been exactly parallel to the progress in social evolution, which has itself been dominated by the progress of subjective morals and conscience. The gods were at first divided into two classes : the beneficent and the maleficent, who ultimately came to be recognized as respectively virtuous and wicked. Then these two classes were absorbed into their respective chiefs, into Ormuzd and Ahriman, into God and Satan, into a principle of good and a principle of evil. Thus by a fresh dualism spirits themselves were separated and ranged into classes, as the spirit itself had previously been separated from the body. Finally the principle of goodness subsisted victoriously under the name of God. He became the personification of the moral law and the moral sanction, the sovereign legislator and judge, in a word, the living law of universal society, as a king is the living law in a human society. To-day God tends to be identified with the human conscience purified *ad infinitum*, and adequate with the universe. For these last and most subtle representations of the religious sentiment, God is no more than a symbol of the moral and the ideal. One may see in this evolution of religious ideas the gradual triumph of sociomorphism, since it is characterized by an extension to the universe at large of social relations which are incessantly progressing toward perfection among men.

*II. The moral sanction in the society which includes gods and men.*

To the personification of the law, religious morals inevitably joined that of the sanction which plays so capital a rôle in every human society. The celestial government

The gods inevitably become protectors of social justice.

has always been a projection of the human government, with a penalty at first terrible and subsequently softened. To say the truth, the theory of a sanction is the systematization of that of a providence. The distinguishing characteristic of a providence is that it awards or recompenses, insomuch that one may bring down upon one's self or avoid its anger, by such and such conduct. Well, the instant a man admits that a divine power is governing him, this power will inevitably appear to him to be exercising a control over his conduct, and, as it were, sanctioning it. This control will at first be exercised only in regard to the personal relations of the individual, with his god and his gods. But the individual will soon recognize that if the gods take an interest in him they may well take an interest also in the other members of the tribe, provided that these last know how to render them propitious; and to injure the other worshippers of a god would be indirectly to injure the god himself, and provoke his anger. All the members of a tribe therefore find themselves protected against each other by their association with the gods, religion lends support to social justice, and whoever violates social justice expects the gods to punish him. This expectation also must have been confirmed by the facts, for if antisocial and unjust conduct had habitually prevailed among men, social life would have been impossible. Injustice must then always on an average have carried its sanction with it, and this sanction must have appeared to be the direct work of the gods, passing judgment from on high on the social conduct of their clients, as Roman patrons did, seated beneath the columns of the atrium.

As religions intermingled and grew in extent, the clientage of a god, at first extended to the members of a single tribe, passed beyond its bounds. Men, of no matter what origin, might become citizens of the celestial city, of the superhuman association which took charge of each of its members, so that the divine sanction tended increasingly to become confounded with the moral sanction, and one understood that God protected justice not only within the bosom of a tribe, but everywhere within the limits of humanity.

*And of human justice.*

While in the matter of the sanction the sociomorphic conception of the world tended thus to become a moral conception, morality itself must have tended, in order to eke out its own insufficiency, to ally itself with religion. Human society, powerless to make itself always respected by every one of its members, inevitably invoked the aid of the society of superior beings which enveloped it on all sides. Man being essentially a social animal, ζῷον πολιτικόν, could not be resigned in the presence of the success of antisocial conduct, and whenever it seemed that such conduct had succeeded humanly, the very nature of mankind tended to make it turn toward the superhuman to demand a reparation and a compensation. If the bees should suddenly see their hives destroyed before their eyes without there being any hope of ever reconstructing them, their whole being would be shaken, and they would instinctively await for an intervention of some kind, which should

*Natural desire to have the scales loaded on the side of rectitude.*

re-establish an order as immutable and sacred for them as that of the stars is for us.   Man, by virtue of the moral nature with which heredity has furnished him, is thus inclined to believe that wickedness ought not to have the last word in the universe ; the triumph of evil and of injustice always stirs his indignation.   This species of indignation is observable in infants almost before they can talk, and numerous traces of it may be found even among animals.   The logical result of this instinctive protest against evil is a refusal to believe in its definitive triumph.[1]

Man, in whose eyes the society in which the gods live corresponds so closely to human society, must almost inevitably imagine the existence among them of antisocial

*Results in victory being given in heaven to principle of light.*

beings, of Ahrimans and Satans, protectors of evil in heaven and on earth, but it is natural that he should give the victory in the end to the "principle of good" over the "principle of evil."   Of all things it is the most repugnant to him to believe that the universe is fundamentally indifferent to the distinction between good and evil ;  a divinity may be irascible, capricious, and even intermittently wicked, but man cannot understand an impassible and cold nature.

The most powerful of the gods had thus served to reconcile force and justice, a barbarous justice appropriate to the spirit of primitive man.

*Gods legitimated by alliance with the moral forces of society.*

Through the idea of sanction grafted thus upon that of providence, religion assumes a really systematic character, and becomes attached to the very fibres of the human heart.   As instruments of goodness in the universe, the gods, or at least the sovereign gods, serve to confirm human morality ;  they become in some sort the life of morality.   Their existence is no longer simply a physical fact ; it is a physical fact, morally justified by a social instinct which relies upon it as its main safeguard.   Henceforth the power of the gods is legitimate.   A divine king, like a human king, requires a certain mystic consecration ;  it is religion which

[1] See the author's *Esquisse a'une morale* (I., iii.) ;   *Besoin psychologique d'une sanction.*

consecrates human kings, it is morality which consecrates the king of the gods.

The notion of a divine intervention to trim the balance of the social order, to punish and to recompense, was at first

*Importance of conception of immortality in the moral evolution of religion.*

altogether foreign to the belief in a continuation of life after death ; it became allied to this belief much later. Even among a people so advanced as the Hebrews in matters of religious evolution, reward and punishment beyond this life played no rôle, and yet there has scarcely ever been a people who believed more heartily in the will of God as directing the life of mankind ; but in their eyes God achieved his victory in this life ; they possessed no need for an immortality as a means of redressing the moral balance of the world.[1] It was only later, when the critical sense had attained a higher development, that it was recognized that the sanction did not always come in this life ; the chastisement of the culpable, the hoped-for recompense of the virtuous, gradually retreated from the present world into a distant future. Hell and heaven were thrown open to correct the manifest imperfections of this life. The notion of immortality thus assumed an extraordinary importance, insomuch that it seemed as if modern life would be destroyed if it were deprived of this belief, which former times had, however, succeeded in doing without. At bottom a clear and reflective conception of a life after death, in which one is rewarded or punished for one's life here, is a very complex and remote deduction from the notion of sanction.

[1] The question whether the Hebrews believed in the immortality of the soul has long been discussed, and M. Renan has been reproached with his negative attitude in the matter ; but M. Renan never denied the existence, among the Hebrews, of a belief in a sojourn for the shadows or manes of the dead ; the whole question was whether the Hebrews believed in a system of reward and punishment after death, and M. Renan was right in maintaining that any such notion is foreign to primitive Judaism. It is equally foreign to primitive Hellenism. Though the living endeavoured to conciliate the dead, they did not envy their fate which, even in the case of the just, was worse than the fate of the living. "Seek not to console me for death, noble Ulysses," Achilles says, when he arrives in Tartarus. "I would rather be a hired labourer and till a poor man's field than reign over all the regions of the dead." (See *Morale d'Épicure*, 3d ed.; *Des idées antiques sur la mort.*)

The religious sanction, being fundamentally an extension of human social relations to the life of the gods, successively assumed the three forms of human penalty. At first it was only vengeance, as in the case of the lower animals and of savage man. It is evil rendered in return for evil. The sentiment of vengeance has subsisted, and still subsists, in the bosom of every religion which admits a divine sanction ; vengeance is confided to God, and becomes only the more terrible. " Do not avenge yourselves," St. Paul says, " but rather give place unto wrath : for it is written, Vengeance is mine ; I will repay, saith the Lord. Therefore, if thine enemy hunger, feed him ; if he thirst, give him to drink : for in so doing thou shalt heap coals of fire on his head." " Our patience," St. Cyprian wrote, " comes from our certainty that we shall be avenged ; it heaps coals of fire upon the heads of our enemies. The day on which the Most High shall number the faithful shall see the culpable in Gehenna, and our persecutors shall be consumed in eternal fire ! What a spectacle for my transports, my admiration, and my laughter ! " And by way of a refinement, one of the martyrs at Carthage told the pagans to look him well in the face so that they might recognize him on the day of judgment at the right hand of the Father, while they were being precipitated into eternal flame.[1]

*Religious sanction at first conceived as a vengeance.*

The notion of vengeance, as it becomes more subtle and passes, so to speak, from the domain of passion into that of intelligence is transformed into the notion of expiation, which is exclusively religious, although spiritualistic philosophers believe that it contains moral and rational elements. Expiation is a sort of naïve compensation by which one fancies one may counterbalance moral evil by accepting physical evil along with it. Expiation is a penalty which possesses no utility in the way of benefiting the culprit or those who might follow his example ; it is neither corrective nor preventive ; it is an alleged satisfaction of the law, the re-establishment of an apparent symmetry for the delight of pure intelligence, a public prosecution pure and

*Then as an expiation.*

---

[1] The most orthodox theologians, of course, mean by fire a veritable flame.

simple. In a singular passage in the *Pensées chrétiennes*, Father Bouhours has clearly and innocently set in relief the inutility of religious expiation: "Penitence of the damned, thou art rigorous, and how useless; could the anger of God go further than to punish pleasure so brief by torments which shall never end? When a damned soul shall have shed tears enough to fill all the rivers of the world, even if he should only have shed one a century, he will be no farther ahead after so many millions of years; he will only have begun to suffer, and even when he shall have recommenced as often as there are grains of sand upon the shores of the sea, he shall even then have done nothing." The highest degree of the notion of expiation is in effect this of eternal damnation. In this theory of the penalty of damnation, and the pains of fire without end, one recognizes the barbarism of former time and the torments inflicted on the vanquished by the vanquisher, on the rebel by the chief of the tribe. A sort of atavism attaches even to the religion of love in this perpetual inheritance of hatred, of the customs of a savage period erected into an eternal and divine institution.

### III. Worship and religious rites.

The cult, which, so to speak, is no more than the religion become visible and tangible, is, like the religion itself, simply the apotheosis of a certain social relation: the exchange of services between men living in society Man, who believes himself to receive benefits from the gods, feels himself obliged to give something in exchange. He conceives a sort of reciprocity of action as appropriate between God and man, a possible return in good or evil conduct; man possesses a certain hold on his God, he is capable of procuring Him a certain satisfaction or causing Him a certain pain, and God will reply a hundred fold in kind—pain for pain, pleasure for pleasure.

*The cult an expression of supposed reciprocity between gods and men.*

One knows how gross the external forms of worship in the beginning were. They simply consisted in a practical application of the social economy: the gods were given to eat and drink; an altar was a butcher's stall or the stall of a wine merchant, and the cult was a veritable commerce between heaven and earth—a sort of a market, in which man offered lambs or sheep and received in exchange riches and health.   In our days, the cult is refined; the exchange has become more and more symbolic, the gift is simply an expression of moral homage, for which the worshipper expects no immediate return; still the principle of the cult is always the same, one believes that an act on man's part possesses a direct influence on the will of God, and this act consists in offerings or prayers fixed on beforehand.

*Is so, even to-day.*

Another principle of primitive cult is proportionality.   One can expect no more from another than a proportionate return; bow three times before him, and he will be better disposed toward you than if you bow but once; offer him a beef, and he will be more grateful than if you offer an egg.   Accordingly, to an uncultivated and superstitious mind, it follows that quantity and number should regulate our relations with the gods as they regulate our relations with our fellow-men; multiply your prayers, and you will multiply your chances of favours; three Paternosters go farther than one, a dozen candles will produce a much greater effect than a single candle.   A prayer that you go to a temple to say in public, a cantique chanted in a sonorous voice, will attract more attention than a silent demand formulated at the bottom of one's heart.   Similarly, if one wishes to obtain rain or sun for the crops, it is into the fields that one must go to offer up one's prayer, in a motley file of chanting worshippers; it is always serviceable to point one's finger at what one wants, and to make the demand in person.   The better to stimulate the memory of one's idol primitive man was accustomed to drive a nail into him, and the custom still survives in Brittany in the form of thrusting pins into the bodies of the saints.   Out of sight, out of mind, holds good both of gods and saints.   To simple minds it would be contrary to the law of proportionate exchange for a simple thought, a silent prayer, to receive such favour in the eyes of the gods as an overt act.

*Governed by the law of the market.*

Every religion insists upon some quite determinate exterior form of worship, a precise manifestation, a creed ; it

Embodied in<br>fixed forms.

endeavours to incorporate itself into a certain number of rites and customs, which are numerous and inviolable in proportion as the religion is primitive. The universality of an external form of worship in the different religions of the world is the consequence and the most striking proof of their sociomorphic origin. Man has always believed that he might be useful and agreeable to his gods so long as he has conceived them as analogous to himself and to his neighbours.

Add that to the notion of seducing the gods that of constraining is soon joined. To the conception of an exchange

Which soon<br>came to be con-<br>ceived as coercive.

of services is soon joined that of a species of coercion exercised in some vague manner by the intermediation of some friendly god or even by some simple magic formula which has once succeeded, once procured the object demanded ! Formulæ consecrated by custom appear to be equally binding on gods and men. Accordingly the cult, at first more or less loose, more or less arbitrary, ultimately becomes minutely regulated ; ultimately becomes what one knows as a rite. A rite, at its lowest, is simply the result of a tendency to repeat indefinitely an act which, at some time or other, has seemed to render a god or a fetich propitious. After propitiation comes mechanical custom. Religion, as Pascal well said, is to a large extent habit. Rites are born of the need to perform again and again the same act, under the same circumstances ; a need which is the foundation of custom, and without which all life would be impossible. Moreover, there is something sacred in every habit whatsoever, and every act, whatever it may be, tends to become a habit and by that fact to become respectable, to be in some sort self-consecrated. Rites, therefore, strike root in the very foundations of our being ; the need for rites manifests itself very early in the life of the child. Children not only imitate other people and themselves, repeat other people and themselves, but exact a scrupulous precision in these repetitions ;

in general they do not distinguish the end from the means by which, and the circumstances under which, it is pursued ; they do not yet possess a sufficiently exercised intelligence to understand that the same line of action may lead to the same result in different ways and under different circumstances.  I once observed a child of from eighteen months to two years old : if I got up from my armchair and paraded about the room for its amusement, and stopped, it was necessary before beginning once more that I should return to my seat ; the child's pleasure was much diminished if the repetition was not exact.  The child was accustomed to be fed by a number of people indifferently ; still if I had given it some one thing—milk to drink, for example—a number of times, it was no longer satisfied to receive milk from anybody else, and insisted that the same person should always give it the same thing.  If, on leaving the house, I took another cane than my own, the child would take it away from me to put it back where it belonged.  It was unwilling that one should wear one's hat in the house or go bare-headed out of doors.  And finally, I saw it achieve a veritable bit of ceremonial on its own account.  It had been accustomed to be told to call a domestic at the top of the servants' stairway ; one day the domestic was in the room when the child was told to call her ; the child looked at her, turned about, went to the top of the stairway where it usually called her, and there only shouted out her name.  All the conduct of life, in effect the most important as the most insignificant, is classified in a child's head, rigorously defined, and modelled on the type of the first act of that kind that has caught its attention, without the child's ever being able to distinguish the object of an act from its form.  This confusion between purpose and form exists in a no less striking degree among savages and primitive peoples, and it is upon this very confusion that the sacred character of religious rites is founded.

The trouble that is apparent in a child or an uncultivated man in the presence of whatever deranges his established association of ideas, has been explained by a pure and simple horror of novelty.  Lombroso has even coined a word to

designate this psychological state; he has called it *misoneism.*
But let us not confound two quite distinct things, a horror of
Primitive man a breach of custom and a horror of novelty; there
possesses a repug- are new perceptions, and habits that may be added
nance not to nov-
elty but to a to the whole body of already existing percep-
breach of custom. tions and habits without deranging them much
or at all; and against these neither the savage nor the child
rebels. Though the child never wearies of listening to the
same tale and becomes irritated the moment one alters its least
detail, it will listen no less passionately to a new tale; and
new toys and new walks delight it. The same taste for
novelty is observable among savages, just in so far as it can be
gratified without disturbing their preconceived ideas. Primitive
man is like the miser who will not part with any of his acquired
treasure, but asks nothing better than to increase it. He is
naturally curious, but he has no desire to push his curiosity to
the point of contradicting what he knows already or believes
he knows. And in a measure he is right, he is simply obeying
the powerful instinct of intellectual self-preservation; his
intelligence is not sufficiently supple constantly to knit and
unknit the associations of ideas which experience has established in him. A black, out of an attachment for Livingstone,
wished to accompany him to Europe; a few days on the
steamer drove him insane. It is, therefore, in obedience to a
certain branch of the instinct of self-preservation that primitive
peoples are so conservative in their customs and rites; but
they show themselves no less willing to appropriate the
customs and rites of other people whenever they can do so
without abandoning their own. The Romans ultimately came
to accept the cult of all the peoples in the world without, however, any abandonment of their national cult; and fêtes, which
are properly survivals of paganism, subsist even at the present
day; one acquires superstition, and customs, much more easily
than one loses them.

The power of example contributes also to lend an additional
stability to the public cult; an individual becomes hardened
in a practice which he finds universal in the society in
which he lives. Thence comes the importance of public

worship; the practice of public worship makes those who abstain from it conspicuous. Public worship is a *viva voce* poll.

Worship in public confirms cult. Everyone sits in judgment upon you, all of your acquaintances become your accusers, and all men who worship God are your enemies. Not to think as everybody else does is comprehensible—but not to act as everybody else does! To wish to break away from the servitude of action which, once established, tends to perpetuate itself! In the end the machine bends; one becomes brutalized. Even among people of superior minds the force of habit is incredible. In the hours of doubt, in his youth, M. Renan wrote to his adviser: "I recite the Psalms; I could pass hours and hours, if I but followed my own inclination, in the churches. . . I experience lively returns of devotion. . . At times I am simultaneously both Catholic and rationalist! When one cuts loose from such beliefs, beliefs which have become a second nature to one, it seems as if one has severed one's self from one's whole past. One has in some sense lived them, and one is attachéd to them as to one's own life; to abandon them is to resolve to die to one's self. It seems as if one's entire strength had come from them and that one will be as feeble as a child when one has lost them; they are to one what Samson's hair was to him. Happily they will grow again."

Priesthood is a consequence of the establishment of rites. The priest is the man supposed to be most capable of influenc-

Priesthood a consequence of established rites. ing the divinity by a minute and learned observation of the sacred rites. Rites, in effect, the moment they become complicated by an accumulation of diverse customs lie beyond the knowledge and power of the ordinary man; it requires a special education to talk to the gods in the complex language which alone they understand, in the formulæ which coerce their wills. Whoever possesses this imagination is a species of magician or sorcerer; and the priesthood arose out of sorcery, of which it was simply the regular organization.[1]

[1] "Sorcery, in the beginning purely individual and fantastic," says M. Réville, "gradually develops into sacerdotalism and by that change, having become a perma-

The externals of worship remain to-day, in special in the Catholic and Greek religions, a collection of traditional, inflexi-

Tendency of priest to become a sacred person. ble formulæ, which could not be trusted to produce their effect if a word or a gesture in them were changed; certain ceremonies are really veritable traditional forms of incantation. Rites resemble the invisible bonds in which Faust held the Devil; but it is God himself in this case that is enchanted, charmed, and overpowered. At bottom the belief which makes the Chinese priest turn his praying machine, the belief which makes the devotee tell her beads, the belief which makes the priest thumb his breviary or say salaried masses for unknown peoples, which in the Midi makes rich people pay beggars to mumble prayers before their doors, all rest upon one and the same principle : they all rest on a faith in a power of the rite, of the traditional formula in and of itself, no matter who pronounces it. The efficacity of the interested prayers does not seem to depend solely on the legitimacy of what one demands but on the form employed in demanding them ; and this form has been determined at bottom by experience ; the majority of devotees perform minute experiments on the comparative virtue of individual prayers, masses, offerings, pilgrimages, miraculous waters, etc. ; they amass the result of their observations and transmit them to their children. The invocation of certain privileged Madonnas, such as the Madonna at Lourdes, is even to-day a vestige of primitive sorcery. The priest inherits all these naïve experiments as to the conditions appropriate to induce a miracle, and he systematizes them. Priests being men picked for their capability in the function which was regarded as the most useful of all others for the preservation of society, necessarily came to constitute a really superior caste and to be personally in some sense the object of the cult which they adminis-

nent public institution, sacerdotal sorcery becomes systematic, develops a ritual which becomes traditional, imposes upon those who aspire to the honour of conducting the conditions of initiation, proof of efficiency, a novitiate, receives privileges, defends them if they are attacked, endeavours to augment them. This is the history of all sacerdotal institutions, which are certainly descended from a capricious, fantastic, disorderly, practice of sorcery in previous ages."

tered.  The perfect type of sacerdotal privilege is hereditary priesthood as it existed in ancient Judaism, as it still exists in India; every Brahman is born a priest and needs no special education.  The thirty-seven great priests of Vishnu in Gujerat are honoured even to-day as the visible incarnation of Vishnu.[1]

Historically the priest has always found a rival, sometimes an adversary, in the prophet, from Buddha to Isaiah and Jesus.  The prophet is not a priest bound to a sanctuary and slave to a tradition, but an individual.  "Prophecy," says M. Albert Réville, "is to religion what lyrism is to poetry."  The prophet and the lyric poet, in effect, both speak in the name of their own inspiration.  The prophet is often a revolutionist, the priest is essentially a conservative; the one represents innovation, the other custom.

*Antagonism between priest and prophet.*

Exterior forms of worship and rites allying themselves with refined and elevated sentiments have in all religions taken on a symbolic and expressive character that they did not possess in the practice of primitive sorcery; they have become æsthetic and by that fact rendered durable.  For whoever looks upon the most ancient religious ceremonies with the eye of an artist, they consist in the reproduction, nowadays too mechanically and unconsciously, of a work of art which once was not without its significance and its beauty.  They are nowadays like a hand-organ playing admirable compositions by some old master.  Pfleiderer, in his "Philosophy of Religion," has shown that the dominant element in the externals of worship is dramatic, the dramatization of some mythological or legendary scenes.  It is especially among the Aryans that this element predomi-

*Dramatic element in cult.*

---

[1] It is an honour for which one pays dear to be permitted to consecrate to them one's soul, one's body, or the soul and body of one's wife.  One pays five rupees for the privilege of contemplating them, twenty for the privilege of touching them, thirteen for the privilege of being whipped by them, seventeen for the privilege of eating betel that they have chewed, nineteen for the privilege of drinking the water in which they have bathed, thirty-five for the privilege of washing their great toes, forty-two for the privilege of rubbing them with perfumed oil, and from one hundred to two hundred for tasting in their company the essence of delight.

nates; the Aryans are especially susceptible to the charm of great epics and dramas. The Semites are lyric rather, and thence arises the importance of prophecy among them; although the lyric element was also represented among the Greek poets and Pythonesses. The dramatic element, on the contrary, is visible in certain symbolic ceremonies of Christianity and Judaism. The Mass was formerly a veritable drama of the Passion in which the spectators also took part; the half pagan, half Christian processions that still subsist to-day possess for the crowd something of the attractiveness of the opera. The Communion is a dramatization of the Lord's Supper. Catholicism especially is distinguished by the possession of dramatic and æsthetic (too often gross) elements, which explain, not less than historical reasons, its victory over Protestantism among the nations of southern Europe, which are more artistic than those of the north, and more sensually artistic. The æsthetic superiority of a religion is not to be disdained by the thinker. It is the æsthetic element in every rite which, as we shall see, is its most respectable characteristic. Moreover, religious sentiment and æsthetic sentiment have always gone hand in hand; and this union has been one of the most important factors in the development of the æsthetic sentiment; it is thus that dramas and epics dealt in the beginning with gods and demi-gods rather than with men; the earliest romances were religious legends; the first odes were sacred chants and songs. Music and religion have always been allied. But in the end, the æsthetic element becomes feeble and is replaced, as religion loses its vitality, by a species of mechanical routine. In the East, even more than among us, this phenomenon is manifest, the whole tendency there is toward monotonous and interminable ceremonials. The Parsees, the representatives of the oldest existing religion, pass six hours a day in prayer. And according to the *Indian Mirror* the following is a description of the festival of the Lord, a part of the cult of Brahmaism, the altogether modern and wholly deistical religion founded by Ram Mohun Roy and Keshub: "At precisely six o'clock a hymn was intoned in chorus in the upper gallery of the *mandir* to announce the day's solemnity. Others followed to the accompaniment of the harmonium, and thus, after a succession of hymns, the sacred office was reached, which, counting in the sermon, lasted from seven to ten o'clock. A part of the congregation then retired to take some rest, but those who remained intoned the *vedi* to demand of the minister explanations in regard to several points of his sermon. At noon, the assembly having convened, four *pundits* came out successively and recited Sanskrit texts. At one o'clock the minister gave a conference." Then came the exposition of a number of philosophical and religious theses, delivered by their respective authors. Hymns, meditations, and prayers in common lasted till nearly seven o'clock, when the initiation of seven new Brahmaists was celebrated. This ceremony, including a sermon, lasted not less than two hours, and the assembly, which, if one may believe the reporter, did not show any sign of fatigue after these fifteen hours of continuous devotion, separated with a hymn to the effect that it had not yet had enough : " The heart wishes not to return home."

#### IV. *Subjective worship—Adoration and love.*

Subjective worship has grown out of, and been a refinement upon, the external cult, which in the beginning was in the eyes of mankind much the more important of the two. To the incantation, to the material offering, to the sacrifices of the victims succeeded subjective prayer and the subjective offering of love, and the subjective sacrifice of egoistic passion. To external homage, to evidences of fear and respect by which one was supposed to recognize the superior power of the gods, as one bows down in recognition of the superior power of kings, succeeded a mental adoration, in which a god is recognized as all-powerful but also as all-beneficent. The mental bowing down of the entire soul before God is the last refinement of ritual ; and ritual itself in the higher religions comes to be the simple sign and symbol of this adoration.[1] Thus the primitive sociomor-

*Subjective worship a refinement on public and external worship.*

[1] Among the Hindus, *Tapas*, that is to say fire, the ardour of devotion, and of voluntary renunciation, signified in the beginning simply the incantation intended

phic character of the cult becomes progressively more subtle :
the semi-material society, consisting of gods and men, becomes
a wholly moral society, composed of men and the principle of
goodness, which still continues to be represented as a person,
as a master, as a father, as a king.

The highest form of subjective worship is love of God, in
which all the duties of religious morality may be regarded as
summed up. Adoration contains in it a vitiating
element of respect for power ; love is a more intimate union. The love of God is a partial manifestation of the need to love which exists in every
human being. This need is so great that it cannot always find
satisfaction in real life ; it tends therefore to stretch beyond,
and not finding upon earth an object which completely suffices
for it, it seeks one in heaven. The love of God appears thus
to be an expression of the superabundance of the love of man.
Our heart sometimes feels too big for the world and seeks to
overpass its limits. Let us not forget, for the rest, that the
world has been strangely contracted by religious ignorance,
intolerance, and prejudice ; the sphere left open to the need
of loving was formerly a very narrow one : it is not astonishing
that the latter should have stretched out its arms toward a
celestial and supernatural being.

The same thing happens when human affections are ship-
wrecked in us, lose their object, no longer find anything to
which they can attach themselves. In France, as
in England and America, the habitual devotion
of spinsters has long since been observed, though
it often coincides with a certain pining away of
the heart. In our times a virtuous unmarried woman is, so to
speak, predestined to devotion ; divine love is for her (on an
average, of course) a necessary compensation. Remark also
that old men are generally more inclined to devotion than
young. There are, no doubt, a number of reasons for it : the
approach of death, the enfeeblement of the body and of the

The love of God
an outlet for the
surplus of human
love.

Nourished by
isolation, feeble-
ness, and misfor-
tune.

to constrain the Devas to obedience, and to deprive them of a part of their power.
Out of a crude conception has grown an extremely refined one. See *Manuel
de l'Histoire des religions*, par C. P. Tiele, p. 19 (translated by Maurice Vernes).

intelligence, the increasing need for a support, etc.; but there exists also a more profound reason. The old man, always more isolated than the young, and deprived of the excitations of the sexual instinct, possesses a smaller outlet for his instinct for affection and for love. Thus there accumulates in him an amount of treasure which he is free to apply as to him seems best ; well, the service of God is that which demands least effort, which is most appropriate to the natural indolence of the old, to their preoccupation with themselves ; they become therefore devotees, partly out of egoism, partly out of a need for some disinterested occupation. A grain of incense burns in every heart, and when the perfume of it can no longer be given to the earth we let it mount to heaven. Note also that the loss of beloved beings, misfortunes of every sort, and irreparable infirmities all provoke an expansion of the heart toward God. In the Middle Ages unhappiness was frequently one of the most important factors of piety ; when a great and unmerited misfortune happened to a man, the chances were that he would enter the Church or else become an atheist ; it depended often on his strength of mind, his habits, and his education. When one strikes an animal it is equally possible that it may bite one or crouch at one's feet. Every time the heart is violently bruised there comes an inevitable reaction ; we must reply from within to the blows from without, and this reply is sometimes revolt and sometimes adoration. The feeble, the disinherited, the suffering, all those to whom misfortune has not left strength enough for rebellion, have but one resource : the sweet and consoling humility of divine love. Whoever does not love, or is not loved completely and sufficiently, on earth will always turn toward heaven : the proposition is as regular as the parallelogram of forces.

Just as we have seen in an error of the senses one of the objective principles of religious physics, so perhaps may we

*Power of mysticism a perversion of love.*

find in a perversion of love one of the most essential subjective principles of mysticism. It is by love that this unction, this penetrating sweetness which makes the mystic tremble to the marrow of his bones, is to be explained. Profound love, even the most terrestrial, tends to envelop the object with respect and veneration ; an effect which is due to a number of causes, and among others to the psychological law according to which desire magnifies the desired object. To love is always a little to adore. If it is a human being that is the object of the love, the divinization incidental to it will be confined within certain limits, but if the love stretch up from the earth into heaven, it may command the full powers of the imagination ; the soul, seeking at a distance for some vague object to which to attach itself, will go out in mystic outbursts of emotion and ecstasy. The soul will personify its ideal, will supply it with figure and speech : its ideal will be Jesus with Mary Magdalene at his feet, or the Virgin weeping at the foot of the cross, or Moses in the midst of the clouds, or the child Buddha before whom the statues of the gods rose and made obeisance. Thus mystical religions are formed of great images and passionate sentiments and the heart of man, the very life blood of which they turn to their profit. What appears often to be the most intellectual of tastes is only love in disguise. The most earthly love is often a religion in its earliest stages. Henri Beyle, visiting the salt-mines at Salzburg, found in a shaft a branch covered with incomparable diamonds scintillating in the light. It was a dead timber on which the salt had crystallized ; in the timber thus transformed Beyle saw the symbol of what happens in every loving heart ; every object one finds there has taken on an extraordinary brilliancy, a marvellous beauty. He calls this phenomenon crystallization ; we should prefer to call it divinization. Love always divinizes its object ; partially and provisionally when this object is placed upon earth and close to one's eyes, but definitively when this object is lost in the distance of heaven. Our gods are like those mysterious beings who spring, in legend, from a drop of generous blood or a loving tear let fall upon the earth ; it is with our own substance that we nourish them ; their beauty, their goodness come out of our love, and if we love them as we do, the reason is that we must love something ; must lift up to the four corners of the

horizon, even if they be deaf, a supreme appeal. This outcome of love and religious sentiment is most visible in exalted
minds, both in the Middle Ages and in our own days. The
true element of originality in Christian literature is that one
there finds, for the first time, a sincere and warm accent of
love, scarcely divined, here and there, by the great spirits
of antiquity, by Sappho and Lucretius. In a page of St.
Augustine one finds the expression of a franker and more
profound ardour than in all the elegant affectations of Horace
or the languors of Tibullus. Nothing in pagan antiquity is
comparable to the chapter in the " Imitation " on love. The
passion, confined and held in check, mounts to heights till
then unknown, like a dammed river ; but it is no less genuinely itself. What shall we say of the visionary mystics of
the people like St. Theresa, and Chantal, and Guyon?
Among them piety, in its most exaggerated form, verges upon
the madness of love. St. Theresa might have been a
courtesan of genius equally as well as a saint. Physiologists
and physicians have often observed, in our days, analogous
pathological cases, in which the religious effusion is simply, so
to speak, a case of mistake in identity.[1]

In Christianity the conception of Jesus, the beautiful, gentle
young man, the Holy Spirit incarnate in the purest and most
ideal form, favours more directly than any corresponding conception in any rival religion this
particular perversion of love. Christianity is the
most anthropomorphic belief in existence, for it

*Worship of
Christ to a con-
siderable extent a
perversion of love.*

is the one of all others which, after having conceived the most
elevated idea of God, abases it, without degrading it, to the most
human of human conditions. By a much more refined, much
more profound paganism than the paganism of antiquity,
the Christian religion has succeeded in making God the object
of an ardent love, without ceasing to make Him an object of
respect. By a myth much more seductive and poetic even than
that of Psyche, we see God, the true God, descended upon earth
in the form of a blond and smiling young man ; we hear him
speak low in the ear of Mary Magdalene at the fall of evening;

[1] Ribot, *de l'Hérédité*, 364 ; Moreau de Tours, *Psych. morbide*, 259.

and then this vision suddenly disappears and we see in the gathering shadow two mutilated arms extended toward us, and a heart which bleeds for humanity. In this legend all the powers of the imagination are called in play, all the fibres of the heart are moved ; it is an accomplished work of art. What is there astonishing in the fact that Christ has been and is still the great seducer of souls ? In the ears of a young girl his name appeals at once to all her instincts, even to the maternal instinct, for Jesus is often represented as a child with the dimpled, rosy cheeks which the Greeks ascribed to Eros. The heart of the woman is thus besieged on all sides at once : her wavering and timid imagination wanders from the cherub to the youth, and from the youth to the pale figure, with the bowed head, upon the cross. It is possible that from the birth of Christianity down to the present day there has not been one single woman of an exalted piety whose heart has not first beat for her God, for Jesus, for the most lovable and loving type that the human mind has ever conceived.

Side by side with its somewhat sentimental element the love of God contains a moral element, which is progressively detaching itself with the march of ideas. God

Moral element in the law of God.

being the very principle of goodness, the personification of the moral ideal, the love of God ultimately becomes a moral love properly so called, the love of virtue, of sanctity at its height. The subjective act of charity thus becomes the religious act *par excellence*, in which morality and subjective worship are identified ; good works and the externals of worship are simply a translation into the outer world of the moral consciousness. At the same time, in the highest speculations of philosophic theology, charity has been conceived as embracing simultaneously all beings in the divine love, and by consequence as beginning to realize the sort of perfect society in which " all exist in all and all in every part." The social and moral character of religion thus attains its highest degree of perfection and God appears as a sort of mystic realization of the universal society, *sub specie æterni.*

# Part Second.

## THE DISSOLUTION OF RELIGIONS IN EXISTING SOCIETIES.

### CHAPTER I.

#### DOGMATIC FAITH.

I. Narrow dogmatic faith—The credulity of primitive man : First, spontaneous faith in the senses and imagination ; Second, faith in the testimony of superior men ; Third, faith in the divine word, in revelation, and in the sacred texts—The literalness of dogmatic faith—Inevitable intolerance of narrow dogmatic faith—Belief in dogma, revelation, salvation, and damnation all result in intolerance—Modern tolerance.

II. Broad dogmatic faith—Orthodox Protestantism—Dogmas of orthodox Protestantism—Rational consequences of these dogmas—Logical failure of orthodox Protestantism.

III. The dissolution of dogmatic faith in modern society—Reasons that render this dissolution inevitable—Comparative influence of the various sciences ; influence of public instruction, of means of communication, of industry even and of commerce, etc.—The disappearance of belief in oracles and prophecies—Gradual disappearance of the belief in miracles, in devils, etc.

### I. Narrow dogmatic faith.

IF faith has not varied especially in and of itself as a mode of feeling, the objects with which it is concerned have differed from generation to generation. Hence the various forms of doctrine which we shall pass in review as showing the evolution and dissolution of faith.

In primitive religions, faith was altogether experimental and physical ; it was not opposed to scientific belief, which, to say the truth, did not exist. It was a credulity rather than a faith ; and religious faith, in our day, is still a credulity, an obligatory credulity, primarily in the authority of superior men, secondarily in that of God himself.

Primitive faith more properly a credulity.

The origin of religious faith has been attributed solely to an appetite for the marvellous and the extraordinary; but we have already shown that religions do everything in their power to regulate the imagination even in the very act of stimulating it, and to bring the unknown to the touchstone of the known. The marvellous must aid in making something at least apparently comprehensible; with marvel for marvel's sake religion holds no commerce. So much so, that primitive people have sought in religion, less to multiply the marvellous, in the modern sense of the word, than partially to suppress it; they have been in search of an explanation of some sort. An explanation by superior powers, by spirits, by occult virtues, seemed clearer to them than an explanation by scientific law.

*Subordination of the marvellous in primitive faith.*

For the rest, any explanation once given, primitive man never dreamed of disputing it, he was essentially a "man of faith." The delicate shades of thought we designate as verisimilitude, probability, possibility, were as little known to primitive man as to children. The voluntary suspension of judgment that we call doubt indicates an extremely advanced state of mind. With children and savages, to conceive and to believe are one; they know nothing about reserving their approbation, or mistrusting their own intelligence or that of others. A certain humility, which young minds do not possess, is necessary before one can say: That may be true but also it may not, or in other words, I don't know. And also one must have patience to verify with care what one believes, and patience is courage of the most difficult kind. Finally, man always feels the need to declare that what is attractive, what satisfies his mind, is real: when one tells an interesting story to a child, he says, "It is true, is it not?" If, on the contrary, it is a sad story he will cry out: "That is not true!" A man of the people to whom one should demonstrate, with the evidence in one's hand, that a thing he thought true was false, would reply with a shake of the head, "If it is not true, it ought to be." All primitive people were like that. In a memorandum on The Development of Language and Intelligence among Children, E. Egger char-

*Rationale of primitive man's faith in the marvellous.*

acterized this state of mind as "rebellion against the notion of doubt and even that of simple probability." Felix, a child of five and one-half years, took a lively interest in sacred history, but he could not understand why all the lacunæ had not been filled in, or why doubtful points should be marked as such. " The actual state of his mind," adds E. Egger, "corresponds in a manner to that of the Greek mind during the period when the effort was made painfully to set in order the chaos of ancient legend." Two years later the same child received a present of a collection of stories. He found in the preface that the author gave the stories out as true; he asked nothing further, and was promptly astonished to find anybody else in doubt. "His trustfulness displayed no disposition to go behind the letter of his text, in especial as the stories sounded to him sufficiently probable." In my own experience with children, I have noticed that nothing irritates them like uncertainty; a thing must be true or false, and generally they prefer that it should be true. For the rest, a child does not know the limits of his own power, and still less that of others; and too, he has no clear sense of the marvellous and the improbable. A child saw a horse galloping by one day, and said to me seriously, "I could run as fast as that." Thus again the little peasant girl, of whom we spoke above, asked her mistress why she might not have made the flowers in the garden. A sense of the possible is lacking in primitive intelligences: because you seem to a child or a savage to be able to do more things than he, he readily comes to believe that you can do everything; so that what we call miracles seem to primitive people simply the visible and necessary sign of superior power; so much so, indeed, that to them a man of mark ought to be able to perform miracles; they expect them from him as their due, and become indignant if they are not forthcoming, as a child is indignant when one does not help him carry a burden that is too heavy for his strength. The Hebrews precisely expected Moses to perform miracles and, so to speak, obliged him to do them. The people believe in their great men, and the belief in miracles is but a corollary from their general confidence.

Moreover, faith reaches a height among primitive nations that it never does among cultivated intelligences: they believe immeasurably things that it is out of all measure to believe at all; the happy *inter utrumque* is as lacking in the belief itself as in the thing believed. Mr. Spencer, in his "Sociology," cites the example of a young woman who attributed to a certain amulet the magical virtue of preserving her against injuries. She thought herself as invulnerable as Achilles. The chief of the tribe, astonished that so precious an amulet should exist, and wishing no doubt to acquire it, asked to have its virtues verified before his eyes. The woman was brought to him, a warrior prepared his hatchet, and in perfect confidence she put out her arm. The blow fell and the woman uttered a cry of astonishment not less than of pain as her hand fell to the ground. Who in our day has such absolute faith? Very few among us would risk his life, or even his hand, to maintain such and such a dogma. This woman belonged to the race of martyrs; her intense credulity bordered on heroism.

*Absoluteness of primitive faith.*

Man's natural confidence in his fellow-men, especially when there is no very evident reason why the latter should mislead him, is the origin of the credence we give to the testimony and authority of those who claim to be inspired; which all seemed very human and natural in the beginning, and only later came to be regarded as supernatural. This spontaneous disposition to believe is an elementary instinct which plays a large rôle in religious sociomorphism. Suspicious as primitive man is when his material interests are at stake, in all other matters he is apt to be credulous to a fault. Moreover, he scarcely knows what one means by *error*, and does not distinguish it from deception; he puts trust in his own judgment and in that of other people. When you tell him something extraordinary, his first thought is that you are making sport of him; he is less inclined to believe that you have deceived yourself, that you have reasoned falsely; sincerity and verity are confused in his mind. It has taken all the experience of modern life to make clear to us the difference between these two things; to

*Confusion of sincerity with verity by primitive man.*

induce us to verify the affirmations even of those whose characters we esteem most highly ; to contradict, without offending, those who are dearest to us. Primitive man never distinguished his belief in the " law " from his faith in the " prophets." Those whom he esteemed and admired seemed to him of necessity to know the facts. Add that man is always inclined to make much of anything that is a material fact, of anything that appeals to his eyes and to his ears. The sacred word, and the sacred writings that embody it, are to him not merely indications, but *proofs* of what they affirm. I overheard it given in a church one day as an incontestable proof that Moses conversed with the Lord that Mt. Sinai is still in existence ; that is the sort of argument that is successful with the people. Livingstone says that the negroes listened and believed from the moment he showed them the Bible and told them that the celestial Father had written His will on the pages of that book ; they touched the pages and believed at once.

In effect, blind confidence in a word, in a sign—precipitate induction from which one infers from the reality of

Inference from reality of the sign to reality of the thing signified the essence of faith in revelation.

the sign to the reality of the thing signified : a second induction to the effect that any doctrine relatively elevated, from the social and moral point of view, and put forth by men one respects, is probably true, even if it be in many points irrational—these are the principal elements of the primitive faith in revelation. And this faith, in all its crudity, exists at the present day. It wins its way through the eyes and ears ; therein lies its power. It is much less mystical than we are inclined to fancy ; it is incarnate in its monuments, its temples, its books ; it walks about and breathes in the person of its priests, its saints, its gods ; we cannot look about us without realizing its existence in one form or another. It has been of great service to human thought, in spite of its pitfalls, thus to have been able to express itself, to fashion objects in its own image, to penetrate marble and stone, to provide that it shall itself be borne back in upon us from without. How can one doubt what is visible and tangible ?

Faith in testimony and authority leads to faith in sacred texts and in the very letter of these texts. This is what one means by *literal* faith. It exists still in our day, among many civilized people. It constitutes the basis of the Catholicism of the masses. " In order to silence restless spirits," said the council of Trent, " it is decreed that no one may, in the interpretation of the Scriptures, . . . deviate from the construction sanctioned by the Church, to seek for a supposedly more exact rendering." Faith lies thus in a renunciation of thought, an abdication of liberty; imposes upon itself a rule not of logic but of morals, and subjects itself to dogmas as to immutable principles. It restricts intelligence beforehand to precise limits, and imposes a general direction on it, with instructions not to swerve from it. It is at this point that faith comes really to be opposed to scientific belief for which in the beginning it was a substitute. According to the council of the Vatican, those who have faith do not believe " because of the intrinsic truth of the things revealed," but " because of the divine *authority* that revealed them." If you reason with a person of that stamp, he will listen, understand, and follow you—but only to a certain point; there he stops, and nothing in the world can make him go beyond. Or rather from that point he will declare himself inexpugnable, and will assure you that you have absolutely no hold on him ; and in effect, no scientific or philosophical reason could turn him from his belief, since he places the object of his faith in a sphere superior to reason, and makes his faith an affair of " conscience." Nothing can force a man to think rightly when he does not propose rectitude of thought to himself as a supreme aim, and nothing can oblige him to follow the dictates of reason to the bitter end, if he believes that the instant he calls certain dogmas and certain authorities in question he is committing a sin. Thus, faith gives a certain sacred and inviolable character to what it sanctions,—converts it into a sacred ark that one may not touch without sacrilege or danger, neither may one look at it too closely nor touch it with one's fingers, even to lend it support now and then when it seems ready to fall. Free-thought and

*Results in "credo quia ineptum."*

science never consider a thing as true except provisionally, and so long as it is not seriously doubted by someone. Dogmatic faith, on the contrary, affirms as true not only the things that are uncontested, but those which, according to it, are conclusively presumed, and therefore above discussion. It follows that, if reasons for belief diminish, faith must be none the less strong. It was this that Pascal endeavoured to demonstrate. In effect, the less a belief seems rational to our finite minds, the more merit there is in lending credence to "divine authority." It would be too simple to believe no more than what one sees or what sounds probable to one ; to affirm the improbable, to believe in what seems incredible, is much more meritorious. Our courage rises in proportion as our intelligence becomes humble ; the more absurd one is the greater one is—*credo quia ineptum ;* the more difficult the task, the greater the merit. The strength of our faith is estimated, in the mysticism of Pascal, by the weakness of its "reasons." The ideal, on this theory, would be to possess no more than the metaphysical minimum of reason for belief, the weakest conceivable of motives, a mere nothing ; that is to say, one should be attached to the supreme object of one's faith by the slenderest of bonds. The Albigensian priests, the *parfaits*, wear a simple white cord around their waists as an emblem of their vow ; all mankind wears this cord, and it is in reality more solid and often heavier than any chain.

Scepticism tends toward a complete intellectual indifference with regard to all things ; dogmatic faith produces a partial indifference, an indifference limited to certain points, determined once for all ; it is no longer anxious on these heads, but rests and delights in established dogma. The sceptic and the man of faith abandon themselves thus to a more or less extensive abstinence from thought. Religious faith is a determination to suspend the flight of the imagination, to limit the sphere of thought. We all know the Oriental legend that the world is held up by an elephant, which stands on a tortoise, which floats on a sea of milk. The believer must always refrain from asking what supports the sea of milk ? He must never notice a

Complete intellectual rest incident to faith.

point of which there is no explanation; he must constantly repeat to himself the abortive incomplete idea that has been given him without daring to recognize that it is incomplete. In a street through which I pass every day, a blackbird whistles the same melodic phrase; the phrase is incomplete, ends abruptly, and for years I have heard him lift his voice, deliver himself of his truncated song, and stop with a satisfied air, with no need to complete his musical fragment, which I never hear without a feeling of impatience. It is thus with the true believer; accustomed as he is in the most important questions to dwell within the limits of the customary, without any curiosity about the beyond, he sings his monotonous little note without dreaming that it lacks anything—that his phrase is as clipped as his wings are, and that the narrow world of his belief is not the universe.

The people who still hold to this kind of faith represent the antique world endeavouring to perpetuate itself without a compromise in the bosom of the new world, the **Wilful blindness of faith.** world of modern society. The barbarian does not wish to yield to the progress of ideas and of manners; if such people formed the majority of the nation they would constitute the greatest danger to human reason, to science, and to truth. Literal faith, in effect, makes naked truth a subject of pudicity; one does not dare to look it in the face or lift the sacred veil that hides its beauty; you find yourself in the midst of a conspiracy, mysterious beings surround you, putting their hands before your eyes and a finger on your lips. Dogma holds you, possesses you, masters you in spite of yourself; it is fixed in your heart and petrified in your intelligence: it is not without reason that faith has been compared to an anchor that has caught on the bottom and checked the vessel in its course, while the open and free ocean stretches beyond as far as the eye can reach. And who shall break the anchor from his heart? When you shake it loose in one place, faith settles to its hold somewhere else; you have a thousand weak points at which it attacks you. You can completely abandon a philosophical doctrine; but you cannot break away absolutely from a collection of beliefs in which

blind and literal faith has borne sway; there is always something left; you will carry the scars and marks from it as slaves
who are freed still carry on their flesh the signs of their servitude. You are branded in the heart, you shall feel the effects
of it always; you shall have moments of dread and shudder-
ing, of mystic enthusiasm, of distrust of reason, of need to
represent things as being other than they really are, to see
what is not, and not to see what is. The fiction that was
early forced upon your soul shall often seem to you sweeter
than the sound and rugged truth, you need to know; you
shall hate yourself for the sin of knowledge.

There is a story of a Brahman who was talking with a European of his religion, and among other dogmas mentioned the
scrupulous respect due to animals. "The law,"
said he, "not only forbids one's doing evil, voluntarily, to the smallest creature even for the
purpose of supplying one's self with food, it even bids one walk
with extraordinary circumspection with one's eyes down, that
one may avoid stepping on the humblest ant." Without trying
to refute this naïve faith the European handed the speaker a
microscope. The Brahman looked through the instrument and
saw on everything about him, on the fruits that he was
about to eat, in the beverage that he was about to drink,
everywhere that he might put his hand or foot, the movement of a multitude of little animals of whose existence he
had never dreamed: creatures that he had totally left out of
account. He was stupefied and handed the microscope back
to the European. "I give it to you," the latter said. The
Brahman with a movement of joy took it and threw it on the
ground, and broke it, and departed satisfied; as if by that
stroke he had destroyed the truth and saved his faith.
Happily, in our day, one may without great loss destroy an
optical or physical instrument, it can be replaced; but what is
to become of an intelligence in the hands of the fanatical
believer? Would he not crush it, in case of need, as the instrument of glass was crushed, and sacrifice it the more gaily
that a more limpid gleam of truth might well filter through

*Intolerance
incident to faith.*

it ? In India we have an example of the philosophical doctrine, very inoffensive in appearance and upheld, with various
modifications, by great thinkers, of the transmigration of
souls, becoming a religious dogma, producing as a direct
result intolerance, contempt of science, and all the usual
effects of blind dogmatism. Dogmatic and absolute faith in
its every form tends to check thought ; thence springs its
intolerance—a consequence that may well be insisted on.

Intolerance is only an outward realization of the tyranny
exercised within by dogmatic faith. Belief in a *revelation*,
which all religion rests upon, is the very opposite
of progressive *discovery ;* the instant one affirms
that the first exists, the latter becomes useless,

And even logic-
ally resulting
from it.

dangerous, and ends in being condemned. Intolerance, first
theoretic, then practical, is the legitimate offspring of absolute
faith of every kind. In all revealed religion doctrine first
appears in the form of *dogma*, then of dogmatic and categorical commandment. There have always been things that
must be believed, and practices that must be observed, under
pain of perdition. The sphere of dogmas and sacred rites
may be widened or narrowed, the discipline may be loose or
so strict that it extends to the very items of one's diet; but
there is always at least a minimum of dogma that is absolute
and of practice that is rigidly obligatory, without which no
truly religious church could exist. And this is not all.
Theological sanction is by its very nature always in extremes ;
it presents one with no mean between absolute good and absolute evil, both conceived as eternal. And this being
granted, how should believers, who are dominated by an
exclusive preoccupation with an ardent and profound faith,
hesitate to employ constraint in case of need when the
matter at stake is so great—is of absolute and eternal good
or of absolute and eternal evil ? For them the only value of
free-will lies in its use—in its use toward its proper object,
which is the fulfilment of the divine will. In the presence of
an eternity of penalties to be avoided, everything seems permissible ; any means seems good provided it be successful.
Possessed of that implicit certitude which is inseparable from an

absolute and explicit faith, what really enthusiastic soul would hold back before the employment of force? Accordingly, as a matter of fact, every religion which is at once new and powerful is intolerant. The appearance of tolerance marks a decline of faith; a religion which allows for the existence of another is a religion in decay. One cannot believe anything " with all one's heart " without a sentiment of pity and even of horror for those who believe differently. If I were absolutely certain of possessing the supreme and ultimate verity, should I hesitate to turn the world upside-down to make it prevail? One puts blinkers on a horse to keep him from seeing to the right or left; he looks straight ahead and runs forward under the whip with the hardiness and vigour of ignorance; it is in the same fashion that the partisans of an absolute dogma move through life. " Every positive religion, every immutable form," says Benjamin Constant, " leads directly to intolerance, providing one reasons logically."

The reply to Benjamin Constant is that it is one thing to believe that one knows the way to salvation and another thing to force others to walk in that way. The priest

Use of force as justifiable in a priest as in a physician.

looks upon himself as the physician of the soul; to wish to minister by violence to an ailing soul, " is quite as if," it has been said, " the physician of the body for greater certainty should take the precaution of having his patient condemned to death or to hard labor in case of disobedience to his prescriptions." [1] Assuredly it would involve a contradiction in terms for the physician of the body to wish to bring it to death; but it in nowise involves a contradiction for the physician of the soul to wish to put constraint upon the body. The objection falls of its own weight. For the rest, let us not deceive ourselves; if the physicians of the body leave their patients free, it is sometimes that they cannot help so doing, simply; in certain grave cases they insist on having the patient under their control in a hospital, which is, after all, a sort of prison. If a European physician had to prescribe for one of those American Indians, whose habit it is in an attack of smallpox, when the fever reaches forty

[1] M. Franck, *Des rapports de la religion et de l'État.*

degrees, to plunge into the water to refresh themselves, the
first thing he would do would be to strap his patient to his
cot. And every physician would like really to be able to proceed after the same fashion, even in Europe, even at the
present day, with people like Gambetta, Mirabeau, and many
others less illustrious, who kill themselves by negligence.

Besides, one must not reason as if the believer could isolate
himself and act only for himself. For example, to a Catholic
what is the meaning of absolute liberty of choice

Intolerance a
perverted charity. in education? It means the right of parents to
damn their children. Is this right thus permis-
sible in their eyes? There are books calculated to destroy faith;
books by Voltaire, or Strauss, or Renan; books which, if
circulated, result in our losing our souls, "a thing far more
grave than the death of the body," as Théodore de Bèze said,
after St. Augustine. Can a nation truly penetrated by a Christian charity allow such books to be circulated on the pretext
of liberty of conscience? No; one must before all else deliver
the very will from the bonds of heresy and error; it is on this
condition only that it can be free. Moreover, one must prevent
the corrupt conscience from corrupting others. We see plainly
that charitable intolerance is justified from an exclusively
theological point of view. It rests on logical reasonings of
which the point of departure alone is vicious.[1]

[1] It is easy to understand the high ecclesiastical authorities in the Catholic
Church, who maintain as an article of faith the right to repress error. Recollect
the well-known pages in which St. Augustine speaks of what good effects he had
observed to result from the employment of constraint in religious matters. "A
great many of those who have been brought back into the Church by force confess
themselves to be greatly rejoiced at having been delivered from their former errors,
who, however, by I know not what force of custom, would never have thought of
changing for the better if the fear of the law had not put them in mind of the truth.
Good precepts and wholesome fear must go together so that not only the light of
truth may drive away the gloom of error, but that charity may break the bonds
of bad custom, so that we may rejoice over the salvation of the many. . . It is
written: 'Bid them to enter in.' . . God Himself did not spare his son, but
delivered Him for our sake to the executioners." Schiller makes the great inquisitor
in *Don Carlos* say the same thing. See St. Augustine, *Epist.* cxiii. 17,5—St.
Paul, *Ephes.*, vi. 5, 6, 9. Lastly, recollect also the reasoned decision of the doctors
and councils. "Human government," said St. Thomas, "is derived from *divine
government* and should *imitate* it. Now although God is all-powerful and infinitely

In order to understand how legitimate religious intolerance appears from its own point of view, we must remember with what perfect calm we forbid and punish acts that

And a half-caste public spirit. are directly contrary to the actual conditions of our social life (for example, the public outrage of good morals, etc.). Now we know that all religion superposes another society upon the actual one ; it conceives men's life as enveloped and bounded by the life of the gods ; it must therefore seek to maintain the conditions of this supernatural society with not less energy than we employ to maintain our human society, and the conditions of this superior society lead to the multiplication of all the prohibitive rules that we have previously imposed on our existence with our fellows ; imaginary walls cannot avoid being added to the walls and ditches already impeding circulation on the earth's surface : if we live with the gods, we must expect to be jostled by them, and curbed in their name. This state of things cannot disappear entirely until we cease to believe we are co-members of a society with the gods, until we see them transmuted into

good, He nevertheless permits in the universe that He has made the existence of evils which He could prevent ; He permits them for fear that in suppressing them more than equivalent goods might be suppressed incidentally along with them and greater evils provoked in their stead. The same is true in human government ; *rulers naturally tolerate certain evils for fear of putting an obstacle in the way of certain goods, or of causing greater evils,* as St. Augustine said in the treatise on *Order.* It is thus that *infidels,* though they sin in their rites, may be *tolerated, either because of some good coming from them, or to avoid some evil.* The Jews observe their rites, in which formerly the truth of the faith that we hold was prefigured ; the result is advantageous in this, that we have the testimony of our enemies in favour of our faith, and that the object of our faith is, so to speak, shown in a reflected image. As for the worship of the other unbelievers, which is opposed in every way to truth and is entirely useless, *it would merit no tolerance* if it were not to avoid some evil, such as the scandal or *the trouble which might result from the suppression of this worship ;* or again as an impediment to the salvation of those who, under cover of this species of tolerance, come little by little into the faith. It is for that reason that the Church has occasionally tolerated even the worship of heretics, and heathens, when the number of infidels was great." (*Summa theol.,* 2 a ; q. x, a. 11.) One readily perceives the nature of *tolerance* in that sense. It does not in the least recognize the right of those who are the object of it : if it does not maltreat them, it is simply to *avoid a greater evil,* or rather because its power is too small, and the number of infidels is too large.

A professor of theology at the Sorbonne has recently contested the charge of

simple ideals. Ideals never necessitate the exclusiveness and intolerance that realities do.

On the whole, one must distinguish two kinds of virtue on which religion has influence. The first are the virtues that Tolerance highly intellectual. may be called positive and active, of the heart and of instinct, like charity and generosity; at all times and in all countries they have existed among men; religion exalts them, and to Christianity the honour is due of having developed them to their highest degree. The second category includes the purely intellectual virtues, whose operation consists rather in checking and confining than in extending the sphere of one's activity—the virtues of self-possession, of abstinence, and of tolerance, which are quite modern really and the result of science, which has brought about a clearer knowledge of its own limitations even. Tolerance is a very complex virtue, much more intellectual than charity; it is a virtue of the head rather than of the heart; the proof of it is that charity and intolerance are often found together, forming an alliance rather than opposing each other. When tolerance is not philosophical

Catholic intolerance. (M. Alfred Fouillée had just spoken of it in his *Social Science.*) He did so for reasons that may be cited as further proof. "Neither to-day, nor *ever, in any epoch of its history*, has the Catholic Church intended to *impose acceptance of the truth by violence.* All great theologians have taught that the act of faith is a voluntary act, which presupposes an illumination of the mind; *but they have also taught that constraint may favour this illumination, and in especial may preserve others from* a bad example, from a contagious darkness. The Christian Church has had no need of the sword to evangelize the nations; if it has shed blood in its triumph, it has been *its own.*" Has it, then, not shed the blood of others? If one counts all the murders committed by intolerance in the name of absolute dogma, in every country in the world; if one could measure all the bloodshed; if one could gather together all the dead bodies—would the pile not mount higher than the spires of the cathedrals and the domes of the temples, where man still goes, with unalterable fervour, to invoke and bless the "God of Love"? Faith in a God who talks and acts, who has a history of His own, His Bible, His prophet and His priest, will always end by being intolerant. By adoring a jealous and vengeful God, one becomes in the end His accomplice. One tacitly approves all the crimes committed in His name and often (if one believes the Holy Scriptures) commanded by Him. One endeavours to forget these things when they are too stained with blood and filth. The monuments of such bloody scenes have been razed, and the places to which the strongest memories are attached have been purified and transformed: the partisans of certain dogmas need to wash their hearts also in lustral water.

and wholly reasoned, it takes on the aspect of a simple good-humour that greatly resembles moral weakness. Really to demonstrate the greatness of tolerance, one must put to the front the objective reasons drawn from the relativity of human knowledge and not the subjective reasons drawn from our own hearts.[1] Up to the present time tolerance has been founded on *respect* for the person and the will of another: "It is necessary," it is said, "for man to be free—free to deceive himself and to do evil, if need be ; " and nothing is truer, but there is another source of tolerance which is more substantial and tends to gain ground more and more rapidly as dogmatic faith disappears. This source is distrust of human thought and conscience, which are not free not to deceive themselves, and to which every article of absolute *faith* must necessarily be also an article of error. So that, at the present day, tolerance is no longer a virtue, but simply an affair of the intelligence ; the further one goes, the more one sees that one does not in the least understand ; the more one sees that the beliefs of one's neighbour are a complement to one's own, that no one of us can be right alone, to the exclusion of all others. By the mere development of the intelligence which makes us aware of the infinite variety of the world and the impossibility of any one solution of eternal problems, each individual opinion comes to have a value in our eyes: it is nothing more nor less than a bit of evidence bearing on the theory of the universe, and it goes without the saying that no one item of evidence can be made the basis of a definitive judgment, a dogmatic conclusion, without appeal.

## *II. Broad dogmatic faith.*

"The aim of most men," as an English writer says, "is to pass through life with as little expenditure of thought as possible :" but what is to become of those who think, and of intellectual men in general ? Even without suspecting it, one will ultimately allow an interpretation more or less broad of the texts to which one has seemed to cling in a narrow and *literal* faith. There is almost no such thing as a perfectly orthodox believer.

Conflict between intelligence and dogmatism.

[1] See A. Fouillée, *Systèmes de morale contemporains.*

Heresy enters by one door or another, and strange to say it is that precise fact that keeps traditional faith alive in face of the progress of science. An absolute and immutably literal faith would be too offensive to last long. Orthodoxy either kills the nations in which it entirely stifles freedom of thought or it kills faith in itself. Intelligence can never stand still; it is a light that moves, like that cast by the sun on the dripping oars as the boat is being lustily rowed along.

The partisans of literal interpretation and authority seem sooner or later to accept two irrational hypotheses instead of one; it is not enough for them that there have been certain revelations from on high, they insist that the very terms in which the divine thought is incorporated shall be divine, sacred, and immutable, and of an absolute exactitude. They divinize human language. They never think of the difficulties that someone might feel who was not a god but simply a Descartes, a Newton, or a Leibnitz, to express his great thoughts in an unformed and half-savage tongue. Genius is always superior to the language that it makes use of, and the words themselves are responsible for many of the errors in its thoughts; and a "divine inspiration," brought down to the level of our language, would be perhaps more embarrassed than an even purely human inspiration. Nothing therefore can be stranger, to those who examine the matter calmly, than to see civilized nations seeking for a complete expression of the divine thought in the literatures of ancient peoples and semi-barbarous nations, whose language and intelligence were infinitely inferior to ours; their god, talking and dictating, would nowadays hardly be given a certificate of competency in a primary examination. It is the grossest anthropomorphism to conceive a divinity not in the type of an ideal man but in the type of a barbarous man. Also, it is not simply that a literal faith (the primitive form of all revealed faith) ultimately appears to be entirely irrational; it is that this characteristic becomes constantly more marked, for the reason that faith stands still, or tries to stand still, while humanity marches on.

*Dogmatism doubly irrational.*

But for a certain number of heresies born and circulated among them, but for a constant stream of fresh thought, people holding by a literal religion would be a *caput mortuum* in history, a little "like the faithful Tibetians of Dalaï-lama," as Von Hartmann says. Literal religions cannot last and perpetuate themselves except by a series of compromises. There are always in the minds of the sincere and intelligent believer periods of advancement and of reaction, steps forward followed by a recoil. Confessors know these sudden changes well, and are prepared to deal with them and keep them within certain limits. They themselves are subject to such changes; how many of them have thought they believed and been suspected of heresy! If we could see into the bottom of their minds what reconciliations should we not perceive, what secret accommodations and compliances! There is in every one of us something that *protests* against literal faith, and if this protestation is not explicit, it is often none the less real. No one can hope to read more exactly than he who reads between the lines. When one venerates and admires everything, it is generally what one simply does not understand. Very many minds positively like vagueness and accommodate themselves to it, they believe in gross and arrange the details to suit themselves; sometimes even, after accepting a thing as a whole, they eliminate one by one all its parts. Generally speaking, those who aspire to literal faith nowadays are divisible into three classes: the indifferent, the blind, and unconscious Protestants.

*Dogmatism is intellectual indifference or death.*

The Protestantism of Luther and Calvin was a compromise replacing a despotism; it was a broad faith, although it is at the same time intolerant and orthodox; for there are certain things even in Protestantism which do not admit of compromise; it contains *dogmas* that it is impious to reject, and which, to the free-thinker, seem scarcely less contrary to calm reason than the dogmas of Catholicism; it contains a system of metaphysical or historical theses regarded not as merely human, but as divine. The most desirable thing in a religion that is to be progressive is

*Protestantism and liberty of conscience.*

that the sacred texts should be ambiguous; and the text of
the Bible is not ambiguous enough.  How are we to doubt,
for example, the divinity of Christ's mission?  How doubt the
miracles?  A belief in the divinity of Christ, and the genuineness of the miracles, are the very foundation of the Christian
religion; Luther was obliged to accept them, and in our day
even they bear down with their full weight on orthodox Protestantism.  So that what seemed at first a generous concession
to liberty of thought amounts in the end to little.  The circle
one moves about in is so contracted!  Protestants, too, are
fettered; the chain is simply longer and more flexible.  Protestantism has rendered services of great importance to law
and to liberty of conscience;  but alongside of the concessions
to liberty that it enforced, it contains dogmas from which the
use of "charitable constraint" may logically be deduced.
These dogmas which are essential to true Protestantism are:
original sin, conceived as even more radical than it appears in
Catholicism, and as destructive of freedom of the will; the
redemption, which recognizes the death of God the Son as
necessary to redeem man from the vindictiveness of God the
Father; predestination in all its rigour; grace and election in
their most fatalistic and mystical form; and last and most important, an eternity of suffering without purgatory!  If all
these dogmas are simply philosophical myths, Christian is a
purely verbal title, and one might as well call one's self a heathen,
for all the myths of Jupiter, Saturn, Ceres, Proserpine, and
the " divinities of Samothrace," are also susceptible of becoming symbols of higher metaphysics; we refer the reader to
Jamblicus and Schelling.  We must thus assume that orthodox
Protestants believe in hell, redemption, and grace ; and if so,
the consequences that we have deduced from these dogmas
become inevitable.  Also Luther, Calvin, Théodore de Bèze,
have preached and practised intolerance for the same reasons
as did the Catholics.  They claimed the right of private judgment for themselves alone, and only in so far as they felt need
of it ; they never raised it to the level of an orthodox doctrine.
Calvin burned Servetius, and the Puritans in America in 1692
punished witchcraft with death.

If Protestantism has in the long run served the cause of liberty of conscience, the reason is simply that every heresy is

Every heresy serves liberty of conscience.

an instance of liberty and of that enfranchisement which brings in its train a series of additional heresies. In other words, heresy is the victory of doubt over faith. By doubt Protestantism serves the cause of liberty; by faith it would cease to serve it and would menace it—if it were logical. But the characteristic of certain minds is precisely to come to a halt halfway between freedom and liberty, between faith and reason, between the past and the future.

Over and above the dogmas admitted in common, the true Protestant demands further some fixed objective expression of his belief: he attempts—he also—to incorpo-

Protestantism a mark of logical feebleness in those who hold it.

rate it in a certain number of customs and rites which create the need they satisfy and incessantly give fresh life to a faith incessantly on the point of a decline; he demands temples, priests, a ceremonial. In the item of ceremonial as well as in the item of dogmas, orthodox Protestants nowadays feel themselves to be much superior to Catholics; and they have really rejected a considerable number of naïve beliefs and of useless rites not infrequently borrowed from paganism. You should hear an excited Protestant, in a discussion with a Catholic, speak of the Mass, that degrading superstition in which "the most material and barbarous interpretation possible" is put upon the words of Christ—*He that eateth me shall live by me.* But does not this same Protestant admit with the Catholic the miracle of the redemption, of Christ sacrificing himself to save mankind? If you admit one miracle, what reason is there to stop with that or any succeeding miracle? "Once more in this order of ideas," says Mr. Matthew Arnold, "and what can be more natural and beautiful than to imagine this miracle every day repeated, Christ offered in thousands of places, everywhere the believer enabled to enact the work of redemption and unite himself with the Body whose sacrifice saves him." A beautiful conception, you acknowledge, for a legend, but you refuse to put faith in it on the ground that it shocks your reason; very good, but you reject in the same breath all the rest of the irrationalities that are part and parcel of Christianity. If Christ sacrificed himself for the human race, why should not he sacrifice himself for me? if he came to a world that did not call him, why should he not come to me who call upon him and pray to him? if God once took on a form of flesh and blood, if He once inhabited a human body, why find it strange that He should be present in my flesh and blood? You want miracles, on condition that you are not to see them; what is the meaning of such false modesty? When one believes a thing, one must live in the heart of this belief, one must see it and feel it everywhere; when one possesses a god, it is in order that he may walk and breathe on earth. He whom we adore must not be relegated to a corner of the heavens, or forbidden to appear in our midst; and they must not be made sport of, who see him, and feel him, and touch him. Free-thinkers may laugh, if they have the courage, at the priest who believes that God is present in the Host that he holds in his hands, and present in the temple when he officiates. They may laugh at the peasant children who believe that Saints or the Virgin present themselves before them to listen to their wants, but a true believer cannot do otherwise than take all this seriously. Protestants take baptism very seriously, and think it absolutely necessary to salvation. Luther certainly believed in the devil; he saw him everywhere, in storms, in fires, in the tumult that his passage along the streets often excited, in the interruptions that occurred in his sermons; he challenged, and threatened all devils, "were they as numberless as the tiles of the roofs." One day he even exorcised the Evil One, who had been vociferating in the person of the audience, so efficiently that the sermon, which opened in the midst of the greatest disturbance, was finished in peace; the devil had been frightened. Why, then, do orthodox Protestants, especially in our day, so genuinely wish to stop arbitrarily short in their faith? Why believe that God or the devil appeared to men two thousand years ago, and at no time since? Why believe in the Gospel cures and not in the naïve legends that are related of the Communion, or in the miracles at Lourdes? All things hold together in a faith, and if you propose outraging human reason, why not do it thoroughly? As Mr. Matthew Arnold observes, the orthodox Protestant doctrine, in admitting that the Son of God could substitute himself as an expiatory victim for man, condemned for the fault of Adam,—in other words that he could suffer for a crime that he had not committed for men who had not committed it either,—is only to accept the following passage literally and rudely: "The son of man is come to give his life as a ransom unto many." From the moment that one holds literally to a single text, why not do the same in regard to others? In introducing a certain share of liberty into their faith, the Protestants have also introduced a spirit of inconsequence; this is its characteristic and its defect. Someone said to me once: "If I should try to believe everything, I should end by believing nothing." This was Luther's reasoning; he wished to make some allowances for enlightenment; he hoped to preserve the faith by minimizing it. But the limits are artificial. Only listen to Pascal, who possesses the French talent for logic, and is at the same time a mathematician, making light of Protestantism. "How I detest such nonsense!" he cries: that is, not to believe in the Eucharist, etc. "If the Gospel is true, if Jesus Christ is God, what difficulty is there in all that?" Nobody saw more clearly than Pascal the things that, as he says, are " unjust " in certain Christian dogmas, that are " shocking," are " far-fetched," the " absurdities "; he saw it all and accepted it all. He accepted everything or nothing. When one makes a bargain with faith, one does not pick and choose; one takes all and gives all. It was Pascal who said that atheism was a sign of strength of mind, but a strength displayed in one direction only. One might turn that round and say that Catholicism implies strength of mind, at least on one point. Protestantism, though of a higher order in the evolution of belief, remains to-day a mark of a certain weakness of mind in those who, having made the first step toward freedom of thought, rest there; it is a halt midway. At bottom, however, the two rival orthodoxies, over which nowa-

days civilized nations dispute, are equally astonishing to those
who have passed beyond them.

## *III. The dissolution of dogmatic faith in modern society.*

Can a dogmatic faith, whether narrow or broad, indefinitely
coexist with modern science? We think not. Science consists

*Dogmatic faith
distanced by
science.*

of two portions: the constructive and the destructive. The constructive portion is already far
enough advanced, in modern society, to provide
for certain desiderata which dogma undertook formerly to
supply. We have to-day, for example, more extended and
detailed information about the genesis of the world than is
found in the Bible. We are attaining by degrees a certain
number of facts relating to the affiliation of species. And all
the celestial or terrestial phenomena which strike the eye are
already completely explained. The definitive *why* has not
been given, no doubt; we even ask ourselves if there is one.
But the *how* has already been in a great part dealt with.
Let us not forget that religions in the beginning took the
place of physics; that physical theories constituted for a
long time an essential and preponderant part of them. Nowadays physics and religion have been distinguished, and
religion has lost by the separation a large part of its power,
which has passed over to science.

The dissolvent and destructive aspect of science is not less
important. The first to present it in high relief were the

*And under-
mined.*

physical sciences and astronomy. All the
ancient superstitions about the trembling of the
earth, eclipses, etc., which were a constant
occasion of religious exaltation, are destroyed, or nearly so,
even among the populace. Geology has overturned with a
single stroke the traditions of most religions. Physics has
done away with miracles. The same almost may be said of
meteorology, which is so recent and has such a brilliant future.
God is still to a man of the people too often the sender of
rain and good weather, the Indra of the Hindus. A priest
told me the other day, in the best faith in the world, that the

prayers of his parishioners had brought the country three days of sunshine.   In a religious town if rain falls the day of a religious procession, and stops shortly before the time of setting out, the people unhesitatingly believe that a miracle has been performed.   Sailors, who depend so entirely on atmospheric perturbations, are more inclined to superstition. The minute the weather can be more or less accurately foretold and guarded against, all these superstitions are doomed. It is thus that fear of thunder is rapidly subsiding at the present day; this fear formed an important factor in the formation of the ancient religions.   By inventing the lightning-rod, Franklin did more to destroy superstition than the most active propaganda could have done.

As M. Renan has remarked, we might even in our day demonstrate scientifically the non-existence of miraculous interference in the affairs of this world and the inefficiency of requests to God to modify the natural course of things; one might, for example, minister to patients according to the same methods, in two adjoining rooms of a hospital; for the one set of patients a priest might pray, and one might see whether the prayer would appreciably modify the means of recovery.   The result of this sort of experiment on the existence of a special providence is moreover easy to foretell, and it is doubtful whether any educated priest would lend himself to it.

*Experiment in miracles.*

The sciences of physiology and psychology have explained to us in a natural way a multitude of phenomena of the nervous system which we were forced until recently to attribute to the marvellous, or to trickery, or to divine influence, or to the devil.

*Religion and physiology and psychology.*

Finally, history is attacking not only the object of religion, but religions themselves, by displaying all the sinuosities and uncertainties of the thought that constructed them; the primitive contradictions, corrected for better or for worse at some later period, the genesis of the precisest dogmas by the gradual juxtaposition of vague and heterogeneous ideas.   Religious criticism, the elements of which will sooner or later find their way into

*Religion and history.*

elementary instruction, is the most terrible weapon that could be used against religious dogmatism; it has produced and will produce its effect in Protestant countries, where theology passionately engages the multitude. Religious faith tends to give place to curiosity about religion; we understand more readily the things we do not so absolutely believe, and we can be more disinterestedly interested in the things that no longer fill us with a sacred horror. But the explanation of positive religion seemed destined to be absolutely the opposite of its justification: to write the history of religions is to write a damaging criticism of them. When one endeavours to come to close quarters with their foundation in reality, one finds it retire before one little by little and ultimately disappear like the place where the rainbow rests upon the earth: one believes that one has discovered in religion a bond between heaven and earth, a pledge of alliance and hope; it is an optical illusion which science at once corrects and explains.

Primary instruction, which is sometimes made, nowadays, a subject of ridicule, is also an altogether recent institution of which in former times there scarcely existed a *Religion under-* trace, and which profoundly modifies all of the *mined by primary* *instruction.* terms of every social and religious problem. The modicum of elementary instruction that the modern schoolboy possesses, in especial if one adds some few notions of religious history, would alone suffice to put him on his guard against a great many forms of superstition. Formerly it was the custom for a Roman soldier to embrace the religion of any, and of every country, in which he was stationed for a considerable space of time; on his return home he would set up an altar to the distant gods that he had made his own Sabazius, Adonis, the goddess of Syria, or Asiatic Bellona, the Jupiter of Baalbec, or the Jupiter of Doliche. To-day our soldiers and mariners bring back from their travels little more than an incredulous tolerance, a gently disrespectful smile in relation to gods in general.

The perfection of means of communication is also one of the great obstacles to the maintenance of a dogmatic faith; nothing shelters a belief like the abyss of a deep valley or the meanderings of an unnavigable river. The last surviving believers in the religions of antiquity were the peasants—*pagani;* whence the word pagan. But to-day the coun-

And by the perfection of the means of communication.

try is being thrown open, mountains are being pierced, the perpetually increasing activity in the movement of things and of people results in the circulation of ideas, in a lowering of the pretensions of the faith, and this levelling down must inevitably continue step by step with the progress of science. In all times it has been observed that the effect of travelling alters one's beliefs. To-day one travels standing still : the intellectual horizon changes for one, whether one will or not. Men like Papins, Watts, Stephenson, have done as much for the propagation of free-thought as the boldest of philosophers. Even in our days the piercing of the Isthmus of Suez will probably have done more for the enlightenment of the Hindus than the conscientious efforts of Râm Mohun Roy or of Keshub.

Among the causes which will tend in the future to eliminate the dogma of a special providence, let us note the develop-

And by the development of commerce and industry.

ment of the arts—even the art of commerce and of industry, which is still in its very beginnings. Merchants and workmen, equally, have learned already to rely upon no one but their own individual selves, to rely each upon his own initiative, his personal ingenuity ; he knows that to work is to pray, not in the sense that his labour possesses some sort of mystical value but because its value is real and within his reach ; and he acquires by that very fact a vivid and increasing sense of responsibility. Compare, for instance, the life of a pointsman (that of a workingman) with the life of a soldier, and you will see that the conduct of the first is of necessity reflective, and develops in him a sense of responsibility, whereas the second—accustomed to march he knows not where, to obey, he knows not why, to vanquish or be vanquished he knows not how—lives among circumstances which naturally inspire in him a conception of irresponsibility, of divine chance, or of hazard. Moreover, whenever industry does not treat the workman like a machine but forces him to act consciously and with reflection, its natural effect is

to enfranchise the mind. And the same thing is true of commerce; although in commerce a more important rôle is played,
by mere lying in wait—mere passivity; the merchant waits
for a purchaser, and his coming or not coming depends upon
something else. The superstitions of commerce, however, will
grow feebler as the functions of personal initiative and activity
become more extensive. Thirty years ago in a very religious
town there existed a number of small merchants who looked
upon it as a matter of duty not to examine their account book
till the end of the year: it would be, they said, a distrust
of God to ascertain too often whether they were losing or
gaining; it would bring bad luck; the less attention you pay
to your income the greater it grows. Add that, thanks to
this sort of reasoning, which for the rest was not altogether
without a certain naïve logic, the merchants spoken of did not
do an especially brilliant business. In modern commerce
the "positive" spirit—restless intelligence and calculation
outstripping chance—tends to become the true and sole
element of success; as to the risks which, in spite of every
precaution, still remain, they are covered by insurance.

Insurance, then, is a conception altogether modern, whose
operation is to substitute the direct action of man for the
intervention of God in private affairs, and which
looks to the recompense for a misfortune
before it has happened. It is probable that
insurance, which dates only some few years back and is
spreading rapidly, will be applied some day to almost every
form of accident to which man is liable, will be adapted to
every circumstance of life, will accompany us everywhere,
will envelop us in a protecting net; and agriculture and
navigation, and those pursuits generally in which human
initiative plays the smallest part, in which one must dance
attendance upon the special benediction of heaven and ultimate success is always contingent, will become increasingly
independent and free. It is possible that the notion of a
special providence will some day be completely eliminated
from the sphere of economics; everything that in any manner
whatsoever is capable of being estimated in terms of money

*And by the
practice of insu-
rance.*

will be covered by an insurance, shielded from accident, made independent of divine favour.

There remains the purely personal sphere, the physical and moral accidents which may befall us, the maladies that may come upon ourselves and those who belong to us. That is the sphere in which the majority of men feel their will most feeble, their perspicacity most at fault. Listen to a member of the lower classes on the subject of physiology or medicine, and you will understand how deep is the abasement of their intelligence in this matter; and often, indeed, even men of a more extended education are possessed of no more knowledge than they on such points. Speaking generally, our ignorance of hygiene and the most elementary notions of medicine is such that we are helpless in the presence of physical evil; and it is because of this helplessness, at the very spot precisely where we most need help, that we seek for an outlet for an embarrassed volition and a restless hope and find it in a petition addressed to God. Many people never think of praying except when ill, or when they see persons dear to them ill. As always, so here, a sense of an absolute dependence provokes a return of religious sentiment. Just in proportion as instruction spreads, just in proportion as the natural sciences become of service, we feel ourselves armed with a certain power, even in the face of physical accident. In more than usually pious families, the physician scarcely assumed formerly any other character than that of an instrument of special providence; one had confidence in him, less on the score of his talent than of his sanctity; that confidence was absolute; one washed one's hands of all responsibility, as primitive people do in the presence of the sorcerers and " priest physicians." Nowadays, however, the physician is beginning to be looked upon as a man like another, who must rely upon himself, who receives no inspiration from on high, and who must, in consequence, be chosen with care, and aided and sustained in his task. It is understood that the remedies employed by him are innocent of mystery, that their operation is uniform, that the matter is altogether one of intelligence in their use; and

*And the progress of medical knowledge.*

instead of putting one's self, like so much brute matter, into the physician's hands, one does one's best to co-operate with him. When we hear someone calling for help and are free to run to him, does it ever occur to us nowadays to fall upon our knees? No; we should even consider a passive prayer as an indirect form of homicide. The epoch is past when Ambroise Paré could say modestly: "I poulticed him, God cured him." The fact is, God does not cure those whom the physician does not poultice properly. The progress of natural science will result really in a sort of preventive insurance, no longer confined wholly to the sphere of economics; and we shall be able some day to insure ourselves, not simply against the economical consequences of such and such an accident, but against the accident itself; we shall foresee it and avoid it, as we not infrequently nowadays foresee and avoid poverty. And finally, in respect even to unavoidable evils, it will occur to no one to rely upon anything but human science and human effort.

Owing to the causes above enumerated, how far we have travelled since the time of the ancients and the Middle Ages! Progress in matters of belief since heathen antiquity and the Middle Ages. In the first place we no longer lend credence to oracles or to predictions. The law at least no longer goes the length of lending credence to them, and even punishes those who endeavour to speculate upon a naïveté of their more innocent neigbours. Soothsayers at the present day are no longer lodged in Temples. And in no case are philosophers and higher personages among their clients. We are far from the time when Socrates and his disciples made a pilgrimage to consult the oracle, when the gods spoke, and gave advice, and regulated the conduct of men, and took the place of attorneys, of physicians, of judges, and decided upon peace and war. If it had been affirmed to a pagan that the day would come when man would find the oracle at Delphi a superfluity, he would have been as frankly surprised as a Christian is to-day when he hears it affirmed that cathedrals, priests, and religious ceremonies will some day become a superfluity.

The rôle which prophecies played in the religion of the

Hebrews is well known. In the Middle Ages certain prophecies, such as that of the millennium, were publicly and miserably put to the proof. Since that time dogmatic religion, in the fear of compromising itself, has stood aloof from oracles and prophecies, preferring increase of security to extent of influence. Thus by degrees authoritative religion has come to renounce its sway over one of the most important portions of human life, which it pretended formerly to possess a knowledge of, and to regulate—the future. It contents itself to-day with the present. Its predictions, ever vaguer and more vague, nowadays bear only on the period beyond the grave ; it contents itself with promising heaven to the faithful—which the Catholic religion indeed goes the length of in some measure securing for them by absolution. And one may recognize in the confessional a certain substitute for the divination of former times. The hand of the priest opens or shuts the door of heaven for the believer kneeling in the shadow of the confessional ; he wields a power in some respects greater than that of the Pythoness who might determine with a word the fate of battles. Confession itself, however, has disappeared in the stronger and younger offshoots of Christianity. In orthodox Protestantism one is one's self the judge of one's own future, and possesses no other clew to one's destiny than the dictum of one's own conscience, with all its uncertainty upon its head. Owing to this transformation dogmatic faith in the word of a priest or a prophet tends to become a simple reliance on the voice of conscience, which becomes ever less and less authoritative, ever more and more feeble in the face of doubt. Faith in oracles and in the visible finger of Providence in this world has become to-day simply a somewhat hesitating reliance upon an inner oracle and an together transcendental Providence. This is one of the items in respect to which religious evolution may be considered as already something like complete, and religious individualism as on the point of replacing obedience to the priest, and the negation of the marvellous as substituted for antique superstition.

The strength of the belief in a personal God has been in all

*Tendency toward simplicity and uniformity.*

times proportionate to the strength of the belief in a devil—
we have just seen an illustration of it in the case of Luther.

**Belief in God falls with belief in devils.** In effect these two beliefs are correlatives; they are the opposite faces of one and the same anthropomorphism. Well, in our days, belief in the devil is incontestably becoming feebler; and this enfeeblement is even especially characteristic of the present epoch; there has at no other time been anything to equal it. There is not an educated person to be found in whom the notion of a devil does not excite a smile. That, believe me, is a sign of the times, a manifest proof of the decline of dogmatic religion. Wherever the power of dogmatic religion by an exception to the general course of things has retained its vitality, and retained it, as in America, even to the point of giving birth to new dogmas, the fear of the devil has subsisted in its entirety; wherever, as in more enlightened regions than America, this fear no longer exists except as a symbol or a myth, the intensity and the fecundity of the religious sentiment decline inevitably in the same degree. The fate of Javeh is bound up with that of Lucifer; angels and devils go hand in hand, as in some fantastic mediæval dance. The day when Satan and his followers shall be definitively vanquished and annihilated in the minds of the people, the celestial powers will not have long to live.

To sum up, in all these relations, dogmatic faith—and in especial, such as is narrow, authoritative, intolerant, and at **Results.** enmity with a spirit of science—seems on every account destined to disappear, or to survive, if at all, among a small number of believers. Every doctrine, no matter how moral or how elevating, seems to us nowadays to lose these attributes and to become degraded from the moment it proposes to impose itself upon the human mind as a dogma. Dogma happily—that crystallization of faith—is an unstable compound; like certain complex crystals, it is apt to explode, under a concentrated ray of light, into dust. Modern criticism supplies the ray. If Catholicism, in pursuit of religious unity, logically results in the doctrine of infallibility, modern criticism in the course of its establishment of the relativity of human knowledge and of the essential fallibility of intelligence in general, tends toward religious individualism and toward the dissolution of every universal or "Catholic" dogma. And on that score orthodox Protestantism is itself menaced with ruin, for it also has preserved in its dogmas an element of Catholicity, and by that very fact of intolerance, if not practical and civil, at least theoretical and religious.

# CHAPTER II.

## SYMBOLIC AND MORAL FAITH.

I. Substitution of metaphysical symbolism for dogma—Liberal
Protestantism—Comparison with Brahmanism—Substitution of
moral symbolism for metaphysical symbolism—Moral faith—
Kant—Mill—Matthew Arnold—A literary explanation of the
Bible substituted for a literal explanation.

II. Criticism of symbolic faith—Inconsequence of liberal Protes-
tanism—Is Jesus of a more divine type than other great geni-
uses—Does the Bible possess a greater authority in matters of
morals than any other masterpiece of poetry—Criticism of
Matthew Arnold's system—Final absorption of religions by
morality.

EVERY illogical position being in its nature unstable, the
very inconsequence of a religion obliges it to a perpetual
evolution in the direction of an ultimate non-re-

*Inevitable tend-
ency of religion
toward non-
religion.*

ligion, which it approaches incessantly by almost
insensible steps. The Protestant knows nothing
of the ordeal of a Catholic obliged to accept everything or to reject everything; he knows nothing of prodigious
revolutions and subjective *coups d'état;* he possesses instinctively the art of transition, his *credo* is elastic. There are so
many different creeds, each a little more thorough-going than
the last, that he may pass through, that he has time to habituate his spirit to the truth before being obliged to profess it in
its simplicity. Protestantism is the only religion, in the Occident at least, in which it is possible for one to become an atheist
unawares and without having done one's self the shadow of a
violence in the process: the subjective theism of Mr. Moncure
Conway, for example, or any such ultra-liberal Unitarian is
so near a neighbour to ideal atheism that really the two cannot
be told apart, and yet the Unitarians, who as a matter of fact
are often simply free-thinkers, hold, so to speak, that they still

believe.   The truth is that an affectionate faith long retains its charm, even after one is persuaded that it is an error and dead in one ; one caresses the lifeless illusions and cannot bring one's self altogether to abandon them, as in the land of the Slavs it is the custom to kiss the pale face of the dead in the open coffin before throwing upon it the handful of earth which severs definitely the last visible bonds of love.

Long before Christianity, other great religions, Brahmanism and Buddhism, which are much more comprehensive and less

Exemplified in the case of Brahmanism and Buddhism. arrested in their development, followed the course of evolution by which a literal faith comes to be transformed into a symbolic faith. They have been reconciled successively with one metaphysical system after another—a process which has been inevitably carried forward with a fresh impulse under the English rule.   To-day Sumangala, the Buddhist high-priest of Colombo, interprets in a symbolic sense the at once profound and naïve doctrine of the transmigration ; he pretends to reject miracles.   Other enlightened Buddhists freely accept modern doctrines, from those of Darwin to those of Spencer.   On the other hand, in the bosom of Hinduism there has grown up a really new and wholly theistical religion, that of the Brahmaists.[1]   Râm Mohum Roy founded, at the beginning of the century, a very deeply symbolical and wide-spread faith ; his successors have gone the length, with Debendra Nâth Tâgore, of denying the authenticity even of the very texts which they were in the beginning most concerned to interpret mystically.   This last step was taken suddenly, under circumstances which it is worth while to detail, because they sum up in a few characteristic strokes the universal history of religious thought.   It happened about 1847.   The disciples of Râm Mohum Roy, the Brahmaists, had been for a long time engaged in a discussion about the Vedas, and, quite as in the case of our liberal Protestants, had been giving especial prominence to texts in which they imagined they found an unmistakable affirmation of the unity of the Godhead ; and they rid themselves of all concern with the passages that seemingly contradicted this notion by deny-

---

[1] M. Goblet d'Alviella, *Evolution religieuse contemporaine.*

ing their authenticity. Ultimately, somewhat alarmed at their own progress, they sent four Pundits to Benares to collate the sacred texts : it was in Benares that, according to the tradition, the only so-called complete and authentic manuscript was preserved. During the two years that the labour of the Pundits covered, the Hindus waited for the truth in the same spirit that the Hebrews had done at the foot of Sinai. Finally the authentic version, or what purported to be such, was brought to them ; and they possessed the definitive formula of revelation. Their disappointment was great, and they took the matter into their own hands, realizing at one blow the revolution which the liberal Protestants are pursuing gradually in the bosom of Christianity : they rejected definitively the Vedas and the antique religion of the Brahmans, and proclaimed in its stead a theistical religion, which rests in no sense whatsoever upon revelation. The new faith must in time develop, not without heresy and schism, but its adherents constitute to-day in India an important element in progress.

In our days very estimable persons have essayed to push Christianity also into a new path. In according the right of interpretation to private individuals, Luther gave them the right of clothing their own individual thoughts in the language of the antique dogmas and the texts of the sacred books. Insomuch that by a singular revolution, the " Word," which was considered in the beginning as the faithful expression of the divine thought, has tended to become for each of us the expression of our own personal thought. The sense of the words depending really upon ourselves, the most barbarous language can be made at a pinch to serve us for the conveyance of the noblest ideas. By this ingenious expedient texts become flexible, dogmas become acclimated more or less to the intellectual atmosphere in which they are placed, and the barbarism of the sacred books becomes disguised. By virtue of living with the people of God we civilize them, we lend them our ideas, inoculate them with our aspirations, everyone interprets the Bible to suit himself, and the result is that the commentary ultimately overgrows and half obscures the text itself ; we no

*Preservation of the letter while tampering with the spirit of the Bible.*

longer read with undimmed vision—we look through a medium which disguises everything that is hideous, and lends a fresh beauty to everything that is beautiful. At bottom the veritable sacred Word is no longer the one which God pronounced and sent forth reverberating, eternally the same, down the centuries ; it is the one which we pronounce or rather whisper—for is it not the sense which one puts upon it that constitutes the real value of an utterance? and it is we who determine the sense. The Divine Spirit has passed into the believer and, at certain times at least, the true God would seem to be one's own thought. This attempt at a reconciliation between religion and free-thought is a masterpiece of tact. Religion seems always to lag a little behind, but free-thought by exercise of a little ingenuity always find means, in the end, of helping it forward. The progress of the two consists of a series of arrangements, compromises, something like what takes place between a conservative Senate and a progressive Chamber of Deputies, honestly in search of a *modus vivendi.*

By a procedure which Luther would never have dared to emulate Protestants have taken the liberty of employing on

Extension of symbolic interpretation to essential dogmas. essential dogmas this power of symbolical interpretation which Luther reserved for texts of a secondary importance. The most essential of dogmas, that upon which all others depend, is the dogma of revelation. If, since Luther's time, an orthodox Protestant feels himself at liberty to discuss at his ease whether the sense of the sacred Word is really this, that, or the other, he never for an instant questions whether the Word itself is really sacred in effect, or whether it really possesses any meaning that can properly be called divine. When he holds the Bible he has no doubt but that he has his hand upon the truth ; he has only to discover it beneath the words in which it is contained, has only to dig for it in the sacred Book as a labourer might dig in a field in search of a buried treasure. But is it then quite certain that the treasure is really there, that the truth lies ready-made somewhere between the covers of the Book ? That is the question which the liberal Protestant is asking himself, and he has already taken possession of Germany, of England, of the United States, and possesses even in France a large number of representatives. Previous to his advent all Christians were at one in the belief that the sacred Word really exists somewhere; at the present day this belief itself tends to become symbolic. No doubt there was in Jesus a certain element of divinity, but is there not in all of us, in one sense or another, a certain element of divinity? "Why should we be surprised," writes a liberal clergyman, "at finding Jesus a mystery, when we are all of us ourselves a mystery?" According to the new Protestants there is no longer any reason for taking anything at its face value, not even what has hitherto been considered as the spirit of Christianity. For the most logical of them, the Bible is scarcely more than a book like another; custom has consecrated it; one may find God in it if one seeks Him there, because one may find God anywhere and put Him there, if by chance He be really not there already. The divine halo has dropped from Christ's head, or rather he shares it with all the angels and all the saints. He has lost his celestial purity or rather we share it with him, all of us; for is not original sin also a symbol, and are we not all of us born innocent sons of God? The miracles are but fresh symbols which represent, grossly and visibly, the subjective power of faith. We are no longer to look for orders directly from God; God no longer talks to us by a single voice, but by all the voices of the universe, and it is in the midst of the great concert of nature that we must seize and distinguish the veritable Word. All is symbolic except God, who is the eternal truth.

Well, and why stop at God? Liberty of thought, which has been incessantly turning and adapting dogma to its progress, has it in its power to make a step beyond. And even to the conception of God. Immutable faith is hemmed in by a circle which is daily shrinking. For the liberal Protestant this contraction has reached its extreme, and centre and circumference are one and the process is continuing. Why should not God Himself be a symbol? What is this mysterious Being, after all, but a popular personification of the *divine* or even of ideal humanity; in a word, of morality?

Thus a purely moral symbolism comes in process of time to be substituted for a metaphysical symbolism. We are

*The result prac-
tically a religion
of morals. Per-
ceived to be so in
Germany.*

close upon the Kantian conception of a religion of duty, resting upon a simple postulate or even a simple generalization of human conduct, to the effect that morality and happiness are in the last resort in harmony. A faith in morals, thus understood, has been adopted by many Germans as the basis of religious faith. Hegelians have converted religion into a moral symbolism. Strauss defines morality as the " harmonization " of man with his species, and defines religion as the harmonization of man with the universe; and these definitions, which seem at first sight to imply a difference in extent and a certain opposition between morality and religion, aim in reality at showing their ultimate unity; the ideal of the species and the purpose of the universe are one, and if by chance they should be distinct, it would be the more universal ideal that morality itself would command us to follow. Von Hartmann, also, in spite of his mystical tendencies, concludes that there is no religion possible except one which will consecrate the moral autonomy of the individual, his salvation by his own effort and not by that of somebody else (autosoterism as distinguished from heterosoterism). From which it follows that, in Von Hartmann's opinion, the essence of religious adoration and gratitude should be one's respect for the essential and impersonal element in one's self; in other words, piety is, properly speaking, no more than a form of morality and of absolute renouncement.

In France, as is well known, M. Renouvier follows Kant and bases religion upon morality. M. Renan also makes of

*Also in
France.*

religion a little more than an ideal morality: " Abnegation, devotion, sacrifice of the real to the ideal, such," he says, " is the very essence of religion." And elsewhere: "What is the state but egoism organized? what is religion but devotion organized?" M. Renan forgets, however, that a purely egoistic state, that is to say a purely immoral state, could not continue to exist. It would be more accurate to say that the state is justice organized ; and since justice and devotion are in principle the same, it follows that the state as well as religion rests ultimately upon morality : morality is the very foundation of social life.

In England, also, the same process of the transformation of a religious faith into a purely moral faith may be observed.

Kant through the intermediation of Coleridge
*Also in England.* and of Hamilton has exercised a great influence upon English thought and upon the course of this transformation. Coleridge brought down the Kingdom of God from Heaven and domesticated it upon earth ; the reign of God for him, as for Kant, became that of morality. For John Stuart Mill, whose point of approach was widely different from that of Coleridge, the outcome of the study of religions was the same—that their essential value has always consisted in the moral precepts they inculcate ; the good that they have done should be attributed rather to the stimulus they have given to the moral sentiment than to the religious sentiment properly so called. And it is to be added, Mill says, that the moral principles furnished by religions labour under this double disability, that (1) they are tainted with selfishness, and operate upon the individual by promises or menaces relating to the life to come without entirely detaching him from a preoccupation with his own interest, and, (2) they produce a certain intellectual apathy, and even an aberration of the moral sense, in that they attribute to an absolutely perfect being the creation of a world so imperfect as our own, and thus in a certain measure cloak evil itself in divinity. Nobody could adore such a god willingly without having undergone a preliminary process of degeneration. The true religion of the future, according to John Stuart Mill, will be an elevated moral doctrine, going beyond an egoistic utilitarianism and encouraging us to pursue the good of humanity in general ; nay, even of sentient beings in general. This conception of a religion of humanity, which is not without analogy to the Positivist conception, might be reconciled, John Stuart Mill adds, with the belief in a divine power—a principle of goodness present in the universe. A faith in God

is immoral only when it supposes God to be omnipotent, since it, in that case, charges him with responsibility for existing evil. A good god can exist only on condition that he is less than omnipotent, that he encounters in nature, nay in human nature, obstacles which hinder him from effecting the good that he desires. Once conceive God thus, and the formula of duty reads simply : Help God ; work with Him for the production of what is good, lend Him the concurrence that He really needs since He is not omnipotent. Labour also with all great men—all men like Socrates, Moses, Marcus Aurelius, Washington—do as they do, all that you can and ought to do. This disinterested collaboration on the part of all men with each other and with the principle of goodness, in whatsoever manner that principle may be conceived or personified, will be, in John Stuart Mill's judgment, the ultimate religion. And it is evidently no more than a magnified system of morality, erected into a universal law for the world. What is it that we call the divine, except this that is the best in ourselves ? " God is good," cried Feuerbach, " signifies : goodness is divine ; God is just signifies : justice is divine." Instead of saying : there have been divine agonies, divine deaths, one has said, God has suffered, God has died. " God is the apotheosis of the heart of man." [1]

An analogous thesis is maintained with great cleverness in a book which caused considerable stir in England : Mr. Matthew Arnold's " Literature and Dogma." The author, in common with religious critics generally, remarks the growing tension that nowadays exists between science and dogma. " An inevitable revolution, of which we all recognize the beginnings and signs, but which has already spread, perhaps, farther than most of us think, is befalling the religion in which we have been brought up." Mr. Arnold is right. At no former period have unbelievers appeared to have so strong a hold in right reason ; the old arguments

*Matthew Arnold's " Literature and Dogma."*

---

[1] Mr. Seeley, in his work entitled *Natural Religion* (1882), takes pains to establish that of the three elements which compose the religious idea—the love of truth or science, the sentiment of beauty or art, the notion of duty or morals—it is the last only that can to-day be reconciled with Christianity.

against providence, miracles, and final causes, that the Epicureans brought into prominence, seem as nothing beside the arguments furnished in our days by the Laplaces and the Lamarcks, and quite recently by Darwin, the " evictor of miracles," in Strauss' phrase. One of the sacred prophets whom Mr. Arnold is fond of quoting once said : " Behold, the days come, that I will send a famine in the land, not a famine of bread, nor a thirst for water, but of hearing the words of the Lord : and they shall wander from sea to sea, and from the north even to the east, they shall run to and fro to seek the word of the Lord, and shall not find it." The time predicted by the prophet Mr. Arnold might well recognize as our own ; might it not with truth be said of the present that it lacks the word of the Eternal, or soon will lack it ? A new spirit animates our generation ; not only are we in doubt whether the Eternal ever did speak or ever does speak to man, but many of us believe in the existence of no other eternity than that of a universe of mute and unfeeling matter which keeps its own secret except as against those who have the. wit to find it out. There are of course, even to-day, some few faithful servants in the houses of the Lord ; but the Master seems to have departed for the far countries of the past, to which memory alone has access. In Russia in the older seigniorial estates, a disc of iron is fastened to the wall of the mansion of the lord of the soil ; and when he returns from a journey, the first night he passes in his dominion, some follower runs to the disc of iron and in the silence of the night beats upon the metal to announce his vigilance and the presence of the master. Who will awaken nowadays the voice of the bells in the church-steeples to announce the return to His temple of the living God, and the vigilance of the faithful ? To-day the sound of the church-bells is as melancholy as a cry in the void ; they tell of the deserted house of God, of the absence of the lord of the soil, they sound the knell of the believers. And is there nothing that can be done to domesticate religion once more in the heart of man ? There is but one means : to see in God no more than a symbol of what exists always at the bottom of the human heart—morality. And it is to this expedient that Matthew Arnold also turns his attention. But he is not content with a purely philosophic system of morals, he aims at the preservation of religion, and in especial of the Christian religion; and to that end he brings forward a new method of interpretation, the literary and æsthetic method, the purpose of which is to glean from the sacred texts whatever they may contain of moral beauty, in the hope that it may incidentally prove to contain also what is true. It aims at reconstructing the primitive notions of Christianity, in whatsoever they possessed of vagueness, of indecision, and at the same time of profundity, and to set them in opposition over against the gross precision of popular views. In matters of metaphysic or religion there is nothing more absurd than an excessive precision; the truth in such matters is not to be rounded in an epigram. Epigram can at best serve, not as a definition, but as a suggestion of the infinities that it really does not circumscribe. And just as the verity in such matters overpasses the measure of language, so it overpasses the personalities and the figures which humanity has chosen as representative of it. When an idea is powerfully conceived, it tends to become definite, to take unto itself a visage, a voice; our ears seem to hear and our eyes to see what our hearts feel. "Man never knows," said Goethe, "how anthropomorphic he is." What is there so surprising in the fact that humanity has personified that which in all climes claimed its allegiance —the idea of goodness and of justice? The Eternal, the eternally Just, the Omnipotent who squares reality with justice, He who parcels out evil and good, the Being who weighs all actions, who does all things by weight and measure, or rather who is Himself weight and measure—*that* is the God of the Jewish people, the Javeh of adult Judaism, as He ultimately appears in the mist of the unknown. In our days He has become transmuted into a simple moral conception, which, having forcibly taken possession of the human mind, has at last clothed itself in a mystical form—has become personified by alliance with a crowd of superstitions that the "false science of theologians" regards as inseparable from it and from which a more delicately discriminating interpretation—an interpretation more *literary* and less *literal*—should set it free.  God having become one with the moral law, a further step may be taken ; one may regard Christ who immolated Himself to save the world as a moral symbol of self-sacrifice, as the sublime type in which we find united all the suffering of human life and all the ideal grandeur of morality.  In His figure the human and the divine are reconciled.  He was a man, for He suffered, but His devotion was so great that He was a god.  And what then is that Heaven which is reserved for those who follow Christ and walk in the path of self-sacrifice ?  It is moral perfection.  Hell is the symbol of that depth of corruption to which, by hypothesis, they will fall who, by a persistent choice of evil, ultimately lose all notion even of goodness.  The terrestrial paradise is a charming symbol for the primitive innocence of the child : he has done as yet no evil, he has done as yet no good ; his earliest disobedience is his first sin ; when desire is awakened in him for the first time, his will has been conquered, he has fallen, but this fall is precisely the condition of his being set upon his feet again, of his redemption by the moral law ; behold him condemned to labour, to the hard labour of man upon himself, to the struggle of self-mastery ; without that contest to strengthen him he would never see the god descend in him, Christ the Saviour, the moral ideal.  Thus it is in the evolution of the human conscience that a key to human symbolism must be found.[1]  Of them must be said what the philosopher Sallust said of religious legends generally in his treatise " On the Gods and the World ": Such things have never happened, but they are eternally true.  Religion is the morality of the people; it shows to them, realized and divinized, the higher types of conduct which they should force themselves to imitate here below; the dreams with which it peoples the skies are dreams of justice, of equality of goods, of fraternity : Heaven pays for earth.  Let us then no longer employ the names of God, of Christ, of the Resurrection except as symbols, vague as hope itself.  Then, according to Mr. Matthew Arnold, and those who maintain the same thesis, we shall be-

[1] Besides Mr. Matthew Arnold, consult M. L. Ménard, *Sources du dogme Chrétien* (*Critique religieuse, janvier,* 1879).

gin to love these symbols, our faith will find a resting place in the religion which before seemed to be but a tissue of gross absurdities. Beneath dogma, which is but the surface, we shall find the moral law, which is the substance. This law, it is true, has in religion become concrete ; it has, so to speak, taken on colour and form. That, however, is simply owing to the fact that people are poets ; they think in images or not at all. You can only attract their attention by pointing your finger at something. After all, what harm is there in the fact that the apostles, opening the blue ether, showed the gaping nations of the earth the thrones of gold and seraphim and white wings, and the kneeling multitude of the elect? This spectacle fascinated the Middle Age, and at times, when we shut our eyes, we seem to see it still. This poetry, spread upon the surface of the moral law, lends it an attractiveness that it did not possess in its bare austerity. Sacrifice becomes less difficult when it presents itself crowned with a halo. The early Christians were not fond of representing Christ as bleeding under the crown of thorns, but as transfigured and triumphant ; they preferred to keep his agony in the background. Such pictures as ornament our Churches would have filled them with horror ; their young faith would have been shaken by the image of the " agony upon the cross," which caused Goethe also a sort of a repugnance. When they represented the cross it was no longer burdened with the God, and they took care even to cover it with flowers and ornaments of every kind. You may see it in the rude figures, the designs and sculptures found in the catacombs. To hide the cross beneath an armful of flowers is precisely the marvel realized by religion. And when religions are regarded from this point of view, all ground vanishes for looking with disdain upon the legends which constitute the material of popular faith. They become comprehensible, they become lovable, one feels one's self enveloped in an " infinite tenderness " for this spontaneous product of naïve thought in quest of goodness, in pursuit of the ideal, for these fairy-tales of human morality, profounder and sweeter than all other fairy-tales. It was necessary that religious poetry should prepare the earth long beforehand for the coming of the mysterious ideal; should embellish the place where it was to descend, as the mother of the Sleeping Beauty, seeing the eyes of her daughter grow heavy with the sleep of a hundred years, placed with confidence at the side of the bed the embroidered cushion, on which the enamoured prince would one day kneel to reawaken her with a kiss.

We have come a long way in all this from the servile interpretation of the blind leaders who fasten upon particular texts and lose sight of their subject as a whole. If one

*Historical religions to be regarded historically.*

approaches a picture too near, the perspective disappears and all the colours lose their proper value; one must stand back a certain distance and see it in a favourable light: and then alone the richness of the colours and the unity of the work appear. Religions must be looked upon in the same way. If the spectator stands sufficiently above them and aloof from them, he loses all prejudice, all hostility, in respect to them; their sacred books come even in time to merit in his eyes the name of sacred, and he finds in them, Mr. Arnold says, a providential "secret," which is the "secret of Jesus." Why not recognize, adds Mr. Arnold, that the Bible is an inspired book, dictated by the Holy Spirit? After all, everything that is spontaneous is more or less divine, providential; whatever springs from the very sources of human thought is infinitely venerable. The Bible is a unique book, corresponding to a peculiar state of mind, and it can no more be made over or corrected than a work of Phidias or Praxiteles. In spite of its moral lapses and its frequent disaccord with the conscience of our epoch, it is a necessary complement of Christianity; it manifests the spirit of Christian society, it represents the tradition of it, and attaches the beliefs of the present to those of the past.[1] The Bible and the dogmas of the Church, having been formerly the point of departure for religious belief, have come nowadays, no doubt, in the face of modern faith, to be in need of justification; and this justification they will obtain; to be understood is itself to be forgiven.

If the New Testament contains at all a more or less reflect-

[1] See M. L. Ménard, *ibid.* (*Crit. relig.*, 1879.)

ive moral theory, it is assuredly that of love. Charity, or rather affectionate justice (charity is always justice, absolutely considered), such is the "secret" of Jesus. The New Testament may then be considered, according to the opinion of Mr. Matthew Arnold, as before all else a treatise on symbolical morality. The actual superiority of the New Testament, as compared with Paganism and with pagan philosophy, is a moral superiority; therein lay the secret of its success. There is no theology in the New Testament unless it be the Jewish theology, and the Jewish theology had proved itself incapable of the conquest of the world. The power of the New Testament lay in its morality, and it is its morality which even in our times survives still, more or less transformed by modern progress. And it is upon the morality of the New Testament that modern Christian societies must of necessity lean, it is in the morality of the New Testament that they will find their true strength; the morality of the New Testament is the principal argument that they can invoke in proof of the legitimacy of religion itself and, so to speak, of God.

*The moral doctrine of the New Testament the main strength of Christianity.*

Mr. Matthew Arnold and the group of liberal critics, who, like him, are inspired by the spirit of the age (*Zeitgeist*), seem thus to have guided faith to the ultimate point beyond which nothing remains but to break definitively with the past and its texts and dogmas.

*Logical outcome of Matthew Arnold's position.*

Religious thought in these pages is bound by the slenderest threads to religious symbolism. At bottom, if one looks close, liberal Christians suppress religion, properly so called, and substitute a religious morality in its stead. The believer of other times affirmed the existence of God first, and then made His will the rule of conduct; the liberal believer of our day affirms the existence, first of all, of the moral law, and cloaks it in divinity afterward. He, like Matthew Arnold, treats with Javeh on equal terms, and speaks to Him almost as follows: "Art Thou a person? I do not know. Hast Thou had prophets, a Messiah? I no longer believe so. Hast Thou created me? I doubt it. Dost Thou watch over me—me in

especial—dost Thou perform miracles? I deny it. But there
is one thing, and one alone, in which I do believe, and that is
in my own conception of morality; and if Thou art willing to
become a surety for that and to bend the reality into harmony
with my ideal, we will make a treaty of alliance; and by the
affirmation of my existence as a moral being, I will affirm Thine
into the bargain." We are far away from the antique Javeh,
the Power, with whom no bargain could be made; the jealous
God, who wished man's every thought to point toward Him
alone, and who would make no treaty with His people unless
He could precisely dictate the terms.

The more distinguished German, English, and American
clergymen thrust theology so far into the background for
the purpose of forwarding practical morality
that one may apply to all of them the words
of an American periodical, the *North American
Review :* that a pagan, desirous of making himself acquainted
with the doctrines of Christianity, might frequent our most
fashionable churches for an entire year and not hear one
word about the torments of hell or the wrath of an in-
censed God. As to the fall of man and the expiatory agony
of Christ, just so much would be said as to fall short of giving
umbrage to the most fanatical believer of the theory of evolution. Listening and observing for himself, he would reach
the conclusion that the way to salvation lies in confessing one's
belief in certain abstract doctrines, beaten out as thin as possible by the clergyman and by the believer, in frequenting
assiduously the church and extra-religious meetings, in dropping an obolus every Sunday into the contribution box, and
in imitating the attitudes of his neighbours. All the terms of
theology are so loosely employed that all those are considered
Christians whose character has been formed by Christian civilization, all those who have not remained total strangers to
the current of ideas set up in the Occident by Jesus and Paul.
It was an American clergyman who had abandoned the narrow
dogmas of Calvin [1] that, after having employed a long life in
becoming more and more liberal, discovered, in his seventieth
year, this large formula for his faith : " Nobody ought to be

*Practical atten-
uation of Christian
faith.*

[1] Mr. Henry Ward Beecher.

regarded as an infidel who sees in justice the great creed of human life, and who aims at an increasingly complete subjection of his will to his moral sense."

II. What is the possible value and the possible duration of this moral and metaphysical symbolism to which it is being attempted to reduce religion?

Let us speak first of the liberal Protestants. Liberal Protestantism, which resolves the very dogmas of its creed into mere symbols, stands no doubt in the scale of progress in about the same relation to orthodox Protestantism as the latter does in relation to Catholicism. But far as it seems in advance of them from the point of view of morals and society, it is inferior to them in logic. Catholicism has been irreverently called a perfectly embalmed corpse, a Christian mummy, in an admirable state of preservation beneath the cold embroidered chasubles and surplices which envelop it; Luther's Protestantism tears the body to shreds, liberal Protestantism reduces it to dust. To preserve Christianity while suppressing Christ the son, or at least the messenger of God, is an undertaking of which they alone will be capable who are little disposed to make much of what is known as logic. Whoever does not believe in Revelation ought frankly to confess himself a philosopher, and to hold the Bible and the New Testament as little authoritative as the dialogues of Plato, or the treatises of Aristotle, or the Vedas, or the Talmud. Liberal Protestants, as Herr von Hartmann, one of their bitterest adversaries, remarks, seize upon the whole body of modern ideas and label them Christianity. The process is not very consistent. If you are absolutely determined to rally round a flag, let it at least be your own. But the liberal Protestants wish, and honestly, to be and to remain Protestants; in Germany, they obstinately remain in the United Evangelical Church of Prussia, where they about as truly belong as a sparrow does in the nest of a swallow. Herr von Hartmann, whose zeal against them is unflagging, compares them to a man whose house is riven in many places and going to ruin, and who perceives and does all that in him lies still further to shatter it, and continues, nevertheless,

*Logical hollowness of the position of the liberal Protestants.*

tranquilly to sleep in it and even to call in passers-by and offer
them board and lodging. Or again—always according to Herr
von Hartmann—they are like a man who should seat himself
in perfect confidence upon a chair after having first sawed
through all four legs of it. Strauss had already said : " The
instant that Jesus is regarded as no more than a man, one has
no longer any right to pray to him, to retain him as the centre
of a cult, to preach the whole year through on him, on his
actions, on his adventures and maxims ; in especial, if the more
important of his adventures and actions have been recognized as fabulous, and if his maxims are demonstrably incompatible with our present views on human life and the world."
To understand what is peculiar in the majority of liberal
communions which always stop halfway, it is necessary to observe that they are generally the work of ecclesiastics who
have broken with the dominant church, and that they preserve
to the end some suggestion of their former belief ; they can no
more think, except in the terms of the formulæ of some dogma,
than we can speak in the words of a language with which we
are unacquainted ; and even when they endeavour to acquire
a new language they speak it always with an accent which
betrays their nationality. For the rest they feel instinctively
that the name of Christ lends them a certain authority, and
they find it impossible to abandon their profession and its
emoluments. In Germany, and even in France, over and above
the liberal Protestants, who in the latter place are few in number, former Catholics have sought to abandon orthodox
Catholicism, but they have not dared to abandon Christianity.
The case of Father Hyacinthe [1] is sufficiently well known. It
is in vain for those who are born Christians to try their hand
at logic, and to make an effort to rid themselves of their faith.
They make one think, in spite of one's self, of a fly caught in a

[1] Dr. Junqua, whose name almost became celebrated a few years ago, also tried
to found a church, the Church of Liberty ; those who entered were at liberty to
believe almost anything they liked, not even the atheist, properly so called, being
excluded. The church in question was to have been purely symbolic : baptism it
was to recognize as the symbol of initiation into Christian civilization ; confirmation
as the symbol of an enrolment among the soldiers of Liberty ; and the eucharist, that
is to say a religious love feast, as the symbol of the brotherhood of man. It is to

spider-web, who has freed one wing and one leg, and only one.

Let us endeavour, however, to enter more intimately into the thoughts of those who may be called the Neo-Christians, and let us seek for the element of truth, if such there be, that their much-criticised doctrine contains.

**Neo-Christianity.**

If Jesus is only a man, they say, he is at least the most extraordinary of men; at one bound, by an intuition at once natural and divine, he discovered the supreme truth necessary to the life of humanity; he is in advance of all times, he spoke not only for his own people, nor for his own century, nor even for a score of centuries; his voice rolled beyond the restricted circle of his auditors, and the twelve apostles, beyond the people of Judea prostrate before him, to us in whose ears it sounds the eternal truth; and it finds us even still attentive, listening, trying to understand it, incapable of finding a substitute for it. " In Jesus," writes Pastor Bost in his work on " Le Protestantisme libéral," " the mingling of the human and the divine was accomplished in proportions not seen elsewhere. His relation to God is the normal and typical relation of humanity to the Creator. . . Jesus stands forever as the model." Professor Herman Schultz in a conference in Göttingen, some years ago, also expressed the same idea, that Jesus is really the Messiah, properly so called, in the sense that the Jews attached to that word. He did found the kingdom of God, not it is true by marvellous exploits like those of Moses or of Elias, but by an exploit surpassing theirs, by the sacrifice of love, by the voluntary gift of himself. The apostles and Christians in general did not believe in Jesus because of the miracles he performed : they accepted his miracles owing to their previous faith in him, a faith the true foundation of which lay in Christ's moral superiority, and that subsists still

be added that these sacraments were not obligatory and that the members might abstain from them entirely if they chose. Still, they would be members of a communion. Their faith would be designated by a common name, they would be in relations with a priest who would comment in their presence on texts of the New Testament, and would talk of Christ if he and they believed in Him. The church of Dr. Junqua might easily have succeeded in England with Mr. Moncure Conway and the secularists.

even if one deny the miracles. Professor Schultz concludes, against Strauss and M. Renan, that "a belief in Christ is wholly independent of the results of a historical criticism of his life." Every one of the actions attributed to Jesus may be mythical, but there remain to us his words and his thoughts, which find in us an eternal echo. There are things which one discovers once for all, and whosoever has found love has made a discovery that is not illusory nor of brief duration. Is it not just that men should group themselves about him, range themselves under his name? He himself loves to call himself the Son of Man; it is under this title that humanity should revere him. It is not destruction but reconstruction that is the outcome of contemporary biblical exegesis, one of the representatives of English Unitarianism, the Rev. A. Armstrong, said in 1883. It adds to our love of Jesus to recognize in him a brother and to see in the marvellous legends associated with him no more than the symbol of a love more naïve than ours, that namely of his disciples. Proof by miracle is but the ultimate form of a temptation from which humanity should escape. In the symbolic story of the temptation in the desert, Satan says: "Command that these stones be made bread;" he urged Christ to be guilty of a miracle, of the prestidigitation which the ancient prophets had employed so frequently to strike the imagination of the people. But Jesus refused. And on another occasion he said to the people indignantly: If you did not see prodigies and miracles you do not believe, and to the Pharisees: "Ye hypocrites, ye can discern the face of the sky and of the earth, . . . and why even of yourselves judge ye not what is right?" It is by the testimony of our own souls, say the Neo-Christians; it is by our own individual conscience, our own individual reason, that we shall find justice in the word of Christ, and that we shall revere it; and this word is not true because it is divine, it is divine because it is true.

Thus understood, liberal Protestantism is a doctrine that merits discussion; only it is sadly in lack of any distinguishing characteristic especially to mark it off from the numerous philosophical sects which, in the course of history, have gath-

ered about the opinions of some man and endeavoured to identify his teachings with the truth and to lend to them an authority more than human. Pythagoras was for
his disciples what Jesus is to the liberal Protestant.
The traditional respect also of the Epicureans for
their master is well known, the sort of worship
they rendered him, the authority that they lent to his words.[1]
Pythagoras brought to light a great idea, that of the harmony
which governs the physical and moral universe ; Epicurus,
another, that of the happiness which is the true aim of rational
conduct, the measure of goodness, and even of truth ; and by
their disciples these two great ideas came to be looked upon
not as parts of the truth but as truth itself in its entirety ; they
saw no ground for further search.   In the same way, in our
own times, the Positivists see in Auguste Comte not a profound
thinker simply, but one who has laid his finger, so to speak, on
the definitive verity, one who has traversed at a dash the whole
domain of intelligence and traced out once for all its limits.
It is rigorously exact to say that Auguste Comte is a sort of
Christ for bigoted Positivists—a Christ a trifle too recent, who
did not have the happiness of dying on the cross.   Each of
these sects reposes on the following belief : Before Pythagoras,
Epicurus, or Comte, nobody had seen the truth ; after them
nobody will ever see it more clearly.   Such a creed implicitly
denies : 1. Historical continuity, the inevitable result of which
is that the man of genius is always more or less the expression
of his century and that the honour of his discoveries is not due
wholly to himself ; 2. Human evolution, the inevitable result
of which is that the man of genius cannot be the expression of
all the centuries to come—that his point of view must necessarily be some day passed by—that the truth discovered by
him is not the whole truth but simply a stage in the infinite
progress of the human mind.   A *deus dixit* is comprehensible,
or if not comprehensible at least conceivable ; but to resusci-
tate in favour of some mere human being, were it Jesus himself,
the *magister dixit* of the Middle Ages, is a bit of an anachron-

*Modern German historical criti-cism and liberal Protestantism.*

---

[1] See the author's work on *la Morale d'Épicure et ses rapports avec les doctrines contemporaines*, p. 186.

ism. Geometers have always held Euclid in the highest respect, but each of them has done his best to contribute some new theorem to the body of doctrine that he left behind ; and is the rule for moral truth not the same as that for mathematical truth ? Is it within the compass of one man's powers to know and to utter all that there is to be known ? Is an autocracy the only form of government in the sphere of mind ? Liberal Protestants speak to us of the " secret of Jesus "; but there are many secrets in this world, and each of us carries his own ; and who shall utter the secret of secrets, the last word, the supreme verity ? Nobody in particular, probably ; truth is the product of a prodigious co-operation, at which all peoples and all generations must work. The horizon of truth can neither be taken in at a single glance nor contracted ; to perceive the whole of it one must move forward incessantly, and at every step a new perspective is laid bare. For humanity, to live is to learn ; and before any individual human being can tell us the great secret, he must have lived the life of humanity, the lives of all existing beings and even of all existing things, which seem scarcely to deserve the name of beings ; he must have concentrated in himself the universe. There can therefore properly be no religion centred about a man. A man, be he Jesus himself, cannot attach the human spirit to himself as to a fixed point. Liberal Protestants think that they have seen the last of the Strausses and Renans and their destructive criticism, because they have admitted once for all that Jesus was not a god, but criticism will object to them that the non-supernatural Messiah that they cherish is himself a pure figment of the imagination. According to the rationalistic exegesis, the doctrine of Christ, like his life, belongs more or less to the domain of legend. Jesus never so much as conceived an idea of the redemption—the very conception that is which lies at the root of Christianity ; he never so much as conceived an idea of the Trinity. If one may rely upon works which stand perhaps shoulder to shoulder with that of Strauss— the works of F. A. Müller, of Professor Weiss, of M. Havet— Jesus was a Jew with the spiritual limitations of a Jew. His dominant idea was that the end of the world was at hand and that on a new-created earth would soon be realized the national kingdom looked for by the Jews in the form of an altogether terrestrial theocracy. The end of the world being near, it was naturally not worth while to set up an establishment on earth for the short time that it was still to exist ; one's entire business was properly with penitence and the amendment of one's conduct, in order not to be devoured by fire at the day of judgment and excluded from the kingdom to be founded on the new-created earth. Moreover, Jesus preached neglect of the state, of the administration of justice, of the family, of labour and of property ; in effect, of all the essential elements of social life. Evangelical morality itself presents to the critics of this school little more than a disorderly mixture of the precepts of Moses on disinterested love with the doctrine of Hillel more or less well founded on enlightened self-interest. The original element in the New Testament consisted less in the logical coherence of its teachings than in a certain unction in the language employed, in a persuasive eloquence which often took the place of reasoning. All that Christ said others had said before him, but not with the same accent. In effect, German historical criticism at once professes the greatest admiration for the numerous founders of Christianity and leads its followers a long way from the ideal man conceived by the Neo-Christians as being the man-God whom primitive Christians adored. There exists accordingly no more reason to attribute an element of revelation or of sacred authority to the New Testament than to the Vedas or to any other religious book. If Christianity is a symbolic faith, the myths of India may quite as well be adopted as a basis of symbolism as the myths of the Bible. And contemporary Brahmaists with their eclecticism, confused and mystic as it often is, must be regarded as even nearer to the truth than the liberal Protestants who still look for shelter and salvation nowhere but under the diminishing shadow of the cross.

Abandoning, then, all effort to attribute a sacred authority to the sacred books and to the Christian tradition, may one ascribe to them at least a superior moral authority ? Do they lend themselves in any especial degree to such a purely æsthetic and moral symbolism as that suggested by Mr. Arnold?

A purely moral symbolism may be regarded from either of two points of view: the concrete, which is that of history; or the abstract, which is that of philosophy. Historically nothing could be more inexact than Mr. Arnold's method, which essentially consists in making a present of the most refined conceptions of our epoch to primitive peoples. It gives us to understand, for example, that the Javeh of the Hebrews was not regarded as a perfectly definite person, a transcendent power altogether distinct and separate from the world and manifesting himself by acts of capricious volition, a king of the skies, a lord of battles, bestowing on his people victory or defeat, abundance or famine, sickness or health. It suffices to read one page of the Bible or the New Testament to convince one's self that a doubt as to the personal existence of Javeh never for an instant crossed the Hebrew mind. So be it, Mr. Arnold will say, but Javeh was in their eyes no more, after all, than the personification of justice, because they believed powerfully in justice. It would be more exact to say that the Hebrews had not as yet a very philosophic notion of justice; that they conceived it as an order received from without, a command which it would be dangerous to disobey, a hostile will forcibly imposed upon one's own. Nothing could be more natural in the sequel than to personify such a will. But is that precisely what we understand nowadays by justice; and does it not really seem to Mr. Arnold himself that he is playing on words, when he endeavours to make us believe all that? Fear of the Lord is not justice. There are matters that one cannot express in the form of legend when one has once really conceived them—matters the true poetry of which consists in their very purity, in their simplicity. To personify justice, to represent it as external to ourselves under the form of a menacing power, is not to possess a "high idea" of it; is not in the least, as Mr. Arnold phrases it, to be aglow with it, illuminated by it; it is, on the contrary, not yet really to have

*Futility of Mr. Arnold's method considered as an instrument of historical criticism.*

formed a conception of justice. What Mr. Arnold regards as the sublimest expression of an altogether modern moral sentiment is, on the contrary, a partial negation of it. Mr. Arnold's aim, as he says, is a "literary" criticism; but the literary method consists in resetting the great works of human genius in the circumstances among which they were conceived; in discovering in them the spirit of the age in which they were written, and not of the present age. If we endeavour to interpret history by the light of modern ideas we shall never understand a jot of it. Mr. Arnold is pleasantly satirical at the expense of those who find in the Bible allusions to contemporary events, to such and such a modern custom, to such and such a dogma unknown to primitive times. A commentator, he says, finds a prediction of the flight to Egypt in the prophecy of Isaiah: "The Lord rideth upon a swift cloud and shall come into Egypt"; this light cloud being the body of Jesus born of a virgin. Another, more fantastic, perceives in the words: "Woe unto them that draw up iniquity with cords of vanity"—a malediction of God against church bells. That assuredly is a singular method of interpreting the sacred texts, but at bottom it is no more logical to look in the sacred texts for modern ideas, good or evil, than to search them for the announcement of such and such a distant event or for a commentary on such and such a trait of contemporary manners. Really to practise the literary method—and the scientific method at the same time—one must a little forget one's self, one's nation, one's century; one must live the life of past times—must become a Greek when one reads Homer, a Hebrew when one reads the Bible, and not desire that Racine should be a Shakespeare, nor Boccaccio a St. Benedict, nor Jesus a free-thinker, nor Isaiah an Epictetus or a Kant. All things and all ideas are appropriate in their own times and circumstances. Gothic cathedrals are magnificent, our small houses to-day are very comfortable; there is no reason why we should not admire the one and inhabit the other; the only thing that is really inexcusable is to be absolutely unwilling that cathedrals should be what alone they are.

Considered not from the point of view of history but purely from that of philosophy, Mr. Arnold's doctrine is much more

**Philosophical insufficiency of Mr. Arnold's position.**

attractive, for its aim is precisely to enable us to discover our own ideas in the ancient books as in a mirror. Nothing could be better, but are we really in want of this mirror? Do we really need to rediscover our modern conceptions embodied in the form of myth and more or less distorted in the process? Do we really need voluntarily to go back to the state of mind of primitive peoples? Do we really need to dwell upon the somewhat narrow conception that they possessed of justice and of morality before we shall be capable of conceiving a justice more generous in its proportions and a morality more worthy of its name? Would it not be much the same sort of thing as for one who was teaching children physics to begin by seriously inculcating the classic theory of nature's abhorence of a vacuum, of immobility of the earth, etc.? The authors of the Talmud in their naïve faith said that Javeh, filled with veneration for the book which he had himself dictated, would devote the first three hours of every day to a study of the sacred law. The most orthodox Jews do not to-day oblige their God to this recurrent period of meditation; might not one without danger permit mankind a somewhat similar economy of time? Mr. Arnold, whose mind moves so easily, although with so plentiful a lack of directness and of logic, criticises somewhere or other those who feel a need of a foundation of fable for their faith, a foundation of supernatural intervention and marvellous legend, and he says that many religious men resemble readers of romances or smokers of opium; the reality becomes insipid to them, although it is really more grand than the fantastic world of opium and romance. Mr. Arnold does not perceive that, if the reality is, as he says, the greatest and most beautiful of things, we have no further need of the legend of Christianity, not even interpreted as he interprets it : the real world, and by the real world I understand the moral not less than the physical universe, should prove abundantly sufficient for us. Ithuriel, Mr. Arnold says, has punctured miracles with his spear ; and did he not at the same stroke puncture symbolism? We prefer to see truth naked rather than tricked out in parti-coloured vestments; to clothe truth is to degrade it. Mr. Arnold compares a too absolute faith to intoxication; one might willingly compare Mr. Arnold to Socrates, who could drain off more than any other guest at the table without becoming intoxicated. Not to become intoxicated was, for the Greeks, one of the prerogatives of the sage. With this reservation they permitted him to drink, but in our days the sages make small use of the permission; they admire Socrates without imitating him, and find that sobriety is still the best means of keeping one's head. One might say as much to Matthew Arnold. The Bible with its scenes of massacre, of rape, and of divine vengeance is in his judgment bread for the soul; the soul can no more do without it than we can ourselves do without eating. The reply is that he has himself proved it to be a dangerous form of nourishment, and that it is sometimes better to fast than to eat poison.

For the rest, if one persists in seeking in the sacred books of by-gone ages for the expression of primitive morality, it is not in the Bible, but rather in the Hindu books that a literary or philosophical interpretation will find the most extraordinary example of moral symbolism. The entire world appears to the Buddhist as the realization of the moral law, since in his opinion beings take rank in the universe according to their virtues or vices, mount or descend on the ladder of life according to their moral elevation or abasement. Buddhism is in certain respects an effort to find in morals a theory of the universe.

*Buddhism more deeply symbolic than Christianity.*

In spite of the partial lapses from logical consistency that have been here pointed out in the theory of moral symbolism, there is one conclusion that is logically insisted on in the books just examined, and in especial Mr. Arnold's book, namely: that the solidest support of every religion is a more or less imperfect system of morals; that the power of Christianity, as of Buddhism, has lain in its moral injunctions, and that if one suppressed this moral

*Dependence of religion upon morality.*

injunction there would nothing remain of the two great " universal " religions brought forth by human intelligence. Religion serves, so to speak, as an envelope for morality ; it protects morality against the period of its ultimate development and efflorescence, but when once moral beliefs have gained strength enough they tend to protrude from this envelope, like a flower bursting out of the bud. Some years ago what was at that time called Independent Morality was much discussed ; the defenders of religion maintained that the fate of morality is intimately bound up with it—that if morality were separated from religion it must decline. They were perhaps right in pointing out the intimate connection between morality and religion, but they were mistaken in maintaining that it is the former that is dependent ; it would be truer to say the precise opposite, that it is religion that depends upon morality, that the latter is the principal and the former the subordinate. The Ecclesiast says somewhere, " He hath set the world in their heart." It is for that reason that man should first look into his own heart, and should first of all believe in himself. Religious faith might more or less logically issue out of moral faith, but could not produce the moral faith, and if it should go counter to the moral faith it would condemn itself. The religious spirit cannot therefore accommodate itself to the new order of things except by abandoning, in the first place, all the dogmas of a liberal faith, and then all the symbols of a more enlightened faith and holding fast by the fundamental principle which constitutes the life of religion and dominates its historical evolution ; that is to say, the moral sentiment of Protestantism in spite of all its contradictions has really introduced into the world a new principle ; it is this, that conscience is its own judge, that individual initiative should be substituted for objective authority.[1] Such a principle includes as a

[1] Toward the end of his life Luther felt an increasing discouragement and disquietude on the subject of the reform inaugurated by him: " It is by severe laws and by superstition," he wrote with bitterness, " that the world desires to be guided. If I could reconcile it with my conscience I would labour that the Pope with all his abominations might become once more our master." Responsibility to one's own conscience was indeed Luther's fundamental idea—the idea which justifies the Reformation in the eyes of history, as formerly in the eyes of its own author.

logical consequence not only the suppression of real dogmas and of mysteries, but also that of precise and determinate symbols; of everything, in a word, which proposes to impose itself upon the conscience as a ready-made truth. Protestantism unwittingly contained in its own bosom the germ of the negation of every positive religion that does not address itself exclusively and directly to private judgment, to the moral sense of the individual. In our days no one is willing to believe simply what he is told to believe; he must accept it independently: he believes that the danger of private judgment is only apparent, and that in the intellectual world, as in the world of civil liberty, it is out of liberty that all authority worthy of respect takes its rise. The revolution which tends thus to replace a religious faith, founded on the authority of texts and symbols, by a moral faith founded upon the right of private judgment recalls the revolution accomplished three centuries ago by Descartes, who substituted evidence and reasoning for authority. Humanity is increasingly anxious to reason out its own beliefs, to see with its own eyes. The truth is no longer exclusively locked up in temples; it addresses itself to everybody, communicates with everybody, gives everybody the right to act. In the cult of scientific truth everyone, as in the early days of Christianity, is capable of officiating in his turn; there are no seats reserved in the sanctuary, there is no jealous God, or rather the temples of truth are those which each of us rears in his own heart—temples which are no more truly Christian than Hebrew or Buddhist. The absorption of religion into morality is one with the dissolution of all positive and determinate religion, of all traditional symbolism and of all dogmatism. Faith, said Heraclitus profoundly, is a sacred malady, ἱερὰ νόσος. For us moderns it is no longer a sacred malady, and it is one from which all of us wish to be delivered and cured.

# CHAPTER III.

## DISSOLUTION OF RELIGIOUS MORALITY.

I. The first durable element of religious morality : Respect—Alteration of respect by the addition of the notion of the fear of God and divine vengeance.

II. Second durable element of religious morality : Love—Alteration of this element by the addition of ideas of grace, predestination, damnation—Caducous elements of religious morality—Mysticism—Antagonism of divine love and human love—Asceticism—Excesses of asceticism—Especially in the religions of the East—Conception of sin in the modern mind.

III. Subjective worship and prayer—The notion of prayer from the point of view of modern science and philosophy—Ecstasy—The survival of prayer.

HAVING traced the dissolution of dogma and religious symbolism it is appropriate to consider the fate of that system of religious morality which rests upon dogma and upon faith. There are in religious morality some durable elements and some caducous ones which stand out in sharper and sharper opposition in the course of the progress of human society. The two stable elements of religious morality which will occupy us first are respect and love; these are the elements indeed of every system of morality, those which are in nowise related to mysticism or symbolism, and which tend progressively to part company with them.

I. Kant regarded respect or reverence as the moral sentiment *par excellence ;* the moral law, in his opinion, was a law of reverence and not of love, and therein lay its pretensions to universality : for if it had been a law of love, there would have been a difficulty in imposing it upon all reasonable beings. I can insist on your respecting me but not on your loving me. In the sphere of society Kant is right; the law cannot provide

Superiority of element of love over that of respect.

# 196 *DISSOLUTION OF RELIGIONS IN EXISTING SOCIETIES.*

that men shall love each other, but only that they shall respect each other's rights. But is the same thing true in the
sphere of pure morality—have not the two great "universal"
religions, Buddhism and Christianity, been right in regarding
love as the controlling principle in ethics? Respect is no
more than the beginnings of ideal morality; in the attitude of respect the soul feels itself restricted, held in check,
embarrassed. And what in effect essentially is respect, but the
ability to violate a right on the one hand and on the other a
right to go inviolable? Well, there is another sentiment which
does away with the very possibility of violence and which
therefore is even purer than respect, that is to say love, and
Christianity has so understood it. Be it remarked also that
respect is necessarily implied in a properly understood moral
love; love is superior to respect not because it suppresses it
but because it completes it. Genuine love inevitably presents
itself under the form of respect, but this conception of respect,
abstractly taken, is an empty form without content; and can
be filled with love alone. What one respects in the dignity
of another person is—is it not?—a personal power held in check,
a sort of moral autonomy. It is possible to conceive a cold
hard respect that is not absolutely free from some suggestion
of mechanical necessity. What one loves, on the contrary, in
the dignity of another person is the element in his character
which beckons and welcomes one. Is it possible to conceive a cold love? Respect is a species of check, love is an
outleap of emotion; respect is the act by which will meets
will; in love there is no sense of opposition, of calculation, of
hesitation; one gives one's self simply and entirely.

Let it not therefore be made a reproach to Christianity that
it sees in love the very principle of relationship between
reasonable beings, the very principle of the moral
law and of justice. Paul says with reason that he
who loves others fulfils the law. In effect, the
commandments: thou shalt not commit adultery, thou shalt
not kill, thou shalt not covet, and the rest, were summed up in:
thou shalt love thy neighbor as thyself. The defect of Christianity—a defect from which Buddhism is free—is that the

**The mistake of Christianity.**

love of men is there conceived as disappearing, in the last analysis, in the love of God. Man is not beloved except in God and for God, and human society as a whole possesses no foundation nor rule of life except in the relationship of men to God. Well, if the love of man for man, properly understood, actually implies respect for rectitude, the same thing cannot be said with the same degree of emphasis for the love of man for God, and in God's sight. The conception of a society founded on the love of God contains the seeds of theocratic government with all its abuses.

Moreover, if in Christian morality love of man resolves itself, in the last resort, into love of God, love of God is always adulterated with fear ; the Old Testament insists upon it with positive complacency. The fear of the Lord plays an important rôle in the celestial sanction, and justice also, which is essential to Christianity, and which more or less definitely antagonizes and sometimes even paralyzes it. It is thus that, after having traced the sentiment of respect itself and of justice to a foundation in love, Christianity suddenly reinstates the former, re-endows it with precedence and that under its most primitive and savage form—the form of fear in man and vengeance in God.

This sanction, we have seen, is a special form of the notion of a Providence. Those who believe in a special Providence dis-

Respect for the welfare of sentient beings in general the essence of morality.

tributing good and evil admit, in the last resort, that this distribution takes place in conformity with the conduct of the receivers and the sentiments of approval or disapproval that that conduct inspires in the divinity. The idea of a Providence, in the natural course of its development, becomes therefore one with the notion of distributive justice, and this latter, on the other hand, becomes one with the idea of divine sanction. The idea of divine sanction has been conceived up to this point as one of the essential elements of morality, and it seems, at first glance, that religion and morality here coincide, that their respective needs here unite, or rather that morality reaches completeness only by the aid of religion. The notion of distributive justice naturally involves the notion of a celestial distributor, but we have seen in a preceding work that the notion of a sanction properly so called, and the notion of a divine penal code, have in reality no essential connection with morality; that on the contrary they possess a character of immorality and irrationality; and that thus the religion of the vulgar in no respect coincides with the highest morality, but that, on the contrary, the very fundamental idea of the religion of the vulgar is opposed to morality.[1] The founders of religion believe that the most sacred law is the law of the strongest; but the idea of force logically resolves itself into the relation between power on the one hand and resistance on the other, and physical force is always, in the sphere of morals, a confession of weakness. The *summum bonum* therefore can contain no suggestion of force of this especial kind. If human law, if civil law be condemned to rely upon a backing of physical force, it is therein precisely that it lies under the reproach of being merely civil and human. The case stands otherwise with the moral law, which is immutable, eternal, and in some sort inviolable; and in the presence of an inviolable law one can in no sense assume an attitude even of suppressed violence. Force is powerless against the moral law, and the moral law has therefore no need on its own side of a show of force. The sole sanction of which the moral law stands in need, the author has said elsewhere, as against the man who supposes himself to have abrogated it, is and ought to be the mere fact of its continued existence face to face with him, rising up before him ever anew, as the giant Hercules believed himself to have vanquished rose ever stronger to his embrace. To possess the attribute of eternity in the face of violence is the only revenge that goodness personified or not, under the figure of a god, can permit itself as against those who violate it.[2] In human societies one of the

---

[1] See the author's *Esquisse d'une morale sans obligation ni sanction*, p. 188, etc.

[2] " If God had consciously created the human will of such essential perversity as to find its natural expression in thwarting Him, He would be impotent in the face of it; could only show Himself compassionate; could only regret His own act in creating it. His duty would not be to punish mankind but to the utmost possible degree to lighten their sufferings, to show Himself gentle and good directly in proportion to this evil; and the damned, if they were truly incurable, would be in greater need of the joys of heaven than the elect themselves. Either the sinner can

distinguishing traits of high civilization is slowness to take offence ; with the progress of knowledge one finds less and less ground for indignation in the conduct of one's fellow-men. When the being involved is by definition the very personification of love the idea of offence becomes ridiculous ; it is impossible for any philosophic mind to admit the bare conception of offending God, or of drawing down upon one, in the Biblical phrase, his anger or his vengeance. Fear of an external sanction, or of any sanction other than that of conscience, is therefore an element that the progress of the modern mind tends to exclude from morality. It is in vain for the Bible to say that fear of the Lord is the beginning of wisdom ; morality does not truly begin until fear ceases to exist, fear being, as Kant said, pathological, not moral. Fear of hell may have possessed in former times a certain social utility, but it is essentially a stranger in modern society, and, *a fortiori*, will be in the society of the future. Moreover, respect for the happiness of people in general is becoming less and less adulterated by any admixture of fear. This respect, mingled with love and even engendered by love, is coming to be an altogether moral,

---

be reclaimed ; and in that event hell would be nothing more than an immense school, an immense house of correction for preparing the culpable with the utmost possible rapidity for heaven ; or the sinner is incorrigible, is analogous to an incurable maniac (which is absurd), and then he is eternally to be pitied and a supreme Goodness would endeavour to compensate him for his misery by every imaginable means by showering upon him every bliss that he was capable of enjoying. Turn it as one will, the dogma of hell stands thus in direct opposition to the truth.

"For the rest, by the very act of damning a soul, that is to say shutting it out forever from His presence, or, in terms less mystical, excluding it forever from a knowledge of the truth, would not God in turn be shutting Himself out from the soul, limiting His own power, and so to speak in some measure damning Himself also ? The penalty of the damnation would fall in part on Him who inflicted it. As to the physical torment of which theologians speak, interpreted metaphorically, it becomes even more inadmissible. Instead of damning mankind God ought eternally to gather about Him those who have strayed from Him ; it is for the culpable above all others that, as Michel Angelo said, God opened wide his arms upon the cross. We represent Him as looking down upon the sinning multitude from too great a height for them ever to be anything to Him but the incarnation of misfortune. Well, just in so far as they are unfortunate must they not logically be the especial favourites of divine goodness ?"—*Esquisse d'une morale sans obligation ni sanction*, p. 189.

and an altogether philosophic sentiment, purified of anything in the nature of mysticism, and in the best sense religious.

II. Having seen how readily the notion of respect became corrupt in Christianity, let us consider the fate of the notion of love. If the importance which it gave to this principle constitutes the chief honour of Christianity is not the God of the Christians, nevertheless, conceived in a manner inconsistent with the very essence of His being? The God of Christianity, or at least of orthodox Christianity, is a conception of absolute love which involves a contradiction and the destruction of all true fraternity. For the love affirmed to be absolute is in fact limited, since it has to do with a world that is marred by evil, metaphysical, sensible, moral. The love is not even universal, since it is conceived as an especial grace more or less arbitrarily bestowed or withheld, according to the dogma of predestination. The doctrine of grace, round which theology has played with such excess of subtlety, completes the highest principle of morality, the principle of love by the addition of the grossest notion of anthropomorphism : that of favour. God is always conceived on the model of absolute kings who accord favour and disfavour capriciously ; one of the most vulgar of sociomorphic relations being chosen, as one perceives, as the true analogue of God's relation to His creatures. The two elements of the notion of grace are antagonistic to each other. Absolute love is in its nature universal, favouritism is in its nature particular. There are, according to theology, a certain number of beings who are excluded from universal love ; the sentence of damnation is in its very essence such an exclusion. Thus understood, divine charity is incompatible with true fraternity, with true charity ; for true charity God does not possess—sets us no example of it. If we believe that God hates and damns, it will be in vain for Him to forbid personal vengeance. We shall inevitably espouse His hatreds, and the very principle of vengeance will find its support and its highest realization in Him. When St. Paul said : " Let thyself not conquer by the instrumentality of evil, but overcome evil by goodness," the precept was admirable. Unhappily God

*Unstable equilibrium of the Christian notion of absolute love.*

was the first to violate it, to decline to overcome evil by good. Do as I bid thee and not as I myself do is the very spirit of Christian teachings. Is it not in the midst of a sort of hymn to charity and forgiveness that the characteristic phrase of St. Paul occurs : " If thine enemy have hunger give him to eat and thou shalt heap coals of fire upon his head." Thus the apparent forgiveness becomes transmuted into a refined form of vengeance, which the divine sanction serves only to make more terrible, and which, under the cloak of benefits, nay even of caresses, pours upon the head of one's enemy an avenging flame; one's very charity sets the torch to the fires of hell. This indelible stain of barbarism on the page of love, this atavistic animal instinct of vengeance ascribed to God, shows the dangerous side of the theological element introduced into the morality of love.

Another danger to which a religion founded upon a divine love is subject is mysticism; a sentiment destined to an increasing antagonism with the modern mind and condemned, therefore, ultimately to disappear. The heart of man, in spite of its fertility in giving birth to passions of all sorts, has nevertheless always concentrated itself upon a small number of objects which find their own level. God and the world are two antagonists between which our sensibility is portioned out. One or the other of them inevitably receives the greater share. In all times religious sects have felt a possible opposition between absolute love of God and love of man. In a number of religions God has shown himself jealous of the affection devoted to others, and thus in a sense stolen from Him. He was not content with the superfluity of the human heart, He was bent on appropriating the soul in its entirety. Among the Hindus, as we know, the very essence of supreme piety lies in detachment from the world, in a life of solitude in the midst of great forests, in the rejection of all earthly affection, in a mystical indifference in regard to all mortal things. In the western world, when Christianity had made its way, this thirst of solitude, this home-sickness for the desert seized once more upon the soul, and thousands of men fled the faces of their fellows, quitting

*Conflict between divine and human love.*

their families and their homes, renouncing all other love but that of God, feeling themselves more intimately in His presence when they were distant from all beings else but Him. The whole of the Middle Ages were tormented by this antagonism between divine and human love. In the end, with the immense majority of men, human love carried the day. It could not be otherwise ; the very Church could not preach complete detachment for everybody under pain of having nobody to preach to. But among scrupulous and strenuous souls the opposition between divine and human love manifested itself in all the circumstances of life. One remembers Mme. Périer's account of Pascal. She was surprised at times that her brother repulsed her, became suddenly cold to her, turned away from her when she approached to soothe him in his pain ; she began to think he did not love her, she complained of it to her sister, but it was in vain to try to undeceive her. Finally the enigma was explained on the very day of Pascal's death by Domat, one of his friends. Mme. Périer learned that in Pascal's opinion the most innocent and fraternal friendship is a fault for which one habitually fails to take one's self sufficiently to task, because one underestimates its magnitude. " By fomenting and suffering these attachments to grow up, one is giving to someone else some portion of what belongs to God alone; one is in a manner robbing Him of what is to Him the most precious thing in all the world." It would be impossible better to express the mystical antagonism between divine and human love. This principle occupied so prominent a place in the foreground of Pascal's mind that, the more readily to keep it always before him, he wrote with his own hand upon a piece of paper : " It is unjust in me to permit anyone to form an attachment for me, however voluntarily, and with whatever pleasure they may do it. In the long run I should deceive them, for I belong to nobody but to God, and have not the wherewithal to satisfy a human affection. . . I should therefore be culpable, if I should allow anyone to love me, if I should attract people toward me. . . . They should pass their lives and employ their effort in pleasing and searching for God." The instant God is conceived as a person and not as a simple ideal, there inevitably arises in souls tinged with mysticism, a rivalry between His claims and those of other persons. How can the Absolute admit any human being to a share of what essentially is His? He must dwell in as absolute a solitude at the bottom of man's heart as on the height of heaven.

The rivalry between divine and human love perceived by the Jansenists, as by many of the early Christians and by mystics generally, exists even to-day for a large number of men. In certain religious houses any excessively affectionate demonstration toward their parents is forbidden to children, and a fraternal or filial kiss is made the basis of a case of conscience. If Protestant education and custom are not at one on this point with Catholic education and custom, the reason is that Protestantism, as has already been observed, has no talent for ultimate logical consequences. Catholicism, on the contrary, holds logic in scrupulous respect. To cite but one example: is not the interdiction of marriage in the case of the clergy a logical deduction from the conception of a religion which is founded on the theory of the fall of man, and whose purpose in the world is essentially anti-carnal? Love for a woman is too absorbing, too exclusive, to coexist in the heart of a priest, side by side with an undiminished love for God. Of all the sentiments of the soul, love is the one which fills it most nearly to the limit of its capacity. It is, in this respect, in diametric opposition to the theological sentiment which consists in the recognition of a sort of subjective void and personal insufficiency. Two lovers are of all the world the beings who are most sufficient unto themselves, they are of all the world those who experience least the need of God. Well, for mystics, love that is not given to God is love wasted. The lightest veil is enough to screen them once and forever from the "intelligible sun." It is of the very essence of such a God to be relegated to some region above the world, exiled in a manner from the soul of man; there are regions of love in which He does not exist and never will exist. He calls me, and if I do not turn my face in His direction precisely, I lose Him.

*Exists at the present day.*

The absolute detachment of the mystic leads to another consequence which is equally in opposition to modern tenden-

**Conflict between mysticism and egoism.** cies; it treats, that is to say, as an absolute zero a being who has at least the value of unity, to wit: the ego.   If I aim at the welfare of all sentient beings indiscriminatingly, I aim also in some measure at my own, who am one of them; and moreover, it is for my own that I can labour to best advantage.   This ego counts for something in this world, it is a unit in the sum.   The pure love inculcated by mysticism, on the contrary, lets the ego go for nothing, after the manner of the muleteer, who, in reckoning his mules, always forgot to count the one he was sitting on; the missing mule never turned up except when he dismounted, so that he ultimately resolved to go forward on foot. The transcendent and chimerical morality of mysticism might be compared to a purely humanitarian theory of politics; it is indeed even more abstract.   Patriotism, no doubt, leans upon a delusion when it regards one's native country as the centre of the world, but does not humanitarianism lean not upon one but upon a whole series of illusions?   In the item of illusions here below one must put up with the least false and most useful.   Well, it is probably not wholly without utility that each nation in the universe should act for itself; if each should attempt to act exclusively for the universe as a whole and for the love of the whole, either it would not act at all or it would conceive the future of the universe practically on the model of its own future and would commit an uninterrupted succession of mistakes.   Very frequently in this world unconscious and indirect collaboration is more efficacious than that which is conscious and direct.   Men often do more for the best aims of humanity by directing their attention in a spirit of rivalry toward needs comparatively immediate but which for that very reason stimulate their efforts and their hopes, than by uniting for the attainment of an object so distant that it discourages them.   In morals and politics one has not only to hit upon the best means of combining the forces of humanity, but also upon what is the best means of exciting human effort; and on that score there is something to be said even for the

love of the parish in which one is born.   One's parish is at least
a definite object: one knows where it is, one cannot lose one's
way, one may entertain a hope, nay even a certitude, of reaching it, and hope and certitude are great allies.   And the same
is true of self-love and love for those with whom one identifies
one's self.   It is precisely this that mysticism ignores and by
that means puts itself in opposition to the scientific spirit.
For mysticism there is no compromise possible between the
fact and its ideal which denies the fact.   Logically mysticism
ought to address its efforts toward total annihilation, much
after the manner of the followers of Schopenhauer and of Hartmann.   It would be better for the world to go off in smoke,
so to speak; to become sublimated like the corpses which the
worshippers of the sun used to expose to its rays, to be converted, as far as possible, into vapour.

Excess destroys itself.   If pleasure ends in disgust, mysticism possesses also its seamy side in a certain disenchantment
with God himself, in a certain home-sickness
for unknown joys, in that sadness peculiar to the
cloister for which Christians were obliged to

*Love of God on
the decline.*

invent a new name, in the Latin language, to designate—*acedia*.
When in the Middle Ages all one's preoccupations and affections
were turned toward heaven, human tenderness was impoverished
to precisely that extent.   The intellectual and moral evolution
of our days has moved in a contrary direction; love of God is
on the decline.   Love of mankind, on the contrary, and love of
living beings in general, is on the increase.   A sort of substitution of the one for the other is taking place.   Does it not seem
as if earth's turn had come, and that much of the force previously
spent in futile adoration, devoted toward the clouds, is being
more and more practically employed in the service of humanity?

Formerly, ideas of human fraternity and loving equality
were promoted in especial by the Christians.   The explanation
is simple: God was conceived by them as an
actual father, a *genitor;* men seemed to the
early Christians all of one family, having a com-

*Love of man to
take its place.*

mon ancestor.   So that divine love and human love were
regarded by them as inseparably bound up with each other.   It

is to be added that Christianity, which made its way into the world through the lower classes of society, had everything to gain by giving prominence to notions of fraternity and equality; it was by this means among others that it conciliated the masses, who were for a long time its main support.   But from the moment it found itself able to rely upon the higher classes of society, how quickly it changed its language is well known, and at the present moment the position of Christianity is precisely opposite to that which it occupied in the ancient world.   Ardent advocates of the ideas of fraternity are often adversaries of religion, are often free-thinkers, sometimes decided atheists.   The system of thought which founded the love of men for each other upon a community of origin is almost universally rejected.   Social doctrines, which in former times were so often based upon the element of socialism in the New Testament, are nowadays being formed and inculcated in complete independence of religious faith and often in positive antagonism to any religious faith whatever.   Religion sometimes presents itself as an additional obstacle, simply, to the brotherhood of man, in that it creates more stubborn divisions among them than differences of class or even of language. By an inevitable evolution religion has to-day come to represent among certain nations the spirit of caste and intolerance, and consequently of jealousy and enmity, whereas non-religion has come to be the recognized champion of social equality, of tolerance, and of fraternity.   Behind God, rightly or wrongly, as behind their natural defender, the partisans of the old order of things, of privilege and hereditary enmities, have ranged themselves; in the breast of the faithful a mystical love for God corresponds to-day as in other days to an anathema and malediction on mankind.   It was long ago remarked that those whose blessing is most fluent can also show themselves at need the most fluent to curse; the most mystical are the most violent.   Nothing can equal the violence of the gentle Jesus himself when he is speaking of the Pharisees, whose doctrines possessed so close an analogy to his own.   Whoever believes himself to have felt the breath of God upon his forehead becomes bitter and obstinate in his relations with mere men;

he is no longer one of them. So that the notion of the divine, of the superhuman tends toward that of the antinatural and antihuman.

The aim of progress in modern societies is to domesticate peace within their limits as well as without, to suppress mysticism, and to concentrate upon the real universe, present or to come, the whole body of our affections; to bind our hearts together in so intimate a union that they shall be sufficient unto themselves and unto each other, and that the human world, magnified by the eyes of love, may gather to itself the totality of things. In the first place the love of family, which scarcely existed at all in ancient times, and which in the Middle Ages was almost entirely absorbed by the conception of authority and of subordination, can scarcely be said to have acquired before our days a considerble hold on human life. It is only since the eighteenth century and the spread of the theory of equality that the father of a family, in especial in France, has ceased to consider himself as a sort of irresponsible sovereign, and begun to treat his wife in some sort as his equal and to exercise over his children no more than the minimum of possible authority. Whenever women shall receive an education almost equivalent to that given to men, the moral equality between them and men will have been consecrated, and as love is always more complete and more durable between beings who consider each other as morally equal, it follows that the love of family will increase, will draw to itself a greater proportion of the desires and aspirations of the individual. In positive opposition to religion, which has undertaken to combat the love of woman by restraining it within narrow limits, the love of woman has attained little by little an intensity that it never possessed in ancient times: it suffices to read our poets to become convinced of it, and it will continue to increase with the intellectual development of women, which will make a closer and more complete union between men and women possible than exists at present. The association of man and woman being capable thus of becoming in a manner a sort of intellectual association and fellowship, it will result in a fertility of

*And also love of family.*

a new species: love will no longer act upon the intelligence solely as the most powerful of stimulants, it will contribute positive elements hitherto unknown. It is impossible to predict the sort of work that the combined labour of man and woman will produce when they possess a preparation for it that will be practically upon both sides equal. Some hint of what one means may be gathered from examples actually under one's eyes. In the present century men and women of talent are tending to come into closer relations with each other; and I might cite the names of Michelet and Mme. Michelet, of John Stuart Mill and his wife, of Lewes and George Eliot, and other names besides. But not to give an undue prominence to great names like these, which are after all exceptions in the human race, it is not too much to assert that from the very top of the social ladder to the bottom the family tends increasingly to become a unity, a more and more perfect organism in which man will one day find scope for all of his powers and capabilities. The importance of the family increases, as that of the city and of the despotic tutelage of the state decreases. This importance, which is almost non-existent in purely military societies (of which Lacedæmon may serve as the accomplished exemplar), becomes greater and greater in free and industrial societies such as those of the future, and thus there opens a new field for human activity and sensibility. The love of men and women for each other and of both for their children, heightened by the growing sentiment of equality, is destined in the author's judgment to create a new and non-mystical sort of religion, the worship of the family. If a cult for the gods of the hearth was one of the earliest religions, perhaps it will also be actually the last: the family hearth possesses in and of itself an element of sacredness, of religion, since it binds together as about a common centre beings so diverse in origin and sex. And thus the modern family, founded on the law of equality, seems by its very spirit, and by the sentiments which it excites, to be in growing opposition to religious mysticism. The true type of the priest, whatever Protestantism may say, is the solitary man, the missionary here below, devoted body and soul to

God ; whereas the type of the practical philosopher and the modern sage is a loving, thinking, labouring man, devoted to those who are dear to him.

A similar antagonism may be seen between the sentiment of mysticism and of allegiance to the state. The citizen who

And love of country.

knows that the fate of his country lies in his arms, who loves his country with an active and sincere love, is a worshipper in a social religion. Great politicians have almost always been large and liberal minds. The ancient republics were comparatively non-religious for their time ; the disappearance of monarchy coincides in general, in the history of mankind, with enfeeblement of faith. When everybody shall feel himself as equally and truly a citizen as anybody else, and shall be able to devote himself with an equal love to the good of the state, there will no longer be so great a store of unemployed activity, of surplus sensibility lying ready to the hand of mysticism. For the rest, let us magnify a little the sphere of human activity ; not only the family and the state are nowadays demanding an increasingly large share of one's attention and affection, but the human race itself is coming to be each day more and more intimately present to the mind of each of us. We find it more and more difficult even in thought to isolate ourselves, to become absorbed either in ourselves, or in God. The human world has become infinitely more human than formerly ; all the bounds which separated men from each other (religion, language, nationality, race) are regarded already by superior men as artificial. The human race itself is coming to be recognized as a part only of the animal kingdom, the entire world claims the attention of science, offers itself to our love and opens for the devotees of mysticism the perspective of a species of universal fraternity. Just in so far as the universe thus grows larger, it becomes less and less insufficient in our eyes ; and this surplus of love, which formerly mounted toward heaven in search of some transcendent resting place, finds ample room upon the surface of the earth and of heavenly bodies not unknown to astronomy. If the mystical tendency of the human mind be not destined completely to disappear, if it possesses any element of permanency, it will at least change its direction, and indeed, little by little is changing it. Christians were in no sense wrong in finding society in ancient times too narrow and the ancient world too cabined and confined under its dome of crystal; the very reason for the existence of Christianity lay in this vicious conception of society and of nature. To-day the one thing needful is to magnify the world till it shall satisfy the needs of man; until an equilibrium be established between the universe and the human heart. The aim of science is not to extinguish the need to love which constitutes so considerable an element of the religious sentiment, but to supply that need with an actually existing object; its function is not to put a check upon the outleap of human affection but to justify it.

And remark, also, that if the love of a personal God mystically conceived tends to become dim in modern societies, the same is not true of the love of an ideal God conceived as the practical type of conduct. The ideal God, in effect, in no sense exists in opposition to the world, He surpasses it simply; He is at bottom identical with the progress of human thought which, with its point of departure in brute fact, outstrips the actual and foresees and prepares the way for perpetual progress. In human life the real and the ideal are harmonized, for life as a whole both is and becomes. Whoever says life, says evolution; and evolution is the Jacob's ladder resting both on heaven and on earth; at the base of it we are brutes, at the summit of it we are gods, so that religious sentiment cannot be said so much to be in opposition to science and philosophy as to complete them; or rather, it is at bottom identical with the spirit that animates them. We have spoken of religion as science,—in its beginnings as unconscious science; in the same way science may be called religion headed back toward reality; headed, that is to say in the normal direction. Religion says to the human race: Bind yourselves together into a single whole; science shows the human race that all mankind are inevitably parts of a single whole already, and the teaching of the two is practically one.

> But the love of a personal God must be distinguished in all this from love of the ideal God.

In effect there is taking place a certain substitution in our affections; we are coming to love God in man, the future in the present, the ideal in the real. The man of evolution is precisely the man-God of Christianity. And this love of the ideal harmonized with the love of humanity, instead of finding its vent in vain contemplation and ecstasy, will fill the limbs with energy. We shall love God all the more that He will be, so to speak, the work of our own hands. And if there be really at the bottom of the human heart some indestructible element of mysticism, it will be employed as an important factor in the service of evolution; our heart will go out to our ideas, and we shall adore them in proportion as we shall realize them. Religion having become the purest of all things—pure love of the ideal—will at the same time have become the realest and in appearance the humblest of all things—labour.

*Summary.*

The natural and practical complement of mysticism is asceticism; and asceticism is another of the elements of religious morality that are becoming daily feebler in the presence of the modern spirit. Austerity is of two kinds, the one quite mystical in origin, despising art, beauty, science; the other founded on a certain moral stoicism, a certain respect for one's self. The latter is in no sense ascetic, it is composed for the most part of the very love for science and art, but it is the highest art only that it loves, and science for science's sake that it pursues. The excess of austerity, to which religions have so often led, bears the same relation to virtue that avarice does to economy. Austerity alone does not constitute a merit or an element of superiority. Life may be much more gentle, more social, better on many accounts among a people of loose manners like the ancient Greeks, than among a people who regard existence as hard and dry, and who make it so by the brutality of their faith and ignore the lightening of the burden of life that lies in smiles and tears. One would rather live with prodigals than with misers. Avarice, however, which may be regarded in the life of a people or

*Mysticism and asceticism.*

*Asceticism in the good and the bad sense.*

of a family as a state of transition, is economically and morally superior to prodigality. The same may be said of excessive rigour. Excessive rigour and avarice are defects which are rendered tolerable by their consequences, which impoverish life in order subsequently, with a freer hand, to enrich it. It is better for the race if not always so for the individual to be economical to excess than to dissipate its resources intemperately. An impulse held in check gathers force. Austerity, like avarice, is a means of defence and of protection, a weapon. Conquerors have often in the course of history been the sons of misers who have amassed treasure and blood for their benefit. From time to time it is good to regard one's self as an enemy, and to live and sleep in a coat of mail. For the rest, there are temperaments that can be held in check by nothing lighter than bars of iron, that find no mean between pure water and pure alcohol; between a bed of roses and a crown of thorns; between moral law and military discipline; between a moralist and a corporal. Still, one must not represent such a state of mind at least as ideal. The ascetic hates himself; but one must hate nobody, not even one's self; one must understand all things and regulate them. Hatred of self springs from feebleness of will; whoever is gifted with self-control need not hate himself. Instead of giving one's self a bad name one's duty is to make one's self worthy of a better. There may well be a certain legitimate element of rigour, of inner discipline, in every system of morality; but this discipline should be reasonable, rationally directed toward an end which explains and justifies it: one's business is not to break the body but to fashion it, to bend it. The savant, for example, should aim to develop his brain, to refine his nervous system, to reduce his circulatory and nutritive system to their lowest terms. You may call that asceticism if you like, but it is a fertile, a useful asceticism; it is at bottom a moral hygiene simply—which ought to be made a part of physical hygiene. A surgeon knows that he must lead a severe and continent life, or his hand will lose its cunning. The very condition of his being able to aid other people is that he in a measure suffer privation himself; he must choose. And to make this choice he experiences no need of a religious injunction, he requires only the voice of conscience. It suffices for him to know enough of moral hygiene to foresee the distant results of his conduct and to possess a sufficient measure of firmness to be self-consistent. It is after this fashion that, in plotting out one's life according to scientific laws, one may regulate it, may render it almost as hard as that of the most self-denying monk. Every profession that is freely chosen is in the nature of a self-imposed discipline. As to the choice of no profession, as to voluntary idleness—that is in and of itself immoral and necessarily leads to immorality, whatever may be the religion that one holds.

The ultimate consequence of excessive rigourism is morbid preoccupation with sin: an obsession which, with the fear of the millennium, is one of the greatest of the futile tortures that have afflicted humanity. It is as dangerous for man to magnify his vices as his virtues; to believe one's self a monster possesses no greater exemption from evil consequences than to believe one's self perfect. Sin in itself, and philosophically considered, is a conception difficult to reconcile with the modern idea of scientific determinism, which, when it has explained everything, goes far, if not toward justifying everything, at least toward pardoning everything. Neither the pangs nor the vanity of sin are permissible to us nowadays when we are hardly certain really that our own sins belong to us. Temptation comes to us in the guise of the reawaking of an hereditary appetite, handed down to us not only from the first man, but from the ancestors of the first man, or more accurately from life itself, from the universe, from the God who is immanent in the world or who transcends it, and has created it; it is not the devil that tempts us, it is God. Like Jacob, of whom we were speaking a moment ago, we must vanquish God, must subject life to thought, must give the victory to the higher forms of life, as against the lower. If we are wounded in this struggle, if we are branded with the mark of sin, if we mount haltingly up the steps of goodness, we ought not to be immeasurably terrified: the essential thing is to go upward. Temp-

*Asceticism results in a preoccupation with sin.*

tation is not in and of itself a blot, it may be even an emblem of nobility so long as one does not yield to it. Our first fathers were not subject to temptation, properly so called, because they yielded to all their desires, because they made no struggle against them. Sin or moral evil is explicable : first by the antagonism between instinct and reflection ; second, by the antagonism between egoistic instincts and altruistic instincts. This double antagonism between instinct and conscious purpose, between egoism and altruism, is a necessary incident of self-knowledge and a condition of progress : to know one's self is to be aware more or less uneasily of a manifold, and succession of inconsistent desires of which the moving equilibrium constitutes life itself ; self-knowledge, and knowledge in general, is the equivalent of temptation. Life is in some sort always sin, for one cannot eat, one cannot even breathe without some measure of affirmation of low and egoistic instincts. Moreover asceticism logically leads nowhere, to negation of life ; the most thorough-going ascetics are the Yoghis of India, who attain the point of living without air or food and of going down alive into the tomb.[1] And in believing himself thus to have realized absolute renunciation, what the ascetic actually realized is complete and perfect egoism, for the last drops of vegetative life which flow in his veins circulate for him alone and not a shiver of his heart is directed beyond himself ; by impoverishing and annihilating his life, he has suppressed the generosity that fulness of life produced ; in his endeavour to kill sin he has slaughtered charity. The real moral and

---

[1] The fact has been verified by the English authorities and has been commented on by the physiologist W. Preyer (*Über die Erforschung des Lebens*, Jena, and *Sammlung physiologischer Abhandlungen*). Yoghis who have attained the highest degree of perfection, and are insensible to cold and to heat and have contracted, by a series of experiments, the habit of breathing almost not at all, have been buried alive and resuscitated at the end of some weeks. When they were reawakened a heightening of the temperature was noticed as in the case of the reawaking of hibernating mammals, and it is indeed to the phenomena of hibernation that this strange voluntary suspension of animation most closely approaches—this mystical return to a life merely vegetative, this absorption in the bosom of the unconscious, where the Yoghis hopes to find God. As a preliminary discipline the

religious ideal does not consist in denying one's self everything in order to deny one's self what is sinful. There is nothing absolutely evil in us, except excess ; when we apply the knife to our hearts, we should have but one aim, the one which the gardener has in view in pruning trees, to increase our real power. Our manifold desires should all be satisfied at one time or another ; we should take example from the mother who forces herself to eat that she may watch to the end at the bedside of her dying child. Whoever purposes to live for others besides himself, will find no time to sulk ; for whoever possesses a heart sufficiently great no function in life is impure. Every moral rule should be a reconciliation between egoism and altruism, original sin and ideal sanctity ; and to accomplish this reconciliation it suffices to show that each of our manifold and mutually exclusive desires, if carried to the extreme, contradicts itself ; that our desires need each other, that when nature endeavours to rise above herself she inevitably falls headlong. To govern one's self means to reconcile all parties. Ormuzd and Ahriman, spirit and nature, are not so hostile to each other as seems to be believed, and either of them indeed is powerless without the other. They are two gods whose origin is the same, they are immortal, and for immortals some means of accommodation must be found. Complete and unremunerated sacrifice never can be adopted as a rule of life ; never can be more than a sublime conception, a spark in some individual existence, consuming the fuel it feeds upon and then disappearing and leaving behind, face to face, the two great principles,

---

Yoghis diminishes little by little the quantity of air and light necessary to his life ; he lives in a cell which is lit and ventilated by no more than a single chink ; he minimizes all movement in order to mimimize the necessity of respiration; he does not speak except to repeat to himself twelve thousand times a day the mystic name of Om ; he remains for hours together motionless as a statue. He practises breathing over again and again the same body of air, and the longer the period between inspiration and expiration, the greater his sanctity ! Finally he carefully seals all the openings of his body with wax and cotton and closes the opening of the throat with the tongue, which certain incisions permit him to fold over backward, and finally falls into a lethargy in which the movements of respiration may be suspended without the thread of life positively being severed.

a conscious reconciliation of which constitutes the moral mean.

The very nature of the conceptions confirms what we have just said respecting temptation and sin. Directly or indirectly, every idea is a suggestion, an incitement to action; it tends even to take exclusive possession of us, to become a fixed idea, to employ us as a means to its own end, to realize itself often in spite of us; but as our thought embraces all things in the universe, high and low, we are incessantly solicited to act in opposite directions; temptation, from this point of view, is simply the law of thought, and the law of sensibility. And ascetics and priests have endeavoured as a means of struggling against temptation to confine human thought, to prevent it from playing freely about the things of this world. But the things of this world are precisely those which are always present, which solicit us most strongly and constantly. And the greater our effort to exclude them from the mind, the greater their power over us. There is nothing one sees more clearly than what one resolves not to look at; there is nothing that makes the heart beat so quickly as what one resolves not to love. The cure for temptation, so persistently demanded by essentially religious people, is not restriction of thought but enlargement of thought. The visible world cannot be hidden, it is folly to attempt it, but it can be magnified indefinitely. Incessant discoveries may be made in it and the peril of certain points of view counteracted by the novelty and attractiveness of certain others, and the known universe lost sight of in the abyss of the unknown. Thought bears its own antidote—a science sufficiently great is more trustworthy than innocence; a boundless curiosity is the cure for all petty curiosities. An eye which reaches the stars will not aim long at a low mark; it is protected by its command of space and light, for light is purifying. By making temptation infinite one makes it salutary and in the best sense divine. Asceticism, and the artificial maturity that comes of a dissolute life, often amount to the same thing. One must keep one's youth and memory green, and one's heart open. "I was not a man before years of manhood," said

*Results a priori from the nature of ideas.*

Marcus Aurelius. Both asceticism and debauchery make men precociously old, wean them from love and enthusiasm for the things of this world. The island of Cythere and the desert of Thebes are alike deserts. To remain young long, to remain a child even in the spontaneity and affectionateness of one's heart, to preserve not in externals, but in "internals," something of lightness and gaiety is the best means of dominating life; for what is more powerful than youth? One must neither stiffen one's self, nor bristle up against life, nor cowardly abandon one's self to it; one must take it as it is, that is to say, according to the popular maxim, "as it comes," and welcome it with an infant's smile without any other care than to maintain one's possession of one's self, in order that one may possess all things.

III. Morality and religion are inseparable in all historical faiths, and the essential act of subjective worship, the fundamental rite commanded by religious morality, is prayer.

Prayer.

To analyze prayer into all its component elements would be very difficult and far from simple. Prayer may be an almost mechanical accomplishment of the rite, the babbling of vain words, and as such it is despicable even from the point of view of religion. It may be an egoistic demand, and as such it is mean, simply. It may be an act of naïve faith in beliefs more or less popular and irrational, and on this score its value is so slight that it may be neglected. But it may be also the disinterested outpouring of a soul which believes itself to be in some fashion or other serving someone else, acting upon the world by the ardour of its faith, conferring a gift, an offering, devoting something of itself to someone else. Therein lies the grandeur of prayer: it is then no more than one of the forms of charity and the love of mankind. But suppose it should be demonstrated that this especial form of charity is illusory, does one imagine that the very principle of charity itself will by that fact receive a check?

Kinds of prayer distinguished.

Many arguments have been urged in favour of prayer, but

the majority of them are quite external and superficial. Prayer, it has been said, as being a demand on a special Providence, is sovereignly consoling; it is one of the sweetest of the satisfactions incident to reli-gious faith. One who had been converted to free-thought said to me recently, " There is but one thing in my former faith that I regret, and that is that I can no longer pray for you and imagine that I am serving you." Assuredly it is sad to lose a faith which consoled one; but suppose that someone believed himself to possess the fairy-wand and to be able to save the world. Some fine morning he finds himself undeceived, he finds himself alone in the world with no power at his disposal more mysterious than that of his ten fingers and his brain. He cannot but regret his imaginary power, but he will labour nevertheless to acquire a real power and the loss of his illusions will but serve as a stimulus to his will. It is always dangerous to believe that one possesses a power that one has not, for it hinders one in some degree from knowing and exercising those that one has. The men of former times, the times of absolute monarchy, who had access to the ear of princes, possessed a power analogous to that which the believers on their knees in temples still believe themselves to possess; this power, in the case of kings, their confidential ministers have lost as the result of purely terres-trial revolutions; and have they thereby been diminished in their dignity as moral beings? No, a man is morally greater as a citizen than as a courtier; one is greater as the result of what one does one's self only, or attempts to do, and not as the result of what one endeavours to obtain from a master.

Will the individual never be able to do without prayers conceived as a constant communication with God, as a daily confession, a faith in Him and before Him? He will probably not renounce it until he is capable of existing without it. Arguments to prove the practical utility of prayer, conceived as a direct communication with one's living ideal, would all hold equally good in favour of Catholic confession before the priest as a realization of the moral ideal. Nevertheless, when Protestants

*Superficiality of most pleas in its behalf.*

*Arguments for its utility equally good for auricular confession.*

supressed the confession they gave a fresh development to moral austerity : the morality of Protestant peoples, which is defended only by the voice of conscience, is not inferior to that of Catholic peoples.[1] Is it any more necessary for the purpose of ascertaining one's faults and curing them to kneel before a personified and anthropomorphic God than before a priest beneath the roof of a church ? Experience alone can decide, and a number of men seem already successfully to have tried the experiment. The scrutiny of a philosophical conscience has been proved to be sufficient.

Finally it has been said that prayer, even conceived as destitute of objective effect, nevertheless justifies itself by the comfort it affords ; one has attempted to argue in its favour on purely subjective grounds, but prayer runs the risk precisely of losing its power as a consoler the instant one ceases to believe in its objective efficiency. If nobody hears us, who will continue to offer up petitions simply to ease the burden of his own heart ? If the orator is uplifted by the sympathy of the assembly which listens to him, does it follow that he will experience the same effect if he deliver his oration in the void with the knowledge that his thought, his word, his emotion, are lost, and spend themselves in space ?

*Prayer as a subjective relief.*

If prayer is really to be its own reward, it must not consist of a demand addressed to some Being exterior to one's self, it must be a subjective act of love, what Christianity calls an act of charity. Charity is the eternal element in prayer. To ask for something for one's self is a thing difficult to justify ; to ask for something for someone else is at least a beginning of disinterested conduct. " How much longer thy prayers grow, grandmama, day by day ! " " The number of those for whom I pray increases day by day." Over and above this element of charity, prayer contains a certain beauty—a beauty which will not disappear with the disappearance of the superstitions which have clustered about it. The moral beauty of prayer is intimately bound up with certain profound human sentiments: one prays for

*Subjective charity the durable element in prayer.*

[1] See below chapter iv.

somebody whom one loves; one prays out of pity or of affection; one prays in despair, in hope, in gratitude; so that the
most elevated of human sentiments sometimes ally themselves with prayer and colour it.   This tension of one's whole
being at such times finds its way out upon the visage, and
transfigures it with the intense expression that certain painters
have loved to catch and to perpetuate.[1]   What is most beautiful and probably also what is best in prayer is, more than all
else, the human and moral element in it.   If there is thus an
essential charity in genuine prayer, charity of the lips is not
enough, that of the heart and hands must be added to it, and
that is to say in the last resort action must be substituted
for it.

Prayer for love and charity tends increasingly to find vent
in action: a verification of this fact may be found in history.

*Increasing ten-
dency for such
prayer to express
itself in action.*

Formerly, in a moment of distress, a pagan
woman would have thought only of appeasing
the anger of the Gods by some blood sacrifice,
by the murder of some innocent member of the
larger mammals; in the Middle Ages she would have made a
vow or founded a chapel—things still vain and powerless to
alleviate the misery of this world; in our days she would
think rather, if she were a person of some elevation of spirit,
of giving money in charity, of founding an establishment for
the instruction of the poor or the care of the infirm.   One sees
in that fact the march of progress in religious ideas; the time
will come when such actions will no longer be accomplished
for a directly interested end but as a sort of exchange with
the divinity, a traffic of kindness; they will constitute a
recognized part of public worship, the essence of worship will
be charity.   Pascal asks, somewhere, why God has bestowed
prayer upon man, why God has commanded man to pray;
and he replies profoundly enough: " To give him the dignity
of seeing himself as a cause "; but if he who demands benefits
by prayer possessed formerly the dignity of being, in his own

---

[1] This, however, is exceptional; in church, during the services, the majority of the
faces remain inexpressive, for the reason that prayer with the majority of the faithful
is almost always mechanical.

right, a cause, how much greater is the dignity of him who by the exercise of his own moral will procures the object of his desire? And if to be the cause of one's own well-being be thus the essence of prayer, of that which brings man nearest to God, of that which lifts man nearest to His level—may one not say that the most disinterested, the most sacred, the most human, the most divine of prayers is moral conduct? In Pascal's opinion, it is true, moral conduct presupposes two terms, duty and power, and man cannot always do what he should; but one must break with the antique opposition established by Christianity, between the sentiment of duty and the practical powerlessness of a man shorn of all adventitious aid—shorn of grace. In reality the sentiment of duty is, in and of itself, the first vague consciousness of a power existent in us, of a force which tends to achieve its own realization.[1] Consciousness of his power for good and of the power of the ideal unite in man, for this ideal is no more than the projection, the objectification, of the highest power within, the form that that power takes in reflective intelligence. Every volition is at bottom no more than a capability of some sort in labour, an action in the stage of germination: the will to do good, if it is conscious of its own power, has no need to await the prompting of external grace; it is itself its own grace; by the very fact of its birth it becomes efficacious; by the very fact of wishing, nature creates. Pascal conceived the moral end, which duty places before us, too much after the manner of a physical and external object, that one might be able to look upon but not to attain. "One directs one's looks on high," says he, in his "Pensées," "but one rests upon the sand and the earth will slip from under one, and one shall fall with one's eyes on heaven." But might not one respond that the heaven of which Pascal is here speaking, the heaven we carry in our own bosoms, is something quite different from the heaven which we perceive spread out above our heads? Must it not here be said that to see is to touch and to possess; that a sight of the moral end renders possible a progress toward it; that the resting point one finds in the moral will, the most invincible of all the forms

[1] See on this point our *Esquisse d'une morale sans obligation*, p. 27.

of volition, will not give way beneath one, and that one cannot fall, in one's progress toward goodness and that in this sense to lift one's eyes toward heaven is already to have set one's feet on the way thither."

There remains one more aspect under which prayer may be considered. It may be regarded as a species of spiritual eleva-

Ultimate claim for prayer.

tion, a communication with the universe or with God.[1] Prayer has in all times been glorified as a means of uplifting the whole being to a plane that it otherwise would have been unable to attain. The best of us, as Amiel said not long since, find complete development and self-knowledge in prayer alone.

One must be on one's guard against a multitude of illusions in this connection, and must carefully distinguish between two

Distinction be-<br>tween religious<br>ecstasy and philo-<br>sophical medita-<br>tion.

very different things: religious ecstasy and philosophical meditation. One of the consequences of our profounder knowledge of the nervous system is an increasing contempt for ecstasy and for all of those states of nervous intoxication or even of intellectual intoxication which were formerly regarded by the multitude, and sometimes even by philosophers, as superhuman, and truly divine. Religious ecstasy, so called, may be a phenomenon so purely physical that it suffices to apply a bit of volatile oil of cherry laurel to induce it in certain subjects, and to fill them with ecstatic beatitude, and make them pray and weep and kneel. Such was the fact in the case of a hysteric patient, a hardened courtesan of Jewish origin; it sufficed even to induce in her definite visions, even such as that of the girl with golden hair in the blue robe starred with gold.[2] The intoxication indulged in by the followers of Dionysius in Greece, like that indulged in by hasheesh-eaters, was no more than a violent means of inducing ecstasy and of entering into

[1] " Oh, God " said Diderot, at the end of his *Interprétation de la nature*, " I do not know if Thou existest, but I shall bear myself as if Thou sawest into my soul ; I shall act as if I felt myself in Thy presence . . . I ask nothing of Thee in this world, for the course of things is necessary in and of its own nature, if Thou dost not exist, and necessary if Thou dost, by Thy decree."

[2] *Report of MM. Bourru and Burot au Congrès scientifique de Grenoble,* August 18, 1885.

communication with the supernatural world.[1]  In India,[2] and among the Christians, fasting is practised to attain the same end, namely a nervous excitation of the nervous systems.  The macerations of the anchorite were, says Wundt, a solitary orgie, in the course of which monks and nuns ardently pressed in their arms fantastic images of the Virgin and the Saviour. According to a legend of Krishnaïsm, the Queen Udayapura, Mira Bai, being pressed to abjure her God, threw herself at the feet of the statue of Krishna and made this prayer: "I have quitted for thee my love, my possessions, my crown; I come to thee, oh, my refuge!  Take me."  The statue listened motionless; suddenly it opened and Mira disappeared inside of it.  To vanish thus into the bosom of one's God is—is it not?—the perfect ideal of the highest human religions.  All of them have proposed it to man, as a prime object of desire, to die in God; all of them have seen the higher life as a form of ecstasy; whereas the fact is that, in a state of ecstasy, one descends on the contrary to a lower and a vegetative plane of existence, and that this apparent fusion with God is no more than a return to a primitive inertia, to a mineral impassibility, to a statuesque petrifaction.  One may believe one's self uplifted in a state of ecstasy, and mistake for an exaltation of thought what is in reality no more than a sterile nervous excitement. The trouble is that there is no means of measuring the real force and extent of thought.  Under normal circumstances the only means that exist are action; one who does not act is inevitably inclined to exaggerate the value of his thought. Amiel himself did not escape from this danger.  Fancied

---

[1] A defender of the use of hasheesh scientifically employed, M. Giraud, who conceives that it is possible to induce ecstasy at will, and to regulate it by medical doses, writes us with enthusiasm: "A bit of hasheesh dispenses with painful mystical expedients to induce ecstasy.  There is no further need of asceticism; the result is an intoxication, but a sacred intoxication, which is nothing else than an excess of activity in the higher centres."  We believe that every sort of drunkenness, far from possessing a sacred character, will constitute for ever and always, in the eyes of science, a morbid state, in no sense enviable from any rational point of view, by an individual in normal health; the constant employment of stimulants will exhaust the nervous system and throw it out of order, as the daily employment of nux vomica will, in the long run, destroy the power of a healthy stomach.

[2] See above what we have already said in regard to the Yoghis and asceticism.

superiority disappears the moment a thought seeks expression of whatsoever kind.   The dream that is told becomes absurd ; the ecstasy in which one retains complete control of one's mind, in which one endeavours to take stock of the confused emotions one experiences, vanishes before us and leaves behind no more than a fatigue, a certain subjective obscurity, like a winter twilight, which precipitates a frost upon the window-panes that intercepts the last rays of the sun.   My most beautiful verses will never be written, the poet says : " Of my work, the better part lies buried in myself." [1]   That is an illusion by which dream seems always superior to reality ; an illusion of the same sort as that which makes us attach so much value to certain hours of religious exaltation.   The truth is that the poet's best verses are those which he has written with his own hand, his best thought is that which has possessed vitality enough to find its formula and its music ; the whole of him lies in his poetry.   And we also, we are in our actions, in our words, in the glance of an eye or the accent of a word, in a gesture, in the palm of a hand open in charity.   To exist is to act, and a thought which is incapable of expression is an abortion which has never really been alive and has never merited to live.   In the same way the true God is also the one who can be domesticated in one's own heart, who does not fly the face of reflective consciousness, who does not show himself in dreams alone, whom one does not invoke as a phantom or a demon.   Our ideal ought not to be some passing and fantastic apparition, but a positive creation of our spirit ; we must be able to contemplate it without destroying it, to feed our eyes upon it as upon a reality.   For the rest this ideal of goodness and of perfection, persisting as it does in the face of inner scrutiny, has no need of an objective existence in some sort material, to produce its proper effect upon the spirit.   The profoundest love subsists for those who have been, as well as for those who are, and reaches out into the future as well as into the present.   Nay, it even in a manner outstretches the measure of existence and develops a power of divining and loving the ideal that shall some day be.   Maternal love is a model now as always for all moral beings, in that it does not

[1] M. Sully-Prudhomme.

await the birth of its object before making the first steps in its
service. Long before the child is born the mother forms an
image of it in her fancy, and loves it and gives herself to it in
advance.

For a truly elevated spirit the hours consecrated to the
formation of its ideal will always be precious hours of patient
attention and meditation, not only upon what
one knows or does not know, but upon what one
hopes and will attempt; upon the ideal seeking
for birth through one's instrumentality, and leaning upon
one's heart. The highest form of prayer is thought. Every
form of philosophic meditation possesses, like prayer, an element of consolation, not directly, for it may well deal with the
saddest of realities, but indirectly because it enlarges the
heart. Every aperture broken open upon the infinite braces
us like a current in the open air. Our personal sorrows are
lost in the immensity of the infinite, as the waters of the earth
are lost in the immensity of the sea.

The highest
form of prayer.

As for those who are not capable of thinking for themselves,
of standing spiritually on their own feet; it will always be
good for them to retrace the thoughts which appear to
them to be the highest and the noblest product of the human
mind. On this account the Protestant custom of reading and
of meditating on the Bible is, in principle, excellent; the book
however is ill-chosen. But it is good that man should
habituate himself to read or to re-read a certain number of
times a day, or a week, something else than a newspaper or a
novel; that he should turn now and then to some serious subject of meditation and dwell on it. Perhaps the day will come
when every one independently will compose a Bible of his own;
will select from among the works of the greatest human
thinkers the passages which especially appeal to him, and will
read them and re-read and assimilate them. To read a serious
and high-minded book is to deal at first hand with the greatest
of human thoughts; to admire is to pray, and it is a form of
prayer that is within the power of all of us.

# CHAPTER IV.

## RELIGION AND NON-RELIGION AMONG THE PEOPLE.

I. Is religious sentiment an innate and imperishable possession of humanity ?—Frequent confusion of a sentiment for religion with a sentiment for philosophy and morals—Renan—Max Müller—Difference between the evolution of belief in the individual and the evolution of belief in the race—Will the disappearance of faith leave a void behind ?

II. Will the dissolution of religion result in a dissolution of morality among the people ?—Is religion the sole safeguard of social authority and public morality?—Christianity and socialism—Relation between non-religion and immorality, according to statistics.

III. Is Protestantism a necessary transition stage between religion and free-thought?—Projects for Protestantizing France—Michelet, Quinet, De Laveleye, Renouvier, and Pillon—Intellectual, moral, and political superiority of Protestantism—Utopian character of the project—Uselessness, for purposes of morals, of substituting one religion for another—Is the possession of religion a condition *sine qua non* of superiority in the struggle for existence ?—Objections urged against France and the French Revolution by Matthew Arnold ; Greece and Judea compared, France and Protestant nations compared—Critical examination of Matthew Arnold's theory—Cannot free-thought, science, and art evolve their respective ideals from within ?

WE have seen the dissolution which menaces religious dogmatism, and even religious morality, in modern societies. And from the very fact of such dissolution certain more or less disturbing social problems arise. Is it really a perilous thing, this gradual enfeeblement of what has so long served as the basis of social and domestic virtue ? Certain people delight in subjecting nine-tenths of the human race to a sort of ostracism. They declare in advance that the people, and all women and children, are incapable of rising to a conception which it is recognized that a large number of men have attained. The mass of the people, it is said, and women and children, must be appealed to on the side of the imagination ; only, one must take care to choose the least dangerous form of appeal possible, for fear of injuring those whom one means to serve. Let us consider to what extent this incapacity of the people, of women and children, for philosophy is capable of demonstration. It is the more necessary in this book, in that it is the sociological aspect of religion that is here the subject of investigation.

### *I. Is religious sentiment an innate and imperishable possession of humanity ?*

In our days, be it remarked, religious sentiment has found defenders among those who, like Renan, Taine, and so many others, are most firmly convinced of the absurd-

Tendency to regard religious beliefs as necessary in proportion to their absurdity.

ities of the dogmas themselves. So long as such men occupy a purely intellectual point of view— that is to say, their real point of view—the whole of the contents of religion, all the dogmas, all the rites appear to them to be so many astounding errors, a vast system of unconscious, mutual deception ; but the instant, on the contrary, they regard religion from the point of view of sensibility—that is to say, from the point of view of the masses— everything becomes justifiable in their eyes ; everything that they would attack without scruple as a bit of reasoning becomes sacred to them as a bit of sentiment, and by a strange optical illusion the absurdity of religious beliefs becomes an additional proof of their necessity ; the greater the abyss which separates them from the intelligence of the masses, the greater their fear of having this abyss filled up. They do not for themselves feel the need of religious beliefs, but on this very account they regard them as indispensable for other people. They say, " How many irrational beliefs the people do have that we get along very well without ! " And they conclude, therefore, " These beliefs must be extremely necessary to the existence of social life and must correspond to a real need, in order thus firmly to have implanted themselves in the life of the masses."[1]

Frequently, along with this belief in the omnipotence of the religious sentiment, there goes a certain contempt for those

Free-thought for an intellectual aristocracy.

who are the victims of it; they are the serfs of thought, they must remain attached to the soil, bound within the limits of their own narrow horizon. The aristocracy of science is the most jealous of aristocracies, and a certain number of our contemporary men of science are bent on carrying their coat of mail in their brain. They profess toward the mass of the people a somewhat contemptuous charity, and propose to leave it undisturbed in its beliefs, immersed in prejudice as being the sole habitat in which it is capable of existing. For the rest, they sometimes envy the people its eternal ignorance, platonically of course. The bird no doubt possesses vague regrets, vague desires, when he perceives from on high a worm trailing tranquilly through the dew, oblivious of heaven; but the bird, as a matter of fact, is always careful to retain his wings, and our superior men of science do the same. In their judgment, certain superior minds are capable of enfranchising themselves from religion, without evil results following; the mass of the people cannot. It is necessary to reserve freedom

---

[1] Moreover when one has passed one's life, or even many years, in any study whatsoever, one is inclined extremely to exaggerate the importance of this study. Greek professors believe that Greek is necessary to the best interests o. humanity. When any question arises of drawing up a curriculum, if the professors of the several studies are interrogated, each wishes to see his own especial branch of science in the first rank. I remember that after I myself had been making Latin verses for some years I would have ranged myself voluntarily among the defenders of Latin verse. Whenever anyone makes an especial study of some work of genius, that of an individual, or *a fortiori* that of a people—Plato, Aristotle or Kant, the Vedas or the Bible, this work tends to become in his eyes the very centre of human thought; the book of which one makes a special study tends to become *the* book. A priest looks upon the whole of human life as an affair of faith simply; knowledge to a priest means simply a knowledge of the Fathers of the Church. It is not astonishing that even members of the laity, who have made religion the principal object of their studies, should be inclined to magnify its importance for humanity, or that the historian of religious thought should regard it as including the whole of human life, and as acquiring, even independently of any notion of revelation, a sort of inviolable character.

of conscience and free-thought for a certain select few; the intellectual aristocracy should defend itself by a fortified camp. Just as the ancient Roman people demanded bread and spectacles, so modern people demand temples, and to give them temples is sometimes the sole means of making them forget that they have not enough bread. The mass of humanity must, as a mere necessity of existence, adore a god, and not simply god in general, but a certain God whose commandments are to be found in a pocket Bible. A sacred book, *that* is what is necessary. We are reminded of Mr. Spencer's saying, that the superstition of the present day is the superstition of the printed page; we believe that some mystical virtue inheres in the four and twenty letters of the alphabet. When a child asks questions concerning the birth of his younger brother, he is told that one found him under a bush in the garden; and the child is content. The mass of the people is a big child simply, and must be dealt with after the same fashion. When the mass of the people asks questions about the origin of the world, hand it the Bible—it will there see that the world was made by a determinate Being, who carefully adjusted its parts to each other; it will learn the precise amount of time that was consumed in the work; seven days, neither more nor less; and it needs learn nothing further. Its mind is walled in by a good solid barrier which it is forbidden to overleap even by a look—the wall of faith. Its brain is carefully sealed, the sutures become firm with age, and there is nothing to do but to begin the same thing over again with the next generation.

Is it then true that religion is thus, for the mass of mankind, either a necessary good or a necessary evil, rooted in the human heart?

The belief that the religious sentiment is innate and perpetual rests upon a confusion of the religious sentiment with the *Confusion of religious sentiment with need for philosophy and morality.* need that exists in mankind for philosophy and morality; and, however closely bound up together philosophy and morality and religion may be, they are in themselves distinct and separate, and tend progressively to become more and more manifestly so.

In the first place, how universal soever the religious sentiment may appear to be, it must be admitted that it is not

**Religious senti-
ment not innate.**

innate.   Persons who have passed their childhood
without any communication with other human
beings, owing to some corporal defect, display no
signs of the possession of religious ideas.   Dr. Kitto, in his
book on the loss of the senses, cites the case of an American
woman who was congenitally deaf and dumb, and who later,
after she was capable of communicating with the people about
her, was found not to possess the slightest notion of a divinity.
The Rev. Samuel Smith, after twenty-three years intercourse
with deaf mutes, says that, education apart, they possess no
notion of a divinity.   Lubbock and Baker cite a great number
of examples of savages who are in the same case.   According
to the conclusions set forth above, in the beginning religions
did not spring ready-made out of the human heart: they
were imposed on man from without, they reached him through
his eyes and through his ears; they contained no element of
mysticism—in their first steps.   Those who derive mysticism
from an innate religious sentiment reason a little after the
manner of those who in politics should derive royalty from
some supposed innate respect for a royal race.   Such a respect
is the work of time, of custom, of the sympathetic tendencies
of a body of men long trained in some one direction ; there is
contained in it no single primitive element, and yet the power
of the sentiment of loyalty to a royal race is considerable.
The Revolution showed as much, in the wars of the Vendée.
But this power wears out some day or other, the cult for
royalty disappears with the disappearance of royalty itself ;
other habits are formed, creating other sentiments, and the
spectator is surprised to see that a people which was royalist
under monarchy becomes republican under republicanism.
The reign of sensibility over intelligence is not perpetual ;
sooner or later, the position of the two must be reversed ;
there is an intellectual habitat to which we must as inevitably
adapt ourselves as to our physical habitat.   The perpetuity
of the religious sentiment depends upon its legitimacy.   Born,
as it is, of certain beliefs and certain customs, its fate is one

with theirs. So long as a belief is not completely compromised and dissolved, the sentiment attaching to it may no doubt possess the power of preserving it, for sentiment always plays the rôle of protector and preserver. The human soul in this respect is analogous to society. Religious or political sentiments resemble iron braces buried in some wall menaced with ruin ; they bind together the disjointed stones, and may well sustain the edifice for some time longer than, but for them, it would have stood; but let the wall once be undermined, so that it begins to give way, and they will fall with it. No better method could be employed for securing the complete and absolute extinction of a dogma or an institution than to maintain it till the last possible instant ; its fall under such circumstances becomes a veritable annihilation. There are periods in history when to preserve is not to save but definitely to ruin.

The perpetuity of religion has therefore in nowise been demonstrated. From the fact that religions always have existed it cannot be concluded that they always will exist ; by ratiocination like that one might indeed achieve singular consequences. Humanity has always, in all times and places, associated certain events with others which chanced to accompany them ; *post hoc ergo propter hoc* is a universal sophism and the principle of all superstition. It is the basis of the belief that thirteen must not sit down at table, that one must be careful not to spill the salt, etc. Certain beliefs of this kind, such as that Friday is an unlucky day, are so widespread that they suffice sensibly to affect the average of travellers arriving in Paris on that day of the week by train and omnibus; a number of Parisians are averse to beginning a journey on Friday, or to attending to business that can be postponed ; and it must be remembered that the intelligence of Parisians, at least of the men, stands high in the scale. What can one conclude from that if not that superstition is tenacious of life in the bosom of humanity and will long be so ? Let us reason, then, in regard to superstition as in regard to mythological religion. Must we not admit that the need of superstition is innate in man, that it is part of his nature, that his life would really be

Post hoc ergo propter hoc.

incomplete if he ceased to believe that the breaking of a mirror is a sign that someone will die? Let us therefore set about finding some *modus vivendi* with superstition; let us combat superstitions which are harmful not by exposing their irrationality but by substituting in their stead superstitions which are contrary to them and inoffensive.   Let us declare that there are political superstitions and instruct women and children in them; let us inoculate, for example, feeble minds with that ingenious Mohammedan aphorism, that the duration of one's life is determined in advance and that the coward gains absolutely nothing by fleeing from the field of battle; if he was fated to die, he will die on his own doorstep.   Does not that strike one as a useful belief for an army to hold and more inoffensive than a great many religious beliefs?   Perhaps it even contains an element of truth.

One might go far along that path and discover a number of necessary or at least useful illusions, a number of "indestruct-
ible" beliefs.   "It is," says M. Renan, "more difficult to hinder mankind's believing than to induce it to believe."   Certainly it is.   In other words, it is more difficult to instruct than to deceive.   If it were not so, what merit would there be in the communication of knowledge?   Knowledge is always more complex than prejudice.   A knowledge sufficiently complete to put one on one's guard against lapses of judgment demands years of patience.   Happily, humanity has long centuries before it, long centuries and treasures of perseverance; for there is no creature more persevering than man and no man more obstinate than the savant.   But it may be said that religious myths, being better adapted than pure knowledge to popular intelligence, possess after all the advantage of symbolizing a portion of the truth; and that on this score one may permit them to the vulgar.   It is as if one should say that the "vulgar" should be permitted to believe that the sun moves round the earth because the common man is incapable of conceiving, with accuracy, the infinite complexity of the motion of the stars.   But every theory, every attempted explanation, however crude it may be, is in

*[margin note:]* That religious beliefs have been useful no reason for retaining them.

some degree a symbol of the truth. It is symbolic of the
truth to say that nature experiences a horror of a vacuum, that
the blood lies motionless in the arteries, that the line of vision
runs from the eye to the object, instead of from the object to
the eye. All these primitive theories are incomplete formula-
tions of the reality, more or less popular efforts to " render " it ;
they rest upon visible facts not yet correctly interpreted by a
completer scientific knowledge ; and does that constitute a
reason for respecting all these symbols, and for condemning
the popular intelligence to fatten upon them? Primitive and
mythical explanations served in the past to build up the truth ;
they ought not nowadays to be employed to obscure it. When
a scaffolding has served its purpose in aiding one to erect an
edifice, one tears it down. If certain tales are good to amuse
children with, one at least should be careful that they are not
taken too seriously. Let us not take outworn dogmas too
seriously, let us not regard them with excessive complacency
and tenderness; if they are still legitimately objects of admiration to us when we reset them among the circumstances to
which they owed their birth, they cease to be so the instant
one endeavours to perpetuate them among the circumstances
of modern life where they are quite out of place.

Like M. Renan, Mr. Max Müller almost sees an example to
be followed in the castes established by the Hindus among
Preliminary ac-
quisition of false-
hood not necessary
to recognition of
truth.
the minds, as among the classes of the people, in
the regular periods or asrâmas through which
they oblige the intelligence successively to pass,
in the hierarchy of religions with which they
burden the spirit of the faithful. For them traditional error
is sacred and venerable ; it serves as a preparation for the
truth ; one must place a bandage on the eyes of the neophyte
in order to be able to take it off again afterward. The tendencies of the modern mind are precisely the opposite ; it
likes to supply the present generation at once, and without
superfluous preliminary, with the whole body of truth
acquired by the generations which have passed away, without
false respect or false courtesy for the errors it replaces ; it is
not enough that the light should filter into the mind through

some secret rift, the doors and windows must be thrown wide open.  The modern mind fails to see in what respect a deliberate effort to inculcate absurdity in a portion of the community can serve to secure rectitude of judgment in the remaining portions ; or in what respect it is necessary to build a house of truth upon a foundation of falsehood ; or to run down the part of the hill that we have already climbed, as a preparation for climbing higher.

If the religious sentiment should disappear, it may be objected, it would leave a void which it would be impossible to fill, and humanity's horror of a vacuum is even greater than nature's.  Humanity, therefore, would satisfy somehow or other, even with absurdities, that eternal need of believing of which we have spoken above.  The instant one religion is destroyed another takes its place ; it will be always so from age to age, because the religious sentiment will always exist as a continuing need for some object of worship which it will create and re-create in spite of all the ratiocination in the world.   No victory over nature can be lasting ; no permanent need in the human breast can be long silenced.  There are periods in human life when faith is as imperious as love ; one experiences a hunger to embrace something, to give one's self—even to a figment of the imagination ; one is a victim to a fever of faith.   Sometimes this mood lasts throughout one's whole life, sometimes it lasts some days only or some hours ; there are cases in which it does not present itself till late, and even very late, in life.   And the priest has taken note of all these vicissitudes ; he is always there, patient, waiting tranquilly for the moment when the symptoms shall appear, and the sleeping sentiment shall awaken and become masterful ; he has the Host ready, he has great temples reverberating with sacred prayers, where man may come to kneel, and breathe in the spirit of God, and arise strengthened.   The reply is that it is a mistake to regard all humanity as typified in the person of the recently disabused believer.   It has often been made a subject of reproach to free-thinkers that they endeavour to destroy without replacing, but one cannot destroy a religion in the breasts of a people.   At some certain moment in its his-

*Transformation of faith inevitable.*

tory it falls of its own weight, with the disappearance of the pretended evidences on which it was resting; it does not, properly speaking, die ; it ceases simply—becomes extinct. It will cease definitely when it shall have become useless, and there is no obligation to replace what is no longer necessary. Among the masses, intelligence is never far in advance of tradition ; one never adopts a new idea until one has by degrees become accustomed to it. It all takes place without violence, or at least without lasting violence ; the crisis passes, the wound closes quickly, and leaves no trace behind ; the forehead of the masses bears no scar. Progress lies in wait for the moment of least resistance, of least pain. Even revolutions do not succeed except in so far as they are purely beneficial, as they constitute a universally advantageous evolution. For the rest, there is no such thing as a revolution, or a cataclysm, properly so called, in human belief. Each generation adds a doubt to those which existed before in the minds of their parents, and thus faith falls away bit by bit, like the banks of a river worn by the stream ; the sentiments which were bound up with the belief go with it, but they are incessantly replaced by others, a new wave sweeps forward to fill the void, and the human soul profits by its losses and grows larger, like the bed of a river. The adaptation of a people to its environment is a beneficent law. It has often been said, and justly, that there is food for the soul as well as food for the body; and the analogy may be pursued by remarking that it is difficult to induce a people to change its national diet. For centuries the inhabitants of Brittany have lived upon imperfectly cooked buckwheat cakes, as they live by their simple faith and infantine superstitions. It may, however, be affirmed, *a priori*, that the day will come when the reign of the buckwheat cake in Brittany will be at an end, or at least will be shared by other, and better prepared, and more nourishing foods; it is equally rational to affirm that the faith of Brittany will some day come to an end, that the somewhat feeble minds of the inhabitants will sooner or later seek nourishment in solider ideas and beliefs, and that the whole of their intellectual life will, by degrees, be transformed and renewed.

It is only those who have been reared in a faith, and then disabused of it, that preserve, along with their primitive sentiments, a certain home-sickness for a belief to cor-

The disenchant-
ment that accom-
panies it
temporary.

respond to these sentiments.   The reason is that they have been violently hastened in their passage from belief to incredulity.   The story of the passing disenchantment with life, which the recent disbeliever experiences, has often been told.   " I felt horribly exiled,"
M. Renan once said, in speaking of the moral crisis through which he himself had passed.   " The fish in Lake Baikal have taken thousands of years, it is said, to transform themselves from salt-water to fresh-water fish.   I had to achieve my own transformation in the course of some weeks.   Catholicism surrounds the whole of life like an enchanted circle with so much magic that, when one is deprived of it, everything seems insipid and melancholy ;  the universe looked to me like a desert.
If Christianity was not true, everything else seemed to me to be indifferent, frivolous, scarce worthy of attention ;  the world looked mediocre, morally impoverished to me.   The world seemed to me to be in its dotage and decadence ;  I felt lost in a nation of pigmies."   This pain incident to metamorphosis, this sort of despair at renouncing everything that one has believed and loved up to that time, is not peculiar to the Christian who has fallen away from Christianity ;  it exists in diverse degrees, as M. Renan well knew, whenever a love of any sort comes to an end in us.   For him who, for example, has placed his whole life in the love of a woman and feels himself betrayed by her, life seems not less disenchanted than for the believer who sees himself abandoned by his God.   Even simple intellectual errors may produce an analogous sentiment.   Archi-
medes no doubt would have felt his life crumble away beneath him, if he had discovered irremediable lacunæ in his chain of theorems.   The more intimately a god has been personified and humanized, the more intimately he comes to be beloved, and the greater must be the wound he leaves behind when he deserts the heart.   But even though this wound be in certain instances incurable, that fact constitutes no argument in support of the religion of the masses, for an illegitimate and

unjustifiable love may cause as much suffering when one is deprived of it as a legitimate love. The bitterness of truth lies less in truth itself than in the resistance offered to it by intrenched and established error. It is not the world which is desert when deprived of the god of our dreams, it is our own heart; and we have ourselves to blame if we have filled our hearts with nothing better than dreams. For the rest, in the majority of cases, the void, the sense of loss which a religion leaves behind, is not lasting; one adapts one's self to one's new moral environment, one becomes happy again; no doubt not in the same manner—one is never happy twice in the same manner—but in a manner less primitive, less infantine, more stable. M. Renan is an example of it. His transmutation into a fresh-water fish was achieved in reality tranquilly enough; it is doubtful whether he ever dreams now of the salt-water stretches of the Bible, and nobody has ever declared so forcibly that he is happy. One might almost make it a matter of reproach to him, and suggest that the profoundest happiness is sometimes not so precisely aware of itself. If every absolute faith is a little naïve, one is not absolutely without naïveté when one is too confident of one's own happiness.

To the surprise and to the disenchantment which a former Christian experiences in the presence of scientific truth may

The essential cheapness of religious speculation.

be opposed the even more profound astonishment which those who have been exclusively nourished on science experience in the presence of religious dogma. The man of science can understand religious dogmas, for he can follow the course of their birth and development century by century; but he experiences, in his effort to adapt himself to this narrow environment, something of the difficulty that he might feel in an effort to enter a Liliputian fairy palace. The world of religion—with the ridiculous importance which it ascribes to the earth as the centre of the universe, with the palpable moral errors that the Bible contains, with its whole body of legend, which is affecting only to those who believe in them, with its superannuated rites—all seems so poor, so powerless to symbolize the infinite, that the man of science is inclined to see in these infantine dreams the repugnant and despicable side rather than the elevated and attractive side.   Livingstone says that one day, after having preached the Gospel to a new tribe, he was taking a walk in the neighbouring fields when he heard near him, behind a bush, a strange noise like a convulsive cough ; he there found a young negro who had been taken by an irresistible desire to laugh by the account of the Biblical legends, and had hidden himself there out of respect for Livingstone, and in the shadow of the bush was writhing with laughter and unable to reply to the questions of the worthy pastor.   Certainly the surprising legends of religion can give rise to no such outburst of gaiety as this in one who has spent his life among the facts of science and the reasoned theories of philosophy.   He feels rather a certain bitterness, such as one feels generally in the presence of human feebleness, for man feels something of the same solidarity in the presence of human error as in the presence of human suffering.   If the eighteenth century ridiculed superstition, if the human mind was then " dancing," as Voltaire said, " in chains," it is the distinction of our epoch more accurately to have estimated the weight of those chains; and in truth, when one examines coolly the poverty of the popular attempts that have been made to represent the world and the ideal of mankind, one feels less inclination to laugh than to weep.

But, however that may be, the evolution of human belief must not be judged by the painful revolutions of individual belief ; in humanity such transformations are subject to regular laws.   The very explosions of the religious sentiment, explosions even of fanaticism, which still occur and have so often occurred in the course of religious degeneration, enter as an integral part into the formula of the very process of degeneration itself.   After having been so long one of the most ardent interests of humanity, religious faith must, of necessity, be slow in cooling. Every human interest resembles those stars which are gradually declining at once in light and heat, and which from time to time present a solid exterior and then, as the result of some inner disturbance, burst through their outer

*Inevitable extinction of fanaticism.*

rind and become once more brilliant to a degree that they had not rivalled for hundreds of centuries; but this very brilliancy is itself an expenditure of light and heat, a phase simply of the process of cooling. The star hardens once more on its surface, and, after every fresh cataclysm and illumination, it becomes less brilliant and dies in its efforts to revive. A spectator who should be watching it from a sufficient height might even find a certain comfort in the triumphs of the very spirit of fanaticism and reaction which result in a prolonged subsequent enfeeblement and a more rapid approach toward final extinction. Just as haste is sometimes more deliberate than deliberation, so a violent effort to reanimate the past sometimes results in hastening its death. You cannot heat a cold star from the outside.

### II. Will the dissolution of religion result in a dissolution of morality among the people?

The general enfeeblement of the religious instinct will set free, for employment in social progress, an immense amount of force hitherto set aside for the service of mysticism; but it may well be asked also whether there are not a number of forces hurtful to society, and hitherto held in check or annulled by the religious instinct, which upon its disappearance will be given free play.

"Christianity," Guizot said, "is a necessity for mankind; it is a school of reverence." No doubt; but less so perhaps than Hindu religions, which go the length of proposing the absolute division of mankind into castes as an object for reverence; however contrary it may be to the natural sentiments of mankind and the operation of social laws. Assuredly no society can subsist if its members neither respect nor reverence what is respectable and venerable; respect is decidedly an indispensable element in national life; the fact is one which we too easily forget in France; but society is barred from progress if one respects what is not respectable, and progress is a condition of life for a society. Tell me what you respect, and I will

*One must respect what is respectable only.*

tell you what you are. The progress of human reverence for objects ever higher and more high is symbolic of all other kinds of progress achieved by the human mind.

But for religion, say the Guizot school, the property-question would sweep away the masses of the people ; it is the Church which holds them in check. If there is a property-question, let us not seek to ignore it; let us labour sincerely and actively at its solution. *Qui trompe-t-on ici?* Is God simply a means of saving the capitalist ? More than that, the property-question is not one which is more intimately bound up to-day with religion than with free-thought. Christianity, which implicitly contains within it the principles of communism, is itself responsible for spreading ideas among the people which have inevitably germinated in the course of the great intellectual germination which distinguishes the present epoch. M. de Laveleye, one of the defenders of liberal Christianity, confesses as much. It was well known that among the first Christians all property was held in common, and that communism was the immediate consequence of baptism.[1] "We hold everything in common except our women," Tertullian and St. Justin say ; "we share everything."[2] It is well known with what vehemence the Fathers of the Church have attacked the right of private property. "The earth," says St. Ambrose, "was given to the rich and poor in common. Why, oh, ye rich! should ye arrogate to yourselves alone the ownership of it ?" "Nature created rights in common, usurpation has created private rights." "Wealth is always the product of robbery," says St. Jerome. "The rich man is a robber," says St. Basil. "Iniquity is the basis of private property," says St. Clement. "The rich man is a brigand," says St. Chrysostom. Bossuet himself cries, in a sermon on the distribution of the necessities of life : "The murmurs of the poor are just: why this inequality of condition ?" And, in the sermon on the eminent dignity of the poor : "The politics of Jesus are directly opposed to those of this century." And finally Pascal, sum-

*Christianity quite the opposite of a defence against communism.*

---

[1] *Acts* ii. 44, 45 ; iv. 32, sqq.
[2] Tertull. *Apolog.* c. 39, Justin., *Apolog.* I, 14.

ming up in an illustration all the socialistic ideas which compose the bulk of Christian doctrine: "'That dog is mine,'
say these poor children; 'that place there is my place in the
sun.' Behold the beginning and the type of the usurpation
of the earth." When "these poor children" are men, they do
not always view the usurpation of the earth with resignation;
from the Middle Ages down they have, from time to time,
risen in revolt and there have been resulting massacres. Men
like Pastoureaux and Jacques in France and Watt Tyler in
England, the anabaptists and John of Leyden in Germany,
are examples of what we mean. But, these great explosions
of popular clamour once at an end, the Christian priest had
always at his disposal, to subdue the crowd, a robust doctrine
of compensation in heaven for one's sufferings on earth; all
the beatitudes are summed up in "Blessed are the poor, for
they shall see God." In our days, owing to the progress of
the natural sciences, anything like certitude on the subject of
compensation in heaven has disappeared; even the Christian,
less sure of Paradise, aspires to see the justice and compensa-
tions of heaven realized in this world. The most durable
element in Christianity is, therefore, less the check that it
imposes upon the masses than the contempt for the established
order with which it inspires them. Religion is nowadays
obliged to call in social science to aid it in its struggle against
socialism. The true principle of private property as of social
authority cannot be religious; it lies essentially in the sentiment of the rights of other people and in an increasingly
scientific acquaintance with the conditions of social and
political life.

But is not religion a safeguard of popular morality? It is
true that immorality and crime are habitually conceived as
associated with non-religion, and as products of it.
Religion not necessary to morality. Criminologists, however, have demonstrated that
no proposition could be less tenable. If one
considers the mass of the delinquents in any country, one will
find that irreligion among them is an exception, and a rare
exception. In unusually religious countries like England
delinquents are not less numerous, and the average of belief

among them is higher ; the greater number, Mayhew says, profess to believe in the Bible.   In France, where non-religion is
so common, it is natural that it should also be common among
the criminal classes, but it is far from being the rule ; it is
most frequent among the leaders, the organizers of crime,
those, in effect, who rise above the mass of their fellows, like
Mandrin in the last century, La Pommerais, Lacenaire.   If
sociologists find themselves obliged to attribute a positive
antisocial bias to certain criminals, it is not surprising that
they should recognize in a number of them an amount of
instruction and a degree of talent amply sufficient to disembarrass them of the superstitious beliefs of the multitude,
which are shared by their companions in crime.   Neither their
talents nor their culture have  sufficed absolutely to check
their evil disposition, but certainly they have not been responsible for it.   Criminologists cite a number of facts which go
to prove that the most minute and sincere practice of religion
may go along with the greatest crimes.   Despine relates that
Bourse had  scarcely finished a robbery and  a  homicide,
before he went to kneel and take part in a church service.   G.,
a courtesan, as she set fire to her lover's house, cried : "God
and the ever blessed Virgin do the rest ! "   The wife of Parency,
while her husband was killing an old man as a preliminary to
robbery, was praying God for her husband's success.   It is well
known how religious the Marquise of Brinvilliers was ; her
very condemnation was facilitated by the fact of her having
written with her own hands a secret confession of her sins
in which she made mention, along with  parricides, fratricides,
arsons, and poisonings without number, of the list of the number of times that she had been  remiss or negligent in confession.[1]   Religion is no more responsible for all these crimes

---

[1] It must not be believed that even prostitutes, who as a class are so closely
allied to criminals, are wholly non-religious.   A case is cited of a number of
prostitutes who subscribed the money to have one of their companions, who was on
the point of death, removed from a house of ill-fame to some place where the
priest might visit her ; others subscribed money for a great number of masses
to be said for the soul of a companion who was dead.   At all events prostitutes are
quite superstitious, and their religion swarms with strange and ridiculous beliefs.

In Italy criminals are usually religious.   Quite recently the Tozzi family of

than non-religion is; the higher elements of both are equally debarred of entrance into the brain of a criminal. Although the moral sense and religious sentiment are in origin distinct, they act and react incessantly upon each other. It may be announced, as a law, that no one whose moral sense is obliterated can be capable of experiencing genuine religious sentiment in all its purity, though such a person may well be more than usually apt to attach a value to the superstitious forms of a cult. The religious sentiment, at its height, always rests upon a refined moral sense, although, when religious sentiment goes further and becomes fanaticism, it may react on and debase the moral sense. On a person who is deficient in moral sense, religion produces no effects but such as are evil—fanaticism, formalism, and hypocrisy—because it is of necessity ill-comprehended and misconstrued.

Catholic countries often supply an unusually high percentage of criminals, because Catholic countries are more ignorant than Protestant countries. In Italy, for example, as many as sixteen out of every hundred deaths in the Papal States and Southern Italy, have at times been deaths by violence, whereas

butchers, after having killed and dismembered a young man, sold his blood, mixed with sheep's blood, in their shop, and went none the less to perform their devotions to the Madonna, and to kiss the statue of the Virgin. The Caruso band, Lombroso says, habitually placed sacred images in the caves and woods in which they lived, and burned candles before them. Verzeni, who strangled three women, was an assiduous frequenter of the church and the confessional, and he came of a family which was not only religious but bigoted. The companions of La Gala, who were imprisoned at Pisa, obstinately refused to take food on Friday during Lent, and when the keeper tried to persuade them to do so, they replied, "Do you think we have been excommunicated?" Masini, with his band, met three countrymen and among them a priest; he slowly sawed open the throat of one of them with an ill-sharpened knife, and then, with his hands still bloody, obliged the priest to give him the consecrated Host. Giovani Mio and Fontana went to confession before going out to commit a murder. A young Neapolitan parricide, covered with amulets, confessed to Lombroso that he had invoked the aid of the Madonna de la Chaîne in the accomplishment of his horrible crime. "And that she really helped me I conclude from this, that at the first blow of the stick my father fell dead, although I am myself personally weak." Another murderer, a woman, before killing her husband, fell on her knees and prayed to the blessed Virgin to give her the strength to accomplish her crime. Still another announced his acceptance of a line of action devised by his companion in these words, "I will come, and I will do that with which God has inspired thee."

in Liguria and Piedmont only two or three out of every hundred are deaths by violence. The population of Paris is not, on the whole, more immoral than that of any other great European city, although it is distinctly less religious; what a difference, for example, between London and Paris! The churches, temples, and synagogues in Paris would not hold one-tenth of the population, and, as they are half empty in time of services, a statistician may with some show of reason conclude that only about a twentieth of the population fulfil their religious duties. Whereas Paris contains only 169 places of worship, London, in 1882, possessed 1231—without counting the religious assemblies which regularly gather in the parks, the public squares, and even under the railway viaducts.

*Ignorance, not Catholicism, responsible for immorality.*

But should not the crimes of the Commune and those of the French Revolution be set down to non-religion? One might, with more show of truth, render religion responsible for the massacres of St. Bartholomew and of the Dragonnades, for, in the wars of the Huguenots, of the Vaudois, of the Albigenses, the issue was a religious issue, whereas in the case of the Commune the issue was wholly a social one; religion was only very indirectly involved in it. The analogy for the Commune is to be found in the wars concerning the agrarian laws of ancient Rome, or in contemporary strikes which are so often accompanied by bloodshed, or in any of the brutal uprisings of the labourer or the peasant against the capitalist or the owner of the soil. Be it remarked, moreover, that in all these and the like contests the stronger party—the representative of society and, it is alleged, of religion—commits, in the name of repression, violences comparable to and sometimes less excusable than those with which they charge the party of disorder.

*Non-religion not responsible for French Revolution and the Commune.*

What demoralizes races and peoples is not so much the downfall of religion as the luxury and idleness of the few and the discontented poverty of the many. In society demoralization begins at the two extremes, top and bottom. The law of labour is open to two species of revolt; the revolt of the discontented working man who curses the law of labour even while he obeys it, and the revolt of the idle noble, or man of fortune, who ignores it simply. The richest classes in society are often those whose lives show a minimum of devotion, of disinterestedness, of true moral elevation. For a fashionable woman, for example, the duties of life too frequently consist in an unbroken round of trifles ; she is utterly ignorant of what it means to take pains. To bear a child or two (to exceed the number of three, one of them has said, is the height of immorality), to have a nurse to take care of them, to be faithful to one's husband, at least within the limits of coquetry—behold the whole duty of woman! Too frequently, in the upper classes, duty comes to be conceived simply as a matter of abstinence, of not being as nasty or as wicked as one might. Temptations to do evil increase in number as one mounts in the social scale, whereas what one may call temptations to do good decrease in number. Fortune enables one to hire a substitute, so to speak, in all the duties of life—in caring for the sick, in nursing children, in rearing them, and so forth ; the rich are not obliged to pay, as the saying is, with their person—*payer de la personne !* Wealth too often produces a species of personal avarice, of miserliness of one's self, a restriction of moral and physical activity, an impoverishment of the individual and of the race. The shopkeeping class constitute the least immoral section of the rich, and that because they preserve their habits of work ; but they are constantly affected by the example of the higher classes, who take a pride in being useless. The remnant of morality, which exists among the middle class, is partly due to the love of money ; money does, in effect, possess one advantage, that it must in general be worked for. Nobles and business men love money but in different ways. Young men of good family love it as a means of expense and of prodigality, people in a small way of business love it for its own sake, and out of avarice. Avarice is a powerful safeguard for the remnants of morality in a people. It coincides, in almost all its results, with a disinterested love of labour ; it exercises no evil influence except in the matter of marriage, where the question of the girl's portion becomes paramount, and in the

*Labour for labour's sake.*

matter of children, of which it tends to restrict the number. All things considered, as between prodigality and avarice, the moralist is obliged to cast his vote for the latter on the ground that it is not favourable to debauchery, and does not therefore tend to dissolve society; both are maladies which benumb and may destroy one, but the former is contagious and is transmitted by contact. We may add that love of expense rarely serves to encourage regular labour: it produces, rather, an appetite for gambling and even for robbery; clever strokes on the stock-exchange amount, in certain cases, to robbery pure and simple. Thence arises a secondary demoralizing influence. Prodigals are necessarily attracted to the more or less shaky forms of financial speculation, by which, absolutely without labour properly so called, more money can be amassed than by labour; the miser, on the contrary, will hesitate, will prefer effort to risk, and his effort will be more beneficial to society. In effect, the only thing that can maintain society in a healthy state is that love of labour for its own sake which is so rarely met with, and which one must endeavour to develop; but this love of intellectual and physical labour is in nowise bound up with religion; it is bound up with a certain broad culture of the mind and heart which render idleness insupportable.

Similarly with the other moral and social virtues which are alleged to be inseparable from religion. In all times humanity has found a certain average of vice, as of virtue, necessary. Religions themselves have always been obliged to give way before certain prevalent habits and passions. If we had been living at the time of the Reformation, we should have heard Catholic priests maintaining, with all the seriousness in the world, that, but for Catholic dogmas and the authority of the Pope, society would dissolve and perish. Happily experience has proved that these dogmas and that authority are not indispensable to social life; the conscience of mankind has attained its majority and no longer needs the services of a guardian. The day will come, no doubt, when Frenchmen will no more feel an inclination to enter into a house of stone and invoke God to the sound of

*Religion the creature of circumstance.*

a hymn than an Englishman or a German experiences to-day an inclination to kneel before a priest and confess to him.

### III. *Is Protestantism a necessary transition stage between religion and free-thought?*

Over and above free-thinkers, properly so called, there exists in every country a class of men who understand perfectly the defects in the religions in force about them, but have not the power of mind necessary to lift them above revealed dogma generally, and every form of external cult and rite. They begin accordingly to dabble in the religions of neighbouring peoples. A religion which is not in force in one's immediate neighbourhood always possesses the advantage of being seen from a distance. At a distance its faults are scarcely distinguishable, and the imagination freely endows it with all excellent qualities. How many things and persons gain thus by aloofness! When one has seen one's ideal, it is sometimes good not to approach it too near if one is to preserve one's reverence for it. A number of Englishmen, indignant at the aridity of the hard and blind fanaticism of the extreme Protestants, cast envious glances across the Channel, where a religion seems to reign that is more friendly to art,—at once more æsthetic and more mystical, capable of affording a completer satisfaction to certain human needs. Among those who are thus favourable to a properly understood Catholicism may be cited Matthew Arnold and Cardinal Newman; and one might even add the Queen of England herself. In France, as might be expected, quite the opposite disposition obtains. Wearied of the Catholic Church and of its intolerance, we should gladly escape its dominion: compared with the objections against Catholicism which assail our eyes, the objections against Protestantism appear to us as trifling. And the same notion has occurred simultaneously to a number of distinguished Frenchmen: why should France remain Catholic, at least in name? Why should not France adopt the religion of the more robust people who have recently vanquished her; the

*Dependence of Catholicism on power.*

religion of Germany, of England, of the United States, of all the young, strong, and active nations? Why not begin again the labour interrupted by the massacre of St. Bartholomew and the Edict of Nantes? Even if one should not succeed in converting the masses, it would suffice, according to the partisans of Protestantism, to propagate the new religion among the élite of the population very sensibly to modify the general course of our government, of our national spirit, even of our laws. The laws regulating the relations of Church and State would promptly be corrected; they would be reconstructed so as to offer protection to the development of the Protestant religion, as they at this moment do in a thousand ways to the outworn religion of Catholicism. Ultimately Protestantism would be declared to be the national religion of France; the religion, in other words, toward which she ought to endeavour to move, and which constitutes her real ideal, her sole hope of the future, the sole means open to Latin nations to escape death, and to outlive, in some sense, themselves. Add that, in the judgment of the authors of this hypothesis, the Protestant religion, once fairly entered in the lists against Catholicism, must inevitably and speedily win the day; the iron pot would make short work of the earthen pot. The partisans of Protestantism invoke history in support of their conclusions; Protestantism was vanquished among us by force, and not by persuasion; its defeat is therefore not definitive. Wherever Catholicism has not employed violence, persecution, and crime to maintain itself, it has always succumbed; its only tenable argument has been to put its opponents to death; to-day this comfortable method of backing the syllogism by the sword is out of date, and Catholicism is condemned the instant it is attacked. It contains, moreover, an essential and irremediable vice, auricular confession. By the confessional it excites the open or secret hostility of every husband and every father, who sees the priest interposing between him and his wife, between him and his children. The confessor is a supernumerary in every family; a member who has neither the same interests nor the same ideas, and who, nevertheless, is perfectly informed of everything the other members do, and can, in a thousand ways, oppose their projects, and, at the moment when they least expect it, bar their path. When one takes into consideration the mute state of war which so often exists between the married man and the Catholic priest; when one analyzes the other causes of dissolution which are working in Catholicism; when one considers, for example, that the dogma of infallibility is simply inacceptable to anyone whose conscience is not absolutely distorted, one must admit that the project of Protestantizing France, how strange soever it may seem at first glance, is worthy of serious attention.

It is not astonishing that it should have won to its side a number of partisans, and should have provoked a certain intellectual fermentation. Michelet and Quinet were desirous that France should become Protestant, at least transitorily! In 1843, during a journey to Geneva, Michelet discussed with some clergymen the means of accelerating the progress of Protestantism in France and of creating a really national church. Two men, whose names are known to all those who have laboured in philosophy or in social science, MM. Renouvier and De Laveleye, are among the promoters of this movement. Convinced free-thinkers, like M. Louis Ménard, acquiesce in it, making use of the names of Turgot and Quinet; and M. Pillon also has sustained the project. Many Protestant ministers have turned the whole of their activity in this channel, have founded journals and written for the reviews; pamphlets, works often remarkable in their kind, have been composed and circulated. Protestants are more disposed than Catholics to propagandism, because their faith is more personal. They feel that in a number of provinces they form an important nucleus which may grow in time like a snowball. A number of villages, of Yonne, la Marne, l'Aude, etc., have already been converted; in spite of all the obstacles raised by the civil and religious authorities, in spite of vexations and annoyances of every sort, the neophytes have finally succeeded in establishing a Protestant pastor among them. Materially considered, these results are small; their consequences, however, may some day be of great importance. One never suspects how many people there are ready to listen

**Proposal to Protestantize France.**

and to believe; how many people there are ready to preach and to convert. It need not be a matter of surprise, some day or other, to see Protestant clergymen fairly rise out of the soil and overrun our country districts. The Catholic clergy, who present an almost unbroken front of incapacity, will scarcely be able to hold their own against a new and ardent adversary.

The most serious opposition to Protestantism in France is not to be looked for from the Catholics, but from the free-thinkers. It is in the name of free-thought that we shall consider the following question: Ought France really to accept as its ideal any religion whatsoever, even though it be superior to the one professedly in possession at the present day? Is not the acceptance of any religion as an ideal precisely contrary to the whole movement of the French mind since the Revolution?

*Contrary to the tendency of French history.*

It has been said that, if the French Revolution was put down before it had produced all of the results which were expected of it, the reason was that it was undertaken, not in the name of a liberal religion, but in antagonism to all religion. The nation rose as a body against Catholicism, but it had nothing to offer in its stead; it was an effort in the void and resulted necessarily in a fall. To address such a reproach to the Revolution, is precisely to fail to recognize its distinguishing peculiarity. Theretofore religion had usually been involved in the political discussions of men; the English Revolution, for example, was in part religious. And when an uprising was, as it happened, wholly religious, its purpose was to pull down one cult and set up another; the aid of a new God had to be called in to expel the old; but for Jesus or some other unknown divinity, Jupiter would still have been enthroned on Olympus. Also the result of these religious revolutions was easy to predict; at the end of a certain number of years some new cult was bound to carry the day, to intrench itself, and to become quite as intolerant as its predecessor; and the revolution was achieved—that is to say, everything was practically in the same state that it was before. A determinate end, close at hand, had been pursued and attained; a little chapter in the history of the universe had

*French Revolution still being accomplished.*

been written, and one was ready to close it with a period and to say that was all. What drives the historian to despair in the case of the French Revolution, is precisely the impossibility of writing a peroration, of reaching a final stop, of saying, "That is all." The great fermentation persists, and passes on from generation to generation. "The French Revolution has come to nothing," it is said; but the reason is perhaps simply that it has not miscarried. The French Revolution is still in its earliest stages; if we are still unable to say where it is leading us, we may at least affirm with confidence that it is leading us somewhere. It is precisely the incertitude and the remoteness of their aim that constitute the nobility of certain enterprises; if one wants something very big, one must be resigned to want something a little vague. One must be resigned also to a settled discontent with everything that is offered one as a substitute for the fleeing ideal that constitutes one's aim. Never to be satisfied—behold a comparatively unknown state of mind in many parts of the world! Some thousands of years ago there were a number of revolutions in China, which brought forth results so precise and so incontestable that they have come down in a state of absolute preservation to the present day. Is China the ideal of those who wish a people to achieve once for all a state of satisfaction, of stable equilibrium, of established environment, of unalterable outline and form? Certainly the bent of the French mind is precisely the opposite of that of the Chinese. Horror of routine, of tradition, of the established fact in the face of reason, is an attribute that we possess to a fault. To carry reason into politics, into law, into religion was precisely the aim of the French Revolution. It is no easy thing, it is even futile, to attempt to introduce simultaneously logic and light into everything; one makes mistakes, one reasons ill, one has one's days of weakness, one succumbs to concordats and empires. In spite, however, of so many temporary divergences from the straight path, it is already easy to recognize the direction toward which the Revolution tends, and to affirm that this direction is not religious. The French Revolution affords an example, for the first time in the world, of a liberal movement disassociated from religion. To wish, with Quinet, that the Revolution should become Protestant is simply not to understand it. Republican in the sphere of politics, the Revolution tends to enfranchise man, in the sphere of thought also, from every species of religious domination, and of uniform and irrational dogmatic belief. The Revolution did not achieve this end at the first attempt; it was guilty even of imitating the intolerance of the Catholics; therein lay its prime fault, its great crime; we suffer from it still. But the remedy does not consist in adopting a new religion, which would simply be a disguised return to the past.

Let us examine, however, the substantial apology for Protestantism, presented by M. de Laveleye. He maintains the superiority of Protestantism principally in regard

Advantages of Protestantism.

to three points: 1. It is favourable to education; 2. It is favourable to political and religious liberty; 3. It does not possess a celibate clergy living outside of the family, and even outside of the country. Let us pass these different points in review. In Protestantism the need of instruction, and therefore of a knowledge of how to read, is inevitable, for the reason that, as has been often remarked, the reformed religion is founded on the interpretation of a book, the Bible. The Catholic religion, on the contrary, rests upon the sacraments and certain practices, such as the confession, and the Mass, which presuppose no knowledge of reading. Luther's first and last word was, "God commands you to educate your children." In the eyes of the Catholic priest an ability to read is not, so far as religion is concerned, an unqualified advantage, it exposes the possessor to certain dangers, it is a path that may lead to heresy. The organization of popular instruction dates from the Reformation. The consequence is that Protestant countries are far in advance of Catholic countries in the matter of popular instruction.[1] Wherever popular instruction attains its height,

[1] In Saxony, Denmark, Sweden, Prussia, Scotland (not England), illiteracy is at a minimum. Even in the most favoured Catholic countries, such as France and Belgium, at least a third of the population are illiterate. In this comparison race goes for nothing ; Switzerland proves as much ; purely Latin but also Protestant cantons Neuchâtel, Vaux, and Geneva are on a level with the Germanic cantons of Zürich and Bern, and are superior to such as Tessin, Valais, and Lucerne.

labour will be directed with more intelligence, and the economic situation will be better ; Protestantism therefore gives rise to a superiority not only in instruction, but in commerce and industry, in order and in cleanliness.[1]

Similarly in civil and political matters, Protestants have always been partisans of self-government, of liberty, of local autonomy, and of decentralization. Side by side with the advance of the Reformation in Switzerland, in Holland, in England and America there went a dissemination of the principles of liberty which later became the articles of faith of the French Revolution. Calvinists, notably, have always been inclined to an ideal of liberty and equality which has rightfully rendered them objects of suspicion to the French monarchy ; they realized

*Protestantism favours self-government.*

---

[1] In Switzerland the cantons of Neuchâtel, Vaux, and Geneva are strikingly in advance of Lucerne, Valais, and the forest cantons ; they are not only superior in matters of education, but in matters of industry, of commerce, and of wealth ; and their artistic and literary activity is greater. "In the United States," says De Tocqueville, "the majority of the Catholics are poor." In Canada the larger order of business interests, manufacturing, commerce, the principal shops in the cities, are in the hands of Protestants. M. Audiganne, in his studies on the labouring population in France, remarks on the superiority of the Protestants in respect to industry, and his testimony is the less suspicious because he does not attribute that superiority to Protestantism. "The majority of the labourers in Nîmes, notably the silk-weavers, are Catholics, while the captains of industry and of commerce, the capitalists in a word, belong to the Reformed religion." "When a family has split into two branches, one of which has clung to the faith of its fathers, while the other has become Protestant, one almost always remarks in the former a progressive financial embarassment, and in the other an increasing wealth." "At Mazamet, the Elbœuf of the south of France, all the captains of industry with one exception are Protestants, while the great majority of the labourers are Catholics. And Catholic working men are, as a class, much less well educated than Protestant working men." Before the revocation of the Edict of Nantes members of the Reformed church had taken the lead in all branches of labour, and the Catholics, who found themselves unable to maintain a competition with them, had the practice of a number of different industries in which the latter excelled forbidden them by a series of edicts beginning with the year 1662. After their expulsion from France the Huguenots carried into England, into Prussia, into Holland, their spirit of enterprise and of economy ; and enriched the districts in which they settled. The Germans owe some portion of their progress to Huguenot exiles. Refugees from the Revocation introduced different industries into England, among others the silk industry ; and it was certain disciples of Calvin who civilized Scotland. (See M. de Laveleye *De l'avenir des peuples catholiques*.)

this ideal only beyond the seas in the American Constitution, which may be regarded, in some sort, as the product of Calvinistic ideas. As early as the year 1633 an American, Roger Williams, proclaimed universal liberty, and liberty of conscience in particular: he proclaimed the complete equality of all modes of religious worship before the law, and on these principles founded the democracy of Rhode Island and the town of Providence. The United States, with the local autonomy and decentralization which characterize its government, still forms the type of the Protestant state. In such a state the widest liberty exists only, to say the truth, within the limit of Christianity: the founders of the American Constitution scarcely foresaw the day when a wider tolerance would be necessary. And it would be to form an extremely false idea of the United States to imagine that the civil power and religion are wholly disassociated. The separation between Church and state is far from being as absolute in America as is often supposed, and M. Goblet d'Alviella very justly corrects the too enthusiastic assertions, on this point, of M. Guizot and M. de Laveleye.[1]

[1] " Public institutions are still deeply impregnated with Christianity. Congress, the State legislatures, the navy, the army, the prisons, are all supplied with chaplains ; the Bible is still read in a large number of schools. The invocation of God is generally obligatory in an oath in a court of law, and even in an oath of office. In Pennsylvania the Constitution requires that every public employee shall believe in God, and in a future state of reward and punishments. The Constitution of Maryland awards liberty of conscience to deists only. The laws against blasphemy have never been formally abrogated. In certain States, more or less stringent Sunday laws are enforced. In 1880 a court declined to recognize, even as a moral obligation, a debt contracted on Sunday, and a traveller, injured in a railway accident, was refused damages on the ground that he was travelling on the Lord's Day. And, finally, church property and funds are in a considerable degree exempt from taxation." (M. Goblet d'Alviella, *Évolution religieuse*, p. 233.)

Similarly, in Switzerland, in the month of February, 1886, the criminal court of Glaris, the chief place in a canton of 7000 inhabitants, at 130 kilometers from Bern, rendered a singular judgment, A mason named Jacques Schiesser, who was obliged to work in water of an excessively low temperature, shivering with cold, his hands blue, made a movement of impatience at the cold, and uttered irreverential words toward God. A *procès-verbal* was made out against him. He appeared before the judges, who condemned him for blasphemy to two days' imprisonment. It is surprising to see Switzerland carried, actually by Protestantism, back to the Middle Ages.

Finally, to the political superiority of Protestantism must be added the intellectual and moral superiority of its clergy.

**Intellectual and moral superiority of Protestant clergy.** The obligation to read and interpret the Bible has given rise, in the universities of Protestant theology, to a work of exegesis which has resulted in a new science, the Science of Religion. The Protestant clergymen are better educated than our priests, and have moreover families and children, and lead a life like that of any other citizen; they are national, because their church is a national church; they do not receive orders from abroad, and, more than all, they do not possess the terrible power which the Catholic priest owes to the confessional; a power which cost France the Revocation of the Edict of Nantes and so many other deplorable measures.[1]

The several advantages which Protestantism enjoys by comparison with Catholicism are so incontestable that, if one must **But Protestant-ism is not a neces-sary step toward free-thought.** absolutely choose between the two religions, one could not hesitate. But such a choice is not necessary; one can avoid both horns of the dilemma. Free-thought is even more intimately dependent upon, and more disposed to favour, science than Protestantism is, for free-thought absolutely depends upon science. Free-thought is more intimately dependent upon practical and civil liberty than Protestantism is, by the very fact that free-thought is the complete realization of liberty in the sphere of theory. Finally free-thought renders the clergy superfluous, or rather to reinstate a mediæval term it tends to replace the priest by the *clerk*, that is to say by the *savant*, the professor, the man of letters, the man of culture, to whatever state of society he may belong. The best thing that has been said about Protestantism in France is M. de Narbonne's remark to Napoleon. "There is not enough religion in France to make two." In-

[1] "By means of the confessional," says M. de Laveleye, the "priest holds the sovereign, the magistrates, and the electors, and through the electors the legislative chamber, in his power; so long as the priest presides over the sacraments, the separation of Church and State is only a dangerous illusion. The absolute submission of the entire ecclesiastical hierarchy to a single will, the celibacy of the clergy, and the multiplication of monastic orders, constitute a danger in Catholic countries of which Protestant countries know nothing."

stead of a national religion we possess in France a national non-religion ; that very fact constitutes our claim to originality among the nations.   In France two-thirds at least of the male population live outside the limits of religious tradition.   In the country, as in the town, there is scarcely one man for every ten women to be found in church, sometimes not more than one for a hundred, and sometimes none at all.   In the majority of the departments, scarcely one man can be found fulfilling his religious duties.   In the great cities, the labourer is the avowed enemy of religion, in the country the peasant is simply indifferent.   The peasantry displays a certain respect for the exterior forms of worship ; but the reason is that the peasantry comes in contact with the priest, its intercourse with him is constant, it generally fears or esteems him enough not to laugh at him, except behind his back.   The results of the French Revolution cannot be arrested in this country ; sooner or later they will suffice to give birth to a complete religious, political, and civil liberty : even to-day in politics it is not in the direction of a lack of liberty that our failure lies, it is quite the reverse.   For the French, it is useless to talk of adopting Protestantism under the pretext that it is favourable to civil and political liberty, to diffusion of modern ideas and science.

There remains the consideration of public morality in France.   But it is impossible to demonstrate that the morality of Protestant people is superior to that of Catholics ; nay, in respect to a certain number of items, statistics tend rather to prove the contrary, if anything can be proved of morality by statistics.   Drunkenness, for example, is a much less terrible scourge among Catholic peoples who inhabit climates in which alcohol constitutes a much smaller temptation.   Illegitimate births are much more frequent in Germany than in France ; no doubt because of the laws that regulate marriage.   The average of crimes and offences is not very variable from country to country, and such variations as there are, are attributable to difference of climate, of race, of greater or less density of population, and not to differences of religion.   To-day, on account of the increasing perfection of means of

*No sufficient evidence that Protestant countries are more moral than Catholic.*

communication, vice tends to find its level.   Vices spread like contagious diseases : everyone whose system is in a state which is favourable to poison becomes contaminated, to whatsoever race or whatsoever religion he may belong.   The effect of any given religion upon the morality of any given people is certainly not to be overlooked, but it is altogether relative to the character of the people in question, and proves nothing as to the absolute moral quality of the religion itself.   Mohammedanism is of great service to barbarous tribes, because it prohibits drunkenness, and travellers generally agree as to the moral superiority of Mohammedan tribes as compared with tribes converted to Christianity ; the first are composed of shepherds and relatively honest merchants, the second are composed of drunkards, whom alcohol has transformed into beasts and pillagers.   Does it follow that we must all become converted to Mohammedanism, or even that the prohibitions of the Koran, all-powerful as they are over the savage mind, would act with the same force upon a drunkard of Paris or of London ?   Alas, no ! and in the absence of any such possibility one may take refuge in this means : sobriety is even more important for the masses of the people than continence, its absence borders more nearly on bestiality ; moreover the labouring man and especially the peasant possesses less opportunity to run to excesses of incontinence than of drink, for the simple reason that women cost more than drink.   Even among the followers of Mohammed, the poor are obliged to restrict themselves to one wife.

And finally religion does not constitute the sole cause of morality ; still less is it capable of re-establishing a morality which is on a decline ; the utmost it can do is to maintain morality somewhat longer in existence than it otherwise would be, to confirm custom and habit by a backing of faith.   The power of custom and of the accomplished fact is so considerable that even religion can scarcely make head against it.   When a new religion takes possession of a people it never destroys the mass of the beliefs which have taken root in their hearts ; it fortifies them rather by adapting itself to them.   To conquer

*And religion is not the sole factor that determines morality.*

paganism, Christianity was obliged to transform itself: it became Latin in Latin countries, German in German countries. Mohammedanism in Persia, in Hindustan, in the island of Java serves simply as a vestment and a veil for the old Zoroastrian, or Brahman, or Buddhistic beliefs. Manners, national characters, and superstitions are more durable than dogmas. The character of northern peoples is always hard and all of a piece, to an extent that produces a certain external regularity in their lives, a certain submission to discipline, sometimes also a certain savageness and brutality. The men of southern Europe, on the contrary, are mobile, malleable, open to temptation. The explanation is to be looked for in their climate, not in their religion. The rigid fir-tree grows in the north ; flexible, tall reeds in the south. The discipline of the Prussian army and administration does not result from the religion of Prussia, but from the worship of discipline. Throughout the whole life of the north there runs a certain stiffness which shows itself in the smallest details, in the manner of walking, of speaking, of directing the eyes ; and the northern conscience is brusque and rough, it commands, and one must obey or disobey ; in the south of Europe it argues. If Italy were Protestant, there would probably be few Quakers. We believe therefore that the effect is often taken for the cause, where a preponderant influence is attributed to the Protestant or Catholic religion on public or private morality, and, that is to say, on the vital power of a people. This influence formerly was enormous, it is diminishing day by day, and it is science to-day which tends to become the principal arbiter of the destinies of a nation.

If it be so, what must one think of the doubts, as to the future of France, which seem to be entertained in certain quarters? Those who regard religion as the condition *sine qua non* of life and of superiority in the struggle for existence among nations, must naturally consider France as in danger of disappearing. But is this criterion of national vitality admissible?

Is the possession of a religion indispensable for the best interests of humanity.

We find ourselves here once more in the presence of Mr. Matthew Arnold. In his judgment, the modern world has been made what it is by the influence of two peoples, the Greeks and the Jews, representing respectively two distinct and almost opposed ideas, which are contending with each other for the possession of the modern mind. For Greece—the brilliant, but in spite of its subtlety of spirit, somewhat superficial Greece—art and science fill the measure of life. For the Hebrews life might be summed up in one word, justice. And by justice must not be understood a rigid respect for the rights of others, but a willingness to renounce one's own interest, one's own pleasure, a self-effacement in the presence of the eternal law of sacrifice personified in Javeh. Greece and Judea are dead; Greece faithful to the last moment to its belief in the all-sufficiency of art and science, Judea faithless at the last moment to its belief in the all-sufficiency of justice, and falling by reason of that very infidelity. Mr. Matthew Arnold finds the two nations symbolized in an Old Testament story. It was before the birth of Isaac, the veritable inheritor of the divine promise, who was humble but elect. Abraham looked upon his first son Ishmael, who was young, vigorous, brilliant, and daring, and implored God: "Oh, that Ishmael might live before Thee!" But it could not be. Greece, the Ishmael among nations, has perished. Later the Renaissance appeared as its successor; the Renaissance was full of vitality, of future; the dream, the sombre nightmare had passed away, there was to be no more religious asceticism, we were to return to nature. The Renaissance held in horror the tonsured and hooded Dark Ages, whose spirit was renouncement and mortification. For the Renaissance itself the ideal was fulness of life, growth of the individual, the free and joyous satisfaction of all our instincts, of art and science; Rabelais was the personification of it. Alas! the Renaissance fell, as Greece fell, and the natural successor of the Renaissance, in Mr. Matthew Arnold's judgment, is George Fox, the first Quaker, the open contemner of arts and sciences. Finally, in our days, a people in Europe has taken up the succession; the modern

*Matthew Arnold's theory.*

Greece, dear to the enlightenment of all nations, the friend of art and science, is France. How often, and with what ardour, has this prayer in its favour been raised to God in heaven: "Oh, that Ishmael might live before Thee!" France is the average sensual man, and Paris is his city, and who of us does not feel himself attracted? The French possess this element of superiority over the Renaissance, that they are more balanced than other peoples, and though France has aimed to liberate mankind and to enfranchise them from the austere rule of sacrifice, she has not conceived man as a monster, nor liberty as a species of madness. Her ideas are formulated in a system of education which lies in the regular, complete, and harmonious development of all the faculties. Accordingly the French ideal does not shock other nations, it seduces them; France is for them the land of tact, of measure, of good sense, of logic. We aim in perfect confidence at developing the whole human being without violence to any part of it. It is in this ideal that we have found our famous gospel of the rights of man. The rights of man consist simply in a systematization of Greek and French ideas, in a consecration of the supremacy of self, as against abnegation and religious sacrifice. In France, Mr. Matthew Arnold says, the desires of the flesh, and current ideas, are mistaken for the rights of man. While we are pursuing one ideal, other peoples, more tightly chained to Hebraism, continue to cultivate that justice which is founded on renouncement. From time to time they look with envy out of their own austere and dull life, and with admiration upon the French ideal which is so positive, so clear, so satisfying; they are half inclined at times to make a trial of it. France has exerted a charm on the entire world. Everyone at some period or other of his life has thirsted for the French ideal, has desired to make a trial of it. The French wear the guise of the people to whom has been intrusted the beautiful, the charming ideal of the future, and other nations cry: "Oh, that Ishmael might live before Thee!" And Ishmael seems to grow more and more brilliant each day, seems certain of success, is on the point of making the conquest of the world. But at this moment a disaster occurs, the Crisis, the Biblical judgment arrives at the moment of triumph ; behold the judgment of the world ! The world, in Mr. Matthew Arnold's opinion, was judged in 1870 : the Prussians were Javeh's substitute. And once more Ishmael, the spirit of Greece, the spirit of the Renaissance, the spirit of France, free-thought, and free conduct were conquered by Israel, by the spirit of the Bible, by the spirit of the Middle Ages. A brilliant but superficial civilization was crushed beneath the weight of the barbarous and unyielding asceticism of a more or less naïve faith. Javeh is even in the present century the god of battles, and woe to the individuals who do not believe, with the ancient Jew, that abnegation constitutes three-fourths of life, and that art and science together barely fill the other fourth.

Rightly to estimate this philosophy of history let us occupy Matthew Arnold's point of view, which is not without some

Victorious superiority of Hellenism.

shade of truth. Assuredly Greece and Judea, although their ideas dissolved into and became a part of Christianity, are, so to speak, two antithetical nations representing respectively two opposed conceptions of life and of the world. These two nations have unceasingly struggled against each other in intellectual battle, and one may accept as most honourable for France the rôle that Mr. Arnold has assigned to her, that of being the modern Greece, of representing the struggle of art and science against mystical and ascetic faith. Greece and France were conquered, it is true, but it does not follow from that fact that the spirit of Greece and France, of art and science, has been conquered by faith. The battle is on the definitive issue still uncertain. If one must trust to a calculation of probabilities, all the probabilities are in favour of science ; if the French were conquered in 1870, it was not by German religion but by German science. In general it is very difficult to say that a doctrine is inferior because the people who maintained it have been vanquished in history. History is a succession of events whose causes are so complex that we never can affirm that we know absolutely all of the reasons which produced any given historical fact. There are, moreover, in the life of any people a number of currents of thought running side by side, and sometimes in opposite directions. The land of Rabelais is also that of Calvin. More than that, in other nations we see a species of official doctrine professed by a series of remarkable thinkers, which seems more or less in opposition to the more unconscious doctrine of the people, in which the conduct and thoughts of the great multitude may be regarded as summarized. What, for example, is to be considered as the true doctrine of the Jewish people? Is it the passionate faith of Moses, of Elijah, or of Isaiah; is it the scepticism of the Ecclesiast, already foreshadowed in the book of Job; is it the explosion of sensuality in the Song of Songs? It is difficult to decide; it may be affirmed with some show of truth that the temperament of the Jewish people as a whole is rather more sensual than mystic. The official doctrine handed down to us in the Bible may be regarded as a reaction against popular tendencies; a reaction whose violence is the measure of the strength and stubbornness of the tendencies against which it was directed. The great days of the Hebrew people were rather those when, under the reign of Solomon, the arts of ease and life were flourishing than those when the prophets were bewailing the disappearance of so much splendour. Or what was really the spirit of the people in the Middle Ages? Is it to be found in the mystical books of the monks of the times? And are the Middle Ages, apart from the Renaissance, to be regarded as constituting a great and completed epoch? Even if we supposed, with Mr. Matthew Arnold, that every brilliant age, such as the Renaissance, every age of art and science, harbours in its own bosom the germs of death, does that fact constitute a reason for lowering one's estimate of such epochs of intense life, and is it not better for a people to have lived, even though but for a few years, than to have slept through centuries?

Nothing is eternal. When a nation has enjoyed a brilliant life during a certain number of years or centuries, when it has produced great artists or great scholars, there necessarily comes a period of comparative exhaustion. Religions also are subject to the law of birth, maturity, and decay. Where does

the responsibility lie ?  On the very laws of life, which do not
permit plants to blossom eternally, and which in general provide, in all the kingdoms of the natural world,
that there shall be nothing so fragile as a flower.
But if all human things are transitory, to labour
for the efflorescence of intelligence, to regard

*Analogy be-
tween life of
nation and that of
individual.*

art and science as the supreme aim of life, is precisely to
pursue that which is least perishable.  Art, science, the last
achievements of the human mind do not decay ; man alone,
the individual disappears, and the ancient adage is eternally
true : " Art is long, and life is short."  As to true justice, it
also is surely eternal ; but if by true justice be understood the
hard law of Jehovah, the worship of this law has always fallen
upon the insignificant epochs of history, and precisely upon
the epochs of injustice and barbarism.  Therein lies the explanation of the fact that that cult has flourished at periods when
nations were the most robust and difficult to subdue.  The
manners of such nations are ferocious, their life at bottom is
quite contrary to the ideal of justice, and their religious faith
resembles their manners, and is violent and savage, and inclines
them to intolerance, to fanaticism, to massacre ; but all these
elements of injustice none the less constitute, in the people that
unites them all, so many additional chances of victory over
other people.  Later, when manners become more civilized,
when faith diminishes and art and science are born, a nation
often becomes weaker, directly as it becomes nobler ; the finer
an organism is, the more delicate it becomes, the easier it is to
break.  Renouncement of self, submission of the weak to the
strong, and of the strongest to an all-powerful priest, the species
of hierarchy that obtained in Judea, in India, and Europe
during the Middle Ages, formerly gave a people a superiority
in the struggle for existence, like that of a rock over a vegetable, of an oak over a sensitive-plant, of a bull or an elephant
over man ; but is precisely that kind of effectiveness the ideal of
humanity, and the aim to be proposed to human effort ?  To
raise art and science to their highest possible development
exacts a considerable expense of force ; art and science fatigue
and exhaust the people who give them birth.  After epochs

of effervescence, follow epochs of repose and of recuperation, epochs, so to speak, of intellectual lying fallow. These alternations of repose and productivity, of sterility and fecundity will continue to recur until some means be found of maintaining the human mind continuously in its state of highest vitality, as one fertilizes the earth, and, so to speak, thus secures a constant flow of sap and a perpetual efflorescence. The day perhaps will come when the psychic analogue of the rotation of crops may be discovered. However that may be, the greatness of a people has in the past too often exhausted it. But it does not follow, from that fact, that history must be read backward, and that periods of mere preparation and barbarism and despotism must be regarded as those which are the incarnation of the law of justice and have saved the race of mankind.

If greatness kills it is beautiful to die for greatness ; but when it is the death of a nation that is in question, mortality is never complete. Which is the more completely alive to-day, whatever Mr. Matthew Arnold may say, Greece or Judea? Which will be more alive to-morrow, France, which to-day seems trampled underfoot, or the nations which seem to be France's superiors? If we were perfectly sure that France, better than any other nation, represents art and science, we might affirm with perfect certitude that she will possess the future, and say with confidence that Ishmael will live. It is true that, in Mr. Matthew Arnold's opinion, Ishmael represents not only the man of intellect but the man of the senses, of the desires of the flesh. Of a truth it is strange to see anyone regarding the conquerors of France as Quakers, and Paris can lay no better claim than London or Berlin to being dubbed the modern Babylon. Mr. Matthew Arnold's mystic terrors in this connection are really deserving of raillery. What is just in his position is that the French, even in the pursuit of pleasure, display a certain moderation and measure, display a degree of art that is unknown to other people ; and by that very fact they achieve, if not the substance, at least the form of morality, which is, as Aristotle has said, a just mean between two vicious

*Hellenism contains the cure of its own evils.*

extremes. In Mr. Matthew Arnold's judgment, however, this specious morality serves simply as a cloak for the lowest degree of immorality, that namely of seeking one's rule of life not in God but in human nature, with all its diverse tendencies, high and low. This immorality constitutes in its turn a sort of social danger, that of a softening or enfeeblement of the national character of a people. This danger appears to us illusory, or rather, if one may so speak, it is a question which belongs rather to hygiene than to morals; what is really wanted is that science itself should discover in the matter a rule of conduct. In reality, genuine men of science actually are those who know best how to direct themselves in life, and a whole people of men of science could leave little to desire on the score of conduct; and that fact shows that science itself contains an element of practical wisdom and morality. Note also that there exists an antagonism between cerebral labour and the violence of the physical appetites. The prohibitions which are based upon a mystical law too often season desire simply, as it is easy to prove by examples drawn from the clergy of the Middle Ages. A much more certain method may be employed, namely, to extinguish desire, to substitute a sort of intellectual disdain in place of religious terror. The Mohammedan religion prohibits the use of wine; but it is very easy to distinguish between wine and alcohol, which Mohammed did not formerly forbid for the sufficient reason that he was unacquainted with its existence. Moreover, religious faith is not only subject to subtleties of interpretation, it is subject to periods of weakness; but if, on the contrary, you issue no mystical prohibition but cultivate a man to a certain degree of intellectual development, he will simply not desire to drink; education will have transformed him more perfectly than religion could have done. Far from diminishing the value that individuals set upon pleasure, religions in reality frequently augment it considerably, because, over and against such and such a pleasure, and, as it were, holding the balance level against it, they establish an eternity of pain. When a religious devotee yields to temptation, he conceives the desired indulgence as, in some sort, of an infinite value, as condensing into an instant such an eternity of joy as may compensate an eternity of suffering. This conception, which unconsciously dominates the entire conduct of the believer, is fundamentally immoral. Fear of chastisement, as psychologists have frequently remarked, lends a certain additional charm to the forbidden pleasure ; magnify the chastisement, you heighten the charm. Therein lies the explanation of the fact that, if a devotee is immoral at all, he is infinitely more so than a sceptic ; he will indulge in monstrous refinements in his pleasures, analogous to the monstrous refinements in which his god indulges, in the item of punishments, and his virtue, consisting largely in fear, is itself fundamentally immoral. In epochs of scientific development this mystical and diabolical heightening of pleasure will disappear. The man of science is acquainted with the causes of pleasure, they fall into place in his scheme of things, in the general network of causes and effects ; a pleasure is a desirable effect, but only in so far as it does not exclude such and such another equally desirable effect. The pleasures of the senses take their legitimate rank in the classified and subordinated list of human aims. A man of large intelligence holds desire in check by means of its natural and sole all-powerful antagonist—disdain.

To sum it all up, Ishmael is quite capable of regulating his own conduct without Jehovah's help. Justice is salvation, said the Hebrew people ; but science also is salvation, and justice too, and justice not infrequently more just and more certain than any other kind. If Ishmael sometimes strays into the desert, sometimes loses his way and falls, he knows how to get up again; he has strength enough in his own heart to help himself, and to make him independent of Jehovah, who left him alone in infinite space without even sending to his aid the angel mentioned in the Bible. If France has really, as Mr. Arnold says, formulated the new gospel of Ishmael, this profoundly human gospel is indubitably destined to outlive the other, for there is often nothing more provisional, more unlasting, more fragile, than what men have crowned with the adjective divine. The

*Hellenism more just than justice.*

surest method of finding what is really eternal is to look for
the best and most universal elements in the human character.
But the gospel of the rights of man, Mr. Arnold objects, is the
ideal of the average, sensual man only. One wonders what
the meaning of the word "sensual" in this place can be, and
what sensuality can have to do with an unwillingness to dis-
regard the rights of other people or to have one's own rights
disregarded by other people. As if the rights of man had anything to do with sensuality! Mr. Arnold forgets that the
word "right" always implies some measure of sacrifice. But
the sacrifice is precisely proportionate—it is not the sacrifice
of all for the benefit of one or of the few; it is not a sterile
sacrifice, it is not a vain expense of force, it is the partial
sacrifice of all for the benefit of all, it is the renunciation in
our own conduct of everything which might interfere with like
conduct on the part of other people; so that, instead of being
a waste of social power, it is in the best sense an organization
and an increase of social power. The people who first truly
realize the gospel of the rights of man will not only be the
most brilliant, the most enviable, the happiest of peoples, but
also the justest of peoples, with a justice which will be not
only national and passing, but, so to speak, universal and
indestructible; not even the hand of Jehovah will be able to
shiver its power, for what is really divine in power will dwell
in its own heart. The French Revolution was not so purely
sensual and earthly as Mr. Matthew Arnold affirms. It was
an uprising not in the name of the senses but of the reason.
The Declaration of Rights is a series of formulæ *a priori*, constituting a sort of metaphysics or religion of civil government,
founded upon a revelation by the human conscience. It is
easily comprehensible that positive and empirical thinkers,
such as Bentham and John Stuart Mill and Taine, should have
a word of blame for this novel species of religious Utopia; but
a person like Mr. Matthew Arnold, who prides himself on
being religious, ought not to draw back from it, ought even to
admire it. Theodore Parker, a Christian not less liberal than
Mr. Matthew Arnold, did so. Writing on the subject of the
French Revolution, Theodore Parker said: that the French

were more transcendental than the Americans. To the intellectual conception of liberty and to the moral conception of equality they joined the religious conception of fraternity, and thus supplied politics as well as legislation with a divine foundation as incontestable as the truths of mathematics. They declare that rights and duties precede and dominate human law. America says: " The Constitution of the United States is above the President; the Supreme Court is above Congress." France says: " The constitution of the universe is above the Constitution of France!" That is what forty millions of men declare. It is the greatest proclamation that a nation has ever made in history.

What we may reasonably be reproached with is not our love for art and science, but our love for a facile art and a superficial science. We may rightfully be reproached also with a somewhat Attic lightness, a lack of perseverance and of seriousness. Naturally, one does not mean that we should imitate the superstitious Slave who attributes an involuntary burst of laughter to the devil, and who, after having laughed, expectorates indignantly to exorcise the sweet spirit of gaiety whom he regards as a spirit of evil. If French gaiety is one of our weaknesses it is also one of the elements of our national strength; but let us be quite clear about the sense to be put upon the word. The gaiety which is genuine and charming consists simply in highheartedness and vivacity of mind. One's courage is strong enough, confident enough, to be able to afford not to look at things on their painful side. Everything has two handles, says the Greek sage; and by one handle it is light and easy to manage; it is by that handle that the French are fond of taking destiny and fortune. Gaiety of that kind is simply a form of hope; thoughts which come from the heart, great thoughts are often the most smiling. What one calls *aptness*, that swift fitness and appropriateness in which the French delight, is itself an evidence of mental detachment, an affirmation to the effect that things which appeared at first so enormous really possess slight importance, a mark of high courage in the face of disaster; it is simply a less theatrical rendering of the

*Good and evil sides of French gaiety.*

ancient *non dolet*.  A French officer, in a guerilla war (in New Caledonia, I think), felt himself struck in the breast by a bullet; "Well aimed, for a savage," he said, as he fell.  That is French heroism; not going the length of ignoring the fact, but maintaining a just appreciation of it as it is.  But there is a gaiety that cannot be too much blamed or too steadily repressed, a gaiety undistinguished by subtlety or high courage, and one to which other peoples are quite as inclined as the French, the gross laugh which follows horse-play like an echo, and inhabits taverns and *cafés chantants*.  That species of gaiety is the vicious gaiety of peasants out for a holiday, of commercial travellers at dinner.  It is undeniable that the Gaul has a weakness for *gaudriole*.  I know a promising young physician who was obliged to leave Paris, where he had won a name as a hospital surgeon, obliged to quit work and to go to a distant country for his health; in a moment of expansion he confided to me that what he regretted most were the jolly evenings at the Palais-Royal.  There are thousands of distinguished young men subjected to this species of education, of discipline in "chaff," and it is inevitable that it should result in a loss, for them, of something that is fine.  The Palais-Royal, the vaudeville, *cafés-concerts* are places which corrupt the taste as the palate is corrupted by drinking wood eau-de-vie.  It is difficult to be a really remarkable man and at the same time to possess a serious taste for the gross pleasantry of second-class theatres.  The two are irreconcilable.  And it is a melancholy thing to think that the pick of the young men of France should be exposed to precisely that influence, should pass a number of years in such an environment and lose their taste as surely as their ear for music.  Whatever is anti-æsthetic in laughter is degrading; witticisms must be spiritual, must really expand the heart with healthy mirth; laughter should positively embellish the face.  *Nihil inepto risu ineptius est;* the reason is that in such cases laughter is simply an explosion of silliness.  The wise man, says the Bible, laughs with an inner laugh.  Laughter should illuminate and not disfigure the visage, because it reveals the soul, and the soul should be beautiful, should resemble an outburst of frankness, of sincerity.

The charm of laughter lies, in a great measure, in the sincerity of the joy which renders us, for the time being, transparent to those about us. Human thought and the human heart, with the entire world that they contain, may be embodied in a tear.

Parisian wit, which in some quarters is regarded as the very type and ideal of French wit, is in some respects no more than an epitome of its defects; among the working classes it consists in chaff, what they call *blague;* among the upper classes it consists in a superficial varnish, an inability to fix the mind on a logical succession of ideas. In the salon frivolity is a convention, it has positively attained the height of being good manners. My attention was attracted a minute ago by a fly buzzing about my window, its transparent wings described curve after curve on the luminous surface that arrested its flight. Its graceful and futile progress reminded me of the conversation of a lady to whom I had just been listening in the salon, and who for an hour had described a series of scarcely larger circles, upon the surfaces of everything, and beneath the surface of nothing. The whole world of Parisian frivolity was typefied by the shimmering flight of the fly on the window-pane, ignorant of the open air, playing with stray rays of the great sun toward which it was unable to mount.

*Parisian wit an epitome of all that is evil in French gaiety.*

But must one be serious to the point of ennui? Certainly not, it is not necessary. It does not belong to our temperament. Let us recognize, however, that to be enduring of ennui is a great power; it is the secret of slow, patient, painstaking labour, which spares no detail, which guarantees solidity in the foundations and remote and hidden elements of knowledge; it is the secret of the superiority of men of northern race over men of southern. In the south, owing to an impatience of what is tedious, there is manifested an inability to stick to one thing, to follow one pursuit, to venture into the darkness beyond where the light stops. Tasks pursued with obstinacy in the certitude of an ultimate success, indefatigable labour at the desk, reading understood as the absolute appropriation of every word and thought between the covers of the book in hand, are unknown

*True inwardness.*

to those superficial intelligences which are quick to take a birds-eye view of a subject in its entirety, but are impatient of details and of course among others of essential details.   There are races of men who are incapable of anything exacting more attention than "skimming"; they skim their books, they skim the world, they turn the leaves of life.   Neither true art nor true science is within their reach.   "Live inwardly," says the "Imitation."   It is an ideal which Frenchmen, who are particularly inclined to lose themselves in external details, might well pursue.   But true inwardness does not necessarily consist in sterile meditation on a dogma.   "Live inwardly" should signify, be serious, be yourself, be original, independent, and free; bestir your own powers of thought, take a pleasure in developing them and yourself; bloom inwardly like certain plants which lock up within themselves their pollen, their perfume, their beauty; but give out your fruit.   The natural expansiveness which leads a Frenchman to be so communicative is one of his good qualities; the bad side of it, where there is a bad side, consists simply in not having anything serious to communicate.

Our defects are curable, and their remedy does not lie in a sort of religious asceticism, but in a more profound and complete understanding of the great objects of love that have always attracted the French mind— science, art, law, liberty, universal fraternity. There is a Japanese legend of a young girl who procured some flower seeds and was surprised to find them nothing but little black prickly grains; she offered them to her playmates, who would not accept them; then she sowed them, in some anxiety as to the results, and by and by a superb flower sprang from every grain and all her playmates begged for the seeds that they had refused.   Philosophic and scientific truths are just such seeds; they are unattractive at first, but the day will come when mankind will prize them at their just worth.

Remedy for French levity.

# CHAPTER V.

## RELIGION AND NON-RELIGION AND THE CHILD.

I. Decline of religious education—Defects of this education, in especial in Catholic countries—Means of lightening these defects—The priest—The possibility of state-action on the priest.

II. Education provided by the state—Primary instruction—The schoolmaster—Secondary and higher instruction—Should the history of religion be introduced into the curriculum.

III. Education at home—Should the father take no part in the religious education of his children—Evils of a preliminary religious education to be followed by disillusionment—The special question of the immortality of the soul : what should be said to children about death.

## *I. Decline of religious education.*

THE religious education given to children by the priest possesses defects and even dangers which it is important to set in a clear light, and which explain the gradual decline in secular education. An opinion regarded as divine is an opinion which is as unfit for purposes of education as for purposes of science. The great opposition which obtains between religion and philosophy—in spite of their outward resemblances—is that the one is seeking and that the other declares that it has found ; the one is anxious to hear, the other has already heard ; the one weighs evidence, the other puts forth assertions and condemnations ; the one recognizes it as its duty to raise objections and to reply to them ; the other to shut its eyes to objections and to difficulties. From these differences result corresponding differences in methods of instruction. A philosopher, a metaphysician, aims to convince, the priest inculcates ; the former instructs, the latter reveals ; the former endeavours to stimulate and to train the reasoning, the latter to suppress it or at least to turn it aside from primitive and

*Unfitness of religious dogma as material for education.*

fundamental dogmas; the former awakens the intelligence, the latter in some measure lays it asleep. It is inevitable that revelations should be opposed to spontaneity and liberty of mind. When God has spoken man should be silent, in especial when the man is a child. And errors, which are often inoffensive if taught by a philosopher, are grave and dangerous if taught by a priest who speaks in the name and with the authority of God. In the first instance the remedy lies always at hand : an insufficient reason may always be made to give way before a sufficient reason; the child holds the standards of weight and measure in his own hands. And indeed it is not always easy to teach error at all by reason and reasoning : to attempt to give reasons for a prejudice is an excellent means of making its essential untruth prominent. It has always been some attempt on the part of humanity to demonstrate its beliefs that has resulted in their disproof. Whoever endeavours to examine a dogma is close upon the point of contradicting it, and the priest, who regards contradiction as a failure in faith, is always obliged, in the nature of things, to avoid an examination of it, to interdict a certain number of questions, to take refuge in mystery. When a priest has filled a brain with faith he seals it. Doubt and investigation, which are the life of philosophy, the priest regards as a mark of distrust and suspicion, as a sin, as an impiety; he lifts his eyes to Heaven at the bare notion of anybody's thinking for himself. God is both judge and party in every discussion; at the very time when you are endeavouring to find reasons for believing in his existence, He commands you to affirm it. The believer who hesitates at a dogma is a little in the position of the sheep in the fable, who wished to reason with the wolf and to prove to him that the water was not muddy; he proved it indeed, but he was eaten up for his pains; he would have done just as well to hold his peace and yield. Also there is nothing more difficult than to shake yourself free from a faith that was fastened upon you in your childhood and that has been confirmed by the priest, by custom, by example, by fear. Fear, in especial, is a capital guardian to watch over the interests of positive religion and a religious education, a guardian who is always on the *qui vive ;* but for it the body of belief which is known as dogma would soon fall into decay and blow away in dust. One person would reject this, another that ; everybody would rise in open revolt, running hither and thither gaily like a lot of school-children out for a holiday. Happily they are always accompanied by a tutor, who keeps them in order and brings them home like a flock of lambs to the sheepcote. What power can reasoning have over anybody who is afraid? How can you be expected to see anything as in itself it really is, if you have been accustomed from childhood to walk with your eyes closed? Truth becomes for you as variable and unstable as your own sensibility. At an audacious moment you deny everything, the next day you are prepared to affirm more than you were before. It is very easy to understand ; nobody is obliged to be brave always, and, more than all, one's conscience is involved. Conscience, like government, is conservative ; it is naturally inimical to revolution and change. It is early taken in hand, and taught its little lesson ; it becomes uneasy the instant you call in question a line on the map ; you cannot take an independent step without some inner voice crying out to you to take care. Accustomed as you are to hear people anathematized who do not think as you do, you shudder at the thought of incurring such anathemas yourself. The priest has corrupted to his interest every sentiment in your soul—fear, respect, remorse ; he has fashioned your soul, your character, your morals to his hand. Insomuch that if you call religion in question, you call everything in question.

Subsidence of thought, benumbment of the spirit of liberty, love of routine, of blind tradition, of passive obedience, of

Impropriety of suppressing the clergy. everything, in a word, which is directly opposed to the spirit of modern science are the results of a too exclusively clerical education. These dangers are being more and more distinctly felt, especially in France—perhaps too much so. We go the length of demanding that religious education shall be suppressed and that immediately, as being hostile to liberty and to progress. An irresistible movement has begun toward lay education, a movement to which Catholics must some day or other adjust themselves. But it should be done slowly, transition should not be pushed too rapidly. To suppress at a blow the whole clergy who once had complete control of the national education, and still have charge of some portion of it, ought not to be the aim of free-thinkers ; the clergy will suppress themselves if they are but given time ; they will simply become extinct. At bottom it is not a bad thing that fifty-five thousand people should be or appear to be occupied with something else than their personal wants. No doubt one never lives completely up to one's ideal, and the ideal of disinterestedness that the priest proposes to himself is rarely realized ; still it is good that a certain number of men here below should labour at a task which is above their strength ; so many others labour at tasks only which are beneath them.

It must be confessed, however, that no religion is at its best in a country in which it reigns supreme ; really to estimate it, A religion at its best only in competition. one must see it struggling for supremacy against some rival faith, Catholic against Protestant, for example. Under such circumstances the priest and the pastor in a sense run a race with each other, compete with each other in activity and intelligence. One may see the results in the Dauphiné, in Alsace, and in a number of foreign countries. The zeal of the priest profits immensely by some such struggle for existence on the part of the religion to which he belongs ; whoever does the most good, gives the best advice, the best education, to the children in his charge, wins a victory for his faith. The result, which is easy to foresee, is that a mixed population of Protestants and Catholics is better instructed, more enlightened, is possessed of a higher morality than many other countries wholly Catholic.

One very desirable step in Catholic countries is that the priest should be given complete civil liberty, should be allowed Proposed reform in Catholic countries. to leave the Church if he choose, without becoming an outcast in society, should be free to marry, and to enjoy absolutely all the rights of citizenship. A second desirable step, and an essential one, is that the priest, who is one of the schoolmasters of the nation, should himself receive a higher education than he does to-day. The state, far from endeavouring to diminish the income of the priesthood—a very slight economy—might well, at need, augment it and exact diplomas analogous to those demanded of other instructors, and sufficient evidences of competence in extended historical and scientific inquiries and in religious history.[1] Already a number of priests in country districts are studying botany, mineralogy, and, in some instances, music. The ranks of the clergy contain a great quantity of live force, which is neutralized by a defective primary education, by lack of initiative, by lack of habits of freedom. Instead of endeavouring to separate church and state by a species of surgical operation, free-thinkers might well take their stand on the concordat, and profit by the fact that the state controls the income of the clergy, and endeavour to reawaken the priesthood to the conditions of modern life. In sociology, as in mechanics, it is sometimes easier to make use of the obstacles to one's advancement than to try to batter them down. Whatever is, is in some measure useful ; from the very fact that clerical education still maintains its existence it may be argued that it still plays a certain rôle in maintaining the social equilibrium, even if it be but a passive rôle, the rôle of counterpoise. But whatever possesses some degree of utility may well acquire a higher degree ; whatever is may be transformed. We must not endeavour to destroy the priesthood but to transform it ; to supply it with other practical and theoretical pursuits than the mechanical handling of the breviary. Between the literal religion which the majority of the French clergy teach, and a national and human ideal, there exist innumerable degrees which must be achieved successively and slowly, by a gradual intellectual progress, by an almost insensible widening of the intellectual horizon. Meanwhile, until the priest shall have passed through these successive degrees and have become aware of his essential superfluousness, it is good that he should make himself

---

[1] Would it not be possible at once to raise the income of all priests who are possessed of certain lay diplomas such as those of bachelor, licentiate, etc., and who, by that very fact, would be plainly competent to conduct a lay or religious education in a more modern and scientific spirit ?

useful in the manner in which he still believes himself capable of being of use: but one thing should be exacted of him, that he should not make himself harmful by stepping outside of the limits within which he is properly confined.

## II. *Education provided by the state.*

The task undertaken by a state that is endeavouring to substitute a lay for a clerical education is one of increasing importance. The law ought, no doubt, to rec-
State neu-
trality in reli-
gious matters.
ognize all religions as equal, but, as has been remarked,[1] there are two ways in which this recognition may be conducted: the one passive, the other active. The government may stand neutral simply, and abstain from either refuting or from giving comfort to the pretensions of any given system of theology ; or it may be actively neuter, that is to say, it may pursue its task of scientific and philosophical achievement in complete indifference to any and every system of theology.[2] It is a neutrality of the latter sort that should be practised in primary and secondary instruction, and that should govern the conduct of the instructor.

The schoolmaster has always been a mark for raillery, and sometimes justly so ; to-day he is slightly regarded by everyone with any pretensions to high acquirements.
Importance of
the schoolmaster.
Renan and Taine, and partisans generally of an intellectual aristocracy, can scarcely suppress a smile at the mention of this representative of democracy, of science for small children. University professors show small tolerance for the pedantry of their humble assistant, who is sometimes ignorant of Greek. Men of culture, with any tincture of poetry or of art, regard the man as something very prosaic and utilitarian whose main ambition is to instruct some thousands of peasants in the alphabet, grammar, and the names

[1] M. Goblet d'Alviella.

[2] " Lay education," said Littré, "ought not to avoid dealing with anything which is essential ; and what could be more essential in considering the moral government of society than the religions which have dominated or still dominate it ? "

of the principal cities of Europe, and of the geographical localities from which we obtain pepper and coffee. And yet this despised schoolmaster, whose importance is daily increasing, is the sole middle-man between the belated masses and the intellectual élite, who are moving ever more and more rapidly forward. He has the advantage of being necessary and the disadvantage of knowing it; buried in his remote village, his accomplishments impress him almost as much as they do the children and the peasantry about him; the optical illusion is a natural one. But if an exaggerated estimate of his own importance sometimes gives rise in him to an offensive pedantry, it supplies him with the sort of devotion that enables a humble functionary to rise to the height of the duties to which he has been called. And who, after all, but society, is responsible for the fashioning and instruction of the schoolmaster? And cannot society raise the level of his intelligence in proportion as it increases the magnitude of his task? A little knowledge makes a pedant, much knowledge makes a scholar. There will always be schoolmasters who will be as well educated as one could wish, provided only that their salaries are raised side by side with the list of required studies. It is strange that a society should not do its best to form those whose function it is in turn to form it. The great question of popular education becomes in certain aspects a question of shillings and pence. The practical instruction of schoolmasters has already been carried to a certain degree of perfection; he has been initiated into an apprenticeship, and introduced, as it were, into the kitchen of certain sciences; he has been supplied with notions on agriculture and chemistry which often enable him to give excellent advice to the peasantry. It would be very easy a little to perfect his theoretical knowledge, to give him a broader knowledge of the sciences which he considers too exclusively on their practical side, to give him some conception of things as a whole, to raise him above an exclusive adoration of the isolated facts of historical or grammatical minutiæ. A little philosophy would make a better historian and a less tedious geographer. He might be introduced to the great cosmological hypotheses, to some sufficient notions of psychology, and in especial of child-psychology, and finally a little history of religion would familiarize him with the principal metaphysical speculations that the human mind has put forth in its endeavour to pass beyond the bounds of science ; he would become, as a result of it, more tolerant in all matters of religious belief. This more extended instruction would permit him to follow at a distance the progress of science ; his intelligence would not stand still, he would not come to his complete maturity somewhere between the ABC-book and the grammar. Moreover, intellectual elevation is always accompanied by a moral elevation which manifests itself in all the conduct of life, and sometimes a word from a schoolmaster may change all the rest of a pupil's existence. The greater one's intellectual, and in especial, one's moral superiority, the greater one's influence over those about one. Even at the present time the very modest amount of knowledge at the disposal of the ordinary teacher gives him a very genuine influence ; he is believed in, his words are listened to and accepted. The peasant—that doubting Thomas—who nowadays shakes his head over what the priest says, is becoming accustomed to consult the schoolmaster ; the schoolmaster has shown him how to make more grain grow in the same amount of ground ; the quivering of a blade of grass in the wind is for a man of the people the most categorical of affirmations ; to accomplish something is to prove : action is ratiocination enough. Moreover the schoolmaster demonstrates the practical power of science by fashioning successive generations of mankind, by converting them into men. It is at the schoolmaster's hands that everyone receives the provision of knowledge that must last him and maintain his strength throughout his whole life ; he prepares one for life as the priest prepares one for death, and in the eyes of the peasant, preparation for life is much more important than preparation for death. Life has its mystery as well as death, and in the former case the fact of one's capability is certain ; the schoolmaster often determines the future of the pupil in a manner that is visible and verifiable ; and nothing like so much can be said for the priest. The power of the latter also has diminished with the change that has taken place in the popular notion of punishment after death. The priest's power lies in ceremonies, in propitiatory or expiatory sacrifices ; the virtue of sacrifices of both kinds equally is to-day looked on sceptically. Knowledge is better than prayer, and the priest is gradually losing his ascendency over the people. The schoolmaster is often the butt of raillery, but the country priest, whom it was so much the fashion to idealize at the beginning of the century, is to-day a mark for open mirth. The reaction was natural and in some measure legitimate ; perfection is not of this world, and dwells neither in the state nor the school, but the rôle of the schoolmaster and the priest in humanity is important, for they are the sole dispensers of science and metaphysics to the multitude. We have seen how much it is to be hoped that the priest, who is so ignorant to-day in Catholic countries, will soon receive a better education, will soon begin to create a reason for his continued existence in modern society. If he falls too far behind the intellectual movement of the times, he will drop out simply, and the schoolmaster will inherit his power. After all there are all kinds of apostles, in blouse and frock-coat as well as in priestly robes ; and the proselytism of some of them is based upon a mystical disinterestedness, and of others on a certain practical aim ; there are some who travel about the world, and some who sit by the fire and are none the less active for all that. What may be affirmed safely is that in all times apostles have been even more disposed to address little children than men, and it is notable that the modern Vincent de Paul was a schoolmaster-Pestalozzi.

What is taking the place of religious education, in existing societies, is moral education. The moral sentiment, as we

*Moral educa- tion the legitimate successor of reli- gious education.* know, is the least suspicious element in the modern religious sentiment, and metaphysical hypotheses, based in the last resort upon moral conceptions, are the ultimate and highest outcome of religious hypotheses. To the elements of philosophic morality it has been proposed to add, in secondary and even in primary instruction, some notion of the history of reli-

gions.[1]  If this proposition is to be made acceptable it must
be reduced within just limits.  Let us cherish no illusion ; M.
Vernes is wrong if he believes that a professor, and in especial
a schoolmaster, ever could dwell with insistence upon the history of the Jews without coming into conflict with the clergy.  A
truly scientific criticism of the legends which are usually taught
children under the name of sacred history positively batters
down the very foundations of Christianity.  Clergymen and
priests would not endure it ; they would protest and with some
show of reason against it, in the name of religious neutrality :
religion is not less certain in their eyes than science, and the
ignorant faith that distinguishes many of them has not yet
been tempered by a habit of free criticism ; so that anything
like a genuine historical education which should openly con-
trovert portions of the traditional theology must be considered
in advance as impossible.  There must be no question in the
matter of openly refuting anybody ; the course of instruction
must simply be such as to furnish those who follow it with a
criterion of truth, and to teach them to make use of it.  We
believe therefore that if the history of religions is ever made a
part of the regular course of instruction, it will deal principally
with everything but the history of the Jews.  It might furnish
elementary instruction on the moral system of Confucius, on
the moral metaphysical notions involved in Indo-European
religions, on the antique Egyptian religion, on the Greek
myths, and finally on the religious and moral atmosphere in
which Christianity took its rise, and on which it in some sort
depended and throve.  It would be well even to make scholars
in primary schools acquainted with the names of some of the
great sages in the history of the world, with their actual or
legendary biography, with the moral maxims which are attributed to them.  What harm could it do to instruct our
children in the aphorisms uttered by Confucius, Zoroaster,
Buddha, Socrates, Plato, and Aristotle, and to let them see
something of what humanity really believed before the time
of Christ ?  One cannot destroy the old faith openly and in a
minute, but one may do much to undermine and justly to

[1] By M. Maurice Vernes (approved by Littré, and later by M. Paul Bert).

undermine it by showing where and how it borrowed much of all that is best in it—that it is not an exception in the history of human thought nor even, in all respects, unsurpassed in its kind.

The Church possesses two means of educating children in its dogmas, and only two; the first is that of patristic or ecclesiastical authority : 'The fact is thus and such because I say so'; the second is the testimony of miracles.    These two, even at the present day, constitute the whole effective contents of the priests' armoury. The moment they step outside this little circle of ideas they lose their power.    And to destroy these two arguments it suffices to show : 1st, that other men have said something different from the teachings of Christianity ; 2d, that other gods than Jehovah have also performed miracles; or, in other words, there are no miracles whatever that have been scientifically ascertained. A number of French schools were founded in Kabail, and were prospering, when by degrees they were abandoned.    In one of them, which was the last deserted, some exercises of the pupils were discovered : they dealt with a story about Frede-gunde.    This anecdote illustrates current notions on instruc-tion in classical history : History means facts, and facts often monstrous and immoral ;  not content with teaching them to young Frenchmen we export them to Kabail ; but we do not export our ideas, nor even employ them at home.    We should have done better to teach the young Algerians what we know about Mohammed and his religion and about Jesus and the other prophets, the divinity of whose inspiration Mohammed himself admitted.    The slightest traces that a really rational education should leave in a half-savage mind would be more useful than a heap of absurd facts perfectly remembered.    At bottom it is more important even that a French child should know something of Mohammed or Buddha than of Fredegunde.    Although Mohammed and Buddha never lived on French soil, their influence on us is infinitely more great and their relation to us infinitely closer than that of Chilperic or Lothaire.

The place in which the history of religions really belongs, is

*Helplessness of religion in the face of argument.*

in the higher education. It is not enough to have introduced it with success into the Collège de France, and quite recently to have secured its recognition in a small part of the higher studies in the École. If we should replace our faculties of theology by chairs of religious criticism we should do no more than follow the example of Holland.[1] Mr. Max Müller introduced the science of religions into the University of Oxford with success. Similarly in Switzerland at the organization of the University of Geneva, in 1873, there was created in the faculty of letters a chair of the history of religions, although there already existed in the university a faculty of theology. In Germany the history of religions is taught independently, notably at the University of Wurtzburg, under the name of Comparative Symbolism. Just as a complete course of instruction in philosophy should include the principles of the philosophy of law and the philosophy of history, it will some day include also the principles of the philosophy of religion. After all, even from the point of view of philosophy, Buddha and Jesus possess a much greater importance than Anaximander or Thales.[2]

*Place of religion in state education.*

[1] Some years ago, as is well known, on the 1st of October, 1877, the faculty of theology in the three state universities of Leyden, Utrecht, and Groningen, and in the Communal University of Amsterdam, was declared to be a lay faculty and was freed from all association and connection with the Church, and was required to give purely scientific and philosophic instruction on the history of religion, without practical discipline. (See M. Steyn Parvé, *Organisation de l'instruction primaire, sécondaire et supérieure dans le royaume des Pays-Bas*, Leyden, 1878, and M. Maurice Vernes, *Mélanges de critique religieuse*, p. 305.)

The following is the programme of this faculty: 1. General theology; 2. History of doctrines concerning divinity; 3. History of religions in general; 4. History of the Israelite religion; 5. History of Christianity; 6. Literature of the Israelites, and the ancient Christians; 7. Old and New Testament exegesis; 8. History of the dogmas of the Christian church; 9. Philosophy of religion; 10. Ethics.

[2] As M. Vernes has remarked, the preparation for teaching the history of religions might well be the same as that for teaching philosophy, history, and letters. It should include the studies in the upper classes, of the philosophical section of the *école normale*, and a preparatory course in the divers other faculties: a real *normal* course. In this course the professor should point out the general principle of the history of religions and should confine himself to indicating them very summarily in the case of the religions of Greece and Rome, to which a general literary education

It has been said, after M. Laboulaye, that a professor of the history of religion should be at once an archæologist, an epigraphist, a numismatist, a linguist, an anthropologist, and versed in Hindu, Phœnician, Slavonic, Germanic, Celtic, Etruscan, Greek, and Roman antiquities; he should be nothing less than a Pico della Mirandola. At that rate one might show also that neither schools nor colleges can be expected to include a course on natural history or on the political history of some seven or eight nations—nay, even that it is impossible to teach children to read : the art of reading is so difficult in its perfection ! Really is it necessary that the historian of religion should be a master of all the historical sciences? He is under no obligation to discover new materials, he has simply to make use of those which philologists and epigraphists have put at his disposal ; such materials are now abundant enough and well enough ascertained to require a course specially devoted to them. There is no need for the instructor to master such and such a particular division of the history of religion ; he is simply required to furnish students in our universities, in the course of one or two years, with a general view of the development of religious ideas in history. The professor will no doubt encounter certain difficulties in dealing with religious questions because of the amount of feeling that such problems always involve, but the same difficulty is met with in every course which deals with contemporary questions, and almost every course does deal with them. A professor of history has to deal with contemporary facts, to describe the successive changes in the form of government in France, etc. A professor of philosophy has to deal with questions of theodicy and morals ; and even in pure psychology, materialistic and deterministic theories have to be passed upon ; even a mere professor of rhetoric is obliged, in treating of literature and of Voltaire and of

*Education of instructors.*

---

will have given the pupil access ; he should deal, without excessive attention to detail, with the other Indo-European religions (those of India, Persia, etc.), with the religions of Egypt, of Assyria, of Phœnicia, of Islam ; and should spend his greatest efforts on the criticism of Judaism and the early stages of Christianity, on the history of the principal Christian dogmas and their development.

the eighteenth and nineteenth centuries, to touch on questions which are burning.  Similarly, a professor in the law school must find a thousand occasions for praising, or blaming, or criticising the laws of the State.  And must one, because of dangers of this sort which are met with at every step, cease teaching history, philosophy, and law?  No, and we do not believe that one should be debarred from teaching religious history.  The whole question is one of fact rather than of principle ; it should be the master's business to avoid digressions beyond the limits of pure science, and to be on his guard against seeming to mean something more than he says, and masking a criticism of the existing order of things under a course on abstract theory.[1]

The aim of this impartial course of instruction should be to supply each religion with its proper historical setting, to show how it was born, developed, opposed to others ; it should be described, not refuted.  The bare introduction of historical continuity into the course of religious thought is itself a considerable step in advance ; whatever is continuous ceases to be marvellous. Nobody is astonished at a brook which gradually becomes bigger ; our ancestors adored great rivers of whose sources they were ignorant.

*Legitimate object of religious instruction.*

## III.  *Education at Home.*

It has often been asked, as a question of practical conduct, whether the head of a household ought not to have a religion,

[1] Works in religious criticism would naturally find their place in the school and college libraries.  They might be supplemented by a more or less extensive museum of religious curiosities, beginning with the fetiches of savage tribes and extending down to the present day.

To the mass of the French public the solid results already achieved by an independent criticism of the Bible constitute a *terra incognita ;* they must be disseminated.  M. Lenormant's effort might serve as an example for other efforts of the same kind.  In order to make it apparent at a glance how the Pentateuch has been formed, by the combination and fusion of the earlier sets of documents, M. Lenornant undertook to publish a translation from the Hebrew, in which he distinguishes the extracts from the respective sets of documents by different kinds of type.  Thus one has before one the natural explanation of the way in which all the episodes in Genesis are presented in the two parallel versions, sometimes juxtaposed, sometimes mingled.

at least if not for himself, for his wife and children, and if his wife is religious ought he to abandon the education of his children to her?

We believe it is the duty of the head of a household to rear his family in the ideas in which he believes. Whatever

Father's duty in regard to religious instruction. solution of the religious problem he may have attained, he ought to hide it from no one, and in especial not from his family. Moreover, even if he should wish to keep his opinions secret, he would be unable to do so, at least for the whole of his life. His dissimulation would simply result in such an association in the minds of his children between moral precepts and religious dogmas that the chances would be that they would stand, or rather fall, together. Of all people in the world the child is precisely the one who is likely to suffer most from a belief that religion and morality are inseparably bound up together. Of all human beings children are least philosophical, least metaphysical, least familiar with scientific ideas, and therefore of all others the most easily biassed once for all by the inculcation of false or doubtful notions presented as certain. In China, at the periodical conferences, certain mandarins dilate upon the following theme in the presence of the more notable among the inhabitants: "Do your duty as a citizen and beware of religion." That is precisely what a father ought to say again and again to his children. It is a good principle of education to take it for granted that the child is rational, and to treat it as such, in order ultimately and gradually to develop the spirit of reason in it. What a child lacks is much less intensity of attention than continuity. Very often among country people, and almost always among inferior races (as also among animals), the young are more wide-awake, more curious, more quick-minded than the mature men; but their attention must be seized in transit; teaching them resembles teaching a bird on the wing. Their schoolmaster must have the gifts of a bird-fancier; and it is his fault much oftener than the child's if the latter does not understand, does not ask questions, is inert and incurious. The scientific education of the child should begin with its first question; truth is a debt that one owes to it, and truth accessible to its intelligence. The moment a child asks a question out of its own head, it is at least in part prepared to understand the reply ; the duty of the person interrogated is to reply, as fully and as truly as he believes the child capable of understanding, and if he leaves gaps he must at least never fill them with lies. It is so easy to tell the child to wait until it is bigger. There should be no fear of precociously developing the child's reason in its two essential forms, the instinct of inquiry, of *why* and *how*, and the instinct of perception, of logical cogency in the reply to the "why " and " how." One need not be afraid that the child will fatigue its brain by abstract reasoning ; Pascals are rare. The danger does not lie in a premature development of the reason, which it is always easy moreover to check, but in a premature development of the sensibility. The child must not be encouraged to feel too strongly. To subject it to vain fears such as those of hell and the devil, or to beatific visions and mystic enthusiasms such as young girls experience at the time of the first communion, is to do it much greater harm than to teach it to reason justly and to develop in it a certain intelligent virility. Races become effeminate by excess of sensibility, never by excess of scientific and philosophic power.

It will perhaps be said, with Rousseau, that if the child is not to be trammelled with religious prejudice it may at least

Impossible to leave the child in ignorance. wait for reasoned instruction on religion until it has attained its intellectual maturity. We reply that it is impossible to do so in the present state of society. If the father does not teach his child it will absorb the prejudices of those it associates with, and to disabuse it of them afterward will demand a veritable crisis, which is always painful and often the cause of permanent suffering. The great art of education should consist precisely in avoiding crises of this sort in the orderly growth of the intellect. The father who postpones the decisive moment will be the first person to be surprised at the amount of pain he will be obliged to subject his child to in order to root up the error which he has placidly permitted to grow under his very eyes.

M. Littré has given an account of a case of conscience of this kind ; after having voluntarily held aloof from the religious education of his daughter till she had reached years of discretion, he found her at last so sincerely convinced, so completely fashioned by religion for religion, that he recoiled before so thorough-going a change; like a surgeon whose hand should tremble at the thought of an operation upon a body that love had rendered sacred to him ; like an oculist who should feel that light was not worth the pain that he would have to inflict on eyes that were dear to him. The intellectual operator has not at his command even the resource of chloroform; he must practise his surgery upon a subject who is fully conscious and even excited by attention and reflection. Prevention is better than expectant treatment, which allows the disease to develop in the hopes of curing it afterward. The competent educator, like the competent physician, may be known by his ability in avoiding the necessity of operations. It is a mistake to allow a child to grow up in complete belief in religious legends, with the intention of undeceiving it afterward. It will be undeceived not without regret nor without effort. And often the effort put forth will itself be too great, will overshoot itself, and from excess of faith the child will pass at a bound to sceptical indifference and will suffer for it. Treasures in heaven are treasures in fiat money ; the disappointment which must some day come, when one learns the truth, will be bitter. It would be better always to have known that one was poor. A child may early be accustomed to the conception of the infinite; it makes up its account with it as with the notion of the antipodes, or of the absence of an absolute up and down in the universe. The first sensation one experiences when one learns that the earth is spherical is of terror, a fear of the void, of tumbling off into the abyss of open space. The same naïve fear lies at the bottom of the religious sentiment in certain minds, and is due to factitious associations of ideas which are a matter of education wholly. A fish born in an aquarium becomes accustomed to its habitat, as the ancients were accustomed to the inverted crystal ball of the heavens; it would be

*One must begin early.*

lost in the ocean. Birds reared in the cage often die if they are abruptly given their liberty. A period of transition is always necessary, one needs time to become accustomed to intellectual expanses as well as to expanses of air and water. If mankind is to live without religion it must receive a non-religious education, and this education will spare it a great deal of the suffering that those who have been educated in the faith and have subsequently broken away by their own efforts have undergone. The wood-cutter's child experiences no sentiment of fear in the solitude and obscurity of the forest, in the arched lanes and alleys, among the trees among which it was born. A town-born child would feel lost in such a place and would begin to cry. The world of science, with its shadowy labyrinths and limitless extent and its numberless obstacles which must be removed one at a time, is such a forest; the child who is born in it will not be frightened, will live in it always happily.

Of all the problems of education which lie on the borders of religious metaphysics the most interesting is, unquestionably, what to say to the child about death and human destiny. When these questions are discussed before him, is a rational and truly philosophical method to be employed? Is he to be informed dogmatically, or is it a matter of indifference what is said to him? This problem has been discussed, in the "Critique philosophique," by M. Louis Ménard, who deals with the hypothetical case of a child that has lost its mother and is cross-questioning its father. That is ingenious, but it is a specious way of raising the problem. When a young child loses its mother we regard it as the first duty of the father to console and spare its delicate organism the strain of all strong emotions. The question is one of moral hygiene, in which philosophy and religion are not concerned, in which the age and temperament of the child are the sole things to consider. Truth is not equally valuable at all periods of life; one does not tell a man abruptly that his wife has just died. The most convinced materialist will hesitate to announce to a nervous child that it will never see its mother again. But the materialist in question would always do wrong to put forth a categorical affirmation in a case in which there exists at best nothing more than probabilities; the most dangerous method of deception is to present as a recognized certainty what is really nothing of the kind. In any event there is one form of immortality, that of memory, and that species of immortality we may ourselves secure by implanting it in the mind of the child.[1] The father ought repeatedly to talk to the orphan child of the dead mother. He can create a recollection in the child as vivid and as detailed as his own ; whether the child behaves well or ill he can always say, " If your mother were but here ! " The child will thus become accustomed to find a recompense or a punishment in its mother's approbation or disapprobation.[2]

To raise the problem more fairly, let us suppose the circumstances somewhat less tragic than those which M. Ménard

Should talk with child as with a grown person. has chosen, and let us ask how, in general, the child must be spoken to about death. When the child is capable of following a more or less complex bit of exposition, toward the age of ten or twelve for example, I confess that I see no reason why its questions should not be answered exactly as if they were those of a grown person. At that age it will no longer believe in fairies, it will no longer need to believe in legends, not even in those of Christianity. The scientific and philosophic spirit will have begun to develop and must not be either checked or distorted. If its intelligence leads it toward philosophical problems, so much the better ; one must meet its need as simply as if the problems in question were historical. I have seen a child much tormented by a desire to know whether such and such an historical personage died a natural death or was poisoned. The child was told that the thing was doubtful, but

---

[1] " Memory is no doubt an affliction for the grown man much more than for the child, but it is also a consolation. Cultivation of one's memories supplies powerful means of moral education for all ages, and for nations as well as for individuals. It was quite to be expected that we should find an ancestor worship in the early history of every people." (Felix Henneguy, *Critique philosophique*, 8th year, vol. ii. p. 218.)

[2] *Ibid.*

that the probability was so and so. The same method should be pursued in reference to more important problems.

But how, it may be asked, is one to form replies, that the child can understand, to questions which relate to the life

No difficulty in making the child understand.

beyond the grave? Is not the sole language that it understands that of Christianity, which deals with men raised to heaven, with happy souls seated among the angels and the seraphim, etc? We reply that people in general seem to have a strange conception of the child's intelligence; they expect it to understand the most refined subtleties of grammar, the most unexpected turns and shifts of theology, and are afraid to say a word to it of philosophy. A little girl of twelve years, of my acquaintance, replied with much ingenuity to this unexpected question: What is the difference between a perfect and an imperfect Christian? It was evident that she would not have experienced greater difficulty in replying to a metaphysical question. I recollect having myself followed, at the age of eight, a discussion on the immortality of the soul; nay, I even pronounced an interior judgment in favour of him who was maintaining the cause of immortality. Our system of education is full of contradictions, which consist at once in mechanically burdening the child's memory with things it cannot understand, and in depriving its intelligence of subjects in which it might take an interest. "But," M. Ménard will object, "a child must not be put into a position of being able to oppose its father's belief to that of its mother or of its grandmother." Why not? It happens, necessarily, every day. There are, on all subjects, incessantly going on in the bosom of the family a series of discussions, of small disagreements which in nowise fundamentally disturb the harmony of the household; why should it be otherwise when more important and uncertain questions simply are involved? "But the child will lose respect for its parents." It is certainly better that it should lose respect for them than that it should believe everything they say, even when they deceive it. Happily, respect for one's parents is not at all the same thing as belief in their infallibility. Children early make use of liberty of judgment, they may early be taught to sift out the truth from a mass of more or less contradictory affirmations, their judgment may be developed instead of being supplied, as is at present attempted, ready and completely made. The essential thing is to avoid rousing their passions and converting them into fanatics. The child needs an atmosphere of calm for the harmonious development of its faculties ; it is a delicate plant that must not be too soon exposed to wind and weather ; but it does not follow that it should be kept in the obscurity or half light of religious legend. The sole means of sparing the child the trouble of passion and fanaticism is to place it outside of all religious communion and to habituate it to examine things coolly, philosophically ; to take problems of religion for what they are ; that is to say, for problems simply, with ambiguous solutions.[1] Nothing serves better to awake the intellectual spontaneity of the child than to say to it : This is what I believe, and these are my reasons for believing it ; I may be wrong. Your mother, or such and such a person, believes something else for certain other reasons, right or wrong. The child acquires thus a rare quality, that of tolerance ; its respect for its parents attaches to the diverse doctrines that it sees them professing ; it learns, in its earliest years, that every sincere and reasoned belief is in the highest degree respectable. I am intimately acquainted with a child that has been reared in this way, and it has never had any occasion for anything but satisfaction with the education it has received. It has never been presented on the subject of human destiny, or the destiny of the world, with any opinion in the nature of an article of faith ; instead of religious certitudes it has heard only of metaphysical possibilities and

---

[1] Among the greatest causes of difficulty with a child, let us note the following : the father is apt to be a free-thinker, the mother a Catholic. It hears every day at Church that those who do not practise their religious duties will go to hell : the child therefore reasons that if its father dies it will never see him again, unless it goes to hell with him, and then it will never see its mother again. A full and complete belief in annihilation would be less painful and less annoying than this belief in eternal damnation. Add that in this respect many Protestant clergymen, in especial in England and in the United States, are not less intolerant than Catholic priests.

probabilities. Toward the age of thirteen and a half the problem of the destiny of mankind was abruptly suggested to it; the death of a very dear aged relative caused it to do more thinking than is customary at that age, but its philosophic beliefs proved themselves sufficient. They still are sufficient, although the child in question has been obliged several times to face the possibility, and the immediate possibility, of its own death. I cite the example as an experiment which bears on the question under discussion.

How then should death be spoken of to a child? I reply confidently, as one would speak of it to a grown person,

Summary.

allowing for the difference between abstract and concrete language. I naturally suppose the child to be semi-rational, more than ten years old, and capable of thinking of something else than its top or its doll. I believe it should then be talked with openly, and told what we ourselves think most probable on these terrible questions. The free-thinker who leans toward naturalistic doctrines will say to his son or his daughter that he believes death to be a resolution of the person into its constituent elements, a return to a blind material existence, a fresh beginning in the perpetual round of evolution; that all that we leave behind is the good that we have done and that we live in humanity by our good actions and our good thoughts, and that immortality is productivity for the best interests of humanity. The spiritualist will say that, owing to the distinction between the soul and the body, death is simply a deliverance. The pantheist or the monist will repeat the formula consecrated by the use of three thousand years: *Tat tvam asi*—Thou art that; and the modern child will recognize, as the young Brahman does, that beneath the surface of things there lies a mysterious unity into which the individual may fade. Finally the Kantian will endeavour to make his child understand that the conception of duty involves something anterior and superior to the present life; that to be aware of the moral law is to be conscious of immortality. Everyone will say what he believes, and take care not to pretend that his opinion is the absolute truth. The child, thus treated like a human being, will early learn to make up its own mind, to provide itself with a creed without having received it from any traditional religion or any immutable doctrine; it will learn that a really sacred belief is one which is reflective and reasoned and seemingly personal; and if at times, as it advances in age, it experiences a greater or less anxiety about the unknown, so much the better; such an anxiety, when the senses are not involved and thought alone is concerned, is in no sense dangerous. The child who experiences it will be of the stuff out of which philosophers and sages are made.

# CHAPTER VI.

## RELIGION AND NON-RELIGION AMONG WOMEN.

Are women inherently predisposed toward religion and even toward superstition?—The nature of feminine intelligence—Predominance of the imagination—Credulity—Conservatism—Feminine sensibility—Predominance of sentiment—Tendency to mysticism—Is the moral sentiment among women based upon religion?—Influence of religion and of non-religion upon modesty and love—Origin of modesty—Love and perpetual virginity —M. Renan's paradoxes on the subject of monastic vows—How woman's natural proclivities may be turned to account by freethought—Influence exercised by the wife's faith over the husband—Instance of a conversion to free-thought.

AMONG free-thinkers themselves there are a certain number who believe that women are by the very nature of their minds devoted to superstition and to myth. Is the incapacity of the female mind for philosophy more demonstrable than that of the child's mind to which it has so frequently been compared?

We are not obliged to decide the question whether women's mental powers are or are not inferior to those of men.[1] We are obliged to consider only whether the limits of female intelligence are so tightly drawn that religion, and even superstition, are for it inevitable. Those who maintain that women are in some sort condemned to error argue from certain essential elements in

Woman's attention to details.

[1] As a general rule, Darwin says, men go farther than women, whether the matter be one of profound meditation, of reason, or imagination, or simply of the use of the senses or even of the hands. According to certain statistical investigations it appears that the modern female brain has remained almost stationary, while the male brain has developed notably. The brain of a Parisian woman is no larger than that of a Chinese woman, and the Parisian woman labours under the additional disadvantage of possessing a larger foot.

Admitting these facts one may still refuse to infer from them the existence of a congenital incapacity, for the way in which women have always been treated by men and the education that they have received may well have left results which have

her character; let us examine accordingly the peculiarity of her intelligence and of her sensibility. The female mind, it has been said, is less abstract than that of the male; women are more impressionable on the side of the senses and of the imagination, are more readily appealed to by what is beautiful and striking and coloured: thence arises their need for myths, for symbols, for a cult, for rites that speak to the eye. We reply that this need is not absolute: are not Protestant women content with a cult which does not appeal to the senses? And in any event, an imaginative spirit is not necessarily superstitious. Superstition is a matter of education, not of nature; there is a certain maturity of mind which lends no encouragement to superstition. I have known a number of women who did not possess one superstition among them and were incapable of acquiring one; there was no distinction in this respect to be observed between their intelligence and that of a man; the conception of the world as an orderly succession of phenomena, once really accepted by the human mind, maintains itself by its own power, without aid from without, as the fact in the long run always does.

become hereditary. The education of women has in all times been less strenuous than that of men ; and their mind, perhaps naturally less scientific, has never been developed by direct contact with the external world. In the Orient and in Greece, among the nations from whom we derive our civilization, women (at least in families in easy circumstances) were always restricted to a subordinate rôle, confined to woman's quarters, or withdrawn from all direct contact with the real world. Thence arose a sort of tradition of ignorance and intellectual abasement which has been handed down to us. There is nothing like the brain of a young girl reared at home for gathering to itself completely, and without loss, the whole residue of middle-class silliness, of naïve and self-satisfied prejudice, of strutting ignorance that does not see itself as others see it, of superstition transformed into a rule of conduct. But change the education and you will in a great measure change these results. Even according to Darwin's own theory, education and heredity can in the long run undo anything that they have done. Even if there should remain a certain balance of intelligence in favor of the male, even if the female should prove to be in the end, as Darwin says, incapable of pushing invention as far in advance as man, it would not follow that her heart and intelligence should be filled with another order of ideas and sentiments than those which are beneficial to men. It is one thing to invent and to widen the domain of science, and another thing to assimilate the knowledge already acquired ; it is one thing to widen the intellectual horizon, and another thing to adapt one's eyes and heart to this more open habitat.

A second trait of female intelligence, which has also been made use of, is its credulity—by which religion has so largely profited. Women are more credulous than men,

**Female credulity.** in this sense : they possess a certain confidence in men, whom they recognize as stronger and more widely experienced than themselves; they willingly believe whatever grave men, whom they are accustomed to venerate, men like priests, assert. Their credulity is thus in a great part a mere form of their natural need to lean on some member of the opposite sex. Conceive a religion originated and administered solely by women ; it would be looked upon with great distrust by women, in general. The day men cease to believe, female credulity—in especial that of the average woman, who is accustomed to judge with the eyes and intelligence of someone else—will be profoundly affected. I once asked a maid who had remained thirty years in the same house what were her beliefs. "Those of my master," she replied ; her master was an atheist. The same question was put to the wife of a member of the Institute. She replied: "I was a Catholic until I was married. After I was married I began to appreciate the superiority of my husband's mind, I saw that he did not believe in religion, and I ceased to believe in it entirely myself."

A third trait of the feminine character is its conservativeness, its friendliness to tradition, its indisposition to initiative. Respect for power and authority, Spencer says,

**Female conservatism.** predominates in women, influences their ideas and sentiments in regard to all institutions, and tends to strengthen political and ecclesiastical governments. For the same reason women are particularly inclined to put faith in whatever is imposing; doubt, criticism, a disposition to question whatever is established is rare among them, Mr. Spencer thinks. Women certainly do possess a more conservative disposition than men in religion and in politics ; it has been so found in England where women vote on municipal questions, and in our judgment the rôle that woman should play in this world is precisely that of conservatism ; as a young girl, she must guard her person as a treasure, must be always suspicious of she knows not precisely what; then as a wife she must watch over her child, her house, her husband; must preserve, retain, defend, embrace somebody or something. Is it a thing to be complained of? Is it not to this instinct that we owe our life, and if difference in sex, or sexual functions, involves grave differences in character, must we conclude from this fact that women possess an irremediable civil and religious incapacity? No; conservatism may be of service in the ranks of truth as in the ranks of error; all depends on what is given to conserve. If women are more philosophically and scientifically educated, their conservatism may do good service.

A final trait of the feminine mind, very like the preceding, is that women are more given to an absorption in detail, are less courageous, are more capable of dealing with particular details than with general ideas and things as a whole, and are more inclined to narrow and literal interpretations than men. If a woman, for example, is intrusted with any administrative office she will execute every rule to the letter with an exaggerated conscientiousness and a naïve anxiety. The conclusion is that women will always lend comfort to literal religions and to superstitious practices. In our opinion this penchant for minutiæ and for scrupulousness which is so frequently observed among women may become, on the contrary, an important factor of incredulity when women are sufficiently instructed to perceive at first hand the innumerable contradictions and ambiguities of the texts they are dealing with. An enlightened scruple is a keener instrument of doubt than of faith.

Female timidity.

We confess we do not yet see that the differences, native or acquired, between the male and the female brain suffice to constitute women a sort of inferior caste, devoted by their birth to religion and the service of myth, while men are reserved for science and philosophy.

Let me now examine the more profound reasons based on the nature of women's sentimental proclivities. In general, it is said that women are dominated not by reason but by sentiment. They respond quickly to a call made in the name of pity or of charity, and not so quickly to one made in the name of equity. But is sentiment the exclusive possession of

**Is sentiment a badge of servitude to error?**

religions? And are there not also men of sentiment as well as men of thought? And are the first on that account condemned to a life of error while the second live in the presence of the truth?

But it is insisted that in women sentiment naturally tends toward mysticism. Among the Greeks, Spencer says, the

**Women and mysticism.**

women were more accessible than the men to religious excitation.[1] It may be replied that the greatest mystics have not been women. St. Theresas have been much less numerous than men like Plotinus (it was Plotinus who first gave the word ἔκστασις its current sense), Porphyry, Iamblicus, Dionysius the Areopagite, St. Bonaventure, Gerson, Richard de Saint Victor, Eckhart, Tauler, Swedenborg. Mysticism develops in proportion to the restriction of the individual's activity. Women's life, which is less active than that of men, allows more space for the development of mystic impulses and exercises of piety. But activity cures the diseases of contemplation, in especial of vain and empty contemplation in which only average and ignorant minds can take delight. Woman's religious activity will diminish in proportion as a wider field of activity is opened up to her, and in proportion as an intellectual and æsthetic education is supplied to her and she becomes interested in all the human questions and realities of this world. It has been desired even to render political life accessible to woman, to restore to her the rights which have hitherto been denied her. M. Secrétan has recently advocated this measure, which was formerly advo-

---

[1] Sir Rutherford Alcock says also, that in Japan it is very rare to see any other worshippers in the temples than women and children ; the men are always extremely few in number and belong to the lower classes. At least five-sixths and often nine-tenths of the pilgrims who come to the temple of Juggernaut are women. Among the Sikhs the women are said to believe in more gods than the men. These examples, borrowed as they are from different races, and at different epochs, show sufficiently, in Spencer's opinion, that, when we find an analogous state of things in Catholic countries, and even in some measure in England, we are not to attribute it solely to the education of women ; the cause, he thinks, is deeper, lies in their nature. (See Spencer's *Study of Sociology.*)

cated by John Stuart Mill.   To do so at the present moment would be to hand over politics directly to the priesthood, who at present control women.   But when by gradual degrees women's religious emancipation shall have been completed, it is possible that a certain political emancipation may be the natural consequence of it.   Her civil emancipation in any event is only a matter of time.   The equality of women before the law is a necessary consequence of democratic ideas.   When they shall be forced thus to occupy themselves more actively in the affairs of this world the new employment of their energy will protect them more and more from mystical tendencies.

If an opportunity be given them to influence society they will no doubt exercise it philanthropically.   Well, pity is one of the most powerful derivatives of mysticism.   Even among religious orders it has been remarked how much less exalted the devotion of the members of the philanthropic orders is than of those who restrict themselves to sterile meditation in the cloister.

If mysticism is no more truly indispensable to women than to men, can it be maintained that their moral sentiment is incapable of subsistence apart from some religion?

*Female moral sentiment.*   Is women's moral power less than that of men, and is it only in religion that they can find the additional increment of strength of which they are in need? Resistance to physical or moral pain supplies a sufficiently exact measure of power.   Well, women show in maternity, with all its consequences, in pregnancy, in childbirth, in nursing, accompanied as it is by continual watchfulness and care, a patience of physical pain which is perhaps greater than anything that the average man is capable of.   Just so in respect to patience of moral pain : women may suffer much from poverty, and sadness follows the flying needle, but love and pity are the great sources of restraint.   As the sphere of her intelligence widens, a large field will be supplied for the exercise of women's power of love which is so highly developed.   The genuine remedy for every kind of suffering is increased activity of mind, which means increased instruction.   Action is always an anodyne of pain.   Therein lies the explanation of the power of charity to calm personal suffering, which is always in some degree egoistic. The best way to console one's self, for women and men alike, will always be to minister to someone else; hope revives in a heart which gives hope to others. Pains become gentle as they become fertile in beneficence, and productivity is an appeasement.

And finally, by way of compensation, there are other respects in which women would suffer perhaps less than men from the disappearance of religious beliefs. Women live more completely in the present than men do, they are somewhat bird-like in their composition, and forget the tempest the instant it is passed. Women laugh as easily as they cry, and their laughter soon dries their tears: they are to be forgiven for at least one aspect of this divine levity. Moreover they have their household, all the tender and practical preoccupations of life, which absorb them more completely, heart and soul, than men. A woman's happiness is probably complete the instant she believes herself to be beautiful and feels that she is loved; a man's happiness is a much more complex product and contains a much larger number of intellectual elements. Women live more wholly within the limits of their own generation than men, and experience a sort of contemporary immortality in the hearts of those they love.

*Best side of female levity.*

Among the most developed sentiments of women there are two which constitute the strength of their disposition to propriety: modesty, the dignity of their sex, and love, which is exclusive when it is true. But for these two powerful causes religious motives would always have weighed lightly with her. If religion exercises a great control over women, it is by taking possession of these two motives: the surest means of making women listen, and almost the sole means, is to awaken their love, or to appeal to their modesty: to give themselves or to refuse themselves are the two great acts which dominate their lives, and immorality among them generally increases directly with the diminution of their modesty. Thence arises a new and delicate problem, whether modesty, that compound of power and grace, is not

*Modesty and love.*

rather a religious than a moral virtue, and if religion has maintained it, would it not disappear with the disappearance of religion, and be enfeebled by a religion increasingly scientific and, in a sense, positive ? Note in the first place, that if the essence of all feminine virtue is modesty, as of all male virtue it is courage, that very fact constitutes an additional reason for doing everything in one's power to make modesty independent of religion, in order that it may stand unaffected by the doubts which necessarily, in the modern world, will overwhelm the latter. Certainly modesty is capable of serving remarkably well as a safeguard for beliefs, and even for irrational beliefs ; it always prevents one from pushing reason, as from pushing desire to the end, but there is a true and a false, a useful and a harmful modesty. The first, as we shall see, is not bound up with religion, either in its origin or in its destiny.

In the first place is modesty of religious origin ? Every young girl feels vaguely that she has at her disposal a treasure which a number of people desire. This sentiment, which

Origin of modesty.

is confused with some obscure consciousness of sex, was necessary to enable the female to attain complete physical development before giving herself. Precocious immodesty must inevitably, in effect has, resulted in an arrested development. It might easily have produced also a comparative sterility. Modesty is thus a guarantee for the continuance of the species, one of the sentiments that natural selection must inevitably have tended to preserve and to increase. It is a condition, moreover, of sexual selection ; if the female had been disposed to give herself indiscriminately, the species would have suffered. Happily desire is checked by modesty, an obstacle which it can remove only on condition of the woman's being strongly attracted by the object desired ; a quality which will subsequently be transmissible to the species. From the point of view of sexual selection there is in modesty a great deal of coquetry—a coquetry which is unaware of its aim, which is half unconscious, and often mistakes for a duty what is really but a bit of management. The art of provisional refusal, and of attractive flight, must inevitably have attained a high development among superior beings, for it is a power-ful medium of seduction and selection. Modesty has de-veloped side by side with it, and really constitutes but a fugitive moment in the eternity of female coquetry. Coquetry originates in the young girl who is yet too ignorant to be really modest, but too much of a woman not to love to attract and to retreat ; and at the other extreme it constitutes the last remnant of modesty in women who really possess none. Finally, modesty is also composed largely of an element of fear, which has been very useful in the preservation of the race. Among animals the female almost always runs some risk in the presence of the male, which is generally stronger than she ; love-making is not only a crisis but a danger, and she must mollify the male before surrendering herself to him, must seduce him before satisfying him. Even in the human race, in primitive times, women were not always safe from violence from men. Modesty secures a sort of expectant love which was necessary in primitive times, a proof, a period of mutual scrutiny. Lucretius has remarked that children, by their weakness and by their fragility, have contributed to the softening of human manners ; the same remark applies to women and to this sense of their own comparative weakness, which they experience so acutely in modesty, and which they to some degree communicate to men. Women's fears and scruples have made man's hand less hard ; their modesty has given rise in him to a certain form of respect, to a form of desire which is less brutal and more gentle; they have civilized love. Modesty is analogous to the species of fright that inclines a bird to flee one's caresses, which bruise it. One's very look possesses some element of hardness for a bird; and is it not a prolongation of touch ? In addition to these various elements there goes, to the composition of a young girl's or a young man's modesty, a higher and more properly human element ; the fear of love itself, the fear of something new and unknown, of the profound and powerful instinct which is awakening in one after having up to that time lain asleep, which abruptly arises in one and struggles for dominance with the other forces and impulses of one's being. The young man, unaccustomed as yet to submit to the domination of this instinct, finds in it something stranger and more mysterious than in any other ; *c'est l'interrogation anxieuse de cherubin.*[1]

To sum up, the sentiment of modesty neither originates in religion nor depends upon it ; it is only very indirectly allied to

**Religious education and modesty.** it. Even from the point of view of modesty a religious education is not above reproach. Among Protestants, is the reading of the Bible always a good school? M. Bruston has contended for the propriety of reading the Songs of Songs in an epoch like ours when marriages are often made out of interest rather than of inclination ; and indeed we agree with him that the reading of the Song of Songs does tend to develop certain inclinations in young girls, but hardly an inclination to a regular and complicated church marriage. Among Catholics how many indiscreet questions the confessor puts to the young girl ! How many prohibitions, as dangerous in their way as suggestions ! And even in the item of modesty excess is a defect ; a little wholesome liberty in education and manners would do no harm. Catholic education sometimes distorts the woman's mind by making it too different from that of the man, and by accustoming it to a perpetual timidity and discomposure in the presence of the being with whom she must pass her life, and by rendering her modesty somewhat too indeterminate and savage, and converting it into a sort of religion.

There is also sometimes manifest a sort of perversion of modesty in the mystical tendencies of woman, which are

**True modesty.** especially strong at the age of puberty. These tendencies, exploited by the priesthood, give rise to convents and cloisters. A Catholic education too often constitutes for young girls a sort of moral mutilation ; one endeavours to keep them virgins, and one succeeds in converting them into imperfect women. Religions are too inclined

---

[1] Shame is usually regarded as constituting the essence of modesty, but shame can have been but one of the elements in its formation ; such shame as actually exists is readily explicable as a sense of the uncleanness attaching, in especial in the case of the woman (of whom the Hebrews required a periodic purification), to certain animal functions. But modesty must have been developed also by the use of clothing and the growth of the habit of covering, first the loins and then more and

to consider the union of the sexes under I know not what mystical aspect, and, from the point of view of morals, as a stain. Certainly purity is a power ; it is with a little diamond point that mountains, and even continents, are nowadays pierced, but Christianity has confounded chastity with purity. True purity is that of love, true chastity is chastity of heart ; chastity of heart survives chastity of body, and stops at the point beyond which it would become a restriction, an obstacle to the free development of the entire being. An eunuch or a young man studying for the priesthood may well be destitute of chastity ; the smile of a young girl at the thought of her fiancé may be infinitely more virginal than that of a nun. Nothing moreover stains the mind like a too exclusive preoccupation with the things of the body ; incessant attention to them necessarily evokes a chain of immodest imagery. St. Jerome in his desert, believing, as he relates, that he saw the Roman courtesans dancing naked in the moonlight, was less pure in heart and brain than Socrates unceremoniously paying a visit to Theodora. A too self-conscious modesty is immodest. The whole grace of virginity is ignorance ; the instant virginity becomes aware of itself it is tarnished ; virginity, like certain fruits, can only be preserved by a process of desiccation. Love and sunshine transform the universe. Modesty is simply a coat of mail which presupposes a state of war between the sexes, and aims at preventing a blind promiscuity ; the mutual self-abandonment of love is more chaste than the modest inquietude and the immodest suspicion which precede it ; there grows up between two people who love each other a sort of confidence that results in their neither wishing nor being able to keep back anything from each other ; self-constraint, suspicion, consciousness of antagonism of interest, all disappear. This is assuredly the characteristic of the most perfect form of reunion that can exist in this world ;

more of the entire person ; and indeed the development of modesty and of the habit of wearing clothes must each have been aided by the other. The habit of going covered gives rise very soon to shame at being seen uncovered. The little negresses whom Livingstone supplied with shifts became, in a few days, so accustomed to having the upper half of their bodies hidden that, when they were surprised in their chambers in the morning, they hastily covered their breasts.

Plato believed that the human body is the prison of the spirit and cuts it off from immediate communication with its fellow-spirits ; paradoxical as it may seem, it is in love that the body becomes less opaque, and effaces itself, and soul communicates with soul. Nay, marriage itself preserves in women a sort of moral virginity, as one may recognize on the scarred and discoloured hands of old women the white line that has been protected for thirty years, by the wedding ring, against the wear and tear of life.

Modesty is a sentiment which has survived, as we have seen, because it was useful to the propagation of the species ; mysticism perverts and corrupts it and enlists it precisely against the propagation of the species.

M. Renan on celibacy.

Between a Carmelite nun and a courtesan like Ninon de Lenclos the sociologist might well hesitate ; socially they are almost equally worthless, their lives are almost equally miserable and vain ; the excessive macerations of the one are as foolish as the pleasures of the other ; the moral desiccation of the one is often not without some analogy to the corruption of the other. Vows or habits of perpetual chastity, the monastic life itself, have found in our days an unexpected defender in M. Renan. It is true he does not regard such matters from the point of view of Christianity. If he has a word to say in favour of perpetual chastity, it is strictly in the name of physiological induction ; he considers chastity simply as a means of heightening the capacity of the brain and of increasing one's intellectual fertility. He does not absolutely blame impurity, he delights in a sense, as he himself says, in the joys of the debauchee and the courtesan ; he possesses the boundless curiosity and the accomplished impudicity of the man of science. But he believes that there exists a sort of intellectual antinomy between complete intellectual development and bodily love. The true man of science should concentrate his entire vitality in his brain, should devote his life to abstractions and chimeras; by this reservation of his entire strength for the service of his head, his intelligence will flower in double blossoms, the monstrous beauty of which, produced by the transformation of stamens into petals, is the achievement of sterility. Love is a heavy tax to pay for the vanities of the world, and in the budget of the human race women count almost exclusively on the side of expense. Science, economical of time and force, should teach one to disembarrass one's self of women and love, and to leave such futilities to the drones. These paradoxes that M. Renan puts forth rest on a well-known scientific fact: that the most intelligent species are those in which reproduction is least active; fertility, generally speaking, varies inversely to cerebral energy. But love must not quite be confounded with sexual activity, unless one is to draw the somewhat strange conclusion that among animals hares are those who are best acquainted with love, and among men Frenchmen are those who know least of it. From the fact that excessive commerce with the other sex paralyses the intelligence, it does not in the least follow that the sentiment of love produces the same effect and that one's intellectual power diminishes with the growth of one's heart.

We believe that love may be sufficiently defended on intellectual as well as on moral grounds. If it in certain respects involves an expense of force, it in others so heightens the entire vital energy, that the expense must be regarded as one of those fruitful investments which are inseparable from the very continuance of life. To live, after all, in the physical as well as in the moral sense of the word, is not only to receive but to give, but above all to give one's self to love; it is difficult to pervert one of the most primitive elements of the human character, without also perverting the heart and the intelligence. Love is above all things a stimulant to the entire being and to the brain itself; it takes possession of the whole man; it plays upon man as upon a harp and sounds the whole compass of his being. It cannot be replaced by coffee or hasheesh. Women not only complete men, and form by union with them a more complete, more rounded existence, more justly epitomizing the possibilities of life; they are capable also, by their mere presence, by their mere smile, of doubling our individual powers and carrying them to the highest point of energy of

Love a cerebral stimulant.

which they are capable. Our manhood leans upon their grace. All other motives which inspire man—love of reputation, of glory, even of God—are slight as compared with the love of a woman who understands her rôle. Even the most abstract passion, the passion for science, often fails to acquire its entire strength until it has called to its aid the love of a woman, which wrings a smile out of the grave alembics and fills the crucibles with the gaiety of hope. Nothing is simple in our being ; all things amalgamate and unite together. They who invented the monk aimed at simplifying human life ; they succeeded only in unnaturally complicating it or mutilating it.

But love does not only play, in the life of the man of science and of the thinker, the rôle of stimulant ; over and above its function in inciting such men to work, it contributes indirectly to rectify the product of their labours. Love lives in reality, and to live in reality helps one to think justly. Rightly to understand the world in which we live, we must not dwell beyond its bounds, must not make a world of our own, an unnatural and frigid world, rounded by the walls of a monastery. "To aim at being an angel is to be a beast," says Pascal ; and not only to be a beast, but in a measure to brutalize one's self, to dim the precision and vivacity of one's intelligence. A complete acquaintance with the details of the lives of great minds would reveal surprising traces of love in the audacity and sweep of great metaphysical and cosmological hypotheses, in profound generalizations, in passionate exactitude of demonstration. Love reaches everywhere ; and as the philosopher who is also a lover pushes audaciously forward in the domain of thought, he moves more easily, more lightly, more confidently, with a heightened faith in himself, in others, and in this mysterious and mute universe. Love inspires one with that gentleness of heart which inclines one to an interest in the smallest things and in their place in the universe. There is great kindliness in the heart of the true philosopher.

*Love makes for sanity.*

Then, too, what is science without art ? The most intimate relations exist between the intellectual and artistic faculties.[1]

[1] See the author's *Problèmes de l'esthétique contemporaine*, livre ii.

Could art exist without love? Love becomes, in matters of art, of the very tissue of thought. To compose verses or music, to paint or model, is simply to transmute love by diverse methods and into diverse forms. Whatever the more or less sincere defenders of the monastic spirit and religious mysticism may say, love, which is as old as the world, is not upon the point of quitting it ; and it is in the hearts and minds of the greatest of mankind that it dwells most securely. " Human frailty ! " someone will murmur. " No," we reply : " source of strength and strength itself." If love is the science of the ignorant it constitutes some part also of the science of the sage. Eros is of all the gods the one on whom Prometheus is most dependent, for it is from Eros that he steals the sacred flame. Eros will survive in every heart, and in especial in every woman's heart, when all religions shall have decayed.

*Love the essence of art.*

We may conclude, therefore, that the characteristic tendencies of woman may be employed in the services of truth, science, free-thought, and social fraternity. Everything depends on the education that is given her, and on the influence of the man whom she marries. Woman must be begun with in childhood. The life of a woman is more orderly and continuous than that of a man ; for that reason the habits of childhood exercise a more permanent influence over her. There is but one great revolution in a woman's life : marriage. And there are women for whom this revolution does not exist ; and there are others for whom it exists in its most attenuated form, as when, for example, the husband's manner of life and his beliefs are practically the same as those of the wife's mother and family. In a tranquil environment, such as the majority of women exist in, the influence of early education may persist to the end ; the small number of religious or philosophical ideas that were planted in a woman's brain in her childhood may be found there years afterward, practically unchanged. The home is a protection, a sort of hot-house in which plants flourish that could not live in the open air ; the film of glass or of veiling behind which women habitually stand to look out

*Importance of early education in woman.*

into the street does not protect them against sun and rain alone. A woman's soul, like her complexion, preserves something of its native whiteness.

In France, in the majority of instances, women are children up to the time of their marriage; and children inclined to regard the man to whom their parents wish them to give their hand with a certain mixture of fear and of respect. Such a woman's intelligence is almost as virgin as her body, and in the first months of marriage the husband may acquire, if he chooses, a decisive influence over his wife, model her as yet imperfectly developed brain almost to his will. If he waits, if he temporizes, he will find his task difficult—the more so as his wife will some day gain over him some such influence as he might at first have gained over her. The instant a woman becomes fully aware of her power, she almost always becomes the controlling influence in the household; if her husband has not formed her, if he has left her with all the prejudices and ignorances of a child, and often of a spoiled child, she will, in the course of time, form or rather deform him—will oblige him at first to tolerate, and ultimately to accept, her childish beliefs and errors, and perhaps in the end, profiting by the decline of his intelligence, with the coming on of old age, she will convert him, and by that fact retard the intellectual progress of the household by an entire generation. The priesthood positively count on the growing influence of the wife in every household; but they are helpless in the first months, or perhaps years, of marriage against the influence that the husband may exercise. And once fashioned by him the wife may continue to exist to the end of her life in his image, and to give him back his own ideas and instil them into his children.

*Husband responsible for wife's education.*

The free-thinker, it is true, labours under a great disadvantage in the work of conversion: a believer may always decline to reason; whenever an intellectual duel seems to him to be disadvantageous he may decline to fight; a high degree of indulgent tenacity and of prudence is necessary in a discussion with anyone who is thus ready to take refuge in flight at the slightest alarm.

*Free-thinker's difficulty.*

What can one do against a gentle and obstinate determination
to say nothing, to intrench one's self in ignorance, to allow
argument to shatter itself against an outer wall. "It seemed
to me," a Russian novelist cries, "as if all my words bounded
off her like peas shot at a marble statue." One of Shak-
spere's heroines proposes to essay matrimony as an exercise
of patience. If patience is, in the management of the household, the great virtue of the wife, the man's virtue should be
perseverance and active obstinacy in an effort to fashion and
create her to his desire and ideal. I once questioned a woman
who had married a free-thinker with a secret intention of converting him. The upshot of the matter was the precise opposite, and I quote below her own account, as she gave it to me,
of the successive phases of this moral crisis. It is of course only
an isolated example, but it may serve to illustrate the character
of women, and the more or less great facility with which they
may be made to accept scientific or philosophic ideas.

" The double aim of every Christian woman is to save souls,
in general, and to save her own in particular. To aid Christ,
**Wife's effort to** by bringing back into the fold the sheep who
**convert her hus-** have strayed away, is her great dream, and to
**band.** preserve her own purity is her constant preoccupation. When the moment came for me to try my
powers, a lively solicitude took possession of me : should I
really succeed in winning over the man to whom I was to
unite my life, or would he succeed in winning me over? Great
is the power of evil, and whoever exposes himself to temptation will perish, but if evil is powerful, God, I assured myself,
is still more powerful, and God never abandons those
who confide in him, and I confided in God. To convince the
incredulous who had systematized their incredulity into a
reasoned whole was no slight task, and I did not hope to
accomplish it in four and twenty hours. My plan was this : to
be faithful in the midst of the unfaithful, immutable and
confident in my religion which was the religion of the humble,
the simple, and the ignorant ; to do the utmost good possible,
according to the first of Christ's commandments ; to practise
my religion in silence but openly; to domesticate it in my house-

hold; to inaugurate a secret, slow, incessant combat which should last, if necessary, till the end of my life. And then to rely upon the infinite mercy of God.

"With this disposition of mind I had no difficulty in standing mute whenever my husband attacked my beliefs. My first object was to prove the uselessness of all discussion, the firmness of my faith. I knew perfectly well that I really was unable to reply, that he knew so much and I so little. But if I had only been a doctor of theology I would have accepted the challenge, I would have heaped up proof on proof! With the truth and God for me, how could I have been vanquished? But I was not in the least like a doctor of theology, and the result was that, fortified in my ignorance, I listened placidly to all his arguments, and the livelier, the more cogent they were, the more profoundly I was convinced of the truth of my religion, which stood erect under so much battering and triumphed in its immunity.

"I was inexpugnable, and the siege might have lasted long if my husband had not recognized the strength of my position and changed his tactics. His object was to force me to discuss, to follow his objections, to understand them in spite of myself, to turn them over in my own mind. He told me that it would be a help to him in his work if I should epitomize sometimes in writing, sometimes *viva voce*, a certain number of works on religion. He put into my hands M. Renan's 'Vie de Jésus,' M. Reville's wise and conscientious little book on 'L'Histoire du dogme de la divinité de Jésus Christ,' often full of abstract inquiries in which the sincerity of the author was evident and contagious, even when the reader was looking for sophisms.[1] I could not refuse to read the books without abandoning my most cherished ambition, which was to aid my husband in his work. My conscience was involved, and I could not consult my confessor because we

[1] "Among the polemical works on Christianity I shall cite one which is perhaps somewhat old, but precious, in that it sums up with great impartiality the whole mass of secular objections, including a large number of modern objections to Christianity, the book of M. Patrice Larroque, entitled *Examen critique des doctrines de la religion Chrétienne.*"

were then abroad; moreover my faith, although profound, had always been, or pretended to be, generous and enlightened. If I was ever to hand my religion on I must not be intolerant; and I read! M. Renan did not especially scandalize me, he was a follower of Jesus, writing of Jesus; his book, which has charmed many women as much as a romance, saddened me without repelling me. I was obliged to make a written abstract of the entire book and had to put myself into the author's place, to see things with his eyes, to think his thoughts; and, in spite of myself, I sometimes saw in my own heart, side by side with the impeccable and perfect Christ God, the figure of the imperfect, suffering, worn man, out of patience and cursing. The other books, which were much more abstract, called for a much greater effort on my part, but the very effort that I put forth constrained me more completely to assimilate their contents. Every day I lost ground, and my once passive faith became slowly transformed into an anxious desire to know, into a hope that a more complete knowledge would re-establish my broken defences.

" One day, my husband said to me abruptly: 'You will not refuse to read the Bible, which is the source of your religion, from one end to the other?' I acceded with pleasure, I did not wait for permission—I was beyond that; it seemed to me that to read the Bible must be the beginning of that profound knowledge which I envied my ideal doctor of theology. It was with trembling fingers that I opened the black-bound book, with its closely printed pages dictated by God Himself, alive still with the divine Word! I held in my hands the truth, the justification of human life, the keys of the future; it seemed to me that the tablets of Sinai had been committed to me as to the prostrate multitude of the Hebrews at the foot of the mountain, and I also would have kneeled humbly to receive it. But, as I made my way through the book, the immorality of certain pages seemed to me so evident that my whole heart rose in revolt against them. I had not been hardened from my childhood, as Protestant girls are, to all these tales. The Catholic education, which does what it can to keep the Sacred Books out of sight, seems to me in this respect, and only in this respect, much superior to the Protestant religion. In any event, it prepares one who reads the Bible for the first time in mature years to feel much more acutely the profound immorality of sacred history. Catholicism often perverts the intelligence; Protestantism might naturally go the length of perverting the heart. Unbelievers have often made the moral monstrosities in the Bible a subject of raillery; I felt nothing but indignation when I came across them, and I closed with disgust the book which I had so long regarded with respect.

"What should I think of it; what should I believe? The words of infinite love and charity which the New Testament contains came back to me. If God was anywhere He must be there, and once more I opened the sacred book—the book which has so often tempted humanity. After all, it was Christ that I had adored rather than the Lord of Hosts. My acquaintance had been almost wholly limited to the Gospel of St. John, which I had learned was of disputable authenticity. I read the Gospels from end to end. Even in St. John I could not find the model man above reproach, the incarnate God, the divine Word; in the very midst of the beauties and sublimities of the text, I myself began to perceive innumerable contradictions, naïvetés, superstitions, and moral failings. My beliefs no longer existed, I had been betrayed by my God, my whole previous intellectual life looked to me more and more like a dream. This dream had its beautiful aspects; even to-day I sometimes regret the consolation that it once afforded me and can never afford me again. Nevertheless, in all sincerity, if I had the chance to sleep once more the intellectual sleep of my girlhood, to forget all that I have learned, to return to my errors—I would not for the world consent to take it, I would not take a step backward. The memory of the illusions that I have lost has never disturbed the line of reasoning by means of which I lost them. When once I had come face to face with the reality, it maintained itself from that moment on, sometimes painfully, but steadily in my imagination. The last thing that a human being can willingly consent to is to be deceived."

# CHAPTER VII.

## THE EFFECT OF RELIGION AND NON-RELIGION ON POPULATION AND THE FUTURE OF THE RACE.

I. Importance of the problem of population—Antagonism between numerical strength and wealth—Necessity of numbers for the maintenance and progress of the race—Necessity of giving the advantage of numbers to the superior races—Problem of population in France—Its relation to the religious problem—Are the reasons for the restriction of the number of births physiological, moral, or economic?—Malthusianism in France—The true national peril.

II. Remedies—Is a return to religion possible?—Religious powerlessness and growing tolerance in the matter—The influence that the law might exercise upon the causes of small families—Enumeration of these causes—Reform of the law in regard to filial duty—(Support of parents)—Reform of the law of inheritance—Reform of the military law for the purpose of favouring large families and of permitting emigration to the French colonies.

III. Influence of public education: its necessity as a substitute for religious sentiment.

ONE of the most important of the problems to which the gradual enfeeblement of the religious sentiment has given rise is that of race fertility and the question of population. Almost all religions have attached a considerable importance to the rapid increase of population. With the diminution of the influence of religions among the superior races of mankind, shall we not lose an important aid in their maintenance and multiplication?

I. In the beginning, for the earliest aggregations of mankind, number was a condition of power and consequently of security.

Antagonism between wealth and population. The power of wealth, which can be concentrated in the possession of a single man, did not, so to speak, exist. In our days wealth has become a power which is sufficient unto itself, and which division and distribution often inevitably dissipate. Therein lies the source of the reasoning which appeals nowadays to the heads of families: "To render a family powerful one must transmit one's capital in as undivided a state as possible; that is to say, one must restrict the numbers of one's descendants to the utmost feasible limits." Capital and capitalistic egoism is therefore the enemy of population, because multiplication of men always implies a more or less minute subdivision of wealth.

Religion has always held the power of capital, in this respect, in check. The Christian, the Hindu, the Moham-

*Importance of rapid increase of population.*

medan religion all correspond to a state of things very different from that of the modern world; to a state of society in which number constitutes a great power, in which large families possess an immediate and visible utility. The greater number of the great religions are at one in the precept: "Increase and multiply." According to the laws of Manou, one of the conditions of salvation is the large number of male descendants. The religious and national tradition of the Jews on the point is well known. Every religion of Jewish origin being thus favourable to increase in the size of the family, and expressly prohibiting means of prevention, it follows that, other things equal, a sincerely Christian or Jewish people will multiply more rapidly than a free-thinking people. The infertility of the higher races, over and above the influence of the opposition between religion and the modern spirit, is induced also by a sort of antinomy between civilization and race propagation: rapid civilization is always accompanied by a certain race corruption. This antinomy must be remedied under penalty of extinction. Life is intense in proportion to the number of young, ambitious people who engage in it; the struggle for existence is fertile just so far as it is carried on by young men rather than by men who are fatigued and who no longer possess an enthusiasm for work; a young and rapidly increasing nation constitutes a richer and more powerful organism, a steam-engine working at a high pressure. One-half, perhaps three-fourths of the distinguished men have come of numerous families; some have been the tenth, some the twelfth child; to restrict the number of children is to restrict the production of talent and genius, and that, too, out of all proportion to the restriction of the family. An only son, far from having, on the average, a greater number of chances of being a remarkable man, really possesses fewer; in especial if he belongs to the upper classes. "Both the mother and father, it has been said, watch over this first child and enfeeble it by superfluous care, and spare it, by yielding to its wishes, all moral gymnastic." Every child who expects to be the sole inheritor of a small fortune will put forth less energy, in the struggle for existence, than he otherwise would. And finally, it is a physiological fact that the first children are often less vigorous and less intelligent; maternity is a function which becomes perfect, as other functions do, by repetition; a mother's first effort is as rarely a masterpiece as a poet's. To limit the number of children is, therefore, in a certain measure to dwarf their physical and intellectual powers.

As an increase of population heightens the intensity of the physical and mental life of a nation, so also it heightens the intensity of the economic life of a nation, stimulates the circulation of wealth, and ultimately increases the public treasure instead of diminishing it. It is happening under our very eyes in Germany and England, where public wealth has increased side by side with the population. In Germany, in a period of nine years (1872–1881), the average annual revenue of each individual increased six per cent., while the population rolled up by millions. The economical doctrine which regards overpopulation as the principal cause of poverty is a very superficial one. As long as there is an available plot of ground unoccupied, and perhaps even after the entire earth shall be cultivated (for science may be able to create new sources of wealth and even of food) a man will always constitute a bit of living capital, of a higher value than a horse or a cow, and to increase the numbers of citizens of a nation will be to increase the sum of its wealth.[1]

*Fallacy of Malthusianism.*

[1] What economists have really established, and what MM. Maurice Block, Courcelles-Seneuil, Paul Leroy-Beaulieu, Othenin d'Haussonville are right in maintaining, is that it is harmful to society to add to the non-working classes, to the number of

Formerly the struggle for existence between two races or nations ended in a single violent crisis: the vanquished were massacred or reduced to slavery, and slavery usually resulted in the gradual extinction of the inferior race; it was a slow massacre. Famine, produced by methodical devastation, achieved what war had begun—whole races disappeared abruptly from the face of the globe and left not a trace behind: the most recent and most striking example is that of the great American empires of Mexico and Peru. Thus the strongest and most intelligent races alone survived, and had only to confirm their victory with all its consequences by clearing the earth before them. Existence was a monopoly in the hands of the strong. It is no longer so. To-day the vanquished are no longer massacred; on the contrary, when an uncivilized country is conquered, it is supplied with good laws, with police and hygiene. Inferior races increase and multiply under the rule of superior races. The Cape negroes, the Chinese, the negroes in the United States, and even the last surviving red-skins, who seem disposed to-day to take heart, are examples of what I mean. Well, the Orient contains, in the Chinese Empire, a veritable reservoir of men, which some day or other will overflow the entire earth. In the face of this compact multitude, which is increasing rapidly, and with advancing civilization will increase more rapidly, the four or five great

*Menace to modern civilization.*

feeble beings who are incapable of labour, to the number of beggars, and of non-combatants generally, whoever they may be. Well, poverty favours the birth of those who are dependent upon society, and the birth of those who are dependent upon society tends still further to increase poverty; that is the circle from which so many economists have believed that the precepts of Malthus offered them an issue. Unhappily, if there is one universal attribute of poverty, it is its fertility; for in all nations the poorest classes are those that have the greatest number of children. Malthus has never been listened to by the poorer classes, but precisely by those only who, from the point of view of a sagacious political-economy, ought to be encouraged to leave as many children behind them as possible, because they alone would educate them well : that is to say, the economical peasantry and the prosperous middle class. Insomuch that a fertility of the poor is absolutely without remedy (except by way of charity or emigration) ; but it constitutes in the end a much less considerable evil than the infertility of a nation as a whole, and is an ultimate evil only because, in the last analysis, it results in a genuine unproductivity. Poverty, especially in the cities, rapidly kills out the most prolific races.

nations of Europe, and the United States and Australia, seem a small matter. The future of humanity depends mathematically upon the proportions in which the more intelligent races are represented in the complex composition of the man of the future. And every son of one of the more highly endowed races of the globe, such as the French, German, or English, commits a positive fault in not labouring for the multiplication of his race; he contributes to lower the future level of human intelligence. Men of science have already established it as a law that the power of reproduction decreases with the increase of cerebral activity, and that intelligent races reproduce themselves with increasing difficulty; to augment this natural difficulty by a voluntary restriction is daily to labour for the brutalization of the human race.

The followers of Malthus, supposing that there at present exists an equilibrium between population and the means of subsistence, look with anxiety upon every new arrival in the world; but even admitting that the struggle for existence has already reached that acute stage, it might still be hoped that only the more intelligent would leave children behind them. Malthus' law should possess no force for the educated men of Europe, who alone are acquainted with it, but only for the negroes or the Chinese, who are absolutely ignorant of it. Malthus' law is not meant for us; in reality it is not meant for anyone. By the very fact that one is acquainted with it, and possesses foresight and self-control enough to put it into practice, one proves that one stands beyond the circle of its applicability. Malthusians, who endeavour to apply to the reproduction of mankind the principles of animal-breeders, forget that the dominant principle in all breeding is to favour the multiplication of the superior species. One Durham bull is worth ten common bulls. What is true of bulls and sheep is true of men: a Frenchman, with the scientific and æsthetic aptitude of his race, represents on the average a social capital a hundred times greater than that represented by a negro, an Arab, a Turk, a Cossack, or a Chinaman. To leave few French descendants, in order that Cossacks and Turks may increase and multiply, is

*Duty of civilized races to multiply.*

to commit an absurdity, even on the principles of a Malthusian. Be it remembered that it was among the Aryans, and in especial among the Greeks, that science and art worthy of the name took their rise ; from them they passed to the other Aryans, and then to the other human races.

Michelet compares the treasure of science and truth, amassed by the human mind, to the egg that a slave carried into the Roman circus, at the end of the entertainment, into the midst of the great lions, who were gorged and asleep. If one of the wild beasts opened his eyes and was seized once more by desire at sight of the man with the egg, which is the symbol of human genius, the slave was lost. In our times genius is infinitely less persecuted than heretofore, and is no longer in danger of the arena or of the headsman, and it seems as if the sacred egg out of which the future is to arise has nothing further to fear; but this is a mistake. Precisely because the human mind is year by year growing richer, its treasure is becoming so considerable, so delicate, and difficult to preserve in its entirety, that it may well be asked whether a succession of people sufficiently well endowed will arise to retain and to augment the acquisitions of science. Up to the present day those truths alone have survived the wear and tear of time which were simple ; at the present epoch the rapidity of the progress of science may well make us anxious as to its permanence. The extreme complexity of science may well make us fear that the peoples of the future may not possess mental elevation enough to embrace it in its entirety, and to add to it by a constant increase. Suppose, for example, that the world should be reduced abruptly to Africa, Asia, and South America, where the Spanish race has not yet produced a single scientific genius; must not the scientific labours of our century inevitably miscarry ? Happily their safety is bound up with that of certain great nations. The Anglo-Saxon and Germanic peoples to-day cover the earth with their children and their colonies. But it is sad to think that one of the three or four great European peoples, which alone count for much in the progress of humanity, should be dancing gaily toward annihilation.

*Bad outlook for the future.*

A fusion of races will sooner or later take place in humanity; it is already taking place in the United States, and the perfec-

**Danger from Asia.** tion of means of communication is hastening its consummation throughout the entire world. Europe is pouring out its surplus upon America, Africa, and Australia; Asia will some day overflow Europe and America; what is taking place to-day, fifty years after the invention of railways, can scarcely give us an idea of the mixture and amalgamation of races which will some day be realized on the earth. Such a mixture, even though it raise the level, in some small degree, of races intellectually ill-endowed, may well abase the level of races intellectually well-endowed, if the latter are greatly outnumbered by the former.

It may be objected, it is true, that the superior races of mankind may remain isolated in the midst of the multiplica-

**Money the modern patent of nobility.** tion of the other branches of humanity in a sort of jealous aristocracy, served and respected by those whom they dominate by their intelligence. This is one of the dreams of M. Renan, who sees in the Chinese the future slave of the Europeans—gentle, docile slaves, with just enough intelligence to be marvellous industrial machines. Unhappily we have learned, to our expense, that the Chinese are also excellent instruments of war. In the industrial society in which we live, money constitutes, in the long run, the basis of aristocracy. To-day money is the true force and title of nobility. To lay up treasures demands a very average intelligence, of which a great number of inferior people are no doubt capable: once rich and they will be our equals; richer, they will be our superiors and our masters. If they have money enough they can purchase every privilege, even that of mixing their blood with ours, even that of marrying our daughters and of confounding our race and theirs. The only means by which intelligence can preserve its power is by means of numbers. Genius itself must leave a posterity behind it, and in spite of prejudice to the contrary, if we are to be eternal it must be by means of our children rather than by our works.

Positivists propose to substitute a religion of humanity for existing and rapidly disappearing religions; there is a still more accessible religion, and more practical, and more useful, which was one of the first religions of humanity: the religion of the family, the worship of the little group of beings bound together by ties of blood and memory and name and honour, which form an epitome of a nation; to permit one's family to die out or to diminish in number is to labour, to the extent that in one lies, to diminish the power of one's native country and of humanity itself. Patriotism has been made a subject of ridicule, but patriotism is a beautiful thing, and befitting in the head of a household. Paternity in its completest sense, that is to say, the responsibility for the education of a new generation from birth to the age of manhood, is, after all, the surest element of patriotism, and is within the reach of everyone.

*Religion of the family.*

In France especially, as we have seen, the population question is an important one, and should be insisted on. It has been said with reason that France to-day is not threatened by a multitude of dangers, but by one only, which actually constitutes a national peril: that of extinction from lack of children.[1] A nation may increase its capital in two ways; 1. By productive expenditure and productive labour; 2. By the utmost possible diminution of both, of labour and of expenditure. France has been employing the second means since the beginning of the present century; she has been economizing in children and diminishing the rapidity of the circulation of national life. She has, by this process, amassed a great treasure, but the results of her economy have been in part consecrated to the payment of an indemnity of five billions, and in part to loans, as in Mexico, Turkey, and Egypt, and to speculation of every kind, and the result of these blind economies has been a gradual impoverishment.

*Gradual impoverishment of France.*

Over and above those who are unreflective, or who simply trust to luck, there exists no considerable class of people in France, except Catholics, Protestants, and Jews, who can be counted on to maintain the race. There exists no doubt a

[1] M. Richet.

certain number of *bons vivants* who are determined to take their pleasure at all hazards, and who find in the restriction

Classes in France that maintain the population.
of the family a limitation of their pleasure ; but they are rare. The disciples of Malthus are nowadays much more numerous than those of Rabelais. People who have children, not out of pleasure nor by chance, but out of patriotism and philosophy, are so rare that they need not at present be taken into account. The more the property in France is subdivided, the greater the number of small proprietors, the fewer children there are. Since 1866 the agricultural inquiry has demonstrated the invasion of Malthusianism and the progress of voluntary infertility in almost every department *side by side with the subdivision of the soil*. From that time on the movement has gone forward unchecked. " In certain communes the words brother and sister have almost fallen out of use. Primogeniture, which was abolished in 1789, has been replaced by unigeniture." [1] Labourers only are anti-malthusians, and that out of carelessness for the future. A Malthusian was one day remonstrating with a poor labourer, who was the father of twelve children and ambitious to become the father of a thirteenth. " What will you have ? " said the latter, " it is the only pleasure in the world that I get for nothing ; I would not diminish it on any account."

It has been maintained that a greater or less restriction of the number of births is essentially due, not to a diminution in

Power of religion to stimulate population.
the religious devotion of the people, but simply to an increase of prudence. Whoever does not live simply in the present moment, but takes account of the future, will restrict the number of his children according to the figure of his income. And yet where faith is sincere and rigid, it does not permit one to hesitate on mere grounds of economics. In Brittany prudence neither checks religion nor fertility. Engaged couples, knowing that they will have children after marriage, postpone their union till they shall have laid by a certain amount of money, purchased a house and a plot of ground. In the department of Ille-et-Vilaine, men do not generally become engaged before their twenty-fourth year, nor women before their nineteenth

[1] Toubeau, *La Répartition des impôts*, t. ii.

year. Marriage does not last as long therefore in Brittany as in Normandy ; it lasts on the average twenty-seven years and a half in Normandy and twenty-one in Brittany, and yet the fertility of the women of Brittany, as compared with that of the women of Normandy, is almost as that of a hundred to sixty. In Brittany the result of religion and prudence, before marriage, combined, is a constant increase of population ; in Normandy the effect of incredulity and prudence, after marriage, combined, is a constant diminution of the population ; although, of the two peoples, the Normans are more vigorous, and owing to the greater frequency of twins, naturally more fertile.[1]

The weakness of the French as a nation does not lie in the smallness of the number of marriages. Practically the average number of marriages in France is the same as in Germany, something like eight a year for every thousand inhabitants, so that marriages are about as frequent in France as elsewhere. There is no question of immorality involved, but simply one of the prudence of married people. Illegitimate births are less numerous in France than in Italy or in Germany and in especial in Catholic Germany. In Paris scarcely more than twenty-five per cent. of the children are illegitimate, at Osmultz in Moravia fully seventy per cent. are illegitimate. M. Bertillon has established the fact that, since the beginning of the century, the percentage of marriage has been maintained, and even has increased rather than diminished up to 1865 ; but that the percentage of births has diminished continuously, and regularly. According to statistics every marriage averages five children in Germany, five in England, or almost five, and three only in France.

*Condition of population in France not due to aversion to marriage.*

Certain thinkers have been inclined to believe that the comparative slowness in the increase of the French people was due to a relatively high development of the brain. We have already remarked the antagonism which exists between reproduction and the development of the nervous or cerebral system, but it is somewhat precipitate to apply to a special group of men what is true of

*Nor to degree of civilization in France.*

[1] See M. Baudrillart, *Les Populations rurales de la Bretagne.*

the species as a whole; and there is a touch of fatuity in the notion that the French people have achieved so high a point of development that there exists in certain provinces not only a decrease in the rate of reproduction, but an absolute decrease of population. A statistical investigation has shown, it is true, that members of the Institute do not average more than one or two children apiece, but this statistical inquiry proves simply that members of the Institute have not desired to have large families, and that their conduct, which is generally not influenced by religion, has been comformable to their desire. An ordinarily healthy man could become the father of a hundred children every year; and to imagine that his sexual needs diminish under the influence of intellectual labour to the extent of his having but one child in forty years would be more apropos in a comic opera than in a serious book. Remark, however, that the fertility is less great among peasants, whose cerebral activity is at a minimum, than in our cities, in which it is relatively great; but in cities fertility is balanced unhappily by mortality. The antagonism between fertility and development of the brain should be at its greatest in women; but Frenchwomen, whose education has long been neglected, do not appear to possess on the average any intellectual superiority over the women of other countries. And in our provinces population advances most slowly in Normandy, where the women are so vigorous that the percentage of twins is higher than elsewhere.

Malthusianism therefore is the cause of the evil, and malthusianism is a worse scourge than pauperism; it is in a sense the pauperism of the middle classes. Just as an

Malthusianism the cause.

excessive impoverishment may kill out a whole social class, malthusianism is the death of the middle classes. It is rare to find a middle-class family with more than two or three children; two children, at least, are necessary to replace the father and the mother, and to maintain the population; a certain number of celibates and of married people who are sterile must be allowed for. The middle classes therefore are approaching extinction: the result of restricting their number is suicide.

To sum up, the population question in France is purely and simply a moral question; but more than any other question of the like nature it is closely bound up with religion because, up to the present time, religion has been the sole power which has dared to check popular inclination in this regard. It is in respect to population that lay morality has been most negligent.

II. If the question is really one of a return to some traditional religion or a gradual extinction of the race, free-thinkers may well hesitate between a number of lines of conduct. They may, in the first place, take refuge in resignation: "After me the Deluge." Many of the middle classes and a great number even of economists, who regard the future of their race and of their country as much too distant to be taken into account and consider present comfort as the sole rational aim of man, accept this position. A more radical alternative is to join the Church: both the Catholic and the Protestant churches, in spite of the eccentricity of their legends, are useful as an aid in making a nation numerous and strong and prolific; and the French of all nations needs religion, so that, instead of endeavouring to destroy the Christian faith, it is our duty to endeavour to propagate it. There is an element of hypocrisy and even of cowardice in this effort to revive a bygone error in the name of present utility. And it involves the affirmation that error is at the bottom more useful than truth, and that truth is fundamentally irreconcilable with the continued existence of the human race—an affirmation which is somewhat precipitate. Above all, the effort to arrest scepticism is simply futile—futile for humanity, for a people, for a family. When it is time to regret that certain things have been learned it is too late to set about ignoring them. The French people, in especial, possess a fund of incredulity which is based upon the practical and logical character of their temperament: they rose in 1789 against the clergy, in the name of liberty; nowadays they will struggle with the same stubbornness in the name of comfort against the prescriptions of religion, against the very

*Futility of effort to bring about a return of religion.*

instincts of human nature, and will make themselves sterile in order to become rich without immoderate labour. The re-establishment of religion is simply out of the question ; sincerely religious men themselves, if they happen also to be intelligent, recognize it. This rational sterility, produced by a triumph of the intellect over natural instinct and religious dogma, is a charming theme for declamation ; but declamation is also sterile, and does not date from yesterday ; it was tried before the Revolution and succeeded neither in augmenting religious sensibility nor in diminishing French infertility. In a pamphlet on the Erreurs de Voltaire, the Abbé Nonotte wrote in 1766 : " Present notions and practices on the subject of population are as melancholy for morality as for statesmanship. People are content nowadays with a single heir. Pleasure and libertinism carry the day. The fortunes of a great number of the first families in Paris rest on the shoulders of a single child. It was better in former times ; for families were not afraid of a number of children, and were not so extravagant but that they could provide them with a means of subsistence."

Neither the priest nor the confessor can be counted on. Has the priest ever power enough, even in countries like
*Inability of priest to cope with question of population.* Brittany where devotion is at its height, to suppress the grossest vice ; drunkenness, for example, and that, too, among women ? How can a priest be expected to maintain an influence over men who confess hardly more than once a year—at Easter? How can the priest, under such circumstances, be expected to be really a governor of the conscience, and in especial a physician of the soul? He receives a general confession from each of his parishioners, he is in a hurry, he is obliged to restrict his attention to the most enormous of the sins confessed to him, and the whole ends in absolution, followed by communion. Some days afterward the men get drunk again, and do just as they did before, till the year comes round. Prejudices and habits are stronger than anything else.

They who, with the Abbé Nonotte, regard religion as the cure of all evils, forget that religion itself is very compliant, that it can be made to stand for a multitude of things. If the mass of the French people should allow themselves to be persuaded by the Abbé Nonotte and his disciples to return to the traditional faith, the traditional faith itself would soon cease to be so austere. Confessors would become more discreet. Are they not to-day obliged to tolerate polkas and waltzes, and young people whirling about the room in each other's arms, which was formerly so severely prohibited? The letter of religion remains in vain the same, the spirit of the worshippers changes. At the present day Jesuits willingly close their eyes to the sterility of the family; they have even been accused of whispering to advice for the preservation of certain inheritances. Do you imagine that confessors in the Faubourg Saint-Germain ask especially embarrassing questions? Heaven can be compromised with.

*Pliancy of religion.*

This sort of tolerance, like all tolerance, will grow with time. Even in Protestant families in which a more extreme rigidity reigns, the spirit of the times is dominant. Orthodoxy is everywhere becoming less ferocious, sterility is everywhere on the increase. Even clergymen do not have as large families as formerly. Statistics on this head would be very instructive; one might find in the very bosom of Protestantism sterility increasing directly with liberalism of belief. If Darwin and Spencer have partisans in the English clergy, and among the American Protestants, why should not Malthus also? In especial, since Malthus was a grave and religious man.

*Even of Protestantism.*

The Catholic religion has itself been guilty by its advocacy of religious celibacy. In France one hundred and thirty thousand persons of both sexes are devoted to celibacy.[1] It is to be regretted that Catholicism, which during a number of centuries (in the time when St. Sidonius Apollinaris, the son-in-law of the Emperor Avitus, was Bishop of Clermont-Ferrand) did not impose celibacy upon ecclesiastics, should have felt obliged later to exact it, and should have come to consider absolute

*Decrease of population encouraged by the Catholic Church.*

[1] Dr. Lagneau, *Remarques démographiques sur le célibat en France.*

continence superior to marriage, contrary to all physiological and psychological laws. "Continence as a profession,"
says M. Montesquieu, "has destroyed more men than pestilence and war together. Every religious house constitutes a
family which never gives birth to a child, and which continues
in existence only by adopting children from without. Such
houses are open like so many abysses, to swallow up the future
of the race." Religious celibacy results in another evil consequence : although priests do not to-day constitute the élite
of society, they are still among the most intelligent, the best
educated, the least ill-disposed members of society. And they
gaily consent to be annihilated, to disappear, and to leave, like
the heretics they used to burn, no trace behind. They form
as constant a drain on the body-politic as the victims of the
Inquisition formed during so many years in Spain. If we
should count the sons only of clergymen who have become
distinguished or even great men, from Linnæus to Wurtz and
Emerson, we might see how much we lose by the celibacy of
our priesthood.

But religion apart, sterility may be combated by law, by
morals, and by education.

Religion is the law of primitive peoples ; when it becomes
feeble, its precepts split into two parts : one of which, regarded
as useless, is neglected and loses its entire value,

Legal remedy.

while the other, which is regarded as the guarantee
of social life, becomes formulated into moral or civilized laws
obligatory in character. This is the history of a number of
hygienic measures prescribed by Oriental religion which have
become simple police regulations in the laws of modern
Europe. In the present question it is evident that the law
should take the place that religion once held ; the legislator
should assume the function of the priest. Such a substitution
is not unexampled ; it took place among the Greeks ; the
citizen was obliged, by law, to have children. Socrates in
Athens was obliged by law to take a second wife. In Sparta
the young husband lived at the public table until he had supplied the state with three sons. He was subject to military
service until he had supplied the state with four.[1] Nowadays

[1] Aristotle, *Politica*, ii. 6, 13.

of course such radical laws are not to be thought of, and indeed no simple and direct law could reach the evil; an entire system of mutually completing laws is necessary. The whole series of reasons which prevent the head of a household from having a large family must first be known; then they must be met in detail by a series of laws devised to suppress them or counterbalance them; so that whenever one interest makes for sterility, another and equivalent interest shall make for fertility. It is accordingly in the very bosom of the family that the law, and that progressive reform of morals to which the law is so capable of contributing, must operate.

The head of a family to-day abandons the notion of having many children for a number of reasons, sometimes mutually contradictory, which it is necessary we should make ourselves fully acquainted with before endeavouring to devise means of counteracting them. There exist in the first place, though not very frequently, physical reasons: the ill-health of the mother, the fear of her dying through frequent pregnancies. When this fear is justified in the judgment of a physician it is respectable; it is defensible even from the point of view of society, for children born under such conditions would be delicate and useless as members of society. But in almost the whole number of cases, the grounds of sterility are economical and egoistic. French sterility is an economical, much more than a physiological phenomenon. The head of a family calculates the cost of rearing a numerous family, calculates that instead of being able to lay by money while he is in the vigour of his life, he will have to spend it on his children, and to pass his old age in poverty; having a large family he regards simply as a bit of prodigality. Our budget of 4,200,000,000 represents an average of 113 francs a head; with such taxes, decidedly, if one is to bring up a numerous family, one must have a considerable fortune or must deftly manipulate one's poverty.

*Worship of comfort a reason for small families.*

Also the small proprietor regards the earth somewhat as a savage does his fetich: his field, his house, are sacred entities which he wishes to confide to sure hands. If he has a number of children, it will be necessary to share these treasures and perhaps to sell them in case they cannot otherwise be divided equally. The peasant no more regards such a division of property as possible than a gentleman under the old régime would have admitted the possibility of selling his ancestral chateau. Both of them would regard a mutilation of their family as a less evil than the mutilation of their domain. But to rear a child is to create a bit of capital, and fertility is a form of social economy. Both economists and French peasants admit willingly that to rear a calf or a sheep is to add to one's wealth, and *a fortiori* they should admit that to rear a child is. But there is a difference: the calf, once reared, labours solely for the person who reared it, whereas the child ultimately comes to labour for itself. From the selfish point of view of the father, it is better to raise cattle and sheep. From the point of view of society, it is incontestably better to rear men. In all new countries the French race is prolific, because a large number of children under such circumstances is not a charge but a profitable investment. In Canada sixty thousand Frenchmen have grown into a people of two millions and a half. In Algeria the birth-rate is from 30 to 35 per 1000; in Normandy it is not 20 per thousand. Finally, a striking example of the influence of emigration has been discovered in France itself, in the Department of the Basses-Pyrénées, where the birth-rate varies with the rate of emigration, to fill the places of those who have gone to America.

*Worship of land another.*

Let us consider, on the other hand, the causes which influence women. It is natural that, in a certain stage of society, women should be unwilling to be mothers. Motherhood represents the sole task which it is left to them to perform, and this task they find the harder because fortune has relieved them of every other. They are not even obliged to nourish their children: the maternal breast can find a substitute; they are not obliged either to rear their children or to teach them: governesses can be hired; but nobody can give birth to their children, and in their life of frivolity childbirth is the one serious function

*Women of fashion imitate the demi-monde.*

that remains. They protest against it and they are right. The ambition of women of the *grandmonde* being too often, as has been said, to mimic women of the *demi-monde*, it is well that they should imitate them in this respect as in all others, and that they should endeavour to establish between marriage and prostitution this final bond of similarity—sterility.

Even among the women of the people gestation and childbirth, being, as they are, painful, are also objects of the liveliest repugnance and of protestations of every kind. I have never seen a woman of the people who did not complain at being pregnant and who would not have preferred any other malady. *Ah ! Nous ne faisons pas, nous recevons*—" We women have no voice in the matter," said one of them to me—" if but we had ! " She epitomized in a word the physiological and psychological position of the poor woman. Those who have not had children, far from complaining of it, congratulate themselves, and in any event they rarely desire more than one.

*Women of the lower classes fear labour.*

In Picardy and in Normandy, as M. Baudrillart remarks, a woman who has many children is made the butt of raillery. And if other provinces are less sterile, it is owing to religion or to ignorance. The women have not yet become acquainted with Malthus. They know of but one remedy against an evil that they fear—to keep out of the way of their husbands. The wife of such and such a labouring man prefers a beating to the risk of having another child : but as she is the weaker she often succeeds in bringing upon herself both the beating and the child. Fear of pregnancy is more often than is commonly believed the cause of dissension in poor households, and for that matter in rich households also. The instant a woman reasons, instead of submitting to the law, she inevitably feels the disproportion that exists, for her, between the pleasures of love and the pains of maternity. She must be supplied with a new conception of duty, and that not simply in the way of a religious obligation which the husband can ridicule but of a moral obligation.

*Large families among the poor traceable to ignorance.*

Catholic education, as we have already remarked, does great harm in rearing young girls in a false modesty, in never speak-

Girls should be educated for maternity. ing to them of the duties of marriage for fear of awakening their imagination in the direction of their future husband. The actual result is pre-cisely the opposite of the calculated result. Young girls see nothing in marriage but the future husband and unknown pleasures. They never think of any matter of painful duty which they must accept in advance; they do not consider children as a question of duty but of necessity simply, they are actuated by but one ambition, that of diverting themselves. Girls should be educated and prepared for motherhood; our present education is adapted to the formation of nuns or old maids, sometimes of courtesans, for we neglect early to inspire woman with a feeling of duty for her proper function, which constitutes also a large portion of all that is moral in her life— the duty of maternity. Happily, married women cannot remain sterile simply by wishing it, their husbands must become their accomplices; it is their husbands, who, in the last resort, are responsible. If the husband, out of complaisance to his wife or to his wife's relatives, undertakes to be a Malthusian *malgré lui*, he plays almost as ridiculous a rôle as that of Georges Dandin: the man who permits himself to be dictated to in the matter of not having children is almost as complaisant as the man who acknowledges the children of other people.

Another cause which explains the low birth-rate in France is that paternal and maternal love is more tender and more

Paternal love tends to restrict the number of children. exclusive there than in other countries. The French family, whatever may be said to the con-trary, is much more closely united than the English or German family: in it a sort of fraternity obtains between parents and children. Members of a family separate with regret, and the ideal of the father is to have so few children that he may always keep them by him. We are too refined, too far advanced from a state of nature, to submit with-out suffering to the rupture which puberty naturally brings about in the animal family, to the flight of the young bird whose wings are grown; we have not the courage to accept the dismemberment of the household, far less to wish it as a necessity and, on the whole, a good thing. This affection has of course its egoistic side, and it is on that side that it results in sterility. Parents rear children less for the children's sake than for their own.

Having thus passed in review the principal causes which restrict the number of children in French families let us consider what influence law and morals might exert in counteracting them. Legal reforms should be directed especially toward the two following points: 1. Reform of the law relating to filial duties (maintenance of parents); 2. Reform of the law of inheritance; 3. Reform of the military law, so as to favour numerous families and permit emigration to the French colonies.

*Two legal remedies.*

Rearing children being a considerable trouble and expense it is necessary that it should be made profitable, that it should be converted into a species of loan for a long term of years. The law can bring this about in various ways. French legislation has protected children by a provision that their fathers cannot completely disinherit them; it should also have protected fathers against children's ingratitude. It often happens, in the country especially, that after an aged couple have reared a numerous generation they find themselves dependent upon their sons or upon their sons-in-law and are ill-fed and greeted with abuse. The law provides that children must maintain their parents, no doubt, but maintenance may be supplied in a manner which renders it little better than assassination. The law which has endeavoured to establish the moral independence of the son as against the father might well endeavour to establish on a firm basis the moral independence of the parents themselves. If a father to-day cannot disinherit his son, is it not shocking that a son should be able, in a sense, to disinherit his father—to accept life, nourishment, education from him and to give derision, abusive language, and sometimes blows in return? Observers who have lived among the people, in especial in country districts, uniformly bear witness to the deplorable situation of certain

*Present state of the law does not sufficiently protect parents against ingratitude.*

old men who are obliged to beg on the highroad, or of their
neighbours, for means of support which are refused them in
their own houses. The present French law is helpless in
the presence of filial ingratitude which takes the form, not of
overt act, but of abusive language and disrespectful conduct.
It annuls a donation made to an ungrateful child, but it cannot
annul the donation of life, and ungrateful children benefit by
the inability. A father should be able to count at least on
a certain minimum of revenue from his children, whoever
they may be.[1]

If, as is probable, the principle of social insurance is ultimately to prevail, and if a certain amount of the regular
income of every labourer is to be retained and
laid by to form a provision for his old age, which
his employer or the state will increase in certain
proportions, we believe that it would be equitable to increase
the provision laid by for the father of a family in a larger
ratio than the provision laid by for a celibate. The father of a

*The state owes parents a debt.*

[1] We are not obliged here to enter into details of administration. Perhaps it
would be no more than just to give parents their choice between living with their
children, which is often so painful, and an annual sum, proportional to the salary
and resources of the children. This sum might be taxed by the state or the commune, and paid by it to the father. Every head of a family would at once reflect
that if he some day becomes poor and has but one child he will have but one
source of income, whereas, if he has ten children, he will have ten sources of income,
and ten chances that one of them may be considerable ; as it would be if any of
one's children should have become wealthy. A numerous family would thus
constitute a guarantee of independence for the father ; on the other hand, the more
he expended in educating them, the greater chance he would have of later obtaining
an equivalent return for it. In labouring for the augmentation of the social capital
he would thus be securing an insurance for his old age. Even supposing that the
execution of a law of this kind should be difficult, the right of parents to some
really active gratitude on the part of their children should be recognized and consecrated formally by the letter of the law, which should prescribe a line of conduct
for children and even fix a certain appropriate ratio between their income and the
amount of their remittances to their parents. The law should even do what in it
lies to efface from the language, in especial in their applicability to those who have
generously fulfilled their duties of paternity, the shameful words : *être à la charge
de ses enfants*—dependent on his children for support ; the public should be
made accustomed to consider this sort of dependence not as an accident to the
children, and as a misfortune, and almost a disgrace, to the parents, but as a
natural consequence of the relation of parent and child.

family having done more for the state than the celibate—having contributed to the state his time and trouble and expense in rearing certain members of the new generation—it would be legitimate for the state to make a restitution to him of some small portion of the money he has laid out in a disinterested manner; in a manner which did not benefit him and has benefited the state.

Meanwhile this consummation is somewhat distant, and there is a reform immediately practicable: a tax on celibacy.

**Tax on celibacy.** Whenever this tax has been mentioned it has been made the subject of universal ridicule; it has been represented, as M. Ch. Richet remarked, as a sort of penalty, a fine for not being willing or not being able to marry. This is a very unfair statement of the case; the measure would be simply strict justice. With anything like an equality in the matter of fortune a celibate pays smaller taxes (indirect taxes, taxes on doors and windows, etc.); and the tax of rearing a family, by which the married man serves the state in a number of ways at once, the celibate avoids altogether. The celibate therefore is an altogether privileged person, he avoids almost everything in the way of social duties. In regard to all taxes, direct and indirect, he enjoys dispensations which are not without analogy to those formerly admitted to priests and nobles. The same thing holds good of married people who do not have children; they are, so to speak, encouraged by the law: it is a state of things which should not and cannot last.

By a tax on celibacy one would simply be reverting to the ideas of the French Revolution. The Revolution took care, **In principle identical with certain provisions at time of Revolution.** by a number of laws, to favour the married man at the expense of the unmarried. Thus every celibate was ranked, for purposes of taxation, in a higher class than that to which, according to his income, he would have been placed had he been married. If he demanded assistance for some of the causes for which assistance was granted, he would be given but half the amount that a married man in his situation would have received; if he was more than thirty years old the laws obliged him to pay twenty-five per cent. additional to all ground tax; the taxable value of his property was estimated at fifty per cent. higher than it would otherwise have been. A manufacturer was obliged to declare whether he was celibate or married. The law considered every man a celibate who was thirty years old and was not married, or a widower.[1]

Over and above the special tax on celibacy, a more equitable distribution of the tax on families might be realized. As M.

Parents should be taxed inversely to number of children.

Richet remarks, if the father of a family cannot be assisted by indirect taxes, the direct tax on him should at least be inversely proportional to the number of his children.[2] Not only so, but compulsory road labour—this unpopular tax, which constitutes the last vestige of the *corvée*—might well be suppressed entirely for the fathers of more than four or even of more than three children.[3]

[1] See the *Études sur le célibat en France*, by Dr. G. Lagneau (Académie des sciences morales et politiques, p. 835, 1885.)

[2] " Direct taxes," says M. Javal, " are in a great measure a tax on children : compulsory road labour is forced on young men before they are adult. The tax on doors and windows is a tax on air and light, the inconvenience of which increases directly with the increase in the size of the family and the consequent necessity of occupying a larger apartment. The license itself, which applies to the amount of the rent of one's habitation, is in a great measure proportional to the necessary expenses and not to the resources of the person taxed." (*Revue scientifique*, No. 18, November 1, 1884, p. 567.) " It is well known," says M. Bertillon, " that the city of Paris pays to the state the tax on apartments that rent for less than four hundred francs. In principle nothing could be better, but in practice : suppose two neighbours, one of them an unmarried man, possesses a comfortable lodging of two rooms with the accessories ; one of these two rooms can scarcely be called a necessity for him and is distinctly a simple addition to his comfort, and the city pays his tax. His neighbour has a family and four children, and lives in three rooms which constitute a very narrow, and hardly a sufficient lodging, but the rent of it is five hundred francs and the unhappy man must pay : (1) Six times greater taxes on what he consumes than his neighbour ; (2) A furniture tax ; (3) Some portion of the tax that the city pays on the apartment of the celibate neighbour. Evidently the result is precisely the opposite of what it should be." (Bertillon, *La statistique humaine de la France*.)

[3] If a purse should be given by the state to one of every seven children in the same family (according to a law at the time of the Revolution which has recently been revived and corrected) it would be no more than justice, nay, it would be almost an act of simple reparation ; although it must not be supposed that the practical results would be considerable. The benefit that it would do to the father of the

Everybody is agreed nowadays as to the defects in the law regulating the taxation of inheritances. We believe that it is more than anything else by a modification of this law that the practice of malthusianism can be checked. The tax on every inheritance which is to be divided up among a great number of children ought as far as possible to be reduced, whereas the tax on inheritances which are to go undivided to a single inheritor ought to be increased. The small proprietor who limits himself to one child, in order to avoid dividing his field, would soon learn that he is making a bad calculation if by that very act he subjects his estate to a heavy tax. On the contrary, whoever lays out his fortune in rearing a number of children would at least have the satisfaction of thinking that almost the whole of his fortune could be handed down to them, that the public treasury would take little of it, and that if his property had to be divided after his death it would at least not be seriously diminished ; almost nothing would " go out of the family." [1]

*Injustice of present law of inheritance.*

Every reform of the law of inheritance must make up its account with the two motives which alone inspire a man to amass a fortune : a personal interest, and an interest in his wife and children. So that, whenever a man is a widower without children, his property might be made subject at his death to a considerable tax, without his industry, which society is interested in stimulating, being thereby especially discouraged. A considerable tax therefore on the property left by celibates, and married couples without children, would be evidently equitable, and, no more than in the case of a tax on celibacy, to be regarded as a penalty. The simple fact is that a man who has not

*Tax on inheritances falling to celibates.*

family is too uncertain, and the prospect of such an advantage could influence only a man who had six children and was hesitating about the seventh ; but he who has had six children is not a follower of Malthus and is not likely to be.

[1] Suppose, to take almost the first figures that occur to one, that the law taxed an only son's inheritance twenty per cent. ; it might tax an inheritance to be handed down to two children only fifteen per cent., an inheritance to be handed down to three children ten per cent., to four children eight per cent., to five children six per cent., to six children four per cent., to seven children two per cent., and to any greater number of children nothing. Remark that this gradation actually exists

reared children has expended much less of his income for the benefit of society, and that society has the right during his life-time or at his death to trim the scales against him. Indeed proportionate taxation ought positively to be a matter of conscience with society.

Given the importance of large fortunes in modern society, religion and the patriarchal spirit together devised in former

French law of inheritance tends toward minute subdivision of estates.

times a compromise between the necessity of having a large family and of keeping the family possessions undivided ; I refer to primogeniture.

To attempt to re-establish the law of primogeni-ture in nations which have rejected it would be impracticable and unjust, even though one should recognize that the tradi-tional superstition and prejudices on this point were not with-out some justification. But, to reassure those who dislike the thought of the inevitable partition of their territorial pos-sessions, the present laws in regard to inheritances might be made less stringent. Every land-owner, every owner of a factory or a commercial house, might be left free to designate which of his children he considered most competent to succeed him in the possession of such real property, and the law of partition might be considered as applicable to the rest of his property only. It would be a sort of liberty of bequest, within the limits of the family. The authors of our civil code broke the line of succession as it had existed in the families of the nobility ; and they did well, in that they dispersed masses of unproductive capital, and by that very fact rendered them productive ; but they did less well, in that they rendered it difficult to bequeath large farming or manufacturing establish-ments from father to son. They have necessitated the sub-

to-day but inversely, because just in so far as an inheritance has to be divided up among a large number of children, the expenses of the sale and partition tend to increase and the value of the property, which is thus split up into bits, tends to decrease. A number of cases may be cited in which inheritances that had to be divided among seven or eight children have lost, by partition, not only twenty but even twenty-five or fifty per cent. of their value. On the contrary, an inheritance transmitted to a single inheritor is burdened with the direct tax only, and that amounts at most to ten per cent. Here, as elsewhere, the law protects small families and encourages sterility.

division of capitals which were much more productive in their entirety ; and as a result families of farmers and manufacturers who remain, from father to son, for generations in the same pursuit and are thereby enabled to carry it to its highest degree of perfection, have almost disappeared in France. Such commercial or land-owning dynasties constitute the greatness of England and of Germany. A great commercial house or a great farming enterprise is not to be created in a day, and if after one's death one's labour is to be destroyed by partition, so much the worse for the country. Le Play has depicted in lively colours the despair of the farmer who has laboured all his life to perfect a system of cultivation, of the manufacturer who has created a prosperous house, who see their work menaced with destruction if they have a number of children. Such men have but one resource ; to withdraw enough money from their business to satisfy the requirements of the law in regard to the children who are not to succeed them, and thus to prevent the sale of their establishment. The result of this manœuvre often is that the child who inherits this establishment is left too poor to carry on the business and finds ruin where his father found wealth. The law, in its endeavour to divide the produce of the father's labour among his children, too often annihilates the most valuable part of the father's labour ; in the effort to obtain an apparent equity in the partition of the revenues, it destroys the source of them. The law cuts down the tree to gather the fruit.

Military service, which is perhaps the heaviest burden that the state lays on the individual, also constitutes the state's **Large families should be partly exempted from military service.** principal means of influencing him. The most Malthusian native of Normandy would become amenable at once if a question of five years' military service, more or less, were involved. To-day the father of four living children is exempt from the twenty-eight days' military service (the law does not seem to be well known, but ought to be) ; he ought to be exempt from all reserve service, even in time of war. Similarly, as has already been demanded, a family which has furnished two soldiers to the army ought to be exempt from further military duty. The younger sons should be definitively excused from military service by the fact of their two elder brothers having marched under the flag. As a matter of fact, families in which there are more than two sons are so rare that such a measure would hardly diminish the annual recruits.[1] More than that the Budget is unequal to the needs of the whole number of possible recruits even as the case stands; it is therefore irrational to make one's selection from among them by an appeal to chance. Such a device is an appeal to inequality and that under the disguise of equality and law; the future of every society depends upon the decreasing part played in it by the injustices of chance. The military service required of each family should therefore be regulated with some rational reference to the number of children in it.[2]

Emigration tends to augment fertility; emigration must therefore be favoured by law. It is soberly estimated at present that from thirty to forty thousand Frenchmen emigrate each year; the figure is relatively small, but that number of emigrants a year is enough to settle important colonies.[3] It is unscientific to maintain at this late day that the French are incapable of colonizing when they have so powerfully aided in forming the great English colonies in Canada, India, and Egypt and are actually colonizing Algeria and Tunis. What we lack is not the ability to establish colonies, but the habit of emigration. Emigration, in spite of its importance for us, obtains mainly in certain poor districts in France; it is not general enough to

*Emigration to be encouraged.*

[1] M. Javal in 1885 proposed, in the Chamber, to substitute for Article 19 of the commission another article, according to the terms of which when two or three sons of the same family were enrolled they should be held to only three years of service all told, and that when there were more than three brothers enrolled they should each be required to give but one year's service. The amendment was due to the fact that population in France is not increasing.

[2] Young soldiers also, as M. Richet says, might be permitted to marry under certain conditions. They are precisely at the age when fertility is at its greatest.

[3] Rightly to appreciate the ability of France to maintain colonies, this figure must not be compared with the rate of emigration from other countries, but with the average excess of births over deaths in France. Thus considered, the number of forty thousand emigrants (adopted by M. Paul Leroy-Beaulieu) becomes relatively large, since the annual excess of our births is not one hundred thousand.

have any considerable influence, as yet, in raising the birth-rate; the law should here be looked to, to correct the habits of the people. In England out of every family of four sons it is almost to be expected that one of them will go to India, another to Australia, a third to America; there is nothing surprising in it, it is the custom. A sense of distance is almost unknown on the opposite side of the Channel. In France, if a single child leaves the country, even as the secretary of an embassy, he is as solemnly bid good-bye as if he were going never to return, as if he were dying even. There is a great deal of prejudice and ignorance in paternal anguish of this kind. Such and such a sedentary profession, for example that of a physician, is subject to perils that are perfectly well known to statisticians and which we nevertheless do not hesitate to choose for our children precisely because it permits them to live next door to us, rather than at the other end of the world. Such national prejudices will give way before education, the increasing habit of travelling, and the progressively rapid circulation of society; laws might favour it. The spirit of enterprise and colonization, which seems at first sight so foreign to love of family, is capable of being allied with it; nay, becomes, under certain circumstances, the very condition of it. To rear a numerous family is always in a certain sense to colonize, even though all the children live within the limits of their native country. To rear a large family is to launch one's children upon unknown ways, and demands the activity of mind and fertility of resource which are of the essence of colonization. The creation of a numerous family is positively a social enterprise, as the creation of a great commercial house or a great farming industry is an economical enterprise; success in both cases demands constant effort and brings a various profit in return Suppose a couple have reared ten children to labour and honesty; the children form a protecting phalanx about the parents and give them, in return for the rearing, if not gross and direct benefits, at least happiness and honour. We do not wish to disguise the fact, however, that to rear a family involves a certain amount of risk; but every enterprise involves a risk. And indeed the prime need in this whole matter is to develop the spirit of enterprise and audacity which was formerly so powerful in the French nation. A great many people to-day remain celibate for the same reason that they are content to live within a small income without endeavouring to increase their fortune by investing it in commerce or manufacture ; they are afraid of the risks of the family, just as they are afraid of commercial risks. They consume instead of producing, because producing is inseparable from a certain preliminary investment of money and activity. Similarly a great many people, once they are married, endeavour, so to speak, to reduce marriage to a minimum ; they do not dare to have children ; they are afraid of the preliminary outlay, they are afraid of emerging from the shell of their short-sighted egoism.

It is, of course, emigration to French colonies that the law ought especially to favour, and for that purpose there is one respect in which the military law should be reformed. As a matter of fact, in spite of the law of July 27, 1872, the government is obliged to grant pardon to the numerous Basques and Savoyards who emigrate to escape military service. More than that, the sole important current that exists in France flows toward foreign colonies, and often creates on their shores industries which rival our own, while they rarely open advantageous markets for our commerce. Is it not a matter of urgent necessity to make our colonies as attractive to the French emigrants as the colonies of any foreign nationality? If the young man of twenty who has made up his mind to pass some years of his life in Brazil finds himself *de facto* exempt from military service, ought he not to be *de jure* exempt if he wishes to emigrate to Algiers, to Tunis, to Tonquin, to Madagascar? Emigration is itself a sort of military service. Colonists defend and enlarge the frontiers of the countries ; a really rational law should recognize them as a portion of the military power of the country. Fifty-four chambers of commerce in our principal cities, " considering that it is of the greatest importance to encourage, by every means possible, intelligent and well-educated young

*To French colonies.*

people, intending to emigrate, to establish themselves in our colonies," demanded justly "that, in times of peace, young men residing in the colonies should be granted a delay of five years in the call to military service, a delay which should become a definitive exemption after a further residence of five consecutive years. We believe that this period of ten years might be shortened, and that a residence of seven years in the colonies, or even of five in certain distant colonies, like Tonquin, might be infinitely more profitable to the mother country than a three-years' military service at home.[1] We are much less in need of soldiers to guard our colonies than of colonists; indeed our colonies are too often "colonies without colonists." More than that, we travel too little, we are not as well acquainted as we should be with our own possessions; whoever had spent five of the most active years of his life in the colonies would be tempted to return there or to send his friends and relatives there. An amendment, looking to this exemption from military service, was discussed in the Chamber of Deputies in May and June, 1884. If it should ever be passed, it might have a considerable influence upon the destinies of the French people.[2]

[1] The legal minimum of required residence should not be taken as representing the real duration of actual residence : people do not come back from distant countries merely for the wishing ; but the legislature should take advantage of the psychological effect of a definite figure ; an emigrant rarely leaves France without a determination to be gone only so long. The majority of the Basques who emigrate in such large numbers to America expect to return soon ; three-fourths of them become good citizens of the Argentine Republic.

[2] Among the secondary causes which tend to lower the French birth-rate, and which the law might counteract, let us notice that of abortion, which is practised in France not less commonly than in Germany, but bears much worse results here than there, because of the small number of children that are born in France. Paris positively enjoys a reputation for the art of miscarriage, and ladies come there from various parts of the world to be relieved of their children. "One of the professors of our schools said this year, in one of his courses, that a midwife had confessed to him that she produced on an average one hundred miscarriages a year." (Dr. Verrier, *Revue scientifique*, June 21, 1884.) Pajot affirms that there are more miscarriages than births. Might not this state of things be remedied : 1. By the re-establishment of the revolving boxes (*tours*): 2. By a more constant inspection of the books and offices of midwives and accoucheurs, such as furnished lodgings in Paris are subject to.

Among the principal reasons which prevent marriage let us mention the pre-

III. Apart from the laws, the great means of influencing races is public education : it is by that means that the ideas and feelings may be moulded. The French people must be enlightened, therefore, on the disastrous consequences of depopulation ; sentiments of patriotism, of honour, of duty, must in every possible way be appealed to. The schoolmaster, the physician, and the mayor may all be of help. There are a whole multitude of such means of instruction that are being neglected.

*Dangers of de-population should be taught.*

In the first place there are military conferences. Conferences of a half hour each, with striking facts and examples and a few significant figures, might exercise a considerable influence on the army, which is to-day the nation. Military conferences will some day certainly be one of the great means for the dissemination of knowledge ; they have recently been employed with success in Belgium during the strikes, to inculcate notions of political economy in the army and to fortify the military against certain communistic arguments.

*In the army by conferences.*

liminary formalities, which are too numerous even when both parties are French, and are simply numberless when one party is a foreigner. The law of marriages when both parties are French ought to be simplified to the utmost possible extent, so that an impatience of the preliminaries could in nowise influence engaged couples. More than that every effort should be made to facilitate marriages between French subjects and foreigners, unions the results of which are generally good for the race and which are hindered by all sorts of legal obstacles in certain countries ; this last question is a subject to be dealt with by diplomacy. Still other causes that the law might modify operate in France, if not to diminish the birth-rate, at least—what amounts to the same thing—to increase the mortality among children. In the first place is to be reckoned the employment of wet-nurses, who should be subject to a much more rigorous surveillance than they are at present, under the Roussel law. In the second place, there is the deplorable condition of illegitimate children, the mortality among whom is greater in France than in any other country : some of them are reported as stillborn, who medical statistics would go to show are the victims of murder ; others die of hunger in the second week of their birth owing to negligence or cruelty on the part of the mother. The re-establishment of the revolving boxes (*tours*) would here also be of prime service. In the third place, let us mention the exceptional mortality in France of adults from twenty to twenty-five years of age, which must result from bad administration in the army. Legislators and administrators should direct their attention simultaneously to all these points, if they are to check the current of depopulation in France.

Then, in the second place, posters might be used. Certain speeches delivered in the Chamber or the Senate have a much feebler title to be placarded on the walls of remote villages than such and such economical, statistical, and geographical information. In the country placarding might be supplemented by *viva voce* reading by some important functionary of the village, or even by the public crier. The *Bulletin des Communes*, if it were composed more carefully than it is and filled with examples, might be read every Sunday in front of the town hall. If the school-master were intrusted with this function the reading would be the germ of a weekly conference, which considering the emptiness and monotony of country life might well succeed in attracting a certain number of the public. Statistical and economical information on the depopulation of certain provinces; on the dangers of such depopulation; on the enormous growth of the English, German, and Italian peoples; on the social consequences of the enfeeblement of a race—might thus be placarded, read aloud, and commented on in order to call to the attention of everyone the economical and political ruin which is menacing us. The influence of religious instruction is diminishing; it is essential to supply its place by a moral and patriotic education which shall combat prejudice, egoism, imprudence, and false prudence.

*In the country by proclamations.*

One of the commonest psychological illusions that a better education might dispel is the belief that one's children are going to depend for their happiness on precisely the same circumstances that constitute one's own happiness. A miser, whose happiness consists in adding to his wealth, does not perceive that his posterity will not lay the same emphasis that he does on the possession of an immense and undivided capital. The peasant, who has passed his life in rounding out his plot of ground, by obtaining here a bit and there a bit of real estate at the expense of infinite stratagem, conceives his son as finding his highest happiness in a continuation of the same process. His vision does not stretch beyond the hedge that bounds his own meadow, or rather the hedge that bounds the neighbour-

*Tastes of parents and of children not the same.*

ing meadow which he is ambitious to acquire. A village butcher will have but one child, so that he may make him a butcher like himself, and his successor; if he had two, the second might be forced to become a baker or a carpenter or a locksmith. What a misfortune!—how could one consent to live if one were not a butcher! The idle man of leisure, who passes the first forty years of his life between women and horses, dreams of nothing better for his heir than idleness. Those, on the contrary, who feel such and such a thorn in their present mode of life imagine that they are securing perfect happiness for their son if they secure him an immunity from that particular source of suffering. The hard-working day labourer, the small shopkeeper, the functionary who has laboured all his life ten or twelve hours out of every twenty-four, and has never had but one desire in his life—that of taking his fill of rest—imagines that his son will naturally be much happier than himself if he does not have to work so much. Ninety-five per cent. of the human race are bound to hard labour and imagine that the pinnacle of happiness would be to do nothing. The majority are absolutely ignorant of the fact that, other things equal, happiness is never exactly proportionate to wealth, and that, according to one of Laplace's theorems, if fortune should increase by geometrical progression, happiness would increase by arithmetical progression; the millionaire controls but a fraction more happiness than a workman who makes enough to live on. And too, wealth is never known at its best except by the man who has made it, who knows what it is worth, who looks upon it with the satisfaction of an artist contemplating his work, of a house-owner examining his house, of a peasant measuring his field. A fortune is always more precious to the man who has got it together than to his son, who will perhaps dissipate it. If there is one anxiom that fathers ought to take the trouble to master, it is this: A robust, intelligent young man with the advantage of a good education, which to-day is indispensable, runs a greater chance of being happy in life if he is busy, and he will not be busy if a fortune is handed to him when he comes of age. If a young man is to be made happy, the surest means is not to give him a fortune but to supply him with an opportunity of acquiring one, if fortune be his aim.[1]

The peasantry and the middle classes of France, when they become more enlightened, will begin to understand that the universe stretches beyond their village or their street; that their children, when once they have been sufficiently educated, will have a multitude of careers open to them, and notably that of emigration to the colonies. Whenever a limitless field of action is thrown open to a race, its birth-rate increases. People who live near unoccupied land, or who see numerous careers open to their children, are like people who live on the coast in the presence of the wealth of the ocean. What is the explanation of the well-known fertility of the fishing population, even in France? It has been attributed to differences of food; it is more probably due, as has been remarked, to the fact that the produce of fishing is proportionate to the number of fishermen and that the sea is large enough and deep enough for all.

*Relation between ample means of subsistence and population.*

To sum up, the relation of religious beliefs to the maintenance of the race is the foundation of one of the gravest problems that the decline of Christianity gives rise to. If we have insisted at length upon this problem, the reason is that it is almost the only one in regard to which neither morals nor politics have as yet seriously attempted to supply the place of religion. In regard to such questions morals have hitherto been afraid to insist, and politics have been unpardonably negligent. Religion alone is afraid of nothing and has neglected nothing. This state of things must be changed; some solution must be found for so vital a problem—a problem which becomes every year more

*Summary.*

---

[1] We conceive, for example, that a father who proposes to enrich his son might often do well to take as the measure of his generosity the sum that his son can lay by, and does really lay by, during a year of labour. The father might double or even sextuple that sum, but he ought at least to make it the basis of his calculations instead of taking counsel with some vague and often deceptive notion of equality, or with his affection for his child, which is often an extreme instance of inequality. We know a young man who at his twenty-eighth year had already amassed by ten years of labour forty thousand francs; his parents tripled the amount.

and more vital as instinct declines in power and reflective intelligence becomes stronger.[1] Shall we be obliged some day to adopt the most radical imaginable solution ; shall those who have no children be obliged to pay for the rearing and education of the children of those who have many ? No ; before reaching so extreme a point as that a number of palliatives will have been tried, and we have endeavoured to suggest some of them. What is essential is that politics, morals, education, and hygiene should all do their duty in this matter, in especial since religion is nowadays beginning to be powerless in it. Science must do in the future what religion has done in the past ; must secure the fertility of the race and its physical, moral, and economical education.

[1] See *Esquisse d'une morale sans obligation ni sanction*, p. 53, and *Morale anglaise contemporaine*, 2ᵉ partie.

# Part Third.

## NON-RELIGION OF THE FUTURE.

## CHAPTER I.

### RELIGIOUS INDIVIDUALISM.

I. Is a renovation of religion possible? 1. Is a unification of the
great religions to-day existing possible? 2. Is the appearance of
a new religion to be expected?—Future miracles impossible—
Religious poetry not to be expected—Men of genius capable of
sincerely and naïvely labouring in the creating of a new religion
not to be expected—Impossibility of adding to the original stock
of religious ideas—No new cult possible—Last attempts at a new
cult in America and in France—The Positivist cult—Ethical
culture—Can socialism renew religion?—Advantages and defects
of socialistic experiments.

II. Religious anomy and the substitution of doubt for faith—1.
Will the absence of religion result in scepticism? Will the
number of sceptics increase with the disappearance of religion?
2. Substitution of doubt for faith—Genuinely religious character of doubt.

III. Substitution of metaphysical hypothesis for dogma—Difference
between religious sentiment and instinct for metaphysics—Imperishable character of the latter—Sentiment at once of the limits of
science and of the infinity of our ideal—Spencer's attempted
reconciliation of science and religion—Confusion of religion with
metaphysics.

## I.  Is a renovation of religion possible?

WE have seen that the influence of dogma and of religious
morality is on the wane in actually existing societies; but will
not this period of decline be followed by a reaction in the opposite direction?

Such a reaction could take place in two ways
only: 1. By the unification of religions; 2. By the appearance of a new religion.  The unification of existing religions

Is contempo-
rary scepticism
final?

is not to-day to be thought of ; each of them has shown itself to be incapable of assimilating the others. The different Chris-

**Consolidation of existing religions not possible.** tian confessions hold each other in mutual respect, but they do the same with the great religions of the East. Islamism alone has made notable progress among tribes still imbued with primitive animism, and for them it represents a manifest progress. As for Christian missionaries they have never been able to make many prose-lytes among the Mussulmans, the Buddhists, or the Hindus. The Hindu who has been instructed in European science necessarily comes to doubt the revealed foundation of his national religion, but he is not on that account any the more inclined to believe in the Christian revelation. He ceases simply to be religious and becomes a free-thinker. All peoples alike are in that position ; the principal great religions possess an approximate value as symbols of the unknowable, and worshippers perceive no advance in passing from one of them to the other: mankind in general does not welcome change for change's sake. Missionaries themselves to-day lack faith in their religion ; they possess either enthusiasm minus talent or talent minus enthusiasm, and the time is at hand when the spirit of propagandism, which has hitherto consti-tuted the power of religion, will abandon it. Few people can cry to-day in the words of the unbelieving Jesuit missionary : " Ah, you have no conception of the pleasure of convincing men of what you do not believe yourself ! " Where absolute faith is lacking, and absolute faith in the very details of the dogmas is lacking, sincerity, which constitutes the essential power of all propagandism, is lacking too. Bishop Colenso was one day asked, by his neophytes in Natal, some questions on the Old Testament. After having followed him up from question to question they asked him, on his word of honour, if all that was true. Seized by a scruple, the Bishop fell into a profound train of reflection, studied the question, read Strauss and the German commentators, and finally published a book in which he treats Biblical history as a series of myths. To this celebrated example of Colenso among the Kaffirs, must be joined that of Mr. Francis Newman in Syria, and of the Rev.

Adams in India, and of others less well known.  Efficiently to
combat religions as well organized as those of India, for
example, our missionaries would be obliged to become seriously proficient in the history of religion.  But the day they
sincerely study comparative religion in the hopes of converting somebody else, they will themselves undergo conversion,
or at least will rapidly learn to reject a belief in a special
revelation.[1]  The great religions, and principally the " universal " religions, which to-day have attained their full development, hold each other in check.  These vast bodies show
almost no signs of life except within, by the formation of new
centres of activity which detach themselves from the primitive nucleus, as we see daily happening in the bosom of Protestantism, which is constantly being subdivided into new sects ;
as also within the bosom of Hinduism, insomuch that the
only sign of life that these religions give is that they are
beginning to disintegrate.

The increasing multiplicity of sects, for example of the
Protestant sects ; the courageous efforts of certain disciples of
Analogy be-           Comte and of Spencer, the birth of Mormonism
tween nineteenth   in America and of Brahmaism in India, have been
century and time
of the Antonines   regarded as symptoms of a religious fermentation
superficial.          analogous to that which disturbed the world at
the time of the Antonines and very possibly destined, like
that, to result in a renovation.   " All things in nature spring
from humble beginnings, and no one can to-day say whether
the unconscious mission of the fisherman and publicans,
gathered eighteen centuries ago on the borders of Lake
Tiberias about a gentle and mystical idealist, will not to-morrow

---

[1] See M. Goblet d'Alviella, *L'évolution religieuse.*  Anglo-Saxon religious proselytism has achieved the distinction of contradicting and paralyzing itself.  The
Theosophist Society of the United States, in 1879, sent to India certain missionaries, or rather counter-missionaries, who were commissioned "to preach the
majesty and glory of all ancient religions and to fortify the Hindu, the Cingalese,
the Parsee, against all efforts to induce him to accept a new faith instead of the
Vedas, of the Tri-Pitâka and of the Zend Avestâ."   In India and in the island of
Ceylon these counter-missionaries have succeeded in bringing back to the primitive
faith some thousands of converts to Christianity.

be handed on to such and such an association of spiritualists prophesying in a gorge of the Rocky Mountains; to such and such an illuminated gathering of socialists in some back shop in London; to such and such a band of ascetics, meditating, like the Essenes of old on the miseries of the world, in some jungle of Hindustan. Perhaps all they need is to discover on the road to Damascus another Paul, to give them a passport to future ages." [1] These analogies between our century and that of the Antonines are very superficial; between the century which, as a whole, is of an unexampled incredulity and the century which was of an unexampled credulity—which accepted all religion from that of Isis and Mithra to that of Christ; from that of the talking serpent to that of Christ incarnate in the body of a virgin. During the past eighteen hundred years a new thing has been born into the world—science; and science is not compatible with supernatural revelations, which are the foundation of religions.

Will it be objected that miracles still happen? Possibly one or two notable ones in a century! The surprising thing is not that miracles still happen, but that, with millions of believers, including in their ranks thousands of excited women and children, they do not happen frequently. Every day ought to bring forth its duly authenticated miracle, but unhappily daily miracles no longer happen—except in mad-houses and hospitals for the hysterical, where they are observed and reported nowadays by incredulous men of science. When they happen elsewhere, true believers themselves are almost afraid of them and do not care to talk about them. Of old a king forbade God to perform miracles; the Pope has done almost as much to-day; they are regarded as objects of doubt and suspicion, rather than of edification. Among orthodox Protestant nations, miracles do not happen; enlightened theologians among them no longer insist on the marvellous elements in the early Christian tradition; they regard them as more likely to enfeeble than to confirm the authority of the Scriptures. Add that as a means of founding a new religion, or of reviving old

*Attempt to found a religion to-day on miracles desperate.*

[1] *L'évolution religieuse contemporaine*, by M. Goblet d'Alviella, p. 411.

religions, a miracle or two would do no good ; they would rather result in the total destruction of the faith they were intended to establish.   A whole series of miracles would be necessary, a sort of marvellous atmosphere in which the whole face of nature should be transformed, a mystic halo not only visibly resting on the head of the prophet, but reflected on the believers who surround him.   In other words, the Messiah must be in his lifetime quite as wonderful as he is always reported to be afterward, and that without deception or finesse, either on his part or on the part of those who surround him and are supported by his divinity.   Unhappily, in our days great men are immediately taken account of by history, which verifies everything, describes everything, sets down in plain print the contemporary fact, otherwise so likely to settle, with time, into some fantastic shape.   Even the legend of Napoleon, which he himself laboured with all the resources of despotic power and brutal force to establish, did not last thirty years in Europe ; in the East it exists still, transfigured.   Personalities shrink beneath the touch of history.   If Jesus had lived to-day his letters would have been published, and it is impossible to believe in the divinity of anybody after one has read his correspondence.   The slightest facts of an interesting man's life are ascertainable : state records enable us to ascertain important dates, what he did from year to year and even sometimes from day to day ; sometimes a mere appearance in court, such as happened in the life of Shakspeare's father, may serve to fix a date ; and in the life of a prophet there would be no lack of appearances in court since unlicensed assemblies are interdicted. Life to-day is so hemmed in by reality, so disciplined, that it is difficult for the marvellous to find entrance, or to make good its lodgment even if it should get in.   We live in little numbered and windowed boxes, in which the least disturbance attracts attention ; we are watched like soldiers living in barracks ; we have every evening to be present at the roll-call, with no possibility of dropping out of the society of men, of returning into ourselves, of avoiding the big eye of society.   We are like bees living under a glass ; the observer can watch them at work, watch them constructing their hive, watch them making their honey; and the sweetest of honey, even the honey with which the ancients nourished the baby Jupiter, ceases to be marvellous when one has been present at its tardy and painstaking elaboration.

We are far from the time when Pascal could say " Miracles are as a flash of lightning that reveals." The lightning no longer flashes. Science stands ready to explain the first miracle that arises in support of a new religion.

Metaphysical and poetic genius also, upon which religions were so dependent in their earliest stages in the past, have also withdrawn from their service. Read the descriptions of the latest miracles, those at Lourdes, for example: the little girl taking off her stockings to step into the rivulet, the words of the Virgin, the vision repeated as a spectacle before witnesses who saw nothing—all of it is trivial and insignificant; how far we have travelled from the Lives of the Saints, the Gospel, the great Hindu legends! The poor in spirit may see God or the Virgin, but they cannot make others see them; the poor in spirit cannot found or revive religion; it requires genius, and genius, which bloweth where it listeth, bloweth to-day elsewhere. If the Bible and the Gospels had not been sublime poems they would not have made the conquest of the world. Æsthetically considered, they are epics greater than the Iliad. What Odyssey equals that of Jesus? Refined Greeks and Romans did not at first appreciate the simple, impassioned poetry of the Gospels; it was long before they admired the style of the Scriptures. St. Jerome, transported in a dream to the feet of the Sovereign Judge, heard a menacing voice cry: "Thou art naught but a Ciceronian!" After this dream St. Jerome applied himself to the study of the beauties of the Bible and the New Testament, and came ultimately to prefer them to the balanced periods of the great Latin orator: the Sermon on the Mount, in spite of some inconsistencies (in part the work of the disciples), is more eloquent than the most eloquent of Cicero's orations, and the invectives against the Pharisees, authentic or not, are better literature than the denunciations against Catiline. M. Havet, in our judgment,

*Genius has deserted the service of religion.*

entirely misses the point, when he asks how " so great a
revolution could have taken its rise from such commonplace
literature as the New Testament." The literary excellence
of the New Testament is of a new kind, unparalleled among
the Greeks or the writers of the Old Testament; it possesses
the grace of tenderness and of unction, which is well worth
the lyrical fire of the prophets; it is a profound and naïve
manual of popular morality, and every word makes one's heart
vibrate. The literary success of the New Testament was fully
merited. The Hebrew people, who had not produced one
man of science, had evidently produced a succession of
sombre, tender, puissant poets unparalleled among any other
people; a fact which in a great part explains the victorious progress of Hebrew religion. Poetry, like hope, is the
sister of faith, and is more necessary than hope to faith, for
one may forego the distant grace of hope when one is under
the present charm of an illusion.

To found a great religion has demanded and will always
demand the services of men of genius such as Jesus was, or, to

And the condi-
tions in which
alone genius
could succeed are
wanting.

be quite historic, as St. Paul was. But if genius
is to found religion it can do so only under two
essential conditions. It must in the first place
be absolutely sincere; we no longer live in a
period when religion can be benefited by imposture; it
must, in the second place, distinctly impose upon itself;
it must be the dupe of its own inspiration, of its own
interior illuminations, disposed to see in them something superhuman, to feel itself in direct communication with God, or at
least especially designated by God. This second condition was
easy to realize in ancient times when, in their ignorance of
psychological and physiological phenomena, not only men like
Jesus but philosophers like Socrates and Plotinus believed
that they felt within them something supernatural, took their
visions and their ecstasies seriously; and, unable to explain
their own very genuine genius, regarded it as a proof of some
mysterious or miraculous communication with God. Purely
and simply to rank these great men among lunatics would
be absurd; they were simply seeking to explain phenomena

which overtaxed their knowledge and gave what, after all, was the most plausible explanation for the times in which they lived. With the scientific knowledge that we possess nowadays, and which every man who attains a certain intellectual level inevitably will possess, men like Moses and Jesus, men who are inspired, will be obliged, so to speak, to choose between two alternatives; to see in their inspiration simply the natural impulse of genius, to speak in their own name, to make no pretences to revelation or prophecy, to be, in effect, philosophers, or actively to allow themselves to be deceived by their own exaltation, to objectify it, to personify it, to become madmen in downright earnest. At the present day those who are not capable of naming the force that is acting in them and declaring it to be natural and human, and of preserving their self-mastery, are definitively regarded as of unsound mind; prophets who believe in their own prophecies are sent to Charenton. We are familiar with distinctions that were unknown in ancient times, even to the promoters of religious ideas; the great men who founded religions were carried away by the movement they had themselves called into being; were divinized by the God that they themselves had brought to men. Genius is as capable of going to school as stupidity; and, like stupidity, it has been to school in the nineteenth century and is familiar with nineteenth-century science. A time will come—nay, probably has come for Europe—when prophets, apostles, and Messiahs will be extinct among men. It is a species which is dying out. "Who of us, who of us will become a god?" None of us will become a god, and more than that none of us wants to. Science has killed the supernatural in us even in the very centre of our being, in our deepest ecstasies; visions no longer put on the shape of apparition but of simple hallucination, and the day they become so strong that we believe in them we lose all power to make anybody else believe in them, and become, not uncommonly, amenable to the law. The middle term between the man of genius and the fool, the man of inspiration, of revelation, the Messiah, the God, has disappeared.

Add that inspiration nowadays, and forever more, lacks

and will lack its appropriate environment. Intensity of religious emotion in a people, an intensity which sometimes

Dissemination of knowledge has weakened the religious sentiment.

rises to the height of fanaticism, depends, in a great measure, upon ignorance and upon the level of intelligence achieved by average human life. When problems of the origin and destiny, and reason of things, are suddenly presented to an ignorant people, it experiences profound terrors, ecstasies, a general heightening of the sensibility which is due to the fact that a state of metaphysical and philosophical curiosity is utterly unfamiliar to it, constitutes a positive revolution in its ordinary habits of mind. When the average level of intellectual activity is once raised, metaphysical emotion loses its revolutionary character precisely because the whole extent of human existence has become imbued with it. A calm, high, continuous enjoyment takes the place of a brief, stormy ecstasy ; people who pass their lives on the shore of the ocean cease to fear it, or at least do not experience so violent an emotion in its presence as they did at the sight of their first tempest. If we had never looked upon the starry heavens, the first time we lifted our eyes to them we should be filled with fear ; the spectacle of them to-day calms us, gently inspires us. To appease the violence of religious sentiment, it must, when it has been purified, be permitted to permeate the whole of human existence, be always present with us, and domesticate us in the infinite.

A final condition precedent to the success of a new religion would be that it should be really new, that it should contribute

A new religion must be both novel and significant.

a new idea to the treasury of the human mind. Among the wretched attempts at starting a new faith which have been made from one end of the world to the other in our days, nothing original has made its appearance. In America a religion new in appearance, Mormonism, has had some success ; it is, of all modern attempts, the only one which has relied upon miraculous prophecy and revelation, such as are indispensable to a genuine dogmatic religion : it has also its book, its Bible, and even includes in its legend some prosaic tale of marvellous pair of spectacles destined for the deciphering of the book. The God of Mormonism, who is rather better educated than the God of the Bible, possesses some notion of optics. But at bottom Mormonism is simply a modern edition of Jewish ideas and customs: the whole religion is a bit of plagiarism, a resuscitation of superanuated legends and beliefs, to which it has added nothing but what is trivial; it is a religious anachronism. It seems also to have reached the limit of its development, the number of its adherents is not increasing. Hindu Brahmaism is an eclectic and mystic spiritualism without one really new idea. Comtism, which consists of the rites of religion and nothing else, is an attempt to maintain life in the body after the departure of the soul. The spiritualists are charlatans, or empirics, who have been impressed with certain, as yet obscure, phenomena of the nervous system which they themselves are unable to explain scientifically. But charlatanism has never founded anything durable in the domain of religion. To compare American Mormonism or spiritualism to nascent Christianity is to make one's self ridiculous. Humble as the beginnings of Christianity were one must not be the dupe of historical illusion, nor believe that Christianity owed its triumph to a simple concurrence of happy events; that the world, for example, according to M. Renan's hypothesis, might quite easily have become Mithraic. The disciples of a certain Chrestus, mentioned for the first time by Suetonius, could present, as the basis of their as yet vague beliefs, two incomparable epic poems, the Old Testament and Gospels; they introduced into the world a new system of morality, which was admirable even in its errors, and original at least for the mass of mankind; and they contributed, finally, to the common stock of ideas a great metaphysical conception, that of the resurrection, which, combined with current philosophical conceptions, necessarily gave birth to the doctrine of personal immortality. Christianity conquered by its own weight, it was inevitable that it should find its St. Paul; the Old Testament and the Gospels were too eminent to be forgotten, or to remain without influence on human life. There is not a single example in the history of the world of a great masterpiece, at once literary or philosophical, which has gone its way unperceived, without exerting an influence upon the progress of humanity. Every work which is sufficiently endowed with beauty or virtue is sure of the future.

It is among the masses that religious movements have hitherto begun. But a new religion could not come to us to-

No great religion could nowadays take its rise among the masses.

day from the ignorant masses of an Oriental people nor from the lower classes of any country of Europe. In heathen antiquity, all social classes were united in a belief in naïve superstitions. Marcus Aurelius himself was obliged to preside in great pomp over a ceremony in honour of the serpent of Alexander of Abonoteichos which numbered believers among his friends. To-day a bishop in Australia can refuse to order a prayer for rain, and declare that atmospheric phenomena are regulated by inflexible natural laws, and persuade the believers in his diocese, if they want a remedy against drought, to ameliorate their system of irrigation. These two facts indicate the thorough-going difference between the ancient and modern world. The contemptuous title of Barbarians, which the Greeks and Romans applied to all other peoples, was less than exact, for the Hebrews and the Hindus at least possessed a more profound religion than the Greeks and Romans and even in certain respects a superior literature. Greek and Roman civilization is a rare historical example, which proves that religion is not necessarily the measure of the intellectual development of a people. Greece excels principally by her art and science; but the superiority which she conceived herself to possess in other respects was a pure illusion founded on ignorance. The superiority that we attribute to ourselves is demonstrated by our knowledge; we are better acquainted to-day with the religion of most Oriental peoples than they are themselves; and we have earned a right to sit in judgment on them, and admire them, and criticise them, that the ancients did not possess. The distinction between those who know and those who do not is to-day the sole really serious line of demarcation between classes and nations. And the line is one that religion cannot pass, for every complete religion involves a general conception of the world, and no such naïve conception of the world as a man of the people is capable of can ever find acceptance by a cultivated mind. No great religion can germinate and achieve complete development in modern society.

The impossibility of finding anything new in the domain of mythical religion might almost be demonstrated *a priori;*

Impossibility of improving on existing religions in their kind.

nothing more attractive will ever be discovered in the way of a metaphysical myth than the sovereign happiness obtained in this life in the Buddhists Nirvâna, or obtained in the life after death in Christian immortality. In these two conceptions, the metaphysical imagination of humanity has once for all achieved its masterpiece, as the plastic imagination once for all achieved its masterpiece in Greek statuary. Something may be demanded in another order of ideas, one may exact less naïve hypotheses, hypotheses more neighbour to the truth ; but these hypotheses will never seduce humanity nor pass over the world like a wave of light, nor become transfigured in the form of a revelation. The multitude never listens to a revelation that does not announce some glad tidings, some salvation in this world, or the next ; to be a prophet, and to be listened to, imperatively requires one to be a prophet of good augury. Religious metaphysics, after its two immense efforts in Buddhism and Christianity (Mohammedanism is simply a vulgarization of these two), is condemned in the future to sterility or repetition, so long as severe and truly philosophical hypotheses, based on scientific generalization, engage the attention of mankind. Infantine hypotheses, which resolve the problems of the destiny of mankind and of the world in a manner altogether consoling to human vanity, are condemned to uniformity and banality. To discover anything new in the realm of metaphysics, the religious spirit will have to abandon the conditions which have hitherto existed ; will have to deal with ideas that lie beyond the primitive intellectual range of a Hottentot, and even abandon all notion of universality, of Catholicity, in the sphere of speculation.

The same is true in the sphere of morals.  So far as an exalted

and attractive system of morality is concerned, can one go
farther than Christianity and Buddhism, both of which preach
exclusive altruism, absolute self-abnegation? All
that one can do is really to take a few steps backward to moderate certain exaggerated outbursts
of devotion in the void, to fit Christian and Buddhistic morality to the real world, to supply this beautiful
mysticism with a material body; but for such a task a new
Messiah would be powerless, simple good sense does not charm
humanity; the cold, humble, commonplace duties of everyday
life cannot be made the basis of a great popular movement.
Common-sense is not contagious after the fashion of religious
exaltation, which passes from man to man like wildfire. Moral
sentiment may well, in the course of time, filter into us, pass
slowly from man to man, rise like a rising tide, but so gradually as scarcely to be perceptible. The most lasting approaches
to perfection are often the most unconscious. It is a difficult
matter by a simple impulse of faith to climb sheer up on the
ladder of civilization. True moral perfection is often the precise
opposite of heroic paroxysm. As the passion for goodness
becomes triumphant, it ceases to be a passion : it becomes, and
must become, a portion of our normal life, of the flesh that the
mystics curse, the man must become good from the roots of
his hair to the soles of his feet. Thus Buddhism and Christianity, in many respects, have miscarried. If the first apostles,
who preached these religions, should return among men, how
unchanged and untransmuted they would find humanity, after
so many thousands of years! There has been, no doubt, an
intellectual progress which has confirmed a certain number of
moral ideas, but this very complex intellectual progress has
not entirely been effected by religions. There was as yet no
sign of it in the small number of simple-hearted people
gathered about the " new word " in which the apostles saw their
moral and religious ideal realized. As the primitive virtues of
this small knot of wholly religious and not at all scientific
people overspread humanity, they necessarily became corrupt :
and a morality of exalted self-abnegation could not succeed beyond a small group, a family, a convent, artificially sequestered

from the rest of the world; it necessarily failed when it undertook to appeal to all mankind. The great world is too inhospitable and shifting a soil; one does not sow seed in the sea. A revival or a repetition of the religious epics of Christianity or of Buddhism would to-day meet with an immediate check; for it is the very essence of their influence to develop the heart disproportionately to the brain, and, such an effect being a sort of disturbance of equilibrium, a sort of natural monstrosity, can be produced in individuals indeed, but not in races. The investigator to-day, who adds the least item of truth to the mass of scientific and philosophic knowledge already acquired, performs a much less brilliant but probably more definitive work than the purely religious work of a Messiah. He is of those who construct not in three days, but during successive ages, the sacred edifice which will not fall.

The most essential incident of every dogmatic religion, the cult, is not less foreign to the spirit of modern society than

Growing antagonism to externals of worship. dogma itself is. The foundation of outer forms of worship, as we have seen, is a crystallization of custom and tradition into the form of rites. Well, as has been said, one of the characteristic marks of the innovating spirit, and of intellectual superiority, is the power of breaking up associations of ideas, of liberating one's self in a measure from established collocations of ideas, of being slow to contract invincible habits of thought, of precisely not possessing a ritualistic mind. If such be one of the great signs of superiority in an individual, it is none the less so in a people. Progress in humanity may be estimated by the degree of perfection that the faculty of psychic disassociation has achieved. The instinct for novelty is then no longer held in check by the instinct for ritualism; curiosity may be pushed to its extreme without any sense of innovating impiety such as primitive peoples regard it with. The importance of ritualism in the material and religious life of a people indicates the predominance among them of obscure and unconscious associations of ideas, their brain is caught and enveloped in a closely woven network of tradition, in a tissue impenetrable to the light of conscience.  On the contrary, the progress of reflection and of conscience which is manifested among modern people is accompanied by an enfeeblement of established custom, of unconscious habit, of the discipline and power of the past.  There is often a certain danger, on the practical side, in this change, because reflection becomes strong enough to dissolve habits before it is capable of making head against the passions of the moment.  The power of disassociation is intellectual, and is not in itself adequate to the moral domination and direction of the individual, and whatever may be the objections, from the point of view of morals, to the progress of reflection, it is certain that it sooner or later strips rites, religious ceremonies, and the whole machinery of worship, of their sacred character.  Etiquette in the presence of kings and gods alike is destined to disappear. Whatever is an observance ceases to be a duty, and the rôle of the priest by that fact is seriously changed.  The distant ideal toward which we are marching includes among other things the disappearance of the priesthood, which is rite personified ; the god of the priesthood, who in certain respects is no more than an apotheosis of custom, has to-day grown old and maintains his power only by the prestige of the accomplished fact.  It is in vain for men like German, English, or American clergymen, or Hindu deists, who still possess a religion, to endeavour to throw over revelation and dogma, and reduce their faith to a system of personal and progressive beliefs, to be accompanied by a ritual.  The ritual is an excrescence simply, an almost superstitious habit, mechanically practised and destined to disappear.

The movement which, in certain countries, inclines religion to be shy of dogmas and rites, is in reality a movement of disintegration, not of reconstruction.  Human beliefs, when they shall have taken their final form in the future, will bear no mark of dogmatic and ritualistic religion, they will be simply philosophical.  Among certain people, it is true, every philosophical system tends to assume the practical and sentimental form of a system of beliefs and aspirations.  The ideas of Kant and

The liberal movement in religion a movement of disintegration.

Schelling, when they passed into America, gave birth to Emerson's and Parker's transcendentalism ; Spencer's theory of evolution became, in America, a religion of Cosmism, represented by Messrs. Fiske, Potter, and Savage. But all such alleged religions are simply the moving shadow, in the domain of sentiment and action, of the substance of intellectual speculation. It is not enough to be of the same opinion on some sociological or metaphysical theory and then to congregate to the number of ten or a hundred in some theatre or temple, to found a new religion and a new cult. The majority of these pretended religions, which are simply philosophies and sometimes very bad philosophies, are open to Mark Pattison's observation on the congregation of Comtists in their chapel in London : " Three persons and no God."

The defects of these modern cults appear in their most exaggerated form in secularism, which had its hour of success

Secularism.

in England. Secularism is a purely atheistic and utilitarian religion, which has borrowed all it could from the ritual of the English Church. This contradiction between the outer form and the inner void resulted in a positive parody.[1]

In France the Comtists have made the same attempt to preserve the rites, without the background, of belief. The

Comtists.

Comtist doctrine of fetichism contains a certain amount of truth as characterizing primitive religion, but it is insufficient in its application to actual, existing religions. The religions of the present day have developed, gradually, from a primitive system of physics to a complete system of metaphysics : the fetiches have been transmuted into symbols of the First Cause, or of the Final Cause. Positivism can offer us no symbol of this kind ; its " Great Fetich " is genuinely a fetich, and appropriate for primitive peoples only. " Humanity " does not afford complete satisfaction to one's conception of causality, nor to one's conception of finality. In regard to the first, humanity is a simple link in the infinite chain of phenomena ; in regard to the second, humanity constitutes an end which is

---

[1] See the secularist version of the *Ite missa est.*

practically inexact and theoretically insufficient: practically inexact because almost the whole of one's activity relates to such and such a restricted group of human beings and not to humanity as a whole; and theoretically insufficient, because humanity looks small in the presence of the great universe. Its life is a point in space, a point in time; it constitutes a contracted ideal, and to say the truth, it is as vain for a race to regard itself as its own end as for an individual. One cannot eternally contemplate one's own image and cannot, in especial, eternally adore it. Love of humanity is the greatest of virtues and the most ridiculous of fetichisms. The marriage of positive science and blind sentiment cannot produce religion; the attempt to return to fetichism is an attempt to foist the religion of a savage upon the most civilized of mankind. Moreover, what we believe destined to subsist in the future in a multitude of forms, and to replace religions, is not pure and simple sentiment, but sentiment roused by metaphysical symbols, by speculation and thought. Religious metaphysics may consist in involuntary illusion, in error, in dream; but unmetaphysical fetichism consists in voluntary illusion, in cherished error, in day-dream. Auguste Comte seemed to believe that we should always need as the centre of our system of worship, an imaginary personification of humanity, a great Being, a great Fetich; such a fetichism would be a species of new category, in the Kantian sense. Fetichism has never imposed itself upon humanity after that fashion; intellectually considered, it was based on reasons which can be shown to be false; emotionally considered, it was based on feelings which can be shown to be perverted, and can be rectified. If love sometimes stretches out toward personification, toward fetiches, it is only in default of real persons and living individuals; such in our opinion is, in its simplest form, the law which will gradually result in the disappearance of every fetichistic cult. We must find gods of flesh and bone, living and breathing among us—not poetical creations like those of Homer, but visible realities. We must discover the kingdom of heaven in the human soul, a future providence in science, absolute goodness in the foundation

of life.  We must not project our ideas and subjective images
of things into the outer world, and beyond the limits of the
outer world, and love them with a sterile love ; but must love
the beings of this world with an active affection in so far as
they are capable of conceiving and realizing the same ideas as
we.   Just as patriotism, in so far as it is an abstract love, tends
to disappear, and to resolve itself into a general sympathy for
all our fellow-citizens, just so far the love of God tends to
overflow the surface of the earth and to include all living beings.
To know living beings is to love them ; and thus science, in so
far as it is science of the observation of life, is one with the sentiment which constitutes what is best in religion, is one with love.

Another religion of humanity, or rather a religion of ethics,
has recently been founded in New York by Mr. Felix Adler,

**Ethical Culture Society.** the son of an American rabbi ;  but Mr. Adler,
who is more consistent than Comte, has deter-
mined to do away with religious ceremonial, not
less than with religious dogma.  He has abandoned almost
everything in the way of ceremony ; he has abandoned the cate-
chism, and professes allegiance to no sacred book.  As a
metaphysician he is a follower of Kant, rather than of Comte,
but makes no positive affirmation on the subject of God and
immortality ; he admits only the existence of an unknowable
noumenon, of an ultimate reality which lies behind all appearances, and is responsible for the harmony of the world.  So
long as divergence in matters of belief continues to become increasingly great, Mr. Adler regards it as necessary to concentrate attention on the moral law itself, apart from any theory
of its origin or justification.  Men have so long disputed, he
thinks, about the basis of the law, that the law itself has not
received its due share of notice.  His movement is essentially
a practical movement and appeals to the conscience, a cry for
more justice, an exhortation for the performance of duty.

The primary aim of the society should be, according to Mr.
Adler, to reform the lives of its own members.

**Its object.** He has founded : 1. A Sunday-school, where
instruction is given in practical morality, in the history of the
most important religions, and in the elements of the philosophy

of religion ; 2. A public kindergarten organized on the Froebel method ; 3. A school, for working people's children between the ages of three and nine.[1]

Mr. Adler's following at first consisted of Jews; subsequently a number of people, without distinction of race,

Is of a type destined to survive.

gathered about him. They are left entirely free in the matter of their personal beliefs, and are united only in an ardent desire for the regeneration of mankind. Every Sunday the faithful congregate, to listen to a discourse and then disperse ; none but members of the society are permitted to join in the management of the institutions founded and maintained by the society. This religion, which is, *à l'américaine*, wholly practical, is acceptable to the philosopher ; at bottom it is simply a great mutual aid temperance society. The only objection that can be urged against it is that it is somewhat prosaic, but it is certainly one of the forms of social activity which are destined to succeed ritualistic religions.

Certain partisans of religious revival regard socialism as their last hope. Socialistic ideas ought, in their judgment, to

Antiquity of faith in socialism as a panacea.

give religion a fresh start and supply it with an impetus hitherto unknown. This conception wears an air of originality, but, as a matter of fact, it is quite the reverse of original. The great catholic religions, Buddhism and Christianity, were in the beginning socialistic, they preached universal partition of goods, and poverty ; it was by means of so doing that they were in part enabled to spread with such rapidity. In reality the instant that the period of propagandism succeeded the period of struggle for permission to exist, these religions did everything within their power to become individualistic even at the expense of inconsistency ; they ceased to promise equality on earth and relegated it to heaven or to Nirvâna.

---

[1] Indigent pupils are clothed and fed ; the instruction is gratuitous ; the school contains at present one hundred pupils, having begun with eight. An industrial museum is attached to it. The society also sends out district nurses to attend the sick in the poorer quarters of New York.

Do we therefore believe that socialistic ideas will play no part in the future, and is it not conceivable that a certain

Socialism un-<br>realizable except<br>by a select few. mysticism might form an alliance with socialism, and both lend and borrow force by so doing ? A mystical socialism is by no means unrealizable under certain conditions, and, far from constituting an obstacle to religious free-thought, it might become one of its most important manifestations. But what has hitherto rendered socialism impracticable and utopian is that it has aimed at subjugating the whole of mankind, rather than some small social group. What has been aimed at is state socialism; the case has been the same in the matter of religion. But systems of socialism and of religious doctrine must, in the future at least, be addressed to small groups and not to confused masses ; must be made the basis of manifold and various associations in the bosom of society. As its most earnest partisans recognize, socialism presupposes for its success a certain average of virtue, that may well obtain among some hundreds of men but not among some millions. It endeavours to establish a sort of special providence, which would be quite incompetent to manage the affairs of the world but may well watch over the interests of a neighbourhood. Socialism aims more or less at playing the part of fate, at predetermining the destiny of the individual, at supplying each individual with a certain average amount of happiness which he can neither increase nor diminish. Socialism is the apotheosis of state interference, and the world in general is not disposed to worship it ; its ideal is a life which is completely foreseen, insured, with the element of fortune and of hope left out, with the heights and the depths of human life levelled away—an existence somewhat utilitarian and uniform, regularly plotted off like the squares on a checker board, incapable of satisfying the ambitious desires of the mass of mankind. Socialism is to-day advocated by the rebels in society. Its success, however, would depend on the most peaceable, the most conservative, the most bourgeois people in the world; it supplies no sufficient outlet for the love of risk, of staking one's everything, of playing for the height of fortune against the depth of misery, which is one of the essential factors of human progress.

Practical experiments in socialism are being made every day; there is in France the phalansterian association of M.

Godin; in America there are the associations by the followers of Cabet, not to speak of others of a more purely religious character, such as those of the Quakers, Shakers, etc.; and finally, there are co-operative societies of various kinds. These avowedly or unavowedly socialistic experiments have never succeeded except when their promoters were willing very rigorously to limit their numbers; certain intellectual and moral defects in the members must inevitably in every case have proved fatal to them. Socialism is possible only in a small society of the elect. Even the theorists who once regarded profit-sharing as the universal panacea recognize to-day that profit-sharing constitutes a remedy in some cases only; that the labouring classes are not, as a whole, either patient, or painstaking enough to fulfil the very simple conditions that profit-sharing demands. They are unfit for corporate life, they are hard repellent individuals, they are elements of disintegration; when a small socialistic society finds them on its list of members, it excludes them; if mankind as a whole formed one great socialistic society, it also would be obliged to exclude them. To universalize socialism is to destroy it.

*Experiments in socialism.*

Every scientific discovery passes through three distinct stages: the stage of pure theory, of application on a small scale in the laboratory, of application on a grand scale in the world of business. It frequently happens that the development of an idea is arrested in the sphere of theory, that it does not enter into the sphere of practice at all, or that, completely successful in the laboratory, it miscarries when the attempt is made to apply it to business. If this holds true of scientific ideas, of devices that depend for their success upon the plasticity of inert matter only, which we may bend to our will, *a fortiori* it must be true of sociological ideas, of experiments, of devices that depend for their success on the plasticity of so variable, so heterogeneous a substance as human nature. Socialism is still, for the most part, at the theoretical stage; and even as a

*Future of socialism.*

theory socialism is very vague and not very consistent and, when the effort is made to put it into practice, the difference between experiments in the laboratory, among conditions that the experimenter can in a measure determine and control, and in the great world in which everything is determined and controlled for him, must be remembered. The state which yields to the seduction of some charming socialistic theory, and endeavours, as it will endeavour, to realize it, will inevitably be ruined. Social experiments cannot be attempted by the state—not even if they are experiments in religion, or rather in especial not if they are experiments in religion. Some experiments may at most be observed by the state and followed with interest by it ; nay, the state may even in certain cases encourage the most interesting of them and subsidize them as it does certain industrial enterprises. We are persuaded that socialism in the future, like religion in the past, will appear in many different forms. There will arise a number of conceptions of an ideal society, each of which is realizable in special circumstances, and by people of some special disposition. Human society which to-day, beyond the limits of convents and monasteries (which consist in artificial groupings of individuals of the same sex), presents a certain uniformity of type, may well at some later date, owing to complete liberty of association, and to the spread of personal initiative, present a great variety of types. Socialism will not result in the founding of a religion, but it may well result in the founding of a number of associations dominated respectively by some metaphysical or moral idea. Socialism will thus contribute to that multiplicity and diversity of beliefs which does not exclude but rather encourages their practical application.

The future, therefore, will leave the human mind, as time goes on, more and more at liberty ; will permit the individual to do increasingly as he likes so long as he does not violate the rights of anybody else. What is the highest social ideal ? Does it lie purely and simply in the practice of the necessary virtues or of a half conscious morality, an unreflecting benignity, compounded of ignorance and custom ? This social ideal is realized

*Necessity of allowing for a multiplicity of conflicting ideals.*

in certain countries in the Orient, where Buddhism is dominant, and the people are so gentle that years pass without a homicide ; and yet life in these countries in nowise appeals to us as ideal. To this sort of morality must be added some satisfaction of the principal desire of mankind, of the desire for economic ease and for practical happiness, and even that would not be enough ; for that much is realized in corners of Switzerland, of Portugal, in primitive countries like Costa Rica, where poverty is unknown. Artists dream of a life devoted entirely to art, to the beautiful, of a life which is hostile to prosaic and practical virtue, and this ideal was realized in the Renaissance : the Renaissance was distinguished by an extraordinary efflorescence of æsthetic instinct and moral depravity, and we in nowise desire to return to it. And if science, which is the modern ideal, should become absolute, we should see a society of·*blasés* Fausts which would not be more enviable perhaps than other societies. No ; a complete social ideal must neither consist in bare morality nor in simple economic well-being, nor in art alone, nor in science alone—it must consist in all of these together ; its ideal must be the greatest and most universal conceivable. This ideal is that of progress, and progress cannot take place in one direction only at a time ; whoever advances in one direction only will soon retreat. A point of light shines in all directions simultaneously. The excellence of religion cannot be demonstrated by showing that it favours some one species of human activity ; morality, for example, or art. It is not enough to make man moral as Christianity and Buddhism did, nor to excite his æsthetic imagination as Paganism did. Not one but all of his faculties must be stimulated, and there is but one religion that can do it ; and that religion each must create for himself. Whoever feels attracted by a life similar to that of a priest will do well to become a Christian and even a Quaker, and the artist will do well to become a pagan. What is certain is that no one of the deities which mankind has created and worshipped is all-sufficing; mankind needs all of them and something more, for human thought has outgrown its gods.

Under the sounding domes of old cathedrals, the echoes are so numerous that an immense screen has sometimes to be stretched across the nave to break the reverberations and enable the priest's voice alone to reach the faithful. This screen which is invisible from below, which isolates the sacred word and deadens all other sound, is stretched not only across the cathedral nave but across the heart of every true believer. It must be torn away; every voice and word must be free to attain the ear of man; the sacred word rises from no one throat, but is the symphony of all the voices that sound beneath the dome of heaven.

*Liberty the condition of knowledge.*

I was talking one day with M. Renan upon the gradual decrease in the power of religion, on the silence that has fallen on the divine word, which formerly drowned all other sounds. To-day, it is the word of nature and humanity, of free-thought and free sentiment, which is taking the place of oracles and of supernatural revelation, of dogmatic religion. M. Renan, with the openness of mind which is habitual with him, and which partakes indeed largely of scepticism, took up at once my point of view. "Yes," he said, "we are all marching toward non-religion. After all, why should not humanity do without religious dogmas? Speculation will take the place of religion. Even at the present day, among advanced peoples, dogmas are disintegrating, the incrustations of human thought are breaking up. Most people in France are already non-religious; men of the people hardly believe more than professed men of science; they possess their little fund of ideas, more or less profound, on which they live, without help from the priest. In Germany the work of decomposition is far advanced. In England it is only in its beginnings, but it is moving rapidly. Christianity is everywhere giving place to free-thought. Buddhism and Hinduism are doing the same; in India the mass of intelligent men are free-thinkers, in China there is no state religion. It will take a long while, but religion will in the end disappear, and one may already imagine for Europe a time when it will be a thing of the past. . . Islam is the one black spot on the horizon. The Turks are narrow, rebellious

*Decline of the power of religion.*

against reasoning, hostile to everything that lies beyond literal faith . . . but if they will not follow us we shall simply leave them behind, and I think we shall be obliged to do so." We should add that, if some Christians and Buddhists show themselves as backward as the Turks, we shall leave them behind also. Those members of mankind who think, see, and move forward, are always obliged to drag a long train of those who neither see, nor think, nor wish to move forward. They do move forward, however, in the long run. Professed advocates of the different positive and dogmatic religions count every day for less and less among the truly active members of the human species; and we ask nothing better. Whoever does not count for progress practically does not exist, and ultimately will not exist. Activity of thought is becoming more and more a condition of existence; the preponderant rôle that religions played in the past is to be explained by the fact that religion offered almost the sole field of intellectual and moral activity—the sole issue for the most elevated tendencies of our being. At that time there lay beyond the limits of religion nothing but the grossest and most material occupations; there was no known middle ground between heaven and earth. To-day this middle ground has been discovered—the ground of thought. Science and art are born; and open before us an infinite perspective, where each of us may find an opportunity to employ the best of our gifts. Science offers a field for disinterestedness and research, but does not tolerate vagaries of the imagination. It encourages enthusiasm, but not delirium, and possesses a beauty of its own, the beauty of truth.

## II. *Religious anomy and the substitution of doubt for faith.*

I. We have proposed as the moral ideal what we have called moral anomy—the absence of any fixed moral rule.[1] We

Religious anomy.

believe still more firmly that the ideal toward which every religion ought to tend is religious anomy, the complete enfranchisement of the individual in all religious matters, the redemption of his thought, which is more precious than his life, the suppression of dog-

---

[1] See our *Esquisse d'une morale sans obligation ni sanction.*

matic faith in every form. Instead of accepting ready-made dogmas, we should each of us be the makers of our own creed. Whatever Montaigne may say, faith is a softer pillow for idleness than doubt. Faith is a species of nest in which idleness lies in shelter, and hides its head under the warmth and darkness of a protecting wing; nay, it is a nest prepared in advance, like those that are sold in the markets and made by men, for birds that are kept in cages. We believe that in the future man will be increasingly unwilling to live in cages and that, if he needs a nest, he will construct it himself twig by twig in the open air, and abandon it when he is weary of it, and remake it, if necessary, every springtime, at each new stage of his thought.

Is religious anomy, or the absence of religion, synonymous with scepticism? Since the disappearance of Pyrrhonism and

Religious anomy and scepticism. Ænesideinism, scepticism is simply a word which serves as a label for the most dissimilar doctrines. Greek sceptics were fond of calling themselves seekers, Ζητητικοί; a name which is appropriate to every philosopher as distinguished from believer. But how the term scepticism in its modern negative acceptation is abused! If you do not belong to some definite system of thought, you are at once set down as a sceptic. But nothing is further removed from a superficial scepticism than the sympathetic mind which, precisely because it embraces so large a horizon, refuses to confine itself to some one narrow point of view, as in a glade a hundred feet square or in a diminutive valley between two mountains. "You are not dogmatic enough," the philosopher is sometimes told. "To what system do you belong?" "In what class of thinking insects do you belong?" "To what card in our collection must you be pinned?" A reader always wants to ask an author a certain number of conventional questions. What do you think of such and such a problem? Of such and such another? You are not a spiritualist; are you then a materialist? You are not an optimist; are you then a pessimist? One must reply, yes or no, without explanatory amplification. But what I think is of small importance, even for myself; my point of view is not the centre of the universe.

What I am seeking to learn, what you are seeking to learn, is the contents of human thought in all its variety and complexity. If I study myself it is not because I am myself, but because I am a man like other men. If I watch my own little soap bubble, it is because it contains a ray of the sun; my object is precisely to pass beyond the limits of my own horizon and not to remain within them. More than that, people whose ideas are fixed, clear-cut, absolute, are exactly those who have no ideas of their own. Revelation, intuition, religion, categorical and exclusive affirmation, are notions hostile to modern thought, which is in its very essence progressive. There are two sorts of men: those who remain on the surface of things and those who sound the depths of things. There are superficial minds and serious minds. In France almost all those whom we designate as sceptics or as blasés are superficial minds, with an affectation of profundity. They are also often practical Epicureans. There will always be people ready to say, with a certain hero of Balzac's: "A good fire, a good table; behold the ideal of human life!" Waiting for dinner is the sole occupation of the day. But there will always be other people for whom life consists in an indefatigable activity.

The number of sceptics will not necessarily be increased by the final decay and disappearance of religious scepticism, which is a compound of lightness and ignorance,

Feebleness of scepticism.

resting on the same foundation as religious prejudice, on the absence of a solid philosophical education. Really serious minds are either positive or speculative; a too positive, common-sense spirit might, if it became general in society, menace it with a certain intellectual debasement; but religion would not hinder its development: witness America. The true means of checking the positive spirit is to cultivate the sense of beauty and the love of art. To speculative minds, on the other hand, belongs the future of humanity; but far from being dependent upon dogma, speculation can flourish only in its absence. It is the life of speculation to ask questions about the deepest concerns of human life; dogma provides ready-made answers, and speculation cannot accept them. The disappearance of positive religions will give scientific and metaphysical speculation a fresh impulse. The speculative spirit is the extreme opposite both of the spirit of faith and of the spirit of absolute negation. An inquirer may suspect his own resources, may recognize his own powerlessness, but he will never give up the search. Strong minds will never be discouraged or disgusted, will never be followers of Mérimée or Beyle. In active mental labour there is something which is worth more than faith and doubt together, as there is in genius something which is worth more at once than the somewhat silly admiration of the multitude and the disdainful criticism of pretended connoisseurs; excess of criticism and excess of credulity are alike powerless. It is good to be aware of one's own weakness, but from time to time only; one must turn one's eyes toward the limits of human intelligence, but not rest them there, on pain of paralysis. "Man," says Goethe, "should believe firmly that the incomprehensible will become comprehensible; but for that he would cease to scrutinize and to try." In spite of the number of ideas which make their entrance into and exit from the human mind, which rise and set on the human horizon, which flame up and burn out, there is, in every human mind, an element of eternity. On certain autumn nights one may observe a veritable shower of aerolites; hundreds of stars detach themselves from the zenith like luminous flakes of snow; the dome of heaven itself seems to have given way, the worlds hung above the earth seem to have broken loose, and all the stars at once to be descending and about to leave the great firmament of night unvariegated, opaque; but the falling stars go out one by one, and the serene brilliancy of the fixed stars still remains; the storm has passed beneath them and has not troubled the tranquil splendour of their rays, nor the incessant appeal of their fixity and glory. The appeal is one that man will always respond to; under the open sky and the pressure of the problem brought home to him by the great stars, man does not feel himself feeble unless he pusillanimously shuts his eyes. Humanity will lose none of its intellectual power by the disappearance of religious faith; its horizon will grow wider simply, and the luminous points in the immensity of space will grow more numerous.  True genius is speculative, and in whatever environment true genius is placed it will speculate; it has speculated hitherto despite of all that orthodox faith could do, it will speculate still more actively in spite of all that scepticism can do.

And the practical side of human life has nothing to fear from the growth of the speculative spirit.  Given minds sufficiently large, and the fact that they look down
*Speculation and practice.* upon the earth from a height, does not prevent them from seeing human life as it is and as it should be.  Decidedly one must be a man, a patriot, a "tellurian," as Amiel said, with some contempt; to be so may appear to be a small function in the totality of things, but an upright spirit will not fulfil it with less exactitude because he perceives its limits and its restricted importance.  Nothing is in vain, and *a fortiori* no being is in vain; small functions are as necessary as great.  If a man of intelligence happens to be a porter or a scavenger, he should apply himself to that profession with as much devotion as to any other.  To do well what one has to do, however humble it may be, is the first of duties.  An ant of genius ought not to bring to the ant-hill a grain the less, even though he were capable of taking cognizance of the eternities of time and space.

II. Although the suppression of religious dogma does not lead to scepticism, it decidedly does lead to doubt, and we
*Doubt as distinguished from scepticism.* believe that the modern sense of doubt represents a higher stage of civilization than the faith in dogma that distinguished former times.  Religious faith is distinguished from philosophic belief by a subjective difference.  If the man of faith is not altogether blind, at least he perceives but one point in the intellectual horizon; he has focussed his intelligence upon some one plot of ground, and the rest of the world does not exist for him; he returns day after day to his chosen corner, to the little nest he has made for his thoughts to dwell in, as we said above—returns as a dove returns to the dovecote and sees but it in the immensity

of space. Fanaticism marks a still further degree of contraction in one's intellectual vision. On the contrary, the greater the progress of reflection in the history of the human race, the more completely religious faith becomes merged in, and subordinated to, philosophic conviction; the two cease to be distinguishable except by a difference in the degree of doubt that they involve, a doubt which itself rests upon a clearness in one's vision of things. As reflection becomes more profound, it manifests here as everywhere its destructive influence upon instinct; everything that is instinctive, primitive, and naïve in faith disappears, and, along with it, disappears everything that constituted its strength, that made it so powerful in the human heart. True strength lies in the human reason, in complete self-consciousness, in a consciousness of the problems of life, of their complexity, of their difficulties.

Faith, as we have seen, consists in affirming things not capable of objective verification, with the same subjective satisfaction as if they could be verified; in attributing to the uncertain as great a value as to the certain—nay, perhaps a greater value. The ideal of the philosopher, on the contrary, would be a perfect correspondence between conclusiveness of evidence and degree of belief. The intellectual satisfaction that we take in our beliefs, the degree of tenacity, with which we hold them, should vary precisely with the completeness and certainty of our knowledge. A primitive intelligence cannot be content to remain in suspense, it must decide one way or the other; it is the mark of a more perfect intelligence to remain in doubt in reference to what is doubtful. Credulity is intellectual original sin.

*Ideal gradation of faith.*

Employing the word certitude strictly for what is certain, and meaning by belief what is plausible or probable only, when one is investigating some mere matter of fact, one may in the end be able to say positively such and such is certain, is what the future will affirm on this point; but, when the degree of certitude involved amounts to no more than to probability or even possibility, and to metaphysical possibility at that, it is ridiculous to say:

*Uncertainty of metaphysics.*

" I believe such and such a thing ; such and such is therefore the dogma that everybody ought to adopt." Such positive basis for metaphysical inductions as exists is too uneven not to result in a divergence in the lines of the hypotheses which rise from it into the obscure heights of the unknown ; no two of our glances toward the infinite are parallel ; our attempts at solving metaphysical problems are little more than rockets shot capriciously into the sky. The philosopher can do little more than take cognizance of the divergence of rival hypotheses, and of their equality and equal insufficiency in the eye of reason.

But the problem of action presents itself to the philosopher no less than to the rest of mankind. For purposes of conduct

Postulates for purposes of prac- tice.

some one among the diverging lines of human speculation must be chosen ; philosophic thought must be left to describe its curves and circles above our heads while we walk, if not sure-footedly at least in some definite direction, upon the earth. One is sometimes for practical purposes obliged to rely on doubtful premises as if they were certain. Such a choice, however, is simply an inferior and exceptional means of choosing among hypotheses which one has neither the time nor the power exactly to test. One cuts loose from one's doubts, but the expedient is a purely practical one ; cutting the Gordian knots of life cannot be adopted as one's habitual intellectual procedure. Faith which leans with an equal sense of security upon the certain and the uncertain, the evident and the doubtful, should be but a provisional state of mind forced upon one by some practical necessity. One ought never, so to speak, to believe once for all, to subscribe one's allegiance forever. Faith should never be regarded as more than a second best, and a provisional second best. The instant that action is no longer necessary, one must revert to one's doubt, to one's scruples, to all the precautions of science. Kant did violence to the natural order of things when he ascribed to faith and morals a predominance over reasoning ; when he gave to the practical reason, whose com- mandments may be the expression simply of acquired habits, control over the critical and scientific reason. His moral philosophy consists in erecting a foregone conclusion into a rule, whereas, as a matter of fact, one ought not to make up one's mind definitely until all the evidence is in, until every alternative choice has been considered and rejected, if at all, on good grounds; our beliefs should be relied upon in practice exactly in proportion to their probability in the actual state of our knowledge. Alternatives do not exist in the outer world, they do not exist in a state of complete knowledge. The moral ideal is not to multiply them, nor to make a leap in the dark the habitual method of intellectual procedure. There is no such thing as a categorical imperative or a religious *credo* for the traveller under unknown skies; he is not to be saved by faith but by active and constant self-control, by the spirit of doubt and criticism.

Doubt is not, at bottom, as profoundly opposed as might be believed to what is best in the religious sentiment, it is even a

Doubt and the religious sentiment.

product of the religious sentiment. For doubt is simply a consciousness that one's thought is not absolute—cannot seize the absolute either directly or indirectly; and so, consequently, doubt is the most religious attitude of the human mind. Even atheism is often less irreligious than a positive belief in the imperfect and inconsistent God of religion. To be in doubt about God is a form of the sense of the divine. Moreover, the constant inquiry that doubt provokes does not necessarily exclude the erection of an altar to the unknown God, but it excludes everything in the nature of a determinate religion, the erection of an altar that bears a name, the establishment of a cult that consists in rites. In the cemeteries in Tyrol, a little marble basin rests on each tomb; it gathers water from the rain and the swallows from the eaves of the neighbouring church come and drink from it; this clear water, that comes from on high, is a thousand times more sacred, more deeply blessed than that which sleeps in the holy-water vessel in the church, and over which the priest has stretched his hands. Why should religion, so to speak, sequestrate, retire from public circulation, everything it touches? That alone is truly sacred which is consecrated to the use of mankind as a whole, which passes from hand to hand, which is worn out in process of time in the service of humanity. There has been enough and to spare of closed houses, closed temples, closed souls—of cloistered and walled-in lives, of smothered or extinguished hearts; what is wanted is an open heart and life under the open sky, under the incessant benediction of the sun and clouds.

Philosophy is often accused of pride because it rejects faith, but it was the father of philosophy, Socrates, who first said: "I know but one thing, that I know nothing."

Modesty of doubt.

It is precisely because the philosopher knows how much he does not know that he is not certain in regard to all things, but is reduced to remain in doubt, to wait anxiously and reverentially for the germination of the seed of truth in the distant future. To regard as certain what one does not positively know is to violate one's intellectual conscience. From the point of view of the individual, as from the point of view of society, doubt is in certain cases a duty—doubt, or if you prefer, methodical ignorance, humility, self-abnegation in matters intellectual. Where philosophy is ignorant it is morally obliged to say to others and to itself: "I do not know; I doubt, I hope, nothing more."

The most original, and one of the most profoundly moral products of the present century, of the century of science, is precisely this sincere sense of doubt, of the

Morality of doubt.

seriousness of every act of faith, of its not being a matter to be undertaken lightly, of its being a graver engagement than many others that one hesitates to assume; to give in one's faith to an opinion has come to be like attesting one's allegiance to it by the mediæval signature, which was written in one's blood and bound one for all eternity. At the point of death especially, which is the very period when religion says to a man, "Abandon thyself for an instant, yield to the force of example, of custom, to the natural disposition to affirm as certain what thou dost not know, to fear of damnation, and thou shalt be saved"—at the point of death when a blind act of faith is a last weakness and a last cowardice, doubt is assuredly the highest and most courageous position the human thought can assume: it is a fight to the finish without surrender; it is death with all one's wounds before, in the presence of the problem still unsolved, but faced to the end.

## III. *Substitution of metaphysical hypotheses for dogma.*

Beyond the limits of science there lies still a field for hypothesis, and for that other science called metaphysics, the aim of which is to estimate the comparative value of hypotheses; to know, to suppose, to reason, to inquire, are of the essence of the modern mind; we no longer need dogma. Religion, which in the beginning was a naïve science, has ultimately become the enemy of science; in the future it must give way before science or must become merged in some really scientific hypothesis; an hypothesis, that is to say, which acknowledges itself to be such, which declares itself to be provisional, which measures its utility by the amount it explains; and aspires to nothing better than to give place to an hypothesis that shall be more inclusive. Science and research outweigh stationary adoration. The eternal element in religion is the tendency which produced there the need of an explanation, of a theory that shall bind mankind and the world together; the indefatigable activity of mind which declines to stop at the brute fact which produced in former times the tangle of contradictory myths and legends now transmuted into the co-ordinate and harmonious body of science. What is respectable in religion is precisely the germ of the spirit of metaphysics and scientific investigation, which is to-day proving fatal to religions.

*Scope of metaphysics.*

Religious sentiment properly so called must not be confounded with the instinct for metaphysics, the two are utterly distinct. The first is destined to decline with the extension of knowledge; the other, under some form or other, will always continue. The instinct for free speculation corresponds in the first place to an indestructible sense of the limits of positive knowledge: it is an echo in us of the undying mystery of things. It cor-

*Distinction between metaphysical and religious sentiment.*

responds to an invincible tendency in the human mind to the need for an ideal; to the need, not only of the intelligence but of the heart, to pass beyond the limits of the visible and tangible world.    The wings of the soul are too long to fly close to the earth, the soul is formed to move in long swoops and circles in the open sky.    All it needs is to be lifted above the earth; often it is unable to do this of itself, and its long wings beat and trail in the dust.    And to what power is it to look for its preliminary start?    To its very desire for unknown spaces, to its desire for an infinite and insecure ideal.    Nature, as positive science reveals it to us, is, no doubt, the sole incontestable divinity, the *deus certus*, as the Emperor Aurelius called the Sun; but its very certitude constitutes an element of inferiority. Sun-light is not the most brilliant light; the reality can have no lasting pretensions to be regarded as divine.    The ideal God is necessarily the *deus incertus*, a problematical, perhaps even fictitious God.

This sense at once of the limits of science and of the infinity of human aspirations makes it forever inadmissible for man to

Persistence of metaphysical problems.

abandon all effort to solve the great problem of the origin and destiny of the universe.    The child, Spencer says, may hide his head under the bed-clothes, and for an instant escape consciousness of the darkness outside; but in the long run the consciousness subsists, the imagination continues to dwell upon what lies beyond the limits of human conception.    The progress of human thought has consisted less in discovering answers to ultimate problems than in discovering more precise methods of formulating the problems themselves; the enigmas are no longer stated in primitive terms.    This change in statement is a proof of the progress and growth in the human mind; but the problems unhappily are as difficult as ever to solve.    Up to the present moment no sufficient answer has been suggested, the mystery has simply been transposed from one place to another; so much so that Spencer says the scientific interpretation of the universe is as full of mysteries as theology; and he compares human knowledge to a luminous globe in the midst of infinite darkness.    The larger the globe becomes the greater the depth and extent of darkness that it reveals, insomuch that increase of science but enlarges the abyss of our ignorance.

One must, however, be on one's guard against exaggeration. The universe is infinite, no doubt, and consequently the

*Possible finiteness of the unknown.* material of human science is infinite, but the universe is dominated by a certain number of simple laws with which we may become continuously better and better acquainted. Many generations of men would be necessary to master in all their complexity the vedic epics, but we are able even to-day to formulate the principles which dominate them, and it is not impossible that we may some day be able to do the same for the epic of the universe. We may be able even to go the length of achieving precision in our ignorance, of marking in the infinite chain of phenomena the links which must forever be hidden from us. It is not accurate, therefore, to say that our ignorance increases with our knowledge, although it may be considered as probable that our knowledge will always be aware of something that escapes it, and may come in time to be able more and more distinctly to define, however negatively, the nature of this residuum. The infinity of the unknowable, even, is no more than hypothetical. We perhaps flatter ourselves in the belief that we possess anything that is infinite—even ignorance. Perhaps the sphere of our knowledge is like the terrestrial globe, enveloped by but a thin atmosphere of the unknowable and unknown; perhaps there is no basis and foundation of the universe, just as there is no basis and foundation of the earth; perhaps the ultimate secret of things is the gravitation of phenomena. The unknown is the air we breathe, but it is perhaps no more infinite than the earth's atmosphere, and one's consciousness of an unknowable infinity can no more be regarded as the basis of knowledge than the atmosphere of the earth can be regarded as the foundation upon which the earth rests.[1]

---

[1] The notion of the unknowable has been the subject of a lively discussion in England and in France. See on this point the work of M. Paulhan in the *Revue philosophique*, t. vi. p. 279.

Unknowable or not, infinite or finite, the unknown will always be the object of metaphysical hypotheses. But is to

Distinction be-<br>tween religion<br>and metaphysics. admit the perpetuity of metaphysical hypotheses to admit the eternity of religion? The question involves an ambiguity of words. Spencer defines religious thought as that which deals with all that lies beyond the sphere of the senses, but that is precisely the field of philosophic thought; philosophy in its entirety, therefore, and not religion only, is included in Spencer's definition. Nay more, science itself is in part included in Spencer's definition, for science, which takes cognizance of everything within the reach of perception and reasoning, by that very fact undertakes to fix the limit of their power, and thus indirectly touches upon the field of the unknowable—if not to enter it, at least to outline it, and that itself constitutes a sort of negative acquaintance with it. Knowledge is essentially critical and self-critical. The eternity of philosophy and of science must, no doubt, be admitted; but the eternity of religion, as that word is usually understood, in nowise follows from that admission.

According to Spencer, the unknowable itself is not absolutely unknowable. Among the mysteries, which become more mysterious as they are more deeply reflected

Spencer's un-<br>knowable. upon, there will remain, Spencer thinks, for man one absolute certitude—that he is in the presence of an infinite and eternal energy which is the source of all things. The formula of human certitude is open to discussion. The man of science is more inclined to believe in an infinite number of energies than in an infinite energy, in a sort of mechanical atomism, a subdivision of force *ad infinitum* rather than in monism. Moreover, no religion can stop with the bare affirmation of the existence of an eternal energy or infinity of energies. It must maintain the existence of some relation between these energies and human morality, between the direction of these energies and that of the moral impulse in mankind. But a relation of this sort is the last thing in the world that can be deduced from the doctrine of evolution. Hypotheses in regard to the matter may of course be devised, but, far from possessing a character of certitude, such hypotheses would rather, from the point of view of pure science, display a positive improbability. Human morality, if it be considered scientifically, is a question that concerns the struggle for existence and not a question that concerns the universe. What distinguishes the natural forces, with which science deals, from gods, is precisely that the former are indifferent to the morality or immorality of our lives. In spite of our increasing admiration for the complexity of the phenomena of the world, for the solidarity that obtains among them, for the latent or active life which animates all things, we have not yet demonstrably discovered in the world a single element of divinity. Science does not reveal to us a universe spontaneously labouring for the realization of what we call goodness : goodness is to be realized, if at all, only by our bending the world to our purposes, by enslaving the gods that we once adored, by replacing the reign of God by the reign of man.

The alleged reconciliation of science and religion in Spencer's pages is not made out except by virtue of an ambiguity in terms. Partisans of religion have, however, hastened to welcome these apparent concessions in their favour and have based on them an argument for the perpetuity of dogmas. Jouffroy has told us how dogmas become extinct ; recently one of his successors at the Sorbonne endeavoured to show " how dogmas come into being again," and he took his stand with Spencer on an ambiguity in terms. By dogmas M. Caro meant the principal points of the original doctrine of the soul—as if one could apply the name dogma to philosophical hypotheses, even though they be eternal hypotheses! The important thing, however, is to understand each other; if problems which constantly recur, and constantly receive hypothetical solutions, are to be called dogmas, then dogmas do come to life again, and may be expected always to do so ; *multa renascentur quæ jam cecidere, cadentque.* . . But if terms be employed as a philosopher should employ them, with precision, how can metaphysical conclusions be regarded as dogmas? Examine the writings of Heraclitus, the evolutionist; Plato, the contemplator of ideas;

*Spencer's followers in France.*

Aristotle, the formulater of the laws of thought; Descartes, the inquirer who sought in an abyss of doubt for the absolute criterion of truth; Leibnitz, who regarded himself as the mirror of the universe; Spinoza, lost in the heart of infinite substance; Kant, resolving the universe into thought and thought into the moral law; where are the dogmas in these great metaphysical poems? They are not systems of dogma, they are systems marked by the individuality of genius, although containing something of the eternal philosophy, the *perennis philosophia* of Leibnitz. Every system, as such, is precisely the means of demonstrating the insufficiency of the central idea which dominates it, and the necessity for the human mind of passing beyond it. To systematize is to develop a group of ideas to their logical conclusion, and, by that very fact, to show how much they do not include, how far they fall short of exhausting human thought as a whole; to construct is to demonstrate the weight of the material one is building with, and the impossibility of piling it up to heaven. Every system requires a certain number of years to bring it to completion, and then, when the edifice is achieved, one may one's self mark the points where it will begin to crack, what columns will yield first, where its ultimate decay will begin. To recognize that the subsidence and decay of a thing is rational, is to be resigned to it and in some measure consoled for it; but whatever is useful is necessarily transitory, for it is useful for an end; and it is thus that the utility of a system implies that it will some day make way for something else. "'Ανάγκη στῆναι," says dogma; "ἀνάγκη μὴ στῆναι," the philosopher says. Systems die and dogmas die; sentiments and ideas survive. Whatever has been set in order falls into disorder, boundaries become obliterated, structures fall into dust; what is eternal is the dust itself, the dust of doctrine, which is always ready to take on a new form, to fill a new mould, and which, far from receiving its life from the fugitive forms it fills, lends them theirs. Human thoughts live, not by their contours but from within. To understand them they must be taken, not as they appear in any one system, but as they appear in a succession of different and often diverse systems.

As speculation and hypothesis are eternal, so also is the instinct for philosophy and metaphysics which corresponds to them eternal, though it is perpetually changing. It appears at the present day as something widely different from the intimate certitude of dogma, of confident and placid faith. If independence of mind and freedom of speculation are not without their sweetness, their attractiveness, their intoxication, they are not without their bitterness and disquietude. We must make up our minds to-day to accept a certain modicum of intellectual suffering as inseparable from our treasure of intellectual joy; for the life of the spirit, like that of the body, follows a just mean between pleasure and pain. Intense metaphysical emotion, like intense æsthetic emotion, possesses always an element of sadness.[1] The day will come when the graver moods of the human heart will sometimes demand satisfaction as they demanded and found satisfaction in Heraclitus and Jeremiah. It is inevitable that there should be an element of melancholy in the emotional setting of metaphysical speculation—as there inevitably is in the perception of the sublimity we feel ourselves incapable of attaining, in the experience of doubt, of intellectual evil, of moral evil, of sensible evil which are mingled with all our joys, and of which doubt itself is but a reverberation in consciousness. There is an element of suffering in all profound philosophy as in all profound religion.

*Instability of metaphysics.*

One day when I was seated at my desk my wife came up to me and exclaimed: "How melancholy you look! What is the matter with you? Tears, *mon Dieu!* Is it anything that I have done?" "Of course it is not; it is never anything that you have done. I was weeping over a bit of abstract thought, of speculation on the world and the destiny of things. Is there not enough misery in the world to justify an aimless tear? and of joy to justify an aimless smile?" The great totality of things in which man lives may well demand a smile or a tear from him, and it is his conscious solidarity with the universe, the impersonal joy and pain that he is capable of experiencing, the

*Communion with the universe.*

[1] See our *Problèmes de l'esthetique contemporaine*, 1st part.

faculty, so to speak, of impersonalizing himself, that is the most durable element in religion and philosophy. To sympathize with the whole universe, to inquire the secret of it, to wish to contribute to its amelioration, to overpass the limits of our egoism and live the life of the universe, is the distinguishing pursuit of humanity.

Religion, therefore, may pass away without in the least affecting the metaphysical instinct, or the emotion which accompanies its exercise. When the Hebrews were marching toward the promised land they felt that God was with them, God had spoken and had told them what lay beyond, and at night a pillar of fire lighted them on their way. The pillar of fire has burned out, and we are no longer sure that God is with us ; we possess no other fire to light us on our way through infinite night but that of our intelligence. If we could but be sure that there is a promised land—that others may attain it as well as we—that the desert really has an end ! But we are not certain even of that ; we are seeking for a new world and are not positive that it exists ; nobody has journeyed thither, nobody has returned thence, and our sole hope of repose lies in discovering it. And we shall go forward forever, the puppets of an indefatigable hope.

Summary.

# CHAPTER II.

## ASSOCIATION. THE PERMANENT ELEMENT OF RELIGIONS IN SOCIAL LIFE.

SOCIAL ASPECT OF RELIGIONS—RELIGIOUS COMMUNITIES AND CHURCHES—
IDEAL TYPE OF VOLUNTARY ASSOCIATION—ITS DIVERSE FORMS.

I. Associations for intellectual purposes—How such associations
might preserve the most precious elements of religions—Societies for the advancement of science, philosophy, religion—
Dangers to avoid—Popularization of scientific ideas ; propagandism in the interests of science.

II. Associations for moral purposes—Tendency of religion in the
best minds to become one with charity—Pity and charity will
survive dogma—Rôle of enthusiasm in moral propagandism—
Necessity of hope to sustain enthusiasm—Possibility of propagat-
ing moral ideas : 1. Apart from myths and religious dogmas ;
2. Apart from any notion of a religious sanction—Baudelaire's
conception of a criminal and happy hero—Criticism of that conception—Worship of the memory of the dead.

III. Associations for æsthetic purposes—Worship of art and
nature—Art and poetry will sever their connection with religion
and will survive it—Necessity of developing the æsthetic sentiment and the worship of art, as the religious sentiment becomes
more feeble—Poetry, eloquence, music ; their rôle in the future—
Final substitution of art for rites—Worship of nature—Feeling
for nature originally an essential element of the religious sentiment—Superiority of a worship of nature over worship of human
art—Nature is the true temple of the future.

THE most durable practical idea in possession of the religious
spirit, as of the spirit of reform, is that of association.  In the
beginning, as we have seen, religion was essen-
tially sociological, by its conception of a society
of gods and men.  The element of various
religions that will survive in the non-religion of the future is
precisely this conception, that the ideal of humanity and even

of nature consists in the establishment of closer and closer
social relations between all kinds of beings. Religions, therefore, have justly chosen to call themselves associations and
*églises*, that is to say, assemblies. It is by force of assemblies,
secret or open, that the great Jewish and Christian religions
have conquered the world. Christianity has even resulted in the
notion of an universal church, first militant, then triumphant,
and united in love ; although, by a strange aberration, instead
of regarding universality as an ideal, as the inaccessible limit
of an indefinite evolution, Catholicity has been presented as
already realized in a system of dogmas which there was nothing to do but to disseminate, and that, if need be, by force.
This mistake has been the ruin of dogmatic religions, and it
still subsists, even in religions which have transmuted their
dogmas into symbols ; for an universal symbol is less conceivable than an universal dogma. The only universal thing is and
should be precisely the liberty accorded to individuals of conceiving the eternal enigma in any manner whatever that
appeals to them, and of associating themselves with those who
share the same hypothesis.

The right of association, which has hitherto been checked
by law, by ignorance, by prejudice, by difficulties of communication, etc., had scarcely begun to manifest
its full importance till in the present century.
Associations of every kind will some day cover
the globe, or rather everything, so to speak, will be accomplished by associate enterprise ; and within the limits of the
great body of society innumerable groups of the most diverse
kinds will form and dissolve with an equal facility, without
impeding the general movement. The ideal type of every
form of association is a compound of the ideal of socialism and of the ideal of individualism—such a form of association, that is to say, as will afford the individual at once
the maximum of present and future security, and the maximum of personal liberty. Every insurance company is an
association of this kind ; the individual member is protected
by the immense power of the association ; his contribution to
the associate funds is of the slightest, he is free to join the

*Ideal type of association.*

association or to withdraw from it, and to lead his life absolutely as he chooses.

The mistake of religions, and of systems of socialism also, as
we have already remarked, is that they presuppose a society
of individuals morally and intellectually of the
same type. But human beings are, neither within
nor without, copies of each other ; the comparative psychology and physiology of races and nations, sciences
which are still embryonic, will one day demonstrate the
diversity which exists between different divisions of the human
species and, owing to atavisms of various kinds, even between
individuals of the most strictly homogeneous divisions and
groups. Religious, metaphysical, and moral sentiment will
one day appear in very various forms, and give rise to associations of every kind—some individualistic, some socialistic—
so that men of the same stamp may mutually aid and encourage
each other, under condition, however, of preserving their complete independence, their perfect right to change their beliefs
when they will. Union and independence should go hand in
hand ; everything should be shared, but nobody should be
compelled to give or to receive ; minds may be made transparent without losing their freedom of movement. The future,
in a word, belongs to association, providing it be voluntary
association, for the augmentation, and not for the sacrifice of
personal liberty.

*Its various forms.*

If we pass from these general principles to their particular
applications we find three essential kinds of voluntary association that seem destined to survive religions: associations for intellectual purposes, for moral purposes, for emotional purposes.

### I. Associations for intellectual purposes.

It will always be possible for men of science to associate for
the purpose of verifying and collecting evidence in regard to
doctrines and beliefs which they themselves recognize as provisional only. There are divisions and
subdivisions in the world of thought, which
resemble the geographical division of the earth ; these divisions
practically result from the division of labour ; each person has

*Associations for the advancement of research.*

a distinct task to fulfil, a distinct object to which he must
apply his intelligence. The whole body of labourers united in
one and the same effort of thought, and turned toward the
same point in the intellectual horizon, tend naturally to
gravitate toward each other ; every form of co-operation tends
to become an association. We all of us belong to some intellectual province, we have all of us a mental native land, in
which we find our fellow-citizens, our brothers toward whom
we are impelled by a natural sympathy. This sympathy is
explicable as a vague consciousness of the solidarity existing
between the whole body of intelligent human beings who
inevitably take an interest in each other, who love to share truth
or error, as they love to share pleasure or pain : it is good to see
men draw together and agree, providing they do not thereby
lose flexibility ; providing their solidarity becomes a condition
of progress and not of immobility. Men will always delight in
contributing their store of ideas to the common stock, as the
disciples of Socrates brought their dinners and shared them in
the little house in Athens ; knowledge, supposition, or prejudice,
in common, draws people together like a common love. Our
hearts should go out first to those who are nearest to us, to those
who are our neighbours in the field of intelligence. Labour
not only fashions the object it is expended on, it fashions the
labourer ; similarity of occupation pursued with the same
ardour ends by producing similarity of heart. Companionship
in labour, of whatsoever kind it may be, constitutes one of the
strongest ties among men. In our days associations are formed
among men of science or investigators, as among journeymen
following the same trade. There are societies for the pursuit
of scientific, medical, biological studies, etc. ; and societies for
the pursuit of literary and philological studies, of philosophical,
psychological, and moral studies ; of economic and social
studies, and finally of religious studies. These societies are
genuine *églises*, churches, but churches for community of labour
and not for associate repose in a conventional faith ; and they
will increase in number with the subdivision and specialization
of each of these several branches of study. Such associations
are typical of future associations generally, religious associations

included.  Community of inquiry, which no less than community of faith gives rise to a feeling of fraternity, is often
superior to community of faith and more fertile than it.  The
highest religious associations will, no doubt, some day be associations for the pursuit of religious and metaphysical studies.
Thus the best elements of individualism and socialism will be
reconciled.  The infinite extensibility of science, the opportunity that it offers inquirers of appropriating the results of
each other's labours, make association for the acquisition of
knowledge the type of a perfect association, of an association
that exists for the benefit both of the individuals and of the
society.

There is one thing, however to be avoided.  Opinions, and
in especial opinions on morals, social matters, or metaphysical
subjects, acquire, like the sticks in the fable, a prodigious power,

Scientific
fanaticism.

when a number of people holding them in common once associate, which is out of all relation to
the intrinsic value of the opinions themselves.
Novalis said : " My faith gained an infinite value in my eyes
the moment I saw it shared by someone else."   The psychology of that remark is just ; it calls attention to a dangerous
illusion against which precaution should be taken ;  for in a
certain state of the emotions it is easier for two people, and
even for a thousand, to make mistakes than for any one of
them separately.  Science has its enthusiasts, and also its
fanatics, and might have at need its advocates of intolerance
and violence.  Happily it carries the remedy for all this with
it ; increase science, and it becomes the very principle of tolerance, for the greatest science is best aware of its own limits.

While distinguished minds will thus associate and carry on
their labours and speculations in common, men who are

Association for
purposes of propa-
gandism.

occupied rather with manual labour will associate
for the communication of their more or less vague,
more or less irreflective beliefs, which, however,
will be increasingly free from all element of the supernatural
as instruction spreads among the people.  These beliefs,
which among certain peoples will be metaphysical, among
certain others, such as the Latin nations, will be social and

moral. Such associations will be of every possible kind, according to the opinions which preside over their formation; they will, however, possess this trait in common, that they will more and more rigorously exclude anything in the nature of dogma and of revelation. They will aim also at becoming like the associations of thinkers and men of science of which we have just spoken. It will be the duty of people of education, in such societies, to hand on the results of the scientific and metaphysical inquiries conducted by associations higher in the intellectual scale. Every temple will thus be built in stages, nave on nave, as in certain ancient churches, and the highest of these temples from which the inspired word will descend will be open to the sky and inhabited not by believers but by unbelievers in every limitation of research—by minds restlessly active, in quest of a more extended and demonstrable knowledge: *ad lucem per lucem.*

One of the principal effects of association for intellectual purposes, thus conducted, would be the diffusion of scientific ideas among the people. If religions may be considered as so many expressions of the earliest scientific theories, the surest means of combating the errors and of preserving the good sides of religion would be the dissemination of the established principles of modern science. To disseminate is in a sense "to convert," but to convert the believer to a faith in indubitable virtues; the task is one which is most tempting to a philosopher; one is sure that truth can do no harm, when it is handed on in all its purity. A really capital bit of statement, a really capital book, is often better than a good action; it carries farther, and if an imprudent act of heroism sometimes has a melancholy ending, words that speak to the heart never have. There are already in existence books for children, and for the people, that are masterpieces; they supply the public, for which they are intended, with ideas on morality and on certain sciences and supply those ideas undisfigured; and such books constitute more or less scientific catechisms, which are altogether superior to religious catechisms. At some future day such books will be written in regard to the great cosmological and metaphysical

*Association for the dissemination of useful knowledge.*

theóries, epitomizing in simple language, made simpler by telling illustrations, the body of acquired facts or of probable hypotheses on the prime subjects of human interest. The dissemination of knowledge, standing thus on the middle plane between original inquiry and research and popular ignorance, will take the place held by religions, which are themselves founded on a collection of exoteric notions—a gross and symbolic epitome of what once was profound, and to-day is naïve, in the realm of knowledge. Modern science, if it is to progress, must be popularized ; like a great river, if it is to grow larger, its bed must be deepened and widened.

One of the great advantages of science is that it can employ half talent and modest capacity—a manifest advantage for it

Scientific research open to everybody.

as compared with art. A mediocre poet is a zero in the universe—at least sometimes ; but a very ordinary mind may be capable of rendering a genuine service by some almost insignificant improvement in the method of covering the wires in an electric coil or in the gear of a steam-engine ; it will have done its work in this world, will have paid its tribute, have won its place in the sun. Art cannot endure mediocrity, science may rely upon it—and find collaborators everywhere. Owing to that fact, science is capable of a degree of democratization that art does not always possess—and that religion alone has equalled. Art is capable of being and remaining aristocratic ; science disdains nothing, gathers together all kinds of observations, makes use of all kinds and grades of intellectual power. Like the great Buddhistic and Christian religions, science favours equality, needs the support of the multitude, needs to be named legion. No doubt a small number of commanding men of genius are always necessary to conduct the work, to synthesize the materials in their totality, to make the more fundamental inductions. But if these men of genius were isolated, they would be powerless. Every man must contribute a stone, somewhat at haphazard, and the construction settles firmly on its foundation beneath the added weight of all of them, and becomes really indestructible. Dikes made of irregular stones are the solidest of all. When one walks along such a dike, one feels the sea

rumble and break not only near one but under one's very feet;
the water plays vainly against the uncemented, undressed
blocks of stone without being able to detach them, bathes
them all and destroys none; such, in the history of the human
mind, is science, which is formed of a multitude of little facts,
gathered in very much at haphazard, which generations of
mankind have piled up in disorder, and which ultimately
become so solidly united that no effort of the imagination can
disjoin them. The human mind, in the midst of its eternal
ebb and flow, feels something solid and indestructible in its
possession that its waves beat against in vain.

## II. *Associations for moral purposes and moral propagandism.*

There is another element of religion that will survive.
Men not only associate for intellectual purposes, they will
Association for<br>uplifting the<br>masses. continue to do so for the purpose of minister-
ing to human suffering, of correcting errors,
of disseminating moral ideas.   Such associations,
like those for intellectual purposes, are based on a consciousness of the solidarity and fraternity of mankind, although,
of course, so far as the future is concerned, there will be
no question of a fraternity conceived superstitiously, or anti-
philosophically, as arising out of a community of origin,
from the same terrestrial or celestial father, but only of a
rational and moral fraternity, arising out of an identity of nature
and interest.   The true philosopher should say not only,
" Nothing that is human is strange to me;" but also, " Nothing
that lives, suffers, and thinks is strange to me."   The heart
feels at home wherever it finds another heart, though it even be
in a lower order of being, and *a fortiori*, if it be in an equal or
higher order of being.   A Hindu poet, says the legend, saw
a wounded bird fall struggling at his feet; the heart of the
poet, sobbing with pity, struggled with the struggles of the
dying bird: it is this fluttering of the heart, this measured
and modulated rhythm of pain, which was the origin of verse.
Like poetry, religion also originated in the highest and most
beautiful manifestation of pity.   Human love for human
beings does not demand, as a condition precedent, perfect

spiritual accord ; it is love itself that produces such accord as is necessary.   Love one another, and you will understand one another ; light springs from the true union of hearts.

Universal sympathy is a sentiment which is destined increasingly to develop in future societies.   Even to-day, as
the result of an inevitable evolution, religion has
Love of man-<br>kind in the future. come to be confounded in the best minds with
charity.   Hard and sterile among primitive peo-
ples, little more than a collection of formulæ of propitiation, religions have come, through their alliance with morality, to be one of the essential sources of human tenderness.   Bud-hism and Christianity have headed, first and last, the principal charitable organizations established among mankind.   Fatally condemned as they are, at the end of a longer or shorter period, to intellectual sterility, these two religions are endowed with the genius of the heart.   Men like Vincent de Paul have little by little come to replace men like St. Augustine or St. Athanasius, not without profit to humanity.   This evolutionary process will, no doubt, continue ; to-day, for example, few really talented theological works are produced by the priesthood,[1] but a great many practical charities are excellently conceived and executed by them.   The day, no doubt, will come when the experience of personal suffering will always result in a desire to relieve the suffering of others.   Physical pain usually produces a need of physical movement; æsthetic instinct introduces rhythm into the movement, transforms disorderly gestures into a beautiful regularity, and discordant cries into songs of pain ;[2] moral instinct turns this need of movement toward the service of other people, and every misfortune thus becomes a source of pity for the misfortunes of others, and grief is transmuted into charity.

As in the case of artistic sentiment, religious sentiment at its best must be productive, must stimulate one's activity.
Religion, according to St. Paul, means charity,
Must find ex-<br>pression in action. love ; but there is no charity that is not charity
for someone, and a really rich love cannot be confined within the limits of contemplation and mystic ecstasy, which, scientifically considered, are simply perversions

[1] None in France.          [2] See the author's *Problèmes d'esthétique*, i. 3.

and, as it were, spiritual miscarriages. True love must act.

The ancient opposition between faith and works is thus effaced. There is no powerful faith without works, any more than there is any such thing as a sterile genius or an unproductive talent for art. If Jesus preferred Mary, who was motionless at his feet, to Martha, who was moving about the house, it was, no doubt, because he perceived in the former a treasure of moral energy in reserve for the service of some great devotion ; in reserve and therefore only waiting ; silent, with a silence of sincere love which speaks more fervently than words.

Charity will always constitute the point of meeting between the most audacious theoretic speculation and the least audacious practical activity. To identify one's self, thought and heart, with someone else is to *speculate* in the most charming sense of the word, is to stake one's all. And the risk of staking his all is one that man will always wish to run. He is pushed to it by the most vivacious impulses in his nature. Goethe said that a man is not really worthy of the name till he has " begotten a child, built a house, and planted a tree." The details chosen are somewhat trivial, but the aphorism embodies the need for productivity which is inherent in every being, the need to give or to develop life, to found something; the being who does not obey this impulse is *déclassé*, is degraded below the rank of man; he will suffer from it some day or other, and die of it body and soul. Happily absolute egoism is less frequent than is believed ; to live solely for one's self is a sort of utopia that may be summed up in the naïve formula : Everybody for me and I for nobody. The humblest of us, the instant we undertake a work of charity, come into possession of a completer self ; we belong at once wholly to the enterprise, to the idea involved in it, to an idea more or less impersonal ; we are drawn forward in spite of ourselves, like a swimmer by the current of the stream.

The promotion of every enterprise great and small and of almost every human work depends on enthusiasm, which has

*Charity.*

played so important a rôle in religion. Enthusiasm presupposes a belief in the possible reality of an ideal, an active belief
**Enthusiasm.** to be manifested in effort. There is generally but one way of demonstrating what is merely possible, and that is by realizing it, by converting it from possibility into actuality. Excessively matter-of-fact minds—minds immersed in matter—are condemned to short-sightedness in the realm of the possible; analysts distinguish too exactly between what is, and what is not, to be able to be of the best service in the labour of increasingly transforming the one into the other. There is, no doubt, a point of junction between the present and the future, but pure intelligence finds it difficult to lay its finger on it: it is everywhere and nowhere, or rather it is not an inert point but a flying point, a *direction*, a volition in pursuit of an end. The world belongs to the enthusiast, who deliberately deals with the " not yet " as the "already," and treats the future as if it were the present; the world belongs to the synthetic mind, which confounds the real and the ideal in its embrace; the world belongs to men of the voluntary type, who do violence to reality, and break up its rigid outlines, and force it to yield up from within what might beforehand, in pure reason, have with equal justice been pronounced the possible and the impossible. The world belongs to the prophets and messiahs of science; enthusiasm is necessary to mankind, it is the genius of the masses and the productive element in the genius of individuals.

The essence of enthusiasm is hope, and the basis of hope is manliness, is courage. Courage of despair is not so intense
**Courage.** a phrase as courage of hope. Hope and true and active charity are one. If Hope alone remained in the bottom of Pandora's box it was not because she had lost her wings and was unable to desert the society of men for the open spaces of the sky; it was that pity, charity, devotion, are very elements of her nature; to hope is to love, and to love is to wish to minister to those who suffer. Upon the half-open box of Pandora, from which Hope in her devotion to mankind refused to make her escape, should be inscribed, as upon the leaden coffer in the "Merchant of

Venice," "Who chooseth me, must give and hazard all he hath."

The object of enthusiasm varies from age to age: it was once religion, it may be scientific doctrine and discovery, it may, above all, be moral and social beliefs. It results therefrom that the spirit of proselytism, that seems so peculiar to religion, is destined to survive religion: it will be transformed simply. Every sincere and enthusiastic man with a surplus of moral energy is at heart a missionary, a propagandist of ideas and beliefs. Next to the joy of possessing a truth or a system which seems to be true, is that of disseminating this truth, of feeling it speak and act in us, of exhaling it with our breath. There have been more than twelve apostles in the history of humanity; every heart that is young, and strong, and loving is the heart of an apostle. There is not an idea in our brain that does not possess some element of sociality, of fraternity; that does not struggle for expression. Propagandism will be as ardently pursued, in the society of the future, as discovery. Moral proselytism will aim at communicating enthusiasm for the good and the true, at uplifting the moral level of mankind as a whole and mainly of the masses of the people.

*Proselytism.*

But here we shall be met by an objection; we shall be told that independently of religion it will be difficult to disseminate a system of practical morality, conformable to the scientific ideas of our times. A professor of the Sorbonne was one day maintaining, in my hearing, that in the present crisis anything like systematic moral instruction is gravely in danger. Abstract theories cannot be taught, for they end in scepticism; absolute precepts cannot be taught, for they are false; nothing can be taught but facts, but history: one may be certain about facts. That is to say, morality cannot be taught at all.

*Morality apart from religion diffi- cult to teach.*

We believe, on the contrary, that, even at the present day, the various theories in regard to the principles of morals possess a certain fund of ideas in common, which might well be made the subject of popular instruction. Even the most sceptical and egoistic moral theories admit that the individual cannot live by himself and for himself solely; that egoism involves a narrowing of the sphere of human activity that results in the impoverishment of life. To live fully and completely one must live for others. Our actions are like a shadow which we project upon the universe; the shadow can only be contracted by a diminution of our height; and the best way to enlarge it is to become generous—the principle of egoism is interior littleness. The idea and the sentiment which lie at the bottom of all human morality are the idea and sentiment of generosity; even the systems of Epicurus and of Bentham become generous and philanthropic when they are looked at from a certain height. It is this spirit of generosity which is inherent in every system of morals that a moralist ought always to endeavour to elicit and to communicate to his auditors. What, after all, constitutes the outcome of the years of instruction to which we devote our youth? Abstract forms? More or less scholastic ideas inculcated with so much difficulty? No, that sort of thing fades rapidly away; what subsist are certain sentiments. From history one acquires a certain cult for the past and for our natural tradition, which is useful but may become dangerous if it is carried to extremes; from the study of philosophy we acquire a certain openness of mind, a disinterested preoccupation with the causes of things, a love of hypothesis, a tolerance for difference of opinion; and from a study of ethics we acquire—what? A generosity of heart that causes us, if not to forget ourselves, at least not to forget other people. Other studies enlarge the mind, this one enlarges the heart. It is unreasonable, therefore, to be appalled by diversity of moral systems, for they are all of them obliged in one way or other to beat up to the physiological and psychological verity of love, which is the principle of all altruism and presents mankind with this alternative: to desiccate or to expand. Exclusively egoistic conduct is a rotten fruit. Egoism is eternal illusion and avarice, afraid to open its hands, ignoring the necessity of mutual credit, and the productivity of wealth in circulation. In morals as in political economy, circulation is necessary; the individual must

But not impossible.

share in the life of the society. Moralists have been wrong, perhaps, in overestimating self-sacrifice. It may be denied that virtue is at bottom, in any rigorous sense of the word, a sacrifice, but it cannot be denied that it is at bottom an enlargement of one's self, a form of generosity. And this sentiment of generosity, by means of which one embraces all humanity and the universe, is what constitutes the solid base of all great religions, as of all systems of morality; and therein lies the reason why one may, without danger, study the infinite diversity of human beliefs in regard to the moral ideal—the *summum bonum*. There is a unity in the variety, a unity that centres in the idea of love. To be generous in thought and deed is to be at the centre of all great speculation on morals and religion.

For the rest, is there any need of calling in the aid of mythical and mystical ideas in our effort to understand human society and its necessities, and among them the necessity of disinterestedness? The profounder one's intelligence becomes, the more adequately one perceives the necessity, the inherent rationality of the function one accomplishes in human society; the more absolutely one understands one's self and one's self as a social being. A functionary above reproach is always ready to risk his life for the accomplishment of the duty with which he is charged, even though it be a relatively humble one—that of a policeman or a customs officer, of a signal man, of a railway employee or telegraph operator. Whoever does not feel himself ready to die at a given moment is inferior to these. One may sit in judgment on one's self and on one's ideal, by asking one's self this question: for what idea, for what person would I risk my life? Whoever has not a reply ready has an empty or vulgar heart , he is incapable either of sympathizing with or of achieving anything that is great in life, for he is hidebound to the limits of his own individuality; he is feeble and sterile, and lives in his egoism like the tortoise in his shell. On the contrary, he who is conscious of a willingness to face death for his ideal is willing and anxious to maintain his ideal to the height of this possible sacrifice, and finds in the fact of

*Necessity of disinterestedness.*

the risk a supreme and constant tension, an indefatigable energy and power of will. The sole means of being great in life is to be conscious of indifference to death. And this courage in the presence of death is not the privilege of religions; its germ exists in every intelligent and loving volition, in the very sense for the universal which gives us science and philosophy; it shows itself in the spontaneous impulses of the heart, in the moral inspirations (which are as truly inspirations as those of the poet) that art and morality seek to give rise to in us. Independently of any religious conception, morality is privileged to belong to the poetry of the world and to the reality of the world. This poetry, instead of being purely contemplative, exists in action and in movement, but the sentiment of the beautiful is none the less one of the essential elements of it. A virtuous life, as the Greeks said, is at once both beautiful and good. Virtue is the profoundest of the arts, is that in which the artist and the work of art are one. In the old oak choir stalls in our churches, lovingly sculptured in the ages of faith, the same slab of wood sometimes represents on one side the life of a saint and on the other a pattern of roses and flowers, so arranged that each event in the saint's life corresponds to a petal or the corolla of a flower; his self-sacrifice or his martyrdom lies on a background of lilies or roses. To live and to flower side by side, at once to suffer and to blossom, to unite in one's self the reality of goodness and the beauty of the ideal, is the double aim of life; and we also, like the saints in the choir stalls, should present both sides.

It will be objected that if the dissemination of moral ideas should be attempted in independence of religion, it will lack an element of sovereign power: the idea of a sanction after death, or at least the certitude of that sanction. It may be replied that the moral sentiment in its purity implies precisely doing good for its own sake. And if it be rejoined that any such notion is chimerical, we reply that the power of the moral ideal in future societies will be proportionate to its height.[1] It is commonly believed that the highest ideals are those which it is least easy

Religious sanction a superfluity.

[1] See the author's *Esquisse d'une morale*, pp. 236, 237.

to disseminate among the masses; the future will, we believe, demonstrate the opposite. Everything depends on the talent of the propagandist. Jesus and the evangelists did more to diffuse morality by embodying moral ideas in a form at once simple and sublime than by menacing men with divine vengeance and the flames of Gehenna. "Love ye one another; by this shall all men know that ye are my disciples, if ye have love one to another." In this admirable and eternal precept there is more of inexhaustible, practical power than in : ye shall be cast into the fire; there shall be wailing and gnashing of teeth. Even in the past, it is by favour of great sentiments that great religious revolutions have been achieved; and these great sentiments will persist in the future, shorn of the superstitions with which they have long been associated. Thousands of martyrs have gone gaily to death for religion; and martyrdom to simple honesty and goodness of heart is, no doubt, more difficult though not less realizable than martyrdom to death. Morality will lose none of its practical power by revealing itself more and more as it is ; that is, as the supreme end that a man can propose to himself. The true ideal of morality is charity, and charity is absolute disinterestedness, which looks for a recompense neither from man nor God. Recompense ought never to enter into one's calculations in life nor into the hopes with which one regards the future ; besides, the calculation would probably be bad. Recompense should be taken, when it comes, as a gift; as something distinctly over and above what one has earned. It is even good and reasonable never to do right with any other expectation than that of ingratitude, and to resign one's self to receiving after death no reward of merit. The most practical religious instruction is an appeal to generous sentiments.

To maintain the necessity of the idea of sanction in moral instruction and propagandism, the following argument has been employed. Baudelaire, it is said, in the last days of his intellectual life, sketched a great drama, destined to astonish the partisans of middle-class morality. The hero of the drama, stripping himself of vulgar prejudice, was to commit one after another, and

*Baudelaire's triumphant criminal.*

with an equal success, the crimes which are supposed to be the most terrible—was to kill his father, to dishonour his brother, to violate his sister and his mother, to betray his country, and finally, his work in the world accomplished, in possession of fortune and reputation, was to retire to some charming site, under some soft sky, and to exclaim with all the tranquillity in the world : " Let us now enjoy in peace the fruits of our crime." What reply could you make, it is asked, to such a man and to those who might be tempted to imitate him, if you had not at hand the menaces of religion and the prospect of future punishment ? How could you disturb the criminal's promised joy ?

Let us consider first in what the criminal's promised joy can consist. Baudelaire's hero is naturally incapable of appreciat-
His life pun-<br>ishes itself. ing the pleasures of the hearth ; a man who has killed his father can find little delight in the birth of a son. He is equally incapable of appreciating a love of science for science's sake, for the man who could love science for science's sake would never be tempted to become a great criminal, and as for pure æsthetic pleasures, moral delicacy and æsthetic delicacy in general go hand in hand ; it is not probable that a being incapable of remorse and insensitive to all the shades and varieties of the moral life would be apt to be sensible of all the shades and varieties of beauty and of æsthetic enjoyment. The capacity for a sincere admiration of the beautiful corresponds always to a possibility of strong repugnances to the ugly, and repugnance for the ugly is scarcely conceivable apart from a repugnance for what is ugly in immorality. It is true that Byron depicted certain satanic heroes accomplishing the blackest of crimes without any loss to their elegance, to their good manners, to their high spirit and courage, but his heroes, not to raise the question of their possibility in real life, are extremely unhappy ; they, like Byron himself and his disciples, are the victims of a refined remorse, distaste of life, misanthropy ; the only art that lies within their range is pessimistic art, which but aggravates their malady. Their æsthetic joys are veritable agonies. Or if, Byron and Byronism apart, one keeps close to the truth, one

may well doubt whether true æsthetic pleasures are more within the reach of a genuine criminal than of an educated butcher's boy.  His pleasure would be confined to the monotonous round of wine, women, and play ; and he could not take wine with a light heart, for men talk under the influence of wine ; and he must play but little, for men ruin themselves at play ; so that there remains nothing but women who constitute, as a matter of fact, the habitual consolation of criminals.  In all times police have looked for criminals, and found them, the day after their offence in places of ill-repute.  Very well, the defence of society apart, we see no reason for depriving the poor wretches of the restricted joys that remain to them. It would be doing too much honour to Baudelaire's hero to give him an immortality in the next life, simply as a means of making him pay dearer than he has already done in this for the few kisses that he has purchased with his blood-stained gold.  He suffers enough as it is, the only additional suffering that could be wished for him is that of remorse, but remorse is a sign of superiority.  Real criminals, temperamental criminals, those who are the victims of what is known as moral insanity, are absolutely ignorant of remorse, because they are perfectly adapted to crime ; they are made for the immoral environment in which they live, and live at ease, and experience no desire for a change.  To perceive that a door is low, one's stature must be great.  If Lady Macbeth's hand had been rude and her eye dull, she never would have desired to wash off the drop of blood.  To suffer is to pass beyond the bounds of one's environment ; the criminal who experiences remorse has strayed less far from the human type than the one who does not feel remorse.  The first may become a man once more, the second is incapable of crossing the line of demarcation which separates man and beast, for he is incapable of perceiving it ; he is walled in with his crime, and is a brute or a madman.

But, it will be objected, if this brute or this madman sees no divine menace above his head, would not many people regard his situation as enviable, and labour as they are labouring, to destroy the moral and human instincts in themselves, to place themselves precisely in the position of Baudelaire's hero? We do not believe that faith in a religious sanction

And will in the future be viewed with horror. could greatly change anybody's attitude toward such an abnormal being. Crime offers man but one attraction, that of wealth; but wealth, whatever value it may have in the eyes of the people, is but one among the good things of the world. Offer a poor man a million dollars coupled with the gout, and if he had an atom of common-sense he would refuse. Propose to make him rich, on condition of his being bandy-legged or humpbacked, and he would probably refuse also; in especial, if he were young. All women would refuse. The difficulty experienced in finding people to fill certain situations which are in themselves well paid—that, for instance, of public executioner—demonstrates that, even in the eyes of the people, money is not everything. If it were, no menace of punishment after death could prevent men generally from becoming assassins.[1] I know women, and men also, who would refuse a fortune if they were obliged to acquire it by becoming butchers—so great are certain repugnances, even purely sentimental and æsthetic repugnances. The moral horror of crime, which is in the generality of cases stronger than any other repugnance, will always separate us from criminals, whatever the prevailing beliefs as to life after death.

This horror will be still stronger when for the habitual hatred, anger, and desire for revenge, that the presence of a criminal

And with pity. now causes us, shall be substituted by degrees a feeling of pity—the pity which we feel for inferior or malformed beings, for the unconscious monstrosities of nature. One may sometimes envy the life of what one hates; but one can never envy the life of what one pities. Hatred signifies the presence of some element of attraction in the

---

[1] M. de Molinari has calculated the chances of death to which the profession of assassin is exposed, as compared with certain dangerous occupations, as that of miner. He reaches the following result : that an assassin runs less risk of death than a miner ; an insurance company might demand a smaller premium of assassins than it would be obliged to demand of miners. (See *Esquisse d'une morale*, the chapter on *Le risque et la lutte*, i. 4.)

object hated ; but pity is the highest and most definitive moral barrier that can exist between two beings.

The sole respectable and durable element in the idea of sanction is neither the notion of recompense nor of penalty,

**The durable element in this notion of sanction.** but that of the ideal of goodness as possessed of sufficient force to impose itself upon nature, and to envelop the world ; it seems to us good that the just and gentle man should have the last word in the universe, but this kingdom of goodness of which humanity dreams does not need for its establishment the procedure of a human kingdom. The moral sentiment may be considered the great power in the universe. The inherent tendency of morality gradually to subdue nature to its purposes by the instrumentality of mankind is the most striking fact in the realm of philosophy, and the one which is, of all others, the most appropriate to excite the spirit of proselytism. No myth is necessary to arouse an ardour for goodness and a sense of universal fraternity. What is great and beautiful is self-sufficing.

Whatever may be the beliefs that men will one day hold on a life after death, and the conditions which render possible the

**Cult for the dead.** final triumph of goodness, the notion of such a triumph is an ultimate moral and social idea, which will always lend itself readily to propagandism, because it is the foundation of all religions without being in any wise essentially bound up with religious dogma ; it is in essence a cult for memory, for veneration and love of ancestry, for respect for death and for the dead. Far from necessarily declining with the decline of religion, a reverence for the dead may rapidly increase because the metaphysical sentiment of the unknown in death will increase. The spirit of democracy itself inclines the masses to an uneasy admiration in the presence of death, the great democrat, the great leveller who wanders incessantly about humanity, and planes down equally all excesses of misery and happiness ; casts us, without distinction of persons, into the great abyss from the depths of which the attentive ear has caught no sound of an arrested fall.

The Greeks, who of all ancient people are supposed to have been the least religious, were of all ancient people those who
Among the Greeks. showed most reverence for the dead.  The most irreligious city in modern times, Paris, is that in which the fête for the dead is most solemn, in which the entire people rise to celebrate it, and that also in which we see the most flippant street Arab take off his hat in the presence of a funeral and salute the visible image of the eternal enigma.  A respect for the dead which binds the generations of mankind together, which is the essence of the most certain form of immortality, that of memory and example, will not disappear with the decay of religion.  Corpus Christi may be forgotten, but All Souls' Day will be observed till the end of human time.

*III. Associations for æsthetic purposes—Worship of art and nature.*

I. The third notion which is destined to survive historic religions, and which has been as yet imperfectly realized, is
Association for enjoyment of products of æsthetic genius. that of voluntary association for the purpose of enjoying in common some æsthetic pleasure of a high and morally refining kind ; therein lies what will survive of the ceremonial of diverse religions.  The artistic elements pent up in various religions will disengage themselves, will become independent of tradition, of symbolism taken seriously, and of superstition. Science, metaphysics, and morals all have their poetical side, and in so far are analogous to religion.

The pure abstraction by which the thinker escapes beyond the limits of sentiment is an unstable and unlasting state
Destined prevalence of admiration. of mind ; abstraction contains something fictitious, for nothing abstract exists in nature ; abstraction is of value only as an instrument ; its aim is to grapple with some one side of the reality, to enable one subsequently more easily to embrace the reality as a whole.  Every general result that abstraction can achieve may sooner or later become the object of a sentiment.  The progress of science, as Mr. Spencer says, has always been accom-

panied side by side by a corresponding progress in the faculty
of admiration ; this faculty must inevitably develop, in the
future, when man will have attained a less fragmentary and more
genuinely synthetic conception of the universe.   Admiration
is one of the surviving elements of the religious sentiment.
Man will always be subject to astonishment, and will always
contemplate the universe in a spirit of wonder, although, no
doubt, the time must come when he will cease to kneel.
Artistic genius, even when inspired by great philosophical
and cosmological ideas, remains essentially different from
religious genius properly so called, the distinctive character of
which is to be dogmatic.   The Greeks were of all peoples the
most poetical and the least religious.   Poetry, like metaphysics,
consists in constructions in the realm of imagination and
thought, which are capable of infinite variety and tend to
overrun the whole compass of the human mind.   Dogmatic
religion, on the contrary, tends continually to limit the fertility of the imagination and of philosophic thought ; it implies a certain poverty of mind to cling always to the same
conception, to feel no desire to pass beyond it, to create.
Metaphysical hypothesis, unshackled by dogma, gifted with
variety and liberty, must inevitably be fertile even in the
domain of art ; it cannot dwell forever among abstractions, it
must produce a corresponding sentiment, a poetic sentiment
which will not be the naïve assurance of faith but the proper
emotional reaction in the presence of a transformation of the
real world under the influence of thought conceiving the ideal.
For the philosopher, as for the poet, every surface that
science touches, every form and figure in the world that the
finger of knowledge taps, gives forth a sound, not of the
void, but, so to speak, of the "essential inwardness of life."
They resemble the marbles in Italy which give forth, beneath
a blow, a sound as harmonious as their forms.   There is an
inner harmony that may well go along with harmony of
surface ; science shows us the laws of surfaces, philosophy
and poetry put us into sympathy with what lies below
the surface.   If it is impossible to deny, as pure idealists
attempt to deny, the objective character of the world in

which we live, one can, at least, not say where objectivity begins and subjectivity ends. Between Naghiri and Yarkand there exists an almost unknown tribe called Hunza, whose language presents a peculiarity which it is impossible to separate from one's notion of humanity; one cannot, in their speech, express the idea of a horse simply, but must say my horse or thy horse or his horse. Our language is more perfect than that of the Hunza, but we are absolutely incapable of conceiving things in abstraction from all notion of human personality; in especial, when we are dealing, not with individual, external objects, but with the cosmos as a whole. There is no such thing as a world existing in isolation; there is only your world, my world, the human world. Man is so inseparably associated with his conception of the universe that it is impossible to know what our universe would be apart from us, or what we should be apart from it. The metaphysician and the poet are at one in celebrating the projection of humanity into all things. At their highest points poetry and philosophy coincide. Metaphysics is the poetry of pure reason, poetry is the metaphysics of the senses and of the heart. The two supply us with our conception of the world, and, after all, since we are the product of the world, it must be in some sense akin to all that we contain. The fundamental secret of things lies at the bottom of human thought. Poetry is a light and winged creature, Plato says, but he was speaking of the poetry of the poet, of his sonorous and harmonious words; but the poetry of the metaphysician, the poetry of profound ideas and hidden causes, is also a winged thing, but winged not to be enabled to skim the surfaces of things as a land bird skims the surface of land and sea, but to be enabled to dive as " divers " do when they plunge into the limpid waves, and, at the risk of asphyxia, walk upon the opaque bottom of the sea and tear it up with their beaks in search of food and come up shaking their feathers from none knows where. Sometimes their search has been in vain, sometimes they bring up buried treasure; and they alone of all beings employ their wings not to skim and to touch the surface of things, but to penetrate to the depths of them. The last word of poetry, as of thought, will be to dive beneath the moving flood and sweep of things, and seize the secret of the material universe which is also the secret of the spiritual universe.

II. The more feeble dogmatic religions become, the greater the necessity for a stronger and higher art. Humanity needs

*Art in a meas-ure to take the place of religion.* a certain amount of distraction, and even, as Pascal said, of "diversion." A human beast, such as an English or German labouring man, knows but one distraction in the world : eating and drinking, especially drinking. Many English labourers never go to the theatre or to church, never read, know nothing of the pleasures of home ; the gin-palace and gin take the place of art, religion, and the family. Opium plays the same rôle in China. They who do not know how to amuse themselves brutalize themselves ; self-brutalization is, at least, a change, an element of variety in the monotony of life, a break in the continuity of the chain of misery. Oblivion from time to time is imperative. One of the ancients said that he would rather be a master in the science of oblivion than in that of memory. The only porches of forgetfulness that are open to the more debased portions of mankind are sleep and intoxication ; people at a higher stage of civilization may approach art and adoration ; and these two forms of distraction are the highest and sweetest.[1]

The amount of activity devoted by men to religion and æsthetics may appear at first sight useless and even harm-

*Art as a diver-sion.* ful ; but it must be recognized that humanity is always possessed of a surplus which must be ex-pended in some way or other. Prayer and reli-gious exercises, regarded as occupations simply, are of the least harmful of pastimes, are of the least vain of the various forms of distraction. Prayer and the church have hitherto been the art and theatre of the poor. No doubt art and prayer cannot be made to constitute alone the whole of life ; mystics have believed that it is practical life that is the diversion, and that the serious element in things is religious contemplation.

[1] Slaves, exiles, and unfortunates generally drink. The Irish and Poles are, according to statistics, the most drunken peoples in Europe.

Precisely the opposite is true : preoccupation with art and metaphysics should dominate human life, but not absorb it. Religion in especial, with its myths, is too generously compounded of illusion and downright fiction to be made the centre of life ; religion is a radiant coloured cloud that wreaths the summit of the mountain. If we climb up into it we perceive that it is empty and sombre within, that it is a cloud, damp and cold like other clouds and radiant only from below.

The poetry of religion may survive the dogmatism of religion ; as articles of faith, religious ideas are to-day anachronisms; as practical and philosophical conceptions they are, like all works of art, in a measure imperishable. Who, asks Lange, could wish to refute a Mass of Palestrina or accuse the Madonna of Raphael of error? Religions have inspired literary and artistic labours—products which will survive them at least in part, and will constitute ultimately their best justification. What remains of the Crusades to-day? Among the best things that they gave us must be counted certain flowers that they brought back with them and propagated among us, for example, Damascus roses, and certain colours and perfumes which have survived the great rising of Europe against Asia in support of certain ideas and passions which are to-day forever extinct.

*Æsthetic element in religion.*

Looked at from a certain point of view, priests are the artists of the people, but the genuine artist ought to move with the times, understand new motives and not repeat indefinitely, from generation to generation, the same musical or poetical theme. The feeble side of religious æsthetics is that its repertoire of incident and mystery is severely limited, that it has repeated itself for centuries. It must enlarge the number of its pieces, must abandon those it has. Nothing could be better than to assemble for the purpose of experiencing in common an emotion at once æsthetic and serious, seeing and hearing something beautiful ; but it is impossible that this emotion should be indefinitely prolonged by a repetition of the same stimulus. Rites are irreconcilable with the double aim of art : variety

*Defects of æsthetic side of religion.*

and progress in the expression of the emotions themselves. Sooner or later the rudimentary art of ritual must give place to genuine and progressive art, just as the instinctive and eternally monotonous architecture practised by bird and insect has become the infinitely varied architecture which has produced and will produce masterpieces of the most varied kind, from Notre Dame de Paris to the Alhambra.

In general, men gather together to listen. Conferences, sermons, songs are the most permanent features in religious cult. They will probably exist in some form or **Transformation of the sermon.** other in future associations as in those of the past. One point will become increasingly important in every spoken word addressed to the people, and that is the instructive aspect of what is said; if one is to address the people, one must teach them something. Well, there are three kinds of instruction, scientific, literary and moral, or metaphysical. The first will have to be more and more generously given, not only in school but wherever adults congregate. The two other sorts may be given simultaneously by lectures. The most interesting elements in many sermons and conferences are the texts and citations brought to the hearers' attention by the speaker. The choice of these texts, the manner in which they are expounded and introduced to the comprehension of the multitude, constitute the value of the sermon. In other words, the best sermon consists simply in the reading and exposition of some choice page from a good book. In Germany, in England, in the Indies preachers of certain liberal sects choose their texts indifferently from among the whole number of the sacred books of humanity. A still more liberal epoch may be conceived, when texts will be selected not only from among the writings of the poets of ancient times but also from among the writings of men of genius of all times; every great work will be read and commented on as a sacred book. The most complete expression of the so-called religious sentiment, apart from the vast Hindu or Jewish epochs, is, after all, to be found in certain profane masterpieces, from the works of Plato and Marcus Aurelius to Kant's " Hymn to Duty "; from the dramas of Æschylus to the "Hamlet" of Shakespeare, to the "Polyeucte" of Corneille, and the "Contemplations" of Victor Hugo.

Religious prophets, like priests, will be replaced by great poets, great metaphysicians, great men of science. Each of us will be able to choose our prophet, to prefer the genius which is best adapted to our personal intelligence and best serves as an intermediary between us and the eternal truth, and each of us will be in the last resort our own priest.[1]

**Transformation of the prophet.**

Apart from poetry and eloquence, the most religious of the arts, the most capable of inspiring the multitude with an elevated sympathy has been, and will be music. Wagner was not absolutely wrong in his notion that music will be the religion of the future, or, at least, the cult of the future. We do not speak of instrumental music only, but also and in especial of vocal music, of choruses such as are often met with in Germany, in which many voices unite in producing the same chant, in beating the same rhythm which has been regulated in advance by genius. Thus conceived, music is truly religious and socially significant.[2]

**Music.**

For the rest, almost every art is reconcilable with the gravity of religious sentiment, for every art at its best awakens, no less than poetry and music, a contemplative and philosophical mood. One may agree with Strauss that religion will gradually be transmuted into art, and even at the present day profane art and sacred art are rather different than opposed. These differences will always subsist; it is evident that a *pas redoublé*, for example, can never be the symbol of a really profound idea of nature or of humanity or of the infinite. Religious æsthetics, even though it be-

**Kinship of æsthetic and religious sentiment.**

[1] " Prophecy is not dead, it flourishes under another name. Religious reforms, emancipation from oppressive authority, war against corrupt institutions, religious poetry, philosophy of history—are all represented under various titles in the modern world. The old trunk has branched again simply." (M. Albert Réville, p. 229, *Prolégomènes de l'Histoire des religions.*)

[2] Music at the present day forms a part of the cult; but either it is supplied by members of the faithful, in which event it is sufficiently bad, for the majority of the faithful are ignorant of music ; or it is provided by mercenaries, and it is then

comes continuously larger and more tolerant, will exclude to the end certain inferior forms of art.

If art is to take the place of religion, it must progress in certain directions, not only in its forms but in its material methods of appeal. Note how much better church services are presented, from the point of view of hygiene, than art exhibitions are. Moderation is practised in the matter of light; the rooms are large and well supplied with fresh air, are of an almost constant temperature; and the æsthetic services are restful rather than exhausting. Compare with all this the entertainment given in concert halls and theatres, where multitudes are packed together under unnecessarily brilliant lights, where the spectators are wrought up and excited and exhausted in a hundred ways and pass out, finally, fatigued, enfeebled, nervously keyed up, and pursued by a host of sensual images. Church architects are infinitely more conversant with hygiene than those who build our theatres; they understand that if the heavens are to be shut out at all, space enough must be shut in to give the heart and chest room to expand. Among the Greeks, where art really did form a sort of religion, the theatres were open to the sky so that the spectators might really repose in body while they gave up their minds to be played upon by the poet.

*Necessary reforms in lay art.*

Just as existing profane art must undergo certain transformations before it can be expected fully to satisfy a sane and well-balanced nature, so religious art, if it is to be true to its highest tendencies, must transform itself, must rid itself of precisely the elements which to-day seem distinctively to constitute it, namely its marvellous subject-matter and conventional handling. The marvellous in

*In religious art.*

more commonly good, but is generally ill chosen. Musical education will one day probably be much more wide-spread than it is to-day; it would not be more difficult, and would always be more useful, to teach children the elements of music than to teach them the mystery of the Incarnation. More than that, if religious music were chosen not only from so-called sacred works but from the works of classical masters generally, one might be certain of hearing good music, varied in style and movement, and capable of pleasing all those in whom the æsthetic sense is developed.

art was long necessary, as we have seen, to capture men's attention; contemporaneous art does not need to make this appeal. All art took its rise from convention, from ceremonial, but has enfranchised itself by degrees. It might even be established as a general law that the more perfect, the more expressive, arts become—the more, that is to say they seek precisely to body forth the sentiment of the artist; and the more expressive they are the less conventional and less pompous they must be. Amplification and exaggeration are suppressed. The artist occupies toward his emotions the same relation that the translator of a great work does to his text: his translation will be regarded nowadays as perfect in proportion as it is close, as it follows the text, line by line and word by word; formerly the tradition was otherwise, and every translator felt himself obliged to amplify. Art possesses *great* means of inspiring emotion, but not *gross* means. Public speakers at the present day make much less frequent use of gesture; the actor no longer steps out on the stage in the cothurnus; the language of verse is approaching the language of ordinary life; music is breaking away from the conventions of counterpoint. What is true of the diverse arts is true also of religious æsthetics, which will one day abandon the fictitious ornaments and vain ceremonies of ritualism. If an æsthetic expression of some profound sentiment is to be true and durable, it must itself be profound, must be like what it expresses, must be murmured rather than articulate. What renders certain verse eternal is its simplicity: the more overcharged an art is the more caducous it proves, like the architecture of the Jesuit style, which is to-day so ridiculous, with its gilding and false ornaments. Ceremonies, properly so called, will become more and more simple in religious or moral associations; the day will come, no doubt, when they will not be employed at all except to celebrate the three great events of human life: birth, marriage, and death; nay, perhaps they will disappear altogether as emotion becomes too profound to be translated by any objective device, by any conventional ceremony whatever.

" Une larme en dit plus que vous n'en pourriez dire."

In cemeteries the tombs of distinguished people may be recognized by their simplicity, by their freedom from conventional ornament. A marble slab under a wreath of flowers is enough to produce upon the passer-by a more vivid impression than crosses, burning lamps, images of the saints, infantine gewgaws, and ridiculous inscriptions. Eternal enigmas need not be supplied with excess of language; they are quite capable of making themselves heard without raising their voices. The silence of the stars is more impressive than speech, and the highest religious instruction could not do better than teach men to listen to such science. Meditation, which, after all, is recommended by every religion, implies the negation of rite.

III. A feeling for nature was, in the beginning, an important element in the composition of the religious sentiment. *Enjoyment of natural beauty.* Hindu ascetics went up into the valleys of the Himalayas, St. Antoine went into the desert at Thebes, St. Bruno went to La Grande Chartreuse, in search of something more than simple solitude; they all of them experienced an ill-defined need to eke out monotony of contemplation by admiration of the beautiful in nature; a need to fill the void of ecstasy with harmonious and powerful sensations. They were unconscious poets, painters without hands, astronomers without special knowledge, and their sentiment for nature made part of their religious sentiment; the profane mingled with the divine, and they ascribed to God alone the intense emotion that forest and mountain summit had given rise to in them. To-day, the æsthetic sentiment exists apart from religious sentiment; although every æsthetic sentiment of an especially elevated kind is both contemplative and philosophical, it contains no suggestion of any particular religion: no tabernacle can roof in heaven; æsthetic sentiment is foreign to the definite and anthropomorphic notion of a personal God. When we contemplate nature we have no sense of communion with the personality of God; the artist has definitively supplanted the religious hermit. The power of theological sentiment has weakened ; the power of sympathy for nature has increased.

This sense of natural beauty, which is so strong in many men at the present day, is destined to a much greater future. Like æsthetic faculties generally, a sense for the beauty of nature must be cultivated and developed by a well-directed education. No germ of it apparently is to be found in certain cases among the peasantry, where a mechanical habit of life has dulled the emotions, nor among dwellers in cities, in whom antagonistic tastes have been developed. A genuine Parisian cares little for the country; he can pass an hour or two in the fields, as he might in the Bois de Boulogne. An open-air landscape would not so readily appeal to him as a picture of it in a gold frame; his eye is not educated for dealing with the dimensions of nature.

*Should be cherished.*

Of all æsthetic sentiments, love of nature possesses the advantage of being the one which, even though pushed to excess, does not disturb the equilibrium of body and mind. Love of nature is the sole emotion which is absolutely hygienic. One may die of an exaggerated love of the theatre, of music and so forth; one simply becomes healthy from an exaggerated love of nature. Air and light! The Greeks were right, were they not? to philosophize in the open air, in gardens and groves. A ray of sunlight sometimes helps one more to understand the world than an eternity of meditation in some gray room in the midst of open volumes.[1]

*The most wholesome form of enjoyment.*

[1] Every library reading room ought to open on a garden where one could read and write on fine days in the open air. For all men whose labour is physical—for example, for a factory hand—the proper recreation is repose in the open air, and, if need be, intellectual labour in the open air. For men who work with their minds, the proper recreation is bodily exercise in the open air, in the sunlight. For children every holiday ought to be spent in the country. Lighted rooms, children's entertainments in the house even on Sunday afternoons, theatrical representations, are, hygienically speaking, absurdities. All boarding-schools, moreover, ought to be beyond the city limits and if possible on some commanding height. If there existed in France, as in Germany for example, great colleges in country districts hard by forests, or still better, in the highlands of Dauphiny or the Pyrenees, such places would ultimately be adopted by the better classes for their

Compare the appeal that nature makes to the æsthetic sense with that made by human art, and you will at once perceive the superiority of the former. Art,

**Superior to enjoyment of human art.**

even great art, even that which seems closest to the truth, can never be more than a very insufficient representation of the real world, because it is forced to a selection; it is forced to ignore nine-tenths of life in order to set in a clear light what is extreme, what appeals to laughter or to tears. Average human life is neither ridiculous nor tragic; life, as it appears in art, is generally one or the other. The reason is that art subordinates truth to interest, while life is truth. Thence results the movement toward pessimism in art, and in especial in modern art; the more masterly the artist is, the more he will be inclined to seek for the ridiculous or the melancholy aspects of life; his aim is to move pity or mirth, and existence in his pages must take the form of tragedy or comedy. To live too exclusively in the world of art is to live in a factitious environment as if one should pass one's whole existence in a theatre. The most beautiful poem, the most beautiful work of art, contains pitfalls which one must avoid. The imagination usually plays with loaded dice. Whoever lives too exclusively on human art becomes, therefore, a little unhealthy, a little unbalanced. The great source of æsthetic appeal is and should be nature, which is always sincere, always shows for what it is, without deception and ornament. A higher æsthetic culture will increase one's sensibility to natural beauty, and it is in a contemplation of the cosmos that æsthetic sentiment, and a purified religious sentiment, will find it possible most completely to coincide. The emotion that arises from the contemplation of a landscape, of a sunset, of a stretch of blue sea, of a snow-capped mountain outlined against the sky, or even the blue dome of the sky itself, is absolutely pure, sane, neither too depressing, nor too immoderately gay. In the presence of nature one's æsthetic

children's education, and thus might be combated the degeneracy of the middle class, which is so much more rapid in France than elsewhere, because the custom of restricting the number of children interferes with natural selection.

sensibilities become the means of refreshing and resting one instead of fatiguing one—nature smiles but never grimaces; and its smile penetrates the soul as the sunlight penetrates the eye; and if nature has its moods of sadness, they contain a touch of the infinite which enlarges the heart. The immensity of nature and of the all-enveloping heavens becomes, for those who feel it, a constant source of a certain stoical serenity.

# CHAPTER III.

## THEISM.

### REVIEW OF THE PRINCIPAL METAPHYSICAL HYPOTHESES WHICH WILL REPLACE DOGMA.

I. Introduction—Progress of metaphysical hypothesis—Metaphysical hypotheses destined to increasing diversity in details, and increasing agreement on essential points—Importance of the moral element in metaphysical hypotheses—The part played by conscience in human morality will not diminish, as Mr. Spencer says—Sympathetic groups under which divers systems of metaphysics will be ranged.

II. Theism—1. Probable fate of the creation hypothesis—The author of the world conceived as a prime mover—Eternity of movement—The author of the world conceived as a creator properly so called—Illusion involved in the conception of nothing —Criticism of the creation hypothesis from the point of view of morals : the problem of evil and of the responsibility of the creator—Attempts to save optimism—Hypothesis of a God creating free agents, "workmen" and not "work"—Reciprocal determinism and the illusion of spontaneity—Immorality of the temptation—Hypothesis of the fall, its impossibility—God the tempter—Lucifer and God—2. Probable fate of the notion of Providence—Hypotheses to explain a special Providence and miracles thus insufficient—Hypothesis of a non-omnipotent God proposed by John Stuart Mill—The God of Comtism—Religion should be not solely human but cosmic—The fate of the philosophical idea of God—Rational religion proposed by the neo-Kantians—Ultimate transformation of the notion of Divinity and of Providence—Human Providence and progressive Divinity in the world.

## I. Introduction—Progress of metaphysical hypothesis.

To say that humanity, in its search for a plausible explanation of the world, finds itself in the presence of a great number **Trend visible in metaphysical speculation.** of hypotheses among which it must choose does not mean that these hypotheses should be regarded with a benevolent neutrality, that they are equivalent in the eyes of reason. Far from it : we believe that metaphysical hypotheses already are following a certain general direction and will continue to do so in the future. Our conception of the unknown will become precise as our knowledge of the knowable becomes complete. Even morals, which vary so markedly from country to country, tend to approach a single type and to become identical among all civilized peoples. The same may be said of the practical part of all religions. Rites become every day simpler, and dogmas do the same, and metaphysical hypotheses will do the same. By the progress of human thought, the avenues that lead to truth will be better known. We regard it as certain, for example, that all effort will be abandoned, if it has not been abandoned already, to conceive mankind's ideal as embodied in the jealous and evil God of the Bible.

The angle at which different human beings look out upon the ideal will continually diminish ; and as the angle diminishes, the power of vision will increase, and this unexpected result will follow : that metaphysical hypotheses concerning the world and its destiny will never be less numerous nor less varied, in spite of the increasing convergence. Human thought may even become more personal, more original, fuller of delicate distinctions, and at the same time less inconsistent as one passes from mind to mind. As mankind approximates the truth its details will become more various, and the beauty of the whole more marked. An approach to certitude augments the dignity and probability of the possible hypotheses without diminishing their number. Astronomy, for example, has increased the sum of the known truths about celestial bodies and at the same time multiplied the number of possible hypotheses concerning them ; the most definite knowledge may thus be the most fertile in views of every sort, even of obscure ones. As the human mind progresses it will see the aspects of nature diversify and the laws of nature unify. This evening from Sermione, the peninsula dear to Catullus, I saw on the surface of Lago di Garda the reflection of as many stars as I could have seen had I lifted my eyes to heaven. Each star reflected in the lake was in reality nothing but a brilliant drop of water, close to my hand ; each of the stars in heaven is a world

*Number of metaphysical hypotheses not destined to decrease.*

separate from me by an infinite reach of space; the stars of
heaven and of the lake were, however, to me the same.
The real distance of things and the depth of the universe
escape the human eye. But science corrects the eye,
measures distances at their just worth, probes ever deeper into
the vault of heaven, distinguishing objects from their reflec-
tions. Science takes account at once of the place of the ray
in the water and of its origin in the sky. It will perhaps one
day discover, in an infinitely magnified expanse of thought,
the primitive and central spring of light which as yet communicates with us only by reflection and broken rays and
flying scintillations from some unstable mirror.

Since the Stoics and Kant, metaphysical hypotheses have
come to be regarded from a new point of view. What to-
day has come to be the great charm of such
Moralism.     hypotheses is that they endeavour to lend a moral
significance to the world, to impress upon the course of universal evolution a direction conformable to that of our conscience as affectionate and sociable beings. The future history
of religion may be summed up in this law: that religious
dogmas, transformed at first into simple metaphysical conjec-
tures, reduced later to a certain number of definite hypotheses,
among which the individual made his choice on increasingly
rational grounds, ultimately came to bear principally on the
problem of morals. Religious metaphysics, in effect, will
result in a transcendental theory of universality, an ideal
sociology embracing in its sweep all the beings that constitute
the universe; and this sociology will be founded, not upon
physical inductions, like that of the earliest religions, nor
upon ontological inductions like that of the first system of
metaphysics, but upon the moral conscience of mankind.
Animism, theism, pantheism, are destined to fall under the
domination of what may be called moralism.

Such diverse solutions as may be given of the moral problem thus understood will always interest mankind, but they
will occupy a smaller and smaller place in its practical life;
they will lose the extraordinary influence that religions have

often possessed over the conduct of men. As society progresses the moral agent will find less and less need to appeal

Increasing
interest in
moralism

for support in the conduct of life to metaphysical
hypotheses and systematic uncertainty. Positive morality will more and more completely suffice for the ordinary exigencies of life. Generosity of heart
will be less dependent on the intelligence for its adventurous
impulses; it will produce them unassisted. Metaphysical
speculations will tend to become, like the highest æsthetic
products, a luxury; they will be sought for their own sakes,
and for the general elevation of mind that they bestow,
rather than for guidance in particular matters of conduct. The destiny of the world will interest us quite apart
from any question of our own destiny, and our voyages into
the unknown will be prompted not by selfishness but by disinterested curiosity.

We do not believe, however, with Mr. Spencer that the part to
be played by the reflective conscience in human life is destined

And in reflective
rectitude.

to diminish, nor that man will come to do what
is right in obedience to a blind instinct—to rush
into the fire or throw himself into the water to
save the life of a fellow-creature almost as irreflectively as he
would lift his hat to a friend in the street. On the contrary,
man will become more and more reflective and philosophical
in all things, and among others, in regard to the directing
principles of his conduct. And there is no room in all this for
the belief that the dissolving influence exercised by reflection
upon primitive instincts will seriously hinder the growth of the
social instinct. Intelligence paralyzes instincts only when it
is obliged to oppose them, when it does not justify them, when
it aims really at displacing them.[1] But speculative thought
will always justify social instinct, even considered purely from
the scientific and positive point of view. As we have shown,
the most extraordinary manifestation of the social instinct,
devotion, belongs to the general law of life, and does not in
the least possess the abnormal character that has sometimes

[1] See upon this point the author's *Problèmes d'esthétique*, p. 139 (*De l'antago-
nisme entre l'esprit scientifique et l'instinct.*)

been attributed to it; to run a risk for someone else is not to be purely unselfish, for one is attracted by the sublimity of danger and of risk, and a capacity for this attraction has been developed and rendered powerful by natural selection in the higher species of the animal kingdom; the desire to expose one's self is almost normal in a morally well-constituted individual. In morals as in æsthetics sublimity is allied to beauty.[1] The speculative instinct will, therefore, not counteract the social instinct; it will rather fortify it, and human disinterestedness generally, for speculation itself is the most disinterested act of the mental life. Generally speaking, reflective conscience is always more disinterested than irreflective action, which is typified in reflex action; it is less directly useful to life on its simplest terms. Parallel to the development of conscience and of speculative intelligence there goes always a development of our moral activity. The more truly intelligent a human being is the more active he is; and the more active he is, the less self-sufficing he becomes, the greater his need to live for someone else. Antisocial beings are almost always mentally and physically dawdlers, who are incapable of continuous mental or physical labour. Activity of mind must inevitably, therefore, indirectly fortify the moral instincts. Sociality is developed by thought.

Although by the progress of analysis the complication of the great mental and moral hypotheses must increase, it is possible, even at the present day, to foresee the main synthetic groups under which the several systems will be classifiable.

**Possible to classify the diverse systems of future.**

This book is not a treatise on metaphysics: an exposition and criticism of these systems will not, therefore, here be expected; but their characteristic spirit, which has also been the spirit of the great religions, is of interest to us here, and, for us, constitutes their value. It is this spirit which is at once speculative and religious, in the true sense of the word, that it is important, accordingly, to elicit, and that wholly without dogmatical or polemical aim of any kind. Absolute sincerity,

**Present interest in such systems.**

[1] *Esquisse d'une morale sans obligation*, p. 215.

impersonal and passionate sincerity, is the first duty of the philosopher. To arrange the world according to one's personal preferences, to be on the lookout, not for the most probable, but for the most consoling hypotheses, is to resemble a merchant who should count his credits only when he is making up his books and should indulge in none but consoling additions. The strictest probity is demanded of him who balances the great book of life ; the philosopher should hide nothing either from others or from himself. We shall endeavour, therefore, to set forth, what are in our judgment the diverse aspects under which the knowable as a whole, and therefore also the unknowable, or if you prefer, the great unknown, present themselves to-day. We shall endeavour to interpret the great metaphysical systems sympathetically, without, however, any illusions in regard to their incompleteness and their errors. In a certain church in Verona sacred texts are inscribed on the marble slabs of which the floor is composed ; they interpret and complete each other, and, however obscure at first, gradually become plain as one advances under the high arched roof ; thus it is in life : the religious and philosophical beliefs in the midst of which we live seem to us at first enigmatical and mysterious, we trample them under foot without understanding them ; but, as we advance, we discover their hidden meaning, their naïveté, and their profoundity. At every step in life a new perspective into the heart of humanity is thrown open to us ; to live is to understand, and to understand is not only to tolerate but to love. Such love, however, is not incompatible with clearness of vision, nor with an effort to transform and ameliorate the beloved object ; on the contrary, a really active love ought to be, more than all else, a desire for transformation and for progress. To love a being or a belief is to seek to make it better.

## II. Theism.

The majority of people scarcely see any possible alternative to such and such a determinate religion except atheism. The fact is, of course, quite otherwise. Religious thought

manifests itself in a hundred forms; why should free-thought
be restricted to a single conception of the universe? I have

Theism and re-<br>ligion distinct. known a multitude of free-thinkers who believed
more sincerely in the existence of God, in the
immortality of the soul, and, in general, in spiritual principles than a great many professed worshippers.
Were they right to do so? Was Voltaire, for example,
who based his affirmation of the existence of God upon the
splendour of a sunrise, somewhat naïve, and inclined to mistake an emotion for a bit of proof? It makes little difference;
what we wish to set in relief is that faith in a priest is not
necessarily part and parcel of faith in a God, and that the
disappearance of the former may lend an increase of power
and of refinement to the latter. No single philosophic doctrine is to be regarded as standing alone in opposition to the
whole body of religions; religions and philosophies together
are all philosophic doctrines, all hypotheses, and none of
them above discussion. We say to the individual: "Weigh
and choose." And among these hypotheses we include that
of which modern religions constitute the symbolic expression,
theism. If the religious anomy which we regard as the ideal
implies the suppression of everything in the nature of an
external revelation, it does not on that account exclude a
subjective and personal intuition of divinity. Even mystics may
find their account in the religious individualism of the future.
Intuition, however, in metaphysics as in morals, is every day
losing ground. The progress of ideas will result in the
gradual triumph of scientific induction over alleged natural
intuition, of probability over faith. Subjective revelation will
disappear as objective revelation is doing, and give place by
degrees to reasoning. Dogmatic theism, like all dogma, is
doomed; but what is purest in the theistic spirit may survive.

I. Let us first consider the probable fate of the dogma of
the Creator, which belongs to the great Jewish, Christian, and
Islamite religions. Science follows the law of parsimony;
nature economizes force, science economizes ideas. The first
economy to be undertaken might well relate precisely to the
idea of the creation. The author of the world may be con-

ceived as the universal motor. But the conception of cause as a source of movement, or as a prime motor, is full of contradictions and is becoming more and more foreign to modern philosophy. For the conception of a first cause implies a pre-existing state of repose, and repose is no more primitive and absolute than nothingness. Nothing is in repose, nothing has ever been in repose. The most motionless atom in the atmosphere describes in its vibration, according to Clausius, four hundred and forty-seven metres a second in a space of ninety-five millionths of a millimetre; it receives during this time four billion seven hundred million shocks. The vibrating atom of hydrogen describes one thousand eight hundred and eighty-four metres in a second. Repose is an illusion of the human mind, and the conception of a divine first mover is a second illusion based on the first. The eternal movement that stirred the molecules of the primitive substance, later grouped them into spheres, and the spheres began whirling of their own accord in the ether without need of a preliminary push from the sacred beetle (as the Egyptian legend has it) that rolls his sacred ball, which is the image of the universe. Where, as Strauss remarked, Newton felt called upon to assume a "divine first impulse," and Buffon was obliged to resort to the hypothesis of a comet colliding with the primitive sphere and breaking it up into the fragments which now constitute the earth and the planets, we need invoke nothing but the fixity of natural laws. Since Kant, Descartes, and Laplace, we possess an approximate explanation of the formation of the stars, which are alternately produced and dissolved by the concentration and resolution of material masses—are born to be "devoured," as Kant said, in the abyss of eternity. One and the same cause, resistance of the ether, explains the agglomeration of nebulous matter into nucleï, and the slowing down of the motion of the spheres thus formed, and the ultimate fall of these spheres upon some neighbouring centre of attraction and the resulting dispersion into nebulæ.

More than that, by the progress of physiology and natural history, the organic and the inorganic worlds have come to be

*God conceived as prime mover a superfluity according to modern physics.*

conceived as so closely related that a true explanation of the first would probably include a true explanation of the second.

The chasm that once existed between life and
And with<br>physiology. what sustains life has been closed. If our laboratories do not enable us to catch spontaneous generation in the act, the reason is simply that their resources are not equal to those of nature, that they have not the same means at their disposal, that the so-called primitive beings that we endeavour to produce in the laboratory are really not primitive. Men of science who have attempted such experiments resemble the followers of Darwin who have tried to transform an anthropoid ape into a human being. Nature permits of an infinite convergence of forces upon a determinate point, that cannot be realized in a laboratory. More than that, time, which we are always inclined to neglect, is a necessary factor in the evolution of things; what is natural is slow. To find the earliest stages of organic life, as to find the early stages in the formation of a star, we must go far back into the remote past.

If there is no necessity for the conception of God as a prime mover, is there any necessity for the conception of God as the
God conceived<br>as a Creator<br>worse than<br>superfluous. Creator of the universe? A creative cause seems to the modern mind less and less needed for the explanation of the world, for the fact of existence stands in no need of explanation; what rather needs explanation is non-existence. Death, repose, are all relative and derived. Death implies life, and is itself only a provisional stage, an interval between two metamorphoses. There exists no *punctum mortuum*, no one really dead point in the universe. It is by a pure artifice of thought that religions have conceived the universe as beginning in annihilation, in death (which is a remote consequence of life), in order to afford an opportunity for the intervention of a creative power: creation is a resurrection following on a fictitious death.

The real state of the case is not that existence springs from non-existence, but that non-existence is a simple aspect of existence, or rather an illusion of thought. The notion of creation will be more and more widely displaced by that of evolution and variation. Different worlds are eternal varia-

Nothingness an aspect of existence.

tions on the same theme, the *tat tvam asi* of the Hindus tends to become a scientific variety. A substantial unity of the world and the solidarity of all the beings in the world will, undoubtedly, be more and more clearly demonstrated.

The creation may be considered, since Kant's time, as a demonstrably indemonstrable and even inconceivable hypoth-

God responsible for evil.

esis; but Kant did not stay to inquire whether the Biblical dogma of the creation will not tend to appear to us increasingly immoral; a tendency which, according to Kant's principles, would suffice to cause it to be rejected in the future. A doubt, which some thinkers of antiquity felt keenly, has come to be widely diffused in our days; a Creator is a being in whom all things find their reason and their cause, and who, consequently, is ultimately responsible for everything. He is responsible for all the evil in the universe. As the idea of infinite power, of supreme liberty of action became inseparable from the conception of God, God was deprived of every excuse, for the Absolute is dependent upon nothing. Everything, on the contrary, depends on Him and finds its reason in Him. In the last resort He alone is culpable; His work, in the manifold series of its effects, presents itself to modern thought as one sole action, and this action, like any other, is capable of being sat upon in moral judgment; the author is to be judged by his work, the world passes judgment on God. Well, as evil and immorality in the universe, with the progress of the moral sense, become more shocking, it seems that to admit the creation hypothesis is to centralize, to concentrate, all the immorality of the world in one being, and to justify the paradox: "God is evil." To admit the doctrine of a Creator is, in a word, to banish evil from the world to God, its primordial source; to absolve men and the universe and accuse the author of both.

There is something still worse than referring the source of all evil thus to a creative will, and that is, for the purpose of exculpating the Creator, to deny the evil itself, and to declare that this world is the best of all possible worlds. Such is the choice that Leibnitz and the theologians made. Religions are obliged to apologize for the universe, to profess an admiration for the divine plan; they hold in reserve excuses for the existence of injustice, and labour unconsciously to falsify the moral sense, in order to relieve God of his responsibility.

*Evil of denying the existence of evil to exculpate God.*

Many hypotheses have been devised in the service of optimism to excuse the Creator, without compromising the moral sense, and mankind's instinct for progress. Physical evil (suffering), intellectual evil (error and doubt), have been declared to be a condition *sine qua non* of moral good; which would justify them. Moral evil would thus remain the sole verifiable evil in the universe, and as moral evil consists simply in evil intentions on the part of men, men alone, on this hypothesis, would be responsible. The universe itself, that is to say, would contain no evil except in the person of the man who is purposely evil by his own free choice, and the possibility of moral evil might be considered as a supreme condition of moral goodness, the latter presupposing freedom of choice, a selection by the will, and an alternative to be refused. The evil in the universe would thus be compensated for by morality, suffering would be compensated for by virtue, mistakes by good will. The world itself would be simply a means of producing morality and, in its apparent imperfection, it would be the best world possible, because its apparent imperfection would be necessary to produce what is best in it.

*Doctrine that physical or intellectual evil are conditions of well-being.*

The world, it has been said, cannot be in every respect absolute, for it would then be God; it must always be in the position of a recipient; the less it receives—the more it acts in independence of external aid, the more it develops from within, and the more it approaches the Absolute, insomuch that the very poverty of the earth constitutes its grandeur, since it is the condition of its real wealth, a wealth not borrowed from another but acquired by its own effort. Everything, therefore, becomes transfigured according to this hypothesis, every

*Doctrine that the dignity of the world lies in its spontaneity.*

suffering becomes a merit; God wished to create the most spontaneous world possible, that is to say at bottom to create as little as possible, to leave as large an initiative as possible to his creatures. *Laissez faire* is God's device, as it is the device of all good government. A small result, but obtained by spontaneity, is superior to a greater result obtained by mechanical artifice. " Divine art," says a philosopher, in commenting on some doctrines of Plato, "is infinitely superior to human art ; it creates individuals who are ends unto themselves and self-evolved. These individuals are not, as Leibnitz believed, automata . . . true perfection is autonomous. If God is only a demiurge, he may be accused, and ought to be accused, of being a bad workman. Is the world not full of unsuccessful attempts, of unfortunate combinations, of ends either missed altogether or ill achieved? The critics of Providence will always have enough to say, but these unfinished sketches are the work not of God but of his creatures, of the forces and individual souls that he has set in operation. In a word God is not a workman who produces works, but a workman who creates workmen."[1] This formula sums up in a striking manner what may be called transfigured optimism. The new hypothesis does not deny evil, but, on the contrary, hastens to admit it ; but by converting evil into a consequence of spontaneity, it subordinates it to good itself, makes it labour in the service of its opposite; the most fragmentary sketch becomes respectable when it is a step, and a necessary step, toward a masterpiece.

The hypothesis in question is certainly one which, within the realm of theism, may well continue to be long the most plausible. It gives rise, however, to a great many difficulties. In the first place it assumes the superiority of what is spontaneous to what is not ; of what, so to speak, does itself, as compared with what is done. Be it so, but in what respect can beings in this world be said to lead a spontaneous existence ; in what respect can I be said to lead a spontaneous existence ? Am I not the result of a multitude

Criticised.

---

[1] A. Fouillée, *Philosophie de Platon*, t. ii. p. 639. See also M. Secrétan, *Philosophie de la liberté*, and Vallier, *L'Intention morale*.

of causes? I was born and am maintained by the consilience of a multitude of little cellular or atomic volitions. Should I be less than I am if I were the result of a single volition, and that a divine volition? Over and above myself there always exist my antecedents, the causes of me; my true cause does not lie within the limits of myself: what difference does it make to me, therefore, whether those causes lie within the universe or beyond? Whether the world is the more or less harmonious work of a multitude of blind spontaneities or the work of a single intelligent will, neither diminishes nor increases the value of any given individual that is the product of the world. My ancestors are indifferent to me the instant I become dependent upon ancestors at all. Should the statue of Pygmalion reproach the sculptor with having made it beautiful, and having made it with his own hands, and definitively fashioned it for life? Providing it lives and is happy, it matters little whence its life comes. Obscurity lies behind, light and life lie before, and it is forward that one's face is set.

In the new Platonic hypothesis, transfigured as above, the organization of the individual always becomes, in the last resort, the work of a reciprocal determinism. According to the ordinary hypothesis, it is the work of a single, absolute, determining will; but the absolute or relative character of the determining principle in nowise affects the nature of what is determined. The actual world is no more passive, if it is produced directly by the operation of the first cause, than if it is produced indirectly by the intermediation of a multitude of derivative causes, even if these causes present individually the character of spontaneity. After all, since the individual must always be solidary, solidarity between it and divine perfection is preferable to solidarity with derivative imperfection.

There is, however, in the Platonic and Aristotelian notion of spontaneity an element of profundity and of verisimilitude, but it leads precisely to the refutation of the doctrine of creation: once carry the hypothesis of the spontaneity of existence to its ultimate conclusion, and the original fund of existence must be impoverished until nothing but nude un-

*Results in de-
terminism*

qualifiable substance be left; but that is to say, one must go back to Aristotle's pure force, to Hegel's pure being, which is identical with not being; the masterpiece of spontaneity would be self-creation. The instant such a spontaneity is possible God is a superfluity; it is easier to say that becoming arose out of the identity of being and not being, or rather that becoming is eternal on its own account. Becoming thus becomes God and theism becomes atheism or pantheism.

*And contradicts itself.*

To sum up, the Creator unable to create bare, virtual substance, must have created beings endowed with some real quality; but, if so, they are once for all his works and not simply independent workmen. More than that, such a substance with such qualities once created, such and such effects necessarily follow; qualities are determinations which determine subsequent determinations in their turn. Behold therefore the present, big with the future. The world becomes a determined succession of "works" which develop fatally from their earliest stage.

*Summary.*

M. Secrétan will tell us that God simply created free wills but not substances; but it must be confessed that these free wills have been immersed in a deterministic universe which leaves them little liberty of action. Why, therefore, did He not create us freer and still freer and as free as Himself? But we should have been gods, it is objected:—so much the better, might be replied; there could not be too many gods; we do not see why God should have reduced himself to a unity, "as if the laws of number constituted a limitation of His power." [1] It does not appear why the Creator should be unable to create a double of Himself; why He should be obliged to hand on the divine life, that He wishes to share, on lower terms only; we do not see why God's productivity should involve a certain degeneration.

*Doctrine that God has created beings free to choose criticised.*

---

[1] M. Fouillée has effectively stated this in his *Systèmes de morale contemporains*, where he in some measure attacks the hypothesis that he had incidentally proposed in his commentary on Plato.

In any event, in default of other attributes, we ought to be given the maximum of possible liberty; admitting that we could not be created free and equal to God, our liberty should differ from His by a minimum.

A maximum
of liberty.

This minimum, being susceptible of infinite diminution, might become less than any conceivable difference; it might become, that is to say, infinitely little, practically zero; but we are far from any such exalted station, and if God gave us liberty He was very miserly about it.

To say the truth, it is only by an abuse of language that any such ideal liberty is ascribed to us as is attributed to God, and regarded as of infinite value. The freedom that religion ascribes to us is freedom of the will, power to do evil or good, a power the very consequence of which is irreconcilable with the notion of God.

An abuse of
language to call
us free.

Without entering upon a consideration of what such a power would be and of its moral worth, why does our free-will exist in the midst of conditions so unfavourable to it, so calculated to render it ineffective? The sole response is the classic theory of the temptation. The temptation, as an explanation of the world, practically involves the hypothesis of a father exposing his children, as a means of testing their virtue, to temptations of vice and crime, and knowing beforehand that they will succumb. Morally, the conception is simply inadmissible; is worthy of the distant times when hearts were harder than they are to-day. More than that, the only beings that could in any proper sense be put to the proof are truly conscientious beings, for they alone are capable of entertaining a moral alternative. A reflective conscience is so rare in the world! By virtue of what temptation resisted are minerals and vegetables permitted to exist in unconsciousness and sleep, while animals are torn by the miseries of life and death without being able to convert their sufferings into a confirmation of the moral will or amelioration of their lot?

The supreme resource of Christianity and of religions generally is the doctrine of the fall, but this explanation of evil as the result of a primitive imperfection is an explanation of evil by evil. The fall must have been preceded by some defect in the will itself, or the will would not have failed. Original sin is not an ultimate; one does not stumble if there is no obstacle in the way, and one's legs are well made, and one is walking in the eye of the Lord. Sin involves temptation, and the doctrine of the temptation necessarily implies that God was the first tempter; morally, it was God himself who fell in the fall of His creatures by Him planned. To explain original sin, which is the root of all sin, the sin of Lucifer, theologians have resorted not to a temptation within the realm of sense, but to a temptation within the realm of intelligence. It was by pride that the angels fell. Their sin rose thus out of the very centre of their minds. But pride is incidental only to short-sightedness. Complete science is aware of its own limitations. Pride, therefore, results from insufficiency of knowledge. The pride of the angels was due to God. One may have reasons for wishing to do and for doing evil, but reasons do not hold in the face of reason itself. If, according to the partisans of free-will, human intelligence is capable by virtue of pride and inner perversity of creating out of nothing motives for evil-doing, it is at least incapable of so doing except in so far as its knowledge is limited, ambiguous and uncertain. Practically, nobody hesitates except in the absence of absolute knowledge. There is no such thing as rationally and consciously flying in the face of reason. Lucifer was, therefore, by his very nature impeccable. The will to do evil is borne of the opposition which an imperfect intelligence fancies it perceives, in a world hypothetically perfect, between its own advantage and the advantage of everybody else. But if God and his works are really perfect, such an antinomy between the good of the individual and the universal good, which even to the best human intelligences appears provisional only, would *a fortiori* appear so to one of the archangels of the intelligence, to the Light-bearer of thought. To know is to participate in the supreme truth, in the divine conscience; to possess all knowledge would be to possess, among other things, the moral insight of God; and how out the midst of all that divinity should anything Satanic arise?

Doctrine of the fall.

To-day, when a sin is committed among men and it cannot be traced to any fault of education, or of environment, or of
God always responsible in the last resort. overwhelming temptation, men of science look for the explanation among the ancestors of the guilty person, in the conviction that they must be in the presence of a case of atavism. No such explanation could exist in the case of God's firstborn. When the world was young and beautiful and good, original sin was as wonderful as the first appearance of the world itself; it was a veritable creation of something out of nothing. Satan's creation was superior to God's. His moral *fiat nox* was greater in genius and creative power than God's *fiat lux.* In effect, every religious explanation of evil ultimately leads to the ascription of it to God himself or to a being more powerful than God, and in both cases equally the Creator is debased. That fact constitutes the principal reason that compromises the creation hypothesis, properly so called, for every philosophical mind.

II. The second notion of theism is that of Providence, which may be either general or special. Along with the
Special Providence and miracles. notion of a special Providence governing the world from without, we have seen that the notion of miracle must be included. The sole means by which these two decrepit conceptions can be defended are the following: Conceive, with Pascal, two worlds, a physical world and above it the moral world enveloping it, and in places penetrating it. The points of intersection, so to speak, between the moral and physical world are miracles. They are not so much breaches in the laws of nature as affirmations of superior laws. Such is the argument; but we reply that the so-called superior laws are inevitably, in certain respects, contradictory to those of nature, in the very respects in reference to which the miracle has happened. One cannot, for example, suppose that a saint, precipitated from the height of a rock, resists the law of gravitation and floats up to heaven, without a manifest contradiction, so far as natural laws are concerned; without a destruction, indeed, of those laws. More than that, a moral law is such precisely in so far as it differs in the lines of its

applicability from natural law; just in so far as a conflict between it and natural laws is inconceivable. Only a natural law can suspend (and that apparently only) the operation of a natural law.

It has been fancied that the difficulty about miracles may be done away with by conceiving that Providence acts, not Attempt to limit its activity to the subjective side. upon the material universe, but upon human thought, by means of suggestion, inspirations from on high, providential ideas; but contemporary science has established so intimate a connection between motion and thought that it is impossible to distinguish between an influence exerted in the spiritual and an influence exerted in the material world. It is hopeless to attempt to immaterialize Providence in order to save it. The special intervention of Providence must be material or not at all.

The old conception of miracles and of the supernatural and special Providence was therefore, in a certain sense, logical. Universal Providence. Religions had not been mistaken; they had perceived that the day Providence became too exclusively universal religion would be absorbed in metaphysics, and this result, in effect, will be produced in the future. Religions have never supported the theory of a general Providence, and it is certain that if a general Providence sufficed for the abstract reason of a Malebranche, with his sense of order, symmetry, and law, it would not suffice for the human heart, with its sense of justice and its desire, if it is to sacrifice itself for God, to find in the God at least a defender and a benefactor. A benefit loses its value as such by being too indirect; humanity has little understanding of justice in general which treats the individual as a means of securing the good of the whole and sacrifices him at need—at least, for a time. Charity, like justice, it seems to him, should be individual and special. A universal Providence is so universal that no traces of it exist in the details of life, and in especial in the particular evils and sufferings which form so large a part of life. The God of Malebranche, who is incapable of showing His effective benevolence to any of us individually, is paralyzed, as Louis XIV. was, by His very greatness. He is the sole being who cannot move without breaking a natural law, and who consequently is condemned to eternal immobility. The least of His interventions being a miracle, He cannot employ the means that other beings employ without derogating from His dignity and His power; so that God is reduced, if He is to remain God, either to standing inert or to contradicting our intelligence. By that very fact He ceases to be lovable, unless one pretend to love Him precisely for what He cannot do, for the benevolence that He cannot show, as for the prayers He cannot grant. Pity is the sole sentiment that can be roused in us by a being who is so good that He cannot wish evil, and so powerless that He is obliged to see nothing but evil accomplished in the world. No human misery could be comparable to a divine misery like that. The very height of suffering must be experienced by a God who should at once be conscious of His own infinity and should feel the distance which separates Him from the world which He has created. Only the clear and profound vision of such a God could penetrate the abyss of evil to the bottom, and it is He of all beings in the world who would suffer from an eternal vertigo.

What is most unacceptable in the traditional notion of Providence is the attribute of omnipotence. In the first place, divine omnipotence is inconsistent with the existence of evil; in the second place, it leads logically to the possibility of supernatural intervention in this world, which, if it is to be of any service, must be special and not general. To avoid these implications of the conception of Providence, John Stuart Mill has conceived a superior and divine being who should not be all-powerful. This being would be the principle of good, acting in the universe according to natural laws, but hindered and retarded in his action by these laws themselves, which bring suffering and death. The existence of such a being once established, religion would be saved and morality confirmed. Virtue would consist in a sort of co-operation with this great unknown being, who is struggling against evil. The good man would feel that he was aiding God and that God was aiding him in so far as He found it possible.

This amended conception of Providence is more admissible and more reconcilable with the real and imperfect world that

Non-omnipotent God.

we are familiar with. But it must be confessed that the amendment amounts to an almost complete cancellation. If Providence is to be reduced thus simply to one of the forces at work in nature, to the force that makes more or less partially and provisionally for goodness, there is nothing to distinguish it from the power that makes for evolution, from natural selection, or from any other beneficent natural law. To personify such laws is futile scientifically; and, practically, is it so very useful? Or conceive the being as existent side by side with these laws and watching their operation, but unable to contravene it; but so to do is to return to the conception of an ineffective, immobile God. The prime condition of existence for a God is to be good for something; a non-omnipotent God soon comes to be an impotent God. The actual world marks the extreme limits of the power of such a God, and at some stage in the course of evolution the unconscious forces of nature, leagued together against the principle of goodness, may succeed in paralyzing it entirely.

More than that, is a non-omnipotent God to be conceived as eternal? If not, He is in no very striking respect superior

Is such a God to be conceived as eternal?

to man. His power is so slight that He has not even been able to make it very clearly manifest to mankind that it exists at all. Or if He is eternal, and eternally present in all things, then His lack of power is growing and becoming radical. One may in any event congratulate one's self that a blind and indifferent universe has, among all possible combinations, fallen by chance into the one which constitutes our present world; but a God who has pursued goodness conscientiously through a whole eternity demonstrates His complete incapacity, if He has succeeded in producing nothing better than such a miscarriage of the ideal as this universe. The judgment that may fairly be passed upon the world is altogether dependent upon the ques-

tion who made it and who created life; if the world is self-
evolved, it may well appear to us as possessing a certain
beauty, as giving an earnest of better things; but if it is the
work of an intelligent will, present in all things, and persisting
in its designs throughout the eternity of the past, it is inevitable that one should feel that this volition has not been possessed of great power, that the importance of the victory is
not in proportion to the duration of the struggle, that such a
God does not constitute a very solid support, and that His existence is a matter of indifference to the future of the universe.
Is such a God more powerful than humanity, or even so powerful? His eternity is but a proof of voluntary or forced
inaction; far from dignifying Him it debases Him. On the
surface of the earth there are many species of insects which
were probably in existence before the race of man. In the
transparent amber that belongs to tertiary strata may be seen
the little corselet of the melipones caught and held there these
past five hundred thousand years. Are these distant predecessors of the human race on that account more venerable?

John Stuart Mill, a disciple of Auguste Comte, put forth
this theory of a non-omnipotent Providence, conceived on the
model of the human will, with a certain mental
reservation; his real meaning was that for many
cultivated men such a being, labouring for goodness, according to the utmost of its limited power, would be
confounded with humanity, taken as a whole. Humanity is,
in effect, according to Comte, a great being of divine aspirations, to whom one might, with all one's heart, render homage;
in especial, if one leaves out of account the individuals who
are, properly speaking, only parasites, and do not co-operate
for the production of the common result, whom progress
consists precisely in excluding from society. Religion, on this
theory, is the state of spiritual unity resulting from the convergence of all our thoughts and all our actions toward the
service of humanity. This, as Mill said, is a genuine religion,
quite capable of resisting sceptical attack and of undertaking
the labour of the older cults. According to this doctrine,

*The religion
of humanity.*

Providence is simply humanity, looking after the interest of its individual members. Such a Providence, regarded as one with human volition, might assuredly be accepted by any philosopher; it marks, as we shall see later, the extreme limit of which the development of the notion of a Special Providence is susceptible, the point at which this notion and the conception of human morality become one. The precept to love mankind in God becomes transformed into the precept to love God in mankind. For a philosopher who identifies God with his ideal, both precepts are equally true and beautiful. We have ourselves shown how the religious sentiment in the course of its evolution tends to become one with the respect and love of humanity, and how religious faith tends to develop into a moral faith, and a simple and active hopefulness in the triumph of moral goodness.

John Stuart Mill's and Comte's ideas are thus shielded against criticism so long as they are taken in a general and almost metaphorical sense; but if they are to be interpreted literally and made the basis of a cult and a religion of humanity, they are puerile simply. Precisely because Providence can be realized by humanity, the cult for Providence, with all its ceremonies, invocations, adorations, which are manifest and ridiculous paganism, must be suppressed. Every organism exemplifies a certain sort of Providence—even the social organism, which is the equilibrium of the laws of life. The totality of an organism is truly admirable, and one may readily understand how any individual member, if he is endowed with consciousness, might admire the whole to which he belongs; but how could he make it the object of a cult? The cellules which constitute me might well be interested in the preservation of what I call myself and help each other, and by that very fact help me to that end, but they could not adore me. Love of humanity is one thing, and idolatry of humanity, or sociolatry, according to Comte's term, is another. A really sincere and enlightened love of humanity is the very opposite of such idolatry; would be by it compromised and corrupted. The cult for humanity reminds one of the antique, naïve cult for the family, for the

*Criticised.*

lares, for the hearth, for the sacred fire kept alive beneath the ashes.  To preserve respect and love to-day does not require a resuscitation of all these superstitions; respect and love pass from heart to heart without need of ceremonial as a medium. The Positivist religion, far from being a step in advance, is a step backward toward the superstitious beliefs which have been banished because they were useless, and consequently harmful.

Religion ought to be not only human but cosmic, and such it will be by the very nature of the case as the result of reflection.  Theism will be obliged, if it is to subsist
**Religion must be cosmic.** at all, to confine itself to the vaguest possible
affirmation of a principle analogous to the soul as the mysterious origin of the world and of its development. The essential character of this principle must be that it is not really separate from the world nor opposed to its determinism. Beliefs in the creation and in a special Providence will give place more and more to belief in some spontaneous action, which is essential to beings generally, and in especial to those who are endowed with consciousness.  Religion has gradually come to be a metaphysics of immanent finality, consisting in the single general proposition: the world possesses a signifi-cance, and is making toward an end and aim of its own;[1] the world is a society of beings who may come to discover in themselves an identity of moral impulse.[2]  God is the term by which we designate what renders the movement of the world toward a state of peace, concord, and harmony *possible*. And since for human intelligence the possible and the real[3] are confused, a belief in the possibility of a better world becomes the belief in something divine which is immanent in this world.

Between idealistic theism and atheism the distance may be diminished *ad infinitum*.  Many atheists, language to the contrary notwithstanding, are already at one with theists, in-toxicated with God.  If the actual existence of God be called in question, at least His progressive existence, the progres-

[1] Kant's *Kritik der Urtheils-Kraft.*
[2] See M. A. Fouillée, *Les systèmes de morale contemporains.*
[3] See Aristotle, *Metaphysica*, and Hegel's *Logik.*

sive realization of an ideal, the gradual descent of Christ from heaven to earth, may be admitted. The presentiment of progress thus becomes merged in a sense of the actual presence of the divine. The ideal seems to live and palpitate in the world about one ; it is as if an artist's vision of his work should be so intense that it should seem to float out of his brain and take its place upon the untouched canvass before him.

*Theism and atheism insensibly pass into each other.*

The power of words is limited ; there are shades and subtleties of thought that cannot be expressed in language. What possible verbal reply can be given to questions like those that Marguerite asks of Faust ? "It is a long time since thou wert at mass . . . dost thou believe in God?" "My beloved," replies Faust, "who would dare to say I believe in God?" . . . "So thou dost not believe in Him? . . . Who would dare to say that he does not believe when he listens to the voice of his heart, when a sense of tenderness and happiness fills his soul? Pronounce the first words that occur to thee. What difference what thou callest it : happiness, heart, love, God? The feeling is everything, the word is vain." The deist philosopher who holds words cheap seems to the superficial multitude to be simply a hypocritical sceptic ; whereas the rigid atheist displays the narrowness of a sectary. What is certain is that the name of God has sometimes been associated with the greatest of human conceptions, sometimes with the most barbarous. The theistic hypothesis cannot continue to subsist unless it be freed once for all from puerile and gross associations.

*Theism must be furnished with a new vocabulary.*

It is toward this consummation that theism, at its best, and in particular what Kant calls religion, within the limits presented by reason, is tending. It merits a special examination.

*Rational religion.*

The neo-Kantian religion ascribes the supreme place to moral goodness as the directing principle of every reasonable will. From that premise the neo-Kantians deduce "moral liberty" as the condition of goodness. For goodness, in their judgment, is simply freedom conceived as appearing to itself in its intellectual purity, and dominating

*Neo-Kantianism.*

the phenomenal self.   Freedom thus conceived occupies a place above phenomena, which belong essentially to necessity and to determinism.   Kantians found also implied in the notion of absolute liberty, subject to the condition of time, the attribute of eternity.   They say, with Spinoza: " I feel, and I know that I am eternal; eternity is one with divinity. Is it not the eternal that all the nations of men have adored? I feel God therefore present in myself.   He reveals himself to me in the moral ideal.   But is this God that my conscience reveals to me really myself?   Is he each of us, and must one believe that the universe in the last resort is, as has been said, a republic of free-wills—that there are thus as many Gods as in-dividuals, and that we are all Gods?   Or does this multiplicity of individuals and of personalities exist only in appearance, and is the universe at bottom the expression of a single will? Theism may choose between these two hypotheses—between a sort of metaphysical and moral polytheism and a sort of monotheism, and may subsequently arrange to its liking the relations which it may suppose to exist between the absolute will and the world of phenomenon.   But a belief in a moral ideal does not in the least involve anything more than a belief in something eternal and divine, as shaping the universal course of things.   One cannot bend it to the service of any one determinate religion, rather than of any other.   Within certain limits, however, it may lend some support to the moral and religious sentiments.   The most acceptable form of theistic doctrine in the future will, no doubt, be some moral philoso-phy analagous to that of Kant.   Kantianism itself, however, is too closely bound up with the notion of duty, properly so called, and with the categorical imperative.   It, like Judaism, is a religion of law.   Instead of the law, one will content one's self, in all probability, in the future, with an ideal conceived as supreme above all things, and as exercising upon our thought and will the highest attraction that can be exercised by what has been called the power of an ideal.[1]

A belief in the divine will then no longer consist in passive adoration, but in action.   A belief in Providence will no longer

[1] See the criticism of Kantianism in the *Systèmes de morale contemporains*, by M. Alfred Fouillée.

consist in a justification of the existing world and of its evils in
the name of the divine intention, but in an effort to introduce
Belief consists    by human intervention a greater amount of justice
not in worship,    and of goodness into the world.   We have seen
but in action.      that the notion of Providence was based among
ancient peoples on the conception of an exterior finality, forcibly
imposed upon things, of a secret and transcendent aim, which
the universe was warped to serve by force of some unknown will.
With such a theory of things, man was incessantly checked in his
activity, since he conceived it to be impossible to prevent the
course of the world from achieving its aim.   The world seemed
to him to be organized definitively ; he had no hope, except in
prayer and miracle ; everything about him seemed to him to be
sacred ; the inviolability of nature was both a principle and a
consequence of the notion of Providence thus understood.
And, as we have seen, science was long regarded as sacrilegious.
It created both surprise and scandal to see science intervene in
the affairs of this world, disturbing everything, changing the
direction of natural forces, transforming the divine rulers of the
world into humble ministrants to human wants.   In our days,
however, science is coming to be more and more held in
honour.   For the past century nature has been, to the best of
human ability, turned upside down.   Humanity's long quietism
has been succeeded by a feverish activity.   Everybody wishes
to lend a hand in the universal mechanism, and to contribute his part in the modification of the direction of the
whole ; everybody wishes to bend things to his own views,
and to become, so far as in him lies, a minor Providence.

Just as the individual is coming to feel himself more and more
a citizen of the state, so he is coming to feel himself more and
more a citizen of the universe, inseparably bound
Increasing        by relations of cause and effect with the universal
power of man-
kind in the        sum of phenomena.   He recognizes that there is
universe.          nothing in the world that does not concern him,
and that on every side he can exert an influence, great or
small, and leave his mark on the great world.   He perceives
with astonishment the extent of the power of his will and intelligence.   Just in so far as his rational faculties establish a

connection between phenomena, they establish by that very fact a connection between phenomena and himself, and he no longer feels himself alone in the universe. Since, according to a celebrated theory, the centre of the world is in each and every distinct being, it follows that if this centre were exhaustively self-conscious it would see all the rays in infinite space focussing in it, and all the chains of phenomenal causation meeting in it, and the effects of its volition stretching out into infinity, and its every action possessing an influence upon the totality of things. It would perceive itself to be a sort of universal Providence.

If human beings are not so exhaustively self-conscious as all that, the progress of science is carrying them forward in that direction. A portion of the government of nature is in our hands, some part of the responsibility for what takes place in the universe is on our heads. At the beginning man conceived himself as living in a state of dependence on the world, in a state which ancient religions symbolize ; at present he perceives that the world is equally dependent upon him. The substitution of a human providence for the omnipresent influence of a divine providence might be given as being, from this point of view, the formula of progress ; the increasing independence of mankind, in the face of the natural universe, will thus result in an increasing inner independence, in a growing independence of mind and thought.

*A consequence of liberty of thought.*

The vulgar conception of a special and exterior providence which, as we have seen, is so closely bound up with the conception of man's place in the universe as one of subjection—nay, even the most refined conception of providence as transcendent and distant and as assigning to each being its determinate place in the totality of things—may thus, without ground of regret, be displaced in the mind of humanity. We shall some day perceive that we are stronger when we stand on our feet, shoulder to shoulder, hand in hand, than when we kneel with bowed heads and implore the unfeeling sky. Among the ancient Germans, when one of the faithful was about to enter a sacred forest he had his hands bound together as a symbol of his subjection to the

*Mankind to be its own special providence.*

gods; if he had the misfortune to fall as he was making his way into the forest, he did not dare to get up again; so to do would have been an affront to the gods; he was reduced to squirming and rolling like a reptile out of the immense temple. To this primitive conception of religious servitude, the modern conception of mankind as free in the presence of its God, of its beloved ideal, of its conceived work in the world, of its dream of progress, is more and more opposed. Even at the present day a true sense of the divine may be recognized by its giving man a consciousness of his liberty and his dignity rather than his subjection; the true gods are those who make us lift our heads higher in the struggle for existence; adoration no longer consists in prostration but in standing upright.

To borrow once more from the classic land of symbolism, from India, whence our German or Gallic ancestors came, the great epic of Ramayana tells us of a sainted

Story of the anchorite.

and sage anchorite who exemplified in his own person the whole sum of human virtue and piety. One day, confiding in the justice of heaven, he was invoking Indra and the whole chorus of the gods, and the gods were capricious and did not listen to him; his prayer fell back from the heavens unheard. The man, perceiving the indifference of the gods, was moved with indignation; and gathering together the power that he had hoarded, by his sacrifices and renunciation, and, feeling himself more powerful than his gods, more powerful than Indra himself, began to issue forth commands to the high heavens. And at his voice new stars rose and shone in the crystal sphere; he said, " Let there be light!" and there was light; he refashioned the world; his goodness became a creative providence. Nor was this all : he conceived the notion of creating new and better gods; and Indra himself was trembling toward his fall, for not even he that commands the air and the skies shall prevail against sanctity. Indra, the powerful, therefore hastened to yield and cried out to the saint, " Thy will be done!" and he left a place in the heavens for the new stars, and their light bears eternal witness to the omnipotence of goodness, which is the supreme God and object of adoration among men.

# CHAPTER IV.

## PANTHEISM.

As theism becomes immanent, the personality of God
comes to be more and more vaguely conceived. It is the
Conception of<br>God being disan-<br>thropomorphized. very existence of God's personality that pantheism either denies or confounds with that of the
universe. According to Mr. Spencer and Mr.
Fiske, the movement which led humanity to conceive its God
anthropomorphically will be succeeded by a movement in the
opposite direction; God will be deprived of all of His human
attributes, will be disanthropomorphized. He will first be
shorn of His lower impulses, and then of everything which is
analogous to human sensibility; the highest human senti-

ments will be regarded as too gross to be attributed to Him. Similarly with the attributes of intelligence and will; every human faculty will in its turn be abstracted and divinity, as it becomes relieved of its limitations, will lose, one after the other, every item of its significance to the intelligence; it will be conceived ultimately as a vague unity simply, which eludes the forms of distinct thought. Pantheism lends itself to this notion of an indeterminate and indeterminable disanthropomorphized divinity. Nevertheless, the crudest and most naïve speculations, anthropomorphism and fetichism, in Mr. Spencer's judgment, contained a part of the truth, namely, that the power that manifests itself in consciousness is simply a different form of the mysterious power that manifests itself beyond consciousness. The last result attained by human science, Mr. Spencer thinks, is that the unknown force which exists outside of consciousness is, if not similar to the known force that exists in consciousness, at least a simple mode of the same force, since the two are convertible into each other. So that the final result of the line of speculation begun by primitive man is that the power which manifests itself in the material universe is the same as that which manifests itself in us under the form of consciousness.

If pantheism goes the length of denying the personality and individuality of God, it is by way of compensation inclined to attribute a sort of individuality to the world. In effect, if God is present in every atom of the universe, the universe is a veritable living being possessing an organic unity, and developing, like an embryo, according to a determinate law. What distinguishes pantheism from this point of view is, therefore, the substantial unity that it ascribes to the world.

*Pantheism.*

But, of course, pantheism is a very indefinite doctrine, susceptible of many interpretations according to the manner in which the universal energy, the omnipresent unity, and in especial, the fundamental ground of its activity, which some regard as determinism simply and others as the orderly achievement of a final cause, are conceived. Nay, more; both necessity and the orderly

*Different forms of pantheism.*

achievement of a final cause may be conceived optimistically or pessimistically.

## *I. Optimistic pantheism.*

The first kind of pantheism, then, that which conceives a single substance as developing in an infinity of modes with no final cause in view, may be typified by the purely intellectualistic pantheism of Spinoza. This doctrine shows us, as existing in the totality of things, the immanent logic which presides over its development. The essence of human nature is reason, since reason is the essence of man. The proper function of reason is understanding, and to understand is to perceive the necessity of things, and the necessity of things is nature, or, if you will, God. Reason serves no other purpose than to enable us to understand; and the soul, in so far as it employs reason, regards that alone as useful which leads to understanding. To conceive the absolute necessity of eternal nature is to conceive that which, being subject only to the law of its own being, is free; it is, therefore, to conceive eternal freedom. And by that very fact it is to participate in eternal freedom, to identify itself with it. A consciousness of necessity is thus one with the fact of freedom. Human thought thus identifies itself with divine thought and becomes a consciousness of eternity. This consciousness, which is supreme joy, is love of God. The mystic Hebrew and Christian idea thus proves one with the moral theories of antiquity in Spinoza's vast synthesis. Intellectual intuition is self-conscious nature; the intellectual liberty, as the Stoics taught it, is consciousness of necessity, and nature possessing itself; and mystic ecstasy, by which the individual is absorbed in universal being, is nature returning to itself and rediscovering its eternal existence beneath its passing modes.[1]

The objection that moral and religious philosophy urged, and always will urge, against Spinoza's pantheism, considered as a possible substitute for religion, is that it is an optimistic fatalism, that regards everything as achieved by the mechanical and brutal operation of efficient causes, and excludes the

*Spinozism.*

---

[1] See the chapter on Spinoza in the author's *Morale d'Épicure*, p. 230.

possibility of any conception of final cause or of progress, properly so called. The evolution of the modes of substance, even when it results in pain, death, and vice, is divine; and the question arises, why this universe, which is alleged to be perfect and incapable of progress, should not be wholly motionless, and why this eternal, aimless agitation in the bosom of absolute substance should exist?

An optimistic fatalism.

In Mr. Fiske's judgment, Spinozism is the only pantheism, properly so called. The remark seems to us unduly to restrict the application of the term. Every system of theism that involves the notion of a final cause tends to become pantheistic when it denies the transcendence and admits the organic unity of the universe, which is the *Deus vivens*, the *natura naturans*, with a law of progress which is superior to the necessary laws of pure logic and mathematics and mechanics. The exclusion of any notion of the immanence of a final cause in things is not essential to pantheism. One might even conceive a sort of moral pantheism which should recognize a certain moral significance in the world, or at least what Mr. Fiske himself calls a dramatic tendency toward a moral dénouement. The instant men feel it to be a god that is labouring in the universe, they feel, rightly or wrongly, reassured as to the destiny of the moral ideal; they feel that they have an aim to march toward, and seem to hear, in the shadow of things, a multitude marching with them. They no longer have a sense of the vanity of life; all life, on the contrary, becomes divine, if not as it is, at least as it tends to be and ultimately will be.

Fiske's theory of a dramatic movement in the universe.

This system, according to its partisans, may be regarded as an induction which is justified by the modern doctrine of evolution. Mr. Fiske even goes the length of saying that Darwinism has done as much to confirm theology as to weaken it. Unhappily, nothing is more problematic than such an interpretation of modern science. Science reveals no element of divinity in the universe, and the process of evolution, which results in the incessant construction and destruction of similar worlds in an endless round, moves toward

Criticised.

no conscious or unconscious natural end, so far as we can discover. Scientifically, therefore, the notion of a final cause of
the universe may be no more than a human conception, than
a bit of abstract anthropomorphism. No scientific induction
can justify one in ascribing to the universe as such a conscious
purpose. And it is equally rash to conceive the universe as a
whole possessing a psychical and moral unity, since the universe, as science reveals it to us, is an infinity in no sense
grouped about a centre. Materially speaking, the universe
may perhaps be regarded as the expression of a single power,
but not as possessing any moral or psychic unity. Whatever is
organized, living, feeling, thinking, is, so far as we know, finite,
and the equivalence of forces in the universe possesses nothing
in common with the centralization of these forces. It is, perhaps, precisely because the forces of the universe are not moving in the same direction that the struggle and contest which
are the life of the world exist. Who knows but that for the
universe to become a unity and a total would involve its
becoming finite, involve the acquisition of a centre, and by
that very fact, perhaps, of a circumference which would arrest
the eternal expansion of matter and life in infinite space.

What constitutes the charm of pantheism, for a number of
its followers, is precisely this conception of unity in the world;
but when one endeavours to make the concep-
tion precise, it proves so evanescent that it ultimately resolves itself into the absolute indeter-
mination of Hegelian Non-Being. The more one examines
it, the more one asks one's self whether the unity that pantheism ascribes to the universe is not as purely a bit of anthropomorphism as is the design that pantheism attributes to the
universe. The character of definiteness and of totality that
the universe seems to possess may be simply a form that the
human mind imposes upon the world of experience. Project
on a wall—the wall of Plato's cavern—shadows of numberless
confused objects, of revolving atoms and formless clouds, and
they will all fall into some certain figure; will look like the fantastic shadow of certain human constructions: will present
the outline of towers and cities, animals and what not.

*No unity in the so-called universe.*

The unity and figure of the world are perhaps simply of the same nature. Apart from our conception of it, the world is perhaps infinite, and infinity can never mean anything else to the human mind than formlessness, for we are, by the very nature of the case, unable to describe its contours. The unity of the world is perhaps realized only in our minds; it is, perhaps, only from our minds that the mass of things obtain such unity as they seem to possess. Neither the world nor humanity are totals except in so far as we think of them as such, and act upon them, and group them about our thought and action as a centre.

To sum up, if the need of unity seems to justify pantheism, this need receives, at least, but an illusory satisfaction in the two principal forms of pantheism, and, in espe-

**Summary.** cial, in the deterministic form. Either the primordial and finite unity of the world is abstract and indeterminate and therefore purely subjective; or it becomes determinate in attributes which are as human as those of the god of atheism. The will which Schopenhauer makes the basis of his system is either the human will or simply force (which itself is human or animal), or the sense of effort, or, finally, pure abstraction. The same is true of the eternal force which Mr. Spencer regards as immanent in the universe. Such conceptions are more meagre in content but not necessarily more objective than those of the God of love, the World-Spirit, the World-Thought.

## II. Pessimistic pantheism.

Pantheism has travelled from Spinoza's optimism to Schopenhauer's pessimism; its most recent form, and in some respects one of its most ancient forms. The pessimistic

**Pessimism.** interpretation of religions with death or Nirvâna regarded as the redemption, is making incessant progress in Germany. Pascal long ago said: "Of all creatures that inhabit the earth, the Christian alone avoids pleasure and willingly embraces pain." Germany, after having resuscitated Buddhism with Schopenhauer, Von Hartmann, Bahnsen, is in a fair way to supply us with a sort of pessimistic edition of

Christianity which will far outdo Pascal.   But for evil and sin,
religion would not have existed, Von Hartmann thinks, and
as evil is of the essence of existence annihilation is the sole
salvation possible.   Bahnsen, in his philosophy of despair
reaches an analogous conclusion.   The most interesting representative of the new doctrine is Philipp Mainlaender, the
author of the " Philosophy of the Redemption " (Die Philosophie der Erclösing).   He was the son of parents of an exalted
piety, and grandson of a mystic who died of nervous fever in
his thirty-third year, and brother of another mystic who,
on his arrival in India, was converted to Buddhism and
died soon after, exhausted by the intensity of his mental life.
Mainlaender found his Damascus in Italy ; the heavens opened
upon him in a bookshop in Naples where he discovered the
writings of Schopenhauer.   After having composed his system of pessimistic philosophy, he supervised the printing of
the first volume, and the day he received his first copy (March
31, 1876) he hanged himself.[1]   The sincerity of this pessimist's conviction cannot be denied, nor the power of abstract
ideas implanted on a brain prepared for them by heredity,
and by the intellectual tendencies of the times.   Mainlaender
regarded philosophy as some day destined to replace religion,
but the philosophy is to be pessimistic ; Mainlaender declared
himself a Christian even while he was founding a scientific
system of atheism.   Freedom to commit suicide is the
modern substitute for the beautiful illusion of immortality.
Salvation by death will, Mainlaender thought, take the place
of salvation by eternal life.   The tree of science will thus become the legendary fig-tree of Timon the misanthrope, the
branches of which were weighted every morning afresh by the
bodies of the dead, who had come in search of oblivion from

Must find the       the evil of life, and had found it in self-destruction.
causes of pessi-          I. To estimate the value and probable duration
mism.               of the pessimistic sentiment, which has in some
cases at the present day been identified with the religious sentiment, one must first consider its causes.

[1] See in the *Revue philosophique*, June, 1885, an article by M. Arréat on Mainlaender.

Different reasons have brought about this transformation of pantheism, which after having divinized the world,
now inspires the individual to dream fondly on his
annihilation and reabsorption into the unity of
things. The first cause is the progress of panthe-

The growth of
pantheistic meta-
physics.

istic metaphysics. After having adored nature as the product of
immanent reason, pantheists have come to regard it as a work of
immanent unreason, as the degeneration of an indeterminate
and unconscious unity in the misery and conflict of phenomenal
selves, of conscious beings condemned to suffering. At the very
least, nature is indifferent to man. Eternal force, which is so
much spoken of to-day, is no more comforting and reassuring to
us than eternal substance. Right or wrong, the metaphysical
instinct, which is identical at bottom with the moral instinct,
demands not only the presence of life in all things, but of life
in pursuit of an ideal of goodness and universal sociality.

I was lying one day in the mountains, stretched on the grass ;
a lizard came out of a hole and mistook my motionless body for
a rock, and climbed up on my leg and stretched
himself out to bask in the sun. The confiding
little creature lay on me enjoying the light,

Persistence of
anthropomor-
phism.

untroubled by any suspicion of the relatively powerful stream
of life which was flowing noiselessly and amicably beneath
him. And I, for my part, began to look at the moss and the
grass on which I was reposing, and the brown earth and the
great rocks ; was I not myself, after all, a lizard simply as compared with the great world, and was I not perhaps a victim
of the same mistake ? Was there not a secret life throbbing
everywhere about me, palpitating beneath my feet, sweeping
forward confusedly in the great totality of things ? Yes, but
what difference did it make if it was simply the blind egoistic
life of a multitude of atoms, each striving for ends of its own.
Little lizard, why have I not, like thee, a friendly eye in the
universe to watch over me ?

The second cause of contemporary pessimism is the rapid
progress of positive science, and the revelations it is making in
regard to the natural world. The movement has been so precipitate, new ideas have been produced with such rapidity, that

the intelligence has found it difficult to adapt itself to them ;
we are going too fast, we find it as difficult to get our breath as
The progress of science. the rider of a runaway horse, or an aeronaut swept
away at a dizzy speed by the wind.  Knowledge
causes thus, at the present epoch, a sense of dis-
comfort which is due to a disturbance of the inner equilibrium ;
consciousness of the world, so joyous in its beginnings at the
time of the Renaissance, making its first appearance in the
midst of Rabelais' uproarious fun, has come to be almost melancholy.  We have not yet become domesticated in the infinities of the new world which has been revealed to us, and we feel
a little lost ; therein lies the secret of the melancholy of the
present epoch, which was melodramatic and rapid in the pages
of Chateaubriand and the youngest children of the century ;
and has come to be serious and reflective in the pages of Leopardi and of Schopenhauer and of the pessimists of the present
day.   In India the Brahmans are distinguished by a black
point between their eyes ; our men of science, our philosophers and artists, carry this black point on their foreheads.

The third cause of pessimism, which results from the two
preceding, is the suffering caused by the exaggerated develop-
Exaggerated development of thought. ment of thought at the present day, and the dis-
proportionate place that it occupies at present in
human life.  We are suffering from a sort of
hypertrophy of the intelligence.  Those who work with their
brains, who meditate upon life and death, who philosophize,
ultimately experience this suffering ; and the same is true of
artists, who pass their life in endeavouring to realize a more or
less inaccessible ideal.  One is drawn all ways at once by the
sciences and arts ; one wishes to devote one's self simultaneously
to all of them, and one is obliged to choose.  One's whole
vitality sets in toward one's brain ; one has to check it, to beat
it back, to resign one's self to vegetating instead of to living !
One does not resign one's self—one prefers to abandon one's self
to the inner fire that consumes one.  One's thoughts gradually
become feebler, the nervous system becomes irritable, becomes
feminine ; but the will remains virile, is always on the stretch,
unsatisfied, and the result is an eternal struggle, an endless

dissatisfaction with one's self; one must choose, must have
muscles or nerves; be a man or a woman; and the thinker and
artist are neither the one nor the other. If by a simple
immense effort we could but express the world of sentiment
and thought we carry within us, with what joy, what pleasure
we should do it; even if the brain should be torn asunder in
the process! But we must give it out by small fragments,
squeeze it out drop by drop, submit to all the interruptions of
life, and little by little the organism becomes exhausted in
the struggle between mind and body, and the intelligence
flickers like a light in a rising wind, until the spirit is vanquished and the light goes out.

Modern thought is not only more clear-sighted in matters of
the external world, but also in matters of the internal world.
John Stuart Mill maintained that introspec-
tion and the progress of psychological analysis
possess a certain dissolving force that, along with
disillusionment, induces sadness. We come to be
too well aware of the source of our feelings and the details of
our character; what an antagonism between being gifted
enough in matters of philosophy or poetry to create a world
to one's own mind, to embellish and illuminate the real world,
and, nevertheless, being too analytic and introspective to profit
by the pleasing illusion! We build airy palaces of cards and
are the first to blow them down. We are without pity for our
own hearts, and sometimes wonder whether we should not
have been better off without them; we are too transparent to
our own eyes, we see the hidden springs of our own activity,
we have no sincere faith in objective reality, nor faith enough
in the rationality of our own joys to enable them to attain
their maximum.

At the same time that the intelligence is becoming more
penetrating and reflective with the progress of knowledge,
sensibility of every kind is becoming more
delicate; even sympathy, according to the pessimist, is coming to be an instrument of torture
by annexing the suffering of others in addition to our
own. The echo and reverberation in us of the sufferings of

*Dissolving effect of subjective analysis on the emotions.*

*Heightened sensibility.*

other people, growing with the growing sociality, seem to be greater than the echo and reverberation in us of human joys. Social needs themselves, which have been so magnified at the present day, are so far from being satisfied that pessimists are asking whether they ever can be satisfied and whether humanity is not destined to become simply more numerous in the struggle for existence, and more wretched and more conscious of its wretchedness.

And, finally, a last cause of pessimism is the enfeeblement of the will, which accompanies an exaltation of the intelligence and the sensibility. Pessimism is in some sort a metaphysical suggestion engendered by physical and moral powerlessness. Consciousness of lack of power produces a disesteem, not only for one's self, but for everything; a disesteem which, in certain speculative minds, must inevitably crystallize into *a priori* formulæ. It has been said that suffering embitters one; and the same is true in an even greater degree of a sense of powerlessness. Recent psychological observations confirm this conclusion.[1] Among the insane, and among hypnotic subjects, periods of satisfaction and optimism, which are periods of benevolence and amenity, coincide with a heightened muscular power, whereas periods of discontent and malevolence coincide with a state of depression of the will which is accompanied by a lowering of the muscular powers, sometimes by one-half. One may say, with M. Fréré, that people in good health, at the maximum of their muscular vitality, are incessantly disposed to estimate the world in terms of their own vigour, whereas the degenerate, the physically or mentally enfeebled, are incessantly disposed to estimate the world and its possibilities in terms of their own slackness and incompetency. Add that, being themselves unequal to the struggle with the universe, it seems to them, by a natural illusion, that the universe is unequal to their ideals and demands upon it; they fancy that it is they that tip the scale, whereas the fact is precisely the opposite.

In all the experiments in hypnotism a sense of powerlessness engenders dissatisfaction; the patient who finds himself

*Depression of vitality.*

[1] M. Ch. Fréré, *Revue philosophique*, July, 1886.

unable to obtain possession of a desired object endeavours to explain his inability by seeking in the object itself some quality which renders it repulsive. We are inevitably in-clined to objectify the limitations of our own power instead of recognizing them for what they are.

Once started in this path, hypnotic patients would certainly, if they were competent, go the length of construct-ing a metaphysical system to justify their state of mind.[1]

Pessimism thus probably originates, for the individual, in a sense of lack of power. Sometimes this sense possesses indis-putably a certain element of universality; a con-sciousness of the limits of human power, as of human intelligence, must as inevitably increase by the very progress of our knowledge and capacity. Pessi-mism is not, therefore, pure madness, nor pure vanity; or, if it is madness, the madness is natural, and is induced sometimes by nature itself. At certain periods nature seems to go in-sane, to revel in folly, although the power of logic, which is identical in the last resort with the overruling principle of things, always has the last word in the universe, as it ought to have also in the human mind.

To sum up: in this century of transition, of religious and moral and social transformation, of reflection and dissolving analysis, causes of suffering are abundant and ultimately assume the guise of motives of de-spair. Every new step in intelligence and sensibility brings new modes of suffering within our reach. The desire of

*Relation be-tween power-lessness and pessimism.*

*Sense of power-lessness destined to increase.*

*Summary.*

[1] A woman somnambulist was induced to believe that she could not lift her wor-sted neckerchief off the back of a chair; her shoulders were cold and she wanted it; she put out her hand, and finding herself unable to overcome the subjective ob-stacle, she translated it into the outer world and declared that the neckerchief was unclean, or of an offensive colour, etc., and ultimately became violently terrified. Another subject, also a woman, was persuaded that she could not pull open a drawer; she touched the button and then let go of it shivering, and exclaiming that it was cold. "No wonder," she added, as a rational justification of her repulsion, "it is of iron!" She was given an iron compass; she endeavoured to handle it, but soon dropped it. "You see," she said, "it is as cold as the handle, I cannot hold it." Thus the objective explanation of a subjective fact, once entertained, tends by force of logic to become general, to include a whole class of similar phenomena, to become a system, and, if need be, a cosmological and metaphysical system.

knowledge, in especial, which is the most dangerous of all human desires, because the object of it is really infinite, becomes every day more insatiable and enslaves not only isolated individuals, but entire nations; it is the desire of knowledge that is the disease of the century, a disease which is growing, and becoming for the philosopher the disease of humanity. The seat of the disease is in the head; it is the brain of mankind that is attacked. We are far from the naïveté of primitive people, who, when they are asked for the seat of thought, point to the stomach or the bosom! We are well aware that we think with our heads, for it is in our heads that we suffer from a preoccupation with the unknown, with the ideal, with an incessant endeavour to overtake the progress of a winged and devouring thought. On the mountains of Tartary one sometimes sees a strange animal pass through the morning mist at a breathless speed; its eyes are those of a frightened antelope, and while it gallops with a foot that trembles as it strikes the soil, two great wings stretch out from the sides of its head and seem on the point of lifting it from the ground each time that they pulsate. It sweeps down the valleys, and its path is marked by traces of blood, and suddenly it falls, and the two great wings rise from the body, and an eagle, which was feeding leisurely upon its brain, takes its way off into the sky.

II. Is pessimism curable? A sense of evil constitutes a legitimate element in the metaphysical or religious sentiment;

Is pessimism the last word of philosophy? but is that a sufficient reason for recognizing it not simply as a part, but as the whole of metaphysics and of religion? Such is the problem.

Von Hartmann has endeavoured to discover in all religion a basis of pessimism. To do so is to judge all humanity too narrowly, according to one's observation of it at

Pessimism only part of the truth. the present day. To maintain that religion is founded on a radical pessimism is like affirming that medicine is based not on a theory of the curability, but of the incurability of disease. Schopenhauer's pessimism, like Spinoza's optimism, contains, no doubt, a certain indestructible element of truth, but immensely overstated and magnified. If science cannot regard the world as divine, neither can it regard the world as diabolical. There is no more ground for cursing the objective universe than for adoring it. And the subjective causes of unhappiness, which we have analyzed, are provisional simply. Human knowledge, which at present is so considerable in its dimensions that it actually embarrasses the brain, may well come to be so organized (as, indeed, in some cases, it is even now) that it will produce a sense of well-being and of largeness of life only. There is need, however, for a wholly new science, that of intellectual hygiene, of intellectual therapeutics, a science which, once created, might prevent or cure the mental depression which seems to result from exaggerated nervous excitation, such as pessimism seems to be incidental to, and such as Greece was unacquainted with.

For the rest, the desire of knowledge, which is, as we have seen, among the most profound of the desires of the century, may become the source of, perhaps, the most trustworthy and most infallible cure for a great number of human ills. Some of us, certainly, who are of the physically and mentally disinherited, may cry : " I have suffered in all my joys." *Nescio quid amari* was present for us in the first draught of pleasure, in the first smile, in the first kiss, and yet the present life is not without its sweetness when we do not rebel against it, when it is rationally accepted. What makes up for the bitterness of knowledge is the definiteness and clearness that it lends to the world. As science becomes more perfect it may some day inspire the soul with something of the serenity that is everywhere incidental to unfaltering clear light. Therein lies the secret of Spinoza's intellectual calm. If his objective optimism is indefensible, his subjective optimism is not without an aspect of truth in the consciousness of inner peace that belongs to breadth of intelligence and harmony of thought.

*Resignation.*

So far as introspection is concerned, and the dissolving force it exercises upon our joys, introspection is destructive, really, of none but irrational joys, and by way of compensation, it is destructive also of irrational griefs. Truth resists analysis; it is our business to seek in truth not only for the beautiful, but for the good. Take it all in all, there is as much solid and enduring truth in enlightened love of family, of country,

*Analysis de-* of humanity, as in the most unquestionable scien-
*stroys irrational* tific fact, or in certain physical laws, like that
*joys only.* of gravitation. The great remedy for excessive analysis, such as Amiel, for example, suffered from, is a little to forget one's self, to widen one's horizon, and, above all, to do something. Action, by its very nature, is a realized synthesis, a decision which necessitates the solution of a certain number of problems, or the recognition that their solution is not indispensable. Action is something too trenchant and provisional, no doubt, but men must remember that they live in the provisional and not the eternal, and that of their life, after all, what is least provisional is action, motion, the vibration of an atom, the undulation which traverses the great whole. Whoever lives immersed in the conduct of life has no time for self-pity or self-dissection. Other forms of oblivion are involuntary and sometimes lie beyond one's power, but one may always forget one's self. The cure for all the sufferings of the modern brain lies in an enlargement of the heart.

It has been urged, it is true, that we suffer increasingly from a growing sympathy and pity for each other. The problem of

*The problem* individual happiness, owing to the increasing
*of distribution* sense of the solidarity of mankind, is more than
*of wealth.* ever dependent to-day upon the happiness of society at large. Not only our immediate and personal griefs, but the griefs of other people, of society, of humanity, present and to come, influence us. So be it. To discuss the future would be endless. We have not Macbeth's privilege of being brought face to face with the file of future generations, and cannot read in advance the destiny of our descendants in their faces. The mirror of human life shows us nothing but an image of ourselves, and in this image we are inclined, like the poets, to emphasize the lines of pain. The labour problem, which at present distresses us, is infinitely complex; but we believe that the optimists have even more right to regard it with tranquillity than the pessimists have to declare it insoluble; in especial when one considers that it has assumed a

threatening aspect only during something like the last half century.

The labour problem involves two distinct questions, one of them relating to a conflict of interests, the other to a conflict of intentions. We believe that the strictly economic problem will one day be solved by a simultaneous increase in the difficulty of the industrial situation and in the knowledge of how to deal with it, which will lead the well-to-do classes to perceive that by endeavouring to save everything they are running the risk of losing everything, and will lead the lower classes to perceive that by endeavouring to obtain too much they are running the risk of gaining nothing and of seeing society's coveted wealth melt away before their eyes, and that dividing capital is like dividing a germ, and results in sterilization. The remedy for socialism lies in science—even though the first effect of a wider dissemination of knowledge would be to increase the strength of socialism. Out of the very intensity of the crisis the solution will come. The moment different interests are completely conscious of their real points of antagonism, they are close upon a compromise. War is never the result of anything but an incomplete knowledge of the comparative powers and respective interests of the opposing parties; people fight when they can no longer calculate, and the march of armies and pitched battles may themselves be regarded as a sort of higher arithmetic.

*How the economic half of the problem will be dealt with.*

When it has once come to be understood that there is no fundamental conflict of interest between the classes, the sense of antagonism between them will gradually diminish. The most reassuring promise of a complete solution of the industrial problem lies in human sociality. All asperity of temper in the matter will be smoothed away by the incontestable growth of sympathy and altruism.

*The human half will settle itself.*

If sympathy, love, labour in common, recreation in common, sometimes seem to augment the pains of life, they more than proportionately augment the joys. Moreover, as is well known, to share trouble is to lessen it; sympathy is itself a pleasure ; poets know it, dramatic poets in especial ; even when pity is accompanied by a lively realization of another's pain it nevertheless induces love, and to that extent still pre-

*Love and admira-*
*tion the panacea*
*for pessimism.*

serves a certain charm. That creature suffers, therefore I love it; and there are infinite joys in love; it multiplies the value of life in one's own eyes, by giving it a value in the eyes of other people, a social value, which is in the best sense a religious value. Man, Wordsworth says, lives in admiration, hope, and love, but he who possesses admiration and love will always possess an abundance of hope. He who loves and admires will possess the lightness of heart that carries one through the day without fatigue. Love and admiration are the great remedies of despair. Love, and you will wish to live. Whatever may be the value of life from the point of view of sensibility—knowledge and action, and principally action in behalf of another, will always constitute reasons for living. And it is mainly one's reasons for living that justify one's tenacity of life.

Pessimism sees only the sensitive side of life; but life presents also an active and an intellectual side; over and above

*Pessimism an*
*optical illusion.*

the agreeable there exist the great, the beautiful, and the generous. Even from the mere point of view of pleasure and pain, pessimism is based on calculations which are as open to discussion as Bentham's hedonistic arithmetic. We have seen elsewhere[1] that happiness and unhappiness are *ex post facto* mental constructions that are based upon a multitude of optical illusions. Even the disillusionment of pessimism is itself a sort of an illusion.

Leopardi hit upon an ingenious empirical argument in favour of pessimism in his dialogue between an almanac seller and a passer-by:

*Almanac Seller.* Almanacs! New almanacs! New calendars! Who wants new almanacs?

*Passer-by.* Almanacs for the new year?

*Almanac Seller.* Yes, sir.

*Passer-by.* Do you think this year will be a happy one?

*Almanac Seller.* Yes, to be sure, sir.

[1] *Esquisse d'une morale sans obligation ni sanction*, p. 89.

*Passer-by.* As happy as last year?

*Almanac Seller.* Much more so.

*Passer-by.* As the year before?

*Almanac Seller.* Still more so, sir.

*Passer-by.* Why, should you not like the new year to resemble one of the past two years?

*Almanac Seller.* No, sir, I should not.

*Passer-by.* How many years have gone by since you began to sell almanacs?

*Almanac Seller.* About twenty years, sir.

*Passer-by.* Which of the twenty should you wish the new year to be like?

*Almanac Seller.* I do not know.

*Passer-by.* Do you not remember any particular year which you thought a happy one?

*Almanac Seller.* Indeed, I do not, sir.

*Passer-by.* And yet life is a fine thing, is it not?

*Almanac Seller.* So they say.

*Passer-by.* Should you not like to live those twenty years, and even all your past life from your birth, over again?

*Almanac Seller.* Ah, dear sir, would to God that I could!

*Passer-by.* But if you had to live over again the life you have already lived, with all its pleasures and sufferings?

*Almanac Seller.* I should not like that.

*Passer-by.* Then what other life would you like to live? Mine, or that of the prince, or whose? Do you not think that I, or the prince, or anyone else would reply exactly as you have done, and that no one would wish to repeat the same life over again?

*Almanac Seller.* Yes, I believe that . . .

*Passer-by.* And it is clear that each person is of opinion that the evil he has experienced exceeds the good; . . . but with the new year fate will commence treating you, and me, and everyone well, and the happy life will begin . . .

*Almanac Seller.* Almanacs! New almanacs! New calendars![1]

[1] Dialogue cited by M. Caro in *Pessimisme.*

Many of us no doubt would reply to the poet as the almanac seller did—we should not wish to begin our life over again—

*Persistent novelty in the universe.*

but it is not to be concluded from that that our past life, taken as a whole, has been unhappy rather than happy.    It is to be concluded simply that it has lost its novelty, and with its novelty a great part of its charm.    Man, in effect, is not a purely sensitive being.    His pleasures are, so to speak, not blind.    He not only enjoys, he knows that he enjoys, and knows what he enjoys, and each of his sensations constitutes an addition to his treasures of knowledge.    Having once begun to amass this treasure, he desires incessantly to augment it, though he cares little enough futilely to handle and to contemplate the wealth already acquired.    Our past life, therefore, is to some extent tarnished and deflowered. The number of hours that were so rich, so full that we could not exhaust them at the time and desire to repeat them, is not great ; and, barring such hours, the principal charm of the rest of our past existence lay in estimating its details, in comparing them with each other, in exercising upon them our intelligence and our activity, and ... lightly passing them by ; they were not worth lingering over ; they resembled the tracts of country that the traveller does not feel tempted to turn and look back upon.    If novelty possesses for mankind a certain charm, if a repetition of identically similar circumstances rarely affords as great pleasure the second time as the first, the fact is owing in part to the very laws of desire, but in part to the superiority of the human mind ; the desired object should always offer something new to the intelligence.    Every desire contains an element of philosophic and æsthetic curiosity that the past cannot satisfy ; the flower of novelty cannot be gathered twice from the same branch.

But Leopardi might reply, What is the charm of novelty but an illusion ?    For everything on earth is really old : the future is but a repetition of the past and ought

*And genuine novelty.*

logically to be as repugnant as the past.    Abstract formulæ, and precipitate inductions like that, offer no resistance either to reason or to experience. Whatever pessimistic poets may say to the contrary, nothing is a repetition of anything else, either in human life or in the universe. There is always something new under the sun, if it be no more than the budding leaves on a tree or the changing colour on a cloud. No two sunsets are the same. Fairy-stories tell of a marvellous picture book, the pages of which one may turn forever without weariness, for the instant the picture has been looked upon and the page turned, its place is taken by a new picture. The universe is such a book; when one wishes to turn back to a familiar page it is no longer the same nor are we ourselves the same, and if we consider the matter narrowly, the world should always possess for us its first freshness.

The distinctive sign of a really superior, really human intellect is to be interested in everything in the universe, and in the difference between things. When we look straight before us without, properly speaking, seeing anything, we perceive resemblances only; when we look with attention, with affectionate love of detail, we perceive an infinity of differences; an intellectual activity, always awake, finds everywhere objects of interest. To love anything is to find in it, incessantly, elements of novelty.

Perception of difference the mark of high intelligence.

When pessimists maintain that the charm of the future is an illusion, it may be retorted that the illusion is theirs, that they do not look at the world closely enough to see it as it is, and do not love it because they do not know it. If one could view the Alps from the surface of a passing aërolite, the Rigi, the Faulhorn, Mont Blanc, Monte Rosa would all look alike, would all appear to be indifferent points on the earth's rind; but what shall be said of the naïve traveller who confounds them, and professes to have seen the whole of the Alps when he has climbed the Rigi? Life, also, is a perpetual ascent, of which it is difficult to say one has seen the whole because one has climbed the first peak. From childhood to old age, the horizon grows larger and changes and is always new. Nature seems to repeat itself only to a superficial gaze. Each of its works is original, like those of genius. Æsthetically or intellectually

The world inexhaustibly interesting.

considered, discouragement is voluntary or involuntary blindness. If poets have wished to forget past experiences which were too painful, even in memory, no true scholar or man of science has ever expressed the desire to forget what he knew, to make a blank space in his intelligence, to reject the knowledge so slowly acquired—unless, indeed, it were for the refined pleasure of learning it all over again and of owing nothing to the labour of previous generations. Beneath every human desire, we repeat, there exists this thirst for truth, which is one of the essential elements of the religious sentiment, and all other desires may be satiated or fatigued, but this one still subsists; one may be weary of life without being weary of knowledge; even those who have been most bitterly wounded by the conditions of life may still accept them for the light that the intelligence brings them at the price of pain, as a soldier, whose eyes have been injured by some chance splinter, nevertheless strains them beneath his eyelids to follow the course of the fight about him.

In effect, the analysis that pessimism is based upon is, in many respects, superficial. Even the word pessimism is inexact, for the doctrine ascribes no progress from bad to worse, from *pejus* to *pessimum;* it maintains simply that the world is bad and must be recognized as such, and that this recognition is the consequence and the condition of progress, of intellectual power and of knowledge.

*Summary.*

The practical rules for the conduct of life that pessimism prescribes from its principles are still more open to discussion. Granted the wretchedness of life, the remedy that pessimists propose is the new religious salvation that modern Buddhists are to make fashionable. This novelty, which is older than Sâkya-Muni itself, is one of the most ancient of Oriental ideas; it to-day proves attractive to a number of Occidental peoples, as it has several times proved attractive to them in former days, for traces of it may be found among the Neo-Platonists and the Christian mystics. The conception is that of Nirvâna. To sever all the ties which attach you to the external world; to prune away all the young offshoots of desire, and recognize that to be rid of them

*Suicide as a resource.*

is a deliverance; to practice a sort of complete psychical circumcision; to recoil upon yourself and to believe that by so doing you enter into the society of the great totality of things (the mystics would say of God); to create an inner vacuum, and feel dizzy in the void and, nevertheless, to believe that the void is plentitude supreme—Πλήρωμα—these have always constituted temptations to mankind; mankind has been tempted to meddle with them, as it has been tempted to creep up to the verge of dizzy precipices and look over. The pantheistic or monistic notion of Nirvâna eludes criticism precisely because it is void of all precise content. Physiologically speaking, Nirvâna corresponds to the period of repose and quietude which always follows a period of tension and of effort. One cannot stop and take breath in the eternal forward march that constitutes the phenomenal life of humanity; it is good sometimes to feel lassitude, it is good a little to understand the comparative cheapness and vanity of everything one has hitherto attained, but good only on condition that such an understanding of our past constitutes a spur to fresh effort in the future. To rest content with lassitude—to believe that the deepest existence is the meanest, the coldest, the most inert—is equivalent to a confession of defeat in the struggle for existence. Nirvâna leads, in fact, to the annihilation of the individual and of the race, and to the logical absurdity that the vanquished in the struggle for existence are the victors over the trials and miseries of life.

It would be interesting to perform a practical experiment in Nirvâna. One of my acquaintances pushed the experiment as far as a European of scientific tendencies could.

Trial of Nirvâna. He practised asceticism to the point of rejecting all variety in his diet, he gave up meat (as Mr. Spencer also did for some time), wine, every kind of ragout, every form of condiment, and reduced to its lowest possible terms the desire that is most fundamental in every living being—the desire of food, the excitation of the famished animal in the presence of appetizing dishes, the moment of heightened expectation before dinner which constitutes for so many people the event of the day. For the protracted meals that are customary, he substituted a certain number of cups of pure milk. Having thus blunted his sense of taste and the grosser of his appetites, having abandoned all physical activity, he sought to find a recompense in the pleasures of abstract meditation, and of æsthetic contemplation. He entered into a state which was not that of dreamland, but neither was it that of real life, with its definite details. What gives relief and outline to the life of each day, what makes each day an epoch for us in our existence, is the succession of our desires and our pleasures. One has no idea what a blank would be produced in one's existence by the simple omission of some hundreds of meals. By a similar process of elimination, employed in regard to pleasures and desires generally, he secured for his life a certain savourless, colourless, ethereal charm. The whole universe recoiled by degrees into the distance, for the universe was composed of things that he no longer came into forcible contact with, that he no longer handled vigorously, and that, therefore, came less violently into contact with him, and left him, therefore, more indifferent to them. He entered the cloud in which the gods sometimes envelop themselves, and no longer felt the firm earth beneath his feet, but he soon found that, if he no longer stood upon firm earth, he was not on that account the nearer heaven ; what struck him most was the enfeeblement of his thoughts precisely at the time when, owing to his complete detachment from all material cares, he was inclined to believe himself most intellectually competent. The instant that thought ceased to rest upon a foundation of solid reality it became incapable of abstraction ; the life of thought as of our whole being is contrast, and it gathers power by dealing from time to time with objects which seem least readily to lend themselves to its purposes. An endeavour to purify and to sublimate thought robs it of its precision ; meditation gives place to dream, and dream gives place to the ecstasy in which mystics lose all sense of the distinction between ἓν καὶ πᾶν; but in which a mind accustomed to self-possession cannot long remain without a sense of vapidity. Then a feeling of revolt supervenes, and one begins to understand that abstract thought needs, if it is to achieve its highest point of lucidity and concentration, to be spurred on by desire. Such at least was the experience of the friend mentioned above, and I suggest his experiment for imitation to those who speak of Nirvâna from hearsay only, and have never practised absolute renunciation. The only danger to fear is lest renunciation produce a certain brutalization, lest one lose one's self-control and be overcome by a sort of vertigo before having measured the depth of the abyss, and having perceived that it is bottomless. The safest paths in the mountains are those that have been trodden out by asses and mules. "Follow the asses," is the advice of the guides. The advice is often good in real life; the good sense of the multitude opens the way which must be followed, whether one will or not, and philosophers may well at times "follow the asses."

Absorption in infinite substance, renunciation of the desire to live, and inert sanctity will always constitute the ultimate form and expression of human illusion. If all is vanity, nothing, after all, is more vain than to be completely conscious that all is vanity ; if action is vain, repose is still more vain ; life is vain, death is vainer. Even sanctity is not the equal of charity, the equal, that is to say, of what binds the individual to other individuals, and by that fact renders him once more the slave of desire and of pleasure—if not of his own desires and pleasures, at least of those of other people. One must always serve someone, must always be in bonds to something, even if only to the flesh. One must drag a chain, if one is to draw others after one. Nobody forms a sufficient end and aim for his own activity ; nobody can emancipate himself by living ' in and in,' by forming an ideal circle like the coiled serpent, by reflecting eternally, according to the Hindu precept, on his navel ; nothing is more like servitude than liberty that is confined within the bounds of self. The perfect sanctity of the mystics, Buddhists, and pessimists is a subtler egoism simply ; and the sole genuine virtue in the world is generosity, which does not fear to set its foot in the dust, in the service of another.

We do not therefore believe, with Schopenhauer and Von Hartmann, that pessimism will be the religion of the future.

*Sanctity and egoism.*

Life will not be persuaded to seek death, nor movement to prefer immobility. We have said elsewhere that what renders existence possible renders it also desirable ; if the sum of the pains of human life were greater than the sum of the pleasures, the species would become extinct by a gradual decrease in the vitality of each succeeding generation. Occidental nations, or rather the active people in the world, to whom the future belongs, will never become converts to pessimism. Whoever acts, feels, has power, and to be strong is to be happy. Even in the Orient, when their pessimism, the great religions, is addressed to the multitude, it is very superficial ; commonplace maxims on the ills of existence, and on the necessity for resignation, result as a matter of fact in a *far niente* which is appropriate to the manners of the Orient. And, when it is addressed to thinkers, pessimism is only provisional—it points to its own remedy in Nirvâna ; but Nirvâna as a panacea and salvation by negation, or by violent self-destruction, will not long captivate modern common sense. It is ridiculous to attribute to man the power to destroy the sacred germ from which life, with all its illusions, has sprung, and will always spring, in spite of ascetics and partisans of individual suicide, and even, if Von Hartmann will, of " cosmic suicide." It is perhaps less difficult to create than to annihilate, to make God than to destroy Him.

*Pessimism not destined to prevail.*

# CHAPTER V.

REVIEW OF THE PRINCIPAL METAPHYSICAL HYPOTHESES
WHICH WILL REPLACE DOGMA—*Concluded.*

IDEALISM, MATERIALISM, MONISM.

I. Idealism—Different forms of idealism : subjective idealism,
objective idealism : The whole of existence resolved into a mode
of mental existence—Value of idealism considered from point of
view of the religious sentiment—Most specious of contemporary
idealisms : Possibility of universal progress on the hypothesis of
radical spontaneity and of " freedom "—Reconciliation between
determinism and the conception of freedom—Moral idealism as a
possible substitute for religious sentiment : Dependence of the
universe on the principle of goodness.

II. Materialism—Difficulty in defining absolute materialism: Matter,
—The atom—Nebular hypothesis—Hydrogene—Necessity of
supplementing materialism by some theory of the origin of life—
The latest conception of materialism : Conception of infinite
divisibility and infinite extensibility.

III. Monism and the fate of worlds—Current of contemporary systems toward monism—Scientific interpretation of monism—The
world conceived monistically as a becoming and as a life—Scientific
formulæ for life—Progress consists in the gradual confusion of
these two formulæ—That the rise of morality and religion can be
accounted for without the presupposition of any final cause—
Metaphysical and moral expectations in regard to the destiny of
the world and of humanity it may be founded on scientific
monism—Facts which appear to be inconsistent with these expectations—Pessimistic conception of dissolution that is comple-
mentary to the conception of evolution—Is the immanence of
dissolution demonstrable ?—Natural devices for the perpetuation
of the "fittest "—Rôle of intelligence, of numbers, etc.—Calculation of probabilities—Is eternity *a parte post* a ground of discouragement or of hope—Probable existence of thinking beings
in other worlds: the planets, possibility of the existence of beings
superior to man—Survival of the conception of gods—Hypothesis
of intercosmic consciousness and of a universal society.

IV. Destiny of the human race—The hypothesis of immortality

from the point of view of monism—Two possible conceptions of immortality—Eternal or untemporal existence and continuation of life in some superior forms—I. Hypothesis of eternal life—its function in antique religions, in Platonism, and in the systems of Spinoza, Kant, and Schopenhauer—Eternal life and the subsistence of the individual—Distinction made by Schopenhauer and various other philosophers between individuality and personality—Eternal life problematical and transcendent—Aristocratic tendency of the theory of eternal life—Hypothesis of conditional immortality—Criticism of the hypothesis of conditional immortality ; incompatibility of this notion with that of divine goodness—II. Hypothesis of a continuation of the present life and its evolution into some superior form—What sort of immortality the theory of evolution permits us to hope for—Immortality of one's labours and conduct—True conception of such immortality—Its relation to the laws of heredity, atavism, natural selection—Immortality of the individual—Objections drawn from science—Protestations of affection against the annihilation of the person—Resulting antinomy—III. Modern opposition between the conception of *function* and the conception of simple substance, in which ancient philosophy endeavours to find a proof of immortality—Peripatetic theory of Wundt and modern philosophers on the nature of the soul—Immortality as a continuation of function, proved not by the simplicity, but by the complexity of consciousness—Relation between complexity and instability— Three stages of social evolution—Analogy of conscience with a society, collective character of individual consciousness—Conception of progressive immortality—Last product of evolution and natural selection : (1) No necessary relation between the compositeness and complexity of consciousness and its dissolubility : indissoluble compounds in the physical universe—(2) Relation between consciousnesses, their possible fusion in a superior consciousness—Contemporary psychology and the religious notion of the interpenetration of souls—Possible evolution of memory and identification of it with reality—Palingenesis by force of love— Problematic character of those conceptions and of every conception relative to existence, of consciousness, and the relation between existence and consciousness—IV. Conception of death appropriate to those who, in the present state of evolution, do not believe in the immortality of the individual—Antique and modern stoicism—Acceptance of death : element of melancholy and of greatness in it—Expansion of self by means of philosophical thought, and scientific disinterestedness, to the point of to some extent approving one's own annihilation.

NATURALISM consists in believing that nature, together with the beings which compose it, make up the sum total of exist-

The problem of the immanence of being.

ence. But even from this point of view there still remains the problem, what existence essentially is, and what special mode of existence is most typical. Is nature material, or mental, or both? The problem of the essence of being is one that cannot be escaped.

The theory that seems to-day to be dominant is the "double-aspect" theory—the theory of two inseparable correlatives subjective and objective, of consciousness

The double-aspect theory.

and of motion. We have, as M. Taine[1] would say, two texts of the eternal book instead of one. The question is, which of the two texts is original and sacred? Sometimes that which is furnished by introspection alone, sometimes that which objective science endeavours to decipher, are respectively held to be primitive. Thence arise two opposed tendencies, not alone in psychological but in metaphysical speculation; the one toward idealism, the other toward materialism; the one toward what lies within, the other toward what lies without. But these two aspects may and should be conceived as possessing a certain unity; there is an inevitable tendency in the human mind to follow out two converging lines to their point of intersection. There are, therefore, three forms of naturalism: idealism, materialism, monism. These three constitute the three genuine systems of thought from which theism, atheism, and pantheism are respectively derived.

## *1. Idealism.*

If the words thought and idea be interpreted as Descartes and Spinoza understand them, as designating the entire life

Idealism defined.

of the mind, the sum total of the possible content of consciousness, idealism may be defined as the system which resolves all reality into thought, into psychical existence, insomuch that to be is to think or to be thought; to feel or to be felt; to will or to be willed; to be the object or subject of a conscious effort.

[1] M. Ribot holds the same doctrine.

It is evident that idealism is one of the systems which is capable of affording a certain satisfaction to the religious sen-

Idealism and the religious instinct. timent, because the religious sentiment is allied to the instinct for metaphysics, and the instinct for metaphysics finds itself at home among all things of the spirit, of thought, of the moral world. The foundation of theism, as we have said, is *moralism ;* the belief, that is to say, that the true power in nature is mental and moral. God is simply a representation of this power, conceived as transcendent. Pantheism itself, after having divinized and materialized the universe and resolved all things, so to speak, into God, tends to become idealistic, to resolve God into the thought which has conceived Him, to deny Him all existence over and above that which He possesses in thought, and for thought, and by virtue of thought. According to the Hindu compari- son, the human mind is like the spider that can build its man- sion out of materials drawn from its own body, and then reabsorb them.

But how shall the mind itself, the central fund of thought that is the origin and end of all things, be conceived ? Is it

Subjective idealism criticised. individual or impersonal ? English subjective or egoistic idealism, as Mr. Huxley defines it in his " Life of Hume," replies, that in spite of all dem- onstration to the contrary, the collection of perceptions which constitute our consciousness may be simply a phantasmagoria which, engendered and co-ordinated by the ego, unrolls its successive scenes upon a background of nonentity. Mr. Spencer retorts that, if the universe is thus simply a projec- tion of our subjective sensations, evolution is a dream ; but evolution may be formulated in idealistic quite as well as realistic terms : and a coherent dream is as good as reality. Subjective idealism is therefore difficult to refute logically ; but in spite of that fact it will never have many followers. For this apparent simplification of the world is in reality a complication. For subjective idealism involves the ridiculous hypothesis of a chance agreement between the impressions of any given individual and of all other individuals : a difficulty much harder to explain away than the preliminary one of the

simple reflection in us of an external world. Mental phenomena are always more complex than material phenomena.

The reduction of the external world to subjective terms, the
explanation of the optical illusion of objectivity, demands a
much greater display of vain ingenuity than any theory of
simple perception. More than that, the least effort with the
resistance that it encounters is a refutation of egoistic, or as
the English again say, solipsistic idealism. In the fact of
resistance, subjective sensation and the perception of an objective reality coincide. Even if the manner in which our sensations of resistance are combined in tridimensional space may
be conceived as subjective, it is difficult to admit that the
materials out of which the structure is made are, as it were,
suspended in mid-air. To explain the fact of resistance
requires us absolutely to pass beyond the limits of consciousness, for even in the cases in which the sensation of
resistance seems to be due to hallucination, the cause of hallucination is always found to be some instance of actual resistance, of friction or stress inside the body. The mistake of a
madman, who sees an unfamiliar form take shape and rise
before his eyes, is not that of considering the power as existing outside of himself, but of locating it at the extremities of
his nerves of touch ; whereas it is really in his brain, at the
point where the nerves intersect with the cerebral centres.
He is right in his sense of the presence of an enemy, but
wrong in the direction in which he looks for it.

We are obliged, therefore, to admit the hypothesis of a multitude of microcosms, of mine, of yours, of everybody's, and of
a single macrocosm the same for everybody.
Truth in subjec-
tive idealism. What is true is that between the great world and
every little world there is an incessant communication, by means of which everything that passes in the one
is echoed in the òther. We live in the universe, and the universe lives in us. The statement is not metaphorical, but
literal. If we could look into the consciousness of a school
child, we should see a more or less faithful image of all the
marvels of the world : skies, seas, mountains, cities, etc.; we
should perceive the germ of every elevated sentiment, of

every kind of complex knowledge that the human brain contains. If we could look into the consciousness of some great man—some thinker, some poet—the spectacle would be quite different. It would embrace the whole of the visible and invisible universe, with its facts and its laws; it would embrace what is best in the whole of humanity. If the traces left by experience on the nervous system could be read, like the writing in a book, the earth might disappear, and its image and history be handed down in certain chosen human brains.

Active and practical humanity will always believe in realism to the extent of insisting that the world possesses an existence which is independent of any individual thought.
Realism destined to prevail.
We shall dwell no further on subjective idealism, which is more important as a metaphysical curiosity than for any comfort it gives to the religious sentiment.

Of objective idealism the same cannot be said. In objective idealism, too, all material existence is regarded as a mode of mental existence; being is identified either
Objective idealism.
with the ideal law which presides over the development of the universe, or with the genuine foundation of our consciousness, our sensations, our desires. The world, as Emerson has said, is a precipitate of the soul.

This hypothesis is certainly one of those that may best serve as a substitute for theism, if theism should ever disappear.
Criticised.
But idealism, thus understood, is open to the following objection: Is it of any special use to objectify the soul, if the existence of evil, which Plato identified with matter, is thereby left unchanged? It is in vain to translate evolution into psychic terms; no difficulty can be avoided by so doing. The mysterious imperfections of the exterior world are transported bodily into the mind; evil is spiritualized simply. Identifying things with the intellectual law which presides over their evolution in nowise excuses us from explaining why that law is in so many respects bad, and why the intelligence that directs the universe is so often self-contradictory and feeble.

In spite of this objection, which will, perhaps, never receive a sufficient reply, it is certain that, so far as our moral and social instincts are concerned, idealism offers us greater ground for hope than either of the remaining systems of thought. In spite of evil and pain, the desire of progress and of salvation, which is the basis of all religious speculation, may rely upon thought as its last re-source. But thought, if the doctrine of objective idealism is to be made acceptable, must be understood as including not only intelligence, but also sentiment, desire, and volition, and, in effect, the purely intellectual idealism of a former time is at the present day being succeeded by an ideal-ism that regards the will as the fundamental element in the universe.[1] Universal sensibility is an incident of universal power of will, whereas intelligence, properly so called, at least in so far as the function of intelligence is regarded as repre-sentation, is more superficial than sensibility or volition.[2] These three inseparable forms of psychic life[3] constitute the great forces to which moral and religious sentiment must always turn for support.

*Objective ideal-ism relatively capable of satisfy-ing the moral instincts.*

Idealism, thus understood, constitutes one of the most tempting of the solutions of the problem of evil. Optimism being, as we have seen, indefensible, and pessi-mism being a caricature, the most plausible religious and metaphysical hypothesis at the present day is the conception of a "possible prog-ress owing to the radical spontaneity of all existing things."[4] The will, according to this hypothesis, with its tendency to indefinite self-expansion, is *par excellence* the primitive power, the central element in man and in the universe. Freedom of the will in man means the consciousness of this progressive power, which is immanent in all things, and this consciousness may be made the foundation of a moral being. This concep-tion of freedom, which is reconcilable with determinism, becomes an additional motive among the other motives that

*Hypothesis of moral progress immanent in the world.*

---

[1] See Schelling, Schopenhauer, Lotze, Wundt, Secrétan, MM. Ravaison, A. Fouillée, Lachelier, and, to a certain extent, M. Renouvier.

[2] See Schopenhauer, Horwicz, and M. Fouillée.

[3] See Wundt's *Psychologie physiologique*.

[4] Alfred Fouillée, *La Liberté et le Déterminisme*, 2d edition, pp. 353, 354, 356.

govern man's life, and tends to be realized by the very fact
that it is conceived and desired. Through the intermediation
of this conception, reality possesses a progressive freedom,
that is to say, a power of constant union with the whole, and
of moral enfranchisement. "In the beginning there obtains
a universal antagonism among the forces of the universe, a
brutal fatality, an infinite reign of shock and counter-shock,
between blind and blindly driven beings; then there arises a
progressive organization that makes the evolution of consciousness, and therefore of volition, possible; there arises a
gradual union and fraternity among the particulars that constitute the universe. Ill-will, whether it originate in mechanical necessity or in intellectual ignorance, is transitory;
good-will is permanent, radical, normal, and fundamental. To
cultivate good-will in one's self is to enfranchise one's self from
the individual and the transitory in favour of the universal
and the permanent; it is to become truly free, and by that
very fact to become truly loving." [1]

Between progressive freedom thus conceived, and the determinism in the midst of which it progresses, there is no opposi-

Reconciliation
between freedom
and determinism.

tion; freedom and determinism constitute two
aspects of one and the same process of evolution.
Determinism essentially consists in a series of
actions and reactions existing between other beings and ourselves; but these very actions and reactions constitute the
manifestation of the development of our, and their, inner
activities. And the source of activity in the universe is none
other than an overflowing power, which is hostile to limitation,
to impediment of every kind; is, in a word, none other than a
self-realizing volition. Freedom, thus understood, may, therefore, be considered in the last resort as the origin of determinism and as one with it. [2] Necessity is, so to speak, the outer
surface of freedom—the point of contact between two or
more free agents. Freedom is inconceivable apart from a resulting determinism, for to be free is to possess power, is to act
and to react, is to determine and to be determined. Deter-

[1] Alfred Fouillée, *La Liberté et le Déterminisme*, 2d edition, pp. 353, 354, 356.
[2] A. Fouillée, *op. cit.*

minism, on the other hand, that is to say, reciprocal action, is inconceivable apart from freedom, from internal action, from a spontaneous outbreak of power that tends to be free. So that one may say, without contradiction, that determinism envelops the world, and that free-will constitutes it.

If the shock of wills in the world is unusually brutal, the reason is that they are as yet but half conscious of their powers; as consciousness develops, contest will give way to concurrence. To avoid violent concussion with obstacles in the way, the free agent has less need of acquaintance with them than of acquaintance with itself. As there is nothing in the universe that is foreign to volition, there is nothing in the universe that is foreign to the ideal that every volition aims at. It is probable that life is always and everywhere accompanied by consciousness in some slight degree; and wherever consciousness exists, desire may exist. Nature's device, as a contemporaneous poet has said, is " I aspire." The human ideal is, perhaps, no more than the conscious formulation of this aspiration which is common to the whole universe. If so, it follows that ideal freedom is the limit of evolution, and that volition, which aims at ideal freedom, is the principle of it.[1]

*Ideal liberty the aim of the universe.*

It has been objected to this idealist theory of evolution that progress implies an aim and the observance of certain principles in its attainment, while evolution does not.[2] But the precise object of the doctrine in question is to supply evolution with a name and appropriate principles, and to extend the notion of progress to the universe as a whole. It has also been objected to this somewhat panthelistic hypothesis ($\theta\epsilon\lambda o\varsigma$), that if everything is free, nothing is free.[3] This objection is not exact, for it would imply, in economics, for instance, that to increase everybody's well-being would increase the well-being of nobody, or that if

*Objections answered.*

[1] " The category of Real Existence does not seem reconcilable with the notion of liberty; the latter in its perfection must be conceived under the category of the Ideal, and in its imperfection under that of Becoming."—A. Fouillée, *La Liberté et le Déterminisme*, conclusion.

[2] M. Franck, *Essais de critique philosophique.*

[3] M. Franck, *op. cit.*

everybody equally should be impoverished, everybody would
equally be enriched.    To universalize a conception is one thing,
to suppress it is another.    The world cannot at the present day
be conceived as distinct from the human race: the two are
vitally and intimately related.    Endow mankind with an un-
biassed freedom of will, and Epicurus would be right in holding
that indeterminism is the basis of all things.[1]    Similarly, suppose mankind endowed with " a radical goodness of will, which is
very distinct from freedom of the will, but nevertheless constitutes a sort of moral freedom in process of formation,"[2] and
the germ of such goodness of will should be found in a more
or less unconscious form throughout the entire universe.    Before the human mind can really produce anything whatever,
the whole universe must be like it in labour.    Partisans of the
theory of goodness of will as the basis of human morality
are therefore logical in regarding it as more or less present in
some degraded form throughout the whole of nature, even in
beings in which intelligence has not yet made its appearance ;
and goodness of will in such cases is to be considered as
accompanied by the obscure beginnings of responsibility, of
implicit merit or demerit—one must return in effect to a sort
of re-reading of the Hindu theory, according to which the
several degrees that exist in nature represent so many stages
in morality.

*Hypotheses fingo* is the mother of metaphysics.    Moral idealism of the kind we have just epitomized from the pages of a

Moral idealism      contemporary author is decidedly no more than a
and the religious   hypothesis, and a hypothesis open to discussion ;
sentiment.          but it is assuredly the form of idealism that is
least incompatible with the theory of evolution, and with the
facts of natural history and of human history.[3]    Moreover, it
affords unusual scope for the religious sentiment, freed from its
mysticism and transcendence.    If the unknown activity which

---

[1] The author argued the point at length, in 1873, in his book on Epicurus.    See
also his *Morale anglaise*, 2 partie, pp. 385–386, 2d edition.

[2] A. Fouillée, *La Liberté et le Déterminisme*, 2d edition.

[3] This form of idealism is equally compatible with the prevailing monistic doctrines, and is in some cases, as notably in that of M. Fouillée, confounded with them.
See below.

lies at the basis of the natural world has produced in the human race a consciousness of goodness, and a deliberate desire for it, there is reason to hope and to believe that the last word of ethics and metaphysics is not a negative.

We have a number of times cited Schleiermacher's definition of religion : the sense of our absolute dependence in regard to the universe and its principle. When the religious sentiment becomes transformed into a moral idealism its correct formula tends to be the inverse of the preceding : a sense of the dependence of the universe upon the determination that goodness shall prevail, of which we are conscious in ourselves and which we conceive to be or to be capable of becoming the directing principle of universal evolution. The notion of the moral and social ideal of freedom is, therefore, according to this doctrine, not a mere superficial accident in the universe, but a revelation and growing consciousness of the most fundamental laws of the universe, of the true essence of things, which is the same in all beings in different degrees and in diverse combinations. Nature represents an eternal ascent toward a more and more clearly conceived ideal, which dominates its progress from beginning to end. As one climbs a height to survey a mountain range, the snow-capped peaks rise silently and take their places side by side along the horizon ; it seems as if the enormous masses rise in obedience to an immense effort which uplifts them ; it seems as if their immobility is only apparent, and one feels borne aloft with them toward the zenith. The heroes in the Indian legend, when they were weary of life and of the earth, rallied their strength for a final effort, and hand in hand scaled the Himalayas, and the mountains bore them away into the clouds. Ancient peoples generally regarded the mountains as a transition between earth and sky ; it was from the mountains that the soul, profiting by the impulse lent it by the last touch of earth, took its freest flight : the mountains constituted a pathway toward the open heavens. And that may be an element of profundity in these naïve ideas which ascribe to nature aspirations which are more properly human. Do there not exist in nature great unfinished

*Religion interpreted in the light of this hypothesis.*

sketches, hints and lines leading upward? Nature has done all that unconsciously, has blindly piled block on block of stone slowly toward the stars. It is man's privilege to read a meaning into her work, to make use of her efforts, to employ past centuries as the materials out of which to build the future; by scaling the heights of nature man will reach the sky.

## II. Materialism.

Properly to estimate idealism it must be contrasted with its opposite, materialism.

We shall say but a few words on the subject of pure materialism, because of all systems of thought materialism is the farthest removed from those which give rise to religious and to metaphysical theories. Absolute materialism is somewhat difficult to define, because matter is one of the vaguest of words. To aim at representing the ultimate elements of matter as wholly independent of thought, of consciousness, of life, is evidently chimerical; such an effort leads straight to the pure indeterminism of matter as conceived by Plato, Aristotle, and Hegel; to an indefinite dyad, to a theory of virtuality and of the identity of non-being. Also materialists are obliged to regard as determinate and material the primitive force of which the world constitutes simply a development. If, for example, according to the most recent theories, all matter should prove to be reducible to hydrogen, materialism would regard hydrogen as constituting a sort of material or substantial unity in the world. Variety would exist only in the forms displayed by the primitive element, hydrogen, or, if you prefer, prehydrogen.

*Materialism difficult to define.*

It must be confessed that this conception is somewhat naïve and nominalistic; the word material or chemical can never express more than the outside, than the exterior properties of the primordial element. The hydrogen atom itself is probably in a high degree composite, is itself probably a world of little worlds, held in place by gravitation. The very conception of an in-

*Materialism criticised.*

divisible atom is philosophically infantine. Thomson and Helmholtz have shown that our atoms are little vortices of energy, and have succeeded in producing experimentally analogous vortices formed of vapour; for instance, of the vapour chlor-hydrate of ammonia. Each vortex is composed always of the same particles; no one particle can be separated from the others; each vortex possesses, therefore, a stable individuality. When the attempt is made to cut the vortices, they fly the blade or bend about it, and prove to be indivisible. They are capable of contraction, of dilation, of partial interpenetration and distortion, but never of dissolution. And certain men of science have thence inferred that we possess thus a material proof of the existence of atoms. And so indeed we do, providing an atom be understood to be something as complex, as little primordial, and as relatively enormous as a nebula. Atoms are indivisible as a nebula is indivisible by a knife blade, and the atom of hydrogen is about as simple as the solar system. To explain the universe by hydrogen is like explaining it by the sun and the planets. The rise of the actual world out of hydrogen can be conceived only on condition of ascribing to the alleged atoms of hydrogen something more than physicists and chemists know them to possess. Materialism, therefore, must enlarge its principle if it is to prove productive : enlarge, as Diderot would say, your atheism and your materialism.

But the instant materialism is "enlarged," the universal element must at once be regarded as alive and is not what is called brute matter. Every generation of physicists, as Mr. Spencer says, discovers in so called brute matter forces the existence of which the best informed physicist would some years previous have disbelieved. When we perceive solid bodies, sensitive in spite of their inertia to the action of forces, the number of which is infinite ; when the spectroscope proves to us that terrestrial molecules move in harmony with molecules in the stars; when we find ourselves obliged to infer that the innumerable vibrations traverse space in all directions, the conception which is forced upon us is not that of a universe of dead matter

*Must be supplemented by some theory to account for life.*

but rather that of a universe everywhere alive; alive in the general sense of the word, if not in the restricted.[1]   The notion of life is perhaps more human and more subjective, but after all more complete and concrete than the notion of movement and of force ; for we cannot hope to discover the truth at any great distance from the subjective, since subjectivity is the necessary form in which truth appears to us.

The second emendation to which materialism must submit, if it is to satisfy the metaphysical instincts of mankind, is to

*Must be supple-
mented by some
sort of mind-stuff
theory.*

include in the primordial element not only life but some germ of mind.   But primitive matter conceived as a force capable of living and ulti- mately of thinking is not what is scientifically and vulgarly regarded as matter, far less as hydrogen.   The pure materialist, thumping the rotundity of the earth with his fist, and relying grossly on his sense of touch, cries : " Matter is everything," but matter is analyzable into force, and force is simply a primitive form of life.   Materialism therefore issues into a sort of animism; in the presence of the circling world, the materialist is obliged to say it is alive.   Nor can he stop there ; the world is force, is action, is life—and something more ; for in and by me the world thinks.   *E pur si pensa !*

Behold us landed once more in idealism.   And, indeed, as Lange and M. Taine have well shown, materialism easily

*Passes readily
into idealism.*

passes to idealism; pure materialism results in an abstract mechanism, which is analyzable into the laws of logic and of thought.   And the basis of this mechanism—atoms and motion—consists in enfeebled sub- tilized and rarefied tactual and visual sensations, taken ulti- mately as the expression of the final reality.   The alleged foundation of objective reality is  simply a residuum of our most essential sensations.   Materialism is advocated in the name of positive science ; but it, not less than idealism, belongs really to the poetry of metaphysics ; its poetry is recorded simply in terms of atoms and motion, instead of in terms of the elements of consciousness.   Materialistic symbols are

[1] Mr. Spencer himself has a little forgotten this fact in a number of his own somewhat too mechanical constructions.

more matter of fact, more neighbour to the visible reality, possess a wider compass and generality, but they are none the less symbols simply. Materialism is in some sort a tissue of metaphor in which scientific terms lose their scientific signification, and gain a metaphysical signification in its stead, transferred, as they are, to a domain that lies beyond the range of experience. The man of science who speculates thus upon the nature of things is, unknown to himself, a modern Lucretius.

And finally, materialism, properly so called, has been invaded by a notion which has been at all times peculiarly

*Materialism and the notion of infinity.* adapted to satisfy the metaphysical and religious aspirations of mankind; the notion of infinity, whether in the direction of greatness or the opposite. Men of science go to the trouble of estimating the number of molecules in a drop of water; they tell us that the thousandth part of a millimeter of water contains 228,000,000 molecules; they say that a pinhead contains the fourth power of 20,000,000 atoms, and that, if the atoms could be counted a billion every second, it would take 253,678 years to complete the task. But all such calculations are simply arithmetical *jeux d'esprit*. These figures, which are so great in appearance, really amount to nothing, and a grain of sand, no doubt, contains literally an infinite number of particles.

The argument against the notion of infinity, based on the logical impossibility of an infinite number, is not decisive;[1]

*Final breakdown of materialism.* it rests upon a begging of the question, namely, that everything in the universe is innumerable— that is to say, is capable of being precisely included within the limits of an intelligence like our own. Logic, on the contrary, insists that in homogeneous matter, like space, time, and quantity, there is no limit to the possibility of division and multiplication, and that, consequently, they may proceed beyond any given number. If so called "purely scientific" materialism does not admit that nature is coextensive with man's conception of what is possible—if it

[1] See Renouvier's arguments and Lotze's and Fouillée's replies to them in the *Revue philosophique.*

denies the parallelism between thought and nature—it by that very fact denies also the rationality of nature, which is precisely the principle upon which every philosophy that pretends to be purely scientific ultimately relies. Whoever rejects the notion of infinity is obliged, in the last resort, to suppose a species of contradiction between the activity of the human mind, which is unable to stop at any given point, and nature, which stops, for no reason in particular, at a determinate point in time and space. The conception of infinity may be said to be forced upon materialism, and that very notion contains one of the antinomies against which intelligence, by the very fact of its employment, is ultimately brought to a standstill; it is precisely in the act of counting that intelligence achieves the conception of the innumerable; it is by exhausting every given quantity that it achieves the conception of the inexhaustible; it is by reaching ever beyond the limits of the known that it comes in touch with the unknowable; and all these conceptions mark the point where we feel our intelligence becoming feeble and beyond which our sight grows dim. Back of matter, which thought takes cognizance of, and back of thought, which takes cognizance of itself, lies infinity, which envelops both of them, and which seems the most fundamental aspect of matter itself. It was not without reason that the ancients called matter, abstractly considered, as independent of its diverse forms, the infinite ἄπειρον. Materialism thus leaves us, as other systems do, in the presence of that ultimate mystery which all religions have symbolized in their myths, and which metaphysics will always be obliged to recognize, and poetry to express, by the instrumentality of images.

By the seaside stood a great, upright mountain that pierced the sky like an arrow-head, and the waves beat upon its base.

Apologue.

In the morning, when the first light of the sun touched the ancient rocks, they shivered, and a voice rose from the gray stones and mingled with the sound made by the blue sea; and mountain and wave conversed together. The sea said: "The heavens have been mirrored in my shifting waves a million years, and in all that time have held as high aloof from me and stood as motionless." And the mountain said : "I have climbed toward the heavens a million years, and they are still as high above me as ever." One day a ray of sun fell smiling upon the brow of the mountain, and the mountain questioned it on the distant heavens from which it came. The ray was about to reply, but was reflected suddenly from the mountain to the sea, and from a scintillating wave back to the heavens from which it came. And the ray is still *en route* across the infinite, toward the nebulæ of Maïa, in the Pleiades, which were so long invisible, or toward some point farther still, and has not yet replied.

### III. Monism. The Fate of Worlds.

The word infinite, ἄπειρον, which the ancients applied to matter, the moderns have applied to mind. The reason, no doubt, is that matter and mind are two aspects of one and the same thing. The synthesis of these two aspects is attempted by monism.

*Monism.*

I. It is not our purpose here to pass judgment upon the theoretical pretensions of monism as a system of metaphysics. We observe simply that the trend of modern thought is toward this system. Materialism is simply a mechanical monism, the fundamental law of which is conceived as capable of being completely formulated in mathematical terms. Idealism is simply a monism the essential law of which is conceived as mental, as pertaining to the intelligence or to the will. This latter form of monism numbers many adherents in Germany and in England. In France it has been advocated by M. Taine, and we have just seen that it is maintained at the present moment under a somewhat different form by M. Fouillée, who regards it as a reconciliation of naturalism and idealism, and no doubt also as a possible reconciliation between what is essential in pantheism and in theism.[1] In our judgment the balance must be more evenly trimmed than the philosophers above cited have done, between the material and mental aspects of exist-

*Monism to-day prevalent.*

---

[1] See the preceding chapter.

ence, between objective science and subjective, conscious knowledge. Monism, therefore, essentially consists simply in a hypothesis that combines the least questionable facts dealt with by science, those which are inseparable from the elementary facts of consciousness. The fundamental unity imported by the term monism is not to be confounded with Spinoza's unity of substance, nor with the absolute unity advocated by the Alexandrians, nor with Spencer's unknowable force, nor with anything in the nature of a final cause, such as is spoken of, for example, by Aristotle. Neither do we affirm the existence of any unity of figure and form in the universe. We are content to admit, by a hypothesis at once scientific and metaphysical, the fundamental homogeneity of all things, the fundamental identity of nature. Monism, in our judgment, should be neither transcendent nor mystical, but immanent and naturalistic. The world is one continuous Becoming; there are not two kinds of existence nor two lines of development, the history of which is the history of the universe.

Instead of endeavouring to resolve matter into mind or mind into matter, we recognize them both as united in this synthesis, *The fundamental conception of philosophy is that of life.* which science itself (and science is a stranger to anything in the nature of moral or religious prejudice) is obliged to recognize: the synthesis known as *life*. Science tends every day still further to extend the domain of life, and there exists no fixed point of demarcation between the organic and the inorganic world. We do not know whether the foundation of life is *will*, or *idea*, or *thought*, or *sensation*, although in sensation we no doubt approach the central point; it seems to us probable simply that consciousness, which constitutes for us everything, should count for something in every mode of being, and that there is, so to speak, no being in the universe which is entirely abstracted from self. But, leaving these hypotheses to one side, what we can affirm with certainty is that life, by the very fact of its development, tends to engender consciousness; and that progress in life ultimately comes to be one with progress in consciousness, in which what is movement in one aspect is sensation in another. Considered from within everything, even the intellectual forms of time and space, is resolvable by the psychologist into sensation and desire ;[1] and, considered from without, everything is resolvable by the physicist into emotion; to feel and to move seem to be the two formulæ that express the entire inner and outer universe, the concave and convex aspects of things ; but to feel that one's self moves is the formula that expresses self-conscious life which is still so infrequent in the great totality of things, but which is becoming increasingly more common. The very meaning of progress in life consists in what is expressed by the gradual fusion of these two. Life means, in fact, development toward sensation and thought.

Side by side with the tendency which life thus displays to take possession of itself by consciousness, it seeks to widen the sphere of its operation by a more and more profound activity. Life is productivity. At the lowest stage of consciousness life leads only to the inner development of the solitary cell ; at the highest stage of consciousness, life manifests itself in intelligent and moral productivity. Expansion, far from being opposed to the nature of life, is in harmony with its nature, is the very condition of life, properly so called, just as in generation the need to engender another individual results in that individual's existence being, as it were, a condition of our own. The fact is that life does not consist in nutrition only, it consists in production, and pure egoism involves not an expansion of self but a diminution and mutilation of self. Also the individual, by the mere fact of growth, tends to become both social and moral.[2] It is this fact of the fundamental sociality of mankind which is the basis of the moral instinct, and of what is most profound and durable in the religious and metaphysical instinct. Metaphysical speculation, like moral action, thus springs from the very source of life. To live is to become a conscious, a moral, and ultimately a philosophical being. Life is activity in one or other of its more or less equivalent forms:

*Life and activity.*

---

[1] See the author's study on *L'idée de temps* (*Revue philosophique*, April, 1885).

[2] See the author's *Esquisse d'une morale*, p. 447, *et seq.*

moral activity, and what may be called metaphysical activity, that is to say, activity of thought, binds up the individual with the universe.

Up to this point we have made no mention of anything in the nature of a final cause. Morality, in our judgment, is as independent as the so-called religious instinct of anything in the nature of a primordial end and aim. Morality in the beginning is simply a more or less blind, unconscious, or, at best, subconscious power. As this power becomes endowed with self-consciousness, it directs itself toward more and more rational objects: *duty* is self-conscious and organized morality. Just as humanity moves blindly forward without in the first instance possessing any notion of its destination, so also moves nature.

*No final cause in nature.*

All this being true, what is the destiny of mankind in the world? Does monism allow a place for the hopes on which the moral and metaphysical sentiments have always relied in their effort to save thought and good-will from the charge of vanity?

*Monism and the problem of destiny.*

If evolution may be conceived as possessing from the beginning a certain aim and as being on the whole providential,—a metaphysical hypothesis which unhappily is guiltless of the smallest trace of scientific induction,—it may also be conceived as resulting in beings capable of proposing to themselves a certain aim, and of dragging nature after them toward it. Natural selection would thus finally be converted into moral and, in some sort, divine selection. Such an hypothesis is, no doubt, as yet a rash one, but is at least in the direction of the trend of scientific thought, and it is not formally in contradiction with present knowledge. Evolution, in effect, can and will produce species and types superior to humanity as we know it; it is not probable that we embody the highest achievement possible in life, thought, and love. Who knows, indeed, but that evolution may be able to bring forth, nay, has not already brought forth, what the ancients called gods?

*Natural selection and the possible evolution of gods.*

Such speculation offers a permanent support for what is best in the religious sentiment for sociality, not only with all

**Possibility of arresting process of dissolution.**

living and knowing beings, but with the creatures of thought and superior power with which we people the universe. Provided such beings are in no sense anti-real, provided they might somewhere exist, if not in the present at least in the future, the religious sentiment may attach itself to them without check from the scientific sentiment. And in so doing it becomes one with the metaphysical and poetic impulse. The believer is transmuted into a philosopher or a poet, but into a poet whose poetry is his life, and who dreams of a universal society of real or possible beings who shall be animated to a goodness of will analogous to his own. The statement that Feuerbach proposed, of what is essential in moral and religious sentiment (the reaction of human desire on the universe), may then be interpreted in a higher sense as referring to a desire and a hope both that, first, the sociality with which we feel ourselves personally to be animated may, as biology would lead us to believe, be discovered in all beings that exist at the summit of universal evolution ; and second, that these beings thus placed at the front by evolution, will one day succeed in securing what they have gained, in preventing dissolution, and that they may thereby permanently establish in the universe the love of social or rather universal well-being.

Thus understood, the religious sentiment may still be regarded as ultra-scientific, but no longer as anti-scientific. It

**The highest possible conception in the realm of morals.**

is, no doubt, taking much for granted to suppose that beings who have arrived at a high degree of evolution may determine from that point on the direction that the evolutionary process is to take, but, after all, since we are unable to affirm with certitude that such is not or may not become the fact, the moral and social sentiment urges us to act in such manner as to turn as far as in us lies the process of evolution in that direction. If, as we have said, morality is a species of productivity, every moral being must turn his eyes toward the future, must hope that his work will not die, must watch over the safety of that portion of himself that he has delivered to someone else—of his love—by which not only he has devoted himself to others, but has made others in a sense his own ; has acquired rights over them, has conquered them, so to speak, by subjecting himself to them. By labouring for humanity and for the universe with which humanity is bound up, I acquire certain rights over the universe. There arises between us a relation of reciprocal dependence. The highest conception of morals and metaphysics is that of a sort of sacred league between the higher beings of the earth, and even of the universe, for the advancement of what is good.

II. What scientific facts may be urged in bar of such hopes as to the destiny of the universe and of humanity?

The most discouraging aspect of the theory of evolution is that of dissolution, which seems to be inevitably incident to it.

Immanence of dissolution.

From Heracleitus to Mr. Spencer, philosophers have regarded these two ideas as inseparable. But does evolution necessarily result in dissolution? Our experience, both of the life of individuals and of worlds, seems, so far as the past is concerned, to make for a reply in the affirmative. Our whole acquaintance has been with worlds which have gone or are going to shipwreck. When the corpse of a sailor is thrown into the sea, his friends take notice of the exact point of latitude and longitude at which his body disappeared in the ocean. Two figures on a bit of paper are all that exists of what was a human life. An analogous destiny may be supposed to be in reserve for the terrestrial globe and for humanity as a whole. They may some day sink out of sight in space and dissolve beneath the moving waves of ether ; and at that period, if some neighbouring and friendly star observe us, it may take the latitude and longitude in infinite space of the point in the celestial abyss where we disappeared—the angle made by the last rays that left the earth ; and the measure of this angle, made by two extinct rays, may be the sole trace to remain of the whole sum of human effort in the world of thought.

Nevertheless, the duty of science being equally in its denials and in its affirmations to keep within the limits of certainty, it

Has been observed in the past only.

is important not to model our conception of the future too absolutely upon our knowledge of the past.

Up to the present time there has been no individual, nor group of individuals, nor world which has attained complete

The future may differ from the past.

self-consciousness, complete consciousness of its life and of the laws of its life. We are unable, therefore, either to affirm or to demonstrate that dissolution is essentially and eternally incident to evolution by the very law of being : the law of laws is to us simply $x$. If thought is ever to understand the law of laws, it will be by realizing the law in its own person. And such a height of development is conceivable ; if it is impossible to prove its existence, it is still more impossible to prove its non-existence. It may be that if complete self-consciousness, if complete consciousness is ever achieved, it will produce a corresponding power great enough to arrest the process of dissolution. Beings who are capable, in their infinite complication of movements in the world, of distinguishing those which make for evolution as against those which make for dissolution, might be capable of defeating the latter and of securing the unimpeded operation of the former. If a bird is to cross the sea it needs a certain breadth of wing ; its destiny depends on some inches, more or less, of feathers. Seabirds that desert the shore before their wings have attained the proper strength are one after another engulfed in the waves, but when their wings are full grown they can cross the ocean. A world also needs, so to speak, a certain breadth of wing to secure its flight in infinite space—its fate depends on some small increments, more or less, in the development of consciousness ; beings may one day be produced capable of traversing eternity without danger of being engulfed, and evolution may be established once for all in security against a recoil ; for the first time in the onward movement of the universe a definitive result may be achieved. According to the profound symbolism of the Greek

religion, time is the father of worlds.  The power of evolution
which the moderns regard as ruling over all things is the
ancient Saturn who devours his offspring.  Which of his
children shall deceive him and vanquish him—what Jupiter
shall some day prove strong enough to chain up the divine
and terrible power that engendered him?  The problem for
him when he shall arise—for this god of light and intelligence
—will be to check the eternal and blind impulse of destruction
without at the same time arresting the impulse of productivity.    Nothing, after all, can justify one in affirming scientifically that such a problem is forever insoluble.

The great resource of nature is number, the possible combinations of which are infinite and constitute the secret of the
eternal mechanism of the universe.    Fortuitous

**The inexhaust-
ible resources
of nature.** combination and selection, which have produced
so many marvels in the past, may give rise to still
greater marvels in the future.    It is on that fact that Heracleitus, Empedocles, Democritus, and later the men like Laplace, Lamarck, and Darwin based their conception of the part
played by chance in the universe, and of the point of union
between luck and destiny.    There is in the history of the
world—as in the history of a people, a belief, or a science—a
certain number of partings of the way, where the least impulse
toward one side or toward the other suffices to destroy or to
preserve the accumulated effort of centuries.  We must happily have passed an infinity of such cross-roads to have attained
our present point of development.  And at each new point of
the kind we encounter once more the same danger and run
the same risk of losing everything that we have gained.  The
number of times that a fortunate soldier has evaded death will
not make the next shot fired at him deviate a millimetre from
its appointed path, but if our successes in the past are no
guarantee of success in the future, our failures in the past do
not constitute a definitive proof of failure in the future.

The gravest objection that can be urged against hopefulness, an objection which has hitherto not been sufficiently
considered, and which M. Renan has omitted to deal with in
his something too optimistic " Dialogues "—is that of the eter-

nity *a parte post*, is the semi-abortion, the partial miscarriage
of a universe which, throughout an infinite past, has proved
itself incapable of a better world than this.[1]  Still,

**Even chances that the future may not resemble the past.** if that fact constitutes a reason for looking with
less confidence toward the future, it cannot
be regarded as a ground for despair.  An in-
finite past has proved to be more or less sterile, but an infinite
future may prove to be otherwise.  Even taking for granted
the total miscarriage hitherto of the labours of humanity and
of the infinity of extra-terrestrial beings who no doubt coöp-
erate with us, there remains, so far as the future is concerned,
mathematically one chance out of every two of success; and
that is enough to debar pessimism forever of an ultimate triumph.  If the mere chances of the dice, by which, according to
Plato, the universe is governed, have as yet produced nothing
but crumbling worlds and caducous civilization, a calculation
of probabilities demonstrates that even after an infinite number of throws the result of the present cast or of the next cast
cannot be foreseen.  The future is not entirely determined by
the past *which is known to us*.  Future and past are recipro-
cally related and the one cannot be absolutely known without
the other, and the one cannot be absolutely divined from a
knowledge of the other.  Conceive a flower in bloom at some
point in infinite space—a sacred flower, the flower of thought:
hands have been groping for it in every direction throughout
an infinite past; some have touched it by chance and then lost
it again before they could seize it.  Is the divine flower never
to be plucked?  Why not?  A negative answer would be simply the outcome of discouragement, not the expression of
probability.  Or conceive, once more, a ray of light following
a straight line through space, not reflected by any solid atom
or molecule of air, and an infinity of eyes in an eternal obscurity seeking for this ray, with no means of discovering how
near to them or how far from them it may, at any moment, be.
The ray pursues its way unimpeded, and innumerable open,
ardent eyes long for it and sometimes seem to feel the presence of the luminous wave moving forward on its victorious

[1] See on this subject the author's *Vers d'un philosophe*, p. 198.

course.   Must their search eternally be vain?   If there is no definitive reason for affirming it, there is still less any categorical reason for denying it.   It is a matter of chance, the man of science might say; it is a matter, also, of perseverance and intelligence, would be added by the philosopher.

The fact that we are to-day capable of stating such problems in regard to the destiny of the universe seems to indicate

*Positive evidence of ultimate success.*

something like an advance in the direction of solving them; thought is unable to advance upon reality beyond a certain point; the conception of an ideal presupposes the existence of a more or less imperfect realization of it.   In the tertiary period no animal speculated about the universal society.   A true conception of the ideal, if the truth about the matter could be known mathematically, would be found to possess, in all probability, an enormous number of chances of being realized; properly to state a problem is to have begun to solve it.   A purely mathematical calculation of the external probabilities of the case does not, therefore, express the real value in the domain of intelligence and morality, because in matters of intelligence and morality, possibility, probability, and the powers upon which the realization of the fact depends, lie in thought which is a concentration of inner and, so to speak, living chances.

Over and above infinity of number and eternity of time, a field of hopefulness lies in the immensity of space, which

*In especial when the infinity of space is taken into account.*

makes it irrational for us to judge too absolutely of the future of the universe solely from our experience of so small a portion of it as our solar, and even as our stellar system.   Are we the only thinking beings in the universe?   We have already seen that, without passing far beyond what science holds to be certain, one may even now reply in the negative.   There very probably exists an infinity of cold or cooling stars, which have arrived at about the same point in their evolution as our earth; each of these stars is physically and chemically analogous to the earth, and they must have passed through analogous stages of vapourization, and condensation, and incandescence, and cooling.   It is therefore probable that they have given rise to

forms of organic life more or less analogous to those that we
are acquainted with. In effect, the homogeneity of the organic
matter of which our stellar system is composed (a fact which
spectral analysis enables us to ascertain in regard to even the
most remote stars) allows us to infer, by an induction which is
not too improbable, a certain similitude in the most fundamental types of organic life. Analogous types of mineralization
and crystallization must have given rise to analogous types of
organization, although the number and richness of the forms
that are possible increase as existence grows more complex.
We do not see why the primordial protoplasm should in such
and such a satellite of Sirius be especially different from that
of our globe; nay, there may even obtain a certain cycle of
forms and "living numbers," as Pythagoras would say, that
periodically recur. It is difficult in the actual state of science
to conceive life as appearing except in some form of matter
analogous to the cellule, and to conceive consciousness as
otherwise than centralized in and manifesting itself by
vibrations such as those to which our nervous systems are
subject. Conscious life implies a society of living beings, a
sort of social consciousness which the individual consciousness
seems, in a sort, to presuppose. Organic and conscious life,
the conditions of which are so much more determinate than
those of inorganic life, must everywhere, in spite of differences
in the circumstances, have assumed in the course of evolution
forms that, in a number of respects, must have been analogous
to animals and human beings such as we are familiar with.
Perhaps the most general of the laws formulated by Geoffrey
Saint-Hilaire on the correlation of organs might be found to
hold good of the animals existing on the satellites of distant
stars of the twentieth magnitude. In spite of the infinite
variety of the flora and fauna of our globe, and the seemingly
inexhaustible ingenuity that nature has displayed in varying
their forms, it may reasonably be surmised that the difference
between the types of life with which we are acquainted and
those with which we are not acquainted is subject to certain
considerable limitations. In spite of differences of temperature, of light, of attraction, of electricity, sidereal species, how

different soever they may be from terrestrial species of living beings, must, by the necessities of the case, have been developed in the direction of sensitiveness and of intelligence, and have gone in that direction sometimes not as far as we, sometimes farther. Note also that even on our globe the excessively odd and monstrous types produced, like those of the tertiary period, as it were in obedience to a sort of apocalyptic imagination, have proved unable to maintain themselves. The most enduring species have generally been the least eccentric, the closest to a uniform and æsthetic type. It is not excessively improbable, therefore, that the universe contains an infinite number of human species analogous to humanity as we know it, in all essential faculties, although, perhaps, very different in the form of their organs and in the degree of their intelligence. They are our planetary brothers. Perhaps by comparison with us they are gods ; and in that fact lies, as we have said, the kernel of possible or actual truth in the ancient beliefs in regard to the divine inhabitants of the skies.[1]

---

[1] To understand the enormous differences which, in spite of the analogies, may exist between the organization of the planetary or stellar beings and our own, it suffices to consider the immense variety which obtains among terrestrial species. Ants have already achieved an advanced state of society with their shepherd, labouring, and warrior castes. Suppose them to continue their intellectual development instead of halting at a mechanical life of instinct ; they might arrive at a point of mental evolution analogous, *mutatis mutandis*, to that of such and such a human society ; for example, that of the Chinese. Who knows, indeed, but that they might rule the earth by virtue of substituting number and intelligence for individual power ? Their civilization would be in some sort Liliputian, and destined, no doubt, to exercise a smaller influence on the course of things than that of which physically stronger beings might prove capable ; or, to pass from one extreme to the other, in the dreamland in which Fontenelle, Diderot, and Voltaire have laboured, conceive a race of human beings developed not from anthropoids, but from the next most intelligent members of the animal kingdom—from elephants. Scientifically, the supposition is not impossible, when it is considered that the elephant's trunk is at once one of the strongest and most delicate organs of prehension known to us, and that to possess a well-developed brain and good organs of prehension are perhaps the prime requisites for success in the struggle for existence. A giant civilization, therefore, quite different from ours in externals, if not in essentials, might well have been achieved on the earth or on some neighbouring star. However repugnant to our instinctive anthropomorphism, we should familiarize ourselves with the thought that if evolution is subject to necessary laws, a simple series of accidents and favourable circumstances may give such and such a

But, it has been said, if other globes than ours are inhabited by intelligent and affectionate beings who live as we do upon the daily bread of science, these beings cannot be notably superior to us, or they would have given us before this time visible signs of their existence. To argue thus is not sufficiently to take account of the terrible power of space to imprison beings in infinite isolation. It may well be doubted whether beings of a relatively infinite intelligence, as compared with us, would not find their power unequal to dealing with such spaces as separate the stars. Our testimony on a question of the existence of such beings has no more value than that of a flower in the polar regions, or a bit of moss on the Himalayas, or a bit of weed in the depths of the Pacific Ocean, would have if it should declare the earth to be void of really intelligent beings on the ground that they had never been plucked by a human hand. If, therefore, the universe somewhere contains beings really worthy of the name of gods, they are probably so distant from us that they are as unaware of our existence as we are of theirs. They perhaps have realized our ideals, and the fact of that realization will perhaps remain unknown to us to the end.

It is to-day admitted that every thought corresponds to a certain kind of motion. Suppose that an analysis more delicate even than that of the spectrum should enable us to record

species the advantage over such and such another, and invert the comparative dignity of the two without the general onward movement of evolution being checked.

Moreover, the development of intelligence in a planet depends much less on the bodily form and number of the inhabitants than on the nature of their life ; and as their life depends upon phenomena of heat, light, electricity, and the chemical modifications that they produce, it is these phenomena that in some sort decide the intellectual future of the planet. Kant threw out the suggestion that in an astronomic system, for example—in our solar system—the intellectual and moral perfection of the inhabitants increases with their aloofness from the central star, and thus follows a lowering of the temperature ; but such a hypothesis is much too simple to account for so complex an effect, and one which is dependent upon many other things than temperature. What is probable, from the phenomena of life as we know them, is that thought could scarcely be developed either in a brazier or a glacier, and that a certain mean is a necessary condition of organic and intellectual development.

and to distinguish, not only vibrations of light but the invisible vibrations of thought in distant worlds. We should,
perhaps, be surprised to see that in proportion as the light and heat of the incandescent stars decrease, there by degrees arises consciousness, and that the smallest and most obscure stars are the first to produce it, whereas the most brilliant and enormous, like Sirius and Aldebaran, are the last to feel these subtler vibrations, but feel them ultimately with greater power, and develop a humanity with faculties and powers proportionate to their enormity.

*Possibility of discovering inhabitants in other spheres.*

The total amount of space which is known to us, from our earth to the farthest nebulæ that the telescope renders visible, and to the dark depths beyond, is no more than a mere point as compared with the totality of the universe—supposing always that there is a totality. Eternity may, therefore, be necessary for progress to traverse the immensity of space, if one conceives progress (if such a thing exists at all) as starting from some one point of departure, from a sort of holy-land and elect people, and spreading from them out in all directions into the infinite. Modern science, of course, scarcely permits one to believe in so privileged a land. Illimitable nature scarcely possesses, after the fashion of God, exclusive election. If the ideal has been achieved in one place, it must also, in all probability, have been achieved in a number of others, although the wave of progress has not yet spread to us. Intellectual light travels less rapidly than solar and stellar light, and yet how long it takes a ray to come to us from Capricornus!

*Slowness of spread of civilization from star to star.*

In our inferior organisms, consciousness does not seem to pass from one living molecule to another unless they are contiguous in space; still, according to the most recent discoveries in regard to the nervous system, and to the propagation of thought by mental suggestion from a distance,[1] it is not contrary to the facts to conceive the possibility of a sort of radiation of consciousness through space by means of undulations of a degree of subtlety as yet unknown to us. It is not utterly unpermissible to con-

*Possibility of mind acting on mind at a distance.*

[1] See the *Revue philosophique*, 1886.

ceive a society of consciousnesses not hemmed into some small corner of the universe, each in a narrow organism which is a prison, but communicating freely with each other throughout the whole expanse of space; it is not utterly unpermissible to conceive the ultimate realization of the ideal of universal sociality which constitutes the basis of the religious instinct. Just as out of a more intimate communication with individual consciousnesses there may arise upon our earth a sort of collective consciousness, so it is not ridiculous to suppose that there may arise, in an infinity of ages, a sort of intercosmic consciousness.

God is patient because he is eternal, theologians are fond of saying. In an all-powerful being patience of evil would be a crime; patience, which can scarcely be ascribed with any propriety to God, belongs however most fitly to a being who is aware of his fundamental unity with the totality of things, and is conscious of his eternity as a member of the human species, as a member of the brotherhood of living beings of which the human species is simply an accident, as a part of the evolution of this globe in which conscious life itself at first appears as no more than an accident, and of the evolution of the vast astronomical systems in which our globe is no more than a point. Man may be patient because, as an inseparable part of nature, he is eternal.

*Patience.*

*IV. The destiny of the human race and the hypothesis of immortality from the point of view of monism.*

Next to the fate of the universe, what interests us most vitally is the question of our own destiny. Religion consists for the most part in a meditation on death. If death were not an incident of life mankind would nevertheless be superstitious, but superstition would probably never have been systematized into religions. The mass of society possesses so slight an interest in metaphysics! A problem must bruise and wound them to attract their attention; and death prevents such problems. Will the gates of the valley of Jehoshaphat, through which the dead

*Theory of evolution and death.*

must pass, open on the heavens like a rainbow made of light and hope, like a joyous triumphal arch, or will it be low as the door of the tomb, and open upon infinite darkness? Such is the great question to which all religions have endeavoured to furnish a response. "The last enemy that shall be vanquished is death," says St. Paul; perhaps that also represents the last secret that shall be penetrated by human thought. The ideas which tend to become dominant in modern philosophy seem, however, to exclude the notion of the perpetuity of the self. The conception of evolution principally is based on a theory of mobility, and appears to result in the dissolution of the in-dividual, with even a greater certainty than in that of the species or the world. The individual form, and the species form, are equally unstable. On the walls of the catacombs may often be seen, roughly designed, the dove, bringing back to the ark the green bough, the symbol of the soul which has passed beyond the ocean and discovered the eternal harbour; at the present day the harbour recoils *ad infinitum*, before human thought; limitless open sea stretches away before it ; where in the abyss of bottomless and limitless nature shall be found the branch of hope. Death is a wider void than life.

When Plato approached the problem of destiny, he did not hesitate to launch out into philosophical hypotheses, and even into poetical myths. It is our present purpose to examine what are to-day the suppositions, or, if you choose, the dreams that may still be enter-tained as to the future by a sincere believer in the dominant philosophy of the present day, the philosophy of evolution. Given the present conception of nature, would Plato have found himself cut off from those beautiful expectations to the charm of which he said we ought to submit ourselves? In Germany, and in especial in England, it is not uncommon to endeavour to discover how much of the antique religious beliefs still subsists, and is, in however problematic and uncer-tain a form, involved in the scientific and philosophic hypoth-eses of the day. It is our purpose to undertake here an analogous inquiry in regard to immortality, recognizing how conjectural any attempt to solve the mystery of fate must be.

*The problem of life after death at the present day.*

Is it necessary to say that we make no pretensions to "demonstrating" either the existence or even the *scientific* probability of a life after death? Our design is more modest; it is enough to show that the impossibility of such a life is not yet proven; even in the presence of modern science immortality is still a problem; if this problem has not received a positive solution, no more has it received a negative solution.

It is our intention further to consider what bold, and even adventurous hypotheses may be necessary to enable one to translate into philosophic language the sacred symbols of religion, or the destiny of the soul.

I. There are two possible conceptions as to life after death; that of eternal existence and that of immortality, properly so called, or continuation and evolution of life under

Death and idealism.

a superior form. The first conception corresponds more particularly to the idealistic theories of the world, which we have analyzed above, which, regarding the basis of things as an eternal thought, a thought of thought, believe that by identifying itself with it mankind might pass out of time into eternity. Thought, which seems at first no more than a reverberation and image of things, idealists believe, turns out in the last analysis to be the very reality of which all the rest of the world is but a reflection; but this conception of an eternal existence is not in the least incompatible with the philosophy of evolution, for evolution in time does not exclude a transcendent mode of existence out of time. Such an existence, however, remains essentially problematic; it corresponds to Kant's Noumenon and Spencer's Unknowable; according to this hypothesis, corporal death is simply a stage in physical evolution, and the final term to be attained by all beings is their fixation in the consciousness of eternity. This point of fixation, accessible to every thinking being, is to be attained only by the highest, most disinterested, impersonal, and universal thought possible.

Such is the hope which lies at the bottom of the great religions, and the great idealistic systems of metaphysics. According to Plato there is nothing durable in us but what

relates to the eternal, and to the universal, and is therefore of the same nature as they are. All the rest is eliminated by Becoming, by perpetual Generation, that is, by

*An eternal ele-
ment in man.* evolution. A flower is, in our eyes, a friend; it owes its colour and charm, however simple, to a ray of the sun; but this ray, to which our affection is due, is wholly impersonal; it creates the beauty of the flower, and passes on its way; and it is the sun that we should love, both for the ray and the flower. Too exclusive and limited affection is always based on some mistake, and is on that account perishable. It insists on our stopping at such and such a link in the infinite chain of causes and effects. It is the principle of the universe, it is the universal being that we must love, if our heart is big enough, and it is that love alone, according to Plato, which is eternal. Is not eternity the very form of existence in the intelligible world, in which Goodness is the sun and the Ideas are the stars? Christian neo-Platonists, over and above Time and its incessant mobility, have dreamed of an intemporal and immutable somewhat, that they call the life eternal: *Quæ enim videntur, temporalia sunt; quæ autem non videntur, æterna.* Spinoza has dealt with the same conception of an existence under the form of eternity, which does not exclude the perpetual development of changing modes. Kant also, by his word *Noumenon*, designated an intelligible, intemporal, transcendent somewhat, that lay beyond the scope of physical evolution. "The eternal evolution of the soul," Schelling has said in his turn, "is not eternal in the sense that it possesses neither a beginning nor an end, but in that it bears no relation to Time." And Schopenhauer, finally, believes in an intemporal, eternal will, which is distinguished from the will to live that belongs to time and to the evolution of temporal forms. "We willingly recognize," says Schopenhauer, "that what remains after the complete abolition of the will is absolutely nothing to those who are still full of the desire of life, but for those in whom desire is annihilated what does our evil world, with its sun and its Milky Way, amount to? Nothing." It is with these words that Schopenhauer closes his book. He brings us once more into the pres-

ence of *Nirvâna*, conceived not only as a refuge from life, but also as a refuge from death; as an existence that shall be placeless and timeless, and, so to speak, *utopian* (in its primary intention) and *achronistic*.

But is this eternal life, the fact of which is, as we have seen, problematic, altogether impersonal or not? No certain reply can be given since we are as ignorant of the essence of individual being as of the essence of universal being, and consequently of the degree to which it is possible for individuality to subsist in universality. Schopenhauer, however, in his endeavour to ascribe to the individual a greater amount of reality than Plato allowed, opposed the principle of individuation to the natural individualities in which it manifests itself, and it may, indeed, be asked, whether genuine consciousness, genuine thought, and genuine volition do not at once pass beyond the individual, and preserve what is most essential in the individual. Individuality is always more or less physical, but it is possible that what makes individuality limited is not of the essence of personality, of consciousness; perhaps what is best in thought and will may become universal, without ceasing in the best sense to be personal like the Νοῦς of Anaxagoras.[1]

*Is such immortality personal or not?*

---

[1] At the very centre of one's being, universality and personality increase side by side; that is to say, the greater the share of existence a being possesses, the greater the amount of existence that it is capable of sharing with other beings. Incommunicability or impenetrability represents the lowest degree of existence; natural existence, the existence of forces as yet blind and fatal, maintains by their mutual antagonism an equilibrium in a state of inertia and torpor . . . The greater one's self-appropriation by intelligence, the greater one's power of taking possession of other beings by thought; the being that best knows itself best knows other beings . . . the spirit, in so far as it is intelligent, should be open, penetrable, participable, and participant. Two minds, in so far as they are perfect, may interpenetrate each other by means of thought (A. Fouillée, *Philosophie de Platon*).

"We must distinguish," M. Janet also says, "between personality and individuality. Individuality consists in all the external circumstances which distinguish one man from another—circumstances of time, place, organization, etc. . . The root of personality lies in individuality, but it tends incessantly to withdraw from it. The individual is centred in himself; personality aspires to rise above itself. The ideal of individuality is egoism, the focussing of the whole in self; the ideal of personality is devotion, the identification of self with the whole. Personality, properly so called, is consciousness of the impersonal" (*Moral*, 573).

Speculate as we may upon individual and universal being, we are all but brought face to face in the end with the same transcendental $x$. Such speculations, however, are not without a certain utility, that of impressing us afresh with the limits of our knowledge. A belief in a transcendent immortality, as Fiske says, can be defined only negatively, as a refusal to believe that this world is everything. The materialist maintains, Fiske says, that when we have described the entire universe of phenomena, of which we are capable of taking cognizance under the conditions of this life, the whole of the story has been told. Fiske himself believes, on the contrary, that the whole has not then been told.[1] We may at least say that it is *possible* that the whole story has not then been told. But to pass from the possible to the probable, no conclusion of the kind can be considered satisfactory that is not based upon more positive reason, psychological or moral ; unsupported metaphysical speculations leave the mind simply in the presence of a problem.

*No positive knowledge to oppose to hypothesis of immortality.*

Theories in regard to an eternal life such as we above mentioned have always proved in history more or less aristocratic and inclined to limit the number of the elect. In Buddhism the sage alone is capable of achieving eternal existence, whereas all the rest of mankind are condemned to life in time and illusion. Spinoza recognizes eternity only in what he calls cognition of the third order, intellectual intuition and love. Such cognition belongs properly to the true philosopher only. The intelligence of the vulgar is passive and perishable. "The instant the vulgar cease . . . to suffer," says Spinoza, "they cease to exist." And Goethe, too, was inclined to regard the eternal life as reserved for an aristocracy.

*The hypothesis of a conditional eternity.*

This theory of inequality is maintainable only in so far as it is based upon an actual ascertainment of the difference in progress displayed by different minds, and of the small number of those who achieve the heights of wisdom. The case is otherwise when such an observed fact of natural or moral inequality is converted into a divine right,

*Criticised.*

[1] Fiske, *The Destiny of Man*, p. 113.

and God is conceived as creating and desiring precisely such a state of things. The latter, however, is the alternative that modern Christian theologians have adopted in their effort to offer a re-reading of the sacred texts. In their judgment the good alone are immortal, or, rather, are immortalized by God; the others are damned, in the sense that they are totally annihilated—an interpretation of the dogma of eternal punishment that seems to them wholly to exculpate the Deity. Any such notion is based upon a metaphysical illusion. The hypothesis of traditional eternity is inconsistent with that of the existence of a creator, since it is forever impossible on that hypothesis, to escape the contradiction involved in the notion of a being's creating only to destroy—of a being's choosing among his creatures a certain number for condemnation to death. Annihilation is simply damnation palliated; it is the substitution of a celestial guillotine for the long miseries that have preceded. This theological hypothesis affords us no way out of the difficulties involved in the doctrine of divine sanction that lies at the heart of all religions; it is the sacrifice of Isaac, or of Jesus, in another form simply. Will it be said that, on the hypothesis of conditional immortality, the immoral being is alone responsible for his own death? Yielding to passion, or even to vice, cannot be assimilated to suicide, for in suicide one knows what one is doing and is responsible for it; one kills one's self because one wishes to die; but one does not wish to die when one abandons one's self to a passion; and, if the result therefore of so doing is annihilation, death comes upon one unforeseen and undesired, takes one by surprise, by a sort of divine ruse, and the responsibility for such annihilation lies and must lie with God. Moreover, how can there exist between two individuals of the same nature a sufficiently great natural or moral difference to justify the one's being wholly annihilated, and the other's being permitted to live *in æternum?* It may be said, with Plato in the "Republic," that, if vice were a disease that is really mortal to the soul, it would kill it in this life. Its destructive influence would be felt long before the occurrence of death, which, so far as vice is concerned, is an accidental circumstance simply.

As the notion of conditional immortality is incompatible with the notion of an omnipotent, omniscient, sovereignly loving creator, so also is it with that of a society of souls, of a spiritual kingdom, from which a certain number of mankind would be excluded forever.

Is incompatible with human fellowship.

An absolutely wicked and hateful soul, unpossessed of any element of humanity, not to say of divinity, and consequently unfit to live, is a pure figment of hate and amounts to transporting the caste of pariah into the celestial city. It is a contradiction in terms to enjoin us to universal charity toward all men without exception, and at the same time to wish us to consent to the absolute annihilation and damnation of some of them. We are naturally and morally too intimately related for certain of us to be condemned definitively to death without the rest of us being impeded on our upward course; we are bound to each other by our love of humanity like Alpine climbers by the cord that passes from waist to waist, and one of us cannot slip but that the rest of us feel it, nor fall without all of us falling. *Nihil humani alienum;* one heart beats in the bosom of humanity, and if it stops forever in a single human breast, it will stop forever in the breasts of those also who are supposed to be immortal. The best of us, those who would be fit to receive baptism into immortality, would do as the barbarous and pagan chief, who, after having washed away his sins in the holy water of the font, with salvation in his hand and Paradise before his eyes, demanded suddenly what would be the fate of his former companions who had died unconverted, and whether he should find them in heaven. "No," replied the priest, " they will be among the miserable and the damned, and thou amongst the blessed." " I will go, then, among the damned, for I wish to go where I shall find my companions in arms. Adieu!" And he turned his back upon the font.

The hypothesis of conditional immortality can, therefore, be maintained only by eliminating from it the doctrine of a creator of absolute merit, of virtue, and of universal and infinite charity; thus diminished, it becomes a belief in a sort of natural or metaphysical necessity to which beings are subject according to their degree of perfec-

Summary.

tion simply. This hypothesis is essentially anti-providential, and in harmony only with systems more or less analogous to that of Spinoza.

In general the notion of eternal life is altogether transcendent and a fit subject for mystical dreams only. Let us, therefore, abandon this high ground and descend to nature and experience. Instead of talking of eternity, let us speak of life after death and of an immortality not conditional, but conditioned by the laws of matter and of mind and attainable by everyone.

II. Let us take our stand in the beginning on positive experience, and consider what sort of immortality the philosophy of evolution permits us to hope for. There exists in the sphere of consciousness, so to speak, a series of concentric circles which lie closer and closer about an unfathomable centre, personality. Let us pass in review the diverse manifestations of personality and see if they contain any imperishable element.

*Does personality contain a permanent element?*

The most external, and, in some sort, the most observable aspect of mankind, consists in their works and actions. Where material works alone are concerned, such as a house that one has built, a picture that one has painted, a statue that one has modelled, it may be felt that the distance between the worker and the work is too great, and that immortality in one's work is too much like a sort of optical illusion. But when intellectual and moral works are concerned, the effect and the cause are more nearly one; therein lies the element of truth contained in the highly impersonal and disinterested doctrine that one lives in one's works. Intellectual and moral labours are more than their mere material effect. The good man's highest wish is to live and live again in his good actions; the thinker's highest wish is to live and live again in the thought that he has contributed to the inheritance of humanity. This doctrine may be found in almost all great religions and is capable of subsistence in the domain of pure science. According to the modern Buddhists of India a man's actions are his soul, and it is this soul that

*One's works immortal.*

survives his death, and transmigration of souls is simply the constant transformation of good into better, and evil into worse; the immortality of one's soul is the immortality of one's actions, which continue to operate forever in the world according to their original force and direction.

Generation after generation labours at the task, and passes the token of hope from hand to hand. *Heri meum, tuum hodie,* yesterday was mine and I spent it in doing

Continuity of human effort.

good, but not enough good; to-day is thine: employ the whole of it, do not lose an hour of it; if an hour dies sterile, it is a chance lost of realizing the ideal. Thou art master of to-day; do what in thee lies to make to-morrow what thou wouldst have it, let to-morrow be always in advance of to-day, and the horizon that men see each fresh morning be brighter and higher than the one they saw before.

The action must be followed into its effects, or into the effect of those effects, and so on infinitely. Our conduct

Nothing lost.

stretches away *ad infinitum,* beyond the reach of our knowledge. Even from the purely physical and physiological point of view, neither intended nor attempted goodness is ineffective, since both thought and desire develop the mind. The very notion of what is to-day chimerical corresponds to a real movement in our brains; it is a mental force which contains its element of verity and influence. We inherit not only what our fathers did, but what they could not do, what they attempted and did not achieve. We are still alive with the devotion and sacrifice of our ancestors, with the courage that perhaps they spent in vain, as we feel in the spring the breath of distant antedeluvian springs and the loves of the tertiary period.

The ability of the present generation has been made possible by the stumbling and mistakes of generations in the past; and

Failure in the past the guarantee of success in the future.

this embryonic and successless past constitutes the guarantee of our future. In the moral, as in the physiological world, there are instances of fertility that are not yet explicable. Sometimes long after the death of the man who first loved her the woman brings forth a child that resembles him; and humanity may bring forth a civilization on the model of some ideal cherished in the past, even when the past seems to be buried forever, if the ideal contains some obscure element of truth and, by consequence, of imperishable force. What has once really lived shall live again, and what seems to be dead is only making ready to revive. The scientific law of atavism is a guarantee of resurrection. To conceive and desire the best is to attempt the ideal, is to predetermine the path that all succeeding generations shall tread. Our highest aspirations, which seem precisely the most vain, are, as it were, waves which, having had the power to reach us, have the power to pass beyond us, and may, by a process of summation with other waves, ultimately shake the world. I am satisfied that what is best in me will survive, perhaps not one of my dreams shall be lost; other men will take them up, will dream them over again in their turn until they are realized. It is by force of spent waves that the sea fashions the immense bed in which it lies.

In effect, in the philosophy of evolution life and death are recognized as relative and correlative conceptions; life is in one sense death, and death is the triumph of life over one of its particular forms. Proteus in the fable could be prevented from changing his shape only by being caught in sleep, which is the image of death; thus it is in nature; fixed form is sleep, is death, is a pause in the eternal fluctuation of life. Becoming and life are alike formless. Form, individuality, species, mark a transitory stoppage in the channel of life; we can neither seize nor hold nature, except when it is laid asleep, and what we call death—my death or yours—is itself a latent pulse of universal life, like one of the secret vibrations that pass through the germ during the months of apparent inertia during which it is making ready for the later stages of its development. The law of nature is eternal germination. A man of science was one day holding a handful of wheat, that had been found in the tomb of an Egyptian mummy. " Five thousand years without sight of the sun! Unhappy grains of wheat, as sterile as death, of which they have so long been the companions, never shall their tall stalks bow beneath the wind on the banks of the

*Death not inevitable.*

Nile. Never? What do I know of life, of death?" As an experiment simply, without much hope of success, the man of science sowed the grains of wheat that he had recovered from the tomb, and the wheat of the Pharaohs received the caress of the sun, of the air, and came up green through the soil of Egypt, and bowed beneath the wind on the banks of the sacred and inexhaustible flood of the Nile. And shall human thought, and the higher life which stirs in us like the germ in the seed, and love that seems to sleep forever in the tomb, not have this reawakening in some unforeseen springtime, and not be brought face to face with eternity, which seems at present to be buried, once and for all, in darkness? What is death, after all, in the universe, but a lesser degree of vital heat, a more or less transitory lowness of temperature? Death cannot be powerful enough to hold life and its perpetual youth in check, and to prevent the infinite activity of thought and of desire.

III. Yes, I and my works shall survive; but is immortality in this sense sufficient to satisfy the religious sentiment? As

Is a more personal immortality possible?

an individual, what do science and the philosophy of evolution promise me or permit me to hope? A somewhat external and impersonal immortality is, as we have seen, possible; is anything in the nature of an internal or personal immortality likewise possible?

Assuredly, it is not of science that the individual can demand proofs of his permanence. The fact of generation is, in

Science answers in the negative.

the eyes of the man of science, in and of itself a negative of individual immortality; the social instinct which opens our hearts to thousands of other beings emphasizes the negation, and the scientific and metaphysical instincts themselves, which cause us to take an interest in the sensitive world, in its laws and destinies, diminish, so to speak, our importance as limited individuals. Thought breaks the limits of the self in which it is confined, and our breast is too narrow to contain our heart. Oh, how rapidly one learns in science and in art to make small account of one's self, and this diminution of self-esteem neither lessens one's enthusiasm nor one's ardour, but adds to them only an ele-

ment of manly sadness such as a soldier might feel who says :
" I count for but one in the battle, nay, for less than that, for
but a hundred millionth, and if I should disappear the result
of the contest would no doubt not be changed, and yet I shall
stay and fight."

Scientifically considered, individuality is a sort of provisional native land, and one's native land is a sort of
magnified individual with a consciousness composed of ideas and sentiments, and one's love
for one's country may be greater than one's
love for such and such an individual.   Such a love does not
prevent us from understanding that our country will not be
immortal as a nation, that it will have its periods of growth
and of decay, that the obstacles which keep peoples apart are
caducous, and that nations incessantly disappear and lose old
elements and take on new.   Why, merely from the fact that
we love our own individuality, should we not consent to the
same reasoning in regard to it ; why should we wish to imprison it forever within the limits of the same individuality ?
If a nation dies, why should not a man ?  If it sometimes
amounts to divination to cry out as one falls on the battlefield,
" *Finis patriæ !* " does it any the less surely amount to divination to cry out in the presence of death, " *Finis individuæ* " ?
Could Kosciusko feel that he himself had a right to live when
Poland and the ideas and beliefs to which he had devoted his
life were no more ?

A young girl, a relative of mine, on the point of death and
unable to articulate, signified her wish for a piece of paper.
When it was given to her, she began to write, " I do
not want——" Death suddenly intervened and
interrupted her volition before it could find expression in words ; the thinking being and the expression of her
thought seemed to be annihilated by the same blow.  The
child's protest, like her life, was interrupted in the middle.
Volition is powerless against death, and it is useless to stiffen
one's will against the final blow.  On the contrary, man's sole
superiority in death consists in acceptance.  Pascal's conscious
reed might not only be constrained to bend like any other

*Counsels
resignation.*

*Dignity of
resignation.*

reed, it might bend consentingly and respect the law that
requires its death.   Next to consciousness of his own power,
the highest of man's privileges is consciousness of the limits
of his power, at least as an individual.   Out of the very disproportion between the infinity that kills us, and the nothing
that constitutes us, arises the sense of a certain greatness in
us; we prefer to be stricken by a mountain rather than by a
pebble; we should rather fall in a struggle against a thousand
than in a struggle against one; so that intelligence, by measuring the greatness of our adversary, deprives us of regret at
our defeat.

To desire to make the individual, who is more or less physical even in his moral nature, eternal, is, in the eyes of the
man of science, a remnant of egoism.   In his
*Desire to sur-
vive egoistic.* judgment, the human mind should accept the
death of the individual by a species of intellectual devotion analogous to that with which we accept the
death of our native country.   Modern men of science may be
defined as those who have no hope, οἱ μὴ ἔχοντες ἐλπίδα, as St.
Paul said; we are *individually* of too small account in the
eyes of science to live always *individually*.

Ought we, therefore, to consent cheerfully to the sacrifice of
self, and to die willingly for the benefit of the universal life?
So far as one's self is concerned, one can make the
*But only when
it relates to one's
self.* sacrifice lightly, but the annihilation of those one
loves cannot be accepted by a conscious and
affectionate being.   It is in vain for scientific and philosophic
stoicism to urge with Epictetus that it is natural for a vase,
which is fragile, to break, and for a man, who is mortal, to die.
The question still remains, whether what is natural and scientific ought, as the Stoics alleged, to satisfy my reason and my
love.   As a matter of fact, when one really loves another person, what one endeavours to love is not the element of fragility,
the vase of clay, but the intelligence and the heart, which
Epictetus declines to consider separately from their perishable
accompaniments.   One attaches one's self to them as to something permanent; one corrects and transfigures nature itself,

and passes in thought beyond the brutality of its laws, and therein lies, perhaps, the very essence of the love of another. If the laws of nature, after seeming for a moment to be suspended and vanquished by the force of one's disinterested love, subsequently break the bond that holds them in check, is it surprising that one's love should still hold out against them? It is not only pain that I experience at being baffled by the laws of nature; it is indignation, it is the sense of injustice. The Stoics regarded pain as a passive affection of the sensibility simply, but moral pain implies a struggle of the will against nature, and an effort, as they themselves admit, to correct it. It is on this ground that pain is not an evil; its rôle is incessantly to impose our moral and social ideal on our physical nature, to force it to perfect itself; pain is the principle of development in life, and if there exists a means of vanquishing death, it is perhaps by virtue of pain that we shall arrive at it. We are right, therefore, in rebelling against nature's powers of life and death, in so far as she exercises them for the purpose of annihilating what is morally best in us and in others.

True love should never be expressed in the language of time. We say: " I loved my father during his lifetime; I was deeply attached to my mother or my sister." Love under the form of eternity. Why locate it in the past? Why not say always: " I love my father or my mother?" Does not, and should not, love lay claim to an eternal present?

How could one say to a mother that there is nothing truly and definitively alive, personal, unique, in the at once smiling and meditative eyes of the child she holds upon Uniqueness of the individual. her knees; that the little being that she dreams of mature, and good, and great, is a simple incident in the life of the species? No; her child is not like any other that has ever lived or that ever will live; none other could possess that look. Nowhere among the generations of men can there exist a fac-simile of the beloved face before one. All nature does not possess the equivalent of the individual, which it can destroy, but not replace. It is not, therefore, without reason that love refuses to consent to the substitution of one individual for another, which constitutes the very movement of life; it cannot reconcile itself to the eternal whirl in the dust of being; it is bent on fixing life, on arresting the world in mid-progress.   But the world does not stop at its bidding.   The future calls to generation after generation, and this powerful force of attraction is also a force of dissolution. Nature gives birth by means of death, and the joy of new loves is composed of the fragments of the old.

This protest of love against death, against the dissolution of the individual, attaches also to the lower animals.   A dog, The protest of love against death not limited to humanity. it seems, has only a market value, and yet can I ever buy again one that shall be the equivalent of this one that has died before my eyes?   He loved me with all the power of his unhappy being, and endeavoured to hold fast to me while he was slipping away, and I endeavoured to hold him fast.   Does not every being that loves acquire a right to immortality?   Yes; the ideal of affection would be to immortalize all conscious beings; nay, more, the poet who is delicately sensitive to the individuality of a flower, or a ray of coloured light, of the drop of dew that refracts it, would wish to immortalize all nature, would wish to view under the form of eternity the rainbow that quivers in a soap bubble; for can any two bubbles ever be the same?   And yet, while the poet aims thus at holding everything fast, at preserving everything, at fixing his dreams, at enchaining the ocean of life, the man of science replies that the eternal flood must be allowed to pulsate, to engulf our tears and our blood, and that the world must be left free.   For the man of science, the flux and reflux and progress of life are more sacred than the love of the individual.

Thus, in the question of individual immortality, two great forces drag human thought in opposite directions.   Science is Antagonism between love and science. inclined everywhere to sacrifice the individual in the name of natural evolution; love is inclined, in the name of a higher moral and social evolution, to preserve the individual.   The antinomy is one of the most disquieting that the philosophic mind has to deal with.

Should science be admitted to be wholly in the right, or must we believe that an element of truth exists in the social instinct which lies at the basis of affection, as there is a presentiment and anticipation of the truth in all great natural instincts? The social instinct possesses a greater value at the present day, because philosophers are beginning to consider even the individual as a society, and to recognize association as a universal law of nature. Love, which is the power of cohesion at its highest degree, is perhaps right in its desire for an element in the association between individuals. Its sole error is that of exaggerating its pretensions and of misplacing its hopes. After all, one must not be too exacting nor ask too much of nature. A true philosopher, even for those that he loves, should not shrink from proof by fire, and death is the flame that purifies while it consumes. If anything survives the ordeal that alone is much, and if what survives is precisely what is best in us, what more can be asked? One may break the vase, of which Epictetus speaks, but the perfume remains, and floats out into the air, and becomes, no doubt, ultimately indistinguishable, but still subsists.

*The best in one may survive.*

The science which seems to offer the strongest opposition to the preservation of the individual is mathematics, which recognizes the existence of nothing in the world but variable and equivalent figures and abstractions. On the contrary, perhaps the most concrete of the sciences, sociology, recognizes everywhere groups of realities; sociology therefore cannot hold relations that arise out of association, nor the terms between which they exist, so cheap. Let us consider whether, from the point of view of a more complete and more concrete science, consciousness, which is the principle of personality, properly so called, necessarily and forever excludes the possibility of indefinite duration that all great sciences attribute to the spirit.

*Sociology and the problem of immortality.*

III. Antique metaphysics gave too much attention to questions of substance, to considering whether the soul is simple or complex. The question amounts to whether the soul is made of indivisible or divisible material; it assumes as the basis of the phenomena of mind, an imaginary and in some sort ex-tended substance. It was upon this doctrine of the simple substance that the demonstration of the immortality of the soul was founded. Evo-lutionist philosophy tends to fix our attention nowadays, not on the substance, but on the way the substance behaves, that is to say, in physical terms, on movements.[1] Con-sciousness is a certain action accompanied by a certain collective unity of movements. If it exists in a substance it is not the duration of this substance that interests us, but that of its activ-ity, since it is that activity which constitutes our consciousness.

*The basis of existence not substance but activity.*

Wundt is one of the contemporary philosophers, who, after Aristotle, Hume, Berkeley, and Kant, has best shown the illusiveness of endeavouring to discover a simple substance underlying consciousness. It is only internal experience, he says, only consciousness itself, that comes to us guaranteed by immediate certainty. And this implies, he adds, "that all these substances which spiritualism regards as the basis of subjective or objective experience are of the highest degree of uncertainty, for in no experience whatsoever are they given. They are deliberate fictions, by the aid of which it has been attempted to explain the unity of experience." The true explanation of this unity should be sought for elsewhere in continuity of function, and not in simplicity of substance. "The consecutive effects of anterior states combine with those which arise later; in this way there is caused a subjective continuity of states which

*Continuity of existence means continuity of function.*

---

[1] "Whoever says that he cannot conceive an action without a substratum con-fesses by his very words that the alleged substratum which he conceives is a prod-uct of his imagination ; it is his own thought that he is obliged to place as a sup-port behind the reality of things. By a pure illusion of the imagination, after one has stripped off from an object the only qualities that it possesses, one affirms that something of it, one knows not what, still subsists." (Schelling, *System of Transcendental Idealism.*)

"To be," said Berkeley, "is to be this or that. Simply to be, without explana-tory addition, is to be nothing; it is a simple conception, if not a word void of sense."

"Berkeley's object was to overthrow the hypothesis of a substance lying beyond the range of spirit, as an imperceptible support of the qualities of which our senses take cognizance." (Félix Revaisson, *La Philosophie en France*, 9.)

See also M. Lachelier, *De l'Induction.*

corresponds to the objective continuity of movement, which is the condition of unity of consciousness." The binding together of successive mental states is lacking in bodies, although they must possess the germ of action and of sensation. For this reason Leibnitz was right in saying that bodies are "momentary spirits," which forget everything immediately, and know only a present, uncomplicated by a past or a future. Conscious life, on the contrary, by the very means of changing elements, realizes a continuity of mental functions, a memory of the past, a certain durability. This continuity is not a result of simplicity, but, on the contrary, of the higher complexity that belongs to mental functions. "On the physical side, as on the psychical side," says Wundt, "the living body is a unity; this unity is not founded in simplicity but in compositeness of a high degree of complexity. Consciousness, with its multitude of combined states, is a unity analogous to that of the bodily organism. The absolute correlation between the physical and the psychical suggests the following hypothesis:[1] that what we call the soul is the internal aspect of what, in its external aspect, we call the body that contains the soul. This way of conceiving the problem of correlation inevitably leads us to the belief that the essence of reality is intellectual, and that the fundamental attribute of being is development or evolution. Human consciousness is the highest point of such evolution; it constitutes the nodal point in the course of nature where the world recollects itself. It is not as a simple being but as a product evolved out of innumerable elements that the human soul is, as Leibnitz says, "a mirror of the world."[2]

From this modern point of view, which is a development of that of Aristotle,[3] the question of immortality amounts to asking how far the continuity of mental functions may be supposed to extend the continuity of one's intellectual being, which is the subjective unity of a complex multiplicity aware of itself as such?

The problem of immortality at the present day.

[1] This hypothesis is identical with that of monism.

[2] Wundt, *Psychologie*, vol. ii.

[3] See M. Ravaisson, *La Métaphysique d'Aristote*, vol. ii., and *Rapport sur la Philosophie en France.*

Note, first, that even in the external world we are not without examples of indissoluble compounds; certain simple atoms are compounds of this sort. The atom of hydro-gen is a vortex of little worlds. Well, is there nothing indissoluble in the universe except so-called atoms, so-called physical "individuals," and is it unpermissible to conceive, on the subjective side, individuals more worthy of the name, whose duration is guaranteed by the very fact of their complexity?

*Indissoluble material compounds.*

According to the reigning doctrines in physiology and experimental psychology, individual consciousness is, as we have said, a compound of the consciousnesses of all the cells that are united in the physical organism.[1] The individual, consisting thus of a society, the problem of death amounts to the question, whether there can exist an association, at once solid enough to endure forever, and flexible enough to adapt itself to the ever-shifting conditions of universal evolution.

*Restatement of the problem.*

This problem, be it observed in the first place, is precisely that which human societies are endeavouring to solve. At the lowest stage of social evolution solidity and flexibility are rarely united. Egypt, for example, was solid but not very progressive. A stage higher in the scale of evolution, in proportion as science advances and personal liberty comes to be recognized, civilization becomes both more solid and indefinitely flexible, and at some period in the future, when scientific civilization shall have once mastered the globe, it will possess a power that the most compact, and, in appearance, the solidest masses cannot equal; it will be firmer than the very pyramids, and will at the same time prove increasingly flexible, progressive, capable of adap-

*The ideal type of association.*

[1] Association or grouping is the general law of organic and inorganic existence. Society, properly so called, is only a particular case, is only the most complex instance, of this universal law. . . A consciousness is rather a *We* than an *I*. It is capable of union with other consciousnesses and of forming, in conjunction with them, a more comprehensive and more durable consciousness, from which it receives and to which it communicates thought, as a star both borrows and communicates motion in the system to which it belongs. (Espinas, *Des Sociétés animales*, 128. See also M. Fouillée, *La Science sociale contemporaine*, l. iii.)

tation to every variation in the environment. The synthesis of complexity and stability will then have been achieved. The very character of thought is increasing adaptivity, and the more intellectual a being is, the greater its power of displaying the qualities which are most advantageous under any given set of circumstances. The eye, which is more intellectual than the sense of touch, furnishes a power of adaptation to a wider and more diversified environment. Thought, which is more intellectual than sight, enables one to adapt one's self to the universe itself, to the immensity of the stars, as well as to the infinite pettiness of the atoms in a drop of water. If memory is a masterpiece of intellectual record-taking, reasoning is a masterpiece of flexibility, of mobility, and of progress. So that, whether individuals or nations are in question, the most intellectual are those which possess at once the greatest amount of stability and of adaptability. The problem of society is to unite these two things, the problem of immortality is at bottom the same; the individual consciousness being, as we have seen, itself a society. From this point of view, it seems probable that the more perfect one's personal consciousness is, the more absolutely it possesses both durability and a power of indefinite metamorphosis. So that, even admitting what the Pythagoreans insist upon, that consciousness is a number, a harmony, a musical chord, we may still ask whether certain harmonies may not become sufficiently perfect to endure forever without, on that account, ceasing to enter as elements into richer and more complex harmonies. A lyre might vibrate *ad infinitum* without its several strings losing their respective tonalities amid the multitude of their variations. There ought to exist an evolution in the organization of consciousness as in the organization of molecules and living cells, and the most vital and durable and flexible combinations should possess the advantage in the struggle for existence.

Consciousness is a collection of associations of ideas, and, consequently, of habits, grouped about a centre; and we know that habits possess an indefinite duration; contemporary philosophy regards the properties of elementary material substances as habits, as instances of indissoluble association. A

vegetable or animal species is a habit, a type of grouping and
organic form which subsists century after century.    It is not
proved that mental habits may not in the course
of evolution achieve a fixity and a durability of
which we possess to-day no example.    It is not
proved that instability is the definitive and eternal characteristic of the highest functions of consciousness.    A philosophic hopefulness in regard to immortality is founded on
the belief that, in the last stages of evolution, the struggle for
existence will become a struggle for immortality.    Nature will
then come to realize, not by virtue of simplicity, but of judi-
cious complexity, a sort of progressive immortality, the final
product of natural selection;  and, if so, religious symbols will
have been simply an anticipation of this final period.    We shall
have wings to support us in our flight through life, Rückert
says, wings to support us in our flight past death;  but the bird
does not learn to fly immediately nor at once;  the hereditary
habit of flight must have been acquired and developed by the
species because of the advantage it brings with it in the struggle for existence.    Survival, therefore, must not be conceived
as completed at a bound, but as slowly perfected by a gradual
and continuous lengthening of the average span of life.    It
must be shown, however, that such a survival would constitute
a superiority, not only for the individual, but for the species.

The last stage
in the struggle
for existence.

And now let us consider consciousnesses in their relations
to each other.    Contemporary psychology tends to the doctrine that different consciousnesses, or, if you
prefer, different aggregates of states of consciousness, may combine, and even interpenetrate, somewhat analogously to what theologians mean by
communion of souls.    And if so, it is permissible to ask
whether, if consciousnesses can interpenetrate, they may not
some day come to possess a continuity of existence;  may not
be able to hand on their existence to each other, and to communicate to each other a new sort of durability instead of
remaining, as Leibnitz says, more or less momentary;  supposing always that such durability would be advantageous to
the species.

Psychology and
the communion of
souls.

Mystical intuitions sometimes contain a certain presentiment of the truth. St. Paul tells us that the heavens and the
Possible frequency of this phenomenon. earth shall pass away, that prophecies and languages shall pass away, but that one thing shall not pass, and that is charity, or love. If this doctrine is to be interpreted philosophically, the bond of continual love, which is of all bonds the least primitive and the most complex, must be conceived as capable of ultimately becoming the most durable of bonds, and as tending progressively to embrace a larger and larger proportion of the whole number of the inhabitants of the celestial city. It is by what is best, what is most disinterested, most impersonal, and most loving in one, that one achieves communion with the consciousness of another, and such disinterestedness must coincide ultimately with disinterestedness in others, with others' love for one's self ; and there will arise thus a possible fusion of souls, a communion so intense that as one suffers in the bosom of another, so, too, one may come to live in the heart of another. To be sure, we have passed here into the limits of dreamland, but it is to be remarked that such dreams are extra-scientific, and not anti-scientific.

Let us conceive ourselves as existing in this problematical, though not impossible, epoch when individual consciousnesses
Vision of the ideal society. shall have achieved a higher degree of complexity and of subjective unity, and along with them a power of more intimate communion than they possess to-day, without the fact of that communion altogether breaking down the bounds of personality. They will communicate thus with each other, as the living cells in the same body sympathize with each other, and contribute each to form the collective consciousness ; they will be all in all, and all in every part. And indeed one may readily conceive means of communication and of sympathy, much more subtle and direct than those which exist to-day among different individuals. The science of the nervous system is in its earliest stages ; we are acquainted as yet with exaltation as a state of disease only, and with suggestion at a distance as an incident merely of hypnotism ; but we already begin to be dimly

aware of a whole world of phenomena that go to show the possibility of a direct communication between different, and even under certain circumstances of a sort of reciprocal absorption of two personalities. Some such complete fusion of two consciousnesses, that however still preserve their individuality, is to-day the dream of love which, as one of the greatest of social forces, ought not to labour in vain. Supposing the power of communion with other consciousnesses gradually to develop, the death of the individual will manifestly encounter a greater and greater resistance on the part of the several minds with which such an individual is in communication. And, in any event, the minds with which an individual is in communication will tend to retain an increasingly vivid, and, so to speak, living memory of him. Memory at the present day is simply an absolutely distinct representation of a certain being—an image, as it were, vibrating in the ether after the original has disappeared. The reason is that there does not as yet exist an intimate solidarity and continuous communication between one individual and another. But it is possible to conceive an image which would be scarcely distinguishable from the object represented ; would be the sum of what such and such an object means to me ; would be, as it were, the prolongation of the effect of another consciousness on my consciousness. Such an image might be regarded as a point of contact between the two consciousnesses involved. Just as in generation the two factors combine in a certain third, which represents them both, so such an animated and beloved image, instead of being passive, would constitute a component part of the collective energy and purpose of one's being ; would count for one in the complex whole that one calls a mind or a consciousness.

According to this hypothesis, the problem would be, to be at once loving enough and beloved enough to live and survive in the minds of others. The individual, in so far as

Personal immortality.

his external accidents are concerned, would disappear ; but what is best in him would survive in the souls of those he loves who love him. A ray of sunlight may for a time record upon a bit of dead paper the lines of a face that no longer exists among the living; nay, human art may go farther, and impart to canvas or to stone the minutest resemblances to human life; but art has not yet succeeded in imparting a soul to Galatea. Love must be added to art to achieve that miracle—men must love each other so completely that they become identified in the universal consciousness. When that consummation has been reached, each of us will live completely, and without loss, in the love of our fellows. The power of love is not limited, like that of light, to giving permanence to the outward appearances of life; it is capable of lending stability to life itself.

Separation on such an hypothesis would be as impossible as in the case of those atomic vortices of which we spoke above, which consisted each in a single individual, in the sense that no force could break them up into their elements; their unity lay not in their simplicity, but in their inseparability. Just so in the sphere of consciousness, a manifold of conscious states may conceivably form a luminous ring that can neither be broken nor extinguished. The atom, it has been said, is inviolable, and consciousness may come to be inviolable *de facto*.

Elimination of death.

Nay, one's secondary and reflected life in the minds of other people might even come to be more important than the original of which it is a copy, insomuch that a gradual process of substitution might take place, a substitution of which death would simply mark the definitive and tranquil accomplishment. We might feel ourselves, even in this life, entering into possession of an immortality in the hearts of those who love us. Such an immortality would be a species of new creation. Morality, and religion even, are in our judgment simply the outcome of moral productivity; such an immortality would be simply an ultimate manifestation of the same thing. And if it were once achieved, the opposition that the man of science to-day perceives between the continuation of the species and the immortality of the individual would have disappeared in a final synthesis. Death closes one's eyes, but love stands by to open them again.

Triumph of love.

The point of contact might thus be found between life and immortality. At the beginning of evolution, death was the end of the individual and the light of conscious-

*Complete sur-*
*vival of the* ness ended in obscurity. By virtue of moral and
*individual.* social progress, one's friends tend to remember one after death with increasing intensity and for longer and longer periods; the image that survives the original fades only by degrees, and more and more slowly, as the course of evolution advances. And it may be that, at some time in the future, the memory of beloved beings will so mingle with the life and the blood of each new generation, and will be so passed on from one to the other, that it will become a permanent element in the current of conscious existence. Such a persistent memory of the individual would be a gain in power for the species, for they who remember love more dearly than they who forget, and to love dearly is advantageous to the species. It is not, therefore, unpermissible to conceive a gradual increase in the faculty of memory by natural selection. The day may come when the individual will survive in as detailed and complete a fac-simile of what he was in his lifetime as can well be imagined, and death may become less significant than a period of absence ; love will endow the beloved object with the mystery of eternal presence.

Even at the present day individuals here and there are sometimes so deeply loved that it is doubtful whether or no

*Exemplified* what is best in them does not survive their
*to-day in isolated* death, and their minds, unhappily subject to the
*cases.* weaknesses of humanity and unable as yet to break through the limitations of the physical organism, do not really succeed, by virtue of the love that surrounds them, in achieving an almost complete immortality even before their death. It is in the hearts of those who love them that they really live, and in all the world the corner that it really concerns them to be able to call their own lies in the affections of two or three people.

This phenomenon of mental palingenesis, which is at present isolated, may gradually come to be extended to the whole of the human species. Immortality may be an ultimate pos-

session acquired by the species, as a whole, for the benefit of
all of its members.   Every individual consciousness may come
to survive as a constituent part in a more comprehensive consciousness.   Fraternity may, at
some time in the future, be universal, render soul
transparent to soul, and the ideal of morals and of religion be
realized.   Every soul will be reflected and mirrored in every
other; although it will not suffice for that purpose simply to
look into each other's eyes unless one's heart positively shines
through them.   One must project one's own image into the
mirror of the sea, if one is to find it there.

*Destined to be-
come common.*

It must, of course, be admitted that, if such speculations do
not positively stretch away beyond the limits of possibility,
they certainly do stretch away beyond the limits
of actual science and experience, but precisely
what renders all such hypotheses uncertain renders them also forever possible : namely, our irremediable
ignorance of the basis of consciousness.   Whatever discovery
science may make in regard to consciousness and its conditions, it will never ascertain its essence, nor, consequently, the
limits of its possible subsistence.   Pyschologically and meta-
physically considered, what are conscious action and volition?
Nay, what is unconscious activity, what is force, what is
efficient causality?   We do not know, we are obliged to define
subjective activity and power in terms of objective motion,
that is to say, in terms of their effect, and it will always be
permissible for a philosopher to deny that motion, as a simple
change of relations in space, constitutes the whole of an action,
and that there are no uncaused movements, no relations between non-existent terms.   And, if so, how are we to know
precisely to what extent activity is essentially enduring as the
emanation of a subjective power of which motion is, as it
were, the visible sign, and of which consciousness is the immediate and intimate " apprehension."   Neither word nor act expresses all of us, something always remains unsaid, and will,
perhaps, remain unsaid to the end of our lives—and beyond.
It is possible that the foundation of personal consciousness is

*Possibility of a
still more literal
immortality.*

a power as incapable of being exhausted by any amount of activity as of being confined to any variety of forms.

In any event the matter is, and always will be, a mystery, which arises from the fact that consciousness is *sui generis*, is

Can never be<br>disproved. absolutely inexplicable, and at bottom forever inaccessible to scientific formulæ and a fit subject, therefore, of metaphysical hypotheses. Just as being is the supreme genus, *genus generalissimum*, in the objective world, so consciousness is the supreme genus in the subjective world; so that no reply can ever be given to these two questions: What is being, and what is consciousness? Nor, therefore, to this third question, which depends upon the two preceding: Will consciousness continue to exist?

On an old dial, in a town in the south of France, may be read the legend: *Sol non occidat!* May the light not fail! Such is, indeed, the proper epilogue to *fiat lux*. Of all things in this world light is the one upon which we are most dependent; it, of all things, should have been created once for all, εἰς ἀεί; should pour down from the heavens through all eternity. And the light of the mind, which is more powerful than the light of the sun, may ultimately succeed in eluding the law of destruction which everywhere in the book of nature immediately follows the law of creation, and then only will the command, *fiat lux*, have been accomplished. *Lux non occidat in æternum!*

IV. But, it will be asked, what consolation and encouragement is there in all this for those who do not feel the charm of

Stoicism the<br>last resort. these remote hypotheses concerning the outer limits of existence, for those who see death in all its brutality, and lean, as you yourself probably do, in the present state of the theory of evolution, somewhat toward purely negative conclusions? What can be said to them when they stand, as they believe they do, on the brink of annihilation? Nothing better could be said than the simple and somewhat unfeeling words of the ancient Stoics, who, be it remarked also, were themselves disbelievers in the immortality of the individual: "Be not a coward!" Deeply in the wrong as Stoicism was in the presence of death, in its insensibility to the pain of love which was the condition of its power and of its progress among mankind, when it interdicted attachment and commanded impassibility, it was right when it recommended insensibility to one's own death. A man needs no other consolation than to feel that he has lived a complete life, that he has done his work, and that mankind is not the worse, nay, is perhaps the better for his having existed; and that whatever he has loved will survive, that the best of his dreams will somewhere be realized, that the impersonal element in his consciousness, the portion of the immortal patrimony of the human race, which has been intrusted to him and constitutes what is best in him, will endure and increase, and be passed on, without loss, to succeeding generations; that his own death is of no more importance, no more breaks the eternal continuity of things, than the shivering of a bit of a hand-glass does. To gain a complete consciousness of the continuity of life is to estimate death at its proper value, which is perhaps that of the disappearance of a kind of living illusion. Once more, in the name of reason, which is capable of understanding death, and of accepting it as it accepts whatsoever else is intelligible —be not a coward!

More than that, despair is grotesque because it is useless; cries and groans, at least such as are not purely reflex, originally served their purpose in the life of the species

**Dignity of resignation.**

of arousing attention or pity, or of summoning aid; it is to the fact that it was once useful that the existence and propagation of the language of pain are due; but as there is no help against the inexorable, and no pity to be asked for in a matter that is in harmony with the interests of the totality of things and conformable to the dictates of our own thought, resignation alone is the proper attitude of mind, or rather a certain inner assent, or still better, a smile of detachment and intelligence and comprehension, and interest even in our own extinction. What is beautiful in the natural order of things cannot definitively excite despair.

If anyone who has experienced the pangs of death should make light of the sort of consolation here referred to, we reply
Of considering<br>one's own case<br>impersonally. that we are not ourselves speaking in absolute ignorance of the visage of the supreme moment. We have ourselves had occasion more than once to look death in the face, less often no doubt than a soldier in active service ; but we have had more time to consider it at our ease, and we have never found reason to desire that it should be veiled by an irrational belief. It is better to see and to know the truth ; it is better not to tread the brink of the precipice with bandaged eyes. To disguise death is to pay it too great a compliment. We have had more than one example of it under our eyes. We have seen our grandfather, who, by the way, was himself not a believer, stricken down by successive attacks of apoplexy, and he said to us, smiling in the intervals of his pain, that he felt but one regret, and that was that so many superstitions should be in existence, and that Catholicism in particular (it was at that time when France was aiding the Papacy) should still be in power. Note also that the progress of science—in especial, of physiological and medical sciences—tends to increase the number of instances in which death is foreseen and is waited for almost with serenity. The least stoical of mankind sometimes feel the inclination toward an act of heroism, which, though in a measure forced upon them, is nevertheless not without its dignity. In the course of certain cases of protracted disease, such as consumption or cancer, the patient, if he possesses the necessary scientific qualifications, can calculate the probabilities of his life and determine within a few days at what time he will die. Bergot, whom I knew, was such a patient; Trousseau was another, and there have been many more. Knowing one's self to be condemned, feeling one's self to count for but one in the infinity of the universe, one can consider one's self and one's progress toward the unknown in a sense impersonally.

If such a death is not without its bitterness, it is nevertheless the one which, of all others perhaps, is likely to prove attractive to a philosopher, to a mind with a passion for clearness, for foresight, for comprehension. For the rest, in the ma-

jority of cases, death takes its victims in the height of their
vigour, in the midst of the struggle for existence ; it is a matter
of a few hours, like birth ; its very suddenness ren-
Sudden death a
blessing. ders it less redoubtable to the majority of mankind,
who find it comparatively easy to be brave in the
presence of a danger that is brief, and they hold out against
the supreme enemy with the same obstinate courage that they
would display against any other. On the contrary, when death
approaches slowly, and deprives us of our strength by degrees,
and each day leaves us in possession of something less than
the day before, another source of consolation is open to us.

It is a law of nature that diminution of vitality brings with
it a proportionate diminution of desire ; a man cares less
Decline in in- keenly for what he feels himself less capable of
terest in life with attaining. Illness and old age always make us
decline in vitality. set less value upon the joys of which they deprive
us which they first render bitter and then impossible ; and
the last joy of all, that of bare existence, is as subject to the
law as its predecessors. Consciousness of one's inability to
live brings with it inability to desire to live ; it becomes a
burden to draw one's breath. One feels one's self dispersing,
falling into dust, and no longer possessing the strength to
check the process of decay. Moreover, egoism declines with
declining strength ; as we approach the grave we gain a power
of estimating ourselves more nearly at our just value, of understanding that a faded flower has no right to live ; that, as
Marcus Aurelius said, "a ripe olive *ought* to fall from the
tree." One sentiment alone survives, a sense of weariness,
of extreme weariness. We long for rest, long to relax the
tension of life, to lie at ease, to have done with it once for all.
Oh ! to be no longer on one's feet. The dying well know the
supreme joy of looking forward to their last resting place !
They no longer envy the interminable file of the living whom
they perceive, as it were in a dream, vainly marching and
countermarching upon the surface of the earth where they
sleep. They are resigned to the solitude and abandonment
of death. They are like travellers in the desert—worn with
fever, and fatigue, and unwilling to make another step in ad-

vance; they are no longer borne up by the hope of revisiting familiar skies; they are unable to surmount the remaining difficulties of the way and request their companions to leave them, to march on without them, and, stretched upon the sand, watch without a tear, without a desire, the departing caravan creeping away toward the horizon.

Naturally, some of us will always shrink before death, and wring our hands, and lose our self-possession. Some temperaments are subject to vertigo, to a horror of abysses, and in especial to a horror of the great abyss toward which all paths converge. Montaigne counsels such people to throw themselves blindly over the verge; others counsel them to fix their eyes till the end on some small mountain flower in the crevice of the rock. The manliest of mankind will give their attention to the depths of space and to the heavens, will fill their hearts with the immensity of the universe, will magnify their souls to the limits of the abyss, will subdue the rebellious individuality in themselves before it is forcibly subdued for them, and will scarcely be aware of the precipice till they have fairly passed beyond its brink. And for the philosopher, who is essentially a worshipper of the unknown, death possesses the attraction of novelty; birth only excepted, it is the most mysterious incident in life. Death has its secret, its enigma, and we are haunted by a vague hope that, as the final touch of irony, it may be revealed to us at the last moment; that the dying, according to the ancient belief, divine it and close their eyes only to shield them from an intolerable brightness. Man's last agony and his last pulse of curiosity are one.

*Persistence of curiosity.*

KANSAS SCHOOL OF RELIGION
University of Kansas
1300 Oread Avenue
LAWRENCE, KANSAS 66044